# AP*

## WORLD HISTORY

### 6TH EDITION

**JOHN McCANNON, Ph.D.**

Department of History

Southern New Hampshire University

Manchester, New Hampshire

BARRON'S

## About the Author

John McCannon earned a Ph.D. in history from the University of Chicago in 1994. He has taught Russian, European, and world history at several universities in the United States and Canada and is a former editor of the *Canadian Journal of History*. He has worked as an Advanced Placement Reader for the College Board and is the author of *Red Arctic: Polar Exploration and the Myth of the North in the Soviet Union* (1998) and *A History of the Arctic: Nature, Exploration, and Exploitation* (2012). He is currently an associate professor of history at Southern New Hampshire University.

## About the Contributor

Pamela Jordan received a Ph.D. in political science from the University of Toronto in 1997. In addition to her academic background, she has worked as a news writer for Facts on File News Services, Inc., and as executive director of a nongovernmental organization affiliated with the United Nations. Dr. Jordan is the author of *Defending Rights in Russia: Lawyers, the State and Legal Reform in the Post-Soviet Era*.

## Acknowledgments

Both the author and contributor would like to thank Jennifer Giammusso, David Rodman, and Anna Damaskos, whose editorial supervision has made the preparation of this manuscript's various editions a smooth and successful process. We are also grateful to those assisting with art direction and production assistance and to the anonymous reviewers who have commented insightfully on this manuscript as it has evolved over the years.

*All inquiries should be addressed to:*
Barron's Educational Series, Inc.
250 Wireless Boulevard
Hauppauge, New York 11788
**www.barronseduc.com**

ISBN: 978-1-4380-0272-9 (book only)
ISBN: 978-1-4380-7383-5 (book with CD-ROM)

ISSN 1937-8874

PRINTED IN THE UNITED STATES OF AMERICA
9 8

**10%
POST-CONSUMER
WASTE**
Paper contains a minimum
of 10% post-consumer
waste (PCW). Paper used
in this book was derived
from certified, sustainable
forestlands.

# CONTENTS

## UNIT TWO: TECHNOLOGICAL AND ENVIRONMENTAL TRANSFORMATIONS (600 B.C.E.–600 C.E.)

## UNIT THREE: REGIONAL AND TRANSREGIONAL INTERACTIONS (600–1450)

## UNIT FOUR: GLOBAL INTERACTIONS (1450–1750)

# UNIT FIVE: INDUSTRIALIZATION AND GLOBAL INTEGRATION (1750-1900)

# UNIT SIX: ACCELERATING GLOBAL CHANGE AND REALIGNMENTS (1900 TO PRESENT)

## MODEL TESTS

As you review the content in this book to work toward earning that **5** on your AP World History exam, here are five essential points you should focus on.

*Barron's*
*Essential*
**5**

**1** **Know the course themes.** As important as factual knowledge is, you can't and won't be able to know every detail about the history of the world, nor will the exam focus on fact memorization. You need to think about how the facts fit into the wider contexts addressed by the themes. Not only will the multiple-choice questions be geared in this way, the essay questions will be theme-inspired. As a reminder, the official course themes are: interaction between humans and the environment, development and interaction of cultures, state building, expansion, and conflict, creation, expansion, and interaction of economic systems, and development and transformation of social structures.

**2** **Understand historiography.** Historiography, the study of how historians think and write about history, is a topic of importance. What topics do historians choose to focus on? What sources and documents do they use as evidence, and how do they evaluate the strengths, weaknesses, and biases of that evidence? How do historians determine what causes a major event or development? How do they decide when historical eras begin and end? A number of multiple-choice questions will ask you to analyze images, quotations, and excerpts from historical writing. The document-based question (DBQ) is designed expressly to make you think like a historian.

**3** **Know and understand the method of periodization chosen by the course.** One of the most basic historiographic skills is periodization: identifying key dates in the history of a country or region, or in the history of a topic or theme, and using those dates to define historical periods that make logical sense and organize facts and details in a way that makes them easier for students to learn. It is helpful to know major dates when they serve as key dividing points. It is even more helpful to know why such dates are considered important. How the periodization was chosen by the AP World History course was meant to help you organize your studies. Understanding this will help you both on multiple-choice questions and all essays.

**4** **"How" and "why" (and "how are they alike?") are more important than "who" and "when."** Names, dates, and other such details are never unimportant in the study of history. Mastery of facts can earn you extra points on essay questions and increase your chances of answering multiple-choice questions correctly. However, the exam is far more likely to emphasize how things were done, or why they happened, rather than who did them or when. Causes and effects matter greatly as well. Also, as you study any topic, always consider how it *compares* with similar topics in other times and places.

**5** **Focus on interactions.** Note the number of times the word "interaction" appears in the course themes and historical periods. This is a topic of major interest, and you should concentrate on it throughout your studies. Note that interaction can take place on several levels—local, regional, interregional, and global—and in many forms.

# INTRODUCTION

# How to Use This Book

## TO TEACHERS AND STUDENTS

This book can be used in one of two ways. For those taking (or teaching) a course in world history, or for those who have recently taken such a course, it can serve as a helpful supplement to coursework. For readers who are not taking, or have never taken, a course in world history, this book can serve as an independent study aid.

This introductory unit offers strategies for the various question types encountered on the AP World History exam. These include multiple-choice questions and the free-response (or essay) questions, which include the document-based question (DBQ), the continuity and change over time (CCOT) essay, and the comparative essay.

Units One through Six contain content-based review chapters. Each unit is dedicated to one of the major historical periods covered by the exam, and each is divided into Short Cut and Scenic Route sections. The Short Cut sections should suffice for those readers who need (or only have time for!) a quick review. The Scenic Route sections allow readers to explore topics in more detail, should they so desire.

This book also contains two full-length model exams.

## TO THE TEACHER

This book's review chapters can be used to summarize or reinforce particular classroom or homework assignments. The Short Cut sections, with their unit overviews, allow students to examine historical events from a broad perspective. They are based on the course framework's major themes, and they also place events and developments in the comparative context that the AP curriculum emphasizes.

The model exams can be used near the end of the academic year as the culmination of an AP World History course—and as good practice for the actual AP exam.

This introductory unit should be covered with students at the beginning of an AP World History course and then at several points afterward. The sooner students are familiar with how AP exams work, the more comfortable they will be with the exam experience itself. This is particularly important with respect to the free-response (essay) portion of the exam, where familiarity with the rules and procedures is indispensable.

## TO THE STUDENT

This book can be used for independent review, whether or not you are taking, or have ever taken, a course in world history. *How* you use it will depend on your circumstances.

**Short Cuts vs. Scenic Routes.** To serve students with different needs, this book divides each content-based unit into two sections: a Short Cut overview, suitable for quick review, and a series of in-depth chapters called the Scenic Route.

Which path should you choose? It depends.

Perhaps you are using this book in conjunction with an AP course in world history, or at least over a long period of time. If so, you can take full advantage of the Scenic Route chapters in each unit, along with the Short Cuts. The more time you give yourself to study, the more thoroughly you will be able to absorb information and ideas. Even if AP questions don't tend to test factual knowledge for its own sake, the more you know, the easier you will find it to eliminate incorrect answers on the multiple-choice questions, or to come up with evidence and supporting details for your essays. The Scenic Route chapters can assist you with that.

However, if you have taken a world history course and simply need a refresher, or if you have limited time to study and are cramming at the last minute, you should focus mainly on the Short Cuts, along with the practice exams *and* the "strategies" sections of this introductory unit.

No matter how much time you have to study, be sure to focus not just on *what* the exam covers, but also on *how* to take the exam itself. Knowing the exam process is arguably as important as knowing the course material.

## Suggested Timelines

Different students master material at different paces, and your own circumstances may leave you with more or less time to prepare. Three possible timelines for study are provided here. Adapt as necessary to your own situation and abilities.

### 7-DAY TIMELINE

With such limited time, it is best to concentrate on test-taking methods and big-picture issues.

- **DAY 1**    Read this introductory unit carefully. Take one of the model exams to get a sense of how ready you are.

- **DAY 2**    Read and study the Short Cut sections for Units One and Two.

- **DAY 3**    Read and study the Short Cut section for Unit Three.

- **DAY 4**    Read and study the Short Cut section for Unit Four.

- **DAY 5**    Read and study the Short Cut section for Unit Five.

- **DAY 6**    Read and study the Short Cut section for Unit Six. With any time remaining, review all the Short Cut sections.

- **DAY 7**    Review the introductory unit. Take the second model exam.

### 4-WEEK TIMELINE

Having roughly a month to prepare will allow you some time to examine topics in depth, in addition to focusing on essentials.

- **WEEK 1**    Read this introductory unit to learn how the AP exam works. Then study Units One and Two, focusing on the Short Cut sections. If time permits, or if you have specific knowledge gaps to fill, turn to the Scenic Route chapters as needed.

**WEEK 2**    Study Units Three and Four, using the same approach as above.

**WEEK 3**    Study Units Five and Six, using the same approach as above.

**WEEK 4**    Take the model exams. Review this introductory unit, as well as the Short Cut sections for Units One through Six.

### SCHOOL-YEAR (9-MONTH) TIMELINE

This is the ideal scenario. Here, you are likely using this book as a supplement to a world history course. If so, proceed at the same pace and in the same order as your teacher and classmates. Otherwise, the following will give you a good grounding.

**MONTH 1**    Read this introductory unit. Study Units One and Two.

**MONTH 2**    Study Unit Three. Use extra time to review the Short Cut sections for Units One and Two.

**MONTH 3**    Study Unit Four. Use extra time to review the Short Cut section for Unit Three.

**MONTH 4**    Study Unit Five. Use extra time to review the Short Cut section for Unit Four.

**MONTH 5**    Study Unit Six. Use extra time to review the Short Cut section for Unit Five.

**MONTH 6**    Review the Short Cut section for Unit Six. Take the first model exam. Assess your strengths and weaknesses.

**MONTH 7**    Skim Units One through Six, focusing on weak points. Use the Short Cut sections to help you think about themes and comparisons.

**MONTH 8**    Continue reviewing the Short Cut sections. Reread the introductory unit.

**MONTH 9**    Take the second model exam. Review as needed. Skim Short Cut sections and the introductory unit a final time.

## General Notes

Dates are given according to the standard Western calendar, with one exception. The abbreviations B.C.E. ("before common era") and C.E. ("common era") are used, rather than the traditional B.C. ("before Christ") and A.D. (*anno domini*, or "year of our Lord"). This usage shows more respect to non-Christian cultures. The Western calendar is only one of many systems used worldwide to measure time. According to the Hebrew calendar, for example, year 1 is the equivalent of 3760 B.C.E. Year 1 of the Muslim calendar, by contrast, is 622 C.E.

Dates with no designation—those that appear simply as numerals—are assumed to be C.E.

Names and terms from a variety of languages are used throughout this book. Many, such as Russian, Chinese, Arabic, Japanese, and Hebrew, use alphabets different from the Latin script used by English speakers. There is no single, consistent way to convert one alphabet to another. Consequently, when referring to people or terms transliterated from non-Latin scripts, this book will try to use versions that are both linguistically accurate and easily recognizable. Be aware that certain well-known names and terms have several variants. This includes Genghis Khan versus Chinggis Khan (or Jenghiz Khan), Mao Tse-tung versus Mao Zedong, Mohammed versus Muhammad, or Sundiata versus Son-Jara. Be prepared to encounter different versions like this in different textbooks and readings.

# THE ADVANCED PLACEMENT EXAM IN WORLD HISTORY: AN OVERVIEW

## Format

Advanced Placement exams are typically administered every May. The AP World History exam lasts a total of 3 hours and 5 minutes.

Students are allowed 55 minutes to complete 70 multiple-choice questions.

The free-response (essay) portion of the exam lasts for 130 minutes. It includes the following questions:

- **DOCUMENT-BASED QUESTION (DBQ):** Roughly 50 minutes, including a mandatory period of 10 minutes to read documents.
- **CONTINUITY AND CHANGE OVER TIME (CCOT) ESSAY:** Roughly 40 minutes, devoted to how a specific aspect of one of the five course themes did and did not change over time. Spans at least one of the course's standard time periods.
- **COMPARATIVE ESSAY:** Roughly 40 minutes, devoted to likenesses and differences in how one of the five course themes played out in two or more societies or geographical regions.

The free-response portion of the exam begins with the 10-minute document-reading period mentioned above. During this time, you may make notes on the document sheets, but you are not allowed to work on actual essays. Once the document-reading period ends, you have 2 hours to write your essays. You may complete them in whatever order you like, and you must decide for yourself when to finish one essay and move on to the next. It is strongly recommended that you allow 5 or so minutes per question to plan and outline your answers.

## Grading

Grades for the exam are calculated according to a complex formula that converts a raw score (zero to 120) into a final standard score ranging from 1 (the worst) to 5 (the best):

- Half of the raw score (up to 60 points) derives from the 70 multiple-choice questions. Each correct response earns 1 point. (Incorrect answers, which used to earn a quarter-point penalty, now count for zero, as do any answers left blank.) This zero-to-70 total is converted into a zero-to-60 result that makes up this half of the overall raw score.
- The other half of the raw score (up to 60 points) is based on the three free-response questions. Each essay receives a grade of zero (the worst) to 9 (the best). The zero-to-27 total for all three essays is converted into a raw score of zero to 60, which is added to the raw score from the multiple-choice section.

Another calculation converts the zero-to-120 raw score to a standard score of 1 through 5. This is what students see when they receive their results. Scores can be interpreted as follows:

- **5: EXTREMELY WELL QUALIFIED.** Accepted by the majority of colleges and universities for some kind of academic credit or benefit. Earned by roughly 10 percent of students.
- **4: WELL QUALIFIED.** Accepted by many colleges and universities for some kind of academic credit or benefit. Earned by roughly 15 percent of students.
- **3: QUALIFIED.** Accepted by many colleges and universities for some kind of academic credit or benefit, but often of a limited nature. Earned by roughly 25 percent of students.

**2: POSSIBLY QUALIFIED.** Accepted by a few colleges and universities for academic credit or benefit, generally quite limited. Earned by roughly 25 percent of students.

**1: NO RECOMMENDATION.** Not accepted anywhere. Earned by roughly 25 percent of students.

Universities and colleges have widely varying policies regarding AP exams. You should contact the school of your choice to determine what benefit, if any, a particular score will give you.

## Time Frame

The AP World History exam focuses on human history worldwide, from the Stone Age to the present. The percentage of multiple-choice questions pertaining to each era is approximately as follows:

- to 600 B.C.E.: 5 percent of questions
- 600 B.C.E. to 600 C.E.: 15 percent of questions
- 600 to 1450: 20 percent of questions
- 1450 to 1750: 20 percent of questions
- 1750 to 1900: 20 percent of questions
- 1900 to present: 20 percent of questions

## Themes

The AP World History exam is broad in scope and seeks to test critical and interpretive skills, not just the mastery of facts and data. The study of world history challenges students to examine questions from a big-picture point of view, as well as to draw meaningful comparisons between different societies and time periods.

Five overarching themes form the heart of the AP World History course.

- **STATE BUILDING, EXPANSION, AND CONFLICT.** What political forms do societies adopt, and who rules whom in any given time and place? How and why do revolutions take place, and what impact do they have? Beyond monarchies, empires, and nation-states, what regional and international bodies—such as the United Nations—have exerted influence throughout history? How have war and diplomacy affected world history?

- **DEVELOPMENT AND INTERACTION OF CULTURES.** What do societies believe religiously, philosophically, and politically? What artistic and intellectual traditions do they develop? How do scientific insights and technological innovations fit into their worldviews? How and when does the interaction of peoples lead to cultural sharing—or to cultural clashes?

- **CREATION, EXPANSION, AND INTERACTION OF ECONOMIC SYSTEMS.** How do people in a society make a living, and what resources do they use? How do trade and commerce affect societies and the way they interact? What systems have societies used to organize labor throughout history? What distinguishes hunter-forager, pastoral, and agricultural societies from each other—and from modern systems such as industrialization, capitalism, and socialism?

- **DEVELOPMENT AND TRANSFORMATION OF SOCIAL STRUCTURES.** Who has power and status within a society, and why? What roles are played by family, kinship, and social class? Why do some societies lean more toward hierarchy and others toward social mobility? What roles do cities play in social and economic development? How are gender relations governed? How are ethnic and racial minorities defined and treated?

- **INTERACTION BETWEEN HUMANS AND THE ENVIRONMENT.** How has the natural world shaped the development of human societies, and how have humans, seeking resources and using various tools and technologies, shaped the natural world in return? Where have human societies migrated and settled, and how and why did they do so? How have diseases and ecological changes affected humans throughout history?

No more than 20 percent of multiple-choice questions will cover topics dealing exclusively with European history. U.S. history will rarely be discussed in its own right, but generally in comparative contexts or in relation to global trends.

Basic understanding of world geography is crucial for success on the AP World History exam. You must be able to identify major regions according to the terminology used by the AP World History course: not knowing the difference between "East Asia" and "Southeast Asia," or between "Central Asia" and "the Middle East," will lead to harmful errors. For more information on the geographical labels used by the AP course, see Chapter 1, as well as the appendix (Map of Selected World Regions) included at the end of this book.

## HISTORICAL THINKING SKILLS

A key purpose of the AP World History course is to foster certain skills used by professional historians and emphasized in university-level courses. Nine of these, grouped below under the headings used by the AP course, are especially important. Although it helps to command as much factual knowledge as possible, it is crucial to *use* facts in the following ways in order to do well on the AP exam.

### Crafting Historical Arguments from Historical Evidence

- **SKILL 1: ARGUMENTATION:** Can you identify and analyze another writer's thesis? Can you craft an effective and persuasive thesis of your own?
- **SKILL 2: USE OF EVIDENCE:** Can you weigh and measure the strengths and weaknesses of various sources and other pieces of evidence?

### Chronological Reasoning

- **SKILL 3: CAUSATION:** Can you identify and explain cause and effect? Do you know the differences between causation (one thing causing another), correlation (one thing happening along with another in a way that is related, but not necessarily because of it), and coincidence (things happening together by chance)? Can you distinguish between long-term, medium-term, and short-term causes? Or between competing explanations for why something happens?
- **SKILL 4: CONTINUITY AND CHANGE OVER TIME:** Can you trace a trend or development over a long period of time? Can you discuss which elements of that trend or development remain largely the same, and which change as time passes?
- **SKILL 5: PERIODIZATION:** Do you understand how and why historians divide time into different historical periods? Are you aware of competing methods of periodization, and can you evaluate their strengths and weaknesses?

### Comparison and Contextualization

- **SKILL 6: COMPARISON:** Can you draw useful comparisons over time (one specific trend or geographical region in different historical eras) or place (two or more regions during the same time period)? Are you aware that genuine comparison involves analyzing likenesses *and* differences?
- **SKILL 7: CONTEXTUALIZATION:** Can you connect specific events and facts to wider settings and to broader trends?

### Historical Interpretation and Synthesis

- **SKILL 8: INTERPRETATION:** Can you read and analyze pieces of historical evidence with an eye to point of view and possible bias? Do you understand the various ways that different forms of historical evidence (including myths and oral traditions, works of art and architecture, graphs and charts, diaries and autobiographies, government documents, and so on) can be taken advantage of? Can you discuss how the historical consensus about a key event or trend might change over time or vary from country to country?
- **SKILL 9: SYNTHESIS:** Can you bring together various—and even contradictory—sources, explanatory theories, and pieces of evidence to arrive at a useful and convincing understanding of a historical problem or argument? Do you have a sense of how insights from other scholarly disciplines, such as archaeology, statistics, and the environmental sciences, can aid historians in their research?

## MULTIPLE-CHOICE QUESTION STRATEGIES

The AP exam will require you to answer 70 multiple-choice questions. Each question includes four answer options; you will pick the one that BEST answers the question.

You will have 55 minutes to complete this section of the test.

The percentage of questions devoted to each historical period is the same as described before. Questions will NOT appear in chronological order, so be prepared to shift suddenly from one era to another.

One point is awarded for each correct answer. Incorrect answers, whether blank or wrong, are not penalized. For an overall AP score of 3, you need to answer approximately 50 percent of the multiple-choice questions correctly (assuming an acceptable performance on the free-response, or essay, portion of the exam). To receive an overall AP score of 4 or 5, you should aim to answer at least 70 percent of the questions (roughly 50 out of 70) correctly.

### Tips for the Multiple-Choice Questions

Things to bear in mind for the multiple-choice section of the exam:

- **KEEP YOUR PACE BRISK.** On average, you have 45 seconds to work on each question. While you should read each question as carefully as possible, you will not have time to think deeply about any given one. A good way to keep from bogging down is to take a first run through the entire exam, skipping anything you cannot answer quickly and confidently. Return to the more difficult questions by going through the exam a second time. Even during this second reading, don't spend too much time on any single question. As described in the following text, if something seems too hard, make the best possible guess and move on.

- **LEAVE NOTHING BLANK.** AP exams used to penalize wild guessing by deducting a quarter point for every wrong answer. This is no longer the case, so leaving anything unanswered only hurts you. Once you've completed the questions you're sure about and guessed intelligently at the harder ones, use the last minute or so of your time to fill in every remaining blank, even if you do so randomly.
- **START BY ELIMINATING INCORRECT ANSWERS.** Every distractor, or wrong answer, is supposed to sound at least somewhat plausible. Still, a quick but careful reading generally allows you to eliminate at least one wrong answer, if not two. This is the first thing you should you do. If you can quickly pick the correct answer from the two or three that remain, do so. If you can't, flag the question and come back to it during your second run through the exam.
- **MAKE EDUCATED GUESSES.** Especially during your second run through the exam, if a question proves too difficult, make an educated guess and move on. Obsessing over one stubborn question, even if you get it right, is a bad investment of your time—which would be better spent working on several medium-hard questions. (Remember: You don't need to answer *all* the multiple-choice questions to get a 4 or 5 on the exam! Instead, use your time to ensure that you get 50 to 60 of them right.)
- **TRUST YOUR INTUITION—TO A POINT.** Most experts say that the answer you choose first is generally the correct one, *if* you know the material and have read the question carefully. Unless you have a concrete reason to change your mind, go with your instinct. (But don't use this as an excuse for lazy reading or sloppy thinking!)

## Sample Multiple-Choice Questions

Multiple-choice questions on the AP World History exam will test the historical thinking skills described above, rather than raw factual knowledge. Some questions will ask you to interpret maps, images, quotations, graphs, and charts.

Often, clues to the correct answer are contained in the question itself. This is not always the case, though, and while factual knowledge may not be tested directly, the more of it you possess, the easier you will find it to eliminate incorrect distractors in favor of correct answers.

Below are examples of possible multiple-choice questions, along with answers and explanations.

1.  The support given to Confucianism by Qing China's emperors and the support given to Catholicism by kings in medieval Europe were similar in that both aimed to
    (A)  motivate their people to conquer neighboring lands.
    (B)  encourage an individualistic worldview among ordinary citizens.
    (C)  stimulate good works and charitable donations.
    (D)  increase public respect for political authority.

ANSWER: **D**

This is a classic exercise in comparison. While Catholicism was sometimes used to justify wars, Confucianism was generally not, making A a bad choice. Confucianism emphasizes hierarchy, so B can be eliminated easily. Although neither faith would object to the good works referred to in C, you should recall the standard state-building technique of using official religions to strengthen the legitimacy of political regimes. That would point you in the direction of D.

2. How did the rising influence of Timbuktu affect West Africa during the period 1250–1450?
   (A) Trade in salt and gold brought the region into closer contact with Eurasia and other parts of Africa.
   (B) Native religious leaders objecting to Islam convinced many in the region to revolt against it.
   (C) The city's hostility toward foreigners plunged the region into isolationism.
   (D) Agricultural overdevelopment caused widespread desertification throughout the region.

ANSWER: **A**

This answer is principally about causation. As a flourishing center of commerce and Islamic learning, Timbuktu stimulated trade and cultural exchange with numerous far-off places, making B and C false and leaving A as the obvious choice. Although human-caused environmental pressures can cause desertification, the Sahara had become desert long before the rise of Timbuktu, so you can safely ignore D.

3. Which of the following occurred when Neolithic societies shifted from hunting and foraging to pastoralism?
   (A) They adopted sedentary lifestyles.
   (B) They witnessed a significant improvement in the status of women.
   (C) They placed greater stresses on the environment.
   (D) They transformed fixed points of settlement into cities.

ANSWER: **C**

This is another question dealing with causation. Although pastoral societies tend to be more organized and more hierarchical than hunter-forager communities, they herd animals for a living and are therefore highly mobile, making A and D false. There is no evidence for B; by contrast, the environmental pressures placed on herding grounds by large numbers of migrating animals are well documented.

4. Indonesian foreign policy during the immediate post-World War II decades resembles that of India during the same time period, in that both countries
   (A) established right-wing dictatorships and allied with the United States.
   (B) resolved not to align themselves with either Cold War superpower.
   (C) expelled European colonists by means of long, bloody conflicts.
   (D) moved firmly into the Soviet Union's diplomatic orbit.

ANSWER: **B**

This question involves comparison. Although Indonesia ended Dutch colonial rule by force and, in later years, developed a pro-Western dictatorship, A and C never applied to India. India enjoyed cordial relations with the USSR, but not a formal alliance, so D is not true of it (or of Indonesia). For a time, both countries led an effort to form an association of newly decolonized and non-aligned states.

5. Which of the following best justifies the argument that the early 1800s ushered in a new period in the history of Latin America?
(A) The industrialization of sugarcane production
(B) The U.S. proclamation of the Monroe Doctrine
(C) The emancipation of slaves throughout South America
(D) The Latin American wars of independence

ANSWER: **D**

This question tests your understanding of periodization. Not only must you identify which answers are relevant to the time frame identified in the question, you must decide which would convince most scholars to acknowledge a major historical shift. Answers A and C do not apply to the early 1800s, but to later decades. Answer B fits the time frame and is important, but the wars of independence, by turning European colonies into New World nation-states, fundamentally transformed Latin America.

6. Nothing is more moving, in medieval history, than the omnipresence, almost at times the omnipotence, of religion. . . . Then, above all, the world needed a creed that would balance tribulation with hope, soften bereavement with solace, [and] redeem the prose of toil with the poetry of belief. . . . It was a God-intoxicated age.

— *Will Durant, world historian, 1950*

When we are in the tavern,
We don't worry about turning to dust,
But we hurry to have a good time,
Which always makes us sweat . . .

The mistress drinks, the master too,
The soldier and the priest both do . . .
The sister drinks, the brother drinks,
The grandma drinks, the mother drinks,
This one drinks, that one drinks,
A hundred drink, a thousand drink.

*The song* In taberna quando sumus, *circa 1300*

The second passage does not support the first passage because the second passage
(A) explicitly rejects the teachings of medieval Catholicism.
(B) shows that medieval Europe's worldview was not universally religious.
(C) communicates an exclusively secular understanding of the world.
(D) demonstrates widespread sinfulness among medieval Europeans.

ANSWER: **B**

This question calls on four skills: argumentation, contextualization, interpretation, and synthesis. Although the second passage, a Goliardic student poem from the *Carmina Burana* collection, has a decidedly secular tone, it does not actively contradict or criticize Christian doctrine—and although it describes a secular activity, you cannot safely conclude from this that the poet's views are *completely* secular. So A and C are not good guesses. Nor is there any indication that the poem represents the thinking of all or even many Europeans, making D doubtful. What the poem *does* do is undermine the first passage's implication that Europe's medieval era was principally an age of faith, as many historians have tended to think of it.

7.  Although the empire was conquered on horseback, it cannot be governed from horseback.

> *Adapted from an older saying by the Chinese*
> *official Yelü Chucai (Ye-lu Chu-tsai) and given as*
> *advice to the Mongol khan Ögedei, circa 1230 C.E.*

Yelü Chucai's comment is meant to convey which of the following messages?
(A)  A warning that the conquering Mongols had overextended themselves
(B)  A suggestion that states must develop reliable institutions if they wish to endure
(C)  A call for the Mongols to give up their warlike ways in favor of Buddhist pacifism
(D)  A note of protest against the Mongols' brutal takeover of China

ANSWER: **B**

This question is about interpretation and use of evidence. Yelü Chucai's words contain no hint of religiosity or discontent, so C and D are unlikely. Although the Mongol empire eventually grew unwieldy and broke apart into separate states, Ögedei was only the second Mongol khan, directly succeeding Genghis Khan (even if you don't know that piece of information, this statement doesn't seem to have the tone of alarm you might expect if A were true). This is in fact one of the most famous comments on how warrior states tend to be short-lived unless they learn how to shift from conquering to state building.

8.  The photograph below of a figurine carved in West Africa between the 1200s and 1400s C.E. most likely illustrates which of the following?

(A)  The use of industrial machinery for the mass production of goods
(B)  The cultural diffusion of European artistic techniques to Africa
(C)  The handcrafting of folk art for ritual purposes
(D)  The commissioning of a likeness of a loved one by a private patron

ANSWER: **C**

This question tests contextualization. Answer A does not fit the time frame. Visual examination should be enough to dismiss B, and D is typical of later time periods and more socioeconomically developed societies. General knowledge about African art would bring you immediately to C, but process of elimination can get you there as well. In general, image-based questions ask you to solve problems more complex than simple identification—indeed, the identifying information is often provided. But not always, and it is worth knowing the main features of major artistic and architectural styles. Sometimes, knowing the difference between East Asian and South Asian architecture, or between Renaissance and abstract art, is exactly the clue you need.

9. The map below depicts what significant historical development?

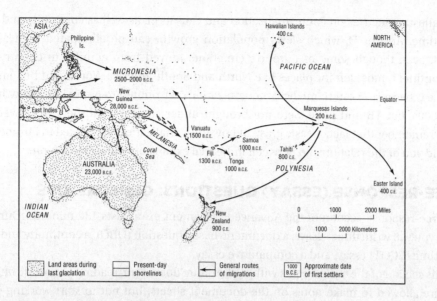

(A) The expansion of Chinese trade routes
(B) European voyages of discovery
(C) Japanese imperialism in the South Pacific
(D) The migration of Polynesian peoples

ANSWER: **D**

The relevant skills here are contextualization and periodization. The dates provided on the map allow for the easy elimination of B and C. In choosing to reject A or D, you might draw on factual knowledge that the premodern Chinese did not trade so far to the east. You might also note that the lines on the map do not go back and forth to China, as one would expect with trade routes.

10. Which of the following developments in the period 1800-1900 best explains the population growth experienced by the cities included on the chart below?

| Year | Cities (Pop. in thousands) | | | | |
|---|---|---|---|---|---|
| | London | Paris | Antwerp | Berlin | Moscow |
| 1800 | 960 | 600 | 60 | 170 | 250 |
| 1850 | 2,700 | 1,400 | 90 | 500 | 360 |
| 1900 | 6,500 | 3,700 | 280 | 2,700 | 1,000 |

(A) The rise of industrial production encouraged urbanization.
(B) Large numbers of Europeans emigrated to foreign countries.
(C) Effective vaccines eliminated diseases such as tuberculosis and polio.
(D) Advanced forms of birth control became more widely available.

ANSWER: **A**

This question focuses on contextualization and causation, as well as continuity and change over time. Answer D, which slows population growth, can be eliminated right away. So can B: even though some of Europe's emigrants moved from country to country within the continent, most left for places like North and South America. You might be tempted to choose C because Western medical modernization contributed to population growth during the 1800s, but TB and polio were not brought under control until the 1900s. Even if you don't remember that fact, a basic grasp of how industrialization proceeded in Europe should remind you of the relationship between industrial expansion and urbanization.

## FREE-RESPONSE (ESSAY) QUESTIONS: GENERAL TIPS

The free-response section of the Advanced Placement exam lasts 130 minutes. During this time, you will write three essays: a document-based question (DBQ), a continuity and change over time (CCOT) essay, and a comparative essay.

This section of the exam begins with a 10-minute document-reading period, during which you are allowed to make notes on the document sheets, but not to start working on your essays. Once these 10 minutes are up, you can write the essays in whichever order you wish, and you can use the remaining 120 minutes however you please—no one will tell you when to finish one essay or start another. You should try to divide your time evenly, spending roughly 40 minutes on each essay, including 5 or so minutes to organize and outline each response. Time management is crucial: students often fail to complete all three questions because they have not practiced writing essays in 40 minutes or less.

A widely agreed-upon guideline is to write the DBQ first. The documents will be fresh in your mind, and because the DBQ operates according to the most complicated rules, it will be good to have it out of the way. Just make sure to leave enough time for the other essays!

### From Basic Core to Expanded Core: Follow the Directions!

Unlike the multiple-choice questions, which are graded by machine, your essays are evaluated by human beings: high-school teachers, university professors, and other specialists who gather every June to serve as AP readers. In about a week, the average AP reader will mark literally hundreds of essays. In 2012, for example, more than 208,000 students took the AP World History exam, and approximately 1,100 readers assessed their work. AP readers are careful and well-trained. Still, they read so many essays in such a short time that special care is needed to ensure that the quality of your work stands out.

The first step toward doing this is to follow the directions! Each essay has its own set of rules, outlined in an official rubric, and AP readers are trained to judge your work according to the rubric. You will lose points if you don't observe the rules. (The actual rubrics are included in sections to come.)

How does the scoring system work? An AP reader will give each of your essays a score of zero through 9. Using the appropriate rubric, the reader will determine whether your essay meets five or six elementary requirements (the **basic core**); you can earn up to 7 points this way. If you fulfill the basic core, the reader will check your essay against a list of advanced requirements (the **expanded core**). Here you can earn an additional 1 or 2 points.

The basic core is an all-or-nothing deal: you can't earn any expanded-core points unless you first earn all the basic-core points. Think of this as opening a gate with five or six locks.

Until you unlock all of them, you can't go any farther. The good news is that if you perform well on each part of the basic core, you're already doing most of what you need to do to score the extra expanded-core points.

## THE THESIS: HALF THE BATTLE

Your essay should begin with a short and easy-to-spot **thesis**: a capsule statement of your central argument or insight. *The thesis is NOT your subject, but the interesting thing you're going to say ABOUT your subject.* All three rubrics require an "acceptable" thesis as part of the basic core and an "analytical, clear, and comprehensive" thesis to satisfy the expanded core. The first thing any AP reader will do is to search for your thesis, and if he or she can't find it or doesn't like it, your entire essay is in trouble. If you start with a good thesis, not only will you earn points right away, you'll put your reader in the kind of receptive mood that boosts your chances of getting even more points.

So it's worth taking time and trouble to craft a good thesis. Here are some general guidelines to help you do so. (Additional suggestions are provided in the essay-specific sections that follow.)

- **PUT IT FRONT AND CENTER.** Your thesis should appear in the first paragraph. In fact, it should *be* the first paragraph. (The thesis can consist of more than one sentence, as long as the sentences are consecutive.) Technically, you're allowed to state your thesis in the conclusion, but this is a bad idea. Don't make your reader hunt around.
- **KEEP IT SHORT.** Your thesis paragraph should contain no more than two or three sentences. Not only are you racing the clock, but for the most part, any material that contributes to the thesis statement can't be counted toward the points you're hoping to earn for evidence, analysis, and context. Extra material will be wasted—so save it for the essay's main body.
- **ADDRESS ALL ASPECTS OF THE QUESTION.** How you do this depends on which essay you're writing, but no matter what, the thesis must touch on all aspects of the question. These include the time period, the geographical area(s), and the things you're comparing or whose changes and continuities you're tracing. It can also include causes *and* consequences if you get a DBQ that takes that approach. "Address" does NOT mean simply restating the question.
- **BE SPECIFIC AND ANALYTICAL.** Vague language weakens your thesis. As noted above, restating the question is not helpful. Neither is relying on lazy and unspecific assertions like "industrialization proved important in Europe and Japan during the 1800s" or "religious life in India changed substantially between 600 B.C.E. and 600 C.E." Analysis, which your reader will want to see, involves discussing HOW and WHY something happened and the RESULTS and EFFECTS that followed. The more concrete you can be, the better.

## OTHER REQUIREMENTS: THOROUGHNESS, EVIDENCE, THE SPECIAL FUNCTION, AND ANALYSIS

Although each essay is unique in its way, the rubrics for all three of them require you to do four things beyond generating a thesis. As you build the main body of your essay (the three to five paragraphs that follow your thesis), think constantly about how you can fulfill these requirements.

### Thoroughness

This word does not appear in any of the rubrics, but the concept is present in the requirement that you "address"—and, for the expanded core, "analyze"—"all parts of the question." This means *all* the documents for the DBQ, it means change *and* continuity over the entire time period for the CCOT, and it means differences *and* similarities for the comparative essay (and paying roughly equal attention to the two things being compared).

### Evidence

Don't just say it, prove it! Concrete details help you make your case, and this is where you can put factual knowledge to good use. Who traded which goods with whom? Who enacted which policies? What environmental or medical disasters had a bearing on your question—or which new technological innovations, artistic trends, or religious developments? Not only do specific nuggets of relevant information make your general comments more convincing, AP readers are told to look for a minimum number of them before awarding points. That number varies from question to question, but the more you include, the better you'll do.

### The Special Function

As with "thoroughness," this phrase does not appear in the rubrics. Instead, it refers to the specialized task associated with each essay type. Your DBQ answer will be judged on how well you group your documents and think about them. The CCOT essay asks you to focus on "relevant world historical context." The comparative essay requires "at least one direct, relevant comparison" between or among the societies you're comparing. Whatever the task, you must complete it properly and in a way that's obvious to the reader. Detailed advice is provided in the essay-specific sections below.

### Analysis

Your entire essay, of course, should be analytical. But to get actual points for analysis, you must clearly *explain* how or why something functioned or happened the way it did. You must do this at least once, and preferably more than once. The bar here is quite high: what you choose to explain must be central to the question's topic, and what you say about it has to be reasonably sophisticated. (On the DBQ, focus your analysis on the documents themselves, and do so as often as possible.) AP readers often struggle to find ways to give students credit for analysis. Don't let this happen to you.

## Miscellaneous Points

Other things to remember as you write your essays:

- **DOING WHAT THE QUESTION ASKS.** Before answering any essay question, look at the question's action verb—what is it asking you to do? Most often, it will ask you to **analyze** something. This involves identifying that thing's key elements and explaining how it worked, or how and why it happened, or what larger impact it had. It does NOT mean simply telling a story or listing facts! Directions for the CCOT and comparative essays are predictable: the former nearly always requires you to "analyze changes and continuities," whereas the latter generally asks you to "analyze similarities and differences." (Sometimes the wording reads "compare A with B," but the meaning is the same.) The DBQ is more complex: you must "Use the following documents" to accomplish one of several different possible tasks, which can include comparison and the analysis of change over time. OTHER THINGS to watch out for? Double-check the time period(s) you're being asked to write about. Also, if the questions allows you to choose between time periods or from a list of regions, be sure you understand the terms of the choice. Is it either/or? Do you pick two items from a list of three? Are you supposed to provide examples from at least two of whatever it is the question is asking you about? And so on.

- **ACCEPTABLE LENGTH.** There is no hard-and-fast rule for how long your essay should be. Page length may vary depending on how large your handwriting is and whether you write concisely or need more words to make your point. As a rule, high-scoring CCOT and comparative essays run 2.5 to 3.5 pages long—assuming normal-sized handwriting and no skipping of lines. Because of their complexity, DBQ essays tend to be longer, with high-scoring examples averaging 4 to 5 pages in length. Whatever the type, any essay shorter than 2.5 pages is unlikely to score well. (If you wish to judge by word count, rough equivalents would be 600–700 words for CCOT and comparative essays, and 900–1,000 words, sometimes slightly more, for DBQs.)

- **PARAGRAPHS.** Dividing your essays into paragraphs will organize your thoughts and make your prose easier to read. Indent clearly. You should end up with four to six paragraphs, depending on how many main points you make in the body of your essay and on whether you add a formal conclusion. Your DBQ will almost certainly contain more paragraphs than your other essays.

- **CONCLUSION . . . OR NOT.** Formal papers generally feature a conclusion that restates the thesis and expands upon it. If you have time to write one, it adds an elegant touch—but it's not strictly necessary, and it won't by itself add points. If you're pressed for time, you're better off strengthening your essay's main body. If you do write a conclusion, don't waste time simply repeating what's in your introduction. Use it to squeeze in more evidence or to make an extra contextual or analytical point.

- **LEGIBILITY.** AP readers do their best to decipher sloppy handwriting. However, neatness makes it easier to appreciate your work. Write quickly, but try your best to be legible.

- **GRAMMAR, SPELLING, AND STYLE.** Substance matters more than style on the AP exam, and readers are not meant to concern themselves with misspellings or grammatical mistakes. Still, fluent prose free of errors makes a better impression, and the more sophistication you display in your writing, the likelier you are to earn expanded-core points.

- **PLAN . . . AND PAY ATTENTION.** Although it's been said several times, it deserves repeating: before writing each essay, take some time—approximately 5 minutes—to plan your answer. And pay attention to the clock!

## DOCUMENT-BASED QUESTION (DBQ) STRATEGIES

Although you are allowed to choose differently, the DBQ, as noted earlier, should be the first essay you write. Its elaborate rules make it the one essay you don't want to be working on if you start running short on time.

Unlike the other essays, the DBQ requires you to perform well on two fronts. Not only does the essay itself have to be solid (complete with a good thesis), but you must demonstrate skillful handling of the documents. The procedure for this is complex enough that you must familiarize yourself with it and practice it ahead of time. Also, if there is one essay where it might be a good idea to take 10 minutes rather than 5 minutes (in addition to the 10-minute document-reading period) to organize your thoughts before writing your answer, the DBQ is probably it.

# Approaching the Document-based Question

When the essay portion of the AP exam begins, you will be shown a set of four to ten documents. Many, if not most, will be written texts, but at least some will be image-based (photographs, cartoons, artworks) or consist of charts and graphs. The documents and their creators may or may not be well-known. You will have 10 minutes to examine them. During this document-reading period, you may make notes on the document sheets and organize your thoughts, but you may not start writing any of your essays.

Taken together, the documents address a particular theme or issue, typically with a fairly narrow focus when it comes to era, geography, and topic. For example, a DBQ might ask about industrialization in nineteenth-century Asia or European imperialism in a specific part of the world. Or it may ask about a noteworthy cultural trend, technological innovation, trade network, or sociological development. A DBQ will require you to use the documents in one of several possible ways: you may be told to compare and contrast two things, to trace continuity and change over time, to analyze causes and consequences, or to analyze the relationship between one thing or another. You will organize the documents into **groups** (typically **three** of them). You will discuss their authors' and creators' **points of view**. Also, to test your understanding of how documents can sometimes be of limited usefulness, the DBQ will ask you to **identify additional documents** that, if provided, would shed further light on the question.

Below is the official AP scoring guide for the DBQ.

**Generic Scoring Guide for AP World History**
**Document-Based Question**

| Basic Core | Points | Expanded Core | Points |
|---|---|---|---|
| 1. Has an acceptable thesis. | 1 | Expands beyond the basic core of 1–7 points. A student must earn 7 points in this core area before earning points in the expanded-core area. | 0–2 |
| 2. Addresses and shows understanding of all (or all but one) of the documents. | 1 | | |
| 3. Thesis is supported by evidence from all documents or all but one. (Supported by all but two documents.) | 2 (1) | Examples:<br>• Has an analytical, clear, comprehensive thesis.<br>• Demonstrates careful and insightful analysis. | |
| 4. Analyzes point of view in two or more documents. | 1 | • Makes convincing use of documents as evidence.<br>• Discusses point of view in most or all documents. | |
| 5. Analyzes documents by grouping them in two or three ways. | 1 | • Compares, groups, and synthesizes the documents in additional ways.<br>• Employs useful external historical content. | |
| 6. Identifies one type of additional document and explains why it is needed. | 1 | • Identifies and explains the need for two or more additional document types. | |
| Subtotal | 7 | Subtotal | 2 |
| TOTAL 9 | | | |

How do you put all this together for a good score?

**The DBQ thesis.** First, match your thesis to the task the question is asking you to perform (comparison, discussion of causes and consequences, examination of changes and continuities, analysis of the relationship between one thing and another). Second, it is not enough just to develop a thesis about the historical subject(s) covered by the question. Your thesis must be something the documents can support as well.

---

**MATCHING YOUR DBQ THESIS TO THE DOCUMENTS**

If your DBQ is about East Indian diaspora communities in Africa, and the documents concern the role of East Indians in African trade networks, it would be a mistake to base your thesis on the question of whether East Indians experienced racial prejudice in Africa. As interesting as that question might be, it would not allow you to use the documents properly. On the other hand, you might be able to introduce the issue in the main body of the essay as "outside" historical content, as long as you show how it relates to your main subject.

---

### Addressing and Understanding the Documents (magic number = all documents)

At some point during your essay, EVERY document should be addressed meaningfully. This does NOT mean simply listing or describing the documents or parroting the information contained in their captions. You must demonstrate some understanding of each document's purpose, the historical context in which it was written or created, and the way it can be used as evidence (discussed below). Where possible, consider the author/creator's point of view (also discussed below). As your AP reader goes through your essay, he or she will carefully count references to the documents to make sure you've included them all.

---

**CITING DOCUMENTS**

How should you cite the documents? The AP rules for attribution used to be more elaborate. These days, it is enough to refer to document number, title, and/or author. In other words, if the source for Document 5 is "Gloria Steinem, American feminist, 'Far from the Opposite Shore' (1978)," you can cite it any of the following ways: "Steinem," "Far from the Opposite Shore," "Document 5," or "Doc. 5."

---

### Evidence and "Outside" Historical Content (magic number = all documents)

Part of "addressing" the documents involves using them as evidence to support your thesis. You must do this by drawing relevant information and/or messages from EVERY document. (The directions allow you to do so from "all but one," but you should ignore this.) ANOTHER way to support your thesis is to bring in "outside" historical content—things you already know about the topic that aren't specifically mentioned in the documents. "Outside" content isn't required by the basic core, but it's one of the easiest ways to earn expanded-core points.

### Point of View (minimum number = 2, magic number = most or all . . . if possible)

At least twice, and preferably more than that, you must analyze the point of view of a document's author or creator. What perspectives, biases, or motivations do the documents express? Can a given document be considered wholly or even partly reliable? Analyzing point of view is easiest if the author/creator is famous and you can bring in "outside" factual knowledge about him or her. Often, though, the author/creator is not well-known, and in some cases is not even identified. You will have to make judgment calls about how an author/creator's occupation, social-institutional status, nationality, gender, religion, or political views might shape his or her point of view. You don't need to go on at length, but you must show some insight. To satisfy the basic core, you must do this two times. To earn expanded-core points, point of view is required for "most or all" of the documents. If you're running short of time, try for at least three or four.

## Grouping the Documents (magic number = 3)

All documents must be sorted into groups—this is the most important demonstration of your ability to analyze them. Each group must contain at least two documents, and no document can appear in more than one group. Unless you have a compelling reason to do otherwise, you should sort documents into THREE GROUPS. Two may seem unconvincing unless the quantity of documents is very small, and anything more than three will be difficult to handle. How should you group your documents? Every DBQ is designed to allow more than one "correct" way to do this, although some approaches work better than others. The weakest method is to group according to chronology or national origin. It's much better to consider factors like the type of document, the perspective and attitudes of the author/creator, the policy or trend a document illustrates, or the side of a debate an author/creator appears to come down on. The groups you come up with will depend on the key elements of the actual question.

---

**MAPPING DBQ GROUPS**

During the 10-minute document-reading period (and during the 5 or 10 minutes you take afterward to continue planning your answer), it's worth sketching out a chart that sorts all of the documents into the three groups you've come up with. This will keep you from forgetting any of the documents as you write. Also, you might jot down notes about (a) point of view for as many documents as you can and (b) where you'd like to identify the need for additional documents (see below). As a bonus, mapping your groups will automatically give your essay the proper structure: thesis paragraph + paragraph for group 1 + paragraph for group 2 + paragraph for group 3 + a conclusion (if you have time for one, or if this is where you choose to identify your additional documents).

---

## Identifying Additional Documents (minimum number = 1, magic number = 2).

To test your understanding of the strengths, weaknesses, and uses of various historical sources, the DBQ requires you to comment on what's missing from the documents you have available: if you had access to ADDITIONAL documents, what would you choose and why would you choose it? To fulfill the basic core, you must answer this question at least once; doing so twice counts toward the expanded core. It's most helpful to think either about what TYPE of source could supplement the documents you have (raw statistics versus a memoir, for example, or a government report versus an artwork or literary excerpt) or about what POINT OF VIEW might be missing (is only one gender represented? or one social class, religion, or nationality? or one side of a controversy?). Be sure to explain WHY the extra documents would be helpful.

## Sample Question

The following question is based on the accompanying Documents 1–10. (The documents have been edited for the purpose of this exercise.)

This question is designed to test your ability to work with and understand historical documents. Write an essay that:

- Has a relevant thesis and supports that thesis with evidence from the documents.
- Uses all of the documents.
- Analyzes the documents by grouping them in as many appropriate ways as possible. Does not simply summarize the documents individually.
- Takes into account the sources of the documents and analyzes the author's point of view.
- Identifies and explains the need for at least one additional type of document.

You may refer to relevant historical information not mentioned in the documents.

1. Using the following documents, analyze the consequences of Russia's communist revolution, from 1917 to 1939. Identify and explain one additional type of document and explain how it would help your analysis of the Russian revolution.

### Historical Background

Communist rule in Soviet Russia began with the October Revolution in 1917. The first Soviet leader, Vladimir Lenin, remained in power until his death in 1924. After a brief succession struggle, Joseph Stalin took his place, governing between 1928 and his own death in 1953.

### DOCUMENT 1

*Source: Rosa Luxemburg, Polish-German communist,* The Russian Revolution, *1918.*

> The basic error of the Lenin-Trotsky theory is that they, too, oppose dictatorship to democracy. They decide in favor of dictatorship over democracy, and thereby in favor of the dictatorship of a handful of persons. [This is] far removed from a genuine socialist policy. Yes, dictatorship! But it must be the work of the *class* and not of a little leading minority in the name of the class—it must be under the masses' direct influence.

### DOCUMENT 2

*Source: Vladimir Lenin, Soviet leader, "Advice to Workers and Peasants," in the official newspaper* Pravda, *February 6, 1918.*

> You must organize and consolidate Soviet power in the villages. There you will encounter kulaks [rich, landowning peasants] who will hinder your work at every step. Make it clear to ordinary peasants that the kulaks must be expropriated in order to achieve a fair and equitable distribution of goods. The bourgeoisie are hiding in their coffers the riches they have plundered. We must catch the plunderers and compel them to return the spoils, otherwise we shall perish.

## DOCUMENT 3

*Source: Poster entitled "What the October Revolution Has Given Female Workers and Peasants,"
1920. Captions on the buildings in the background read: "House for Mothers and Children"
[daycare facility], "Council of Female Workers and Peasant Deputies," "Adult Education,"
"Kindergarten," "Library," "Dining Hall," and "Workers' Club."*

## DOCUMENT 4

*Source: Lyrics to the popular song and air force anthem "Ever Higher," by Pavel Gherman and
Julius Khait, 1920.*

We were born to make fairy tales come true,
To overcome distance and space,
Our reason has made steel wings of our hands,
And given us throbbing motors in place of our hearts.


Casting our willing airplanes into the skies,
Or completing unprecedented flights,
We feel our air force growing stronger,
Our workers' air force, the first in the world . . .

## DOCUMENT 5

*Source: Dmitrii Debabov, "Construction at Magnitogorsk," 1930.*

## DOCUMENT 6

*Source: Letter from a Soviet construction worker to his uncle in Leningrad, 1931.*

Hello, Uncle Fedya. Greetings from Magnitogorsk. They did a poor job of meeting us here. The first night we slept on the bare ground; so began our camp life. They don't give us work since nobody knows when the machine installation will begin. For days we did nothing, or sat in tents, or walked around looking for the bosses. A large number of us leave to go back to where they came from every day. It's very hard to get out of here, but no matter what I'm coming back since life here is impossible: the chow is awful, we're living in tents, and the weather is cold and rainy all the time. When we were being sent off, we heard pretty, sweet words. The project can't proceed without you, they said. But in fact there is such a mess here that you wouldn't be able to make heads or tails of it. Our big shots here are nothing but bureaucrats. There's complete confusion, you can't find anything.

## DOCUMENT 7

*Source: Miron Dolot, Ukrainian farmer and famine survivor, from his memoir* Execution by Hunger, *1987.*

> To safeguard the 1932 crop against the starving farmers, the Party and government passed several strict laws. One of the cruelest laws was enacted on August 7, 1932. This law declared that all collective farm and cooperative property such as the crops in the fields, livestock, and so forth were to be considered as state-owned. The penalties for theft were execution by firing squad, and confiscation of all property of the guilty one. There could be no amnesty for these so-called felons.

## DOCUMENT 8

*Source: Operational order of July 30, 1937, issued by Nikolai Yezhov, USSR People's Commissar of Internal Affairs (head of Stalin's secret police).*

II. On Means of Punishment of Those to Be Repressed, and the Number of Those Subject to Repression

1. All repressed kulak [rich, landowning peasant], criminal, and other anti-Soviet elements are to be divided into two categories:

   a) The first category are the most hostile of the enumerated elements. They are subject to immediate arrest, and after their cases have been considered by a three-person tribunal they are TO BE SHOT.

   b) In the second category are the other less active though also hostile element. They are subject to arrest and imprisonment in a camp for 8 to 10 years, and the most evil and socially dangerous of these to incarceration for the same period in prison, as determined by the three-person tribunal.

2. In accordance with data determined by the people's commissars of the republic-level NKVD [People's Commissariats of Internal Affairs] the following numbers of individuals are subject to repression.

|  | First Category | Second Category | Total |
|---|---|---|---|
| 1. Azerbaijan Soviet Socialist Republic | 1,500 | 3,750 | 5,250 |
| 2. Armenian Soviet Socialist Republic | 500 | 1,000 | 1,500 |
| 3. Belorussian Soviet Socialist Republic | 2,000 | 10,000 | 12,000 |
| [ ... ] | | | |
| 39. Leningrad region | 4,000 | 10,000 | 14,000 |
| 40. Moscow region | 5,000 | 30,000 | 35,000 |
| [ ... ] | | | |
| [ ... ] | | | |
| Total | 72,950 | 177,500 | 250,450 |

III. The operation is to begin on August 5, 1937, and to be completed in four months.

## DOCUMENT 9

*Source: "International Communist Women's Day," celebratory article in the official newspaper* Pravda, *March 9, 1939.*

Yesterday, on March 8, a celebration of International Communist Women's Day took place in the Bolshoi Theater. Comrade K. I. Nikolayeva talked about the heroic and energetic path taken by the women of our country, and about the concern for women shown by the Soviet government and by the party of Lenin and Stalin. Her speech showed how the Soviet woman has secured an honored place in the political and public life of our country. Deputies to the Supreme Soviet include 189 women. What a clear example of the political maturity of the Soviet woman! Comrade Nikolayeva spoke about the heroism of Soviet women and the unforgettable [record-breaking polar] flight taken by pilots Valentina Grizodubova, Polina Osipenko, and Maria Raskova. The heroines were located right there, and the hall greeted them with warm applause. Comrade Nikolayeva cited the example of Zinaida Troitskaya, who successfully mastered the complex craft of driving a locomotive engine, became an engineer, and now is the director of the Moscow regional railway. Her success was recognized with warm applause.

## DOCUMENT 10

*Source: Literacy rates among the Russian-speaking population of late Imperial Russia and the Soviet Union, compiled from census data and the Soviet Ministry of Education, 1897-1955.*

|      | **Literacy Rate** |
| ---- | ----------------- |
| 1897 | 24%               |
| 1917 | 45%               |
| 1926 | 56%               |
| 1937 | 75%               |
| 1939 | 81.1%             |
| 1955 | 99.9%             |

## SAMPLE ANSWER

Russia's communist revolution created one of the modern era's worst dictatorships, but was originally motivated by a utopian desire to overcome the injustice and backwardness of the tsarist regime. Between 1917 and 1939, the USSR gave more rights to certain groups (Docs. 2, 3, and 9). It also modernized rapidly (Docs. 4, 5, and 10). However, because the Soviet state relied so much on force to bring about change, these improvements came at the cost of inefficiency and repression that was heavier than under tsarism (Docs. 1, 6, 7, and 8).

*[In three sentences, this paragraph states the thesis. It identifies the question's major elements (the subject, time period, and task, which involves causes and consequences). It also qualifies the causes and consequences by indicating specifically what will be said about them. Finally, it provides analysis by explaining how utopian intentions went awry in the long term.*

*REMEMBER: Vague language = weak thesis! Be as specific as possible—but without getting swamped. Don't forget that your thesis shouldn't be too long or contain too much detail.*

| Group | Document Nos. | Category | Points of View |
|---|---|---|---|
| 1 | 2, 3, 9 | making certain groups better off | Lenin; poster artist; official media |
| 2 | 4, 5, 10 | modernization | officially approved songwriters; photographer (official media); government statistics |
| 3 | 1, 6, 7, 8 | dictatorship/inefficiency | communist opponent of Lenin; private letter from ordinary worker; memoir of ordinary farmer; high-level gov't official |
| | additional document 1 | | |
| | additional document 2 | | |

*The chart above maps out how this essay will organize the documents. It also leaves room for notes about each document's point of view and the two additional documents that need to be identified and explained (although these are left blank in this case). You should create such a map when you write your own DBQ.*

*Keep in mind that other groupings are possible. For example, one could write about gender (3 and 9), modernization (4, 5, 10, and 6 as an illustration of how not everything went well), and dictatorial tendencies (1, 2, 7, and 8). Or industrial and social progress (3, 4, 5, 6, 9), the countryside (2 and 7), and dictatorial tendencies (1 and 8). In both of these cases, document 6 could conceivably be moved to the "dictatorial tendencies" group. Be open-minded about how to group the documents!]*

In theory, Marxism's goal is complete social and economic equality: tearing down traditional hierarchies and giving more rights and wealth to ordinary people. In his newspaper *Pravda*, Lenin, the revolution's leader and an ideological extremist, calls on lower-class peasants to end economic inequality by using force against wealthier peasants. Although the justifiability of such violence is debatable, Lenin's government largely erased the tsarist-era gap between Russia's old elite and its working classes. Russian revolutionaries also claimed to champion the cause of women's rights, a priority illustrated in Documents 3 and 9. Under tsarism, Russia had been one of Europe's most patriarchal societies. Women got the vote shortly after the tsar's fall, and Soviet women worked in greater numbers than anywhere else in interwar Europe. Doc. 3, in poster form, reminds Soviet women of all the advantages that communism had supposedly given them in just three short years, including jobs and better education. Doc. 3 is official propaganda, so while it may not be actually lying, its purpose is to portray women's conditions as positively as possible. The same is true of the *Pravda* article about International Women's Day in Doc. 9. Here, the accomplishments of female politicians, pilots, and engineers are celebrated, and while these successes were real, the article's purpose is to give credit for them to Stalin and his government.

*[This paragraph covers the first group of documents. Note that it doesn't describe the documents' content in detail. Instead, it uses information from the documents to (a) support the thesis, (b) bring in "outside" content, and (c) illustrate point of view for all of the documents.*

*Other pieces of "outside" content could have been included here. Lenin's "Advice" was written during the early days of the Russian Civil War, which further explains the harsh tone. Especially during the Lenin years, the Soviet regime appointed a number of women to prominent positions, such as Nadezhda Krupskaya (Lenin's wife, who helped form national educational policy) and Alexandra Kollontai (the first woman to serve as ambassador from a major European power). This paragraph includes more general bits of "outside" content (the patriarchalism of tsarist Russia, the high percentage of Soviet women in the workplace, and when Russian women got the vote). The more you know about a particular topic, the better off you'll be, but no matter what the question is about, try to add relevant information whenever you can.*

*What about additional documents? Because the sources pertaining to women were both written from an official perspective, this would have been a good opportunity to talk about the usefulness of having private testimony from a Soviet woman, perhaps in the form of a diary or a letter to a friend, to see whether ordinary women felt they had really been treated as well as the propaganda suggests. This sample essay is structured in such a way as to save discussion of the additional documents for the final paragraph. But this can also be done as you go along—you should do what makes you most comfortable.]*

Before the revolution, Russia had lagged far behind the rest of Europe economically and socially. Lenin spoke often about narrowing this gap, and Stalin's famous Five-Year Plans were intended to industrialize Russia overnight. One aspect of this modernization effort involved aviation, one of the world's newest and most exciting technologies, as demonstrated by the international enthusiasm for record-breaking flights like Charles Lindbergh's. The 1920 song "Ever Higher" links the creation of the Soviet air force not just with questions of defense, but with the larger utopian goal of using technology to instill pride and achieve all of humanity's dreams—or, as the lyrics put it, "to make fairy tales come true." Without words, Dmitrii Debabov's photo of a Soviet worker in 1930, when the First Five-Year Plan was at full steam, makes the construction of Magnitogorsk, a brand-new industrial plant, look heroic as well. Documents 4 and 5 are produced by artists with their own creative vision, but also under a censorship system that required their work to be approved by the state, so the picture of progress they paint is not objective. A more reliable indicator of Soviet modernizing success is presented in Document 10. Although Soviet statistics are not entirely trustworthy, the steady rise in literacy after 1917 speaks to the USSR's ability to outperform the tsarist regime in terms of public education.

*[This paragraph deals with the second group of documents. As before, the point of view is discussed in each case. Bits of "outside" content include the mention of Lindbergh to contextualize the symbolic importance of aviation and the reference to Stalin's Five-Year Plans. Other "outside" knowledge about Magnitogorsk or the Plans' other "hero-projects" (major railroads, canals, metallurgical plants, or hydroelectric dams) could have been included here.*

*Note that Document 6, which also has to do with Magnitogorsk, could have been included here as a pessimistic counterpart to Document 5. As far as additional documents go, it might be helpful to have diary or memoir evidence from an ordinary citizen to see if public enthusiasm for aviation was as high as "Ever Higher" suggests and, if so, whether that enthusiasm translated into positive feelings for the Soviet regime. Also useful might be discussion of the role played by forced labor in the completion of many of the USSR's industrial projects. As noted above, this essay will include additional documents in a separate concluding paragraph, but you may wish to discuss them as you go along.]*

Whatever progress the Soviets made toward their utopian goals, the price was frequent disillusionment and growing dictatorship. The frustration expressed by the anonymous worker in Document 6 (the only document that communicates a sincere and privately-held opinion) exposes the gross inefficiency that characterized the building of Magnitogorsk—a project portrayed officially as such a grand cause in Document 5. The Soviet state's dictatorial tendencies were apparent from the very start, as seen in Rosa Luxemburg's comments on the Russian revolution during its earliest days. A fellow communist, Luxemburg was happy to see Lenin come to power, but feared that his interpretation of the "dictatorship of the proletariat" concept would lead not to the empowerment of the masses, but to the permanent concentration of power in the hands of a small Party elite—a prediction that turned out to be correct. Documents 7 and 8 illustrate the brutality of the resulting dictatorship. Stalin's Five-Year Plans were accompanied by the collectivization of peasant communities into state-run farms and the wholesale confiscation of grain, a policy that caused a horrific famine.

Miron Dolot was one of the millions of Ukrainians who suffered through this experience, and his memoir shows how the regime treated peasants, especially uncooperative ones, with unbelievable cruelty. Worst of all is the order given by Stalin's secret police chief in Document 8, at the height of the great purges carried out by the Soviet government in the late 1930s. Yezhov, a high-level henchman, calls for the execution and imprisonment of tens of thousands of people on grounds that they are "anti-Soviet" threats. Stunningly, what Yezhov (or the regime he is speaking for) seems most concerned about is not the question of guilt or innocence, but how many people can be arrested from the USSR's different regions—as if it were a quota system, almost like the Five-Year Plans.

*[And now the final group of documents. Again, point of view is consistently addressed. The documents are not simply listed or described, but mined for information that supports the thesis. Bits of "outside" information include mention of the collectivization campaign (and its role in causing famine) and the great purges. If you happened to know more about these events and had time to include more information about them, that would help to earn expanded-core points.]*

As rich as the current selection of documents is, additional perspectives would shed more light on the causes and especially the consequences of Russia's revolution. Particularly when it comes to the positive changes supposedly brought about by the Soviet regime, the documents available to us give mainly the regime's point of view. Did ordinary people feel that the revolution had improved their lives? A letter or diary entry written privately by a woman would tell us more about whether Soviet women would have agreed with the propaganda put forward in Documents 3 and 9—or whether their feelings would have contradicted them the way that the author of Document 6 contradicts the message expressed in Document 5. Also, excerpts from diaries, letters, or memoirs might help to determine whether Soviet citizens were truly inspired to love the regime by technological exploits like aviation, the way Document 4 implies they were.

*[What should you do in your last paragraph? If you have enough time, and if you've already dealt with TWO additional documents in your earlier paragraphs, you could wrap things up with a formal conclusion. You can restate your thesis, although you shouldn't simply repeat your introduction. You might carry the argument forward by mentioning that the same tension between modernization and dictatorship continued all throughout the rest of the Soviet period. Or that the balance between the two improved somewhat after Stalin's death in 1953.*

*That's one approach. This essay illustrates another, which is to forego a formal conclusion (which by itself doesn't directly earn points) and concentrate separately on the two additional documents. This provides the feel of a finishing touch, because you're reflecting on—and adding to—what you've just written. It also draws more attention to your analytical thinking about sources than if you shoehorn discussion of additional documents into other paragraphs. The major risk, of course, is that if you leave this till the end and run out of time, you won't do it at all. So if you adopt this approach, budget your time wisely!]*

# CONTINUITY AND CHANGE OVER TIME (CCOT) ESSAY STRATEGIES

Another type of essay required by the AP exam is the continuity and change over time (CCOT) question. This tests your ability to trace a broad trend—related to one of the five course themes (see page 7)—over a long period of time.

In most cases, you will be asked to focus on a particular nation or region, although you may be allowed to choose one from a list of two or more places. Other CCOT questions may ask you to illustrate a certain trend by drawing on examples from one or more regions, but without specifying which ones. Sometimes the CCOT focuses on the relationship *between* two regions. See the box below for how these options may be presented.

---

**SAMPLE CCOT QUESTIONS**

1. Analyze changes and continuities in the formation of diaspora communities in the period between 600 and 1750 c.e. Include examples from at least TWO different world regions.

2. Analyze changes and continuities in trade networks between Asia and Africa from 300 to 1450 c.e.

3. Analyze changes and continuities in the formation of labor systems in ONE of the following regions between 600 b.c.e. and 600 c.e.

   North and South America
   the Middle East

---

## Approaching the Continuity and Change Over Time Essay

The CCOT is less complicated than the DBQ, but certain tasks still need to be accomplished just the right way to fulfill the basic core and move on to the expanded core.

As with the other essays, aim to spend roughly 40 minutes writing the CCOT essay. This includes the 5 or so minutes you should give yourself to think about the question and outline your answer.

Perhaps the key thing to remember about the CCOT essay is that **continuity is as important as change**. And yet students either forget to cover it adequately or find it harder to write about. Also, the examples you provide should **cover the entire time period** in question. This, too, can be difficult unless you put your mind to it. You will have to include a **minimum number of pieces of evidence**. At least once, you must demonstrate a **clear instance of analysis**, and you must also connect your essay to a larger **world historical context**.

On the following page is the official AP scoring guide for the CCOT.

## Generic Scoring Guide for AP World History
## Continuity and Change Over Time Essay

| Basic Core | Points | Expanded Core | Points |
|---|---|---|---|
| 1. Thesis deals acceptably with the global issues and time period(s) in question. | 1 | Goes beyond the basic core of 1–7 points. A score of 7 must be earned before a student can gain expanded-core points. | 0–2 |
| 2. Deals with all parts of the question, though not necessarily evenly or completely. | 2 | Examples: | |
| (Deals with most parts of the question; for instance, change but not continuity.) | (1) | • Begins with an explicit, analytical, and comprehensive thesis. | |
| 3. Backs up the thesis with appropriate historical evidence. | 2 | • Analyzes all aspects of the question: global issues, chronology, causation, change, continuity, content. | |
| (Partially backs up thesis with appropriate historical evidence.) | (1) | • Gives ample historical evidence to back up thesis. | |
| 4. Uses historical context to explain continuity and change over time. | 1 | • Creatively links topic to relevant ideas, trends, and events. | |
| 5. Analyzes the process of change and continuity. | 1 | | |
| **Subtotal** | **7** | **Subtotal** | **2** |
| **TOTAL 9** | | | |

## THE CCOT THESIS

The CCOT thesis must identify and qualify at least one thing about the question's main subject that changed during the time period in question, AND at least one thing that stayed the same. ("Qualify" means NOT simply restating that there was change and continuity, but saying specifically what changed and what stayed the same.) The thesis should allude to the time period itself, and it should take an analytical approach.

An effective way to give your thesis analytical weight is to concentrate on the cause(s) and effect(s) of the changes and continuities. Other angles may occur to you, but any thesis based on "how" or "why" is an obvious and usable one.

By contrast, remember that vagueness = weakness! Don't just say that "many things changed during this period, but many things also stayed the same." Neither is it useful to argue that "change outweighed continuity during these years," or that "we see more continuities than changes during this period." This sort of non-thesis will annoy your reader.

Keep continuity real. Identifying continuity can be difficult. But whatever you do, DON'T resort to the common fallback of claiming that "a key continuity is that things constantly changed"—or other variations on this theme. Change is not continuity, and readers will be irked if you say it is.

Don't overdo! As always, keep the thesis short and straightforward. The thesis cannot earn you basic-core points for evidence, context, or analysis (even though it should *be* analytical). So save that sort of material for the essay's main body.

## Thoroughness: Change and Continuity

Not only should the thesis refer to change and continuity, the main body of the essay must do the same. The best way to do this is to devote one of your paragraphs to continuities and another paragraph to changes. That puts two basic-core points automatically in your pocket.

## Evidence (magic number = at least 5 or 6)

To earn points, enrich your essay with as much concrete (and relevant) information as possible. Readers are told to look for a minimum number of pieces of evidence as they tally up basic-core points. (This changes from year to year, but you should aim to include at least five pieces of evidence to fulfill the basic core.)

To begin with, your evidence must be APPLICABLE. In other words, it must relate to the question's main topic. Obviously, this means avoiding errors or irrelevancy. (For example, talking about the elimination of foot-binding—a Chinese practice—as evidence of change in the status of women in sub-Saharan Africa would do you no good.) But applicability can be trickier when a CCOT question deals somehow with relationships between two regions. In that case, each piece of evidence must apply to both regions, not just one. (For instance, if you're writing about trade between Asia and Africa between 300 and 1450 c.e., mentioning the Silk Road—a Eurasian trade route—will do you no good unless you discuss how goods traded along that route made their way to and from Africa.)

Another rule is to BE SPECIFIC when presenting evidence. If you're describing technological innovations that facilitated the growth of maritime networks between 600 and 1450 c.e., don't settle for saying that "shipbuilding and navigational techniques improved." Mention concrete items like the lodestone compass, the lateen sail, the dhow, the junk, the ability to predict weather patterns like the monsoon season, and the adoption of the sternpost rudder. Not only is this more likely to impress your reader, you'll probably be credited with more pieces of evidence (for more on this, see the point below).

Make each piece of evidence look DISTINCT. You don't want your reader lumping together items that you consider to be separate bits of evidence. This can happen, though, if you present evidence lazily—as in this description of the Columbian Exchange: "Among the items that passed back and forth between the Old and New Worlds were corn, potatoes, coffee, the horse, tomatoes, bananas, and sugarcane, not to mention diseases like smallpox and measles." That's a lot of evidence, right? Maybe . . . but a reader might just count it as ONE piece of evidence, under the heading of "items passing back and forth," or perhaps two pieces (food items + diseases). See how a fairly easy repackaging improves things: "The global impact of the Columbian Exchange proved astounding in many ways. High-yield crops like corn and potatoes traveled from the Americas to Afro-Eurasia, <u>where they improved diets and boosted population growth</u>. The horse, transplanted to the New World, <u>dramatically altered the lifestyle of many Native American peoples</u>. Bananas, sugarcane, and coffee from the Old World grew well in the New World, <u>giving rise to plantation agriculture and long-term dependence on slavery</u>."

See the difference? Even if the underlined passages weren't there, breaking one long list into three distinct sentences increases the chance of earning credit for three pieces of evidence. As for what the underlined passages can do for you, see the next item.

## Analysis

At least once, and preferably more than once, you will need to demonstrate a high-level understanding of cause and effect. HOW and/or WHY did something change or stay the same? What was the CONSEQUENCE or IMPACT of that change or continuity? You will probably find it easier to analyze change, although you should look for opportunities to do both. What is a good way to earn this point? EVERY TIME you include a piece of evidence, try to think of a "how" or "why" issue it's related to. Look at the underlined passages in the box above on the Columbian Exchange: they enable each piece of evidence to do two jobs at once. Not only does each one *show* that change took place, but each one *explains* the change's impact and importance.

## World Historical Context

This item frequently prevents students from completing the basic core, and AP readers often struggle to find ways to give credit for it. At some point, you must CONNECT one of the changes OR continuities discussed in your essay with a larger (and relevant) GLOBAL TREND that applies to most or all of the time period in question (generally interpreted to mean at least half of the time period). This cannot be a quick or casual reference; you must spell it out explicitly. One technique is to use your final paragraph to do this, although if you can touch on context in the main body of the essay, it can't hurt to do that as well.

As you plan your CCOT answer, think about what trends are unfolding worldwide during the era you're writing about. Whatever you choose can relate to any of the AP World History themes—environmental-technological, cultural, political, economic, or social—although it has to be broad enough to cover at least half the time period. Does your topic fit into that general trend? If so, how? If not, does it run against the grain of that general trend in an interesting way?

Some examples:

- Growth of trade networks in Africa from 600 to 1450 C.E. (change) > expansion of Islam (context)
- Rise of the Atlantic slave trade (change) > growing appetite for cheap labor caused by exploitation of colonies, plantation monoculture, and early industrialization (context)
- Cultural and intellectual advancement in Europe during the Renaissance (change) > general flourishing of arts and culture in technologically advanced societies worldwide between 1000 and 1750 C.E. (context)
- The fall of a particular empire (change) > does it relate to a larger migratory pattern? or a widespread environmental trend? or something else? (context)
- The rise of religious fundamentalism in the modern era (change) > does this contradict or run counter to the general tendency for modern societies to become more secular? (context)

Spelling it out: As noted above, you really want your reader to NOTICE it when you address context. Whether you do this in the final paragraph or in the main body of your essay (or both), it can't hurt to draw attention to this part of your essay. Feel free to use phrases such as "Concerning the world-historical context . . . ," or "If we look at the global context . . . ," or "To place this trend in a worldwide context. . . ."

## Sample Question

You are to answer the following question. You should spend 5 minutes organizing or outlining your essay. Write an essay that

- Has a relevant thesis and supports that thesis with appropriate historical evidence.
- Addresses all parts of the question.
- Uses world historical context to show continuities and changes over time.
- Analyzes the process of continuity and change over time.

2. Analyze changes and continuities in the status and treatment of women in ONE of the following places from 1000 to 1750 C.E.

    India

    Japan

    Sub-Saharan Africa

**SAMPLE ANSWER**

As Japan underwent political and religious change between 1000 and 1750 C.E., so too did the place of women in Japanese society. The greatest continuity during these years was that, throughout this period, Japanese women were relegated to secondary roles and positions. On the other hand, and arguably with greater impact, the rise of samurai regimes and the growing influence of belief systems like Neo-Confucianism caused a steep decline in the status of Japanese women, especially those of the upper classes.

*[As all opening paragraphs should, this paragraph briefly* identifies *the question's subject, time period, and task (in this case identifying* one continuity *and* one change*). It also* qualifies *the change and continuity by formally defining them. Finally, it provides* analysis, *both by stating what caused the change and by asserting that change outweighs continuity. (A thesis based only on the latter would fail, but here it's presented as one aspect of a more complicated issue.)]*

At the beginning of this period, Japan was ruled by the culturally refined Heian dynasty, which collapsed in the late 1100s and gave way to a series of decentralized, feudal samurai regimes from the 1200s through the 1500s. These were followed by the Tokugawa shogunate, which reunified Japan at around 1600 and reigned until the mid-1800s. But no matter who governed, certain things remained the same for Japanese women. Whatever their social class, they remained subservient to men. Although during earlier periods of Japanese history, a number of empresses reigned, women during the Heian era onward enjoyed political influence only if they were able to exercise personal influence over powerful husbands. At all points during this period, male children were more highly prized than daughters, and female infanticide was not uncommon. The need to provide daughters with dowries made it expensive for any family to arrange marriages for them, and it was always easier for husbands to divorce their wives than vice versa. A final continuity is that women of the lower classes were less restricted in their behavior than those of the upper classes, who were more constrained by rules of "proper" conduct.

*[A standard way to structure the CCOT essay is to dedicate one paragraph to continuity and another to change, ensuring that you earn both basic-core points for "dealing with all parts of the question." Whether you tackle continuity before change—as shown here—is up to you, but you should consider doing so. Not only is continuity generally harder to discuss, and therefore better to get out of the way, putting it first naturally allows you to set a* baseline—*what were things like at the beginning of the time period in question? Notice how the paragraph opens with a brief political overview: this provides a framework for the rest of the discussion, and by showing a detailed understanding of the basic background, it may earn you expanded-core points.*

*Continuity is clearly dealt with, and* evidence *of it is provided several times. They are not as specific or analytical as those used in the next paragraph to demonstrate change, but they are sufficient to meet the basic core and have placed this essay well on the way toward the expanded core.]*

Important as these continuities were, however, the changes were more dramatic and, particularly for upper-class women, quite negative. With its emphasis on cultural grandeur, the Heian regime offered aristocratic women many opportunities for education. It prized their wit and artistic accomplishments, allowing them a great deal of social and even political influence. Lady Murasaki, the Heian-era author of *The Tale of Genji*, remains the best-known of Japan's early novelists, male or female. But civil war ended the Heian era and led to centuries of samurai conflict. During these centuries, a new warrior ethos, embodied by the feudalistic code of Bushido—which, like chivalry among medieval European knights, stressed loyalty, honor, and military prowess—took hold, and women's intellectual and cultural pursuits were sharply devalued. Women of the samurai class were now expected to obey their husbands without question, and could be put to death if they did not. Nor did the unification of Japan under the Tokugawa improve conditions for women. Tokugawa society was extremely hierarchical, a trend reinforced by the shoguns' attraction to Neo-Confucian ideology after 1600. As it had in China for many years, Neo-Confucianism stressed obedience and staying in one's "place," and it greatly reduced the status of women throughout East Asia. As for non-elite women, although no one would call them free to do as they pleased, they were less burdened by most of these changes—although they found that social stratification under the Tokugawa shoguns made dowries more costly than before, and divorces even harder to obtain.

> [This paragraph focuses on change, mustering several pieces of evidence to demonstrate it. Evidence here is more specific than in the continuity paragraph. Analysis is provided as well—more than once and strong enough to satisfy, and go beyond, the basic core. There is one comparative note, where Bushido is linked with European chivalry, and this may help earn expanded-core points.]

Placed in global context, gender-related trends in Japan paralleled those that played out in many societies during this era. Virtually nowhere could women be said to have attained equal status between 1000 and 1750 C.E. In fact, elite classes the world over tended to restrain women's conduct more when their societies experienced transitions to militarized feudalism, as in medieval Europe during most of this era, or toward increased social stratification. Also, religion in multiple regions played a role in defining women's positions as secondary: Neo-Confucianism in Japan (and other parts of Asia), Catholicism in Europe, South Asia's Hindu caste system, and so on. As a final note, the unequal treatment referred to above prevailed in Japan long after the era under question: equal rights for women took a long time to come to Japan—not until the 1900s—and one could argue that the influence of this traditional sexism is still felt today.

> [While one could try to add a formal conclusion to this essay, it would be better to use the time to (a) address world historical context, which is done here, and (b) try to score expanded-core points for "providing links with relevant ideas, events, trends in an innovative way"—the point of the link to recent and present times. This also provides a graceful epilogue to finish off the essay.]

## COMPARATIVE ESSAY STRATEGIES

Of the AP exam's three free-response questions, the comparative essay is generally thought to be the least complicated. Most students save it for last, and while that may make sense for you as well, don't make the mistake of treating it with complacency. Because they are often rushing to beat the clock by the time they get to the comparative essay, students sometimes perform more poorly on it than they expect. Don't let this happen to you.

Fundamentally, the comparative essay will ask you to compare *and* contrast the way a trend or development unfolded in at least two regions or societies over the same period of time. The trend or development will be related to one of the AP World History curriculum's five themes.

## Approaching the Comparative Essay

The comparative essay may seem to be the most straightforward of the free-response questions, but you must still follow correct procedures to break out of the basic core and into the expanded core.

As with the other essays, aim to spend roughly 40 minutes writing the comparative essay. This includes the 5 or so minutes you should give yourself to think about the question and outline your answer.

The easiest thing to forget about the comparative essay is that **comparison** in this sense means to **compare and contrast**—or, in the language most commonly used by the exam, **analyze similarities and differences**. As with the CCOT essay, you will have to include a **minimum number of pieces of evidence**, and you must demonstrate at least one **clear instance of analysis**. For expanded-core points, it is desirable to connect your essay to a larger global context and to demonstrate some knowledge of parts of the world other than those you are comparing.

Below is the official AP scoring guide for the comparative essay.

### Generic Scoring Guide for AP World History Comparative Essay

| Basic Core | Points | Expanded Core | Points |
|---|---|---|---|
| 1. Opens with acceptable thesis. (Compares the issues or themes specified.) | 1 | Goes beyond the basic core of 1–6 points. The basic core score of 7 must be earned before a student can gain expanded core points. | 0–2 |
| 2. Deals with all parts of the question, perhaps not evenly or thoroughly. | 2 | Examples: | |
| (Deals with most parts of the question.) | (1) | • Opens with an analytical, clear, comprehensive thesis. | |
| 3. Backs up thesis with appropriate historical evidence. | 2 | • Analyzes relevant parts of the question: comparisons, chronology, causation, connections, themes, interactions, content. | |
| (Partially backs up thesis with appropriate historical evidence.) | (1) | • Gives ample historical evidence to back up thesis. | |
| 4. Provides one or two relevant, direct comparisons between or among societies. | 1 | • Links comparisons to larger global context. | |
| 5. Analyzes one or more reasons for a difference or similarity discussed in a direct comparison. | 1 | • Draws several direct comparisons between or among societies. | |
| | | • Regularly analyzes the causes and effects of the resullts of key similarities and differences. | |
| **Subtotal** | **7** | **Subtotal** | **2** |
| **TOTAL 9** | | | |

## The Comparative Thesis

The comparative thesis must identify and qualify at least one similarity AND at least one difference. ("Qualify" does NOT mean vaguely asserting that there were similarities and differences but saying specifically what those similarities and differences were.) The thesis should allude to the time period itself, and it should take an analytical approach.

---

**MAKE YOUR THESIS MEANINGFUL**

Just as on the CCOT, a vague thesis is a weak thesis. Certainly you should not base your thesis solely on whether there were more similarities than differences or vice versa (you can raise this point, but it shouldn't be your only point). Find a "how" or "why" question to focus on.

As with the other questions, don't overdo! Keep your thesis short and straightforward. The thesis cannot earn you basic-core points for evidence, context, or analysis (even though it should *be* analytical). Save the extras for later.

---

## Thoroughness: Similarities and Differences (rule of thumb = at least 2 apiece)

Not only must the thesis compare *and* contrast, the essay's main body has to do the same. An easy way to do this is to devote one of your paragraphs to similarities and another to differences. By itself, that earns two basic-core points. You should try to give equal weight to likenesses and similarities, although you do not have to be exact about this. The same is true of the two regions you are comparing: the rules say that you do not have to deal with each of them evenly, but it's a good idea to aim for something close to a 50-50 split.

## Evidence (magic number = at least 5)

To earn points, enrich your essay with as much concrete (and relevant) information as possible. Readers are told to look for a minimum number of pieces of evidence as they tally up basic-core points. (This changes from year to year, but you should aim to include at least five pieces of evidence to fulfill the basic core.)

---

**RULES OF EVIDENCE**

As with the CCOT essay, your pieces of evidence must be APPLICABLE. In other words, they must relate to the question's main topic and avoid errors and irrelevancy.

Also like the CCOT, the comparative essay becomes stronger if the evidence it contains is as SPECIFIC as possible, and if each piece is presented as a DISTINCT item.

When it comes to the first four or five pieces of evidence presented, the comparative essay requires an EVEN SPLIT, or at least fairly close to an even split, between similarities and differences, and between the two regions or societies being compared.

---

## Analysis

As with the CCOT essay, the comparative essay will call upon you to show at least once that you have a sophisticated understanding of cause and effect (how, why, what consequence, etc.). For the basic core point, you need to analyze ONE similarity OR difference. You'll be better off if you can analyze one of each, and much more so if you can include more analysis than that.

## Direct, Relevant Comparison

The rubric for the comparative essay calls for a "direct, relevant comparison" between the two regions or societies covered by the question, BEYOND those mentioned in the thesis. If you address enough similarities and differences in the main body of your thesis (at least two apiece), you may well fulfill this requirement—just make sure that not everything you include in the main body is alluded to in the thesis! Another possibility is to use your final paragraph not for a formal conclusion, but to make one last comparison that goes beyond what you've already done.

## Sample Question

You are to answer the following question. You should spend 5 minutes organizing or outlining your essay. Write an essay that

- Has a relevant thesis and supports that thesis with appropriate historical evidence.
- Addresses all parts of the question.
- Makes direct, relevant comparisons.
- Analyzes relevant reasons for similarities and differences.

3. Analyze similarities and differences in how TWO of the following regions modernized between 1900 and 1945.
    Latin America
    East Asia
    The Middle East

### SAMPLE ANSWER

The first half of the twentieth century brought immense changes to many parts of the globe. Among these was increased modernization in a number of non-Western regions, including Latin America and the Middle East. Both places faced similar obstacles, such as relative socio-economic backwardness, heavy influence from outside powers, and limited success in the past with representative government. There were, however, key differences as well. Latin American states, with their generally longer history of independence, tended to be more modern already. Traditional religion was less of a barrier to change in Latin America than in the Middle East, and events like the world wars and the Great Depression affected both areas differently. On the whole, these differences outweighed the similarities, causing Latin America to make more progress toward modernization than the Middle East.

*[As with the opening paragraphs for the DBQ and CCOT, this paragraph briefly identifies the question's subject, time period, and task (referring to at least one similarity and one difference). It also qualifies some similarities and differences by spelling out precisely what they are. Finally, it provides analysis by making an assertion about the outcome of the trend in question—and by explaining WHY things turned out the way they did.]*

At the beginning of this period, both Latin America and the Middle East suffered from social and economic underdevelopment. Wealthy elites, whether colonial, corporate, or royal and aristocratic, benefited from the unbalanced exploitation of a handful of commodities. In Latin America, these included foodstuffs (beef, coffee, bananas, and other fruit) and natural resources such as copper, steel, fertilizer, and, in some countries, oil. Oil was even more central to the economies of the Middle East, just as it is today. This "banana republic" overexploitation of resources discouraged the healthy diversification of economies and kept societies rigidly stratified, with small upper classes dominating large, impoverished majorities. Although some of this changed between 1900 and 1945, it limited modernization throughout the period. Another similarity is that Latin American and Middle Eastern states tended to be heavily influenced by outside powers, both before and during this half-century. Prior to World War I, much of the Middle East was ruled by the Ottoman Empire or fell into European spheres of influence—and even though the Ottomans fell after WWI, European spheres of influence grew even larger when the post-WWI mandate system placed much of the Middle East, especially the Ottomans' former Arab possessions, under French and English custody. Most Latin American states had been free since the wars of independence of the early 1800s, but foreign investors (like America's United Fruit Company) wielded much power over Latin American governments, and the U.S. government regarded the region as part of its political sphere of influence. The Pan-American Union and even Franklin Roosevelt's Good Neighbor Policy were instruments of U.S. diplomatic interests throughout Latin America. Even when these outside interests did not deliberately oppose modernization (and they often did), it was rarely in their interest to actively support economic diversification, and because dealing with cooperative elite classes was easier than negotiating with elected governments representing a range of popular interests, they did not necessarily support democracy either.

*[This paragraph deals with similarities. Note that it does NOT attempt to give a complete narrative account of either region's history during this period. Instead, it compares two points directly and in detail. It uses several pieces of concrete evidence to illustrate the comparisons, and it balances its coverage of both regions—not only is roughly equal attention devoted to each (not strictly necessary, although it's a good idea), but the pieces of evidence are evenly split between them (this IS a requirement). Pieces of evidence are not merely listed, but contribute to analysis by concentrating on HOW and WHY modernization was slowed by the two factors dealt with in this paragraph.]*

On the other hand, important differences moved Latin America farther down the path toward modernization. To begin with, Latin American states, although non-industrialized by the standards of Western Europe and North America, had undergone more industrialization than most parts of the Middle East. With this kind of foundation to build on, countries like Mexico and Argentina, for example, found it easier to create sizable industrial sectors after

WWI. Latin American states also had a tradition of constitutional rule stretching back to the era of Simón Bolívar in the early 1800s, and while those constitutions were not always perfectly followed, they created a more favorable climate for progress when it came to gender equity, enlarging the middle classes, and reforming electoral systems. Less of this was possible in the Middle East. Another crucial difference involves the role of religion. Although Catholicism was overwhelmingly central to Latin American culture, and although it tended to exert a conservative influence over public life there, by this point in history it was not nearly as much a barrier to social and economic progress as traditional Islam still was in the Middle East. It is no coincidence that the Middle Eastern states that modernized most were the small handful where energetic Westernizing autocrats—most famously Mustafa Kemal Ataturk of Turkey and Reza Khan Pahlavi of Persia (Iran)—defied the will of Muslim clerics, secularized their states, industrialized their economies and educational systems, and, in Ataturk's case, gave women the vote. By the early twentieth century, Latin America could modernize without such fierce conflict with institutional religion. In the Middle East, by contrast, it remains a struggle even today to balance modernization with respect for Islamic tradition.

*[This paragraph moves on to differences, three of which are described. Coverage of the two regions is not exactly balanced 50–50, but it does not need to be. Numerous pieces of evidence are provided, and these ARE more or less divided equally between the Middle East and Latin America. As in paragraph 2, evidence is presented in such a way as to strengthen analysis, and not just to story-tell or to fill the paragraph with raw information.]*

One last comparison that deserves consideration is the prevalence of dictatorship in both regions during these years. Whether they were monarchs or autocratic strongmen, authoritarian leaders in both regions were often the agents of modernizing change. In the Middle East, the primary impulse for economic and social modernization was typically the will of determined authoritarians, such as the above-mentioned Ataturk and Pahlavi. Among the Latin American dictators who promoted industrialization and other modernizing changes were the Perons in Argentina and the Vargas government in Brazil.

*[Rather than compose a formal conclusion, this essay uses the last paragraph to provide one more "direct, relevant comparison." This ensures that the basic core is met, and it also adds extra content that might help with the expanded core.]*

# UNIT 1

## TECHNOLOGICAL AND ENVIRONMENTAL TRANSFORMATIONS (8000–600 B.C.E.)

# Unit 1 Short Cut

## GENERAL REMARKS

Hominid, or humanlike, creatures appeared on earth approximately 3 to 4 million years ago. Modern humans (*Homo sapiens sapiens*) evolved sometime 200,000 years ago. According to most scholars, their birthplace was East Africa. From there, they spread to the rest of the globe, starting around 100,000 years ago.

The period from approximately 2.5 million years ago to 5,000 or 6,000 years ago is referred to as the **Stone Age**. During this time, human communities took shape but remained at a relatively low level of social and technological development. The principal form of social organization was kinship-based **hunting and foraging** (known more traditionally as hunting and gathering). After around 10,000 years ago, or 8000 B.C.E., during the **Neolithic Revolution**, human societies came to use a wider and more sophisticated variety of tools—increasingly made out of metal as well as out of stone—allowing them to populate a larger variety of ecosystems. They learned how to domesticate animals and plants, giving rise to **pastoralism** and **agriculture**. They developed elaborate **religions**, invented systems of recordkeeping (especially **writing**), and devised more complex forms of economic exchange (including **trade**) and social organization (**villages**, then **cities**, with **labor specialization** and **social hierarchies** led typically by **patriarchal elites**). Agriculture, city-building, and **metallurgy** vastly increased humanity's impact on the environment.

By around 5,000 years ago, the earliest **civilizations**—sedentary societies capable of agricultural production, city building, and advanced political organization—took shape. The first of these appeared between 3500 and 2000 B.C.E. All four were born along the banks of major river systems. They were

- The Sumerian-Babylonian civilization of **Mesopotamia** (the Tigris and Euphrates rivers)
- **Egypt** (the Nile River)
- Indus cities like Mohenjo-Daro and Harappa (the **Indus River valley**)
- **Shang China** (the Yellow River, or Huang He)

Also among the world's oldest civilizations were the **Olmecs**, who arose in Central America around 1200 B.C.E., and the **Chavín**, who appeared in the Andes Mountains after 900 B.C.E.

Meanwhile, other developed societies appeared throughout the world. By 600 B.C.E., civilizations had emerged in many parts of Afro-Eurasia and the Americas. Many were connected by trade, warfare, and the **cultural diffusion** of ideas, beliefs, and technologies. Much of this transfer resulted from the interaction of **sedentary communities** with **nomadic peoples**. Several of the world's major religions had been born.

## BROAD TRENDS

| Humans and the Environment | |
|---|---|
| before 8000 B.C.E. | migration out of Africa to most continents<br>ice ages persist until ca. 10,000 B.C.E. |
| ca. 8000–3500 B.C.E. (Neolithic Era) | erosion and overgrazing caused by pastoralism<br>irrigation and forest clearing caused by agriculture |
| ca. 3500–1200 B.C.E. (Bronze Age) | mining<br>increased impact of irrigation and canal building<br>forest and swamp clearing + terracing of hillsides<br>Bantu migrations begin (ca. 1500 B.C.E.)<br>Indo-European migrations begin (ca. 1500 B.C.E.) |
| ca. 1200–600 B.C.E. (Iron Age) | Bantu migrations continue<br>Indo-European migrations continue |

## Humans and the Environment

- Migrations took *Homo sapiens* out of Africa sometime around 100,000 years ago, first to the Middle East and the warmer parts of Asia. By 40,000 years ago, humans had moved into Europe and northern Asia and are believed to have crossed the Bering land bridge into the Americas around 15,000 years ago.

- Key examples of later migrations that spread populations around the globe include the movement of Indo-Europeans across Eurasia and the Bantu migrations throughout Africa.

- For thousands of years, human communities in the Americas (as well as plants, animals, and diseases there) developed in isolation from those in Afro-Eurasia.

- Until approximately 10,000 B.C.E., ice ages prevailed, restricting where Stone Age human communities could live and delaying the discovery of agriculture. The ending of the ice ages began the transition from the Paleolithic era ("early Stone Age") to the Neolithic ("recent Stone Age").

- During the Stone Age, human hunter-foragers learned to use fire. They also created tools and clothing from a variety of materials, allowing them to shape their environment and survive in a wider range of ecosystems. The Neolithic Revolution heightened the effectiveness and environmental impact of these tools.

- The more advanced the form of economic production, the more ecological stress caused by resource consumption, resource extraction, and manipulation of the environment. Pastoral herding often caused overgrazing and erosion. Not only did agriculture deplete soil, but practices such as irrigation, swamp draining, forest clearing, and the terracing of hills and mountainsides radically altered the environment.

- Metallurgy, mining, and city building placed even greater burdens on the environment.

- On occasion, environmental changes destroyed societies or forced them to move elsewhere. Such changes—which included major temperature shifts, drought and desertification, deforestation, and the drying-up or altered flow of rivers—might be human-caused or natural.

| Development and Interaction of Cultures (Including Technology) | |
|---|---|
| before 8000 B.C.E. | cave painting and rock art<br>early music and storytelling<br>burial of dead<br>ancestor veneration, animism, and shamans<br>use of fire<br>weaving and pottery (early) |
| ca. 8000–3500 B.C.E. (Neolithic Era) | ancestor veneration and shamanism<br>polytheism<br>hoes and plows<br>weaving and pottery (widespread)<br>the wheel and wheeled vehicles |
| ca. 3500–1200 B.C.E. (Bronze Age) | *Gilgamesh Epic*<br>*Egyptian Book of the Dead*<br>*Rig Veda*<br>early recordkeeping (cuneiform, hieroglyphs, pictographs)<br>Vedism<br>Hebrew monotheism<br>calendars, astronomy, mathematics<br>urban planning (streets, sewers, walls)<br>monumental architecture (temples, palaces, ziggurats, pyramids)<br>metallurgy (bronze, limited use of iron)<br>horse riding<br>chariots<br>bows and arrows |
| ca. 1200–600 B.C.E. (Iron Age) | *Iliad* and *Odyssey*<br>more recordkeeping (alphabet, quipu)<br>Zoroastrianism (perhaps earlier)<br>iron tools and weapons |

## Development and Interaction of Cultures

- Artistic expression began as early as the Stone Age, with painting, music, and oral traditions such as storytelling.
- Important works of literature included the *Gilgamesh Epic*, the *Egyptian Book of the Dead*, the *Rig Veda*, and the Homeric epics (the *Iliad* and *Odyssey*). Artistic expression also took the form of sculpture, textiles, painting, and monumental architecture (which also served political purposes, as in palaces, or religious ones, as in temples, pyramids, and ziggurats).
- Writing and other forms of recordkeeping emerged in most civilized societies, starting around 3000 B.C.E. The earliest systems of writing were cuneiform, hieroglyphics, and pictograms in places like the Middle East and China. Later systems include the alphabet (Phoenician in origin, adopted by Hebrews, Greeks, and Romans, among others) and quipu (knot-tying in Andean South America).
- Prehistoric societies buried their dead and observed religious rituals. Early religious practices included ancestor veneration and shamanism.

- Organized religions arose during this era, such as polytheistic pantheons, Vedism, Hebrew monotheism, and Zoroastrianism.
- Key technologies and innovations from this era included pottery, hoes and plows, the weaving of textiles, wheels and wheeled vehicles, calendars, metallurgy (bronze, then iron), horse riding, chariots, and bows (recurve and compound) and arrows.
- Ideas, beliefs, knowledge, and technologies were often exchanged between societies through a process known as cultural diffusion. Sometimes they arose within a society as the result of independent innovation.

| State Building, Expansion, and Conflict | |
| --- | --- |
| **before 8000** B.C.E. | no organized states |
| **ca. 8000–3500** B.C.E. **(Neolithic Era)** | villages and other organized communities<br>early city-states |
| **ca. 3500–1200** B.C.E. **(Bronze Age)** | Mesopotamia (Tigris and Euphrates, ca. 3500 B.C.E. +)<br>Code of Hammurabi<br>Egypt (Nile, ca. 3100 B.C.E. +)<br>Mohenjo-Dara and Harappa (Indus, ca. 2600 B.C.E. +)<br>Shang China (Huang He, ca. 1600 B.C.E. +)<br>empires<br>use of religion to legitimize political rule |
| **ca. 1200–600** B.C.E. **(Iron Age)** | Olmec (ca. 1200 B.C.E. +)<br>Chavín (ca. 900 B.C.E. +)<br>Zhou China (ca. 1100 B.C.E. +)<br>origins of "mandate of heaven" concept<br>feudalism<br>bureaucracies |

## State Building, Expansion, and Conflict

- The first states grew out of core civilizations in the Middle East (Mesopotamia and Egypt), the Indus River valley (Mohenjo-Daro and Harappa), China (the Shang), Mesoamerica (the Olmecs), and the Andes of South America (the Chavín).
- With the development of agriculture and fixed settlements, complex forms of political organization began to appear, including the formation of elite classes and bureaucracies. Cities emerged as centers of political leadership.
- Most governments were monarchies (rule by a single leader) or oligarchies (rule by a small elite). Representative forms of government were all but nonexistent.
- Some states had highly centralized governments. In others, the central authority remained comparatively weak, leading to loosely organized confederations or decentralized feudal systems.
- Law codes, such as the Code of Hammurabi in Babylonia, appeared in some states. Although they were typically harsh and often gave extra rights and privileges to elite classes, they represented an improvement over lawlessness and arbitrary rule.
- Religion was commonly used to legitimize political systems. Typically, the ruler was

either seen as divine in his or her own right or his or her rule was said to be justified by the will of the gods.

- Organized warfare became more common as states formed. Some states built conquest states, or empires, by fighting and dominating their neighbors.

- Attacks by nomads and pastoralists caused civilized societies to react by building stronger city walls, adopting weapons like recurved and compound bows, and learning the arts of cavalry warfare and charioteering.

| Economic Systems | |
| --- | --- |
| **before 8000** B.C.E. | hunting and foraging<br>barter and limited trade |
| **ca. 8000–3500** B.C.E. **(Neolithic Era)** | hunting and foraging<br>domestication of animals gives rise to nomadic pastoralism<br>domestication of plants gives rise to early agriculture<br>early regional trade networks |
| **ca. 3500–1200** B.C.E. **(Bronze Age)** | agriculture spreads<br>trade networks become regional and transregional<br>slavery emerges as a labor system (household servitude and hard labor)<br>Mesopotamian-Indus trade<br>Nubian-Egyptian trade<br>Phoenician trade in the Mediterranean |
| **ca. 1200–600** B.C.E. **(Iron Age)** | agriculture spreads further<br>regional and transregional trade networks become more extensive<br>coins first used as currency |

## Economic Systems

- Hunting and foraging emerged as the means of livelihood for most Stone Age peoples. Hunter-forager societies lived at subsistence levels and possessed few goods. Labor specialization was limited, while trade, where it existed, was based on simple barter.

- During the Neolithic Revolution, domestication of animals gave birth to pastoralism, an economic practice based on herding, which made it easier to maintain a constant supply of food. Most pastoral herders were nomadic.

- Also during the Neolithic Revolution, domestication of plants gave birth to agriculture. Even more so than pastoralism, agriculture ensured not just a constant supply of food, but food surpluses that caused profound social changes (including the accumulation of wealth and the concept of private property).

- Trade became more common, first on a local basis, then at the regional and transregional levels. Cities typically served as important points of economic exchange.

- Trade networks extended overland, but tended to follow rivers and coastlines where they could, because large-scale transport was easier by water than by land. Particularly important transregional trade networks include Egyptian-Nubian trade, trade between Mesopotamia and the Indus River valley, and Phoenician trade throughout the Mediterranean.

- Slavery emerged as a labor system during this period. Often debtors or prisoners of war, slaves might be used for hard labor (in fields or mines, for example), as servants, or to perform other functions.

| Social Structures | |
| --- | --- |
| **before 8000** B.C.E. | family and kin-based units (limited hierarchy)<br>limited gender division of labor? |
| **ca. 8000– 3500** B.C.E. **(Neolithic Era)** | some degree of hierarchy and gender division of labor arises from pastoralism<br>labor specialization + greater hierarchy and social stratification thanks to food surpluses<br>the first cities |
| **ca. 3500– 1200** B.C.E. **(Bronze Age)** | more villages and cities<br>hierarchies and elite classes (religious and political) become more complex<br>artisan and warrior classes emerge<br>caste systems appear in certain societies<br>gender division of labor deepens<br>patriarchalism becomes more common<br>slaves come to occupy the bottom ranks of hierarchical societies |
| **ca. 1200– 600** B.C.E. **(Iron Age)** | [the above trends widen and deepen] |

## Social Structures

- Hunter-forager societies tended to be family- and clan-based, and were for the most part not hierarchical or stratified.
- Basic physical differences between the sexes are thought to have led to a gender division of labor among Stone Age hunter-foragers.
- Pastoral societies were marked by a somewhat higher degree of hierarchy and social stratification. It also tended to deepen the gender division of labor.
- Agriculture caused many societies to abandon nomadism in favor of a sedentary, or settled, lifestyle.
- By allowing the accumulation of food surpluses, agriculture enabled some members of society to make a living by means other than growing food. This resulted in labor specialization and the emergence of elite (political and religious) and non-elite (laboring) classes. Social stratification became much more pronounced, leading in some societies to strict caste systems.
- Specialized classes included artisans, warriors, clergy, and merchants/traders.
- Patriarchalism and an increasingly sharp gender division of labor became characteristic of most agricultural societies. In most places, women were relegated to secondary roles, although the degree to which this happened depended on the society in question. Women might have certain rights (divorce, inheritance, ownership of property), and they might also exercise informal influence within their societies or over their families.
- Slavery and other forms of coerced labor became increasingly common.

## QUESTIONS AND COMPARISONS TO CONSIDER

- What roles do geography, climate, and environment play in shaping human societies? How have different societies affected their environments?

- How do technological advancement, resource extraction and consumption, and environmental impact relate to each other? What stresses have been placed on the environment by hunter-foragers, pastoralists, agricultural villages, and cities?

- What features distinguish less advanced societies from civilizations?

- How do agricultural and urban societies compare with hunter-forager and pastoral societies? How do these different societies interact? How did military threats from pastoral nomads influence civilized societies?

- How did the appearance of cities affect the development of ancient societies?

- When and where did cultural interaction and diffusion change societies technologically, scientifically, and culturally? What about independent innovation?

- Compare how different religions and philosophical traditions have supported political regimes. Also, how have they been used to justify class systems, hierarchies, and gender and ethnic discrimination?

- How have different societies organized themselves economically? What role did trade play in the prehistoric and ancient world, both regionally and transregionally? Compare Egyptian-Nubian trade with Mesopotamian-Indus trade.

- What roles did large-scale migrations play in various parts of the world during this period? Consider the passage of Asiatic peoples to the Americas over the Bering land bridge, the Bantu migrations throughout Africa, and the spread of Indo-Europeans throughout Eurasia.

# UNIT 1

## SCENIC ROUTE
### (Chapters 1–3)

# Big Geography and the Peopling of the Earth

1

→ **PREHISTORY**

→ **MAJOR CONTINENTS**

→ **WATER VS. OVERLAND TRANSPORT**

→ **HOMINID DEVELOPMENT AND THE "OUT OF AFRICA" THESIS**

→ **THE STONE AGE (PALEOLITHIC AND NEOLITHIC)**

→ **USE OF FIRE AND EARLY TOOLS**

→ **HUNTER-FORAGER SOCIETIES AND KINSHIP GROUPS**

→ **GENDER DIVISION OF LABOR**

Hominid, or humanlike, life has existed on earth for 3 to 4 million years, and modern humans, with their immediate ancestors, appeared 200,000 years ago. The history of human civilization, however, stretches back only 5,000 to 6,000 years. The vast expanse of time preceding that moment is called **prehistory**. Because written sources from prehistory are rare to nonexistent, much of what we know about it comes from the work of archaeologists, paleontologists, physical anthropologists, and other scholars who specialize in studying the distant past. New discoveries are made on a regular basis, constantly changing our understanding of the prehistoric years.

AP coverage of this time period is limited, but knowing the basics is important. Moreover, familiarity with basic geography is indispensable for a good performance on the entire exam.

## GEOGRAPHIC ORIENTATION

The map in the Appendix at the end of this book will give you a good sense of the geographic labels preferred by the AP World History course. Study it closely.

Of the world's seven continents, Antarctica has no native human population. Australia, the smallest continent, is home to the earth's oldest surviving ethnic group, the Aborigines, but remained largely isolated for most of its history. The thousands of islands in the Pacific Ocean form no continent but are often referred to, along with Australia, as **Oceania**.

**Africa** is considered by most scholars to be the birthplace of humanity. Its northern third is home to the **Sahara**, the world's largest desert. **Asia** is the largest and most populous continent on earth, and it contains the world's most diverse mix of climates, languages, and cultures. Asia's subregions include the **Middle East**, **Central Asia**, **South Asia** (consisting mainly of the Indian subcontinent), **Southeast Asia**, and **East Asia** (whose core is China, Korea, and Japan). **Europe**, a relatively small continent with a large population, is resource-rich and, on the whole, mild and temperate in climate. It is physically joined to Asia, and together the two are referred to as **Eurasia**. From humanity's early days, the populations of Africa and Eurasia interacted constantly, and the AP World History course frequently uses the term **Afro-Eurasian** to describe trends spanning all three continents.

**North** and **South America** were originally settled by migrating peoples from Asia, who crossed a land bridge that existed only temporarily. Until the late 1400s C.E., the Americas developed in cultural and environmental isolation from the Afro-Eurasian world. Abundant in resources and agriculturally fertile in most places, the Americas became home to many advanced cultures. From 1492 C.E. onward, contact with European societies changed the Americas dramatically.

**NOTE**

An older school of historical thought, *geographic determinism*, used to argue that geography was the paramount force behind a society's development, but few subscribe to that view now.

For thousands of years, **water transport** remained easier and more efficient than overland travel. Although large bodies of water were formidable barriers, many early societies were capable of coastline and river navigation. Oceans, seas, lakes, and rivers not only provided food and other resources but enabled the transfer of people, goods, ideas, technology, religious beliefs, and cultural practices. Be sure to acquaint yourselves with key rivers and bodies of water.

Human beings and the environment mutually influence each other. Especially with tools and technologies to help them adapt, humans have built societies in all but the harshest ecosystems on earth. Still, as a general rule, societies were more prone to develop into advanced civilizations if the local geography featured one or more of the following:

- A climate that was not extremely hot, cold, dry, or wet
- A suitable amount of fertile land, preferably flat
- A reliable source of water
- Topography (shape of the land) that permitted reasonably easy movement
- Access to a river, seacoast, or lake for the sake of transport or food supply
- The presence of one or more desirable natural resources
- Proximity to one or more trade routes

Not all these conditions had to prevail. Think of the monsoons of India (extreme weather) or the terraced fields of the Andean civilizations (little or no flat land for agriculture). However, an advanced society is unlikely to develop without at least some of these factors working in its favor.

## HUMAN ORIGINS AND THE FIRST MIGRATIONS

Between 2 to 3 million years ago, members of the genus *Homo*, the primate category to which humans belong, emerged in southern and eastern Africa. Later species within genus *Homo* made basic stone and wooden tools and clothed themselves in skins and furs.

The vast majority of scholars agree that modern humans (*Homo sapiens*) arose in East Africa between 100,000 and 200,000 years ago and then migrated outward. This theory is informally referred to as the **"Out of Africa" thesis**. (An opposing model, the multiregional thesis, proposes that modern humans appeared independently in various places, having descended from earlier hominid groups that had already left Africa—but only a small minority holds to this theory.)

The **peopling of the earth** by *Homo sapiens* began around 100,000 years ago. The first step was the migration of hunter-forager groups from Africa to the Middle East. From there, human populations spread through the relatively warm southern parts of Asia, reaching places like India and Southeast Asia around 70,000 years ago, and China not long after. Around 50,000 years ago, settlers crossed from Southeast Asia to Australia and other parts of Oceania. It took longer for people to move into Europe, Central Asia, and Siberia because of cooler climates caused by the periodic **ice ages** that lasted until approximately 12,000 years ago. Even so, better tools and warmer clothing allowed numerous communities to push into these places by about 40,000 years ago.

Humans most likely moved into the Americas around 15,000 years ago, with settlers from Eurasia migrating across the **Bering land bridge** that spanned Siberia and Alaska during periods of heavy glaciation. (Alternative theories propose earlier dates for the crossing, or that settlers arrived by boat, but none of these has gained wide acceptance.) By 8000 B.C.E., the time of the Neolithic Revolution, humans had settled all but the most inhospitable parts of the globe.

## HUNTER-FORAGER SOCIETIES DURING THE EARLY STONE AGE (PALEOLITHIC)

The earliest humans made tools from many materials, such as wood, bone, and animal skins and sinews. Those most familiar to archaeologists, because they have survived best over time, were made of stone, so the first period of human history is known as the **Stone Age**, which lasted roughly from 2.5 million to 5,000 years ago. The Stone Age is typically subdivided into the Paleolithic ("early Stone Age," ending 12,000 to 10,000 years ago) and the **Neolithic** ("recent Stone Age," beginning around 8000 B.C.E.) The Paleolithic overlapped with the recurring **ice ages** whose end began the transition to the Neolithic.

During the Paleolithic, Stone Age societies supported themselves by **hunting and foraging** (also known as hunting and gathering). Rather than produce food themselves, they lived off resources taken directly from the land: birds, animals, and fish, as well as nuts, berries, and roots. Tools helped them adapt to a variety of climates and terrains, from jungles and forests to deserts, mountains, and tundra. The most favored habitats tended to be grasslands, such as savannas and steppes, which supported large numbers of game animals and enough plant life to supplement the meat gained by hunting.

As they developed **tools**, Stone Age humans were most concerned about food, clothing, and shelter. They used **fire** not just to cook food, but to heat their dwellings (allowing them to expand into colder regions) and protect themselves against predators. Knives, axes, spears, harpoons, and hooks were used for fishing and hunting—and though it is unknown when organized warfare began, most of these tools could be used for self-protection and in combat. (Some archaeologists theorize that the bow and arrow appeared during the late Paleolithic, but if it did, it was not widespread until later.) Mats and baskets were woven to carry foodstuffs, and **pottery** for cooking and storage became common during the late Paleolithic. The earliest clothes were made from furs and animal hides, sewn with bone needles. As time passed, Stone Age people began to use plant fibers, which led to the **weaving** of cloth and textiles. Stone Age humans lived in natural dwellings such as caves, but also built tents, huts, and structures of wood and stone that required advanced skills in carpentry and construction.

Social organization during the Stone Age was based on **kinship** groups, with extended families clustering together to form clans and larger units such as bands and tribes. Hunter-foragers were often **nomadic**, following their favorite game animals on seasonal rounds of migration—or abandoning old hunting grounds for new ones if resources grew scarce.

Hunter-forager societies tended to be relatively free of hierarchy. Chiefs or councils of elders provided leadership, and some figures exercised religious authority. But most members of a given group performed similar functions and had similar skills, even if labor was divided along gender lines. There was little private property and no ownership of land, so few if any distinctions were made between "rich" and "poor." Lack of a complex class structure, however, did not mean lack of social organization. Teamwork on a high level was needed to hunt large creatures. Also, Stone Age groups did not live in isolation but are known to have traded and interacted over great distances, exchanging goods, ideas, and religious beliefs.

Stone Age hunter-foragers enjoyed a rich artistic and religious life. Musical instruments, cave paintings, and carvings date back to at least 30,000 years ago. Stone Age peoples buried their dead and offered sacrifices, and many practiced **ancestor veneration**. Most subscribed to some form of **animism**, a belief system in which all things in the natural world are thought to be animated by spirits. Religious leaders in such societies are generally called **shamans**, who were believed to be able to speak to spirits and heal the sick.

The **gender division of labor** was felt as early as the hunter-forager stage, with various tasks assigned by sex because of basic physical differences. As a rule, men hunted large animals, fought, and performed heavy labor. Women gathered plants and hunted small game, hauled and prepared food that men had hunted, and looked after the home and children. It is unknown whether this division of labor necessarily meant that, during the Stone Age, men's work was valued more than women's, as tended to be the case in later eras. Either way, the division of labor by gender continued long after the Stone Age and gave rise to a long-standing **gender inequality** that in many ways continues today.

# The Neolithic Revolution and Early Agricultural Societies

# 2

- → THE NEOLITHIC REVOLUTION
- → PASTORALISM AND HERDING SOCIETIES
- → AGRICULTURE AND FOOD SURPLUSES
- → CULTURAL DIFFUSION VS. INDEPENDENT INNOVATION
- → SPECIALIZATION OF LABOR AND SOCIAL CLASSES
- → SOCIAL STRATIFICATION AND HIERARCHY
- → PATRIARCHALISM
- → POTTERY AND WEAVING
- → PLOWS
- → WHEELS AND WHEELED VEHICLES
- → METALLURGY AND THE BRONZE AND IRON AGES
- → WRITING AND RECORDKEEPING

The last of the great **ice ages** ended around 12,000 years ago, bringing about the milder conditions and warmer temperatures of the Neolithic era. Wide expanses of tundra were transformed into grassland, and former grasslands became forest. These and other environmental changes profoundly altered the lives of Stone Age humans, who now settled more parts of the earth. Total population rose steeply, from 2 million worldwide during the last ice age to 10 million by 5000 B.C.E., and again to somewhere between 50 million and 100 million by 1000 B.C.E.

Aside from the more congenial climate, the primary cause of this population growth was a key transformation in how communities fed themselves. Although many continued hunting and foraging, certain peoples, starting between 12,000 to 10,000 years ago, discovered how to domesticate animals and plants and thereby produce their own food. These new skills gave birth to **pastoralism** and **agriculture**, and also caused human beings to manipulate their environments more than ever before.

The earthshaking importance of this change has made it traditional to refer to a **Neolithic Revolution**. A few scholars question the validity of this label on the grounds that the "revolution" took place over many centuries and at different times in different parts of the world. But the concept is accepted by most, and the changes, gradual or not, were immense.

## PASTORALISM AND HERDING SOCIETIES

Humankind's **domestication of animals** began during the Stone Age. First to be tamed was the dog, which provided companionship, security, and help in hunting. Next came goats, sheep, and pigs.

As the Neolithic era progressed, more animals were domesticated. Horses, water buffalo, oxen, camels, and, in the Americas, llamas provided transport and labor. For groups involved in agriculture, animal droppings made useful fertilizer. Wool and hides could be turned into clothing. Most important, animals yielded an increasingly steady supply of food. Like goats, sheep, and pigs, cattle and poultry were a source of meat, not to mention milk and eggs.

Groups that domesticated animals but not plants developed **pastoralist**, or **herding**, societies. These emerged most commonly in grassland regions, particularly in Afro-Eurasia. Although not to the extent that agricultural societies did, pastoralists accumulated wealth and experienced **social stratification**. Warrior elites arose more frequently than among hunter-foragers, and the gender division of labor tended to deepen.

Because livestock consumed huge quantities of grass or fodder, pastoralists lived **nomadic** lifestyles. Highly mobile, they were often expert **horseback riders**, and many invented or used **wheeled vehicles** such as carts and **chariots**, pulled by herd animals. Pastoral herders often traded or warred with settled societies, and they played a key role in the process of **cultural diffusion**—helping to spread new technologies (especially the chariot, the **compound bow and arrow**, and **iron weapons**) and religious beliefs.

Pastoralism had a considerable impact on the environment. It led to an artificial selection of certain species over others, and the grazing of large numbers of herbivores taxed the growing capacity of grasslands, sometimes severely. Overgrazing led to erosion and occasionally caused the transformation of grassland to desert.

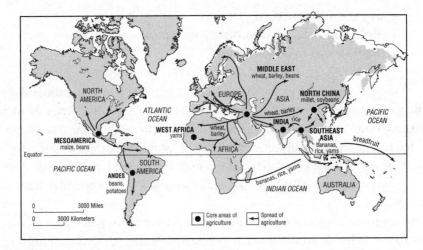

**The Practice of Agriculture, ca. 8000 B.C.E.**
During the transition from the Paleolithic Era to the Neolithic, communities in the Middle East and northern China began to practice agriculture systematically.

## AGRICULTURE

The **domestication of plants**, or **agriculture**, became known in many parts of the globe about 10,000 years ago. Over the next 5,000 years, a combination of **independent innovation** and **cultural diffusion** led it to be adopted worldwide.

Wheat and barley cultivation began in the Middle East around 8000 B.C.E., spreading to Europe, Egypt, and North Africa over the next 4,000 years. Sub-Saharan Africa developed its own agricultural tradition, growing sorghum, plantains, dates, and yams. In Asia, taro was harvested in Papua New Guinea 9,000 years ago, and as early as 8,000 years ago, millet and rice were grown in India. The people of China's river valleys learned to grow millet at the same time, but probably on their own. Rice cultivation began in Southeast Asia around 7,000 years ago and seems to have spread from there to southern China. The peoples of the Americas, starting in the Andes, developed agriculture sometime between 12,000 and 7,000 years ago. Early crops here included potatoes, corn, beans, and squash.

As time passed, seeds, crops, and agricultural techniques were borrowed and handed on from society to society, although the Americas remained isolated from Afro-Eurasia. Most scholars agree that women, already responsible for food collection in most hunter-forager societies, played a vital role in the transition to agriculture.

Agriculture's greatest advantage was that it provided a more dependable supply of food. In exchange, it required intensive labor, cooperative effort, and a shift from nomadism to a sedentary, or settled, lifestyle. Agriculturalists gathered into larger communities, forming **villages** and eventually **cities**. The concept of **private property**, along with sharper distinctions between wealthier and poorer **social classes**, came to seem more natural. **Food surpluses**, which allowed people not directly involved in food production to develop other skills, encouraged the **specialization of labor**. Among the end results were greater **hierarchy** and **social stratification**. Also in most agricultural societies, male-dominated **patriarchalism** tended to be the norm, with **gender inequity** and the **gender division of labor** more pronounced than among hunter-foragers or pastoralists.

The environmental impact of agriculture was likewise heavier than that of hunting-foraging or pastoralism. Plant and animal species selected artificially by humans came to dominate in many regions. Practices such as **forest clearing** and **irrigation** vastly increased humanity's ecological footprint on the land. The same is true of **mining**, as well as engineering projects such as swamp dredging, dam building, canal digging, road building, and **urban planning**— all more common as agricultural communities grew larger and more advanced.

## FROM STONE AGE TO AGES OF METAL: TRANSITIONS TO CIVILIZATION

Because it required greater effort and organization, agriculture promoted closer social ties and the formation of permanent settlements. Such stability proved crucial in civilizing early societies.

In certain areas, the increased social complexity of the Neolithic era led to the emergence of **cities**. Cities offered protection to large numbers of people and served as centers for trade, religious worship, and political leadership. More so than villages, they permitted people with different skills and talents—political elites, professional warriors, artisans, merchants, and farmers—to gather in a single place, bringing about the labor specialization and class distinctions described above. They enabled the exchange of goods, ideas, technologies, religious beliefs, and cultural values. The first cities date back as far as 8000 to 7000 B.C.E. and include Jericho, on the Jordan River, and Çatal Hüyük, in present-day Turkey.

During the Neolithic, technological aptitude improved. Tools invented during the Paleolithic became more refined, and new ones appeared. The crafts of **pottery** and **weaving** spread more widely. In several places during the 3000s B.C.E., the invention of the **wheel**, by permitting the construction of carts, wheelbarrows, and chariots, revolutionized transport and war. Tools like hoes and the **plow** increased labor efficiency and agricultural productivity.

Near the end of the Neolithic, several societies learned the techniques of **metallurgy** (extracting metal from raw ore) and **metalsmithing** (shaping metal into tools). Metallurgy on a large scale began in the Middle East and China between 4000 and 3000 B.C.E. In both places, smiths mixed copper and tin to create the alloy bronze, a strong and versatile material for tool making. As metallurgy spread, both via cultural diffusion and independent innovation, the

Neolithic era gave way to the **Bronze Age** (ca. 3500–1200 B.C.E.). With the development of **iron**, a metal of even greater strength and usefulness, the Bronze Age came to a close.

Another innovation associated with the transition to civilization is **writing**. Ancient societies developed rich **oral traditions**, but the written word enabled people to keep records and pass on learning and information more effectively than before. Perhaps the earliest form of writing was developed in the Middle East, by the Sumerians, between 3500 and 3000 B.C.E., followed by the Egyptians at about 3000 B.C.E., the Indus River people around 2200 B.C.E., and the Chinese before 2000 B.C.E. A handful of cultures, including the Incas, reached a civilized state without the benefit of a written script, but this happened rarely.

Religious practices grew more elaborate. Shamanism, the faith favored by most hunter-foragers, appealed less to the settled societies of the Neolithic and the Bronze Age. Ancestor veneration remained common, and agriculturalists turned also to **polytheism**, the worship of many gods, often organized into complex, formalized pantheons. Permanent sites of worship and ritual were erected, such as burial mounds, megaliths (standing stones, including England's famous Stonehenge, dating to the 3000s), shrines, and temples.

# The Development and Interactions of Early Agricultural, Pastoral, and Urban Societies

# 3

- → **CIVILIZATION**
- → **CITIES AND URBAN PLANNING**
- → **THE RIVER VALLEY CIVILIZATIONS**
- → **THE OLMECS**
- → **ANDEAN CULTURES (THE CHAVÍN)**
- → **SPECIALIZATION AND SOCIAL CLASSES**
- → **STATES (MONARCHIES, OLIGARCHIES, AND EMPIRES) AND STATE-BUILDING**
- → **PATRIARCHALISM AND GENDER INEQUITY**
- → **SYSTEMS OF COERCED LABOR (INCLUDING SLAVERY)**
- → **TRADE AND TRADE NETWORKS**
- → **WRITING AND RECORDKEEPING**
- → **KEY WORKS OF ART, ARCHITECTURE, AND LITERATURE**
- → **SHAMANISM, ANCESTOR VENERATION, AND POLYTHEISM**
- → **VEDISM**
- → **HEBREW MONOTHEISM**
- → **ZOROASTRIANISM**

The first **civilizations** are considered to have formed around 5,500 to 5,000 years ago. The definition of "civilized," as opposed to less flattering terms like "primitive" or "barbaric," has long been a matter of debate, and has changed over time. Still, most agree that civilized societies have certain basic features in common, including most if not all of the following:

- An economic system
- A government
- A social system
- A moral or ethical belief system
- An intellectual tradition
- A reasonably high level of technological aptitude

## CORE/FOUNDATIONAL CIVILIZATIONS AND THE FIRST STATES

Between 3500 and 2000 B.C.E., river systems in the Middle East, India, and China gave birth to the world's oldest civilizations: Mesopotamia, Egypt, the Indus River valley, and Shang China. These, along with the Olmecs and the Chavín, two civilizations that arose in the Americas between 1200 and 850 B.C.E., are considered core, or foundational, civilizations by the AP World History course. The first **states** and **empires** (states that expand by means of military conquest) had their origins in these core/foundational civilizations.

## Mesopotamia

One of the world's two oldest civilizations was the Sumerian-Babylonian culture that arose in the region of **Mesopotamia** (a Greek term meaning "land between the waters"). The rivers giving life to this so-called Fertile Crescent were the **Tigris** and **Euphrates**. Settlement began in this area as early as 8000 B.C.E., and large-scale agriculture by 5000 B.C.E. Between 3500 and 2350 B.C.E., the first true civilization emerged among the **Sumerians**. As time passed, a variety of other groups, especially the Akkadians, **Babylonians** (1900–1600 B.C.E.), and **Assyrians** (911–612 B.C.E.), achieved political dominance. Still, the Sumerians' religion, traditions, and writing system set in place a cultural bedrock that deeply influenced the peoples who later ruled Mesopotamia.

Mesopotamian peoples built many cities, including **Babylon**, which tended to be governed by kinglike figures supported by a small ruling class of priests. Mesopotamia was not always politically centralized, and at certain times, individual **city-states** enjoyed much autonomy. The region's first **empire** was forged by the Akkadian conqueror Sargon, who proclaimed himself "King of Sumer and Akkad" sometime around 2200 B.C.E.

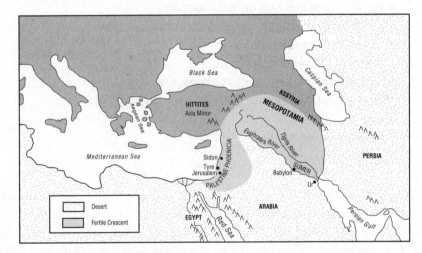

**The Ancient Middle East, ca. 1200 B.C.E.**
Note the importance of bodies of water in giving birth to ancient civilizations. The Fertile Crescent, between the Tigris and Euphrates rivers, encouraged the formation of advanced societies in Mesopotamia. The Nile did the same in Egypt. The Mediterranean Sea was crucial for the movement of people and trade goods.

The Sumerians appear to have been the first people to devise a written script: **cuneiform** (ca. 3300 B.C.E.). Sumerian poems gave rise around 2000 B.C.E. to the *Gilgamesh Epic*, one of humanity's oldest literary works. One of the world's earliest law codes was compiled around 1750 B.C.E. by the Babylonian king Hammurabi. Although **Hammurabi's law code** was quite harsh (death and mutilation were common punishments) and favored elite over lower classes, the idea that society should be governed by a consistent set of regulations, and not the ruler's arbitrary will, was a noteworthy innovation.

The Mesopotamians were skilled builders and craftspeople. Using clay, they erected dozens of large cities and honored their **polytheistic** gods with terrace-stepped temples called

**ziggurats**. They built canals and dams and were accomplished at pottery and metallurgy (bronzeworking began here around 3000 B.C.E.). Keen astronomers, the Mesopotamians developed a high level of mathematical knowledge, originating the **base-60 number system** still used today to measure time and navigational calculations. They traded widely throughout the Middle East and North Africa, and their economic network extended as far east as the Indus River valley. **Mesopotamian-Indus trade** involved boat travel along the Indian Ocean coastline, with the Mesopotamians exchanging wool, barley, and copper for gems and cotton.

During the 1300s and 1200s B.C.E., the **Hittites** came to rule much of Mesopotamia. Adept at **chariot** warfare, they are notable for being among the first to systematically use **iron weapons**. Even more powerful were the **Assyrians**, who, between 911 and 612 B.C.E., created one of the largest of the world's early **empires**. Armed with iron weapons and making good use of horseback warfare, the Assyrians conquered sizable parts of the Middle East, including Mesopotamia and Egypt, holding their empire together by means of a deliberate policy of cruelty.

## Egypt

The other of the Middle East's earliest civilizations appeared in **Egypt**, on the banks of the **Nile**. Surrounded by desert, Egypt depended for survival on the Nile's waters. Agricultural settlements emerged there as early as 5500 B.C.E.

Egypt's history as a civilization is considered to have begun in 3100 B.C.E., when Upper (southern) and Lower (northern) Egypt were united. Its ancient history is divided into several long periods. During the Early Dynastic and **Old Kingdom** (2575–2134 B.C.E.) periods, basic social and political features took shape. Civil war tore Egypt apart during the First Intermediate Period, but a culturally dynamic **Middle Kingdom** arose around 2040 B.C.E. It lasted until 1640 B.C.E., when outside invaders called the Hyksos, armed with **chariots** and **compound bows**, ushered in a Second Intermediate Period. Rebelling against Hyksos rule around 1532 B.C.E., the Egyptians formed a **New Kingdom** that lasted until 1070 B.C.E. Under vigorous leaders, especially Rameses II (ca. 1304–1237 B.C.E.), New Kingdom Egypt conquered a great deal of territory in the Middle East and Africa, including Nubian lands farther to the south on the Nile. Eventually, the New Kingdom collapsed, due to internal disorder and foreign invasions. By the 900s B.C.E., most of Egypt had lost its independence.

Even more so than the Mesopotamians, the Egyptians developed a centralized society presided over by a monarch and a small caste of priests. The monarch, or **pharaoh**, was considered the living incarnation of the sun god. Although their society was less urban than that of the Mesopotamians, and although they did not trade as widely, the Egyptians built many cities and a sizable economic network. **Egyptian-Nubian trade**, which brought gold to Egypt and gave it access to ivory, ebony, and exotic animal skins from sub-Saharan Africa, was crucial but rarely friendly. Egypt raided Nubia for slaves, built border forts to regulate commerce, and conquered Nubia during the New Kingdom period.

Egyptian women, while secondary to men in terms of power and status, enjoyed certain privileges. They managed household finances and the education of children. They had the right to divorce husbands and receive alimony. They could own property, and some managed businesses. Upper-class women could serve as priestesses, and one New Kingdom queen, Hatshepsut, became pharaoh in her own right.

The Egyptians had an elaborate **polytheistic** religion. The chief of their many gods was Ra, the sun deity, and their principal religious text was the **Egyptian Book of the Dead**. Concern about the afterlife gave rise to mummification (the art of preserving bodies) and the building of gigantic tombs, including the **pyramids**, which provided resting places for pharaohs after they died.

The cultural and scientific attainments of the Egyptians were many. Around 3100 B.C.E., they developed the written characters known as **hieroglyphs**. Using the fiber of **papyrus** reeds, they pioneered the craft of papermaking. Talented engineers and architects, they used irrigation to extend the reach of the Nile's waters beyond the river valley itself, and they began to construct pyramids and other impressive monuments around 2600 B.C.E. They made bronze tools and weapons and devised the **365-day calendar** that, with only minor modifications, is still used today.

## The Indus River Valley

Yet another civilization grew up at this time, in what is today Pakistan and northwestern India. This was the **Indus River civilization**, which arose around 2600 B.C.E. and lasted approximately seven centuries. Although the Indus River people had a written language, it has not been deciphered by modern scholars, and while some of their sculptures survive, they left behind little pictorial art. As a result, much about them remains unclear, especially their origins, their culture, and the reasons for their decline.

The Indus River civilization was about the size of modern-day France and was heavily urbanized. Like the Nile in Egypt, the river itself, rich with silt, flooded regularly, allowing irrigation and widespread agriculture. Along a length of nearly a thousand miles, the Indus River people built several hundred cities, the biggest of which were **Mohenjo-Daro** and **Harappa** (the cities' modern names because the original ones are lost to us). Mohenjo-Daro, the larger city, sat on the floodplain, where the Indus empties into the Indian Ocean, while Harappa, 500 miles to the northeast, appears to have been a gateway into the less settled but resource-rich frontier.

Because the layout of most Indus River cities is virtually identical, with streets laid out in extremely straight grids, many believe that the society was unified and highly centralized. It also appears to have been prosperous, based on the fact that most cities feature large baths, central granaries for food storage, and covered drainpipes for sewage disposal. The Indus River people domesticated cattle and water buffalo and grew wheat, barley, and cotton. They traded cotton and precious stones with their neighbors and perhaps with Shang China for jade. **Mesopotamian-Indus trade**, described above, played a significant role in their economy.

The Indus River civilization lasted until approximately 1900 B.C.E. How it ended is a matter of contention. It used to be thought that invasion by outside enemies, the Indo-European Aryans, destroyed the Indus River cities around 1500 B.C.E. However, a majority of scholars now believe that environmental factors—most likely the drying up or diversion of rivers feeding into the Indus—caused the downfall long before that.

## Early China and the Shang Dynasty

The fourth river valley civilization emerged in China, along the **Huang He** (or **Yellow River**) in the north. Western China borders on desert, and much of China's interior is hilly or mountainous. This makes the two east-west rivers, the Huang He and Yangzi (Yangtze), exceptionally important in supporting agriculture, allowing movement, and fostering social and political unity. Small societies formed along the Huang He at around 8000 B.C.E. Wheat and millet were grown in the region's fertile loess soil by 6000 B.C.E., although this required immense amounts of cooperative labor (the same was true of rice cultivation when it began in southern China). By 2000 B.C.E., the Chinese had discovered bronze metallurgy.

China's history between the 1700s B.C.E. and 1911 C.E. is measured in dynasties, or successions of emperors. Although legend speaks of a dynasty called the Xia arising around 2000 B.C.E., the first historically verifiable dynasty and the bedrock of Chinese civilization is the **Shang dynasty**, which emerged on the banks of the Huang He and established a rapidly growing state around 1600 B.C.E. Led by a warrior aristocracy and able to feed and equip an army of tens of thousands, the Shang fought their northern and western neighbors, whom they considered barbarians, and expanded their borders by conquest. Shang armies used **chariots**, which they may have come to know about via contact with the Middle East, and they learned horseback warfare from the steppe nomads they fought in the north. Prisoners of war were typically enslaved.

The Shang traded extensively, and their economic network may have stretched as far as the Middle East—at least indirectly, via trade with the Indus River people, who traded with Mesopotamia. Principal commodities included jade and **silk**, on which the Chinese enjoyed an unbroken monopoly for hundreds of years. The Chinese system of writing, **pictographs**, originated with the Shang, as did two important aspects of early Chinese religion: divination (fortune-telling) and **ancestor veneration** (which reinforced a strong sense of patriarchalism). The Shang considered themselves to be at the center of the world, an idea giving rise to the long-standing tradition of viewing China as a superior "Middle Kingdom." Shang rulers exercised religious as well as political authority, performing sacrifices and rituals of divination.

China's second dynasty, and its longest-lasting, was the **Zhou**, founded in the mid-1000s B.C.E. by a herding society that rebelled against the Shang. The Zhou lasted until 221 B.C.E., although the dynasty slipped into decline long before that, after about 800 B.C.E. Relying more and more on **feudalism** (a form of rulership in which a weak monarch loosely governs a number of decentralized and militarized political units), the Zhou steadily crumbled from within, eventually collapsing after the civil strife of the "Warring States" period (480–221 B.C.E.).

The Zhou preserved knowledge and traditions from the Shang era, but added innovations of their own. Around 600 B.C.E., the Chinese learned to make **iron weapons** and tools. During their period of strength, political sophistication increased. The Zhou made effective use of **bureaucracy** to run their affairs (even China's **polytheistic** pantheon was modeled on a "celestial bureaucracy"), and one of the Zhou's central political principles was the **Mandate of Heaven**, the idea that, as long as a leader governed wisely, he could claim a divine right to rule.

## The Olmecs

A great variety of advanced civilizations appeared in the Americas during and after the 2000s B.C.E. In Mexico and Mesoamerica (Central America), a succession of agricultural societies emerged, some of them deeply influencing the ones that followed. Among the oldest and most significant were the **Olmecs**, who arose between 1400 and 1200 B.C.E. and lasted until 400 B.C.E. The Olmecs are considered to have been a "mother civilization" in Mesoamerica in the same way the Sumerians were in Mesopotamia.

**Olmec Monumental Art**
One of the carved stone heads characteristic of the Olmec cultural style (ca. 1200–400 B.C.E.). Because the Olmec written script has never been deciphered, it is unclear whether these massive sculptures represent deities, political leaders, or some other kind of figure unknown to us.

The chief Olmec cities were located in south-central Mexico. Unlike most other early civilizations, such as the four described above, the Olmecs arose without the benefit of a large river system nearby. Their written language remains a mystery to scholars, but their art, monumental architecture, and religion clearly had an impact on peoples within a large radius, as well as on the civilizations that came after them. The presence of jade and obsidian from faraway places indicates a large trading network, and they were skilled potters and canal builders. As with most peoples in the region, their diet consisted of corn, beans, and squash. They are famous for carving huge stone heads, weighing up to 40 tons, and they constructed tall mounds that seem to be prototypes of the pyramids that later appeared in the region. They passed on to later peoples a fascination with astronomy, a complicated ball game played for ritual purposes, and **polytheistic** deities, including their jaguar god. They probably practiced **human sacrifice**, like the peoples who emerged later in the region.

## Andean Cultures and the Chavín

In northwestern South America, several civilizations rose up in the peaks and valleys of the Andes. It may have been precisely the difficulty of practicing agriculture in such rugged terrain that brought about the social cohesion required for the transition to civilization. The first city in the Americas may have been Caral, founded in central Peru, at around 2600 B.C.E. Most **Andean cultures** were skilled at weaving and metalworking. Also, it is thought that, in the Americas, metallurgy originated in the Andes and then spread northward. Andean societies were urban and class-stratified. Their most important domesticated animal was the **llama**. Like the Olmecs in Mesoamerica, they created advanced cultures without growing up on the banks of a major river. Written languages did not develop here, but a system of recordkeeping called **quipu** evolved, using knots tied into strings.

The most noteworthy of these civilizations was the **Chavín**, who emerged around 1000 B.C.E. and dominated the coastal plain and Andean foothills of what is today Peru. Their chief city, Chavín de Huántar, was located more than 10,000 feet above sea level. Individual clans took responsibility for maintaining roads, bridges, and irrigation systems in the difficult mountain terrain. Trade was conducted between the seacoast and the mountain valleys, and the Chavín subsisted on a diet of fish, corn, quinoa, and potatoes. They worshipped a variety of **polytheistic** gods, including a jaguar deity and a fierce-looking figure identified by archaeologists as the Walking Sticks God. The Chavín are particularly known for their elaborate **textiles**.

The South American plains gave rise to nomadic herders. The rain forests of the Amazon basin were home to innumerable tribes. However, in neither place did large, settled civilizations appear before 1000 C.E.

## Other Cultures and Civilizations

Other peoples from this period to be aware of include the inhabitants of **Nubia**, located to the south of Egypt along the Nile River and settled around 3000 B.C.E. An important corridor of exchange between north and south, Nubia traded with Egypt and sub-Saharan Africa, although Egypt conquered it around 1500 B.C.E. The **Hebrews** of the Middle East emerged around 2000 B.C.E., gained a homeland in Israel around 1000 B.C.E., and developed the first major **monotheistic** religion, Judaism.

In the Mediterranean, the bull-worshipping Minoan civilization took shape on the island of Crete between 2000 and 1450 B.C.E., influencing the Greeks who later emerged nearby. More directly ancestral to the Greeks were the Mycenaeans, who reached their peak between 1600 and 1200 B.C.E. and fought the real-life version of the Trojan War (ca. 1250 B.C.E.) immortalized in the **Homeric epics** (the *Iliad* and the *Odyssey*). Greek culture grew more cohesive between the 1100s and the 500s B.C.E. In Italy, the city of **Rome** is traditionally said to have been founded in 753 B.C.E.

Also worth noting are the **Phoenicians**, a maritime culture that traded and colonized widely throughout the Mediterranean between 1550 and 300 B.C.E. From their home cities in Syria and Lebanon, they harvested cedar and manufactured a famous purple dye from shellfish. Their main legacy is the **alphabet**, a written script in which each sign represents a sound rather than a concept or object, and which was adopted in modified form by the Hebrews, Greeks, and Romans.

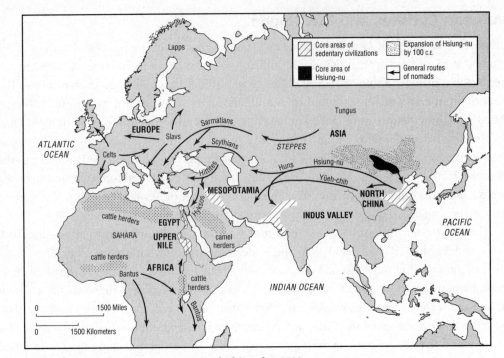

**The Movement of Peoples in Eurasia and Africa after 2000 B.C.E.**
Migration played a major role in the formation and development of early civilizations. Migrations often led to war and conquest, but they also facilitated cultural interaction and the spread of technology, science, languages, and religions.

Even if they did not form civilizations, **migrating pastoralists** influenced those who did. These include the **Indo-Europeans**, thought to have spread throughout Eurasia from Central Asia during the 1000s B.C.E. One Indo-European group, the **Aryans**, is considered by many to have played a foundational role in Indian prehistory by invading from the north around 1500 B.C.E. (Notoriously, Adolf Hitler and the Nazis misinterpreted the Aryans as the Europeans' "purest" ancestors and used this concept to justify their genocidal policies.) It was around 1500 B.C.E. that **Bantu** herders began their long migrations from the Niger River basin throughout most of sub-Saharan Africa. Egypt was conquered by the **Hyksos** people (a Greek term for "shepherd kings") during the 1600s B.C.E., and China's Shang and Zhou dynasties were constantly threatened by steppe nomads from Central Asia. Such pressures typically caused settled civilizations to become more effective at building walls and other defenses, and also to adopt new military techniques like horseback warfare, chariot warfare, and the use of bows and arrows. Conflicts between cities gave rise to increasingly professional armies and the art of siege warfare.

## SOCIETY, TRADE, AND ECONOMICS

All societies exhibit some form of **class distinction**, according to which people are defined by wealth, ancestry, or occupation. Such distinctions are minor in hunter-forager societies and somewhat more noticeable among pastoralists, but far more important in agricultural and settled societies characterized by **specialization of labor**. Specialized occupations in early societies include warriors, priests, artisans, and recordkeepers.

The most common form of government in ancient civilizations, and throughout most of history, was **monarchy**, or rule by a single person. In premodern eras, monarchs were often said to rule by divine will or even to embody a deity. Most monarchs governed with the assistance of a small **elite** class (generally referred to as the **nobility** or **aristocracy**). Also prominent in the ancient world was **oligarchy**, or rule by the few, in which aristocratic elites wield power without a monarch. A government dominated by a religious elite is known as a **theocracy**.

Certain roles, such as political, military, and religious leadership, are more powerful or more valued than others, causing the phenomenon of **social stratification**. A culture's system of ranking social classes is known as a **hierarchy**, and each culture has its own way of deciding how difficult it is for an individual to move from one class to another (the concept of **social mobility**). In earlier periods of history, status was almost always hereditary, and religion often played a role in justifying hierarchies. **Elite classes** were quite small, and social stratification tended to be rigid. Especially strict hierarchies, in which movement between classes is all but impossible, are known as **caste systems**. Elite classes typically enjoyed legal and financial advantages, such as more lenient treatment before the law and immunity from taxation. In most parts of the world since the rise of agricultural and urban cultures, political and religious leadership, as well as important social functions, have been dominated mainly by men, making these societies **patriarchal**. Matriarchal societies are extremely rare.

At the bottom of any hierarchy are those whose labor is coerced. **Slavery**, the most common form of forced labor, was widespread until recent times and still exists in some parts of the world. In ancient times, people fell into slavery in many ways. Some were prisoners of war or captives taken in raids. Many were owned and traded privately, others belonged to the state. **Debt slavery** and **indentured servitude** put people to work for owners who had paid money or taxes they owed. In some societies, slave status was hereditary. Slaves might perform hard labor, such as mining, construction, or agricultural fieldwork, or they might be used for household tasks. The severity of their treatment and the degree to which they had legal protections varied from place to place. **Serfdom**, an institution similar to slavery, compelled peasants to labor for the owners of the land they lived on. **Prison** (or **convict**) **labor**, which often involved especially backbreaking tasks, was utilized in many societies.

The exchange of goods and services, or **trade**, took place on an individual basis (**barter**), but also on local, regional, and transregional levels. Within societies, trade led to the formation of **marketplaces** and strengthened contacts among villages, cities, and rural communities. Connections created by regional and transregional trade spread ideas, beliefs, and technologies over great distances. Trade motivated the development of effective means of **water transport** and **overland transport**, including **caravans**. Until the invention of railroads and modern highways, water transport remained easier than land transport, and trade tended to flourish along rivers, lakeshores, and coastlines.

Key transregional routes during this era include the Nile, a conduit for trade within Egypt and for **Egypt-Nubian trade**. The **Mediterranean** supported a large network of trade among the peoples of North Africa and the Middle East, supported by boats as early as the 4000s B.C.E. Boats also connected the Middle East with the Indian Ocean basin, where commerce, including **Mesopotamian-Indus trade**, flourished among many peoples.

## CULTURE, THOUGHT, AND RELIGION

From earliest times, humans produced art and culture both for individual enjoyment and for social purposes. Civilized societies created works of greater complexity and sophistication. Much of the ancient world's art and architecture served political purposes—impressing populations and foreign visitors with the grandeur of the ruling elite—or religious ones.

Most prominent were works of **monumental architecture**, which required enormous expenditures of resources and labor. Motivations for these mammoth projects include religion, defense, entertainment, and the public display of political power. Examples from this era include tombs like the Egyptian **pyramids**, temples such as Mesopotamia's **ziggurats** and the platformed mounds built by the Olmecs, and the palace of **Babylon**. They also include city walls, paved streets and roads, and sewage and water systems like the ones found in Mohenjo-Daro and Harappa. All cities are the product of **urban planning**, although some are laid out more carefully than others.

**NOTE**

Common forms of art include carving and sculpture, painting, wall decorations, and the weaving of textiles. Familiarize yourself with representative samples of different cultures' artworks, such as the elaborate textiles of the Chavín culture, the purple cloth dyed by the Phoenicians, or the winged bulls carved to decorate the walls and guard the gates of Assyrian palaces.

Most, but not all, civilizations devised systems of **writing**, which allowed for complex recordkeeping and the efficient storage and transfer of ideas and information. The earliest approach to writing was to use symbols mainly to represent concepts and objects, as in the **cuneiform** script invented by the Sumerians around 3300 B.C.E., in which wedge-shaped characters were pressed into clay tablets. This was the same logic behind Egyptian **hieroglyphs** and Chinese **pictographs**. Such forms of writing, in which thousands of characters must be memorized, take great effort to learn. Sometime after 1200 B.C.E., the Phoenicians created the **alphabet**, which represented sounds, not concepts, and allowed the formation of any word from a small set of easily memorized symbols. The Phoenician alphabet was the forerunner of the Aramaic script, which in turn influenced Hebrew and Arabic. It was also adopted with some modification by the Greeks and Romans, who transformed it into the Latin alphabet still used today. In the Andes, no form of writing emerged until after Spain's conquest of the Incas in the 1500s C.E. Instead, a form of recordkeeping arose there known as **quipu**, or "talking knots," by which information was represented by knots tied in strings, with extra meaning added by various color combinations.

The first literary works appeared during this period. Among the world's oldest is Mesopotamia's *Gilgamesh Epic*, compiled around 1800 B.C.E., but based on Sumerian poems dating back to before 2000 B.C.E. The epic is a fictionalized account of a real king from the city-state of Uruk. An oppressor of his people, Gilgamesh is sent by the gods on a series of quests to atone for his wrongdoing. He searches for the secret of immortality and eventually gains wisdom. The **Egyptian Book of the Dead** describes the judgment of souls after death and advises readers on how to ensure a happy afterlife. This involves not just good behavior but the proper mummification and entombment of one's remains. India's *Rig Veda*, a collection of Vedic hymns composed in Sanskrit between 1700 and 1100 B.C.E., is one of the world's oldest Indo-European and one of the earliest Hindu sacred texts. From the early Greeks, at around 850 B.C.E., come the **Homeric epics**, the *Iliad* and *Odyssey*. The first is a fictionalized account of the Trojan War (ca. 1250 B.C.E.), complete with roles for the Greek gods, while the second describes the adventures of the warrior Odysseus as he returns home from the war.

Religions, developed by all societies to address questions of ethics and morality, the possibility of an afterlife, and humanity's place in the universe, grew more complex with the advent of civilization. Religious beliefs crossed borders, sometimes peacefully through trade and **missionary activity**, sometimes by **forced conversion**. Older forms of worship like **shamanism** persisted among hunter-foragers, and **ancestor veneration**, equally ancient, remained popular even in settled communities, for example in China and Rome. Most common in advanced societies was **polytheism**, best illustrated by the Sumerian-Babylonian and Egyptian gods of the Middle East, the Olympian deities worshipped by the Greeks (and borrowed in slightly different form by the Romans), the Vedic gods of ancient India, and the "celestial bureaucracy" venerated in China.

Of the new religions appearing during this era, the most influential were Vedism, the precursor to Hinduism; the Hebrew monotheism that evolved into Judaism; and Zoroastrianism. **Vedism**, a polytheistic faith, is thought to have been brought to India by Indo-European invaders around 1500 B.C.E. The oldest and best-known of its scriptures is the *Rig Veda*. Vedism set into place a rigid **caste system** later adopted by Hinduism. At the top were priest-scholars called **brahmins**, followed by warriors and political rulers, then traders, peasants, and artisans, and finally the lower classes, including servants and laborers. Vedism taught that all creatures possessed a soul that yearned to be reunited with the World Soul (Brahman), in spiritual perfection. Whether or not Vedism originated the concepts of **karma** and **reincarnation**, which were central to Hinduism and Buddhism in later years, is a matter of debate. What is certain is that Vedism placed its greatest emphasis on obedience to the brahmin class and the dozens of gods they performed rituals to, and to accepting one's lot in life—a perfect example of a religion justifying social hierarchy. After about 700 B.C.E. the brahmins' authority was challenged by new ideas that eventually gave birth to Buddhism and Hinduism.

According to Judaic tradition, the **Hebrews**, in the time of **Abraham**, entered into a covenant as the chosen people of the god Jehovah. The resulting religion, **Judaism**, is considered to be the first **monotheistic** faith. It may have arisen around 2000 B.C.E., although the term "Jewish" was not commonly used until after the 900s B.C.E. To the extent one can match Hebrew scripture with historical chronology, the Hebrews migrated to Egypt around 1700 B.C.E., were enslaved, and then escaped under the leadership of **Moses** around 1300 to 1200 B.C.E.—the exodus celebrated during the **Passover** holiday. Moses led the Hebrews to the "promised land" of Canaan (present-day Israel) and is said to have handed down the **Ten Commandments** and the **Torah** ("teaching"), the first five books of the **Tanakh**, or Hebrew scripture. The Hebrew kingdom reached its zenith under **David** (ca. 1000–961 B.C.E.) and his son **Solomon** (ca. 961–922 B.C.E.), the two of whom established a capital at Jerusalem and built the **First Temple** there. After Solomon's death, the Hebrew kingdom split up, then suffered several invasions, starting with the Assyrians in 722 B.C.E. and followed by Nebuchadnezzar's Babylonian Empire in 587 B.C.E. By this stage, many of Judaism's doctrines and customs were in place, but the formalization of Judaism itself would not be complete until the 500s and 400s B.C.E.

The origins of **Zoroastrianism** are difficult to uncover, with the birthdate of its founder, Zoroaster, ranging from 1700 to 500 B.C.E. Most believed that Zoroaster lived around 1000 B.C.E., probably in eastern Iran. Zoroastrian scripture, the **Avesta**, was compiled over many centuries, and the religion emerged as a major faith in Persia by the 500s B.C.E., when it was adopted by Darius the Great to justify his rule as king of kings. Like the Hebrew religion, Zoroastrianism was **monotheistic**, venerating a single god: **Ahura Mazda**, the world's creator and "wise lord." The good deeds of worshippers were said to assist Ahura Mazda in his cosmic struggle against the evil spirit of chaos, Ahriman. An end time of judgment was predicted, with an afterlife promised to those found worthy. Although it is kept alive today by only a few followers—the Parsi sect in parts of Iran, Pakistan, and India—Zoroastrianism influenced much of the Middle East for centuries, and many of its core elements are thought to have found their way into Judaic and Christian doctrines as they evolved.

**NOTE**

Mesopotamian and Greek myths both contain accounts of a catastrophic flood, much like the one described in the Old Testament's tale of Noah. Egyptian legends of the god Osiris, husband of the goddess Isis, speak of how he was murdered by his evil brother Set but brought back to life, a story of resurrection that many historians of religion believe may have influenced the New Testament depiction of Jesus. The Indo-European deities of the Vedic pantheon bear a strong resemblance to the gods of the Greco-Roman and Norse traditions, and are thought by most scholars to have been absorbed and adapted by these cultures, despite the great distances between them. All of these are classic examples of how far-reaching religious borrowing can be.

# UNIT 2

## TECHNOLOGICAL AND ENVIRONMENTAL TRANSFORMATIONS (600 B.C.E.–600 C.E.)

# Unit 2 Short Cut

## GENERAL REMARKS

The period between 600 B.C.E. and 600 C.E. was a time of increased political consolidation, technological aptitude, and social and cultural sophistication. World population continued to rise, and **networks of transregional communication and exchange** widened. Humankind's ability to affect its environment, and often strain it, steadily grew.

Although less advanced societies continued to be found in all parts of the globe, this era saw in many places the emergence of the most powerful and most highly **centralized states and empires** seen to that date. Thanks to effective **bureaucracies** and improved communications, these states were capable of governing large and diverse populations. They regulated systems of **trade**, tax collection, **resource mobilization**, and food supply over great distances. **Cities** played a larger role than ever as venues for political leadership, economic activity, and cultural and artistic dynamism. **Law codes** helped society function less arbitrarily. Increasingly **organized religions**, along with **shared artistic and cultural traditions**, fostered social cohesion and a stronger sense of identity.

In certain parts of the world, the civilizations of this era have come to be thought of as **classical**, in that after they faded, they left behind key cultural, intellectual, and linguistic legacies and golden-age memories of political unity and socioeconomic stability.

Not that instability was a thing of the past. Even the most powerful states broke apart due to **overreach**. As this unit will show, there were many ways to overextend oneself, whether politically, militarily, or economically. Most empires and large states, as they declined and fell, experienced at least one problem associated with overreach, and generally some combination of them. Large-scale **migrations** continued to redistribute the world's population over vast distances, and **war** remained a constant reality.

## BROAD TRENDS

| Humans and the Environment | |
| --- | --- |
| Europe and the Mediterranean | environmental impact of city building and intensive agriculture (deforestation, desertification, soil erosion, silted rivers)<br>appearance of smallpox and bubonic plague<br>aqueducts |
| Middle East | environmental impact of city building and intensive agriculture<br>appearance of smallpox and bubonic plague<br>qanats |
| Africa | environmental impact of city building and intensive agriculture<br>Bantu migration continues |
| East (and Central) Asia | environmental impact of city building and intensive agriculture<br>appearance of smallpox and bubonic plague |
| South (and Southeast) Asia and Oceania | environmental impact of city building and intensive agriculture<br>appearance of smallpox and bubonic plague<br>Polynesian migrations continue |
| Americas | environmental impact of city building and intensive agriculture<br>hillside terracing<br>"floating islands" |

## Humans and the Environment

- Societies and ecosystems in the Americas remained isolated from those in Afro-Eurasia.
- The Bantu migrations through sub-Saharan Africa continued from the pre-600 B.C.E. era into this one.
- The migratory voyages of the Polynesians throughout the Pacific, which may have begun around 1000 or 900 B.C.E., increased in scope.
- Eurasia was swept by a centuries-long wave of migration, consisting of Asiatic and Germanic peoples moving east to west, starting shortly after 1 C.E. and lasting until around 1000 C.E.
- City building and construction skills allowed a growing number of societies to affect their environment in major ways. Monumental architecture, water management (including irrigation, reservoirs, and canal building), the expansion of farming, and other practices made humanity's "ecological footprint" heavier than before.
- Along with pollution, especially important forms of environmental damage included soil erosion, the silting of rivers, desertification, and deforestation.
- Innovations in overland and maritime transport permitted easier and wider travel.
- Diseases and new foods spread more quickly and more widely than before. Some historians argue that this was the case more in Eurasia than in the Americas or Africa because east–west movement (along the same latitude and thus within similar climate zones) was easier there.
- Epidemic diseases, including smallpox, measles, and bubonic plague, played noteworthy roles in the decline of the Roman Empire and China's Han dynasty.

| Development and Interaction of Cultures (Including Technology) | |
|---|---|
| Europe and the Mediterranean | Greco-Roman philosophy, science, and empiricism (600s–200s B.C.E.) (Christianity)<br>Greek drama<br>Greek and Latin as classical languages<br>architecture (columns, domes, Parthenon, Pantheon)<br>wheeled vehicles + saddles and pack animals (horses, oxen) |
| Middle East | formalization of Judaism (ca. 400s B.C.E.; *Tanakh* and *Torah*)<br>Zoroastrianism<br>Christianity (Jesus of Nazareth; ca. 30 C.E.)<br>architecture (Hanging Gardens of Babylon, Great Library of Alexandria)<br>dhow and lateen sail<br>wheeled vehicles + saddles and pack animals (horses, oxen, camels) |
| Africa | ancestor veneration<br>dhow and lateen sail (monsoon winds)<br>wheeled vehicles + saddles and pack animals (camels) |
| East (and Central) Asia | ancestor veneration<br>Confucianism and Neo-Confucianism (Confucius; 500s B.C.E.; *Analects*)<br>Daoism (Laozi; 500s B.C.E.; *Tao-te Ching*)<br>Mandarin Chinese as classical language<br>woodblock printing<br>architecture (Great Wall of China, grid layout of cities, pagodas)<br>horse collar<br>stirrup<br>wheeled vehicles + saddles and pack animals (horses, oxen, camels)<br>Chinese junk |
| South (and Southeast) Asia and Oceania | emergence of Hinduism from Vedism (700s B.C.E.; *Upanishads*)<br>Buddhism (Siddhartha Gautama; 500s B.C.E.)<br>Indian epics<br>Sanskrit as classical language<br>"Arabic" numerals, pi, and zero<br>wheeled vehicles + saddles and pack animals (horses and oxen)<br>dhow and lateen sail (monsoon winds) |
| Americas | polytheism (human sacrifice)<br>ancestor veneration<br>Mayan hieroglyphs and calendar (concept of zero)<br>quipu<br>architecture (pyramids)<br>saddles and pack animals (llamas) |

## Development and Interaction of Cultures

- Existing religions, such as Judaism and Vedism, underwent reform and further codification.
- Major belief systems arising during this time were Hinduism, Buddhism, Confucianism, Daoism, and Christianity.
- Successful religions spread widely across regions and cultures due to trade and missionary activity.

- In some cases, people adopted a new religion but retained some of their older beliefs. The mixing of elements from more than one religion is called syncretism. Examples include the interplay of Buddhism, Confucianism, and Daoism in China and neighboring areas; the persistence of pagan folklore and ritual in newly Christianized parts of Europe; and the Hellenistic blending of Greek imagery with Buddhist art in parts of Asia conquered by Alexander the Great.
- Certain languages, such as Sanskrit, Mandarin Chinese, and Latin became transregionally influential because they were sacred to major religions or the official tongues of large and enduring empires.
- Literature and art were produced on a greater scale, often by clearly identifiable authors and artists. Examples include Chinese poetry, the dramas produced by Greek playwrights, and Indian epics such as the Mahabharata.
- Woodblock printing appeared in China during the 200s C.E. and spread elsewhere, allowing for the faster and wider dissemination of information.
- Distinct architectural styles arose in different regions of the world.
- Philosophy, or the systemization of rational thought, emerged in many regions. Especially in the Greco-Roman world, logic and empirical observation gained prominence, laying the groundwork for a more scientific worldview.
- Key technologies of the era improved maritime transport (lateen sails and boats such as junks and dhows) and increased the efficiency with which pack animals were domesticated (yokes, saddles, and stirrups).

| State Building, Expansion, and Conflict | |
|---|---|
| **Europe and the Mediterranean** | Phoenicia (800s–200s B.C.E.)<br>Greece (1100s–300s B.C.E.)<br>Hellenistic empire (Alexander the Great; 300s B.C.E.)<br>Roman Republic and Roman Empire (ca. 800 B.C.E.–476 C.E.)<br>frontier nomads (Asiatic and Germanic barbarians)<br>bureaucracy (proconsuls)<br>monarchies and oligarchies<br>republic<br>democracy |
| **Middle East** | Phoenicia<br>Persia (Darius the Great; 500s B.C.E.–600s C.E.)<br>Hellenistic empire<br>Rome<br>bureaucracy (satraps)<br>monarchies |
| **Africa** | (Hellenistic empire)<br>Ghana (400s C.E.?+) |
| **East (and Central) Asia** | Qin China (Shi Huangdi; 200s B.C.E.)<br>Han China (200s B.C.E.–200s C.E.; mandate of heaven)<br>frontier nomads (Xiongnu)<br>bureaucracy (civil-service examinations)<br>China's tributary system |

| State Building, Expansion, and Conflict | |
|---|---|
| South (and Southeast) Asia and Oceania | Mauryan Empire (300s–100s B.C.E.; Ashoka) Gupta Empire (300s–500s C.E.) frontier nomads (White Huns) bureaucracy (agricultural tax) |
| Americas | Teotihuacan (100s B.C.E.–750 C.E.) the Maya (250–900 C.E.) Moche (200–700 C.E.) |

## State Building, Expansion, and Conflict

- Most states were still governed by monarchies and oligarchies.
- The expansion of states into empires by means of conquest remained common.
- A few civilizations developed representative forms of government, such as republics and democracies, but these were rare.
- Cities became increasingly important as centers of government and bureaucratic administration.
- Law codes formalized and increased in number. They were not always fair by today's standards, but they boosted political and social stability.
- Many states grew adept at centralizing authority, expanding bureaucracies, and projecting political and military power. Techniques for the latter included diplomacy, the construction of forts and city walls, the maintenance of roads and supply lines, and the effective recruitment of soldiers and officers (both from one's own population and from conquered peoples).
- Armies grew larger, more skilled, and better organized. They equipped themselves with better technology.
- Many of this era's states and empires overextended themselves politically, economically, territorially (becoming victims of their own success), or environmentally. They tended to collapse as a result of this overreach.

| Economic Systems | |
|---|---|
| Europe and the Mediterranean | Mediterranean trade network standard currencies, weights, and measures slavery and corvée intensive agriculture (wheat) |
| Middle East | Mediterranean trade network Silk Road trans-Saharan caravan routes standard currencies, weights, and measures slavery and corvée intensive agriculture (wheat) |
| Africa | trans-Saharan caravan routes Indian Ocean trade network (Mediterranean trade network) slavery |

| Economic Systems | |
| --- | --- |
| East (and Central) Asia | Silk Road<br>Indian Ocean trade network<br>standard currencies, weights, and measures<br>slavery and corvée<br>intensive agriculture |
| South (and Southeast) Asia and Oceania | Indian Ocean trade network<br>standard currencies, weights, and measures<br>slavery and corvée<br>intensive agriculture (rice) |
| Americas | mit'a labor obligation<br>intensive agriculture (corn, potatoes) |

## Economic Systems

- Transregional trade was practiced on a larger scale and over greater distances than before. This change stemmed from innovations in overland and maritime transport.
- Major trade networks of the era included the Mediterranean Sea, the Indian Ocean basin, trans-Saharan caravan routes, and Eurasia's Silk Roads.
- Mobilizing resources and ensuring a steady supply of food became chief priorities for centralized states.
- Infrastructure—which included markets, roads, harbors, and other facilities built and maintained by states—supported local, regional, and transregional trade.
- Cities became increasingly important as centers of trade.
- Tax collection and the gathering of rents became more efficient and intrusive.
- Currency came to be used in a growing number of regions, greatly facilitating trade.

| Social Structures | |
| --- | --- |
| Europe and the Mediterranean | cities (Athens, Rome, Constantinople)<br>class diversification<br>patriarchalism (paterfamilias)<br>plebeians vs. patricians |
| Middle East | cities (Alexandria, Persepolis, Constantinople)<br>class diversification<br>caste system (Persian)<br>patriarchalism<br>diaspora community (Jews) |
| Africa | cities (Carthage, East African ports, Alexandria)<br>patriarchalism (with a handful of matrilineal societies) |
| East (and Central) Asia | cities (Chang'an)<br>class diversification<br>patriarchalism (especially encouraged by Confucianism) |
| South (and Southeast) Asia and Oceania | cities (Pataliputra)<br>caste system (Law of Manu)<br>patriarchalism (sati ritual)<br>diaspora communities (minorities throughout the Indian Ocean trade network) |

| Social Structures | | |
| --- | --- | --- |
| Americas | cities (Teotihuacan) ayllu clans | |

## Social Structures

- Social structures in centralized states grew more complex. A wider array of social classes appeared, including peasants, laborers, artisans, merchants, clergy, and slaves. Elite and ruling classes remained small and generally hereditary.
- Cities grew in size, quantity, and importance and contributed to the diversification of social classes. Major cities included Alexandria, Athens, Carthage, Chang'an, Constantinople, Pataliputra, Persepolis, Rome, and Teotihuacan.
- Most societies were highly hierarchical, with some going so far as to form rigid caste systems.
- Patriarchialism continued to be the norm, with women still generally occupying a secondary status and remaining on the disadvantaged side of the gender division of labor.
- Shared religious, cultural, and linguistic traditions tended to make societies more stable. Diversity and the presence of religious, ethnic, or linguistic minorities could enrich societies, but also presented states and empires with political and organizational challenges. Certain states took an inclusive approach to minority populations, others proved harshly assimilationist or even discriminatory.
- Diaspora communities formed in many places, as refugees, migrants, and traders from one society made new homes far from their points of origin.
- Systems of coerced labor were common to the point of being almost universal. They included slavery, corvée labor, and serfdom.

## QUESTIONS AND COMPARISONS TO CONSIDER

- In what ways did the larger and more centralized states of this era affect their physical environments? In what ways were they affected by their environments?
- What role did disease play in the history of this period? What about the exchange of new crops and foodstuffs?
- Compare the effects of large-scale migration during this period. Consider the movement of nomads into the territory of more settled civilizations. Or the formation of diaspora communities.
- What roles did religion play in supporting or challenging the status quo? In legitimating political regime or shaping social norms and gender relations?
- What was religious syncretism? How and where did it manifest itself?
- Consider the causes and consequences of transregional communication and exchange. What new technologies and techniques enabled the freer movement of people over greater distances? What happened when different regions came into more frequent contact with each other?
- How did the major states and empires of this era organize themselves? What state-building techniques did they use to mobilize resources and maintain political authority?

- How and why did this era's major states and empires decline and collapse? Good comparisons might include Han China and the Roman Empire, or Persia and India. To what degree, and in what forms, did overreach play a role in the fall of states and empires?
- Compare and contrast the major trade routes of the era, focusing on the Mediterranean, the Indian Ocean, trans-Saharan caravan routes, and the Silk Road.
- How did agricultural practice change and expand during these years?
- How did the role of women change from the preceding era? How did women's experiences vary from society to society during this era? To what degree did this depend on one's social class?

# UNIT 2
## SCENIC ROUTE
### (Chapters 4-6)

# The Development and Codification of Religious and Cultural Traditions

# 4

→ **CLASSICAL CIVILIZATIONS**

→ **ANIMISM AND SHAMANISM**

→ **ANCESTOR VENERATION**

→ **JUDAISM**

→ **HINDUISM**

→ **BUDDHISM**

→ **CONFUCIANISM (AND LEGALISM)**

→ **DAOISM**

→ **CHRISTIANITY**

→ **EMPIRICISM AND SCIENTIFIC THINKING**

→ **LITERARY WORKS AND ARCHITECTURAL FORMS**

→ **WOODBLOCK PRINTING**

→ **CULTURAL BORROWING AND SYNCRETISM**

Religions address questions of morality and spirituality. They provide societies with a sense of unity and inspire great works of art and architecture. They influence social and political life by justifying governments, social hierarchies, and gender norms. Less fortunately, religious institutions have at times opposed scientific innovation and social progress, and clashes between different faiths can provoke bigotry and conflict.

The period between 600 B.C.E. and 600 C.E. proved crucial to the development of religions worldwide. Existing faiths reformed themselves significantly, and new religions appeared as well. Also during this era, artistic and literary traditions flourished. Like religions, these provided a sense of social cohesion and shared cultural identity. Many consider this to have been an era of **classical civilizations**, meaning that the literature, art, and architecture produced by states like Han China, Gupta India, or Greece and Rome—as well as the languages used by them—were often much longer-lived in their influence than the actual states themselves.

## THE PERSISTENCE OF OLDER FORMS OF WORSHIP

Among many peoples, especially hunter-foragers, spirit-based belief systems like **animism** and **shamanism** remained popular. Shamans attempted to heal the sick, prayed to the spirits for success in hunting, and enforced taboos, or forbidden behaviors. A rare instance of animism practiced by a more settled society is Shinto, a religion indigenous to Japan, where it survives even today, alongside Buddhism.

Also carried over from earlier times was **ancestor veneration**. Most African peoples placed this at the heart of their religious practice and believed that proper observance of funeral customs and the sacrifice of food and wine would persuade the spirits of departed ancestors to protect their village. Thanks to its importance in China, ancestor veneration spread widely throughout East Asia—and the emergence of Confucian thought, with its emphasis on **filial piety**, reinforced the custom. In the Andes, peoples such as the Inca mummified their ancestors and placed them in special chambers, where they could be consulted for oracular advice (proper treatment was also thought to ensure a steady supply of water). Correct burial of the dead was crucial to the Hebrews and Greeks, and in ancient Rome, families built household shrines to ancestral spirits who, if not ritually placated, could turn spiteful and destructive. Romans also celebrated the yearly festival of Parentalia, or "ancestral days."

In many societies, the blending of old and new religious beliefs was common, as was the mixing of practices from more than one religion. This phenomenon is called **syncretism**, and it is illustrated by the absorption of ancestor veneration into Buddhist and Confucian ritual, by the incorporation of Vedic concepts into the newer religion of Hinduism, and by the persistence of pagan beliefs among newly Christianized peoples.

## REFORMED FAITHS AND NEW RELIGIONS

### Judaism

During this era, the **monotheistic** faith of the **Hebrews** took more solid shape in the form of **Judaism**. Starting in the 700s B.C.E., the Hebrew kingdoms were conquered by a succession of overlords, including the Assyrians, the Neo-Babylonian empire, the Persians, and the Romans. During the 500s B.C.E., the Neo-Babylonians uprooted the Hebrews from their land and tore down the First Temple built by Solomon. Soon after, the Persians allowed the Hebrews to return to Jerusalem, where a second temple was erected, but many chose to remain in their new homes, beginning the **Jewish diaspora**. The Jewish population was scattered even further by the Romans, who responded to Jewish rebellions by destroying the second temple and dissolving what remained of the Jewish state. The main source of Roman-Jewish tension was the Jews' monotheistic refusal to worship the Roman emperor as a living god, as other subject peoples agreed to do.

In the face of conquest and exile, religious adherence helped Jews to preserve their sense of identity. During this period, especially around the 400s B.C.E., rabbis codified Jewish scripture (the **Tanakh**, which included the **Torah**, the first five books of the Hebrew bible), and added their own commentaries on it (the **Talmud**, or "Instruction"). Jewish law operated on a retributive principle—an eye for an eye, a tooth for a tooth—that was common throughout the ancient Middle East. In particular, the **Code of Hammurabi** is thought to have influenced texts like the **Ten Commandments** enumerated in the Torah. Dietary restrictions were strict, and marriage outside the Jewish community was strongly discouraged. Although women were respected in the home, Hebrew society as a whole was patriarchal, and, like neighboring peoples in the eastern Mediterranean, the Hebrews practiced slavery. On the other hand, Jewish scripture insisted on treating slaves humanely and, more generally, placed a premium on charity. Jews also came to believe that a messiah ("anointed one") would someday appear as a savior to free them from foreign oppression.

### From Vedism to Hinduism

In India, where **Vedism** had dominated since around 1500 B.C.E., a religious crisis arose after 700 B.C.E. This resulted from growing discontent with the priestly brahmins, who taught that only through unquestioning obedience to them could worshippers be reincarnated into better lives. By contrast, a series of essays and poems called the **Upanishads** raised the possibility that people could liberate themselves from the cycle of life, death, and reincarnation without relying so heavily on the brahmins. As discussed below, the new faith of Buddhism emerged in the 500s B.C.E. as a result of these debates, but for most people in India, Vedism was not rejected outright, but absorbed into the larger set of beliefs known as **Hinduism**. This process took a long time, but was essentially complete by the 300s B.C.E. Today, the vast majority of people in India are Hindu, and sizable Hindu populations live elsewhere in South and Southeast Asia.

Hinduism recognizes tens of thousands of gods and goddesses, making it the most polytheistic religion in the world. The Vedic gods had their place, but three newer deities attracted the largest followings by the 200s B.C.E. **Brahma** is the masculine personification of the World Soul. **Vishnu** the Preserver is a savior figure and a great friend to humanity. **Shiva** the Destroyer, the dancing god of creation and destruction, reflects the duality of life and death. Hinduism's great mother goddess is Shakti.

From Vedism, Hinduism inherited the concepts of **karma** and **reincarnation**. Another legacy was the **caste system**, thought to have originated after 1500 B.C.E., when Indo-European invaders from the north relegated menial tasks and manual labor to the darker-skinned natives. Already by the 600s B.C.E., this scheme had stratified society into four distinct classes: priests, warriors and rulers, farmers and artisans, and servants and serfs. Over time, the system grew more complex and came to include a category of "untouchables," who performed degrading tasks like the handling of human waste and burial of the dead. The **Law of Manu**, a Hindu text compiled between 200 B.C.E. and 200 C.E., justified the caste system by arguing that acceptance of one's social status was a moral duty: good behavior as a member of a lower caste would result in good karma, increasing the likelihood of rebirth into a higher caste.

**The Practice of Sati.**
The ritual of sati (or suttee) was a long-standing Hindu tradition. When a man of high caste died, his widow was expected to be burned to death on her husband's funeral pyre. Only in the twentieth century was this practice fully abolished.

Hindu society was highly patriarchal. Women were considered legal minors even as adults, with no right to divorce or to own property. It was believed that women could not achieve spiritual union with the Brahman in their lifetimes, but had to wait to be reincarnated as a man. The most extreme form of female subservience was the **sati** (suttee) **ritual**, in which widows of certain castes were required to burn themselves to death on the funeral pyres of their deceased husbands. This practice was discouraged by India's colonial masters, the British, during the nineteenth century and outlawed by the Indians themselves in the twentieth.

## Buddhism

Several movements besides Hinduism arose in India during the transition away from traditional Vedism. One of these was **Buddhism**, based on the teachings of **Siddhartha Gautama** (ca. 563–483 B.C.E.), a nobleman from northern India. Appalled by the pain and poverty suffered by the common people, Gautama abandoned his aristocratic life to seek an answer to the question of human suffering. His search is said to have caused his spiritual **enlightenment**, after which he took the name Buddha, "the awakened one," and began to preach. Followers recorded his teachings in texts called sutras and distributed them widely. Long after Gautama's death, the Mauryan emperor **Ashoka** (269–231 B.C.E.) became a great supporter of Buddhism, spreading it throughout India and beyond its borders. Its influence is felt throughout all of South, Southeast, and East Asia.

Although Buddhism originated with the teachings of one person, the variety of beliefs and practices that fall into the category "Buddhist" is staggering. In its earliest form, Buddhism was less a religion and more a philosophy whose purpose was to correct the worst features of Vedism. Like Hinduism, Buddhism postulates that souls evolve toward spiritual perfection by means of birth, death, and **reincarnation**, and according to the law of **karma**. However, Gautama rejected the caste system and argued that anyone could achieve **nirvana**, or liberation from the wheel of life, without the aid of priests or rituals. All that was needed was to realize the Four Noble Truths and to follow the Eightfold Path of good conduct and the Five Moral Rules. At no time did the Buddha claim to be divine.

After the Buddha's death, the tradition he founded split into various denominations, roughly divided into two major schools. The older is **Theravada** (also referred to as Hinayana). Prominent in South and Southeast Asia, Theravada emphasizes simplicity and meditation and remains closer to the Buddha's actual teachings. The newer school, **Mahayana**, caught on farther to the north, especially in Japan, Korea, and parts of China. Mahayana involves more ritual and symbology than the Buddha spoke of, mainly due to **syncretism**: upon reaching new lands, Buddhism often blended with local beliefs. In some Mahayana denominations, the idea of nirvana came to resemble a heavenly afterlife, and the Buddha came to be seen as divine. Other elements appeared as well, such as the concept of hell and complex pantheons of gods and bodhisattvas (saintlike souls who had achieved nirvana but chose to remain in the earthly realm to help living humans).

> **NOTE**
>
> **The Four Noble Truths are as follows:**
> (1) human existence is inseparable from suffering;
> (2) the cause of suffering is desire;
> (3) suffering is extinguished by extinguishing desire;
> (4) desire may be extinguished by following the Eightfold Path (know the truth; resist evil; do nothing to hurt others; respect all forms of life; work for the well-being of others; free your mind of evil; control your thoughts; practice meditation). In addition to the Eightfold Path, the Buddha described Five Moral Rules (do not kill any living being; do not take what is not given to you; do not speak falsely; do not drink intoxicating drinks; do not be unchaste).

## Confucianism

Like Buddhism, **Confucianism** grew out of a philosophy founded by an individual who made no claim to divinity. A government official who served China's Zhou dynasty, **Confucius** (ca. 551–479 B.C.E.) lived through political chaos and war and, in retirement, began to ponder the proper relationship between society and the individual. His teachings, compiled by followers after his death, are contained in the *Analects*.

Confucianism took for granted the existence of the **celestial bureaucracy** of traditional Chinese gods but was most concerned with wise and ethical conduct in this world. Confucius proposed that **social harmony** could be created by a combination of benevolent rulership from above and good behavior from below. Order and **hierarchy** are paramount, and the well-being of the group comes before that of the individual. As long as the ruler performs his duties well, his people are obliged to obey him. This notion squared well with the **mandate of heaven** ideology that emerged during the Zhou period and remained central to Chinese political thought. Above all, Confucianism stressed **filial piety** and envisioned society as a perfect family, with junior members paying respect to their elders. This made it a good fit with China's longstanding tradition of **ancestor veneration**. A highly **patriarchal** system, Confucianism firmly established women as subservient. Men ruled, fought wars, and received educations. They could keep more than one wife, as well as concubines, and could divorce any woman who failed to produce an heir. Women were exclusively homemakers and mothers. They were allowed a limited education, but they were prohibited from owning property, and brides had no dowry system to provide them with financial security.

In theory, these hierarchical relationships rested on the concepts of reciprocity and mutual respect. Central to Confucian thought was a "golden rule" similar to that found in Christianity; in the *Analects*, Confucius declares, "Never do to others what you would not like them to do to you." (Confucius's assumption that people are inherently good and remain so if treated well contrasted with the logic behind a rival doctrine in China, **Legalism**, which viewed people as innately immoral, and advocated harsh punishments as the only way to control them.) Confucianism coexisted with, and at times competed against, Daoism and Buddhism. Several times it gained, lost, and regained its status as a state-supported code of conduct. By the 600s C.E., a newer variation of the creed, **Neo-Confucianism**, appeared. Even when it was not in official favor, Confucianism's influence persisted. China's traditional emphasis on filial piety, social hierarchy, and respect for authority stems in large part from Confucianism and has lasted into the modern era, even under the communist regime.

## Daoism

Like Confucianism, **Daoism**, a more mystical strain of thought, took shape in China during and after the 500s B.C.E. Its founder is considered to be **Laozi** or Lao-tse (ca. 600 B.C.E.), who may or may not have been an actual historical figure. Daoism's central text, the **Tao-te Ching**, is attributed to Laozi, but was most likely written in the 300s or 200s B.C.E.

Daoist belief maintains that the universe is governed by the **dao** (the "way" or "path"), an invisible yet irresistible force. Daoism is deliberately antirational, using parables to understand the world in non-logical ways. In one famous example, a Daoist teacher asks whether he is a man awakening from a dream in which he had been a butterfly, or a butterfly dreaming that it is a man. Daoists seek harmony with the universe and care little for politics or material possessions.

Flexible and individualistic, Daoism was easily reconciled with **ancestor veneration** and respect for China's **celestial bureaucracy** of gods. It influenced many cultural practices, including traditional medicine, martial arts, and, through its embrace of alchemy and astrology, the sciences of metallurgy and astronomy. Fortune-telling was crucial to Daoism, and the **I-Ching** ("Book of Changes"), one of its key texts, teaches how to read the future. Daoism added a profoundly philosophical tone to Chinese poetry, especially during the Tang dynasty, which produced some of the most beautiful verse in the country's history. Daoist ritual became interwoven with the architectural art of **feng shui**, or harmonious placement, which orients buildings and the items inside them in ways that ensure good fortune. Daoism's most famous symbol is the **yin-yang**, a circle whose dark and light halves are divided by a double-curved line, illustrating that nothing is absolute.

Daoism spread quickly throughout China, and elements of it were transported to the many parts of Asia where China exerted cultural influence. In all these places, it was common for people to blend Daoist, Buddhist, and Confucian practices **syncretically**.

## Christianity

Growing out of the Judaic tradition, **Christianity** was founded by **Jesus of Nazareth** (ca. 4 B.C.E.–29 C.E.)—later known as the Christ, from the Greek translation of the Jewish term "messiah." According to the Christian bible, Jesus was born into a Jewish family of humble background. As a wandering teacher, he sought to reform Jewish laws and traditions. To him, charity and compassion were more important than simply obeying rabbis and observing customs. During his ministry, Jesus claimed to be the messiah foretold by Hebrew prophecy. Although many Jews expected the messiah to restore the Hebrew kingdom politically, Jesus spoke of a heavenly kingdom instead, calling himself the "Son of God," whose teachings would redeem those who followed him.

Christ's teachings proved popular among the common people and the poor. On the other hand, his claims to be the messiah and his questioning of tradition angered conservatives within the Jewish religious establishment, and rumors that he had named himself "king of the Jews"—a misinterpretation of what he meant by being the messiah—aroused anxiety among the Jews' Roman overlords. When Jesus came to preach in Jerusalem during the Passover season, Jewish religious authorities demanded that the Romans arrest him. They did so, putting him to death by crucifixion.

Before his arrest, Jesus had claimed that he would return from the dead before returning to God in heaven. Afterward, his disciples began to preach that this had happened, and a new religion dedicated to him began to spread. Followers believed not just in the Resurrection, but also a Second Coming, when all souls would be subjected to a Day of Judgment—with virtuous Christians admitted to heaven, and nonbelievers damned to hell.

Roman law banned Christianity, and yet the new faith gained a large following over the next three centuries. Crucial to organizing the early church was the apostle **Paul**, who began as a persecutor of Christians, but suddenly converted and, between 45 and 64 C.E., worked with Christ's chief disciple **Peter** to establish new centers of worship. Paul's main contribution was to widen Christianity's appeal beyond its original community of Jewish followers. By decreeing that Christians did not have to observe Jewish dietary restrictions or circumcise male believers, Paul made it easier to convert Greeks, Romans, and other populations within the Roman Empire.

Christianity caught on among many groups, especially those who felt powerless in Roman society: noncitizens, slaves, commoners, and women. The new religion was open to all and held out the hope of a happy afterlife to those whose present lives were drab or miserable. The early church gave women many influential roles, but as it grew more hierarchical, the church took a more patriarchal stance. Many of the church fathers described below used the Old Testament story of Adam, Eve, and the serpent to assign women the blame for humanity's "original sin," and Paul's writings in particular put women in a secondary position. They were to obey men, and they were barred from positions of leadership, including priesthood. Cultures that adopted Christianity were affected by this worldview for centuries to come.

In 313 C.E., Roman persecution ended when the emperor **Constantine** legalized Christianity with the Edict of Milan. By the end of the century, Christianity had become not just the empire's official faith, but the only legally permitted one. During the 300s and 400s C.E., the church formalized its hierarchy of priests and bishops, with the pope at the top, and with men only as priests. Theologians now known as the "church fathers" established a body of dogma, or officially agreed-upon beliefs, with unacceptable views condemned as heresy. They also compiled the books of the **Bible**, combining texts from Jewish scripture (the Old Testament) with the four Gospels and other materials (the New Testament). Among the most famous of the church fathers are Jerome (347–420), who completed the first Latin translation of the Bible, and **Augustine** (354–430), whose *City of God* provided the intellectual basis for further Christian doctrine.

After the collapse of Rome in the 400s C.E., the Christian church drifted apart in terms of leadership and doctrine. In the west, **Roman Catholicism** remained dominant and provided much of Europe with a badly needed force for cultural unity. In the eastern Mediterranean and Middle East, the church, based in cities like Constantinople, evolved into **Eastern Orthodoxy**. The split between the two became final in the Great Schism of 1054 C.E. Despite this rupture, the **Judeo-Christian** tradition was and remained for centuries a bedrock of Western culture.

## THOUGHT AND CULTURE

Many peoples from this era developed an excellent working knowledge of mathematics, astronomy, anatomy, and engineering and also grew more adept at learning **empirically**, or by means of systematic observation. Most, however, attributed the workings of the world to cosmic forces or the will of the gods, rather than underlying scientific principles.

Among the first in the ancient world to move toward **scientific thinking** were the Greeks, between 600 and 200 B.C.E. Heavily influenced by Egyptian learning, Greek scholars, beginning with the so-called "Ionian scientists" (including the mathematician Pythagoras) and continuing with leading figures like Aristotle, Euclid, Ptolemy, and Archimedes, outlined many of the basic laws of geometry, geography, astronomy, medicine, and natural history. Their findings and observations were not always correct, and this was no straightforward shift from religious to secular thinking, for most Greek thinkers continued to believe in the gods at least somewhat. But this was a definite step forward in understanding how the world works. At the same time, the quest to properly define a **decimal system**, complete with the **concepts of *pi* and zero**, was ongoing. In Afro-Eurasia, scholars from Gupta India are generally credited with success here, as well as with inventing the misnamed "**Arabic numerals**." Some Mesoamerican peoples, including the Maya arrived at the concept of zero on their own.

Several civilizations also pioneered the mode of rational thought known as **philosophy**. Generations of Greek thinkers, culminating in Socrates (470–399 B.C.E.), Plato (428–347 B.C.E.), and Aristotle (384–322 B.C.E.) created the intellectual foundation on which most Western thought rests. All three asked fundamental questions about the nature of reality, moral behavior, and, especially in Plato's *Republic*, the best way to govern a society. Among the Romans, the emperor Marcus Aurelius gave powerful voice to the Stoic point of view, which called for courage and virtuous behavior even in the hardest of circumstances. The Greco-Roman blossoming in philosophy can be compared to the explosion of ideas caused in India by the religious debates over Vedism, and in China during the "Hundred Schools of Thought" era that gave birth to Confucianism and other new belief systems.

Scientifically minded or not, this era's major civilizations made great strides in the cultural sphere. Enduring works of literature appeared. In India, famous texts included the **Mahabharata**, composed between 200 B.C.E. and 200 C.E., a grand epic of 90,000 stanzas, making it perhaps the longest poem in the world. It depicts a great war between two royal houses, and its most renowned section is the **Bhagavad-Gita** ("Song of the Lord")—a poetic dialogue between the warrior-prince Arjuna and the demigod Krishna, who lectures Arjuna on the concept of moral duty. Early Chinese literature includes the Confucian and Daoist classics, such as the *Analects*, the *Tao-te Ching*, and the *I-Ching*, as well as *The Art of War* (500s B.C.E.), by Sun Tzu. In ancient Greece, which already had a tradition of epic poems like the *Iliad* and *Odyssey*, the practice of theatrical performance grew out of religious festivals. **Greek dramas** such as Aeschylus's *Oresteia* trilogy, Sophocles's Oedipus trilogy, and the bitter plays of Euripides commented on the role played in the universe by gods versus free will and the rights of the individual balanced against the obligations of belonging to a larger society. The **Aeneid**, an epic poem by Virgil, serves as a foundation myth for ancient Rome, which is depicted as having been founded by refugees from the Trojan War. Certain literary languages, especially if they were also the languages of widespread religions, powerful states, or **classical** civilizations with long-lasting cultural legacies, became historically and transregionally influential. Among these were **Sanskrit**, **Mandarin Chinese**, **Greek**, and **Latin**.

**Woodblock printing** appeared in China in the 200s C.E., allowing for the faster reproduction and dissemination of information. This innovation spread throughout Eurasia and would eventually give rise to the more revolutionary concept of moveable-type printing.

Regionally distinct forms of architecture took shape during this era, typically for religious and political purposes, although military defense was important as well. Large building projects continued in the Middle East, including the **Great Library of Alexandria** in Egypt and the **Hanging Gardens of Babylon**. Greco-Roman architecture made distinctive use of **columns** and facades, with the Romans adding archways and **domes**—requiring advanced engineering skills—to the repertoire. Key works include the **Parthenon** (the temple of Athena in Athens), Rome's **Pantheon** (a temple to all Roman gods) and **Colosseum**, and the Church of St. Sophia built in Constantinople in the 500s C.E. The cultures of Mesoamerica, especially the Maya and Aztecs, remain famous for their large **pyramids**, which were used not as tombs, as in Egypt, but as places of human sacrifice. Representative works from India include huge **cave temples** built in honor of Buddhist and Hindu deities (sometimes both at the same complex). The walls and towers guarding the Mauryan capital of Pataliputra rank as another Indian masterpiece, and numerous **Pillars of Ashoka**, inscribed with Buddhist teachings and Ashoka's own commentary about society and morality, were erected at sites throughout Mauryan India. As Buddhism spread throughout East Asia, temples came to be built in the unique **pagoda** style, and the Chinese practice of planning cities such as **Chang'an** according to meticulous **grid layouts** caught on throughout the wider region.

**The Buddha Guarded by the Greek Demigod Herakles (Hercules)**
This architectural feature, created during the 100s C.E. in the Kingdom of Gandhara, located on the border of present-day Pakistan and Afghanistan, illustrates the unique fusion of Greco-Roman and Buddhist culture that followed the far-ranging military conquests launched by Alexander the Great.

One style unique to this era is the **Greco-Buddhist architecture and sculpture** that resulted from the campaigns of **Alexander the Great** in the 300s B.C.E. and the establishment of a long-term Greek presence in Central Asia and present-day Pakistan, Afghanistan, and India. A striking example of **cultural borrowing**, this fusion of two styles is thought by some to have led to the first artistic depictions of the Buddha in human form—a particular strength of Greek sculpture.

# The Development of States and Empires

**5**

→ **PERSIA**
→ **QIN AND HAN CHINA**
→ **ARYANS AND DRAVIDIANS**
→ **THE MAURYAN AND GUPTA EMPIRES**
→ **THE PHOENICIANS AND CARTHAGE**
→ **THE GREEKS (ATHENS AND SPARTA)**
→ **ALEXANDER THE GREAT AND HELLENISTIC CULTURE**
→ **THE ROMAN REPUBLIC AND ROMAN EMPIRE**
→ **TEOTIHUACAN AND THE MAYA**
→ **THE MOCHE**
→ **ADMINISTRATIVE INSTITUTIONS AND BUREAUCRACIES**
→ **METHODS OF PROJECTING STATE POWER**
→ **ORGANIZATION OF LABOR AND RESOURCES**
→ **IMPERIAL AND STATE OVERREACH**

State building during this era reached new levels of complexity and sophistication. Fielding better-armed and better-organized military forces, and with stronger bureaucratic and recordkeeping mechanisms at their disposal, a number of **key states and empires** brought political, economic, and social unity to wide-ranging territories. Many of these became the **classical** civilization in their part of the world, bestowing a long-lived cultural inheritance to the states that succeeded it.

In a process often referred to as **overreach**, states and empires typically overextended themselves in one or more of several ways, leading to decline and downfall.

## KEY STATES

Among this era's most centralized states are those listed below. As you study them, think about patterns in the way they governed themselves, projected power, and organized labor and resources.

### The Persian Empires (Southwest Asia)

In a very short time, the **Persians** of present-day Iran came to dominate the Middle East, building one of the largest empires in world history. Their first dynasty, the Achaemenid (550–331 B.C.E.), quickly conquered neighbors like the **Lydians** (who invented **metal coinage** around 600–500 B.C.E.), the Neo-Babylonians, and the Egyptians. Under the third Achaemenid ruler, **Darius the Great**, Persia's empire stretched from North Africa to India and measured more than 2 million square miles, making it the biggest state seen in the world to that date.

From two capitals—Susa for administration and **Persepolis**, built by Darius in the Mesopotamian style to impress citizens with his power—the Persians ruled with the help of an advanced postal system, an excellent network of roads, a single currency, and a form of **provincial administration** that divided the empire into 20 or so regions and delegated local authority over them to officials called **satraps**. Persian society was patriarchal and rigidly stratified, with the population divided into several **castes**: warriors, priests called magi, and peasants. The ruler was known as the "king of kings" (*shahan-shah*) and referred to all his subjects as "my slaves." Under Darius, Persia embraced **Zoroastrianism**, but Achaemenid rulers remained relatively tolerant of other faiths.

Achaemenid Persia fought several losing wars with its Greek neighbors to the west in the 500s and 400s B.C.E. In 331 B.C.E, it fell to the Hellenistic conqueror **Alexander the Great**. A new dynasty, the Parthians (247 B.C.E.–224 C.E.), liberated Persia from the regime founded by Alexander's generals after his death. More decentralized than the Achaemenid and Hellenistic empires, the Parthian state combined elements of Greek and Persian culture and grew wealthy from trade along the **Silk Road**. They were powerful enemies of the Roman Empire as it expanded eastward. It may have been in Parthian Persia that **smallpox** first arose, possibly spreading from there to Rome and Han China. Rising up in the Parthians' place was the Sassanid empire (224–651 C.E.), another great rival of Rome and the Byzantine empire that followed it. The Sassanid shahs earned riches from the Silk Road, but also from the commerce generated by **Arab traders**. Like earlier Persian rulers, the Sassanids practiced Zoroastrianism, but made it an official state faith and proved much less tolerant than the Achaemenids had been. The Sassanids were suddenly swept away in the 600s C.E. by the rapid military expansion of **Islam** out of the Arabian Peninsula.

## The Qin and Han Empires (East Asia)

From the 200s B.C.E. to about 600 C.E., a united and steadily growing China was ruled by several major dynasties. The most notable were the Qin (221–206 B.C.E.) and the Han (206 B.C.E.–220 C.E.).

Although short-lived, the **Qin dynasty** was important because of its founder, **Shi Huangdi**, who ended feudal decentralization of the "Warring States" period and, for the first time in the country's history, united northern China with the Yangzi valley in the south. A stern ruler who favored the ideology of **Legalism** (which advocated harsh laws as a way to keep inherently wicked people in order), Shi Huangdi turned the Qin state into a centralized dictatorship, administered by a large and effective **bureaucracy**. He standardized weights and measures and modernized the Chinese army by introducing iron weapons, crossbows, and cavalry warfare. He used forced labor to build thousands of roads and canals, as well as the first of the defensive structures that collectively came to be known as the **Great Wall of China**. The Qin state ended slavery and serfdom, not out of kindness but because free peasants had to pay taxes and serve in the army. The Qin taxed so heavily that, shortly after Shi Huangdi's death, rebellions destroyed the dynasty.

The strong and durable **Han dynasty**, brought to power by these uprisings, built on the Qin state's foundations to create a centralized, efficient empire. Under warrior-emperors like Wu Ti (156–87 B.C.E.), its armies expanded hundreds of miles in all directions, absorbing most of China and parts of Vietnam, Korea, Manchuria, and Mongolia. Where they did not take over directly, the Han rulers established a **tributary system**, exacting payment from neighboring states. **Cavalry warfare** and the **crossbow** gave them military advantages and allowed them to repel **steppe nomads**—especially the worst threat, the Turkic **Xiongnu**.

**The Great Wall of China.**
The so-called Great Wall was actually a network of many walls. Construction began as early as the 200s B.C.E., under the emperor Shi Huangdi, and took centuries. Thousands of the workers, many of them prisoners, died. As impressive a feat of engineering as the Great Wall is, it failed to defend China from attack. Note the state of disrepair depicted in this engraving.

From their capital at **Chang'an**, the Han rulers, like the Qin before them, put into place an efficient postal system, tax-collection system, and **bureaucracy**, staffed by civil servants who had to pass a rigorous **examination system**. They built defensive fortifications (enlarging the Great Wall), canals to link the nation's rivers, and roads. The Han governed less ruthlessly than the Qin, reviving the Zhou ideal of the **Mandate of Heaven**, which proposed that only virtuous rulers deserved to rule. In contrast to the Legalism of the Qin years, the Han turned to **Confucianism**, with its argument that superiors owed kind treatment to their inferiors. Han rulers also expanded China's law code.

During most of the Han period, China's economy was strong, spurred by improved agricultural techniques (including better irrigation and the invention of the **horse collar**, which allowed heavier loads to be pulled) and the country's monopoly on **silk production**, which made it a dominant player in **Silk Road** trade. By 200 C.E., though, the Han state was in decline. Agricultural downturn and an overall economic slump sapped its strength, as did governmental corruption and ineffectual leadership. Bandits, rebels, and nomadic invaders, particularly the Xiongnu, made it difficult for the Han to protect their borders. What appears to have been a **smallpox epidemic**, arriving from the west in the late 100s C.E., also weakened the country. In 220 C.E., Han rule collapsed. Over the next three and a half centuries, China remained mired in anarchy. Not until 589 C.E. did a strong dynasty, the Sui, reestablish order.

## The Mauryan and Gupta Empires (South Asia)

To what degree the Indus River civilization was "Indian" remains unclear, as do the true foundations of Indian culture. Conventionally, these are said to have been laid around 1500 B.C.E., when the **Indo-Europeans** known as **Aryans** invaded northern India. These lighter-skinned horseback warriors conquered darker-skinned natives (collectively known as **Dravidians**), forming a common culture with them as they expanded southward. Variety within this culture was still astounding, however, with dozens of ethnicities and languages evolving throughout the subcontinent.

India's size and diversity kept it broken apart during much of its early history. The first state to unify most of it was the **Mauryan Empire** (324–184 B.C.E.), founded by Chandragupta Maurya and ruled from the capital of **Pataliputra** on the eastern Ganges. The empire, which included all but India's southernmost tip, developed an elaborate **bureaucracy** that collected a 25 percent tax on all agricultural production and maintained a network of informers to spy on its own people and enforce obedience. The Mauryans' powerful army deployed elephants in addition to chariots and cavalry, and their trade network was extensive. They issued a standard currency and traded not just with East and Southeast Asia, but as far away as the Middle East and the eastern Roman Empire. Key exports included salt, iron, and cotton cloth. The best known of the Mauryan emperors was **Ashoka** (269–232 B.C.E.). A successful warrior as a youth, Ashoka became sickened by war after one of his greatest victories. He converted to Buddhism and advocated peace and tolerance, advertising those ideals by raising stone columns carved with Buddhist teachings—the **Pillars of Ashoka**—throughout the country. He encouraged trade with China, especially for its silk, and opened trade routes to the north. He was admired for his justice and wisdom, and remains famous for creating harmony between India's Buddhists, Hindus, and other believers. His efforts to spread Buddhism played a key role in establishing it as a formal religion.

In 184 B.C.E., the Mauryan empire collapsed due to attacks from outside enemies, and for the next five centuries, India reverted to a state of political disunity. Not until 320 C.E. did another large empire rise up, also along the eastern Ganges: the **Gupta Empire**, which controlled most of north-central India, with vassal states to the east and northwest. The Gupta consciously imitated the Mauryan empire. Their first ruler, Chandra Gupta, borrowed his name from the first Mauryan emperor, and chose the Mauryan capital, Pataliputra, as his own. The Gupta empire was smaller and less centralized than the Mauryan, and depended more on diplomacy to maintain its authority. Although the Gupta were Hindu, they practiced religious toleration. Gupta India traded by boat with Malaysia and Indonesia, exchanging cotton, metal wares, and salt for spices, and also with China for silk. Their economic network also included the Arabian Sea and eastern Mediterranean. At least in Afro-Eurasia, Gupta scholars are thought to have originated the **decimal system** (and the wrongly named "**Arabic numerals**"), including the concepts of **zero** and *pi*. As did the Mauryans, the Gupta imposed a 25 percent tax on agricultural products. Not only did the Gupta strengthen the **caste system**, they were more patriarchal than the Mauryans, and the status of women declined. Women lost the right to own property and were forced to become more obedient to males. Among Hindus, the **sati** ritual of burning widows alive with their dead husbands became more common.

The Gupta emperors fell in the mid-500s C.E. As with the Mauryans before them, the main cause was outside military pressure, especially from the nomadic **White Huns** on the northwest frontier. From then until after 1000 C.E., India remained decentralized. Muslim invaders then moved into the subcontinent, decisively reshaping Indian politics and culture.

## Phoenicia, Greece, Alexander the Great, and Rome (The Mediterranean)

In the Mediterranean, the **Phoenicians** reached their peak as a civilization during this era. Originators of the **alphabet** and great seafaring traders, the Phoenicians, starting in the

800s B.C.E., spread westward from present-day Syria and Lebanon to establish city-states throughout the Mediterranean. The most important of these was the North African port of **Carthage**. Like most Phoenician colonies, Carthage enjoyed a high degree of social mobility, electing an **oligarchic** government from a merchant aristocracy that was not restricted by birth. The Phoenicians worshipped a polytheistic pantheon headed by the storm deity Baal, and are known to have sacrificed children to their gods. Carthage possessed a large and technologically advanced navy, and proved a powerful foe to Rome in the 200s B.C.E. The **Punic Wars** between Carthage and Rome determined the destiny of the Mediterranean world for centuries.

Between 1150 and 800 B.C.E., the ancient **Greeks** (or **Hellenes**) formed a distinct culture, united by a common language and the worship of the Olympian gods. In the centuries that followed, and especially during the **classical** period (ca. 500s–300s B.C.E.), they built a society of **Greek city-states and colonies** not just in Greece itself, but throughout the eastern Mediterranean, from Italy to the Turkish coast. (The Greek term for "city-state," *polis*, is the root of our word "politics.") Excellent mariners, the Greeks traded widely in the Mediterranean, exporting olives and wine. Some of Greece's city-states were monarchies, but most were **oligarchies**, in which a small elite class of rich, powerful families ruled. The most influential of the classical city-states were Sparta and Athens. **Sparta** exploited the labor of agricultural slaves called helots and subjected all freeborn males to a regimented, militaristic upbringing—producing the Greek world's finest and most feared army. **Athens** focused on cultural and political advancement, relying on maritime trade for wealth and basing its military might on naval power.

While Sparta handled its helots with infamous brutality, **slavery** was common in all Greek city-states. As much as a quarter of a city's population might be slaves, although many were used not for the most crushing forms of hard labor, but as highly valued household servants and skilled workers. In most Greek city-states, women were treated as distinct social and political inferiors—it was in Sparta, interestingly, that women had the most rights. Despite slavery and patriarchalism, ancient Greece hit upon one of the ancient world's most significant political innovations. This was **democracy**, or rule by the people, which began in Athens in 508 B.C.E. and reached its peak during the 400s B.C.E.—although even in Athens, women and slaves were excluded from political life.

**Hellenic culture**, described in the previous chapter, gave rise to **philosophy**, **scientific thinking**, **Greek dramas**, and some of the world's finest architecture and sculpture. Politically, the Greek city-states remained highly decentralized, although most of them banded together to resist conquest during the **Persian Wars** (492–479 B.C.E.). A generation later, rivalry between Sparta and Athens led to a devastating conflict known as the **Peloponnesian War** (431–404 B.C.E.). Although Sparta and its allies triumphed, both sides were exhausted, leaving Greece open to domination by its neighbor to the north, Macedonia.

It was from this Greek-Macedonian kingdom that the ancient world's most gifted commander, **Alexander the Great** (356–323 B.C.E.), launched one of the most successful military campaigns of all time. Alexander crossed into Asia, toppled the Achaemenid Persian empire, and conquered territory all the way to India's northwest border. Before dying, he had led his army on a journey lasting almost ten years and covering more than 20,000 miles. His generals split his empire among them, preserving Greek-Macedonian rule for many years in places like Egypt, Persia, and Central Asia. More important in the long term than his battle victories was Alexander's promotion of Greek culture and the fusing of it with other societies' traditions to create **Hellenistic** ("Greek-like") **culture**. Hellenistic influences spread across a huge portion of Eurasia, from North Africa and the Mediterranean to the Indian frontier, where the Greco-Buddhist culture mentioned in the last chapter flourished. Alexander's grand capital, the Egyptian city of **Alexandria**, with its **Great Library**, became one of the ancient world's greatest centers of trade, learning, and culture.

As the Greeks' political power waned, a new force emerged not far away: **Rome**, founded around 800 B.C.E. From their homeland in Italy, the **Romans** came to dominate the Mediterranean and the regions adjacent to it, creating one of the largest and longest-lasting empires in history. Rome remained a monarchy until around 500 B.C.E., when rebellion created the **Roman Republic**. From the Latin term *res publica*, or "public thing," a **republic** is a state without a monarch and one in which all or most adult citizens (in premodern times, only males) play some role—although not necessarily an equal role—in the political system. During the republican period, Roman society experienced tensions between the **plebeian** (lower) and **patrician** (upper) classes. Through a long process of struggle and negotiation, the former gained greater, but never complete, equality. The latter controlled the oligarchic Senate and the consuls, two executive leaders elected annually from among patricians. It was during this period that Rome became a Mediterranean empire, first expanding throughout the Italian peninsula, and then fighting three bitter conflicts, the **Punic Wars** (264–146 B.C.E.), against the Phoenician city of Carthage. Victory over Carthage made Rome the strongest state in the western Mediterranean. It then turned east, taking Greece and parts of Turkey, setting the stage for future conquests in Egypt and Asia.

Such rapid expansion caused the **collapse of the Roman Republic** during the first century B.C.E. Small farmers, the closest Rome had to a middle class, went bankrupt, thanks to falling grain prices and the increased use of slave labor by larger landowners. Poverty worsened, and many of the urban poor joined violent mobs. Rome was shaken by a series of civil wars and slave revolts from 91 to 30 B.C.E., and political power began to fall into the hands of individual politicians. The most famous of the late republican leaders was the charismatic general Julius Caesar, who assumed dictatorial powers during the civil war of 49–45 B.C.E. and was assassinated in 44 B.C.E. by aristocratic republicans who feared he would crown himself king. More war followed, ending the republic by 30 B.C.E.

A new regime, the **Roman Empire** (ca. 30 B.C.E.–476 C.E.), was founded by Caesar's adopted son, who renamed himself Caesar Augustus, revived Rome's strength and wealth, and created the position of emperor. Although the Senate continued to function, Rome's emperors became more despotic over time, with some using their power more wisely than others. Despite occasional episodes of political violence, Rome, between the reign of Augustus and the early 200s C.E., experienced an age of peak power and prosperity known as the *pax Romana* ("Roman peace"). Its economic and military might increased, and its huge territory extended from Spain in the west to Asia Minor in the east, from northern Africa in the south to the British Isles in the north. The Romans masterfully administered a huge **bureaucracy**, dividing the empire into provinces governed by regional officials called **proconsuls**, and building a tremendous network of roads, sea lanes, **aqueducts** (to carry water over long distances), and fortifications, including city walls and frontier defense barriers such as Hadrian's Wall in Scotland. The **distribution of grain** throughout the empire, and especially the doling-out of cheap or free bread to the poorer classes in Rome and other large cities, was a key state priority.

After the early 200s C.E., Rome found itself in crisis. Many emperors proved incompetent. Also, already during the late 100s C.E., the **epidemic** spread of what was probably **smallpox** (brought back by soldiers returning from wars in the Middle East) had severely depleted the empire's population and economic production—and **measles** and **bubonic plague** would do the same in later years. During the 300s C.E., the eastern half of the empire split from the western half, becoming the **Byzantine (Eastern Roman) Empire**, headquartered in the city of **Constantinople**. Deprived of the east's wealth and suffering from military and political **overreach**, the western half of the empire found it difficult to govern itself and to pay the ever-larger amounts of money it owed its army. Military uprisings became depressingly common, and migrating waves of **Germanic** and **Asiatic nomads**, whom the Romans called **barbarians**, attacked from the east and north in growing numbers. Although some barbarians settled in Rome and adopted its civilized ways, others did not, and the empire's heartland lay open to them by the 400s C.E. Germanic Goths sacked the city of Rome in 410 C.E., and another wave of Goths took it over completely in 476 C.E.—the year Rome's western empire is considered to have fallen.

Roman society was sharply divided into citizens and noncitizens, with the latter possessing no civil rights. Among citizens, the primary distinction was between upper-class **patrician** and lower-class **plebeian**. **Slavery** was widely practiced—approximately a third of Rome's population was enslaved—and occasional slave revolts, like that of Spartacus in the 70s B.C.E., disturbed the order of things. The role of women changed over time. Republican Rome was strictly **patriarchal**, giving the **paterfamilias** (male family head) absolute power over his wife and children. By the late republican period and early empire, women gained more economic rights and greater freedom to divorce. They still had no vote.

Together with the Greeks, whose philosophy, art, and gods they absorbed, the Romans bestowed to the Western world an immense cultural heritage: **Greco-Roman classicism**, which has remained central to the Western tradition to this day. In their own right, the Romans were master architects and engineers, and many of their roads, **aqueducts**, cities, and fortifications proved useful for centuries to come. They were the first to use large arches and **domes** on a regular basis. Politically, the monarchs of medieval Europe would long attempt to live up to the Roman ideal of unified and centralized rule. **Roman law** remains a keystone of Western legal thought. The concept of "innocent until proven guilty" stems from republican Roman law as codified in the **Twelve Tables**, and the **Justinian law code**, compiled in Byzantium during the 500s C.E., served as the chief model for later law codes throughout Europe. **Latin** remained the common language of Europe's educated classes for hundreds of years. Finally, it was on the Roman Empire's eastern edge that the religion of Christianity was born. By **legalizing Christianity** in the 300s C.E., and then adopting it as their official faith, the Romans ensured the new religion's survival as a major intellectual and cultural force long after the empire itself had disappeared.

## Teotihuacan, the Maya, and the Moche (Mesoamerica and the Andes)

In Mesoamerica, many societies emerged from the religious and cultural foundations left by the Olmecs, who faded around 400 B.C.E. These city-states shared a common culture and interacted economically, but remained disunited and frequently warred with each other. Kings and priests ruled in extremely hierarchical fashion. Women were subject to rigidly defined gender roles, although upper-class women gained status as priestesses or by exerting informal influence over noble husbands, and at least two Mayan kingdoms allowed women to rule. Like the Olmecs before them, many Mesoamericans practiced **human sacrifice**. They built **pyramids** that symbolized sacred mountains with roots in the underworld, but reaching to the heavens as well.

One of these societies arose near present-day Mexico City, centered on **Teotihuacan** (ca. 100 B.C.E.–750 C.E.)—which, with a population of 200,000, ranked as one of the world's largest cities at that time. Politically unusual, in that they governed by means of **oligarchy** rather than monarchy, the Teotihuacan people practiced human sacrifice and built **pyramid** temples to the sun and moon, as well as to the god Quetzalcoatl, a bird-serpent worshipped by other Mesoamericans, including the Mayans. Teotihuacan peasants engaged in **intensive farming**, making the most of limited space by draining swamps, elaborately irrigating their fields, and terracing hillsides. In shallow lakes, they built "floating islands" (*chinampas*), which created more space for crops—the most important of which was corn. They produced pottery and obsidian carvings and traded widely, including with the Maya. They entered into decline around 650 C.E. Their downfall used to be blamed on war, but it is now thought that elite overspending caused social tension that led to violent and crippling revolts.

**Mayan Pyramid of Chichén Itzá.**
The Maya founded the city of Chichén Itzá around 250 C.E. It remains a treasure trove of archaeological evidence of how the Maya lived.

Teotihuacan's period of prominence overlapped with the rise of the **Maya** (ca. 250–900 C.E.), whose culture emerged in present-day Guatemala and spread as far north as southern Mexico. The Mayan lands were governed by approximately 40 city-states and kingdoms. In total, the Mayan population reached three million. Staple crops included corn, squash, beans, cacao (from which chocolate is made), and cotton.

Mayan kings served both as politicians and as priests. The Maya built **pyramids** and satisfied their polytheistic gods—which included jaguar deities and the winged serpent Quetzalcoatl—by means of **human sacrifice**. **Slavery** was common, with most slaves taken as captives during wartime. The Maya devised an elaborate **hieroglyphic** script, the most advanced system of writing in the pre-Columbian Americas. Superb astronomers and mathematicians, they understood the concept of **zero** and invented an intricate and accurate

**calendar**. The reasons for their collapse, indicated by the abandonment of most Mayan cities between 800 and 900 C.E., remain a mystery. Theories include nearby volcanic activity, intercity warfare, disease, and environmental degradation caused by overpopulation or overuse of the land.

Farther to the south, in the **Andes Mountains**, many advanced cultures arose during this era. The most powerful were the **Moche**, who lived in present-day Peru between 200 and 700 C.E. Like other societies in the region, the Moche used the **quipu**, or knot-tying, system of recordkeeping, and they lived in clans called **ayllu**, which owned land communally. As did other political elites in the Andes, the warrior-priests who governed the Moche compelled ayllu to perform labor according to the **mit'a** system, which combined elements of serfdom and corvée labor. Members of an ayllu would typically farm land owned by the elite, tend llama and alpaca herds, or build roads, bridges, or hillside terraces. Those living in the valleys grew quinoa, corn, and potatoes, while coastal settlers fished. Trade with the Amazon river basin provided fruit. The Moche produced excellent ceramics and textiles. Their society was highly stratified, but not politically united under a single state. With no written script available, historians theorize that the Moche culture ended because of a combination of environmental factors (shifting of the Moche River by an earthquake, plus natural erosion caused by heavy rains) and interference with its trade routes by a military rival.

## METHODS OF RULE

Governing large states and empires required a complicated mix of political skill, military strength, and economic judgment. As you study the societies described above, learn how to compare and contrast the techniques they used to deal with key aspects of rulership.

**Administration** and **state institutions** were crucial to rulership. **Centralized government** was the goal of most kings and emperors: among the most successful centralizers were Persia, Qin and Han China, Mauryan India, and Rome. Societies organized on a **city-state** basis, such as Phoenicia, ancient Greece, and the Maya, tended to be culturally unified but politically decentralized. **Law codes** and **courts** enforced rules, although in most premodern states they did not guarantee equal treatment of all classes—elites often received more rights and privileges, and lighter punishment for crimes. **Bureaucracies** enabled rulers to exercise their will over large areas. Among the tasks they performed were **tax collection**, **law enforcement**, the **mobilization of food and resources**, **military defense**, the **regulation of trade** (including the creation of **currencies** and standard weights and measures), and the maintenance of **infrastructure** (roads, canals, postal systems, and so on). Most rulers created **regional** and **local levels of government** and delegated authority to officials at those levels. Persia was subdivided into provinces governed by **satraps**, and large territorial units in Rome were run by **proconsuls**. In Qin and Han China, the empire was organized into large zones called *jun*, and then into smaller counties. Gupta and Mauryan India likewise operated several levels of government.

Other techniques of rule included **religious justification** (the Mandate of Heaven in the case of Han China, the priestly functions claimed by leaders like the Moche and Mayan rulers, the notion in most societies that the ruler was somehow blessed by the gods), **claiming the legacy** of an earlier regime (as the Gupta did in India by emulating the Mauryan empire), and creating a **secret police** or **network of spies and informants** to monitor one's own people. **Official religions** were one way to strengthen feelings of loyalty and social unity, but they could also create resentments in states with diverse populations. Some empires forced their official religion on all subjects, while others, such as the early Persians and India under the Mauryans and Guptas, practiced **religious toleration** to one degree or another. Because it made the task of governing easier, Rome's imperial policy was to allow those it conquered to worship as they pleased, as long as they obeyed Roman gods and respected Rome's gods along with their own. Alexander the Great followed a similar policy.

The **projection of power** often led to **war**, necessitating the effective use of **military force**. China, Rome, Mauryan India, the Greek city-state of Sparta, and the Mayans were known for powerful **land armies**. Although horses were unknown in the Americas, nomadic peoples in Eurasia became especially adept at **chariot** and **cavalry warfare**, practices eventually borrowed by more advanced societies. (Invention of the **stirrup**, most likely by the Chinese in the 300s C.E., made fighting from horseback even more efficient.) It took great wealth and specialized aptitude to excel at **naval warfare**, which tended to be the forte of societies with trade-based, rather than agriculture-based, economies, such as Phoenicia and the Greek city-state of Athens. **Siegecraft**, the art of capturing cities, required knowledge of engineering and was a particular strength of the Romans, Indians, and Chinese. To enlarge their armies without drafting too many of their own farmers and workers, or to acquire troops with particular combat skills (such as archery, siegecraft, or cavalry or naval warfare), states frequently **hired mercenaries** or **recruited soldiers from conquered peoples**.

**Diplomacy** offered a less violent and less costly way to project power. States sought allies, negotiated treaties to end or avoid wars, and tried to keep their rivals divided or, better yet, at war with each other. Mauryan political advisers coined the famous phrase "the enemy of my enemy is my friend," and the Romans originated the slogan "divide and conquer," but all major states operated according to these principles. **Divide and conquer** was particularly useful for empires threatened by multiple nomadic tribes, many of whom disliked each other as much as they did the empire. China dealt with steppe nomads in this fashion, and Rome did the same with the various barbarians on its frontiers. Some states bullied their neighbors into becoming **tributary states**, extorting money from them or dictating policy to them without going to the expense and trouble of conquering them outright. Han China and Gupta India relied on this technique.

The effective projection of force demanded that armies and navies be fed and supplied properly, and that they be able to move efficiently. Advanced states laid out **supply lines** to make sure their forces were not without food or gear. They gained control over **sea lanes**, especially in the Mediterranean, the Indian Ocean, and China's coastal waters. They built **roads**, permitting the rapid movement of troops, and also facilitating trade. Persia's 1,600-mile Great Royal Road could be traveled in less than a week, and Rome's and Han China's road networks were masterpieces of engineering. **Fortifications** in the form of **city walls** protected population centers. They also defended frontiers: two familiar examples are the **Great Wall of China** and **Hadrian's Wall**, built by Rome on the border between England and Scotland.

## SOCIAL STRUCTURES

**Cities** were the hallmark distinguishing civilized societies from less advanced ones. They served as hubs for trade, especially if they were **seaports** or **river ports**. They housed major temples and monasteries, and acted as garrisons and navy yards for military forces. They also provided the seat of government.

Major cities of the era include **Persepolis** (the ceremonial capital of the Persian Empire), **Chang'an** (capital of Han China and a key point on the **Silk Road**), **Pataliputra** (chief city of

India's Mauryan and Gupta empires), **Athens** (birthplace of democracy, and the commercial and naval power of the Greek city-states), **Carthage** (Phoenician port on the North African coast and an early enemy of Rome), **Rome** (the Italian home to the most efficiently centralized state in the ancient world), **Alexandria** (Alexander the Great's capital in Egypt and the Mediterranean world's most cosmopolitan center of learning), **Constantinople** (eastern headquarters of the Roman empire and the Byzantine empire that followed it, situated on the crossroads between Europe and Asia), and **Teotihuacan** (near present-day Mexico City).

Hierarchies grew more complex during this time. **Elite classes** included political leaders (rulers and their closest advisors), **aristocracies** (noble families who shared in running the government), high-ranking members of the clergy, and **bureaucrats**. In most societies, the largest and least-respected class consisted of **cultivators**, or growers of food like peasants and farmers. Also on the lower rungs of the social ladder were **servants** and **unskilled laborers**. In between were more specialized classes, such as **merchants**, **artisans**, and **warriors**.

Most premodern societies were characterized by **low social mobility**, and some, like India and Persia, maintained strict **caste systems** that allowed no mobility at all. Elite status was generally **hereditary**. Even when **merit** played a role in gaining jobs within a bureaucracy (as with the civil-service examinations in Han China), **literacy**, available to very few in any given society, was needed. The wealth of aristocratic classes tended to be based on **land ownership** (often inherited), while merchants generated wealth through **commerce and trade**. A strong merchant class generally meant a higher degree of social mobility, as in Athens and Phoenicia, and to a degree in Rome.

Each society had to choose how to organize **labor** and **food production**. Unfortunately, common solutions included **slavery** and **serfdom**, which yielded servants to perform household tasks and skilled functions and, more important, a labor force for physically burdensome jobs like growing food. Free members of the lower classes paid **rents** to landowners, as well as **taxes** or **tribute** to the state, sometimes in the form of money, sometimes in kind (food or other goods). Serfs and free people alike could be mobilized against their will by states or landlords to provide **corvée labor**, which typically involved large-scale projects like clearing forests, draining swamps, irrigating fields, or building roads. (**Prison labor** was used for these purposes as well.) The **mit'a** system found in the Andes involved elements of serfdom and corvée labor. Military service, or **conscription**, was another form of labor organization, with members of the lower classes drafted to serve as soldiers, sailors, or rowers of galleys.

Most societies maintained a system of **food storage and distribution**, whether for emergencies or for everyday use. Governments built granaries and sometimes—as in the case of Mauryan and Gupta India—collected a portion of every year's harvest to keep in reserve. Rome preserved social order by providing grain, most of it from the breadbasket of Egypt, to its common people at little or no cost. The Romans created lavish entertainments for the same purpose, leading some to speak of **bread and circuses** as a crude way to keep societies under control.

Without exception, major societies during this era were **patriarchal**, although the specifics of how women were treated varied from place to place, and also over time.

## IMPERIAL AND POLITICAL OVERREACH

States and empires collapsed for a variety of reasons and in a variety of ways. The end could come suddenly or gradually, and it could be due primarily to **internal** or **external factors**. Often, the problem stemmed from **overreach**: the state assumed too many responsibilities, spent too much money, or conquered too much territory for its rulers, bureaucracies, and armies to handle.

Pay attention to how each of the states described above met its end. Typically, a combination of factors, and not just one cause, brought about the downfall. Challenges commonly faced by states in decline or crisis include

- Unwise or corrupt political leadership
- Rebellions and social tensions caused by overtaxation or injustice on the part of the elite
- Civil wars
- Conquest of more territory than one could effectively govern
- Economic downturns and disruptions of regional trade patterns
- Neglect of infrastructure, such as roads
- War with one or more advanced states or the sudden appearance of a powerful enemy
- Constant, long-term harassment by raiding or migrating nomads (classic examples: Germanic and Asiatic barbarians attacking Rome, White Huns against Gupta India, and the Xiongnu disturbing Han China)
- External environmental factors, such as climate change, natural disasters, or the appearance of new diseases (such as smallpox, measles, or bubonic plague)
- Self-inflicted environmental problems, such as overpopulation, overuse of wood (deforestation), overuse of water (desertification), or the silting of rivers and erosion of soil caused by overfarming or large construction projects

# Emerging Transregional Networks of Communication and Exchange

# 6

- → **TRANSREGIONAL TRADE**
- → **WATER TRANSPORT VS. OVERLAND TRANSPORT**
- → **COASTAL VS. OPEN-WATER NAVIGATION**
- → **MEDITERRANEAN SEA LANES**
- → **THE INDIAN OCEAN BASIN**
- → **TRANS-SAHARAN CARAVAN ROUTES**
- → **THE SILK ROAD**
- → **DOMESTICATION OF PACK ANIMALS**
- → **SADDLES, STIRRUPS, YOKES, HORSE COLLARS**
- → **GALLEYS, DHOWS, JUNKS, LATEEN SAILS**
- → **INTENSIVE AGRICULTURE AND WATER MANAGEMENT**
- → **EPIDEMIC DISEASES (SMALLPOX, MEASLES, BUBONIC PLAGUE)**

New technologies and greater familiarity with larger parts of the world facilitated the movement of peoples throughout Afro-Eurasia and the Americas—although these two regions continued for the time being to exist in isolation from one another. Such movement gave rise to greater **transregional interaction** among states, as well as between states and nomadic societies. **Networks of communication and exchange** grew in number and size.

Along with **war** and **migration**, the most powerful force driving this process was **trade**. Whatever motivated the spinning of these new and more extensive networks, the consequences were many and profound. They included the transfer of technology and knowledge, the spread and mixing of religious beliefs, the redistribution of plants and animals, the waging of war over longer distances, and the spread of diseases.

## TRANSREGIONAL TRADE ROUTES

In many places, trade operated mainly on the local or regional levels. Sometimes this was because a society did not have the means to travel between regions, but in other cases, where the climate and terrain varied widely, a wide assortment of foods and resources could be obtained from not very far away. This was true, for example, among the islands of Oceania and in the Americas. Many different goods were exchanged among the societies of Mesoamerica, a relatively small space. In the Andes, local trade connected people living on the coast with those living in nearby mountain valleys, and regional trade linked both with the tribes of the Amazon River basin. No horses existed in the Americas as of yet, so the principal pack animal in the Andes was the **llama**.

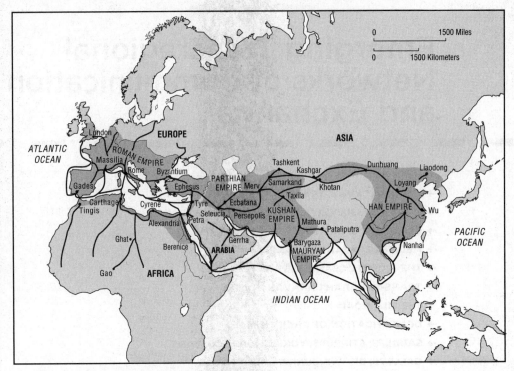

**Principal African-Eurasian Trade Routes, ca. 200 B.C.E.–200 C.E.**
During this time, merchants sold goods along a vast trade network that spanned from England in
the northwest, to western Africa, Central Asia, and as far east as the Han Empire.

**Transregional trade** spanned greater distances and required more effort but was typically
more lucrative. During this era, four major transregional trade routes came into being, thanks
to technological innovations and improved geographical knowledge.

## The Mediterranean

Geographically the smallest of the major trading zones, the **Mediterranean Sea** facilitated
communication and exchange all along the southern coast of Europe, the shores of present-
day Turkey and the Levant, and the entirety of North Africa, including Egypt. The presence of
many islands made navigation here even easier.

Societies that took special advantage of Mediterranean trade during this era were the
Persians, the Greeks (who colonized widely between Italy and Turkey), the Phoenicians
(based in the Levant, but colonizers of southern Spain and North Africa), and the Romans.
During the *pax Romana*, the Mediterranean became virtually a private lake for the Romans,
who used it to move goods, passengers, and armies over long distances with relative ease. Of
crucial importance was the sea connection between Italy and Egypt, a key source of grain for
the Roman Empire. Most Mediterranean mariners relied on **galleys**: oared ships with small
square sails (not uncommonly, the rowing was done by slaves or prison convicts). Suitable
for **coastal navigation**—as opposed to riskier **open-water navigation**—galleys tended to
travel short distances, relying on the growing number of port cities to support trade.

At many points, the Mediterranean trade network meshed with other trade networks.
Many of the trans-Saharan caravan routes led to the southern Mediterranean. The Turkish
straits linked the Mediterranean with the Black Sea to the northeast. Via Egypt and the narrow
land bridge known as the Suez isthmus, traders could pass between the Mediterranean and

the Red Sea to the southeast, and from there to the Arabian Sea and the Indian Ocean basin. From faraway East and Central Asia, Silk Road trade extended to the port cities of the eastern Mediterranean.

## The Indian Ocean Basin

The sea lanes of the **Indian Ocean maritime network** connected East Africa, the Middle East, South Asia, and Southeast Asia with China and Japan. Middle Eastern ports and Egypt's Suez isthmus provided points of indirect connection between this network and trade in the Mediterranean.

Trade within the basin itself was voluminous to begin with, but the network also extended to the South China Sea and the western Pacific, serving an astonishing variety of societies and transporting an equally astonishing array of goods. From East African ports came commodities like ebony, ivory, animal products, and wood carvings. Copper, myrrh, frankincense, and dates came from Arabia. Spices and foodstuffs were traded by India, the Malay Peninsula, and Indonesia, as were jewels and cotton textiles. China, home to the key port of Canton, sold porcelain and silk.

Wherever they were from, traders in this network benefitted from **open-water navigation**, a skill that distinguishes Indian Ocean trade from Mediterranean commerce, where coastal navigation prevailed. Throughout the Indian Ocean, ships like **dhows**, using triangular **lateen sails**, crossed large marine expanses—especially once sailors there learned how to take advantage of seasonal **monsoon winds**. Another difference between Mediterranean and Indian Ocean trade involves the degree to which traders and sailors remained connected with their homelands. The Mediterranean's comparatively smaller size allowed traders to maintain closer ties, whereas greater distances meant greater separation for those trading in the Indian Ocean. Small but vital **diasporic communities** of foreign traders began to settle permanently in cities throughout this trade network. Among the more famous are the Chinese minority who still reside on the Malay Peninsula and the Arab merchants who came to live in China's port of Canton. In general, the cultural, linguistic, and religious interchange encouraged by Indian Ocean trade immensely influenced societies throughout the region.

## Trans-Saharan Caravan Routes

Since becoming desert around 2500 B.C.E., the Saharan expanse has been a barrier to movement and trade between sub-Saharan Africa and the Mediterranean. Animals capable of carrying large loads over long distances through such arid conditions were rare, and specialized knowledge of where to find **oases**, or sources of water, was crucial.

During most of this era, only a handful of routes linked sub-Saharan Africa with the Mediterranean. As it had in earlier centuries, **Nubia** served as an avenue for north-south trade between Egypt and the southern half of the continent. Between the 300s B.C.E. and the 100s C.E., the Nubian city of Meroë, a prosperous producer of iron, profited from this trade until topsoil erosion caused by deforestation plummeted it into decline. In western Africa, a trickle of overland trade made its way from the south to ports like **Carthage**, both before and after its conquest by the Romans.

Several factors boosted trans-Saharan trade between the 200s and 500s C.E. Rome's decline and collapse caused North African societies, which had previously traded with Rome, to look southward for new commercial partners. Organized states, such as **Ghana**, began to take shape in sub-Saharan Africa and wished to trade northward. Most important of all was the domestication of **camels** during the 200s C.E., particularly among the desert Berbers of northwest Africa.

With a pack animal biologically adapted to long-distance desert travel now at their disposal, traders began to map out **trans-Saharan caravan routes**, both in the western and eastern halves of Africa. The first of these were relatively limited, carrying salt and manufactured goods to the south and bringing nuts, oil, foodstuffs, gold, and ivory from the south. They connected sub-Saharan Africa not just with North Africa and the Mediterranean but also with Egypt and the Middle East. In later years, Islam's expansion throughout Africa would cause an explosive growth in the size and importance of the trans-Saharan trade network. As this happened, **slavery** would eventually become a major part of the northbound trade.

## Eurasia's Silk Roads

The most famous overland trade route of premodern times, the **Silk Road**, actually enjoyed two periods of peak prominence: first, between 100 B.C.E. and approximately 800 C.E., and again between the 1200s and 1500s C.E. It came into being gradually, although its "discovery" is commonly attributed to a Chinese explorer who crossed the barren lands north of Tibet and came into the lush Ferghana Valley in 128 B.C.E.

Between 4,000 and 5,000 miles long, the Silk Road stretched from the Middle East and the ports of the eastern Mediterranean to China's Pacific coast. Along the way, it passed through the Persian empire of the Parthians, the Central Asian city-states of Bukhara and Samarkand, and China, whose chief economic hub was the city of **Chang'an**. By extension, the Silk Road was connected to all the networks described above: the cities on its western end lay within economic reach of the Mediterranean and trans-Saharan networks, and goods traveling along the Silk Road found their way to and from the Indian Ocean basin, either via north-south trade between the road itself and South Asia or via maritime traffic between China's Pacific shores and South and Southeast Asia.

Although **overland transport** was harder and more time-consuming than water transport, and although much of the Silk Road passed through perilous wilderness, overland caravans were cheaper—and in this case the only way to gain access to the Central Asian interior, whose cities had their own goods to sell. Spices, jewels, and cotton went west from India and Southeast Asia, as did porcelain and silk from China. Glassware, perfumes, and slaves were transported along the route as well. The Silk Road's impact on the transfer of technology throughout Eurasia and the sharing of cultural traditions and religions—particularly Buddhism and Christianity (and, in later centuries, Islam)—was remarkable.

## INNOVATIONS IN TRANSPORT

Trade and travel were made easier during these years by improvements in geographical knowledge, whose benefits included reliable maps and better understanding of weather patterns. They were also assisted by changes in technology.

**Overland transport** during the premodern era required more time and effort and was more subject to outlawry and political disruption. But it was less expensive and the only way to reach places far from rivers and coastlines. Land movement of large amounts of cargo depended on **domesticated pack animals**. **Wheeled vehicles** like carts and wagons were helpful on roads and on flat ground, but rough terrain rendered them useless, so animals sometimes had to carry the loads themselves. One of Eurasia's first and most versatile pack animals was the **horse**, although it was not as strong as the **ox**, which could haul far heavier loads. In the Americas, where the horse did not exist, the most common pack animal was the **llama**, excellently suited to the Andes and other mountains. **Camels** were vital to trade in the Sahara, the Middle East, and along the Silk Road. Large processions of pack animals and/or vehicles were called **caravans**.

Several technologies from this era heightened the usefulness of pack animals. The **stirrup**, which emerged in Central Asia and China between the 200s B.C.E. and the 100s C.E., added greater stability for those riding camels and horses. (They also transformed warfare by making it easier for horseback soldiers to wear heavy armor and use swords, axes, and lances.) **Yokes** and **collars** allowed animals to pull heavier loads without choking. Specialized **pack saddles**, such as those devised by horsemen in Central Asia or the camel riders of Arabia and the Sahara, enabled pack animals to carry more cargo on their own backs—a crucial function in mountains, deserts, and rough ground that made it hard or impossible to use wheeled vehicles.

Where possible, **water transport** was easier and preferable to overland transport, although it generally cost more to outfit ships than to organize caravans. During this era, changes in **maritime technology** made overseas trade even more efficient. Beforehand, most ships and crews were restricted to **coastal navigation**, and rarely ventured far from land. This was the case in the Mediterranean, where the principal vessel was the **galley**, powered by oars and a small square sail whose rigging did not permit heading into the wind. By contrast, the **dhow**, invented by Arab mariners in the Red and Arabian seas, was suitable for **open-water navigation**. Not only was it constructed more sturdily than the galley (its planks were not nailed together but drilled, tied with ropes, and then sealed), but its tall, triangular **lateen sail** was stronger and more efficiently rigged than the square galley sail. This allowed Indian Ocean sailors to take advantage of seasonal **monsoon winds**, which were forceful enough to propel ships over long distances at great speed. The dhow style of shipbuilding caught on throughout the Indian Ocean, from East Africa to South Asia. Another ship capable of open-water navigation, and of carrying large amounts of cargo, was the Chinese **junk**.

## TRANSMISSIONS: THE EFFECTS OF COMMUNICATION AND EXCHANGE

Common consequences of trade include **technology transfer**, **environmental** and **medical impact**, and **religious** and **cultural borrowing**.

The exchange of crops and foodstuffs over long distances changed people's dietary habits, as well as their farming and irrigation techniques. The cultivation of rice and cotton, for example, spread from South Asia to East Asia and the Middle East. The Silk Road brought new foods, such as spinach, pistachios, and sesame, to China. Spices went west from East and South Asia. The Bantu, as they migrated through sub-Saharan Africa, spread new crops all over the continent.

To handle growing populations and to make the best use of space, many societies turned to **intensive agriculture**, or the use of technology to maximize productive potential of every square foot of a given area. More primitive methods of production, like **swidden** (or **slash-and-burn**) **agriculture**, cleared fields by chopping down trees and bushes, and then burned the foliage to fertilize the soil. Once the soil's nutrients ran out, villagers cleared more forest or moved on to another location. This was relatively easy, but not an efficient use of space. Intensive farming techniques included the **terracing of hillsides** common in Mesoamerica and the Andes, the laborious **rice-paddy cultivation** that originated in

Southeast Asia, the **draining of swamps** and **wetlands**, and the building of **elevated fields** and **"floating islands"** (like Teotihuacan's *chinampas*). The Chinese pioneered use of the **horse collar**, which made plowing easier. Methods of **water management**, always crucial to agriculture, included complex **irrigation** systems, **aqueducts** (most famous in Rome, but also constructed in India and the Middle East), and the **qanat** (originating in Persia, but used widely throughout Eurasia). Qanats sank vertical rainwater shafts in the ground, connecting them to a horizontal (but gently downward-sloping) underground pipe that carried the collected rainwater toward the area to be irrigated. Building aqueducts and qanats required huge investments of money and labor.

The **spread of disease** paralleled the movement of humans, whether they were trading, migrating, preaching new religions, or fighting wars. Populations are especially vulnerable to diseases to which they have not built up immunities, and so initial encounters typically caused mass deaths due to epidemic. Eurasia in particular was a huge alleyway for the spread of illnesses, which over time made people there more disease-resistant than in Africa and the Americas. During this era, **bubonic plague** appears to have spread from India to Southeast Asia and China by the 600s C.E., and even earlier to the Eastern Roman (Byzantine) Empire in the 500s. **Smallpox** and **measles** struck the Roman Empire and Han China in the 100s and 200s C.E., weakening both and contributing to their imperial decline. In each case, the diseases seem to have been borne by nomadic peoples or by Roman and Chinese soldiers returning home from fighting the nomads.

Religions spread as well, sometimes due to gradual **cultural borrowing**, sometimes due to active **missionary activity**, and sometimes due to war and **forced conversion**. Most major religions traveled far from their original birthplaces. Hinduism spread throughout Southeast Asia. Thanks largely to the proselytizing efforts of **Ashoka**, Buddhism burst out of India, eventually reaching much of Southeast and Central Asia and all of East Asia. Confucianism and Daoism influenced religious and philosophical thinking in many parts of Asia besides their native China. Judaism and Christianity (and, soon enough, Islam) came out of the Middle East to shape religious life throughout Eurasia. Trade routes—particularly the **Silk Road**—played an indispensable role in all these developments.

# UNIT 3

## REGIONAL AND TRANSREGIONAL INTERACTIONS (600–1450)

# Unit 3 Short Cut

## GENERAL REMARKS

Between 600 and 1450, newer world civilizations matured, largely on the foundations of older cultures that had collapsed or faded away. It was also during this era that world civilizations vastly increased their **regional and transregional interactions** with each other—economically, religiously, and culturally, as well as by means of diplomacy and war.

Many of the world's **classical civilizations** failed or fell into decline between the 200s and 600s C.E., including the Roman Empire (with the Greek influence it had kept alive), Han China, and India's Mauryan and Gupta Empires. The same process continued up to about 1000 C.E., as other societies considered "classical"—such as Tang China, Heian Japan, and the Abbasid caliphate—weakened or collapsed.

New civilizations built on what remained of these classical cultures. In some cases, as in Europe after the fall of Rome, a lengthy period of backwardness and decentralization followed the collapse of a classical civilization. In others, as in China, the transition was less traumatic or lasted a shorter time. Whatever the case, a myriad of sophisticated cultures, many of them drawing upon the legacy left behind by their classical predecessors, appeared throughout the world during these years.

One important historical question is whether these civilizations are best studied as **nation-states** (countries as formally defined political entities, in the modern sense of the word) or **cultural units** (defined less by political boundaries and more by ethnic similarities, shared cultural traditions, ethnicity, or government by a larger imperial or regional power). Examples of the latter include the Islamic world, which came into being with the sudden **rise and expansion of Islam** during this period, as well as European Christendom, sub-Saharan Africa, and Mesoamerica.

The other central trend of this age was the continued growth of **networks of communication and exchange** between world cultures. (On a related note, **increased productive capacity** became the economic norm in most parts of the world.) Although the Americas remained isolated, vibrant **systems of interaction** arose to link the various civilizations of Africa and Eurasia. Trade, religious influence, technological, and cultural exchange all marked this era. **Diaspora communities**, **migration**, and the **movement of nomadic peoples**, such as the Vikings, Bantu, and Mongols, greatly affected settled societies—and a key question pertaining to this period is how nomadic movement compares to the importance of **cities** as a cause of historical change. Even though the world was not as joined together as it would later become, thanks to the Europeans' encounter with the Americas, it was moving swiftly and steadily toward interaction on a truly global scale.

# BROAD TRENDS

| State Building, Expansion, and Conflict, 600–1450 | | |
|---|---|---|
| **ca. 600–900** | | |
| **Europe** | Byzantium (300s–1453) Constantinople barbarian kingdoms feudalism | |
| **Middle East** | (Byzantium) early caliphates (Medina and Umayyad) Abbasid caliphate (750–1258) Baghdad dar al-Islam and "circle of justice" Sharia law | |
| **Africa** | Ghana (ca. 800–1200) | |
| **East (and Central) Asia** | Sui (589–618) and Tang (618–906) dynasties in China mandate of heaven Chang'an Nara period in Japan (700s) Heian regime in Japan (794–1185) | |
| **South (and Southeast) Asia and Oceania** | disunity in India Khmer (500s–1400s) and Srivijayan (500s–1100s) empires city-states in Southeast Asia | |
| **Americas** | Mississippian culture (ca. 700–1500) Cahokia city-states in Mesoamerica Toltec (ca. 800–1000) | |
| **Global and Interregional** | Islamic expansion into Africa and Asia Islamic conquest of Spain (al-Andalus) battles of Tours/Poitiers (732) and Talas (751) | |
| **ca. 900–1200** | | |
| **Europe** | early nation-states papal-imperial struggle and the ideal of Christendom Italian city-states (Venice) feudalism continues | |
| **Middle East** | political diffraction of Abbasid caliphate dar al-Islam and "circle of justice" Sharia law | |
| **Africa** | Ghana Great Zimbabwe (ca. 1000–1400) Swahili city-states | |
| **East (and Central) Asia** | Song dynasty (960–1279) in China mandate of heaven breakdown of Heian regime in Japan the shogun, samurai daimyo, and feudalism in Japan (1100s–1500s) | |

| State Building, Expansion, and Conflict, 600–1450 | |
|---|---|
| South (and Southeast) Asia and Oceania | disunity in India<br>Khmer and Srivijayan empires<br>city-states in Southeast Asia |
| Americas | city-states in Mesoamerica |
| Global and Interregional | battle of Manzikert (1071)<br>Crusades (Christian Europe vs. Islamic Middle East) |
| ca. 1200–1450 | |
| Europe | nation-states gradually centralize<br>papal power peaks, then weakens<br>Italian city-states<br>feudalism continues<br>Mongol rule over Russia (Golden Horde)<br>fall of Constantinople and Ottoman conquest of Byzantium (1453) |
| Middle East | Mongol Il-khanate (mid-1200s to mid-1300s)<br>Ottoman empire (1299–1922)<br>Ottoman conquest of Byzantium (1453)<br>dar al-Islam and "circle of justice"<br>Sharia law |
| Africa | Mali (mid-1200s to 1600s; Mansa Musa in 1300s)<br>Timbuktu<br>Songhai (mid-1400s to late 1500s)<br>Great Zimbabwe<br>Swahili city-states |
| East (and Central) Asia | Yuan (Mongol) dynasty in China (1271–1368)<br>Chagatai (Mongol) khanate in Central Asia (early 1200s to mid-1600s)<br>Ming dynasty (1368–1644) in China<br>mandate of heaven<br>the warlord Timur (1300s) |
| South (and Southeast) Asia and Oceania | Delhi sultanate (1206–1526) in India<br>Calicut<br>Khmer empire<br>city-states in Southeast Asia and Malay sultanates<br>Melaka |
| Americas | city-states in Mesoamerica<br>Aztecs (Mexica, mid-1200s to 1520)<br>Tenochtitlan<br>Incas (ca. 1300s to early 1500s) |
| Global and Interregional | Crusades end (1290s)<br>Mongol conquests under Genghis Khan (early 1200s) and the pax Mongolica<br>battle of Ain Jalut (1260) |

# State Building, Expansion, and Conflict

- Most forms of rulership remained non-representative. Monarchies and oligarchies were the most common.

- Many states were not nations in the modern sense of the world. Some were decentralized. Others were multicultural empires whose various peoples were joined only by the fact that a single authority had conquered them all.

- When classical empires collapsed, the states taking their places typically made use of traditional sources of legitimacy and power—such as patriarchal authority, religious backing, and the support of landowning elites—but blended them with innovative governing techniques. Examples include Byzantium and the post-Han dynasties (Sui, Tang, and Song) in China.

- New modes of government appeared, among them the Islamic caliphates, the Mongol khanates, city-state systems (as in East Africa, Southeast Asia, the Americas, and Italy), and feudalism (most distinctive in medieval Europe and Japan).

- Imperial expansion, as well as conflict and contact between civilizations, caused cultural borrowing, diffusion, and the transfer of technologies and cultural practices. Europe's Crusades against the Middle East provide one example, while others include the impact of Mongol expansion, the interchange between Tang China and the Abbasid caliphate, the regional impact of Persian culture throughout the Islamic world, and China's wider cultural influence throughout East Asia.

- Cities placed a larger role in the political life of most civilizations.

- The invention of gunpowder technology and its diffusion throughout Eurasia began to change the balance of world power.

| Culture, Science, and Technology, 600–1450 | |
|---|---|
| **ca. 600–900** | |
| **Europe** | papal ideal of Christendom emerges<br>Latin as regional language of religious and educated elite (Greco-Roman foundation of European culture)<br>longboats (Vikings) |
| **Middle East** | birth and expansion of Islam (600s+)<br>Sunni-Shiite split<br>Arabic as religious language (note cultural importance of Persian and widespread use of Turkic languages)<br>astrolabe improved (700s)<br>camel saddle improved |
| **Africa** | spread of Islam via war and trade<br>sculpture, wood carving, weaving, metal-working<br>oral traditions (griots) |
| **East (and Central) Asia** | Neo-Confucianism<br>diffusion of Buddhist culture<br>horse collar improved in China<br>gunpowder invented in China (800s–900s) |
| **South (and Southeast) Asia and Oceania** | diffusion (and mingling) of Buddhist and Hindu culture<br>Borobudur temple<br>outrigger canoes (Polynesia) |

| Culture, Science, and Technology, 600–1450 | |
|---|---|
| **Americas** | earth mounds in North America<br>pyramids in Mesoamerica (polytheism and human sacrifice) |
| **Global and Interregional** | Islam's cultural influence in Africa, South Asia, and Southeast Asia<br>Tang-Abbasid cultural transfer<br>interregional travel = pilgrimage of Xuanzang (600s)<br>influence of Greek and Indian mathematics on Islamic world (algebra in 800s) |
| **ca. 900–1200** | |
| **Europe** | papal ideal of Christendom climaxes<br>great schism between Roman Catholicism and Eastern Orthodoxy<br>scholasticism (partial reconciliation of Christian doctrine with Greco-Roman thinkers like Aristotle and Plato)<br>universities<br>code of chivalry<br>romanesque and gothic cathedrals<br>castle-building |
| **Middle East** | *The Thousand Nights and a Night (Arabian Nights)*<br>Omar Khayyám, *Rubaiyat*<br>expertise in medicine, astronomy, and mathematics<br>madrasas<br>Sufism |
| **Africa** | continued spread of Islam<br>sculpture, wood carving, weaving, metalworking<br>oral traditions (griots)<br>emergence of Swahili as regional language<br>Great Zimbabwe city complex |
| **East (and Central) Asia** | Zen (Chan) Buddhism<br>woodblock printing improved and movable-type concept invented in China<br>compass invented in China (late 1000s–early 1100s)<br>water mills and water clocks in China<br>*The Tale of Genji*, Lady Murasaki<br>samurai culture and code of Bushido in Japan |
| **South (and Southeast) Asia and Oceania** | diffusion (and mingling) of Buddhist and Hindu culture<br>Angkor Wat<br>outrigger canoes (Polynesia) |
| **Americas** | earth mounds in North America<br>pyramids and Toltec/Aztec influence in Mesoamerica (polytheism and human sacrifice) |
| **Global and Interregional** | improved horse collar, compass, and printing spread from China to Middle East and Europe<br>Greek science and philosophy reintroduced to Europe from Muslim Spain<br>European-Islamic cultural transfer during Crusades |

| Culture, Science, and Technology, 600–1450 | |
|---|---|
| **ca. 1200–1450** | |
| **Europe** | Renaissance humanism<br>movable-type printing press (mid-1400s) |
| **Middle East** | Rumi's poetry |
| **Africa** | Islamic influences<br>sculpture, wood carving, weaving, metalworking<br>oral traditions (griots)<br>*Sundiata* epic (Mali, 1300s+)<br>Great Zimbabwe city complex<br>mud-and-timber mosques of Timbuktu |
| **East (and Central) Asia** | Zheng He (1400s) and interregional travel<br>Forbidden City<br>Heian Shrine |
| **South (and Southeast) Asia and Oceania** | diffusion (and mingling) of Buddhist and Hindu culture<br>Islam arrives in India |
| **Americas** | earth mounds in North America<br>pyramids and Aztec influence in Mesoamerica (polytheism and<br>    human sacrifice)<br>Inca influence on Andes culture<br>Temple of the Sun and Machu Picchu<br>quipu |
| **Global and Interregional** | interregional travel = Marco Polo (1200s), Ibn Battuta (1300s), and<br>    Zheng He (1400s)<br>cultural transfer throughout Mongol empires<br>gunpowder acquired by Middle East and Europe (1200s) |

## Culture, Science, and Technology

- Distinct artistic and cultural traditions developed in all major regions. However, cultural diffusion and mutual influence among these traditions became increasingly common, thanks to the expansion of empires, the growing extent of trade networks, the emergence of diasporic communities, and the spread of religious beliefs.
- A new religion, Islam, was born in the Middle East and rapidly spread throughout Afro-Eurasia.
- The civilizations possessing the greatest degree of scientific knowledge and cultural sophistication were East Asia, India, the Middle East, and Muslim Spain (al-Andalus).
- Europe underwent great cultural development, especially during the Renaissance.
- China and India exerted tremendous cultural and religious influence over their neighbors. Buddhism, Hinduism, and art and architectural styles spread from these states to Southeast Asia, Korea, Japan, Tibet, and elsewhere.
- In their own right and because of the knowledge they imported from China and India, the Middle East and Muslim Spain played a large role in spreading philosophy, science, technology, music, art, and architecture to North Africa and Europe. The Middle East's cultural influence on medieval and Renaissance Europe was indispensable.

- Travelers and explorers created links between societies and increased geographical and cultural awareness. Examples include Zheng He, Xuanzang, Marco Polo, and Ibn Battuta.
- In the Americas, major civilizations such as the Toltec, Aztecs (Mexica), and Inca left their cultural and religious imprint on many of their neighbors.
- Certain languages attained regional status, either because of their cultural preeminence, their usefulness as languages of learning, or their suitability as a lingua franca for trade. Examples include Swahili, the Turkic and Arabic languages, and Latin.
- The improvement of block printing in China, as well as the invention of the concept of movable type there, began to alter cultural life not only in Asia, but elsewhere, as this new innovation spread westward. The culmination of this trend was the invention of the movable-type printing press in Europe during the mid-1400s. The resulting information explosion caused a revolution in intellectual life in many parts of Eurasia.
- The invention of gunpowder technology and the magnetic compass in China had global impacts described below.

| Economic Systems, 600–1450 | |
|---|---|
| **ca. 600–900** | |
| **Europe** | open-water navigation improves (impact of Viking longships)<br>feudal manorialism (serfdom) |
| **Middle East** | Mediterranean trade<br>trans-Saharan caravans (Arab-Berber expertise with camels)<br>Silk Roads<br>(connection with Indian Ocean basin) |
| **Africa** | pastoralism continues in many areas<br>Mediterranean trade<br>trans-Saharan caravans (Arab-Berber expertise with camels)<br>Indian Ocean trade continues |
| **East (and Central) Asia** | nomadic pastoralism continues in steppe zone<br>Grand Canal in China<br>China's regional trade network<br>Silk Roads<br>connection with Indian Ocean basin |
| **South (and Southeast) Asia and Oceania** | Indian Ocean trade continues<br>spices, cotton |
| **Americas** | pastoralism continues in many areas<br>mit'a labor system in Andes |
| **Global and Interregional** | general rise in agricultural production (due to technological innovation)<br>new trading cities emerge<br>luxury goods fuel expansion of trade networks<br>minting of coins and printing of paper money spreads<br>credit and banking become more common<br>slavery and serfdom become increasingly common |

| Economic Systems, 600–1450 | |
|---|---|
| **ca. 900–1200** | |
| **Europe** | feudal manorialism (serfdom)<br>revival of European and Mediterranean trade<br>guilds (artisans and craftsmen)<br>Italian peninsula and Mediterranean trade<br>Crusades stimulate awareness of and appetite for goods from the east |
| **Middle East** | Mediterranean trade<br>trans-Saharan caravans (Arab-Berber expertise with camels)<br>Silk Roads partly disrupted<br>(connection with Indian Ocean basin) |
| **Africa** | pastoralism continues in many areas<br>Mediterranean trade<br>trans-Saharan caravans (Arab-Berber expertise with camels)<br>salt, gold, ivory<br>Indian Ocean trade<br>rise of Swahili city-states |
| **East (and Central) Asia** | nomadic pastoralism continues in steppe zone<br>Silk Roads partly disrupted<br>connection with Indian Ocean basin<br>silk, iron, steel, and porcelain industries expand in China<br>feudal landholding in Japan (serfdom) |
| **South (and Southeast) Asia and Oceania** | Indian Ocean trade<br>cotton industry in India<br>spices |
| **Americas** | pastoralism continues in many areas<br>mit'a labor system in Andes |
| **Global and Interregional** | general rise in agricultural production (due to technological innovation)<br>increased craft production<br>new trading cities and merchant classes<br>luxury goods<br>coins and paper money<br>credit and banking<br>slavery and serfdom become increasingly common |
| **ca. 1200–1450** | |
| **Europe** | feudal manorialism (serfdom declining in Western Europe)<br>European and Mediterranean trade intensifies<br>guilds (artisans and craftsmen)<br>Italian peninsula and Mediterranean trade<br>Hanseatic League |
| **Middle East** | Mediterranean trade<br>trans-Saharan caravans<br>(connection with Indian Ocean basin)<br>Silk Road revives |

| Economic Systems, 600–1450 | |
|---|---|
| **Africa** | pastoralism continues in many areas<br>Mediterranean trade<br>trans-Saharan caravans<br>salt, gold, ivory<br>Indian Ocean trade<br>Swahili city-states |
| **East (and Central) Asia** | nomadic pastoralism continues in steppe zone<br>Silk Road revives<br>connection with Indian Ocean basin<br>silk, iron, steel, and porcelain industries expand in China<br>feudal landholding in Japan (serfdom) |
| **South (and Southeast) Asia and Oceania** | Indian Ocean trade<br>cotton industry in India<br>spices |
| **Americas** | pastoralism continues in many areas<br>mit'a labor more extensive under Inca |
| **Global and Interregional** | general rise in agricultural production (due to technological innovation)<br>increased craft production<br>new trading cities and merchant classes<br>luxury goods<br>coins and paper money<br>credit and banking<br>slavery and serfdom become increasingly common |

## Economic Systems

- Economic production increased globally.
- Transregional trade was practiced on a massive scale. Existing routes, such as the Silk Roads, the Mediterranean sea lanes, the trans-Saharan caravan trails, and the Indian Ocean basin, witnessed huge upswings in commercial activity. New routes expanded trade in Mesoamerica and the Andes as well.
- New cities emerged as key centers for interregional trade. They include Venice, Novgorod, Baghdad, the Swahili city-states, Timbuktu, Hangzhou, Melaka (Malacca), Calicut, Cahokia, and Tenochtitlan.
- Trading organizations like northern Europe's Hanseatic League came into existence.
- Demand for luxury goods assumed a more prominent role in interregional commerce. Textiles, porcelain, and spices from the Middle East and East Asia became especially important.
- In Afro-Eurasia trade was made easier and safer by the emergence of new forms of banking and monetization (credit, checking, banking houses), as well as state practices like the minting of coins and the printing of paper money. Customs agencies and standard weights and measures helped to regulate and regularize trade.
- Interregional trade was facilitated by the warmer weather of the medieval climatic optimum and then affected by the global cooling that led to the Little Ice Age.

- Technological innovation played a role in expanding trade, especially in the fields of ship design (including the Viking longboat, the Indian Ocean dhow, and the Chinese junk) and navigation (with the astrolabe and the magnetic compass proving crucial). Also important was the effective adaptation of environmental knowledge (such as Saharan camel herders' knowledge of the desert or Central Asian pastoralists' use of horses for steppe travel).
- Agricultural production increased worldwide, thanks partly to climatic changes, partly to technological innovations (including the horse collar, better terracing, rice cultivation in Asia, and waru waru and chinampa techniques in the Americas).

| Social Structures, 600–1450 | |
|---|---|
| **ca. 600–900** | |
| **Europe** | rise of serfdom<br>Christian doctrine and patriarchy |
| **Middle East** | Jewish diaspora<br>Islam and patriarchy (veiling, seclusion, polygamy)<br>jizya tax for subject non-believers (dhimmi)<br>military slaves (mamluks) |
| **Africa** | greater prevalence of matriarchy and matrilinealism |
| **East (and Central) Asia** | Sogdian merchant diaspora along the Silk Roads<br>An Shi rebellion in China (700s)<br>Neo-Confucianism and patriarchy (foot binding) |
| **South (and Southeast) Asia and Oceania** | Chinese merchant diaspora in Southeast Asia<br>Hinduism and patriarchy (sati, seclusion) |
| **Americas** | mit'a labor system in Andes<br>ayllu clan system in Andes |
| **Global and Interregional** | greater urbanization and trading cities<br>Muslim merchant diaspora in Africa and Indian Ocean basin<br>slavery and serfdom become increasingly common<br>patriarchy continues or deepens |
| **ca. 900–1200** | |
| **Europe** | serfdom vs. free peasantry<br>peasant revolt in Byzantium (900s)<br>craftsmen and guilds<br>moneylending by Jewish diaspora (anti-Semitism)<br>Christian doctrine and patriarchy |
| **Middle East** | Islam and patriarchy (veiling, seclusion, polygamy)<br>jizya tax for subject non-believers (dhimmi)<br>military slaves (mamluks) |
| **Africa** | greater prevalence of matriarchy and matrilinealism<br>Muslim merchant diaspora<br>Arab slavers in North and East Africa |

| Social Structures, 600–1450 | |
|---|---|
| **East (and Central) Asia** | Neo-Confucianism and patriarchy (foot binding)<br>samurai nobility and feudalism in Japan (serfdom)<br>samurai patriarchalism |
| **South (and Southeast) Asia and Oceania** | Chinese merchant diaspora in Southeast Asia<br>Hinduism and patriarchy (sati, seclusion) |
| **Americas** | mit'a labor system in Andes<br>ayllu clan system in Andes |
| **Global and Interregional** | growth of artisan (craftsman) classes<br>growth of merchant classes<br>greater urbanization and trading cities<br>Muslim merchant diaspora in Africa and Indian Ocean basin<br>Jewish diaspora (Middle East, Europe, Indian Ocean basin)<br>slavery and serfdom become increasingly common<br>patriarchy continues or deepens |
| ca. 1200–1450 | |
| **Europe** | serfdom (declining in Western Europe) vs. free peasantry<br>peasant revolts in England, France, and elsewhere (1300s)<br>craftsmen and guilds<br>moneylending by Jewish diaspora (anti-Semitism)<br>Christian doctrine and patriarchy<br>witch hunts (*Hammer of Witchcraft*, 1400s) |
| **Middle East** | Islam and patriarchy (veiling, seclusion, polygamy, the harem)<br>jizya tax for subject non-believers (dhimmi)<br>start of Ottoman millet (religious community) system<br>devshirme (Ottoman slave-recruiting system)<br>military slaves (mamluks and janissaries) |
| **Africa** | greater prevalence of matriarchy and matrilinealism<br>Arab slavers in North and East Africa<br>origins of Atlantic slave trade |
| **East (and Central) Asia** | Red Turban uprising in China (1300s)<br>Neo-Confucianism and patriarchy (foot binding)<br>samurai nobility and feudalism in Japan (serfdom)<br>samurai patriarchalism |
| **South (and Southeast) Asia and Oceania** | Chinese merchant communities in Southeast Asia<br>Hinduism and patriarchy (sati, seclusion)<br>Islam and patriarchy (veiling, seclusion, polygamy) |
| **Americas** | mit'a labor system deepens under Inca<br>ayllu clan system in Andes |
| **Global and Interregional** | greater urbanization and trading cities<br>growth of artisan (craftsman) classes<br>growth of merchant classes<br>Muslim merchant diaspora in Africa and Indian Ocean basin<br>Jewish diaspora (Middle East, Europe, Silk Roads, Indian Ocean basin)<br>slavery and serfdom become increasingly common<br>patriarchy continues or deepens |

## Social Structures

- Population growth continued in all parts of the world.
- Many peoples continued to practice nomadic pastoralism as a form of labor organization.
- Of settled societies, the vast majority remained fundamentally agricultural. In the countryside, the chief forms of labor organization were free peasant production (typically owing rents to landlords or taxes to the government) and serfdom (unfree labor bound to the land and owing labor to the landowner).
- Urbanization, or the growth of cities, proceeded worldwide, although periods of decline were mixed with periods of revival and expansion. In cities, the rise of trade and commerce made merchant classes larger and more influential. Also in urban settings, a key form of labor organization was craft production, with artisans often banding together in guilds.
- Other forms of labor organization include coerced and unfree labor (especially slavery, serfdom, and the mit'a), as well as military conscription. The demand for slaves, whether for domestic labor, agricultural work, or military service, grew substantially.
- Unrest and revolts caused by unfair treatment of workers and peasants became more common in various parts of the world (significant examples during this era include China and Byzantium).
- Along far-reaching trade routes, diasporic communities and foreign enclaves formed in many ports and towns.
- Class hierarchies, social stratification, and caste systems continued to function. Social mobility increased in a few places, often in urban settings where trade and commerce dominated.
- Patriarchalism, often buttressed by traditional religion, continued to be the norm. Still, women's roles varied from society to society. Women's political rights tended to be minimal to nonexistent, and they had sharply defined occupational roles, generally confined to childbearing, homemaking, and low-status jobs such as weaving, food gathering, farm chores, and domestic servitude.
- In most places, women had at least some freedoms and rights (which might include the right to divorce abusive husbands, the right to a dowry, the right to at least some education, or the right to inherit and own property). They also tended to play informal but important roles as they managed households and family finances, supervised the education and upbringing of children, and influenced their husbands.
- In most societies, upper-class women lived easier lives but found themselves more constrained by religious and cultural restrictions on their behavior (such as seclusion or purdah, foot-binding, and veiling). Lower-class women, whose lives were much harder, were often less bound by such restrictions because the rules of "proper" behavior applied less to them.
- In places like West Africa, Japan (during certain periods), the Mongol Empire, and parts of Southeast Asia, women enjoyed more respect than average during this period.
- Gender relations and family structure were frequently influenced by religious change, with Buddhism, Christianity, Islam, and Neo-Confucianism playing especially significant roles.
- In addition to monogamous marriage, practices such as polygamy, concubinage, and harems were permitted in certain places. Terms of divorce varied from place to place, and whether or not children born outside of marriage were recognized as legitimate likewise varied.

| Humans and the Environment, 600–1450 | | |
|---|---|---|
| **ca. 600–900** | | |
| **Europe** | Viking migrations begin (late 700s) | |
| **Middle East** | | |
| **Africa** | Bantu migrations continue (ca. 1500 B.C.E.–1000 C.E.) bananas arrive from Middle East | |
| **East (and Central) Asia** | | |
| **South (and Southeast) Asia and Oceania** | Polynesian migrations (ca. 1500 B.C.E.–1200 C.E.) | |
| **Americas** | chinampa agriculture and terrace farming continue waru waru agriculture in Andes | |
| **Global and Interregional** | medieval climatic optimum migration of Mongol-Turkic horse pastoralists (East and Central Asia, Middle East) | |
| **ca. 900–1200** | | |
| **Europe** | Viking migrations continue cotton, sugar, and citrus spread through Mediterranean | |
| **Middle East** | cotton, sugar, and citrus spread through Islamic world | |
| **Africa** | | |
| **East (and Central) Asia** | Champa rice spreads to China | |
| **South (and Southeast) Asia and Oceania** | Polynesian migrations continue | |
| **Americas** | | |
| **Global and Interregional** | migration of Mongol-Turkic horse pastoralists (East and Central Asia, Middle East) | |
| **ca. 1200–1450** | | |
| **Europe** | black death (mid-1300s) | |
| **Middle East** | black death (early to mid-1300s) | |
| **Africa** | | |
| **East (and Central) Asia** | black death (early 1300s) | |
| **South (and Southeast) Asia and Oceania** | | |
| **Americas** | | |
| **Global and Interregional** | Little Ice Age begins | |

## Humans and the Environment

- The Americas remained cut off environmentally and culturally from Afro-Eurasia.
- Nomadic and migratory populations (especially those of the Vikings, Mongols, Bantus, and Polynesians) continued to have a profound impact on large parts of the world.
- Massive epidemics struck Eurasia. Most famous was the "black death": the wave of plague that swept China, the Middle East, and Europe in the 1300s.
- Human impact on the environment increased dramatically as a result of population growth and the greater capacity of advanced and urbanized societies to carry out large-scale engineering projects (such as China's Grand Canal).
- The increased scale of agricultural production heightened the risks of soil erosion, deforestation, and other forms of major environmental damage.
- Mining, which supported the expansion of industrial production and the increased demand for metals, gems, and jewels, exerted a growing impact on the environment.
- Increased trade activity spread plants and foodstuffs (including bananas, rice, cotton, sugar, spices, and fruits) far from their points of origin.
- A global warming trend, often called the medieval climatic optimum, lasted between 800 and 1300s, greatly affecting patterns of migration, agricultural life, and interregional trade.
- Between the late 1200s and the early 1500s, a cooling trend began, leading to the so-called Little Ice Age, which persisted until the early to mid-1800s.

## QUESTIONS AND COMPARISONS TO CONSIDER

- Differences and likenesses of various interregional trade networks.
- Differences and likenesses among systems of labor organization, both free and coerced.
- What roles did environmental factors, such as the medieval climatic optimum and the Little Ice Age, play in social and economic development? What about diseases?
- Intellectual and cultural developments in different societies, and the intellectual and cultural influences exerted by different societies on each other. Good examples include the Middle Eastern influence on medieval Europe, India's influence on Southeast Asia, the mutual influence between Tang China and the Abbasid caliphate (or between China and its neighbors), and the transfer of technology and knowledge throughout the Mongol empire during the "pax Mongolica."
- Pay attention to explorers, travelers, and diasporic communities as agents of cultural diffusion and change.
- Be aware of the methods and techniques that powerful states and empires used to administer their lands and project power effectively. How did they legitimate their power?
- How did the fall of powerful states and the reconstitution of new ones unfold in different parts of the world? Consider the post-Han dynasties in China or Europe after the fall of Rome, or the rise and fall of the different caliphates.
- How did new technology affect warfare during these years? Travel? Trade? Agriculture?
- How important is the nation-state, as opposed to empires and larger cultural units, as an object of study during this historical period?
- Consider the role of nomadic movement as a cause of change (environmental, social, political) during these years. Do the same for the growth of cities.

- Examine major migratory movements during this period and their various effects.
- What roles did religions play in political development, especially in areas that attempted to create large, multinational civilizations united by religion, such as Christendom and the Islamic caliphates?
- How did religion affect the status of women and the dynamics of family life in various parts of the world?

# UNIT 3

## SCENIC ROUTE

### (Chapters 7–11)

# State Building, Expansion, and Conflict, 600–1450

# 7

- → **DIFFERING TRANSITIONS FROM CLASSICAL REGIMES AND EMPIRES**
- → **EUROPEAN FEUDALISM + BYZANTINE CENTRALIZATION + ITALIAN CITY-STATES**
- → **ABBASID CALIPHATE + OTTOMAN EMPIRE**
- → **GHANA AND MALI + SWAHILI CITY-STATES**
- → **TANG + SONG + YUAN + MING DYNASTIES**
- → **HEIAN JAPAN + MEDIEVAL SHOGUNATES**
- → **DELHI SULTANATE + SOUTHEAST ASIAN CITY-STATES**
- → **INTERREGIONAL CONTACT AND CONFLICT (TANG-ABBASID, CRUSADES, MONGOL KHANATES)**
- → **IDEOLOGIES AND POLITICAL USES OF RELIGION (CHRISTENDOM, DAR AL-ISLAM, MANDATE OF HEAVEN, NEO-CONFUCIANISM)**
- → **WARRIOR CODES (CHIVALRY, BUSHIDO, FURUSIYYA)**
- → **KEY BATTLES (TOURS/POITIERS, TALAS, MANZIKERT, AIN JALUT, FALL OF CONSTANTINOPLE)**
- → **KEY LEADERS (CHARLEMAGNE, HAROUN AL-RASHID, SALADIN, MANSA MUSA, GENGHIS KHAN, KUBLAI KHAN, FUJIWARA CLAN)**

Although most forms of rulership remained non-representative, with monarchies and oligarchies most common, states themselves took widely varying shape during this era.

In many cases, **classical** empires and regimes—such as Rome, Han China, and the Gupta Empire—collapsed, leading to one of several outcomes. In some instances, new states quickly took their place, using some of the old states' traditional sources of legitimacy and power (including patriarchal authority, religious backing, and the support of landowning elites), but blending them with innovative governing techniques. Examples include Byzantium and the post-Han dynasties in China. Sometimes decentralization followed, giving rise in certain places, most famously medieval Europe and Japan, to the system of feudalism. Another alternative was for dramatically new forms of governance to appear, as in the Islamic caliphates, the Mongol khanates, and the city-state systems that emerged in East Africa, Southeast Asia, the Americas, and Italy.

In all cases, pay attention to methods of rulership and administration. Also take note of how states and empires interacted with each other, whether peacefully or violently.

# STATE BUILDING IN AFRO-EURASIA: TRADITION AND INNOVATION

## Europe and Byzantium

After the fall of Rome, European political life varied widely depending on region and time. In the east, the state of Byzantium enjoyed wealth, cultural advancement, and a high degree of centralization. For the rest of Europe, by contrast, the Early Middle Ages (ca. 500–1000) were a time not just of overall backwardness, but of political decentralization and perpetual military threat. During the High Middle Ages (ca. 1000–1300), an era of cultural and economic revival, nations took firmer shape. During the period between 1300 and 1500—the Late Middle Ages for most of Europe, the Renaissance in Italy—states trended toward even greater centralization, although these were also years of constant warfare, social unrest, and crises such as the black death.

In the aftermath of Rome's collapse, no single authority emerged in western or central Europe to take its place. Instead, small and short-lived kingdoms rose and fell. Constantly menaced by migrating barbarians and Muslim invaders, these monarchies were also weakened by decentralization: their rulers lacked the money, military strength, and administrative tools to govern their lands effectively. By the 700s, however, particularly in the Frankish kingdom that eventually spawned Charlemagne's empire, certain leaders hit upon a partial solution. This was the system of **feudalism**, in which monarchs awarded land to loyal followers, or vassals. In exchange, these vassals guaranteed that their parcels of land (fiefs) would be governed, that law and justice would be dispensed, that crops would be grown, and that the land would be protected. Those who received the largest land parcels evolved into Europe's **noble** (or **aristocratic**) **class**, and these nobles typically subdivided (or subinfeudated) their own land, becoming lords to their own vassals. The obligations owed to each other by lords and vassals were formal and contractual—a point of difference between European feudalism and feudalism elsewhere, especially in Japan, where relationships were governed by a more abstract sense of loyalty.

**NOTE**

A key originator of European feudalism was the Frankish war leader Charles Martel, who successfully turned back Muslims invading from Spain at the battle of Tours (732, also known as Poitiers) and thereby limited the Islamic presence in medieval Europe.

**A Medieval Tournament.**
The military and political backbone of medieval Europe's feudal system was the knight. High-born and trained from youth in cavalry warfare, the knight was the state-of-the-art warrior of his era. Knights also made up Europe's noble class. Knights honed their military skills—and cultivated the arts of chivalry—at tournaments such as the one portrayed here.

A key function of the feudal nobility was military. Vassals were required to recruit foot soldiers from the land given them, and they themselves fought as **knights**, or elite armored cavalry, a style of combat that required wealth and lifelong training. In theory, the code of **chivalry**—expressed fictionally in songs and poems like those about King Arthur—was supposed to ensure that knights acted as virtuous, Christian warriors, dealing fairly with the lower classes and treating women with delicacy and respect. Even though the code had some restraining effect in real life, it was often broken. The economic realities of feudalism were also less than pleasant because the system relied on the labor of **serfs**: peasants who were not technically slaves but were tied to a feudal lord's land and had no right to change profession or residence without permission. Serfs spent a certain number of days per month working directly for their lords and also owed their lord a portion of their own crops and livestock. Generally speaking, their living conditions were dismal.

Feudalism remained at the heart of European politics and socioeconomic life for centuries. On the other hand, centralizing tendencies were felt in certain places as early as the 800s and 900s. Much of the need to centralize further had to do with continued struggles against Muslim forces, as well as the wave of attacks launched from the north by Vikings, starting in the late 700s and lasting until approximately 1000. A prime example of an early and successful state-builder is the Frankish king **Charlemagne** (r. 768–814). Not only did he defeat Vikings, Muslims, and barbarians, he sponsored education and culture, created a network of administrators and local officials to supervise his growing territories, and formed the Holy Roman Empire. The very name of Charlemagne's state highlights two key strategies pursued by European rulers during the Middle Ages. One was to legitimate one's rule by association with the Catholic Church—whose political role in medieval Europe was considerable—and another was to hearken back to the Roman Empire as a model of effective government to imitate. Charlemagne's empire was split by his grandsons, but his example was followed by later monarchs.

During the High and Late Middle Ages, European states centralized at different paces and to different extents. Even under the best of circumstances, all of them had to deal with the powerful underlying tension between monarchs (who preferred centralization) and their nobles (who wished to preserve their feudal powers and privileges). Equally important, and equally complicated, was the relationship between European monarchs and the **Catholic papacy**, which claimed and exercised a great deal of worldly power during the Middle Ages. In Western Europe, the most stable states were England and France, whose royal families were intertwined for several centuries, thanks to the **Norman Conquest** of 1066, which brought French-style feudalism to England and fused Latin-based culture with the Celtic and Anglo-Saxon traditions already present in the British Isles. Unusually, England achieved a high degree of centralization while significantly restricting the power of the king. In 1215, the **Magna Carta**, imposed on the king by his barons, guaranteed the nobility certain rights and privileges. Later in the 1200s, England's nobility won the right to form a **Parliament**, which made laws in conjunction with the king and gradually became more representative. Also during this time, England's system of **common law** began providing for jury trials and observing certain personal liberties ("a man's home is his castle," for example). By contrast, the Capetian kings of France, who ruled from Paris, followed the more typical route to medieval state-building, which was to centralize the nation by increasing their own power. The French kings' crucial task during the High and Late Middle Ages was to conquer large and economically important regions that either wished to remain independent (such as Burgundy or large parts of the south, where Paris used religious differences as an excuse to launch a brutal crusade) or were claimed by England (such as Normandy and Aquitaine). It took years of fighting to untangle England's and France's competing claims over French territory. The last and most important of these conflicts was the **Hundred Years' War** (1337–1453), which coincided with social unrest on both sides and the black death. The English enjoyed the upper hand at first. However, the French ultimately won—thanks in large part to the warrior maid **Joan of Arc**—and victory in the 1400s vastly boosted the efforts of the French kings to centralize their power at home. Unlike their English counterparts, French monarchs were not obligated to share their power in any legally meaningful way.

Although important states formed in southern and central Europe, they were less centralized. Sprawling across the middle of the continent—especially the German-speaking parts of Europe—was the Holy Roman Empire, a multicultural monarchy founded in the 900s by Charlemagne's heirs. The emperor was supposed to work in partnership with the pope, although in actuality the two clashed more than they cooperated. Although the emperor's territory was large, his powers were comparatively weak. The position was not hereditary: each new emperor was chosen by the empire's leading noble families. The population was ethnically diverse (Germanic, Slavic, Italian, Hungarian, and more), and the empire itself was a difficult-to-administer patchwork of dozens of duchies, kingdoms, and principalities—almost 200 of them in the 1300s. One centralizing factor near the end of this period was the rise of the **Habsburg family**, which gained permanent control over the imperial throne in 1438. Italy—not even a country at this time—remained even more decentralized. Much of northern Italy was controlled by the Holy Roman Empire, and many parts of the south passed in and out of French, Spanish, Muslim, Byzantine, and even Viking hands. Those areas that remained free were governed by **city-states**: Italy was one of the most urbanized regions of Europe and a major player in the Mediterranean trade network, whose economic prosperity and cultural dynamism made it the birthplace of the **Renaissance** in the late 1200s and early 1300s. The chief city-states of medieval and Renaissance Italy were Florence, Milan, and Venice in the north and Naples in the south. Also important was Rome, the heart of the Papal States. As for Spain and Portugal, their medieval development was shaped above all by their conquest at the hands of the Moors, or Muslim invaders, during the 700s. On one hand, the Moorish presence benefited al-Andalus (as Islamic Spain and Portugal were known): the science, technology, and deep understanding of Greek philosophy brought to Spain by Muslim and Jewish scholars eventually spread to the rest of Europe, and the beauty of Moorish art and architecture is still evident in Spain and Portugal today. On the other hand, both countries spent most of the Middle Ages locked in a long war, the **Reconquista**, against Moorish armies. The Reconquista began in the early 1000s and lasted until 1492, although already by the late 1200s, the Moors had been pushed into Granada, the southernmost part of Spain. One of the Reconquista's legacies was the intense religious hostility shown toward Muslims and Jews by Spanish and Portuguese Catholics, both during and after the war. Another was a tradition of regional autonomy in Spain, where the existence of about half a dozen separate kingdoms, not counting Portugal, delayed full centralization until the end of the 1400s.

By far the strongest and most advanced state in medieval Europe was **Byzantium**, or the Eastern Roman Empire, whose capital, **Constantinople**, sat at the crossroads of Europe and Asia and was home to a million people at its peak. Economically, Byzantium played a role in Mediterranean trade, Silk Road commerce, and, indirectly, the Indian Ocean trade network. Politically, its emperor used **Eastern Orthodoxy** to legitimize his rulership and took advantage of a large and elaborate bureaucracy—a holdover from the days of Rome—to administer and supervise his territory. Byzantine emperors were master strategists, using complex fortifications, naval power, advanced technology, and diplomatic skill to fend off multiple enemies at once. Until the late 1000s, the *theme* system, by which Byzantium granted land to soldiers serving in frontier zones, proved a clever and cost-effective way to protect the empire's borders. In 1071, the Seljuk Turks defeated Byzantium in the pivotal battle of **Manzikert**, setting into process the empire's steady territorial decline. Finally, in 1453, the Ottoman Turks, thanks to effective deployment of gunpowder weaponry, captured Constantinople for themselves and destroyed the Byzantine state.

In both Catholic Europe and Orthodox Byzantium, religion was central to political and cultural life. The relationship between church and state, however, played out differently in each half of Europe. Like the Catholic papacy, the Orthodox patriarchate strictly controlled art, music, architecture, and literature, and it strove for as much influence over politics as it could get. Nonetheless, Orthodox doctrine held the Byzantine emperor up as the supreme authority over worldly and spiritual affairs alike, leaving the Orthodox Church in a weak position on those occasions when it quarreled with the emperor. On the other hand, the Catholic Church promoted the **ideal of Christendom**: the concept of Europe as a single civilization, joined by a common allegiance to the Christian church. By this logic, the political authority of the pope counted for as much as that of any other king or prince, and during the High Middle Ages, the Catholic Church made a concerted effort to argue that the pope's political authority should be higher than that of any monarch. The popes never completely realized this ambition, and yet they gathered into their hands some tremendously important worldly powers. The Catholic Church owned vast amounts of land and had the right to collect tithes from the general population. The popes had the right to determine what was **heresy** and to exclude worshippers from the Catholic Church (**excommunication**), and in 1231, they established the **Holy Inquisition**, a set of special courts with wide-ranging powers, to seek out and punish non-conformity. The popes heavily influenced how European monarchies ruled their countries, and they had the power to declare holy wars, or **crusades**—the most famous of which are described at greater length below.

## The Middle East

Prior to 600 C.E., the dominant civilizations in the Middle East were the Byzantine Empire and Persia. Suddenly, the political and religious landscape of the Middle East was transformed by the appearance of Islam (discussed in detail in Chapter 8).

Mohammed's new religion spread through Arabia and beyond during the 600s and 700s, destroying Persia and threatening Byzantium. A vast territory including Spain, most of North Africa, virtually all of the Middle East, and parts of Central Asia came under Islamic control during these years, and further conquests awaited.

Most people who fell under Muslim rule converted to Islam, but territorial and economic control—not conversion for its own sake—was the main aim of these wars. Islamic theology

**SPECIAL NOTE**

A mix of centralization and decentralization prevailed in Eastern Europe. Much of the region was brutally Christianized and dominated by Teutonic knights from the German states, and then threatened during the mid-1200s by the Mongols' westward push or, during the 1300s and 1400s, the Ottoman Turks' invasion of the Balkans. Still, places like Poland, Croatia, and Hungary flourished for at least a while as stable states. By contrast, the Russian lands were governed during most of this era by a loose confederation of city-states. Although the princes ruling these cities owed allegiance to the grand prince of Kiev, they feuded constantly, leaving them weak and divided when the Mongols arrived in the 1240s. For two centuries, the Russians lived under Mongol rule, after which a more centralized state began to take shape under the leadership of Moscow.

divided the world into two spheres, **Dar al-Islam** ("house of peace"), where **Sharia law** was dominant and Muslims were therefore guaranteed the ability to worship freely, and Dar al-Harb ("house of war"), where Islam was not established. In early times, Muslim authorities viewed it as their duty to expand dar al-Islam as far as possible, but while they insisted on political submission and did not extend full rights or equal treatment to non-Muslims, they did not generally force non-Muslims to change their faith—making them arguably more tolerant than Christian authorities in medieval Europe.

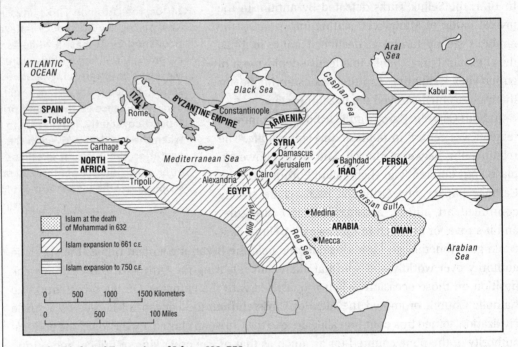

**The Birth and Expansion of Islam, 632–750.**

Born in Arabia, the dynamic new faith of Islam triumphed throughout the Middle East, where it is still dominant. It then continued to expand, both eastward and westward.

**NOTE**

**Compare the ideal of Christendom espoused by Europe's medieval popes with the success enjoyed by the Islamic caliphs in combining religious and political authority, and compare the Middle East's "circle of justice" concept with that of the "mandate of heaven" in China.**

The Muslim world was governed by the **caliph** ("successor"), who combined political and religious power in one person. A key political principle here was the **circle of justice**, which predated the rise of Islam but nevertheless guided the caliphates and the Ottoman empire that followed them. According to this notion of good government, the ruler gives justice to the people, the people pay taxes to the treasury, the treasury ensures that the army receives its salary, and the support of the army allows the ruler to exercise sovereignty—and to give justice to the people, thereby continuing the cycle. The first caliphs, including Mohammed's father-in-law Abu Bakr, ruled from Medina, and presided over the early expansion of Islam. After the civil war that led to the **Sunni-Shiite split** (656–661), power passed to the Umayyad caliphate (661–750), which governed from the Syrian city of Damascus. The Umayyad caliphs continued Islam's military expansion. They also made **Arabic**, the religion's holy language, the official language of the Muslim world, and they started the practice of imposing a tax (**jizya**) on dhimmi, or those subjects who did not convert to Islam. A series of rebellions toppled the Umayyad caliphs.

Following the Umayyad regime was the **Abbasid caliphate** (750–1258), which established a great capital at **Baghdad** and, as described in Chapter 8, presided over the golden age of classical Islamic culture, building many libraries and **madrasas**, or centers of learning, in the process. Up through the 900s, the Abbasid caliphs were strong, applying military force when necessary but for the most part providing peace and stability across the Islamic empire. The first Abbasids halted the westward expansion of Tang China at the **battle of Talas** (751) but then entered into a fruitful relationship of cultural and economic exchange with the Tang emperors. Economic unity prevailed, and Abbasid trade networks linked the Middle East with Europe, Africa, the Indian Ocean, and Asia. Abbasid commerce was stimulated by the rise of credit and the creation of a single, universally respected currency. Muslim manufacturers were among the most skilled in the world at this time, especially when it came to working **steel**. The most famous and best loved of the Abbasid caliphs was **Haroun al-Rashid** (776–809).

Abbasid political unity began to disintegrate during the 900s, owing to geographic overextension, ethnic and cultural diversity (with the Sunni-Shiite split providing added stress), and the chaos caused by nomadic movements in North Africa and the Middle East. Persia, Syria, Egypt, and Spain slipped in and out from under Abbasid rule, and Baghdad fell to the Seljuk Turks in 1055—although the Seljuks kept the caliph in place as a figurehead. Abbasid weakness made it easier for the European **Crusades**, which began in the 1090s, to wreak havoc on the Middle East. The final blow came from the Mongols, who captured Baghdad in 1258 and killed the last Abbasid caliph.

**NOTE**

**The Mongol advance into the Middle East was stopped cold in 1260, when Mamluk cavalry defeated Mongol forces at the battle of Ain Jalut (Goliath Springs) in Syria.**

Political confusion prevailed in the Middle East between the 1000s and the 1300s, with the Seljuk Turks badly damaging Byzantium at the 1071 battle of **Manzikert**, the entire region contending with the Crusades, a **Mamluk** (elite cavalry) state arising in Egypt and Syria in the 1250s, and the Mongols arriving in force, also in the mid-1200s. None of these states proved capable of centralizing the Middle East. The Middle East also suffered during the early 1300s as the **black death** arrived from China. Not until the 1300s did a dominant power begin to emerge in the Middle East: the **Ottoman Turks**, who settled in Asia Minor and founded their own state under Osman I (1280–1326). The Ottomans grew in power, eventually gaining hegemony over the Middle East and moving into southeastern Europe and the islands of the eastern Mediterranean. They also destroyed the Byzantine Empire: the gunpowder armies of Mehmet II brought about the **fall of Constantinople** in 1453—shocking all of Europe and setting the stage for an intense, centuries-long Ottoman-Christian struggle.

## Africa

In Africa during this period, the chief distinction between major societies was whether they adopted Islam or not. The strongest and richest states tended to. Some of these places were incorporated into Dar al-Islam by force. In others, the conversion proceeded peacefully, in many cases facilitated by trans-Saharan trade or Indian Ocean commerce along Africa's east coast.

Most of North Africa, from Egypt to Morocco, converted rapidly during the 600s and 700s, coming under the authority of the caliphates until the Abbasid collapse and under that of the Ottoman Empire in later years. The Mamluk sultanate in Egypt, a breakaway state founded in the 1250s by elite soldiers who had formerly served the Abbasids, was a formidable military power until its conquest by the Ottomans in the early 1500s.

By the 1000s and 1100s, Islam was taking root not just in the Sahara, but also in several parts of sub-Saharan Africa, including the Sahel (the grassland zone that lies just south of the desert). The southward and westward penetration of **Arab traders** played a crucial role in this process—although an unfortunate result of their increased presence was a significant expansion of the **Arab slave trade**, described further in Chapter 9. In West Africa, conversion was also carried out by the **Berbers**, nomadic camel herders and hardened warriors who embraced the new faith with enthusiasm that bordered on the fanatic. From Marrakesh, in present-day Morocco, Berber clans known as the Almoravids extended Muslim authority far to the south.

In West Africa, the states of Ghana and Mali became Islamic, although in different ways. **Ghana**, which had existed in the Sahel since the 500s C.E., emerged as a true power between the 800s and 1000s, thanks to its large deposits of gold and its prominent role in trans-Saharan trade. Ghana welcomed Muslim traders, and many individuals adopted Islam, but in the late 1000s, the state's failure to officially convert triggered an invasion from the north by the zealous Almoravid Berbers. Thus brought within the Muslim orbit, Ghana survived as a gold-trading state until the 1200s. Islam came to **Mali** (mid-1200s to 1600s) with much less violence. Well positioned in the Niger River basin, an important north-south trade route, Mali, like Ghana, was blessed with deposits of gold and other metals. It also traded in salt, ivory, animal skins, and slaves, and emerged as a key point in the trans-Saharan trade network. Mali was founded as a strong state by the conquering chieftain **Sundiata** (whose exploits are praised in a famed epic poem named after him), and its chief commercial and cultural hub, though not its capital, was **Timbuktu**. Not only was the city a stopping point for caravans, it became a renowned center of Islamic scholarship, home to key mosques and madrasas. Mali's peaceful conversion to Islam proved beneficial, enabling good relations with Arab and Berber states and creating a community of educated scholars who served as public servants. Mali's most powerful ruler was **Mansa Musa** (1312–1337), a devout Muslim who gained fame throughout Africa and Europe as one of the world's wealthiest monarchs—a Spanish map of 1375 referred to Mali as home to the "richest and noblest king in all lands." Mansa Musa centralized the government and expanded trade. His hajj, or pilgrimage to Mecca, was an international sensation, not least because he brought so much gold from Mali, that when he spent it in the Middle East, he singlehandedly caused a major devaluation of gold in the region. Mali's might weakened, and its territory shrank, due to foreign attacks in the 1400s and 1500s.

On the shores of East Africa, **Swahili city-states** flourished between 1000 and 1500. Here, nearly forty autonomous, or self-ruling, urban centers were sprinkled along 1,500 miles of coastline. All were heavily involved in the Indian Ocean trade network, and all were multiethnic, with Persians, Arabs, and others migrating here and mixing with the local Africans. Also adding to these cities' populations were migrants from India and Southeast Asia. Islam, along with other religions and traditions, played a prominent role on the East African coast, and a few of these city-states came to be ruled by Arab sheiks or merchant families. Key ports included Mogadishu, Mombasa, Sofala, and **Zanzibar**. The arrival of European colonists and merchants in the early 1500s would change this region beyond recognition.

In the non-Islamic parts of sub-Saharan Africa, a handful of sizable states arose. Among these were Kongo, Benin, and the mighty city of **Great Zimbabwe**. In most of sub-Saharan Africa, though, large and centralized political units developed later and more slowly than elsewhere. Even with a widespread **Bantu** heritage, more than 2,000 languages and dialects are spoken here, and this tremendous ethnolinguistic diversity encouraged the development of distinct societies by small groups. Environmental factors also limited the growth of major states in sub-Saharan Africa. Fluctuating climate and human susceptibility to insect-borne diseases (especially **malaria** and **sleeping sickness**) were obstacles to population growth.

## Asia

For detailed discussion of the Mongol khanates, see the "Afro-Eurasia: Interregional Contacts and Conflicts" in the following section.

After the Han dynasty's fall in 220 C.E., China alternated between periods of political unity and fragmentation. Imperial collapse in China tended not to be as traumatic as the fall of Rome was for Europe, but it did cause turmoil. The first stable dynasty to emerge after the fall of the Han was the short-lived Sui (589–618), which reunified the country and expanded its borders. Even stronger was the **Tang dynasty** (618–906), under which China became larger than it had ever been before. Tang emperors like Xuanzong (712–755) extended China's rule to parts of Central Asia, Mongolia, Manchuria, Tibet, and the Pacific coast. As during the Han dynasty, Tang China forced many of its neighbors into a **tributary system**, in which countries like Korea, Japan, and Vietnam had to make regular monetary payments to avoid punishment. The Tang rulers expanded the **Grand Canal**, which the Sui had built to connect the Yellow and Yangzi rivers, and they stimulated the Chinese economy by taking advantage of Silk Road and Indian Ocean trade. With a near-monopoly on world production, the Chinese **silk industry** generated particularly large profits during the Tang era. Unfortunately, the Tang elite's love of luxury sparked resentment among the common classes and touched off many peasant uprisings—most famously the **An Shi Rebellion**—starting in the 700s and continuing through the 800s. In 906, the dynasty collapsed.

After the Tang breakdown, China fragmented into separate states until the late 1200s. The most durable and advanced of these was the **Song Empire** (960–1279), which ruled east-central China, from the Yellow River in the north to the Vietnamese border in the south. In the 1120s, defeat at the hands of rivals to the north, the Jurchen, forced the Song to give up much of their territory and withdraw to a smaller southern state that survived until the Mongol conquest. Despite its political troubles, Song China enjoyed steady population growth, increased urbanization, thriving trade (with the port of **Canton** becoming one of the world's busiest and most cosmopolitan), and stupendous cultural and technological advancement. It was the Song era that witnessed the invention of **gunpowder** and the **compass**, among other innovations, by the Chinese. Like their Tang and Han predecessors, the Song rulers subscribed to the **mandate of heaven** concept and selected government officials according to the **civil service examination**. They relied heavily on the hierarchical doctrines of **Neo-Confucianism** to legitimate their rule.

Soon after the rise of **Genghis Khan** in the early 1200s, Mongol forces began moving into Chinese territory, conquering most of the west and north by the 1230s. The Song state resisted for several more decades, but fell in the 1270s to **Kublai Khan**, one of Genghis's grandsons, along with the rest of China and parts of Southeast Asia. As the Mongol khanates broke apart, Kublai Khan proclaimed the **Yuan Empire** (1271–1368), and although he called himself Great Khan of the Mongols, he can be considered the first ruler in centuries to have reunified China as a single state. Kublai Khan reigned until 1294 and made Yuan China rich and powerful. Although he attacked Japan and Java without success, his armies forced most of China's neighbors to pay tribute. As they did elsewhere, the Mongols in China adapted themselves to local ways: Kublai Khan embraced Buddhism and made Mandarin Chinese the official language of his court. He rebuilt China's bureaucracy and economy, repaired roads and canals, built new cities, and restored trade with the west. The **Silk Road**, which had declined somewhat, recovered as a vital trade route. **Marco Polo** visited Yuan China, and the court of Kublai Khan himself, in the late 1200s. The Yuan state was not so lucky after Kublai

Khan's death. During the early 1300s, China experienced the first wave of the bubonic plague epidemic known as the **black death**, losing 30 to 40 percent of its population before the disease moved to the Middle East and Europe. Economic decline resulted, and a series of civil wars broke out in the 1340s, leading to the final rebellion which overthrew the Yuan in 1368.

The rebel who brought down the Yuan Empire took the name Hongwu and established the **Ming dynasty** (1368–1644). He and his son **Yongle** (1403–1424) created a solid foundation for the new regime by repairing the damage done by the wars of the 1300s and recentralizing the political and administrative system. The population and the economy both rebounded. To restore imperial legitimacy, Yongle transformed Beijing into a magnificent capital by building the **Forbidden City** as a new seat of power. The early Ming rulers created a large and effective army, using it to expand China's borders and to force neighbors into its traditional tributary system. For a short time, the Ming navy also served as an instrument of diplomacy and intimidation. From 1405 to 1433, the admiral **Zheng He** made seven long voyages to Southeast Asia, India, the Middle East, and East Africa. He expanded trade, learned much about the outside world, and forced 50 states and cities to pay tribute. After Yongle's death, however, the Ming rulers, distracted by the land-based threat of nomads to the north, lost interest in exploration and naval expansion. This was a global turning point: had the Ming continued to exploit their power at sea, China might have begun a wave of worldwide exploration and colonization, as the nations of Europe were on the verge of doing.

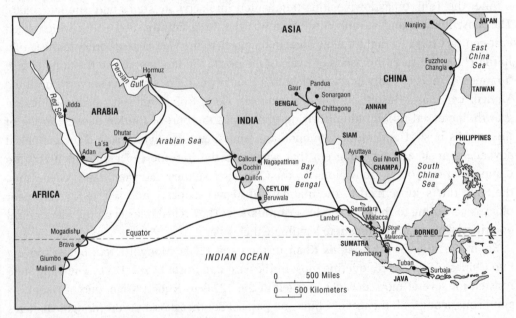

**The Voyages of Zheng He, 1405–1433.**
China's greatest mariner, Zheng He, sailed several times from China to Arabia and East Africa.
He explored, established diplomatic relations, and exacted monetary tribute from weaker states.

At the beginning of this period, Japan's emperors ruled from the city of Nara. Buddhism had recently arrived from China, and the Taika Reforms of the mid-600s imported Chinese bureaucratic methods and legal principles. Japanese urban planning imitated China's, and temple architecture was influenced by Chinese styles. In the late 700s, the emperors shifted their capital to Heian (present-day Kyoto), and this **Heian period** (794–1185) is considered to be Japan's classical era. The Heian regime took an unusual shape: although the emperor remained important as a symbolic figurehead, he lost his political power to the chancellor (*kwampaku*), whose duty it was to serve and protect the emperor. In practice, this meant keeping the emperor in seclusion and ruling in his name. In the mid-800s, the **Fujiwara clan** gained permanent control over the chancellorship, essentially making it Japan's ruling family until the mid-1100s. For many years, the Fujiwara presided over a peaceful, prosperous, and culturally brilliant society. However, the family's pursuit of cultural refinement and their preoccupation with court politics led them to neglect military affairs and to delegate them to warrior clans. During the early 1100s, these clans quarreled among themselves and with the Fujiwara, leading to a terrible civil conflict known as the **Taira-Minamoto War** (1156–1185), in which each side supported a rival claimant to the emperor's throne. The Minamoto drove the Fujiwara from power, defeated the Taira, and created a new form of government: the shogunate.

Minamoto victory marked Japan's transition to medieval **feudalism**. As before, the emperor retained his symbolic importance, but real power now rested with the **shogun**, or "great general." Two shogun regimes, the Kamakura and Ashikaga, ruled between the late 1100s and the late 1500s (the former gave way to the latter in the 1330s), and both coped with highly decentralized conditions. As monarchs in medieval Europe did with their knightly aristocracy, the shogun shared power with noble warlords called **daimyo**, who received control over parcels of land called *shoen*. Both the shogun and the daimyo belonged to the warrior elite known as **samurai**, who were privileged but also bound by a strict code of loyalty, honor, and bravery called **Bushido** ("way of the warrior"). Bushido was even more stringent and hierarchical than European chivalry; the most extreme penalty for violating it was ritual suicide (seppuku, or hara-kiri). Adherence to Bushido was supposed to govern the relationship between lords and vassals in the Japanese system, as opposed to the more formal contracts that were used in medieval Europe. During the 1200s and early 1300s, the Kamakura shoguns kept order in Japan and drove off Kublai Khan's two attempts to invade from China. The Ashikaga shoguns were weaker and allowed greater decentralization. A combination of civil wars and peasant revolts began tearing Japan apart during the mid-1400s, leading to almost complete disunity in the 1500s. Only in the late 1500s and early 1600s would Japan reunify.

Turning to South Asia, India remained in a state of disunity between 550 C.E., when the Gupta Empire collapsed, and approximately 1200 C.E. A quiltwork of small states and independent cities, including the Tamil kingdoms on the Indian Ocean coast and the Malibar city-states (including **Calicut**), governed throughout the subcontinent. In 1206, though, Muslim invaders, who had been battering away at the northwest frontier since the 900s, captured Delhi. Most of northern India fell into the hands of Muslim generals, who established the **Delhi Sultanate** (1206–1526). The key consequence of this victory was to introduce Islam into India, where it would remain long after the sultanate had faded away. The first Delhi Sultans imposed their new faith harshly, and although they became less severe with time, division and tensions continued to characterize the relationship between Hindus and Muslims, who did not tend to mix. Between the mid-1200s and the mid-1300s, the Delhi sultanate expanded to control most of India but then shrank as many states and cities in the south broke away. Also, in 1398, the Central Asian warlord **Timur** attacked Delhi from the north, capturing it and plundering it for a year. The sultanate survived, but barely, and then succumbed to new invaders in the 1520s.

In Southeast Asia, major states emerged before and around 500 C.E. Of especially long duration were the Khmer Empire (500s–1400s) in Cambodia and the Srivijayan Empire (500s–1100s), which governed many of the Indonesian islands and parts of the Malay

**NOTE**

Islam spread to the Indonesian islands in the 1200s and remains a dominant faith there to this day.

Peninsula. Both were strongly influenced by Indian culture—as demonstrated by **Angkor Wat**, the Khmer Empire's architectural masterpiece—and both bore the imprint of Hinduism and Buddhism. Between the 1200s and 1400s, power flowed from these places to kingdoms like Burma, the Thai monarchy, and the Vietnamese states of Annam and Champa. In addition, **city-states** became an important form of political organization throughout this region. The Malaysian port of **Melaka** (Malacca), which sits at a key chokepoint between the Indian and Pacific islands, is a notable example.

## AFRO-EURASIA: INTERREGIONAL CONTACTS AND CONFLICTS

Both within and between regions, contacts among major societies could lead to conflict, but also to important economic, technological, and cultural exchanges. **Viking** migrations and invasions did both, as did the Norman Conquest of England and the Moorish invasion of Spain.

### Tang China and the Abbasid Caliphate

Of special significance was the **Tang-Abbasid interchange** that began in the mid-700s. In 751, at the **battle of Talas**, the newly arisen Abbasid caliphate decisively halted Tang China's westward expansion into Central Asia. With the frontier between them fixed into place, the two states quickly normalized relations, with the caliphate going so far as to lend Arab troops to the Tang emperor to assist against the An Shi rebellion. Trade flourished between the two along the **Silk Road**, and also by sea via the **Indian Ocean trade network**. Muslim **diaspora communities**, already present in Chinese ports and trading cities since the late 600s, grew, and a sizable Muslim minority formed on China's western frontier.

Tang-Abbasid commerce (and similar ties that continued under the Song dynasty) enabled the westward movements of the Chinese innovations discussed elsewhere in this unit, such as improved printing, paper currency, the compass, and gunpowder weaponry.

### The Crusades

In Catholic Europe, the pope's powers included the authority to declare holy wars known as **crusades**. These were fought for many reasons: to convert nonbelievers to Catholicism (as in the Teutonic knights' crusades in Eastern Europe), to crush Christian sects the pope considered heretical (infamous crusades of this sort enabled France's kings to tame independent regions in the south), and to combat non-Christian foreigners (Spain's anti-Muslim **Reconquista**, for example, was at times given the status of crusade).

**TIP**

Compare the Christian notion of crusades with the Islamic concept of holy war, or jihad.

The best-known crusades—the ones generally referred to as "the Crusades"— were those waged against the Muslims of the Middle East and North Africa between 1095 and 1291. The **First Crusade** (1096–1099) was sparked by Byzantine requests for military aid against the Seljuk Turks, who had smashed Byzantine forces at **Manzikert** in 1071, then gone on to capture Jerusalem and the Holy Land. Motivated by a combination of sincere religious fervor, racial prejudice, and a hunger to gain wealth from plunder and land, thousands of crusading knights and their followers gathered in Constantinople, then drove south to Jerusalem, which they besieged in the summer of 1099. In one of the bloodiest slaughters in military history, the Crusaders butchered almost every Muslim and Jew in the city, as well as many Orthodox Christians whom they mistook for Muslims. They then cemented their military and economic presence in the Middle East for the next two centuries by establishing a series of Latin Kingdoms on the Mediterranean's eastern shores. This threw an already politically confused Middle East into deeper chaos.

Lack of unity among Arabs, Turks, and other Muslims was a key reason for the Crusaders' initial success, since neither the weakened Abbasids nor their political rivals were capable of organizing effective resistance. Over time, the Muslims improved their efforts to expel the Europeans, and the many crusades that followed were generally European responses to major Muslim victories. For example, the Kurdish general **Saladin**, one of the most dynamic military leaders in Middle Eastern history, recaptured Jerusalem in 1187 and held back the Third Crusade (1189–1212) which followed. After 1200, the crusades lost their focus (the **Fourth Crusade** of 1202–1204 turned into a Venetian-backed trade war against Christian Constantinople, which was brutally sacked) or failed miserably (like the ill-fated Children's Crusades). The Latin Kingdoms steadily shrank during the 1200s, and the Europeans abandoned their last major outpost in 1291.

Long-term effects of the Crusades include the worsening of the relationship between European Christians and the Muslim Middle East. Also important was the greater awareness of the wider world, especially the lands of the east, that the Crusades stimulated among Europeans. Along with this came an increased knowledge of—and desire for—the economic wealth to be gained by greater interaction with the Middle and Far East. Moreover, the crusading ideal—the notion that Christian warriors were fighting on behalf of a sacred cause—contributed powerfully to the myth of knightly chivalry that emerged in Europe during the Middle Ages. There was also technology transfer, as Europeans learned much about castle architecture from their experience in the Middle East, and also came into contact with some of the innovations that Middle Eastern peoples had adopted from China.

## The Mongol Khanates

During the 1200s, Eurasia was swept by a whirlwind from the Central Asian steppes. The **Mongols**, nomadic horse warriors united by **Genghis Khan**, burst out of their homeland in the 1210s, rapidly creating one of the largest empires in world history. Their brief semi-unification of Eurasia during the 1200s is known as the **pax Mongolica** ("Mongol peace"), and even after the empire broke apart into separate khanates, the Mongols facilitated the transfer of technologies, cultural practices, and trade goods across Eurasia—particularly along the **Silk Road**—during the 1300s and into the 1400s.

The first wave of Mongol conquest lasted until Genghis Khan's death in 1227 and left the Mongols in charge of Mongolia, much of China, and parts of Central Asia, including the city of Samarkand. By the mid-1200s, his heirs had absorbed parts of Eastern Europe (especially most of Russia and Ukraine), portions of the Middle East, and all of China. Their westward drive was halted by Teutonic knights and Hungarians in Eastern Europe and by Mamluk cavalry in Syria, at **Ain Jalut**. They destroyed the Song Empire in China, the Abbasid caliphate, and the Kievan city-state confederacy in Russia, among other states.

Over this massive expanse, the Mongols imposed a single political authority, revived Silk Road trade, and enforced law and order. Although the Mongols are frequently stereotyped as barbaric (and pacified enemies with great bloodthirstiness when they thought it necessary), they maintained their rule not just by force, but by a high level of administrative sophistication. They skillfully organized their army into decimally based units and quickly learned new military techniques—such as siegecraft—from neighbors and conquered peoples. In general, they were adept **cultural borrowers**. They adopted a written script from the Turkic Uighurs, their paper currency and their law code (the *yasa*) from China, and Buddhism or Islam as their religion, depending on where they settled. They used their own aptitude as horse riders to create one of the premodern world's most efficient postal systems (the *yam*). From their subject peoples, the Mongols conscripted or enslaved soldiers, artisans, and others who possessed skills they needed.

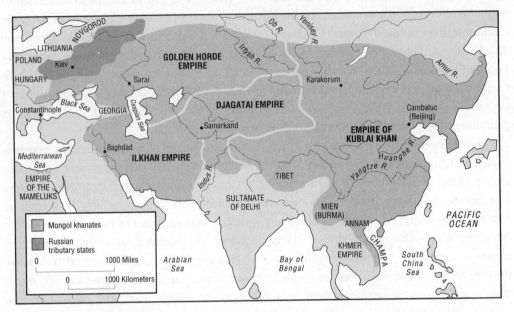

**The Mongol Empires, 1294 C.E.**

By 1294, the Mongols, a nomadic people, had conquered most of Asia and key portions of Europe and the Middle East. Mongol control over these territories had a major and lasting effect on many parts of Eurasia.

Even so, the Mongols were better at conquering than governing. As a Chinese official famously described the Mongols: "One can conquer an empire on horseback, but one cannot govern it from there." The last khan to rule over a united Mongol state died in 1260. After a brief civil war, the empire's four largest units became independent khanates. The homeland, which included Mongolia and Yuan China, went to **Kublai Khan**. The Golden Horde kept Russia under its yoke until the mid-1400s. The Il-Khan Mongols converted to Islam and ruled much of the Middle East until the rise of the Ottoman Turks. The Jagatai khanate governed Central Asia well into the 1400s, becoming Muslims like their Il-Khan rivals.

From 1370 to 1405, the Jagatai khan **Timur** (also known as Tamerlane) attempted to repeat the military triumphs of Genghis Khan, moving into Persia, southern Russia, parts of the Middle East, and northern India. This expansion ceased after Timur's death, but his descendants ruled Central Asia until the 1500s.

# STATE FORMATION IN THE PRE-COLUMBIAN AMERICAS

The geographical isolation of the Americas from Afro-Eurasia continued until the end of the 1400s, when the voyages of Christopher Columbus brought the societies of North and South America into sustained contact with outsiders. In the historiography of the Americas, the period before 1492 is referred to as the **pre-Columbian era**.

## North America

In North America, most Native Americans were nomadic hunter-foragers divided into tribes. Not counting Mexico, two regions of North America became home to more advanced societies. One was the Southwest, where settlement began in the 300s B.C.E., and where the most famous early culture was the **Anasazi**, who inhabited the region from about 400 (perhaps earlier) to 1300. They lived in complex dwellings known as **pueblos**, sometimes built on the open flatland, sometimes in caves high up in the canyons.

To the north and east, sophisticated societies emerged in the Ohio and Mississippi river valleys. The most advanced of these **earth mound**-building cultures was the **Mississippian civilization** (ca. 700–1500). The Mississippians also built cities, the largest of which was **Cahokia**, with a population of over 30,000 by 1200. For unknown reasons, Cahokia was abandoned around 1250, and the culture fell into a long decline. At this time, Native Americans began to form smaller hunter-forager groups that evolved into the major tribes which remain familiar today.

## Mexico and Mesoamerica

In Mexico and Mesoamerica, the city-states of the dominant **Mayan** culture faded away during the 800s C.E.—although whether because of wars among them, outside invasion, social unrest, or depletion of resources is unknown. Taking their place were the **Toltecs**, an aggressive warrior society that ruled much of the region between the 800s and the 1100s.

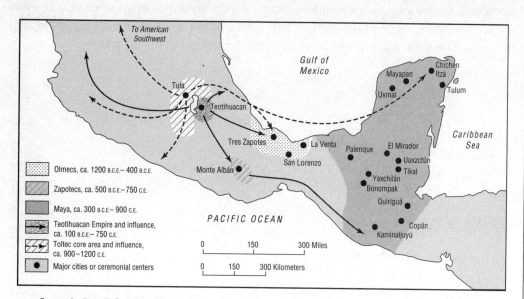

**States in Pre-Columbian Central America, ca. 1200 B.C.E.–1200 C.E.**

This map demonstrates that, in Central America, many civilizations developed, rose, and fell in succession. The Olmecs set the pattern for cultural development here, followed by the Maya, Toltecs, and Aztecs.

The next major group in Mesoamerica—and the last before the Europeans' arrival—were the Mexica, better known as the **Aztecs** (1200s–1500s). Their chief city was the metropolis of **Tenochtitlán**, on the site of what is today Mexico City. At the height of Aztec power, Tenochtitlán had a population of half a million, and its marketplace could hold 60,000 people. Like others in the region, they adopted the cultural and religious practices of **pyramid building** and **human sacrifice**.

The Aztecs were even more warlike than the Toltecs before them. During the 1300s, they conquered an empire of more than 125,000 square miles, ruling a population of 5 to 12 million. Subject peoples were taxed by a **tributary system** that provided the Aztecs with foodstuffs and gold. Aztec rulers built an extensive network of roads for political and economic purposes. The Aztecs thrived until the early 1500s, when the Spanish arrived. Defeat of the Aztecs led to Spanish domination of Mexico and Central America until the 1800s.

## The Andes

In South America's Andes Mountains, several civilizations—including the **Moche** (ca. 200–700 C.E.)—arose during the centuries following the fall of the Chavín around 250 B.C.E. Most of these had certain features in common: a reliance on **terrace farming** and **waru waru** agriculture, the domestication of **llamas** and related creatures for transport and wool, and a hierarchical social system in which clans called **ayllu** cooperated to fulfill the labor obligations placed on them by the stringent **mit'a** system. Writing was unknown here, but many Andean peoples used the knot-tying method of **quipu** to keep records.

All these features were shared by the **Incas** (1300s–1500s), who built a massive empire in less than a century, stretching 3,000 miles from north to south and extending from the Pacific coast to the upper Amazon in the east. Keys to Incan power included a road network measuring more than 13,000 miles, an elaborate bureaucracy, and extreme social stratification. The ruler, known as the Great Inca, was considered the descendant of the sun god. To look at him directly was an offense punishable by death, and he legally owned all property in the Incan state. In addition, Incan rulers transformed mit'a labor into an even harsher and more burdensome system than before. Incan civilization enjoyed its heyday during the 1400s, but was brought down by Spanish conquest in the early 1500s.

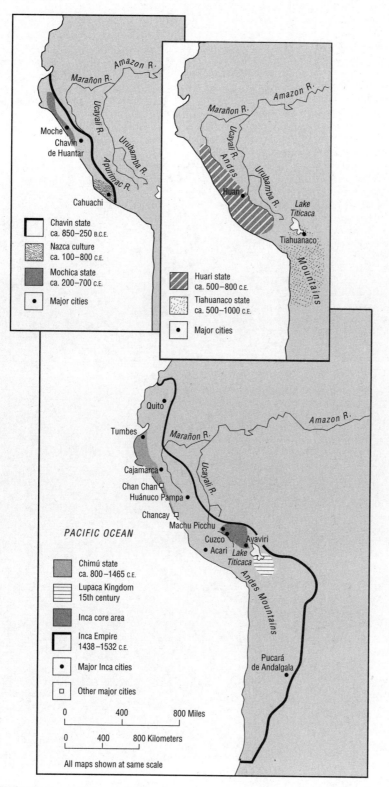

**Andean Civilizations, ca. 850 B.C.E.–1532 C.E.**

The earliest major civilizations of South America emerged in the Andes Mountains, on the continent's western coast. The last and greatest was the Incan Empire.

# Culture, Science, and Technology, 600–1450

## 8

- → **BUDDHIST AND NEO-CONFUCIAN CULTURAL INFLUENCE IN EAST ASIA**
- → **BUDDHIST AND HINDU CULTURAL INFLUENCE IN SOUTH AND SOUTHEAST ASIA**
- → **ISLAMIC CULTURAL INFLUENCE IN THE MIDDLE EAST, AFRICA, AND THE INDIAN OCEAN BASIN**
- → **TRANSNATIONAL LANGUAGES (LATIN, ARABIC, SWAHILI, TURKIC)**
- → **INTERREGIONAL TRAVELERS (XUANZANG, MARCO POLO, IBN BATTUTA, ZHENG HE)**
- → **KEY ARCHITECTURAL MONUMENTS**
- → **KEY WORKS OF LITERATURE**
- → **SCHOLASTICISM TO RENAISSANCE HUMANISM**
- → **BIRTH OF ISLAM (MOHAMMED, THE QU'RAN)**
- → **ALGEBRA AND ARABIC NUMERALS**
- → **ASTROLABE AND COMPASS**
- → **SPREAD OF GUNPOWDER WEAPONRY**
- → **PRINTING TECHNIQUES (WOODBLOCK + MOVABLE TYPE)**
- → **OUTRIGGER CANOES AND VIKING LONGBOATS**

The level of cultural sophistication rose worldwide during this era. Much of this stemmed from the global tendency toward greater interregional connectedness. Trade, migration, empire-building, and cross-cultural mixing led to the diffusion of religious practices, cultural traditions and styles, and scientific and technological innovations. The rise of print technology during this period further accelerated this trend.

At the same time, individual regions experienced their own cultural changes and advancements. Whether they were imported from abroad or home-grown, you should make yourself familiar with the distinct artistic, architectural, and intellectual characteristics of each major culture, as well as the general developments that caused cultures to influence each other.

## CROSS-CULTURAL EXCHANGE AND CULTURAL GROWTH

Key instances of cross-cultural exchange shaped the art, literature, and traditions of many parts of the world during this era.

From China, the influence of **Buddhist culture** spread throughout East Asia, first to Korea, and then to Japan, arriving there most likely in the 500s C.E. Not only were religious beliefs transmitted, but also sacred texts, Chinese pictographs (many of which were absorbed into Korea's and Japan's systems of writing), and artistic and architectural styles. Buddhist temples in Korea and Japan adopted the pagoda-shaped form of Chinese temples, and the old capital of Japan, Heian (present-day Kyoto), was deliberately built according to the same grid layout as Tang China's capital, Chang'an. Also from China, **Neo-Confucian principles** of hierarchy and filial piety spread widely, reinforcing social stratification and gender inequality in East Asian societies.

**Heian Jingu Shrine, Kyoto, Japan.**
Kyoto, the old capital of Japan, still contains many architectural masterpieces from the Heian era (794–1185), when the city was known by that name. Heian was a major center of Buddhist worship and scholarship, and China's cultural and artistic influence was felt heavily there.

A similar pattern unfolded in South and Southeast Asia, where **Buddhist and Hindu influences** radiated outward from India. A renowned example of Hindu culture's regional influence appeared in Cambodia's Khmer state (500s–1400s). In the 1100s, Khmer rulers built the fabulously ornate, 40-square-mile temple complex of **Angkor Wat**, directly imitating architectural styles from south India. Originally designed as a Hindu place of worship, Angkor Wat was converted to use by Buddhists during the 1200s. The long cultural reach of Indian Buddhism is evident as far away as the Indonesian island of Java, where the Srivijayan Empire (600s–1100s) built the temple complex of **Borobudur** between 770 and 825. Taking the shape of a mountain over 100 feet high, Borobudur rises in levels, each of which represents a stage on the path to enlightenment.

**Angkor Wat**

The temple complex of Angkor Wat, built in Cambodia during the 1100s, demonstrates India's cultural and religious influence over much of Southeast Asia. Originally a site of Hindu worship, Angkor Wat became a Buddhist center during the 1200s.

The cultural influence of **Islam**, discussed at greater length below, extended from Spain and North Africa to the Middle East and Persia, and even beyond that—to many places in sub-Saharan Africa (both in the west, in the vicinity of Mali and Ghana, and along the eastern coast), to Central Asia and China's western frontier, and into South and Southeast Asia (as far as India and Indonesia by the 1200s). Arabic and Persian literary, artistic, and architectural styles affected poetry, music, painting, and the building of mosques throughout the growing Muslim world.

In the Americas, as in earlier times, certain core civilizations put their cultural stamp on neighboring peoples, sometimes over a wide radius. Like the Olmecs and Mayans before them, the **Toltecs** (ca. 800s–1100s) and **Aztecs**, or Mexica (ca. 1100s–1500s), perpetuated throughout Mesoamerica a variety of practices, such as **pyramid** building, **human sacrifices**, and the worship of a pantheon of deities that, for centuries, had been venerated in roughly the same form throughout the region. As they came to rule the Andes between the 1300s and 1500s, the **Incas** exerted the same kind of regional cultural influence, including worship of the sun god and the use of **quipu** knot tying instead of a written script for recordkeeping.

Cross-cultural exchange during these years also included pivotal transfers of technology and scientific knowledge. Muslim scholars, who ranked among the era's finest mathematicians and astronomers, derived much of their expertise from encounters with **mathematical writings from India and ancient Greece**. The formalization of **algebra**—an Arabic word—as a mathematical discipline in the early 800s resulted from this dynamic. This familiarity with Greek texts also allowed Jewish and Islamic scholars in Muslim Spain (al-Andalus) to contribute to intellectual revival in medieval Europe. These scholars reintroduced **Greek philosophy and science** (including important medical knowledge and fresh translations of works by Plato and Aristotle), adding to Europe's understanding of the Greco-Roman classics and paving the way for Europe's **Renaissance**. From China, numerous key technologies spread westward throughout Eurasia during this period. Among these were the **astrolabe** and the **compass**, vital for navigation on land and especially at sea, and **gunpowder weaponry**, which revolutionized warfare in the 1200s and 1300s when it reached Europe and the Middle East.

Medieval Europe's expertise in castle building increased by leaps and bounds after 1100, as their Crusades against the Middle East exposed them to the military architecture of the Islamic world, where Muslim armies had long used stone construction to build strong and complex castles. Before this, European kingdoms had built castles mainly with wood, and when they had used stone, they had settled for relatively uncomplicated designs. European crusaders quickly imported Muslim designs for their own use at home.

Perhaps the most revolutionary technology to come out of China was **printing**, which has a long and complex history. The relatively simple technique of **(wood)block printing** had originated as early as the 200s C.E., but not only was it costly and time-consuming, a block, once carved, could be used to print only one text or image, and it could not be corrected. The concept of **movable-type printing**, which allowed individual, reusable characters to be placed in a frame, and then rearranged, arose during the 1000s in Song China and was known in Korea by the 1200s. However, the Chinese used expensive and fragile ceramic tiles, and while the Koreans discovered how to print with cheaper and more durable metal tablets, Asian languages had so many characters that even this more versatile form of printing had less impact than it later did in Europe, where it eventually spread. The first workable and cost-effective movable-type press was designed by the German inventor **Johannes Gutenberg** in the 1430s. Especially because the small number of letters in the Latin alphabet made it easy to mass-produce texts, the Gutenberg press had an explosive effect on literacy rates, the speed at which information spread, the impact of new ideas and scientific theories, and the expansion of libraries and universities. It would also play an indispensable role in Europe's Renaissance and Protestant Reformation.

Many languages were affected by cross-cultural exchange, especially by the migration of peoples and the movement of trade goods. Silk Road commerce helped to spread **Turkic** languages throughout the Asiatic expanse between modern-day Turkey and Mongolia, while the expansion of Islam propelled **Arabic**—the religion's holy language—even farther, giving it a prominent cultural role not just in the Middle East, but all the way from North Africa to the borderlands of India. (**Persian** became similarly important throughout much of Islamic Eurasia.) The migration of the **Bantu** peoples throughout sub-Saharan Africa profoundly affected linguistic development in many parts of the continent. Specifically in East Africa, trade and the mixing of ethnicities (not only African, but from Arabia and the Indian Ocean basin) led to the creation of **Swahili**, the region's widely adopted lingua franca, or common tongue.

## TRANSNATIONAL LANGUAGES

Throughout history, certain languages have risen up to allow communication between cultures whose native tongues are very different. The term *lingua franca* is often used to describe them. Examples include Latin; Arabic; Swahili; the sign language used by Native American tribes on the Great Plains; and, increasingly in our own time, English. A language achieves the status of lingua franca for various reasons. In some cases, it is the shared religious language of people who are ethnically different; in others, it is the tongue that most effectively facilitates trade in a multilingual region. Sometimes it is imposed by a military or imperial power (like Spanish in Latin America or English in India).

## FAR FROM HOME: INTERREGIONAL TRAVELERS

Several interregional travelers from this period became famous for creating important ties between distant societies or, through their writings, raising geographical and cultural awareness.

In the early to mid-600s, the Chinese monk **Xuanzang** journeyed to India to learn more about Buddhism (inspired by similar travels made by the monk Faxian in the 300s C.E.). After more than a decade and a half of visiting holy sites and libraries, Xuanzang returned with wagon loads of Buddhist art and artifacts, as well as hundreds of sacred texts in Sanskrit that he and his followers studied, translated, and distributed throughout China. By promoting greater understanding of South Asian sources, Xuanzang's efforts had a profound impact on Buddhist doctrine in East Asia. He left behind his own record of the journey, entitled *Great Tang Records on the Western Regions*, but even more famous is the epic novel written about him centuries later, during the Ming dynasty. Wu Chengen's beloved *Journey to the West* features Xuanzang as a fictional character who travels to India in the company of the mischievous and magical Monkey King. Here, India's geography and culture are deliberately portrayed unrealistically, to heighten the sense of fantasy and exotic adventure.

One of the first Europeans to cross the breadth of Eurasia, the young merchant **Marco Polo** traveled from Venice to Asia along the Silk Road during the mid- to late 1200s. His journeys occupied nearly a quarter century, and if he is to be believed, he befriended Kublai Khan, the Mongol ruler of China. Although scholars today are not sure how far to trust his autobiography (*Books of the Marvels of the World*, better known as *The Travels of Marco Polo*), Marco Polo's writings played an enormous role in familiarizing medieval and Renaissance Europeans with the riches, luxuries, and cultural advancements of Asia—and in stoking the desire of Europeans to travel and trade there. Christopher Columbus, for example, was merely one of countless Europeans to read Marco Polo's descriptions of Asia with intense interest.

The great explorer of the Islamic world was **Ibn Battuta** of Morocco, who began a pilgrimage to Mecca in 1325 and, instead of returning, embarked on a journey lasting almost 30 years and covering over 70,000 miles. Not only did he visit most of West and North Africa, along with the Middle East, he ventured throughout Central Asia, East and Southeast Asia, and South Asia, going as far as the Indonesian islands. His *Travels* reveal the remarkable diversity of customs and cultural practices among Muslim people, and Ibn Battuta was often surprised, and sometimes shocked, by how different lifestyles could be among various peoples technically joined together by allegiance to a common faith.

Another traveler from this era to be aware of is **Zheng He**, the Chinese captain who took ships of the Ming navy on seven far-ranging voyages through the Indian and Pacific Oceans during the early 1400s. He is described in more detail in Chapter 7.

## OLD AND NEW TRADITIONS: CULTURAL DEVELOPMENTS BY REGION

### Medieval and Renaissance Europe

For years, it was common to view Europe's **medieval period** as the "Dark Ages," an era completely lacking in culture. It is now more standard to recognize the richness of medieval culture—but it remains true that Europe lagged far behind Byzantium, the Middle East, and East Asia in terms of cultural attainment, and that when it did move forward, it was largely due to outside influences. Also, change over time was key: the Early Middle Ages (ca. 500–1000) were backward to the point of barbarism, and it was the High Middle Ages (ca. 1000–1300) that witnessed genuine cultural advancement. For most of Europe, the period between 1300 and 1500 is considered the Late Middle Ages, while Italy was already undergoing the cultural revival known as the **Renaissance**.

The most important factor shaping Europe's medieval culture was the Christian church. During the early medieval chaos that followed the fall of Rome, the Church played an indispensable role in preserving Greco-Roman manuscripts and, at least in Western and Central Europe, promoting **Latin** as an international language of learning. The **ideal of Christendom**, according to which all European nations should be bound together by their allegiance to the Church, played an important role in medieval Europe—even though the

Church split formally after the Great Schism of 1054, which divided **Roman Catholicism** (Latin-based and governed by the Roman papacy) from **Eastern Orthodoxy** (Greek-inspired and headquartered in Byzantium). Throughout the entire medieval period, the Catholic and Orthodox churches alike provided the vast majority of employment opportunities for artists, architects, and musicians. On the other hand, both churches strictly controlled culture and severely punished art, literature, and scientific ideas that fell out of line with church doctrine.

The dominant philosophy of the Middle Ages was **scholasticism**, the attempt by thinkers such as Peter Abelard and Thomas Aquinas to reconcile Greco-Roman learning from the past with Christian teachings. Adaptation of the former was limited for two reasons: it was dangerous to accept Greco-Roman ideas that the Church objected to, and most medieval scholars were less familiar with Greek than with Latin and tended to know Greek thinkers like Plato and **Aristotle** only through Latin translations. Medieval scientific understanding was based mainly on Greco-Roman scientific ideas that the Church found acceptable. While this was of some benefit, it also encouraged some mistaken ideas, especially regarding medicine and astronomy—because the Church chose to adopt the **geocentric theory**, which proposed that the sun revolves around the earth.

The cultural achievements of the medieval era include the architectural sophistication of Europe's **castles** and **cathedrals**, with the relatively simple Romanesque style giving way to the incredibly ornate Gothic style during the High Middle Ages. Icons, or religious paintings, were inspired by Byzantine styles, even in Catholic Europe, and the best-known form of church music was plainsong, or Gregorian chant. Secular music arose in the form of **troubadour poems**, which celebrated love, **chivalry** (the knightly duty to protect and idealize women), and the adventures of heroes like King Arthur, El Cid of Spain and the knight Roland.

**The writings of Aristotle on science, ethics, and politics were at the center of the medieval worldview, but there is some irony to the way Europeans learned from him during the Middle Ages. For one thing, not all of his writings met with the Church's approval. More important, many of the factual errors contained in his scientific writings were unquestioningly accepted by medieval Europeans—even though Aristotle, following a logic similar to the modern scientific method, had argued that scientific views needed to be constantly improved and updated by means of testing and careful observation. This lesson, perhaps Aristotle's most important, was lost on medieval scholars.**

Europe's first **universities** appeared during this time, both as centers of religious training, but also to teach law and medicine. During the Late Middle Ages, two other trends helped to accelerate the spread of learning throughout Europe. One was the increased use by the 1200s and 1300s of native, or **vernacular**, languages instead of Latin by poets and other authors, including Geoffrey Chaucer of England and Dante Alighieri of Italy. This stimulated a growth in literacy and made literature available to a wider range of people. The same is true of the second development: the invention by **Johannes Gutenberg** of the first viable **movable-type printing press** during the early 1400s, as described earlier in this chapter.

By the late 1200s and early 1300s, certain parts of Europe, particularly Italy, began to experience the cultural rebirth known as the **Renaissance**—prominent in Italy between the early 1300s and the early 1500s, and prevalent in the rest of Europe between the late 1400s and the early 1600s. Italy's thriving trade-based economy, its exposure to wider cultural influences throughout the Mediterranean, and the growing familiarity of its scholars with Greek science and philosophy (thanks to cultural contacts with their Jewish and Islamic counterparts in Muslim Spain) all caused significant advancements in art, literature, architecture, and science. The cardinal principles of the Renaissance were classicism (a greater emphasis than before on Greco-Roman influences), secularism (more frequently painting or writing about non-religious subjects, although religion remained important, and Renaissance artists had to take care not to violate Church dictates), and **humanism**—the conviction that to be human is something to rejoice in. This last concept, derived from Greco-Roman culture, ran counter to the prevailing medieval view that to be human was to be tainted with sin and that worldly life was less important than the heavenly afterlife. Prominent figures from the Italian Renaissance include the writers Petrarch and Boccaccio, the political theorist Niccolò Machiavelli, and the artists Leonardo da Vinci and Michelangelo.

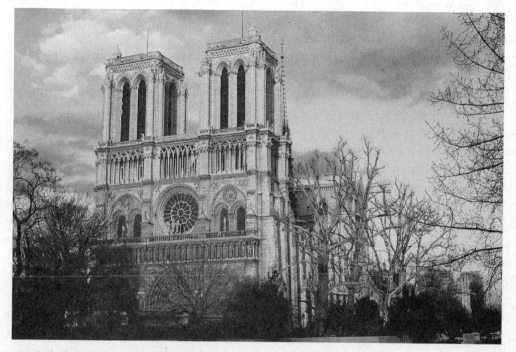

**Cathedral of Notre Dame, Paris, France.**
One of the best-known landmarks of Paris, the Cathedral of Notre Dame provides a quintessential example of the Gothic style of church architecture.

## Islam and the Middle East

Perhaps the most earth-shaking cultural trend of this period was the birth of Islam in the 600s and its rapid expansion throughout—and beyond—the Middle East.

The youngest of the world's major religions, **Islam** is linked with Judaism and Christianity in many ways. Despite their stormy, even tragic, relationships with each other, these three **monotheistic** faiths contain many similarities and possess an eventful shared history.

Islam arose in the Arabian Peninsula due to the efforts of **Mohammed** (also Muhammad, 570–632), a merchant from the town of Mecca. In 610, Mohammed, while meditating in the nearby mountains, experienced a profound vision in which the archangel Jibril, or Gabriel, is said to have delivered the word of Allah (Arabic for "God") to him. With the help of his wife Aisha, his father-in-law Abu Bakr, and his son-in-law Ali, Mohammed preached and formed a religious community. In 622, he and his followers were forced out of Mecca by leaders of the local polytheistic faith and fled to the city of Medina. This flight—the Hegira—marks the beginning of the Islamic calendar. In 630, Mohammed returned to Mecca and converted the city. He died in 632, but his new religion survived and grew. The teachings of Mohammed are contained in the **Qur'an** (Koran), and the holy language of Islam is **Arabic**. **Sharia** is the codification of traditional Islamic law.

Mohammed claimed to be the final prophet in the Abrahamic tradition. While he believed his interpretation of that tradition to be the purest and truest, he respected many figures from Judaism and Christianity as important teachers and therefore instructed Muslims to acknowledge Jews and Christians as "**people of the book**." Muslims are to live by the **Five Pillars of Faith**: to confess one's faith ("there is no god but Allah"); to pray five times daily, facing in the direction of Mecca; to fast during the month of Ramadan; to give alms to the poor; and to attempt a pilgrimage (hajj) to Mecca at least once in one's lifetime. Other traditions include abstaining from alcohol and pork, avoiding the portrayal of human or animal images in art, and supporting polygamy (Muslim men were allowed to take up to four wives, so long as they could support them properly). Islam's holiest city is Mecca, but Medina and Jerusalem (where Mohammed is said to have ascended to heaven) are important as well.

A high degree of **patriarchalism** restricted the conduct of Muslim women, who were often secluded in women's quarters and required to veil themselves when in public. In the past, as today, the degree to which these customs were observed depended on class, region, and individual circumstances. Islam commanded men to treat women with respect, and women in much of the Islamic world enjoyed the right to inherit, have dowries, and own property—but even so, women's status remained distinctly secondary.

As it expanded between the 600s and 800s, early Islam made no distinction between political allegiance and religious affiliation: to be a Muslim meant also to belong to a political and social community, or **umma**, linked by religious belief. After Mohammed's death, the umma was governed by a **caliph**, or "successor," who was both a religious and political leader. The first caliph was Mohammed's father-in-law, Abu Bakr, and the history of the various caliphates is described above, in Chapter 7. Islam did not survive these early years without discord: a succession crisis in the mid-600s led to civil war and the **Sunni-Shiite split**. Sunnis, who comprise more than 80 percent of all Muslims, supported the civil war's victors, the Umayyad caliphs. The followers of Mohammed's son-in-law Ali, who was killed during the war, formed the Shiite movement as a minority denomination. Divisions between the two remain relevant today.

**NOTE**

Islamic theology divides the world into two states: dar al-Islam ("house of peace") and dar al-Harb ("house of war"). The former includes those lands where Islam is the dominant faith. In early times, the expansion of dar al-Islam was encouraged. Many moderate Muslims now consider dar al-Islam to be a wider community including all places where their religion can be practiced freely.

Under the Abbasid caliphate (750–1258), the Middle East enjoyed tremendous artistic and intellectual sophistication, and its cultural contacts with Byzantium, Tang China, and India were extensive. Mathematical, astronomical, and scientific aptitude among Muslim scholars was great—they developed **algebra** and popularized the use of **Arabic numerals** (originally from India)—and the *Canon of Medicine*, by the Persian physician Avicenna (Ibn Sina, 980–1037) became the most authoritative medical text in the Middle East and Europe until the 1600s.

As Christianity did in medieval Europe, Islam decisively influenced cultural life in the caliphate. Muslim authorities determined what was acceptable art or literature. Because the Qu'ran forbids the worship of graven images, for example, Islamic art during these years tended to feature geometric patterns and shapes rather than human or animal figures—although this was not a hard-and-fast rule. The chief centers of learning were **madrasas**, or religious colleges, and a main thrust of Islamic philosophy, as with the scholastics of Christian Europe, was to investigate the relationship between human reason and religious faith. **Averroës** (1126–1198), a doctor from Muslim Spain, translated and analyzed the works of the Greek philosopher Aristotle, a key step in reintroducing his ideas to medieval Europe as a whole. Also from Muslim Spain (and also important in refamiliarizing Europe with Aristotelian thought) was the Jewish thinker **Maimonides** (1135–1204), whose *Guide to the*

*Perplexed* attempted to reconcile the rationality of Greco-Roman thought with Jewish theology.

Classics of Islamic literature from these years include **Ibn Battuta**'s *Travels*, described above, as well as *The Thousand Nights and a Night*, known in the West as **The Arabian Nights** and featuring the famed tales of Sinbad the Sailor, Ali Baba, and Aladdin, among others. Also important is the *Rubaiyat* of **Omar Khayyám**, a mathematician and astronomer who composed this collection of bittersweet, meditative poems in the early 1100s. Increasingly popular during the Abbasid years was **Sufism**, a mystical strain of Islam that emphasizes union with Allah by means of spiritual exercises like chanting and dancing. The Sufi poet **Rumi** gave expression to these ideas in his verses during the 1200s.

**NOTE**

Arabic was both the holy language of Islam and the principal language of cultural and intellectual life, just as Latin was for the Christians of medieval Europe. However, starting in the 800s and 900s, Persian joined Arabic as a major language in Islamic thought and literature.

## Africa

The sheer size of Africa and its amazing ethnic diversity make it difficult to speak briefly about African culture in general. For many centuries, non-Africans tended to view African art as primitive, and to theorize that African societies advanced technologically only by borrowing from other peoples. Recent years have seen a greater acknowledgment of how skillfully produced African arts and crafts are, and also of the fact that most African societies discovered advanced metalworking and architectural techniques on their own.

That said, **Islamic culture** powerfully shaped artistic and intellectual life in many parts of Africa. Most of North Africa and much of the Sahara became part of the Islamic caliphates, and Islam, if not necessarily Muslim rule, came to West African states like Ghana and Mali. Even more strongly than other cultural influences from the Indian Ocean basin, Islam blended with indigenous African traditions in the **Swahili ports** along the East African coast. By comparison, the bulk of sub-Saharan Africa remained less touched by Islamic influence.

THE MOSQUE OF SANKORÉ

**Sankore Mosque, Timbuktu, Mali**
Built in the 1300s, during the reign of Mansa Musa, the Sankore Mosque served not only as a place of worship, but also as a famed library and madrasa, or Islamic university. Its unique mud-and-stick construction demonstrates the blending of Islamic cultural influence with architectural styles indigenous to northwest Africa.

Whether in North Africa or the sub-Saharan zones, African artists produced masterful carvings and sculptures out of wood, ivory, and metal. Their textiles exhibited bold colors and patterns, and they were known for intricate beadwork as well.

Architecture varied across regions owing to diverse cultural influences, both Islamic and indigenous. The **mud-and-timber constructions** of West Africa, best exemplified by the Sankore Mosque in **Timbuktu**, show a unique fusion of Islamic function with local style. The architecture of Zanzibar, on the eastern coast, is distinguished by the use of coral to decorate buildings. The vast walls enclosing **Great Zimbabwe** were constructed so carefully—with each stone set precisely and sturdily in place without mortar—that, for many years, European colonizers insisted that they must have been erected later than they actually were, because they refused to believe that Africans could have built something so impressive without learning how to do so from Europeans.

African literature of this period was preserved by **oral tradition**. Professional storytellers—best-known by the West African term **griots** (or djeli)—chronicled history and social custom. They also acted as entertainers and advised chiefs and rulers. The most famous African epic from these years comes from Mali, dating from the 1300s. This is the *Sundiata*, named after the chieftain who founded the Mali state and relating, in somewhat fictionalized terms, his many exploits.

## Asia and Oceania

China during the Tang (618–906) and Song (960–1279) dynasties was arguably the world's most scientifically and technologically advanced society, with the possible exception of the Abbasid caliphate. The Song Chinese in particular were excellent mathematicians and astronomers. They developed the **compass** during the late 1000s, as well as accurate water clocks and reliable water mills. Also during the Song period, China invented **gunpowder**, popularized the use of **paper currency**, and improved **printing** techniques, making the transition from woodblock to movable-type printing.

NOTE

The most striking example of Song China's scientific and technological expertise was the celestial clock of Su Song (built in 1088), an 80-foot-tall structure that told the time of day, the day of the month, and the positions of the sun, moon, planets, and major stars. It was the first device in world history to use a chain-driven mechanism (powered by flowing water).

During the Song period, and again during the Ming dynasty (1368–1644), there was a great revival of Confucius's teachings—**Neo-Confucianism**—that reinforced China's cultural tendency toward hierarchy and obedience. During the various political crises of the Song years, Neo-Confucianism served as an important unifying factor in a politically divided China, and the Ming emperors relied on it as a tool to justify their rule. As before, most government officials gained their posts by scoring well on rigorous **civil service examinations**, which, among other things, tested knowledge of the Confucian classics. After about 600 C.E., a new form of Buddhism emerged in China: **Chan** (known as **Zen** in Japan), which stressed simplicity and meditation and became very popular, both in China and abroad.

China's Tang emperors were generous cultural patrons. They sponsored the creation of the Han Lin Academy of Letters, a key institution of learning, and the poets who received their patronage are considered to have been extraordinarily eloquent and meditative. As noted above, Tang China interacted culturally with the Abbasid caliphate, and it heavily influenced neighbors like Korea, Vietnam, and Japan, both artistically and religiously. The Ming years remain equally famous as a time of artistic grandeur and intellectual dynamism in China. The architectural masterpiece of the early Ming period is the **Forbidden City**, the imperial residence erected in Beijing during the early 1400s, both to serve as a seat of government and to impress onlookers with the regime's power and grandeur. Great works of classical Chinese literature appeared, including *The Golden Lotus*, a novel about a wicked landowner, and Wu Chengen's ***Journey to the West***, inspired by the seventh-century journey of the monk Xuanzang to India. In addition to the Chinese tradition of manufacturing **silk**, Ming artisans produced some of the most exquisite glassware and **porcelain** that the world has ever seen. Another major art form was scroll painting, which depicted landscapes and other scenes on vertical rolls of silk and paper.

For Japan, the Nara (710–794) and Heian (794–1185) periods, especially the latter, marked a time of cultural brilliance. Japanese religious life was shaped by the importation from China through Korea of Buddhism and, to a lesser extent, Confucianism and Daoism, all of which coexisted with Shinto, Japan's native faith. The poetry, art, and architecture of Tang China had a profound impact on Japanese style: Heian painters reached a high degree of skill, and one of the classics of world literature, ***The Tale of Genji***, a story of love and court life by **Lady Murasaki**, dates to the Heian period.

After about 1000 C.E., the Japanese began to develop a more independent cultural tradition. Things changed even more dramatically after the collapse of the Heian regime in the late 1100s and the rise of the medieval shogunates. As the code of chivalry did with European knights, the code of **Bushido** ("way of the warrior") required samurai not just to be loyal and brave, but also culturally refined; artistic pursuits became less centrally important than they had been during the Heian period. An epic but melancholy work of literature from this era, *Tales of the Heike*, describes the Taira-Minamoto war (1156–1185) that destroyed the Heian regime. New forms of Buddhism arrived: **Zen** (**Chan**), whose emphasis on self-discipline appealed to the samurai elite, whereas Pure Land (Jo Do) promised a heavenly afterlife and gained a large following among the lower classes. The philosophical simplicity of Zen affected several important cultural practices in Japan, such as the *cha-no-yu* tea ceremony, landscaping (rock gardens and bonsai trees), and haiku poetry.

Both the Indian subcontinent and the island chains of Southeast Asia are home to many ethnic groups, dozens of different languages, and many minor and major religions. Key themes here include the cultural fusion throughout the Indian Ocean basin, as well as the wider regional impact of Buddhism (both from China and India) and Hinduism. Architectural monuments like **Angkor Wat** speak to the latter. Also note that Islam arrived in India and elsewhere in South and Southeast Asia during the 1200s.

Much of Oceania was populated during this period by the Polynesian peoples, who migrated throughout the Pacific in their **outrigger canoes**. The environmental impact of these migrations is described in Chapter 11, and the Polynesians also blanketed much of the Pacific with a cultural tradition that remained quite consistent over huge distances. This featured a polytheistic form of worship principally focused on the avoidance of **taboos**—the Polynesian word for ritually forbidden behaviors. Also in Oceania, but farther to the south and living for the time being in isolation from other cultures, were Australia's Aborigines, who followed a form of animism that involved trying to enter and understand a transcendent spiritual state known as the **dreamtime**.

## The Americas

Cultural life in the pre-Columbian Americas was unusual in that the wheel, so fundamentally important in Afro-Eurasia, was essentially unknown, and systems of writing were rare. Despite this, numerous societies reached an advanced state of civilization.

In most of North America, the principal way of life remained hunting and foraging, and the most common form of worship was animism. The most advanced society in what is today the United States was the Mississippian civilization (ca. 700–1500), whose people practiced agriculture, built cities as trading centers, and are remembered for their large **earth mounds**, which they raised for religious and ceremonial purposes.

As before, Mesoamerica was home to highly centralized and urban societies—especially the Toltec (ca. 800–1000) and the Aztecs (1200s–1500s)—and much of the cultural foundation laid down by earlier peoples like the Olmecs was still in evidence. The Aztecs' most distinctive cultural feature was their religion. They built **pyramids** to serve as temples and worshipped many of the same gods as the Mesoamericans who preceded them. Key deities included the jaguar god and the feathered serpent Quetzalcoátl, but most important was the sun god Huitzilopochtli. The Aztecs believed that the sun reappeared every morning only if reenergized by human blood, so they practiced **human sacrifice** on a large scale. Victims included prisoners of war, but also ordinary Aztec citizens, and the victims numbered in the thousands every year.

Andean societies were even more centralized and stratified, particularly by the Incan era (1300s–1500s). As in earlier times, they relied not on writing, but on the knot-tying system called **quipu**, to keep records and accounts. The Incas constructed large cities, including the capital, Cusco (Cuzco), and the fortress and temple complex of **Machu Picchu**. They worshipped a number of deities, chief among them was the sun god, and Cusco's **Temple of the Sun** was their largest place of worship: laid out in the shape of a puma, its interior was lined with gold. The temple was staffed by thousands of *acllas*, or "virgins of the sun." These were young women chosen each year from throughout the empire to serve as acolytes.

# Economic Systems, 600–1450

**9**

→ MODES OF INTENSIVE AGRICULTURE

→ EARLY FORMS OF (PROTO-)INDUSTRIAL PRODUCTION (IRON, STEEL, PORCELAIN, TEXTILES)

→ GROWING DEMAND FOR LUXURY GOODS (SPICES, SILK, GEMS)

→ THE SILK ROAD (CARAVANSERAIS, MONGOL PEACE)

→ MEDITERRANEAN SEA LANES (GALLEYS) + THE HANSEATIC LEAGUE

→ TRANS-SAHARAN CARAVAN ROUTES (CAMEL HERDING, EXPANSION OF ISLAM)

→ INDIAN OCEAN TRADE NETWORK (DHOWS AND JUNKS)

→ ASTROLABES AND COMPASSES

→ MAJOR TRADING CITIES

→ BANKING AND CREDIT

→ CURRENCY (COINAGE AND PAPER MONEY)

→ INFRASTRUCTURE (ROADS, CANALS)

A central trend during this historical period was greater interconnectedness among civilizations. Afro-Eurasia and the Americas remained isolated from one another, but within each of these large spaces, steadily growing networks of exchange spun strong webs of mutual influence—cultural, economic, technological, biological, and political—among varied and often distant regions. At the heart of this interaction was **trade**.

At the same time, economic productivity grew substantially in most parts of the world. Typically this was due to improved or innovative methods and technologies. All the methods of **intensive agriculture** described in Chapters 6 and 11 continued to be used and became more common. In addition, **industrial production** began to appear alongside traditional artisanry and craftsmanship. This was not the full-scale, mechanized industrialization of the modern era, but still involved systematized manufacture, often taking the forms of **cottage industry** or **proto-industrialization**.

## TRADE NETWORKS

Trade expanded significantly during this period, with growth especially prominent along the four major Afro-Eurasian networks that had emerged in earlier centuries. As before, the movement of goods was easier by water than by land, so trade routes tended to follow rivers and coastlines wherever possible, although overland travel was in some cases necessary.

Although it never fell into complete disuse, the **Silk Road** experienced its share of ups and downs during this era. Active from 100 B.C.E. to approximately 800 C.E., Silk Road trade was somewhat disrupted until about 1200 C.E. After that, it flourished again through the 1400s. (Its economic relevance began to fade in the late 1400s, after the 1453 fall of **Constantinople** to the Turks, and it dwindled even more in the 1500s, as European maritime trade took off.) Over the Silk Road's length of nearly 5,000 miles, caravans moved east and west, hauled by a variety of beasts, including horses, camels, and oxen. Stretching from the Middle East and Persia to China and the Pacific coast, the road passed through desert, steppe wilderness, and mountains, especially in Central Asia. Breaking up the journey was a network of oasis towns and **caravanserais** (roadside settlements providing safety and shelter), as well as key cities such as **Baghdad** (capital of the Islamic Abbasid caliphate), the Central Asian metropolis of **Samarkand**, and **Chang'an** (capital of Tang-era China, and once the eastern terminus of the Silk Road). As the name suggests, silk from China remained the best-known commodity traded along this route, but an indescribable variety of other items moved back and forth on it, from raw materials and foodstuffs to luxury goods and manufactured products. China sold porcelain in addition to silk, and also stepped up its industrial production of iron and steel. Cotton, spices, and jewels came from India and Southeast Asia. The Middle East became a source of slaves, metalware, and glassware, with Persia specializing in textiles. The Silk Road also served as Eurasia's principal artery for the transfer of cultural and religious practices, technological innovations, and new diseases. (Thanks to missionary efforts and cultural diffusion, Christianity and Islam moved eastward along the Silk Road, and Buddhism spread along it as well. Printing, gunpowder, and navigational technology proceeded westward from China to the Middle East and Europe—but so did the black death in the 1300s.) Traders and travelers of all ethnicities used the Silk Road or dominated certain sectors of it over time. Especially important during the early part of this period were the **Sogdians** of Central Asia, Zoroastrian and Buddhist merchants from the Samarkand region. Later, after 1200, the revival of Silk Road trade owed much to the **Mongols** and the pax Mongolica ("Mongol peace") they imposed as they created their empire. Muslim, Jewish, and Chinese traders also played prominent roles in Silk Road trade.

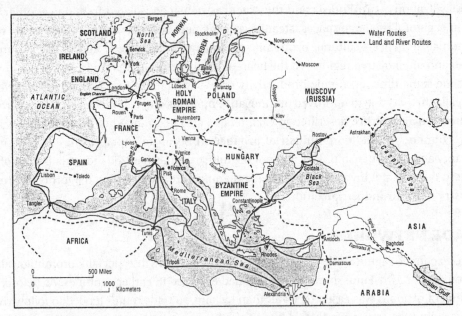

**European and Mediterranean Trade Routes During the Late Medieval Period and Renaissance.**
European desire for more direct access to the goods of East and South Asia prompted the great wave of exploration that began during the 1400s and continued during the 1500s and 1600s.

Likewise, **Mediterranean** sea lanes continued to support large-scale trade between Europe, North Africa, and the Middle East—although here, as with the Silk Road, political disturbances affected commerce. The fall of the Roman Empire, for example, largely disrupted trade in the western Mediterranean and Europe as a whole between 500 and 1000 C.E., while Europe's **Crusades** against the Middle East, between 1100 and 1300 C.E., had their own impact on economic life in the Mediterranean, increasing European awareness of and appetite for goods from Asia and the Middle East. Commerce in the region depended above all on the oared **galley**, well-adapted to coastal navigation. Major centers of Mediterranean trade during these years included the Italian city-states (**Venice** being one of the wealthiest and most powerful), the ancient Egyptian port of **Alexandria**, and **Constantinople**, the seat of the Byzantine Empire and a key crossroads point between Europe, Asia, and the Middle East. As before, Mediterranean commerce tied directly or indirectly into Afro-Eurasia's other leading trade networks, interacting with trans-Saharan caravan trade in northern Africa, with Silk Road traffic in the port cities of the eastern Mediterranean, and with Indian Ocean trade via the Red and Arabian seas.

Trade along **trans-Saharan caravan routes** vastly increased during this period, influenced by dramatic changes like the fall of Rome, the rapid **expansion of Islam** into North and West Africa (both peacefully and by means of forced conversion), and the formation of strong African states like Ghana and Mali. Increased expertise in **camel herding** proved vital to this network's growth, and **Arab traders** played an indispensable role in the Sahara—not just economically, but also religiously, by helping to spread Islam throughout the region. Much of the trans-Saharan trade during this period went north-south, linking North Africa with the sub-Saharan portion of the continent, but east-west trade became more common as well, tying Africa more closely to the Islamic Middle East and, by extension, to the Silk Road and Indian Ocean trade networks. Many of the commodities remained the same as before: ivory, exotic animal skins, and foodstuffs like nuts and fruits flowing northward from sub-Saharan Africa, and **salt** and manufactured goods (such as metalware, pottery, and glass) traveling southward. Two items in particular, though, took on greater importance during this period. One was **gold**, which states like Ghana and Mali supplied in sizable quantities after about 800 C.E., and which many Africans, ironically, found less useful than the copper and iron they received in return. As places like Europe and the Middle East adopted the practice of minting coins, the demand for Ghana's, and then Mali's, gold increased, and when Mansa Musa, the Muslim king of Mali, went on pilgrimage to Mecca in the 1300s, he brought so much gold to the Middle East that he briefly devalued it as a currency there. Sadly, the second newer element in the trans-Saharan network was the expansion of the **Arab slave trade**, controlled largely by Arab merchants, who had transported African slaves across the Sahara since the 600s, but were greatly increasing the volume of trade by the eleventh century. The Arab slave trade caught on in east Africa as well and eventually resulted in the forcible removal of at least 10 million Africans. Major hubs for trans-Saharan commerce included Koumbi Saleh in Ghana and **Timbuktu** in Mali, a famed center for Islamic scholarship, as well as a key site in the salt and gold trades.

**NOTE**

Economic recovery in medieval Europe after 1000 C.E. caused several trade networks to emerge outside the Mediterranean, including along the Rhine River and in the North Sea and English Channel. Especially important was the formation in the 1200s and 1300s of the Hanseatic League, a trading organization that united Germanic and Scandinavian cities in the Baltic Sea, and whose influence stretched from England in the west to Russia in the east—where the city of Novgorod, originally founded as an outpost for Viking trade with Byzantium via Russian river routes, became one of the few points of interaction between Russia and Western Europe.

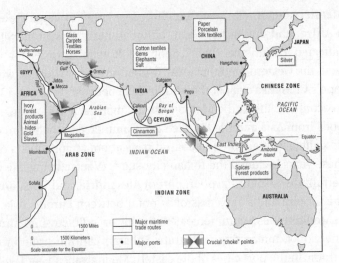

**The Indian Ocean Trade Network Before 1500 C.E.**
The arrival of Portuguese traders just before 1500, then the massive influx of other Europeans, changed the economic patterns of this region forever.

One of the world's most vibrant and culturally diverse commercial economies centered on the **Indian Ocean trade network**, in which **lateen-sailed dhows**, Chinese **junks**, and other vessels plied an expanse wider than 6,000 miles from west to east. In the west, a zone controlled largely by Arab and Persian traders, goods came from East Africa and the Middle East—ivory, diamonds, animal hides, ebony, and gold from the former, and copper, textiles, glassware, and Arabian horses from the latter. The middle zone was dominated by Indian cities and kingdoms. India offered precious gems, elephants, salt, and cotton cloth. From Sri Lanka (Ceylon) came cinnamon, while other spices, as well as exotic woods, came from Indonesia. In the east, China traded silk, porcelain, and paper, and Japan acted as a major source of silver. Key points in this network included the **Swahili city-states** of the East African coast, **Mecca** in Arabia, Hormuz in Persia, the Malibar metropolis of **Calicut** in western India, and the Malaysian city of **Melaka** (Malacca), which dominated the chokepoint between the Indian and Pacific oceans. Also connected to the network were the Chinese ports of **Canton** (**Guangzhou**) and, farther up the coast, **Hangzhou**, located in the Yangzi delta and at the southern end of China's **Grand Canal**. From here and other cities, ships ventured back and forth between China and Southeast Asia, India, and Persia.

> **NOTE**
>
> An interesting site connected with the Indian Ocean trade network was the city of Great Zimbabwe, several miles inland from the East African coast. Zimbabwe flourished from around 1200 to 1400 or 1500, thanks to rich deposits of gold and diamonds. Far enough from the Swahili coast, it remained relatively untouched by Islamic influence. It traded with East African ports. Archaeology gives us an excellent sense of how trade worked here: the presence of Chinese ceramics and Persian artworks in the city's ruins shows how extensive its economic influence was.

Trade routes in the Americas were not as extensive or as interconnected as in Afro-Eurasia, but they, too, expanded during this period. Cities like **Cahokia**, in Mississippian North America arose as a center of wide-ranging exchange. The city-states of Mesoamerica traded heavily, and the Aztec capital of **Tenochtitlan** was among those that benefited the most. A surprisingly elaborate system of roads, paths, and bridges made trade possible throughout the Andes, both before and after the rise of the Incas. Andean communities living on the coast fished and traded with their neighbors in the mountain valleys. Andean peoples also traded with tribal societies living along the Amazon River to the east.

## MAKING TRADE EASIER: TECHNOLOGY, BANKING, AND INFRASTRUCTURE

Especially in Afro-Eurasia, key technologies and practices made the transport of luxury goods and other trade items easier and more efficient. The **astrolabe**, which measured the sun's position in the sky to calculate latitude, came into wider use at sea after the 700s (it had been used on land in previous centuries), and the magnetic **compass**, invented in China during the eleventh century, reached the Middle East and Europe during the late 1100s and early 1200s. Means of transport improved as well. Ships like **junks**, **dhows**, and, in Europe, **Viking longboats** and **sailing ships** (as opposed to oared **galleys**) became larger and more capable of open-water (oceanic) navigation. Overland transport benefited from various improvements in wagons, carriages, and harnesses—better **camel saddles** in the Sahara and along the Silk Road are noteworthy here.

Other innovations facilitated trade as well, both on the private and state levels. Along the major trade networks, where political stability prevailed, commerce was boosted by the rise of **banking** and the extension of **credit** in the form of checks, bills of exchange, and loans with interest. These practices required trust, often over long distances, but allowed for the safer and simpler transfer of wealth. States contributed by policing and regulating trade routes (including with **customs houses** and the enforcement of **standard weights and measures**), as well as by supporting **currencies**, whether that meant **minting coins** or printing **paper money** (a Chinese invention that spread westward). Good **infrastructure**, whether it was built and maintained privately or by the state, also enabled the expansion of trade. **Markets**, trading outposts, and port cities were all vital to the movement of goods, as were the **caravanserais**, or wayside inns and settlements that lined routes like the Silk Road. Networks of **roads** and man-made **waterways** (where rivers did not run or needed to be joined) were just as crucial. The era's most impressive waterway was China's **Grand Canal**, which ran well over a thousand miles and connected the Yellow and Yangzi rivers. Completed by the Sui dynasty (581–618), the canal was improved during the Tang period and ran from Beijing in the north to Hangzhou in the south.

All of Eurasia's major empires helped to enable transcontinental trade during this period. Because trade flourished best under stable and predictable conditions, large empires such as Byzantium, the Islamic caliphates, the Mongol states, and China made it more viable by bringing vast territories under their authority—which typically meant consistent laws and regulations, relative safety from bandits or pirates, mutually-recognized currencies, and proper care for transportational and communications infrastructure. Sometimes, though, rather than trading peacefully, states competed or even warred with each other over trade. In one infamous example, the authorities of Venice persuaded the armies of the **Fourth Crusade** (1202–1204) to attack and pillage Constantinople—a city of fellow Christians, but also an economic rival to the city-states of Italy—instead of pursuing their original war aims against Muslims in Egypt.

# Social Structures, 600–1450

With population growth steady and economic productivity rising during this era, social structures and systems of labor management grew more complicated in most parts of the world. **Social stratification** remained the norm, with old **hierarchies** and **caste systems** still in place and new ones emerging as well. The vast majority of people, wherever they were from, lived in the countryside and earned their keep by means of **agriculture** or **herding**.

On the other hand, the increased scale and importance of trade during these years led to greater **urbanization** and sparked some degree of class diversification and **social mobility**, with trade, artisanry (craftsmanship), shopkeeping, and early forms of (proto-)industrial manufacture allowing more people to work in non-agricultural occupations and giving rise to different forms of labor organization. Depressingly enough, **patriarchy** and **gender inequity** remained as common as they had before, and in some cases worsened due to cultural or religious trends.

## CITIES

As in earlier times, **cities** served as seats of power (political, administrative, and military) and also as centers of cultural and economic activity. The fate of individual cities varied widely during this period: some fell into decline, at least for a time—Rome during the early medieval era is an excellent example—while others prospered due to expanded trade. Overall, the trend worldwide was toward increased **urbanization**, as existing cities grew larger and more cities came into being.

Why did major cities decline or disappear? Common reasons include disease, military pressure from external enemies, the depletion of nearby resources, and agricultural shortages. The advent of the **Little Ice Age** had an impact after about 1300, making it harder for certain urban centers to sustain themselves than it had been during the **medieval climatic optimum** between 800 and the mid-1200s. Among the conditions that encouraged the emergence of cities, or made it easier for them to thrive, were the lack (or end) of a major military threat, proximity to or involvement with a major trade route, favorable agricultural and climatic conditions, a solid population base, and a reliable transportation infrastructure.

Pay close attention to the location and characteristics of the **major cities** referred to in this unit's earlier chapters, as well as to the roles they played in various trade networks. The level of urbanization remained comparatively low in much of Europe and the Americas and in most of sub-Saharan Africa. The world's most heavily-urbanized areas were the Middle East, the shores of the Indian Ocean basin (home to a multitude of independent city-states in East Africa, the Indian coast, and Southeast Asia), and East Asia—especially China, where several cities had populations exceeding a million.

Although the social impact of urbanization varied from region to region, the importance of cities for trade, banking, and commerce tended to make **merchant classes** larger and sometimes more influential—even if elite classes in many areas viewed trade and those involved in it with disdain. City life also fostered **specialization of labor**, created a need for artisans, manual laborers, and a growing number of others who belonged neither to the elite nor to the rural, agricultural population.

Thanks to the enlargement of interregional trade during this period, **diasporic communities** and foreign enclaves formed in ports and cities along far-reaching trade routes. These included travelers and traders of all sorts, but centered on merchant families who took up long-term residence far from home. Diasporas to be aware of from this era include Chinese merchants throughout Southeast Asia, especially in Malaysia and Indonesia; Sogdians along the extent of the Silk Road; Jews throughout the Mediterranean, the Indian Ocean basin, and along the Silk Road; and Muslim traders throughout the Indian Ocean trade network, as far east as China's Pacific coast. Mosques in the Persian style were established in the port cities of Canton and Hangzhou during the 1300s, not just to missionize among the Chinese, but to serve the sizable community of Muslim merchants who had settled there from elsewhere. In all these cases, the diaspora minority introduced its traditions and practices into the host culture.

## SOCIAL STRUCTURES AND LABOR MANAGEMENT

World population grew steadily during this period, and as societies grew larger, the ways they organized themselves and managed their labor grew more diverse. **Hunting and foraging** remained an important way of life in many parts of the world, as did **herding** and **nomadic pastoralism**. Social organization in these communities tended to be relatively egalitarian and non-hierarchical. As a rule, **settled societies**, whether urban or agricultural, had more complex class hierarchies and were more rigidly stratified.

## Hierarchies and Caste Systems

Class hierarchies and caste systems continued to function in settled societies, although details varied from region to region. As with gender relations, organized religions and deep-rooted cultural norms were often used to justify and reinforce social hierarchies.

In a typical society, **elite classes** comprised 10 to 15 percent of the population. They included the royal family if there was one, as well as aristocrats with noble status. **High-level clergy** tended to fall into this category, and the same was sometimes true of civil servants occupying top spots in the **state bureaucracy**. As a rule, the wealth of aristocratic elites derived from their **ownership of land**. They often looked down on trade, and in some cases were forbidden by religion or custom from participating in it.

A small but growing number of **commoners** worked at occupations that would today be considered **professional**: scribes, lawyers, physicians, mid- or low-level bureaucrats, and mid- or low-level clergy. Such jobs might or might not be open to those of low birth, but they generally required **literacy**, something not easily attained during this period. In certain societies, especially in Europe, professions such as these contributed to the creation of what would eventually be called the **middle class**.

**Merchants and bankers** (who also formed part of the emerging middle class) grew in size, wealth, and clout, thanks to the growing importance of trade and urbanization. What spot they occupied within the social hierarchy depended on the society in question. In many places, they sat higher than most commoners: even if elite classes viewed them with scorn, they earned respect by virtue of the riches they generated. However, in much of Asia, where Confucian doctrines influenced social thinking, peasants—no matter how humble their origin—were considered superior to even the richest merchant.

Others among the common classes included **artisans** and **craftspeople**, whose numbers, like those of merchants and bankers, expanded due to urbanization. Also in the cities, but farther down the social scale, were **shopkeepers**, **unskilled laborers**, and other members of the **urban lower classes**. Demand for their services increased during these centuries.

The vast majority of any settled society's population lived in the countryside and worked in agriculture, although these **farmers** and **peasants** labored under a variety of conditions. Their place in most hierarchies tended to be near the bottom, although this was not the case in Confucian parts of Asia, as noted above. At the very bottom of any society's hierarchy were **slaves** and other **coerced/unfree laborers**, along with the **"untouchable"** or **pariah classes** that existed in places like Japan and India.

**NOTE**

To an extent, China's famous civil-service examination system allowed entry into a desirable profession—the mandarin class—by means of merit rather than birth. However, to qualify required a high degree of literacy and learning that only sons from relatively privileged backgrounds stood a realistic chance of passing the exams.

## Social Hierarchies: A Comparison

| Europe | Ottoman Empire | East Asia (Confucian) | South Asia (Hindu Caste System) |
|---|---|---|---|
| royalty | royal/noble elites | royal/noble elites | royal/noble elites |
| aristocracy/ nobility + knights | men of the pen (scholars, civil servants) | scholars + warrior elite (samurai in Japan) | brahmins (priests) |
| merchants | men of the sword (warriors) | farmers | kshatriyas (warriors) |
| artisans and laborers | men of negotiation (merchants, artisans) | artisans | vaishyas (merchants, skilled workers, peasants) |
| free peasants | men of husbandry (peasants, herders) | merchants | sudras (unskilled workers, servants) |
| enserfed peasants | slaves | slaves (+ untouchables in Japanese caste system) | slaves; pariahs and untouchables |

Social mobility tended to be limited during this era, but in some places more than others. In many parts of medieval Europe, for instance, cities served as pockets of relative freedom, where peasants could escape the bonds of serfdom, and where trade and commerce allowed for a certain degree of self-advancement, regardless of birth. By contrast, **caste systems** remained in operation in various parts of the world, eliminating virtually any chance of social mobility—and permanently condemning certain members of society to pariah, or "untouchable," status. The Hindu caste system in India remains the most famous example, but caste systems existed elsewhere as well, including in feudal Japan, which was highly regimented; its own "untouchable" class, the *eta*, handled waste and disposed of the dead.

### MINORITIES AND DIASPORAS

Minority and diaspora populations did not always fit neatly into their host communities' social hierarchies. Depending on time and place, religious and ethnic minorities might find their place in society tolerated or respected—or they might encounter prejudice, even persecution. Make note of the diaspora communities mentioned in the section above. Another noteworthy example of how minorities were treated is that of the Jews in medieval Europe. There, until late in the Middle Ages, Christians were not allowed to charge interest on loans to fellow Christians, leaving it to Jewish moneylenders to provide this necessary—but often bitterly resented—service. This did much to marginalize Jews in a society where religious prejudice against them was already strong. Also be aware of the religious tax (*jizya*) that Islamic states required non-Muslims to pay in exchange for the right to keep their own faith. To this, the Ottoman empire added the millet system, which sorted each non-Muslim group into its own community—permitted to worship as it pleased, but subject to many legal and social restrictions.

## Free vs. Coerced Forms of Labor

Although working conditions might be arduous, burdensome, or even unfair, many of the forms of labor described above left those pursuing them legally free. In less settled societies, these included hunting and foraging, as well as nomadic pastoralism. In settled societies, free forms of labor included merchant trade, the majority of professions requiring literacy, and—in most cases—artisanry and craftsmanship. In urban settings, artisans and skilled workers often banded together in **guilds**. These associations maintained a monopoly on their respective trades. They restricted membership, set prices and standards of quality, and provided pensions. Free peasant production was practiced by those who either owned their land or, more frequently, owed rents to landlords or taxes to the government.

**Slavery** and other forms of **coerced labor** were just as common as free forms of labor, if not more so. Mesoamerican and Andean societies sometimes enslaved their neighbors. The same was true in Africa—and foreigners added to the burden here by arriving from outside to enslave Africans. The **Arab slave trade** in Africa steadily grew during these years, and with the Portuguese moving into West Africa by the early 1400s, the continent felt the first stirrings of what would soon grow into the Atlantic slave trade.

Elsewhere as well, the demand for slaves, whether for domestic labor, agricultural work, or military service, grew substantially. Where they conquered, the Mongols compelled soldiers and skilled workers to serve them, often far from home. Slavery was common in the Middle East, for military purposes as well as civilian ones. As early as the 800s, Muslim armies recruited neighboring peoples from Asia Minor and the Caucasus Mountains as military slaves called **mamluks**. Slavery in this instance was meant less to oppress than to ensure loyalty, and not only did mamluks develop tight-knit bonds and a sense of professional pride, they received many privileges and could attain positions of power. Mamluks were taught to observe the code of **furusiyya** ("equitation"), which involved not just military training, but cultured and honorable behavior. Later, as they rose to power in the Middle East, the Ottoman Turks devised the **devshirme** system, which took young men from non-Muslim (typically Christian) families and groomed them to serve as privileged slaves in the civil service and in the army (the most famous of these troops were gunpowder infantry called **janissaries**, whose status as privileged slave-soldier was similar to that of the mamluks).

**TIP**

Compare the Mamluk code of furusiyya with chivalry in Europe and Bushido in Japan.

Where agricultural labor was not performed by free peasants or slaves, it fell to **serfs**, who were not technically slaves (serfs were not seen as actual property) but were bound to the land. Serfs were not legally free and could not change residence or profession without permission from their landowner. Serfdom was most common in feudal societies. It arose in medieval Europe during the 700s and 800s: it appeared first in Western Europe, fading there by the Renaissance; then it spread to Central and Eastern Europe, persisting there as late as the 1700s and even, in the case of Russia, till the mid-1800s. After Japan descended into samurai feudalism in the late 1100s, its peasants lived in serf-like conditions as well. Although the conditions of serfs' lives varied, they were generally harsh. Serfs had to give a portion of their own crops and livestock to the lord, and they had to spend a certain number of days per month fulfilling labor obligations. These included not just agricultural work, but also **corvée labor projects** such as building roads or cutting down forests. In addition, when knights, samurai, and other feudal landowners were called upon to raise armies for their liege lords, they conscripted serfs from their lands to serve as soldiers.

In the Americas, a similar form of coerced labor was the **mit'a system**, which had already become common practice in the Andes by the Moche period (200s–700s C.E.). Here, commoner clans known as **ayllu** cooperated to fulfill the labor obligations they owed the warrior-priest elites who controlled landownership. As Inca rulers came to dominate the Andes, they strengthened the mit'a system and made it more burdensome. In theory, private property did not exist among the Incas, whose ruler was considered the ultimate owner of everything.

## Social Unrest and Labor-Related Revolts

Whether their labor was coerced or they were technically free but not well-treated, most peasants and laborers had no choice but to accept dreary working conditions. On occasion, though, certain groups stood up to protest unfair treatment or intolerable circumstances. **Labor-related unrest and revolts** became more common in various parts of the world during these years.

Urban populations sometimes rose up in anger. A prominent example from these years was the Wool Carders' Revolt in Florence (1378), sparked by the rage of unskilled workers who had no guild to protect them from being paid too little. Many consider this the first urban labor dispute in European history.

**Peasant uprisings** were more common during these years. They tended to take place either in times of famine or disaster, or when taxes, rents, or military obligations suddenly increased. Byzantium experienced one such uprising, led by **Basil the Copper Hand** in the early 900s, when new agrarian laws accidentally caused terrible food shortages. Several revolts broke out in China's countryside as well. In the mid-700s, the general An Lushan staged the **An Shi Rebellion**, supported by peasants in northern China who resented the contrast between their miserable poverty and the sumptuous luxuries enjoyed by the elite classes. China's Tang rulers quashed the An Shi revolt, but not before hundreds of thousands perished due to violence and famine. Centuries later, during the mid-1300s, China's Yuan dynasty had to contend with the **Red Turban revolt**, provoked by two main causes: the regime's unwillingness to provide peasants with relief from disastrous floods and a sharp rise in the taxes peasants had to pay to support the regime's military spending. During the early 1400s, Japanese peasants regularly rose up against the feudal order and their daimyo landowners.

In Europe, the strain and stress caused by the **Hundred Years' War** (1337–1453) between France and England caused large peasant revolts on both sides. French peasants staged the Jacquerie in 1358, while Wat Tyler led the English Peasants' Revolt in 1381.

## GENDER ROLES

In no part of the world did women in settled societies enjoy gender equality in the modern sense of the phrase. Although gender relations varied over time, and from place to place, and even between classes in a given society, **patriarchy** and **gender inequality** continued to be the norm. As with social hierarchies in general, organized religions and cultural traditions played a key role in shaping relations between the genders.

With respect to social status, upper-class women lived easier lives, but as a rule found themselves more constrained by religious and cultural restrictions on their behavior. In most societies, lower-class women might work harder and endure harsher living conditions, but they were often less bound by such conventions because the rules of "proper" conduct applied less to them.

### Women's Occupations

Wherever they lived and whatever their class, women's occupational roles were more sharply restricted than those of men.

Women from elite classes might occasionally govern states, although this was rare. If they exercised political power, it was generally indirectly, by informally influencing royal or noble sons and husbands. (Politically powerful women from this period include **Wu Zhao**, empress of China during the 700s and the only woman to rule the country in her own right, and **Eleanor of Aquitaine**, who married the king of France during the 1200s, and then the king of England, and influenced politics and culture in both countries.) Elite women often assisted with the supervision of households and estates. They typically had access to education and sometimes distinguished themselves in the arts. (Examples include the Japanese writer **Lady Murasaki** and the German nun-composer **Hildegard von Bingen**.) Religious careers, as nuns or priestesses, were open to women of the upper classes—but like women on lower levels of the hierarchy, elite women often found themselves occupied mainly with childbearing and homemaking.

Among commoners, women might or might not be able to inherit or own **property**, depending on time or place. Wives in merchant or shopkeeper families might help with the running of businesses, and in some cases, although far less often, women might own their own businesses. Farther down the social scale, women from farming and laboring classes were generally confined to low-status jobs such as weaving, pottery, food gathering, farm chores, tending herds, and domestic servitude.

On rare occasions, women fought in wars and even led troops. In the early 1400s, the peasant girl **Joan of Arc** rallied French forces during the Hundred Years' War and defeated their English foes in several key battles. The Mongol armies of **Genghis Khan** allowed women to fight during the 1200s, and one of Genghis's own daughters commanded troops in Central Asia. And although the Chinese saga of the warrior girl **Hua Mulan** arose in the 500s C.E., poems and novels about her reached their peak popularity in China between the 1100s and 1300s.

## Women's (Limited) Rights and Freedoms

In few cases did societies oppress women completely. While in most places they occupied a decidedly secondary status, women tended to enjoy at least some rights and freedoms.

Women could generally inherit and own **property**, although not as freely as men could. These rights, although only partial, existed in Europe, the Middle East, and East Asia. They were more limited in places like the Hindu parts of India and the stratified societies of Mesoamerica and especially the Andes. They were arguably most favorable in parts of sub-Saharan Africa.

If women received a **dowry** or **bride price**, that provided them with some economic security—although in some places and times, it was the woman's family that had to pay a dowry to the husband-to-be, a burden that led many families to view daughters as less desirable than sons. **Divorce**, especially from abusive husbands, was possible in most places, but far harder for wives to achieve than for husbands, who could typically separate for little or no cause. (Unfaithfulness was stigmatized and punished far more harshly when wives were guilty than when husbands were.) Among the upper classes, women were generally allowed to receive some **education**. Before the law and the courts, women enjoyed some **legal safeguards**, but never full equality (in Islamic courts, for example, the testimony of women was not considered as reliable as that of a man). In medieval Europe, the cult of **chivalry** encouraged proper conduct toward women—at least those of noble birth—but was still condescending in how it regarded women as frail and weak, and therefore requiring male protection.

Areas that tended to allow women more freedoms and flexibility include sub-Saharan Africa, especially in the west, where descent was often traced **matrilineally** (through the mother), and where women's labor as farmers, working alongside their cattle-herding husbands, was highly valued. Older women in African societies were also consulted for advice more frequently than elsewhere—and even where Islam penetrated, it tended to restrict women's behavior less than it did in North Africa or the Middle East. The Mongols were surprisingly more respectful of women than other Eurasian societies, and gender relations among the hunter-foragers of North America appear to have been defined comparatively loosely. Japan during the Heian era, prior to 1200, afforded women (at least those from the upper classes) a high degree of respect for their cultural and intellectual attainments—something lost after the rise of Japanese feudalism.

## Restrictions on Women's Lives

Far more famous than rights during these years were the many restrictions placed on women's lives and behavior worldwide. Aside from the **secondary status** they were forced into overall, certain practices stand out as particularly repressive.

Arranged marriages—especially common in places like India and China, but also widespread in other regions—worked almost always to the groom's advantage and often promised young girls as brides to older husbands.

Veiling and seclusion ranked among the most prominent ways to control female conduct. Both are known best for being practiced in the Muslim Middle East (where the harem, or women's quarters, arose, most famously among elites in Ottoman Turkey) and among the Hindus of India and Southeast Asia (where the custom of seclusion was referred to as purdah or zenana). But veiling and seclusion also had a place in Christian Europe, especially in the Byzantine and Orthodox world.

Not only did the terms of divorce vary from place to place, so too did the basic terms of married life. Concubinage, the practice of taking openly-acknowledged lovers in addition to a wife, was a privilege open to men in China and other parts of Asia, as well as in the Middle East. Polygamy, or the taking of more than one wife, was also practiced, most famously in the Islamic world, where up to four wives were permitted. Muslim men, however, were not supposed to marry more wives than they could comfortably support, and polygamy remained more limited in practice than in theory.

Suppression of women's equality sometimes took extreme forms. In medieval and Renaissance Europe, an infamous manifestation of social stress was a sharp rise in the persecution of people thought to be witches, and due to religious and popular prejudice, a majority of those victimized by these witch hunts were women. In many parts of India, the ritual of sati, or the burning of Hindu widows on their husbands' funeral pyres, continued. In China, the subjugation of women expressed itself most obviously in the painful practice of foot binding, which kept women's feet tiny and dainty but in the process crippled them. Firmly established by 1200 and popular among all classes (although especially among elites), foot binding continued into the 1900s.

Organized religions played a crucial role in defining women's roles and justifying their subservience. The majority of Christian theologians, both Catholic and Orthodox, viewed women as subordinate to men, if not inherently more sinful, and refused them positions of spiritual authority. It was the Catholic church that issued *The Hammer of Witchcraft*, a manual to aid in the spotting and trying of witches, in the 1400s. Although Islam proclaimed the desirability of treating women with respect, it also assigned women a secondary status relative to men. Neo-Confucianism encouraged similar thinking in China and East Asia, and Hindu women were highly restricted by the dictates of the caste system.

## WOMEN AND CHANGE OVER TIME IN ASIA 600–1450

Political and religious shifts in Asia caused major change during these years in how women were treated. In India, the arrival of Islam meant that many women were no longer subject to the Hindu caste system or the sati ritual—and came to enjoy more rights than most Hindu women with respect to divorce and property. By contrast, the growing dominance of Neo-Confucianism in China led to the greater subordination of women and contributed to the growing popularity of foot binding. In Japan, the collapse of the Heian regime affected the status of upper-class women. The Heian court had placed great emphasis on cultural brilliance and elaborate manners, and Heian women exerted a certain degree of social and political influence. However, the rougher warrior ethic of the feudal shogunates allowed Japanese women fewer opportunities, and unlike European chivalry, the samurai code of Bushido did little to encourage respectful treatment of women.

# Humans and the Environment, 600–1450

# 11

→ **MIGRATIONS (VIKING, MONGOL-TURKIC, BANTU, POLYNESIAN)**

→ **SPREAD OF BANANAS, COTTON, SUGAR, AND CITRUS**

→ **RICE CULTIVATION (CHAMPA RICE)**

→ **INTENSIVE FORMS OF AGRICULTURE (INCLUDING CHINAMPA AND WARU WARU)**

→ **IMPROVEMENT OF THE HORSE COLLAR**

→ **THE BLACK DEATH**

→ **MEDIEVAL CLIMATIC OPTIMUM VS. LITTLE ICE AGE**

As before, human societies simultaneously adapted to their environment and sought to adapt it to their own needs and desires. Their **environmental impact** dramatically increased during this period—sometimes reaching harmful, even self-destructive, levels—thanks to steady **population growth**, a growing talent for engineering and construction, and a greater willingness and ability to harvest and deplete resources. On the other hand, environmental factors beyond human control, particularly changes in the climate and the movement of disease pathogens, affected many societies during these years.

In keeping with this unit's central theme, much of the relationship between humans and the environment during this period was shaped by the growing trend toward greater interregional interaction.

## MIGRATIONS

Large-scale migrations regularly took place, especially in Afro-Eurasia. They were often caused by environmental factors, such as climate change, the vanishing of food supplies, or overpopulation. In turn, they had their own effects on the environment.

A prominent series of migrations affected Europe, as waves of Asiatic and Germanic peoples continued to move into the region from the east and the north, just as they had during the Roman era. The military threat posed by these invaders forced European states to centralize politically during the medieval era, but they also affected the continent ethnically by settling down, founding their own states, and blending with existing European populations. Among the most influential of these migrating peoples were the **Vikings**. Farther to the east, the migration of **Mongol-Turkic horse pastoralists** had a similar impact on the Middle East, Central Asia, and East Asia.

In sub-Saharan Africa, the **Bantu** peoples continued their continent-wide movements. As they did so, they brought with them new agricultural techniques, which increased the extent of African land under cultivation, with all the environmental impacts that entailed, such as increased reliance on water and the need to irrigate. They also spread the secret of ironworking, which encouraged mining and metallurgy and placed even more stress on African ecosystems.

The 3,000-year **Polynesian migrations**, which had already been underway for some time, populated a 20,000-mile expanse of the Pacific. Beginning in the Indonesian and Philippine islands, these migrations led the Polynesian peoples on long eastward journeys, carried on **outrigger canoes** that allowed them to travel vast distances over water. The original Polynesians were root farmers, growing taro and sweet potatoes and supplementing their diet with pigs, chickens, and fish. They carried these foods—as well as the coconut palm—with them across the Pacific, bringing them to places as diverse as Hawaii and New Zealand (home to the Maori, the largest surviving Polynesian subculture). Unfortunately, the Polynesians badly deforested some of the places they settled—most notably Easter Island, whose civilization was destroyed by environmental stress and tribal war by the 1500s C.E.

Certain trade routes opened or widened because migratory or nomadic peoples traveling upon them adapted to challenging environments. The establishment of trans-Saharan caravan routes depended upon the **camel-herding expertise of Arabs and Berbers** in the Middle East and North Africa, and the excellent **horsemanship of pastoral peoples in the steppes of Central Asia** had much to do with the development of the Silk Road. Between the 800s and the 1100s, the **Vikings**, expert mariners and fierce warrior-traders from Scandinavia, poured out of the north to Iceland, Greenland, the British Isles, northwestern France, and Sicily, as well as to Russia, where, from cities like **Novgorod**, they established a trade route running all the way to **Constantinople** and the Byzantine empire. This far-reaching influence was due to their prowess with **longboats** and their ability—extremely rare in Europe and the Mediterranean at this time—to navigate on the open ocean (a skill they shared with **dhow** sailors in the Indian Ocean basin).

 **NOTE**

During the time of Leif Ericsson, at around 1000 c.e., the Vikings famously became the first Europeans known to have reached the Americas. Although their brief time there had nowhere near the impact that the arrival of Columbus did in the 1490s, it serves as a great testament to the Vikings' navigational skills.

## THE IMPACT OF INDUSTRY AND AGRICULTURE

As described in Chapter 9, economic productivity rose worldwide, both in the industrial (or at least cottage- and proto-industrial) and agricultural spheres. This led to a corresponding rise in the environmental impact of human economic activity.

As they grew in number, size, and political and economic importance, **cities**, discussed at length in Chapter 10, affected the environment by concentrating large numbers of people—and their demand for resources—into small, densely packed spaces. The environmental impact of the construction and engineering that went into building and maintaining cities was likewise heavy.

**Mining** and metallurgy, which supported the expansion of industrial production and a heightened demand for metals, gems, and jewels, represented a particularly intrusive form of resource extraction and exerted a powerful influence on many ecosystems. Increased production of **textiles** created a greater demand for **wool** (requiring the grazing of larger number of sheep) and fibers such as **cotton** (requiring more land to be placed under agricultural production).

Whatever crops were grown, **agriculture** became more efficient and intensive during these years, and more land was used for agricultural purposes. Throughout Afro-Eurasia, improved versions of the **horse collar**, which originated in China, improved agricultural production. In the Americas, greater use was made of **terrace farming** (on the sides of hills and mountains), the Mesoamerican **chinampa** technique of growing crops on "floating islands" in lakes, and the **waru waru** technique: system of interspersing raised seedbeds (where the plants grew) and ditches (which allowed for irrigation and drainage alike), which arose in parts of the Andes as early as the 300s B.C.E. and was more widely adopted during this period. These and all the other techniques of **intensive agriculture** and **water management** described earlier, in Chapter 6, increased the risks of soil erosion, deforestation, and other forms of major environmental damage.

In Afro-Eurasia, increased trade, especially along the routes described in Chapter 9, spread plants and foodstuffs far from their points of origin. **Bananas**, originating in Southeast Asia, reached the Middle East by the mid-600s and took root especially well in Africa between 700 and 1500. Also from Southeast Asia, **citrus** eventually became common throughout the Islamic world and the Mediterranean. **Sugar**, first extracted from the sugarcane plant in New Guinea around 8000 B.C.E., reached the Asian mainland by 1000 B.C.E. and was being produced in crystallized form in Gupta India by the 500s C.E. Buddhist monks traveling from India brought sugar to China, and it reached Persia via the Silk Road by about 600 C.E. During their wars of expansion, Muslim Arabs encountered sugar and spread it even more widely through the Middle East and North Africa. During their Crusades in the Middle East, medieval Europe discovered this "sweet salt" and began growing sugarcane themselves, particularly around Venice. The cultivation of **cotton** became more widespread throughout Afro-Eurasia as well. Around the 900s, important improvements in rice cultivation were imported from Southeast Asia to China and East Asia, in the form of drought-resistant **Champa rice** from Vietnam. Champa rice grew fast enough to permit two harvests per year, substantially increasing food production. In Oceania, the **coconut palm** spread throughout the Pacific, largely due to the migration of Polynesian peoples.

## ENVIRONMENTAL FORCES: DISEASE AND CLIMATE

In certain cases, the environment acted on humans, and not vice versa. Occasionally, natural disasters such as volcanic eruptions, the diversion of rivers, or earthquakes decisively affected societies, or even fatally disrupted them.

Also important were the outbreaks of disease that periodically swept over large parts of Afro-Eurasia. (When pathogens traveled long distances, it tended to be within the same temperature zone, or in east-west directions, rather than north-south ones, meaning that people in the Americas were less susceptible to continent-wide circulation of germs—but therefore had less opportunity to build up natural immunity to the diseases they later encountered upon the Europeans' arrival in the New World.) Already for centuries, **smallpox**, **measles**, and **bubonic plague** had moved back and forth throughout Eurasia, and they continued to do so. The deadliest epidemic to strike Eurasia in the premodern era was the so-called **black death** of the early 1300s. Beginning in China, this particularly virulent outbreak of bubonic plague migrated first to the Middle East, and then by the 1340s to Europe via Mediterranean trade between the Middle East and the Italian peninsula. Each region it visited lost on average a third of its population, resulting in many millions of deaths and making the black death one of the worst medical disasters in world history.

Climate change also affected human populations, especially in the northern hemisphere. Between 800 and 1300, a warming trend called the **medieval climatic optimum** greatly affected patterns of migration (allowing freer movement into northern regions by people like the **Vikings**), agriculture (which became more productive), fishing and whaling, and interregional trade. After the late 1200s, though, the medieval climatic optimum was followed by a general cooling referred to as the **Little Ice Age**. This persisted until the early-to-mid-1800s, making agricultural production more difficult in certain regions and also altering patterns of northern settlement and economic activities such as fishing, whaling, and fur-hunting. The downturn in agricultural production caused by the Little Ice Age may have contributed to the wave of **peasant uprisings** that broke out in places like Europe and China during the mid- to late 1300s.

# UNIT 4

## GLOBAL INTERACTIONS (1450–1750)

# Unit 4 Short Cut

## GENERAL REMARKS

Between 1450 and 1750, the world's civilizations became truly connected for the first time in history. The most significant trend of this era was the emergence of fully **globalized networks of communication and exchange**. Regrettably, much of this interaction consisted of warfare, exploitation, and slavery. Nonetheless, trade, discovery, cultural interchange, and the faster and easier movement of peoples brought the world's societies into greater proximity.

One of the primary causes of this greater interaction was the massive and sustained **European campaign of exploration and colonization**. Driven by scientific curiosity, the quest for power, the hope of spreading Christianity, and a desire for wealth, European explorers during the 1400s and 1500s sought out oceanic trade routes that would link them directly with China, India, Japan, and elsewhere in Asia. They also encountered the Americas: a "New World" that, for thousands of years, had lain outside the bounds of Afro-Eurasian knowledge.

Within decades, European traders, missionaries, and conquerors had spread throughout the world. The Europeans were the first in history to sail around the globe, and they established a presence in many parts of coastal Africa, Southeast Asia, and East Asia. Most dramatically, European colonizers occupied and transformed North and South America. The opening of the Americas to the rest of the world was done brutally and out of greed, but also played a tremendous role in shifting the world's economic, linguistic, religious, and cultural patterns. It changed forever the environments of the Americas, Africa, and Eurasia, as new animals, new foods, and new diseases were passed back and forth in a phenomenon known as the **Columbian Exchange**.

Another trend of this era was the **rise of Europe**, caused by **state rivalries** and **imperial expansion**. Until the 1400s, Europe had been relatively weak and backward, compared with civilizations such as China and the Ottoman Empire. But during the 1500s and 1600s, Europe pulled even with China and the **gunpowder empires** of the Islamic east (Ottoman Turkey, Safavid Persia, and Mughal India) in terms of scientific advancement, global power, and wealth. During the 1700s, Europe overtook these other cultures, becoming the strongest, most technologically adept, and richest civilization in the world. By the middle of the 1700s, Europe was well situated to dominate the vast majority of the globe, militarily and economically—and did so in the 1800s.

Technological development and scientific knowledge increased in many parts of the world at this time. Many societies based their economies increasingly on **commerce**. In some places by the 1600s, **proto-industrial** practices were laying the foundation for fuller industrialization during the late 1700s and 1800s.

In addition, **peasant labor intensified**. In most societies, agricultural production increased, leading to a huge rise in population worldwide—from 350 million in 1400 to 610 million in 1700, the fastest rate of growth seen to that date. It should be noted that the bulk of this era's economic growth depended on **coerced labor** in many forms.

## BROAD TRENDS

| State Building, Expansion, and Conflict, 1450–1750 | |
|---|---|
| **Europe** | absolutist vs. parliamentary nation-states (Louis XIV and divine right theory vs. English Bill of Rights)<br>European age of exploration (Henry the Navigator, Christopher Columbus, Vasco da Gama, Ferdinand Magellan)<br>from Franco-Habsburg rivalry (1500s–1600s) to Anglo-French rivalry (1600s–1700s)<br>Protestant-Catholic religious wars (1500s–early 1600s) + Thirty Years' War (1618–1648)<br>Seven Years' War (1756–1763) |
| **Middle East** | gunpowder empires = Ottoman empire (1299–1922) and Safavid Persia (1501–early 1700s)<br>Ottoman-Safavid rivalry over trade and Sunni-Shiite disputes<br>Ottoman conquest of Constantinople (1453) and campaigns of Suleiman the Magnificent (1520s)<br>Ottoman siege of Vienna (1683)<br>"circle of justice" and Sharia law |
| **Africa** | impact of European arrival (1410s+)<br>Songhai (Askia Mohammed; 1400s–1500s)<br>Kongo and Ashanti kingdoms (1600s+)<br>Omani Arabs in East Africa (1650s) |
| **East (and Central) Asia** | impact of European arrival (1500s+)<br>Ming dynasty (1368–1644) in China and Li Zicheng's revolt (1630s–1640s)<br>Qing dynasty (Kangxi; 1644–1912) in China<br>mandate of heaven<br>daimyo feudalism in Japan (late 1100s–early 1500s)<br>reunification of Japan (late 1500s) and Tokugawa shogunate (Tokugawa Ieyasu; 1603–1868)<br>mandate of heaven |
| **South (and Southeast) Asia and Oceania** | impact of European arrival (1490s+)<br>gunpowder empire = Mughal Empire (Akbar the Great; 1500s to mid-1800s)<br>the Sikh and Maratha states (late 1600s to mid-1800s)<br>joint-stock companies = British East India Company, Dutch East India Company |

| State Building, Expansion, and Conflict, 1450–1750 | |
|---|---|
| **Americas** | impact of European arrival (1490s+) and colonies<br>conquistadors defeat Aztecs and Incas (early 1500s)<br>piracy in the Caribbean (1500s–1700s)<br>joint-stock company = Hudson's Bay Company |
| **Global and Interregional** | greater political centralization and new bureaucratic elites<br>global impact of European age of exploration = trading-post and<br>    maritime empires (1400s+)<br>Dutch and English rivalry with Portugal and Spain over trade routes and<br>    colonies (1500s–1600s)<br>Omani-European competition over East Africa and Indian Ocean basin<br>    (1650s+)<br>global impact of Seven Years' War, especially in Canada and India<br>    (1756–1763) |

## State Building, Expansion, and Conflict

- During the first centuries of this era (the 1500s and 1600s), global might was concentrated in China and the Islamic world's gunpowder empires: Ottoman Turkey, Safavid Persia, and Mughal India.

- The nations of Europe grew steadily more powerful. By the early 1700s, they were overtaking the civilizations listed above in terms of military, scientific, and technological aptitude.

- The most dramatic development of the era was the European campaign to explore (and, where possible, to colonize) the rest of the world. Numerous European states—Portugal, Spain, the Dutch Republic, England, and France, for example—created trading-post empires and maritime empires with a truly global reach.

- European colonization of the Americas, the African coast, and parts of Asia set the stage for a massive burst of imperial activity during the 1800s. It also sparked military competition among European powers for global dominance. Some of the European wars of the 1700s—especially the Seven Years' War (1756–1763), which raged not only in Europe, but also North America and India—can be considered history's first "world wars."

- Several states, including Russia, Ottoman Turkey, Mughal India, and China under the Manchus, created expansive land empires.

- In addition to multicultural and multiethnic land empires, nation-states in the contemporary sense of the word emerged. These were political units with relatively fixed borders, a sense of national unity, and populations that were largely (though never completely) homogeneous in terms of language and ethnicity.

- In many parts of the world, political organization became more centralized and sophisticated. Features of modern government—such as bureaucracies, admiralties, general staffs, treasuries, and state banks—were more commonplace. Rulers devised more reliable and more efficient means to collect taxes and conscript soldiers.

- State-building techniques included impressive displays of architecture and art, as well as continued reliance on religious concepts to legitimate the authority of the regime.

- Most monarchies remained traditionally autocratic or absolutist, but some nations experimented with forms of government that were more representative, including parliamentary monarchy.
- The increased importance of gunpowder weaponry meant that, from this time forward, military strength depended even more on technological aptitude than it had before.

| Culture, Science, and Technology, 1450–1750 | |
|---|---|
| **Europe** | Renaissance continues (late 1200s–early 1600s; Miguel Cervantes, William Shakespeare) <br> baroque style <br> Enlightenment begins (1700s) <br> Protestant Reformation (1500s; Martin Luther) <br> heliocentric theory <br> Scientific Revolution and Newtonian physics <br> improvements in navigational and marine technology (compass, caravel) <br> Versailles (1600s) |
| **Middle East** | widening of the Sunni-Shiite split <br> miniature painting in Persia and Ottoman Turkey <br> carpet-weaving <br> Blue Mosque (1600s) |
| **Africa** | sculpture and carving <br> textile weaving and basketry <br> oral tradition (griots) <br> *Sundiata* epic (1300s+) <br> *The Epic of Askia Mohammed* (1500s+) |
| **East (and Central) Asia** | porcelain <br> *Journey to the West* (1500s) <br> Summer Palace (1700s) <br> kabuki theater <br> ukiyo-e woodblock prints |
| **South (and Southeast) Asia and Oceania** | Sikhism (1500s; Guru Nanak) <br> miniature painting in Mughal India <br> Taj Mahal (1600s) <br> Red Fort (1600s) |
| **Americas** | religious syncretism (Vodun, Latin American cult of saints) <br> creole, mestizo, and other "mixed" traditions <br> Mesoamerican codices (1500s) |
| **Global and Interregional** | growing impact of the printing press <br> increased availability of culture to non-elite classes <br> gunpowder revolution in Eurasian states <br> impact of Europe's age of exploration <br> global spread of Christianity |

# Culture, Science, and Technology

- After the European encounter with the Americas, networks of communication and exchange moved beyond the level of transregional and became truly global. The Atlantic basin itself became a gigantic cauldron of economic, cultural, religious, ethnic, political, and military interaction.

- Most major societies had well-defined artistic and literary traditions. Increased technological aptitude enabled the production of arts and crafts of high quality.

- The level of scientific knowledge and technological achievement was especially high in civilizations such as China, Ottoman Turkey, Mughal India, and Safavid Persia.

- Europe made exceptional strides in terms of scientific knowledge and technological achievement. The Renaissance, Scientific Revolution, and Enlightenment all furthered the intellectual growth of Europe, to the point that, during the late 1600s and 1700s, it overtook the civilizations listed above.

- The steadily increasing influence of the printing press led to the rapid spread of information, scientific knowledge, religious debates, and new ideas. By creating more materials to read—and more incentive to read—the printing press helped to boost literacy rates.

- Aside from printing, the technologies with the biggest global impact during this era were gunpowder weaponry and advances in maritime and navigational technology.

- Art, literature, and drama became more accessible to wider segments of society and popular audiences—including the emerging middle classes, and in some cases the lower classes—not just to elite classes.

- Architecture and art continued to be used for political purposes, especially to show off the power and grandeur of various rulers and regimes.

- New and syncretic religions appeared during this era, including Vodun (voodoo) in the Caribbean, the cult of saints in Latin America, and Sikhism in India.

- Within established religions, schisms appeared or widened. The Sunni-Shiite split in Islam grew more pronounced during this era, as did the influence of Sufism within Islam. Europe experienced a religious earthquake, the Protestant Reformation, that profoundly affected not just matters of faith, but cultural life, military and political affairs, and the way Europeans spread Christianity to other parts of the world.

- The movement of Europeans and Africans (mainly slaves) altered the patterns of North and South American ethnicity, religion, language, art, and music.

- Buddhism and Christianity spread particularly far during these years, thanks to missionary activity, trade, and colonization.

| Economic Systems, 1450-1750 | |
|---|---|
| **Europe** | joint-stock companies (including Dutch East India Company, Hudson's Bay Company, British East India Company)<br>investment disasters ("bubbles"): tulipmania, Mississippi Bubble, South Sea Bubble<br>mercantilism<br>cottage industry and proto-industrialization |
| **Middle East** | decline of Silk Road<br>Omani-European rivalry in Indian Ocean and East Africa<br>Ottoman-Persian competition over Indian Ocean trade<br>carpets |
| **Africa** | arrival of European traders<br>Omani-European rivalry in Indian Ocean and East Africa<br>Arab slave trade continues<br>Atlantic slave trade begins and intensifies |
| **East (and Central) Asia** | decline of Silk Road<br>appearance of European traders<br>porcelain and tea |
| **South (and Southeast) Asia and Oceania** | appearance of European traders<br>Omani-European rivalry in Indian Ocean<br>Ottoman-Persian competition over Indian Ocean trade<br>cotton |
| **Americas** | European piracy and privateering in Caribbean<br>rise of plantation and cash-crop agriculture<br>increased reliance on slavery and coerced labor<br>sugar, cotton, tobacco, coffee, silver |
| **Global and Interregional** | global circulation of trade goods (finished products and raw materials)<br>piracy, privateering, and state competition over trade routes<br>triangular trade in the Atlantic<br>influx of New World silver into world economy<br>increased agricultural production<br>increased manufacturing and the emergence of proto-industrial production<br>increased resource extraction (mining, fishing, hunting) |

## Economic Systems

- The incorporation of the Americas into existing networks of exchange led to the emergence of a truly global economic system, complete with the worldwide circulation of raw materials and finished products.
- The emergence of an Atlantic trade system, combined with the Europeans' ability to circumnavigate the globe, disrupted and altered traditional trade routes, particularly land routes such as the Silk Road.
- Competition over trade routes, especially maritime ones, affected state relations in several parts of the world, including the Atlantic Ocean (and the Caribbean Sea) and the Indian Ocean.

- Agriculture remained dominant as a mode of economic production and as the form of labor practiced by the vast majority of people worldwide. Even so, trade and manufacturing became steadily more important during these years.
- The rise in global productivity and wealth rested on a foundation of coerced labor, which took many forms. The Atlantic and Arab slave trades were extensive. Serfdom was common in Europe (especially Russia) and other parts of the world. Plantation and cash-crop agriculture in the Americas was based on unfree labor, and other examples abound.
- Mercantilism became the dominant economic principle of colonizing states that formed maritime or trading-post empires. Joint-stock companies and monopolies with royal charters helped to finance and carry out much of the exploration and colonization that took place during this era. These include the Muscovy Company, the Dutch East India Company, the Hudson's Bay Company, the Company of New France, and the British East India Company.
- During the 1500s and 1600s, Spanish and Portuguese extraction of precious metals—especially silver—from the Americas affected economies around the world. This huge and sudden influx of coinage into so many economies created a harmful glut of precious metals, leading to severe inflation in places as diverse as China and Europe.
- In several civilizations, primarily Europe, proto-industrial modes of production began to appear, especially during the 1700s. By the late 1700s, the concept of capitalism was emerging as well. Both of these trends would have a profound impact on economic life in the 1800s.
- Interregional trade was affected by the global cooling that led to the Little Ice Age.

| Social Structures, 1450–1750 | |
|---|---|
| **Europe** | serfdom (declining in Western Europe, increasing in Russia) <br> German Peasants' War (early 1500s) + Russian serf and Cossack uprisings (1600s–1700s) <br> rise of the burgher and bourgeoisie (middle) classes <br> elite adjustments for European nobles (nobility of the sword vs. nobility of the robe; Russia's Table of Ranks) <br> Protestant-Catholic religious strife <br> anti-Semitism <br> patriarchy continues, with slightly improved opportunities for women of middle and upper classes |
| **Middle East** | elite adjustments (janissaries and devshirme civil servants) <br> devshirme (Ottoman slave-recruiting system) <br> Arab slave trade <br> jizya tax for subject non-believers (dhimmi) <br> mudarra ("moderation") policy and the millet (Ottoman system for religious minorities) <br> Islam and patriarchy (veiling, seclusion, polygamy, the harem) |
| **Africa** | Arab slave trade in North and East Africa <br> growth of Atlantic slave trade (1400s–1800s; Middle Passage, triangular trade) <br> matrilinear social organization in certain areas <br> impact of the Arab and African slave trades on family structure |

| Social Structures, 1450–1750 | |
| --- | --- |
| **East (and Central) Asia** | intensification of peasant labor (silk)<br>elite adjustments (mandarin bureaucrats in China; salaried samurai in Japan)<br>Li Zicheng's peasant revolt and the fall of China's Ming dynasty (1630s–1640s)<br>serfdom and social stratification in Tokugawa Japan<br>Neo-Confucianism and patriarchy (foot binding)<br>samurai patriarchy and geisha courtesans |
| **South (and Southeast) Asia and Oceania** | intensification of peasant labor (cotton)<br>elite adjustments (zamindar landowners)<br>tolerance and tensions among India's Hindus, Muslims, and Sikhs (Akbar the Great vs. Aurangzeb)<br>Hinduism and patriarchy (sati, seclusion)<br>Islam and patriarchy (veiling, seclusion, and polygamy)<br>role of Southeast Asian women in early encounters between European traders and Asian populations |
| **Americas** | encomienda system (1500s)<br>Spanish adaptation of mit'a system<br>plantation monoculture (plantations and haciendas; sugarcane, cotton, tobacco)<br>growth of Atlantic slave trade (1400s–1800s; Middle Passage, triangular trade)<br>indentured servitude in North America<br>creole and mixed populations (race-based hierarchies in Latin America)<br>role of women in encounters between European arrivals and native populations (Malinche, Pocahontas) |
| **Global and Interregional** | increased agricultural production and increased tax and conscription burdens on peasants<br>greater urbanization and greater class diversification<br>growth of artisan (craftsman) and urban working classes<br>growth and ambiguous status of middle and merchant classes<br>political and economic adjustments for elite classes<br>slavery becomes increasingly common<br>patriarchy continues |

# Social Structures

- Agriculture remained dominant as the form of labor practiced by the vast majority of people worldwide. Most people lived in rural settings.
- As the centralizing power of the state expanded, especially its power to gather taxes and conscript soldiers, pressure on peasant communities increased, occasionally leading to peasant revolts and rebellions.
- New forms of peasant labor (including plantation farming and cash-crop monoculture) arose to take their place alongside traditional methods.
- The rise in global productivity and wealth rested on a foundation of coerced labor, which took many forms. The Atlantic and Arab slave trades were extensive. Serfdom

was common in Europe (especially Russia) and other parts of the world. Plantation and cash-crop agriculture in the Americas was based on unfree labor, and other examples abound.

- Social diversification resulted from the increased importance of banking, commerce, trade, shopkeeping, artisanry, and manufacturing. Growth in these sectors led to the creation of middle and urban working classes. These were small to begin with, but grew in numbers and in cultural and social influence.
- Urbanization continued. This trend was often related to an increase in social mobility.
- Elite classes in many regions faced new challenges, either because of political centralization on the part of their monarchs or because of greater importance now being placed on trade and money-based wealth, rather than on land—which, for centuries, had been the source and measure of power and riches for traditional elites.
- In more societies, merit became important as a criterion for social advancement and even for entry into the elite classes.
- Diasporic communities and foreign enclaves continued to form in many towns and ports, due to the expansion of interregional and global trade.
- Colonization, particularly in the Americas, created mixed populations, such as mulattos, mestizos, and creoles. New hierarchies emerged in Europe's New World colonies.
- Ethnic and religious minorities were treated differently in various parts of the world. In some cases, they enjoyed freedom and equal status. More often, though, they were persecuted, treated as second-class citizens, or restricted in various ways.
- In most parts of the world, women continued to occupy a secondary status in terms of social roles, economic opportunities, and political influence. In parts of Europe, a limited awareness that the treatment of women was unjust began to develop.
- Individual women from small but important segments of society—from the aristocracy or emerging middle class, for example—gained educations, became active in business, made scientific discoveries, and became artists and writers.
- Local women often played crucial roles during economic or political encounters between their own people and European colonizers and traders.

| Humans and the Environment, 1450–1750 | |
| --- | --- |
| Europe | arrival of corn/maize, potatoes, and other crops via Columbian Exchange |
| Middle East | coffee spreads throughout region (1400s–1500s) |
| Africa | arrival of corn/maize, manioc, and other crops via Columbian Exchange |
| East (and Central) Asia | arrival of corn/maize, potatoes, and other crops via Columbian Exchange |
| South (and Southeast) Asia and Oceania | arrival of corn/maize, potatoes, chili peppers, and other crops via Columbian Exchange |

| Humans and the Environment, 1450–1750 | |
|---|---|
| **Americas** | arrival of horses, pigs, cattle, and other animals via Columbian Exchange<br>arrival of sugarcane, cotton, okra, rice, coffee, and other crops via Columbian Exchange<br>Afro-Eurasian diseases (smallpox, measles, and influenza) kill at least 25 to 50 percent of indigenous Americans<br>plantation and monoculture agriculture (sugarcane, cotton, coffee, tobacco)<br>silver mining |
| **Global and interregional** | Little Ice Age reaches its peak (ca. 1500 to mid-1800s)<br>environmental impact of mining, manufacturing, and urbanization increases in many regions<br>environmental impact of fishing and whaling increases, especially in the Atlantic<br>environmental impact of fur hunting increases, especially in Siberia and North America |

## Humans and the Environment

- The European age of exploration brought the Americas into contact with Afro-Eurasia at the end of the 1400s. The transmission of foodstuffs, animal species, and disease pathogens between these geographical areas is known as the Columbian Exchange.
- The introduction of Afro-Eurasian diseases (especially smallpox, measles, and influenza) into the Americas caused a massive demographic crisis, killing at least one-fourth to one-half of the indigenous population, and perhaps much more.
- The importation of corn (maize), potatoes, and manioc dramatically altered the diets and agricultural practices of Europe, Africa, and eventually Asia. Tomatoes had an impact as well, and American-grown crops like tobacco and cacao (from which chocolate is made) were highly desired by Europeans. Populations rose significantly throughout Europe, Africa, and Asia as a result of the new foods.
- To the Americas, Europeans and Africans brought the horse, pigs, and cattle. Afro-Eurasian crops transplanted to the Americas include okra, rice, citrus and other fruits, sugarcane, coffee, and cotton.
- The introduction of European modes of economic production into the Americas, especially plantation agriculture and the cultivation of cash crops like sugar and tobacco, radically altered North and South American ecosystems.
- Fishing, whaling, and the hunting of fur bearing animals—activities with a significant environmental impact—became increasingly important to the economies of European nations, especially as they intensified their efforts to explore and colonize larger parts of the world.
- Manufacturing and mining increased in importance, leading to greater resource extraction and a heavier environmental impact.
- The movement of peoples between Afro-Eurasia and the Americas, whether voluntary or involuntary, ranks as one of the most important migrations in history.
- After a gradual cooling during the 1300s and 1400s, the Little Ice Age hit its peak between the early 1500s and the early to mid-1800s.

# QUESTIONS AND COMPARISONS TO CONSIDER

- Compare one or more major European monarchies from this period with an Asian state, such as Ottoman Turkey, Ming China, Tokugawa Japan, or Mughal India.
- How were states in Africa and the Americas similar to and different from those in Europe and Asia?
- Consider various forms of monarchy during this era, as well as the state-building techniques (use of religious concepts, improvements in bureaucracy and infrastructure, better tax gathering, displays of art and architecture, and so on) they used to maintain and expand their power.
- Compare the emerging Atlantic slave trade with other systems of coerced labor, such as serfdom in Russia, the Arab slave network in Africa and the Mediterranean, the encomienda and hacienda systems in Latin America, and the Ottoman devshirme.
- What technologies and innovations facilitated exploration and imperial expansion?
- What made European exploration different from earlier campaigns of exploration and long-range oceanic navigation?
- Examine the emergence of gunpowder weaponry, the way it spread, and the consequences of its invention.
- Compare elite classes, such as Europe's noble class, zamindars in Mughal India, mandarin civil servants in China, and the daimyo in Japan. What other elites existed or emerged? Did the criteria for elite status include wealth, birthright, or merit? What challenges did traditional elites face during this era, whether because of the increased centralization of states or because of the rising economic importance of trade, commerce, and manufacture?
- What were the social, cultural, and political consequences of the rise of trade and commerce in different regions?
- How did elites in non-European regions interact with European traders and colonizers?
- What were the environmental effects of the European encounter with the Americas? The economic effects? What were the social and cultural consequences? What mixed populations came into being as a result?
- Examine the development of popular and more easily accessible forms of culture, such as drama, or poetry and the novel, or painting.
- Where did literacy improve most quickly? What impact did the printing press have on this development? What were the implications?
- Compare religious developments in various parts of the world. To what degree did religious schisms and disputes affect social and political life more widely?
- Consider key state rivalries during this period. Also consider the way competition over trade affected the global balance of power and patterns of international commerce.

# UNIT 4

## SCENIC ROUTE
### (Chapters 12–16)

# State Building, Expansion, and Conflict, 1450–1750

## 12

→ **THE EMERGENCE OF NATION-STATES**

→ **POLITICAL CENTRALIZATION (BUREAUCRATIC ELITES)**

→ **LAND EMPIRES VS. MARITIME EMPIRES AND TRADING-POST EMPIRES**

→ **EUROPE'S AGE OF EXPLORATION (VASCO DA GAMA, CHRISTOPHER COLUMBUS, FERDINAND MAGELLAN)**

→ **CONQUISTADORS AND THE ENCOMIENDA SYSTEM**

→ **JOINT-STOCK COMPANIES (DUTCH EAST INDIA COMPANY, BRITISH EAST INDIA COMPANY, HUDSON'S BAY COMPANY)**

→ **ATLANTIC SLAVE TRADE AND COLONIAL-ERA FORMS OF COERCED LABOR**

→ **GLOBAL COMPETITION OVER TRADE ROUTES AND OVERSEAS COLONIES**

→ **ABSOLUTISM AND PARLIAMENTARISM IN EUROPE**

→ **ISLAMIC GUNPOWDER EMPIRES = OTTOMAN TURKEY + SAFAVID PERSIA + MUGHAL INDIA**

→ **THE SONGHAI, KONGO, AND ASHANTI KINGDOMS**

→ **THE MING AND QING DYNASTIES IN CHINA**

→ **JAPANESE UNIFICATION AND THE TOKUGAWA SHOGUNATE**

→ **IDEOLOGIES AND POLITICAL USES OF RELIGION (DIVINE RIGHT, DAR AL-ISLAM, MANDATE OF HEAVEN)**

→ **THE MILITARY REVOLUTION THESIS**

→ **MAJOR WARS AND BATTLES (FALL OF CONSTANTINOPLE, EUROPE'S RELIGIOUS WARS AND THIRTY YEARS' WAR, 1683 SIEGE OF VIENNA, OTTOMAN-SAFAVID COMPETITION, OMANI-EUROPEAN RIVALRY, THE SEVEN YEARS' WAR)**

→ **KEY LEADERS (LOUIS XIV, SULEIMAN THE MAGNIFICENT, ASKIA MOHAMMED, KANGXI, TOKUGAWA IEYASU, AKBAR THE GREAT)**

During the first centuries of this era—the 1500s and 1600s—global might was concentrated mainly in states like China and the Islamic world's gunpowder empires: Ottoman Turkey, Safavid Persia, and Mughal India.

However, in one of modern history's major geopolitical developments, the nations of Europe grew steadily more powerful during this era. By the early 1700s, they were overtaking the civilizations listed above in terms of military, scientific, and technological aptitude. Much of this change had to with the European campaign, starting in the 1400s, to explore the rest of the world—and, where possible, to colonize it. Between the 1500s and 1700s, numerous European states—including Portugal, Spain, the Dutch Republic, England, and France—created trading-post empires and maritime empires with a truly global reach.

Another key development of this period involved the incorporation of gunpowder weaponry into warfare as it was practiced by a number of Eurasian states. Both state building at home and imperial expansion in both hemispheres depended on skill in deploying gunpowder infantry, cannon, and gunships, as well as on the ability to build new fortresses and fortified cities capable of defending against gunpowder artillery.

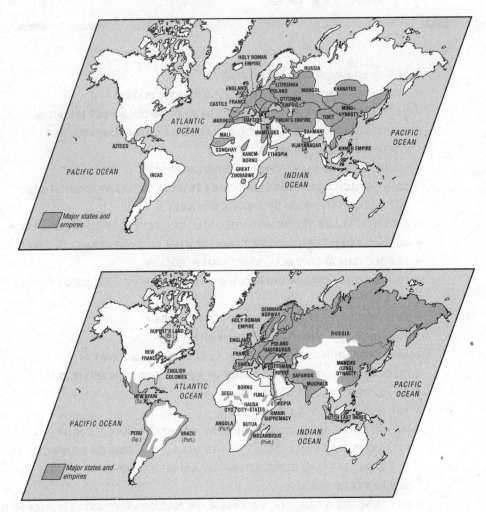

**World Boundaries in 1453 and 1700.**

In 1453, major states and empires were concentrated in Eurasia and small territories in Africa and the Americas. By 1700, large civilizations had spread into Russia, more portions of the Americas, and deeper into Africa.

## STATECRAFT: OLD AND NEW TECHNIQUES OF GOVERNANCE

In addition to multicultural and multiethnic land empires, **nation-states** in the contemporary sense of the word emerged. These were political units with relatively fixed borders, a sense of national unity, and populations that were largely (though never completely) homogeneous in terms of language and ethnicity.

In many parts of the world, **political and administrative centralization** became more sophisticated and led to a higher degree of state organization and efficiency. Features of modern government—such as bureaucracies, admiralties, general staffs, treasuries, and state banks—were more commonplace. Rulers devised more reliable and more efficient means to collect taxes and conscript soldiers.

As in earlier eras, **state-building techniques** included impressive displays of architecture and art. Regimes also continued to rely on religious concepts to legitimate their authority. As detailed in Chapter 15, states during this era grew more adept at handling ethnic and religious groups in ways that placed them firmly under their control, but at the same time kept them economically productive. Examples include the Ottoman empire's treatment of non-Muslim's subjects, the exercise of Manchu authority over ethnic Chinese during the Qing dynasty, and the Spanish treatment of native populations in their New World colonies. Many states also depended on new **bureaucratic elites** to staff administrations that were growing larger and more modern. Examples include the civil servants recruited by the Ottoman **devshirme system**, the **Chinese mandarins** who arose thanks to the Confucian examination system, and various nobles who adapted to civil service in several states—such as Russia (the **Table of Ranks**), Japan (**salaried samurai**), and European nobility (especially **nobles of the robe** in France during the 1600s and 1700s).

Most monarchies remained traditionally autocratic or absolutist, but some nations experimented with forms of government that were more representative, including parliamentary monarchy. While many states established new **land empires** or expanded existing ones, it was the nations of Europe, as described in the section below, which took the lead in building **trading-post empires** and **maritime empires** across the globe.

## EMPIRE-BUILDING: THE AGE OF EXPLORATION AND COLONIZATION

Between the early 1400s and the mid-1700s, the nations of Europe accomplished what no other civilization had done: they explored the wider world around them, discovered how to sail around the globe, and mapped the planet's major oceans and landmasses.

With this knowledge came great power and wealth, but the legacy of European exploration and colonization is mixed. Europe eventually became the dominant civilization on the planet as a result, but it paid a steep moral price in exchange. Exploration and colonization went hand in hand with war, greed, racial and religious intolerance, and slavery. Many parts of the world remained under European rule for centuries, and even now, the tensions left over between Western nations and their former colonies continue to affect international relations.

### Motivations and Capabilities

Why and how did the Europeans become the first to explore the world? For many centuries, European states had been less technologically and scientifically advanced than those in the Middle East and Far East, and their geographical knowledge of other regions was limited until the 1400s. As noted in Chapters 8 and 13, it was China where several key **navigational and maritime technologies** were invented, such as the astrolabe, the compass, and the sternpost rudder. And with the voyages of **Zheng He** in the early 1400s (see Chapters 7 and 8), China had the potential to lead the way in world exploration—although it turned away from that option and lost that opportunity.

Early on, Europe's primary motivation for exploring was economic. Throughout the Middle Ages, **Mediterranean trade**, greater awareness of the Middle East gained during **the Crusades**, and tales told by travelers like **Marco Polo** whetted European appetites for the wealth of eastern locales like China, the Indies, and Japan. Rather than relying on the

**Silk Road** and Middle Eastern middlemen, Europeans increasingly wanted their own direct access to Asiatic goods, such as **silk**, **spices**, and other luxury items.

As the Europeans' interest in exploring grew, so did their ability to voyage farther and more safely. By the 1300s and early 1400s, as described in Chapter 13, the Europeans had adopted, or were in the process of adopting, the abovementioned navigational and maritime technologies that had been developed earlier in Asia: the **astrolabe**, the **compass**, and the **sternpost rudder**. At the same time, the Europeans were developing **sailing ships** capable of long-range oceanic voyaging, with deep keels for stability and advanced rigging systems that permitted ships to sail where they needed to despite the direction of the wind. The most important model was the nimble, three-masted **caravel**, in extensive use by the 1400s.

> **NOTE**
>
> Another reason Europeans ventured outward was to take advantage of rich fishing and whaling grounds in the North Atlantic. Nameless fishers and whale-hunters may have ventured surprisingly close to the Canadian coast during the 1300s and 1400s. Some speculate that they came within sight of the Americas during this time, but there is no concrete proof of this.

**Gunpowder weaponry**, which the Europeans began to use in the 1300s and 1400s, also had an impact on the age of exploration. From the beginning, wherever they went, European sailors and soldiers came equipped with muskets, pistols, and small artillery pieces. Used against less technologically advanced native populations, these weapons allowed for faster and easier colonization. And by the 1500s and 1600s, the Europeans had invented **galleons** and other large **gunships** that allowed them to project even greater quantities of firepower all across the globe.

## The Iberian Wave: Portugal and Spain

The first European nations to systematically explore the wider Atlantic world were Portugal and Spain, on the Iberian peninsula.

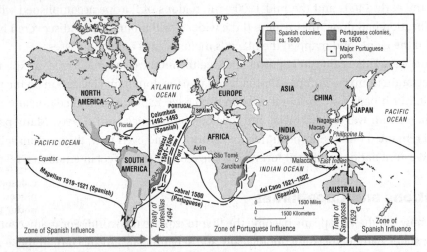

**Spanish and Portuguese Exploration, 1492–1529.**
The first European nations to colonize the wider world were Spain and Portugal. Their successes are attested to in this map. The north–south lines of demarcation were established by the papacy, to whose authority both nations, being Catholic, submitted.

Portugal's exploring efforts, encouraged by **Prince Henry the Navigator**, began in early 1410 with voyages beyond the Mediterranean, well to the west and south. The Portuguese claimed several Atlantic island groups, including the Azores, as well as ports along Africa's west coast. In 1488, Bartholomeu Díaz reached the southern tip of Africa, which the rulers of Portugal named the **Cape of Good Hope**, recognizing this as an important step on the way to India. Over the next decade, the Portuguese made their way into the Indian Ocean basin, capturing East African ports and cities and then crossing the ocean to India itself. The first European to reach India by sea was **Vasco da Gama**, who set out in 1497, landed and traded in Calicut in 1498, and returned home in 1499—earning an immense profit in the process. The Portuguese would quickly take steps to enlarge their presence in Africa and Asia.

In the meantime, the Spanish, distracted by the Reconquista against Muslims in southern Spain, had fallen behind Portugal when it came to exploring. Blocked by their Portuguese rivals from following the African-Indian Ocean route to Asia, Spain's monarchs—King Ferdinand and Queen Isabella—turned to the unusual proposal made in 1492 by the Italian captain **Christopher Columbus**: to sail west to reach the Far East. The boldness of Columbus's plan lay not in the idea that the world was round (a fact well known to educated Europeans), but in his erroneous belief that the globe was small enough that an expedition would be able to sail from Spain to Asia before running out of food or water, or without encountering some other landmass in the way. Columbus set sail in August 1492 and reached the islands of the Caribbean in October.

Columbus himself was convinced that he had found the Indies—hence the mistaken term "Indians" for Native Americans—but the Spanish and Portuguese quickly realized that he had found something completely unknown to them. The two countries turned to the pope to determine who would be allowed to claim which parts of this "New World." In **lines of demarcation** agreed to in 1493–1494 and 1529, the pope gave jurisdiction over most of South America and all of North America to the Spanish. The Portuguese received Brazil, which was discovered in 1500. The lines of demarcation similarly defined Spanish and Portuguese spheres of influence in Asia. In the 1520s, all of Spain's and Portugal's earlier efforts were tied together by **Ferdinand Magellan**, a Portuguese mariner sailing on behalf of Spain. Leader of the first-ever **circumnavigation of the globe**, Magellan left Europe in 1519, traversed the Atlantic, and rounded the tip of South America. His ships made their way across the Pacific and returned to Europe in 1522, although he himself died along the way, in the Philippine islands.

Having reached Africa, Southeast Asia, and the Far East on one hand and the New World on the other, the Portuguese and Spanish established a commercial or colonial presence wherever they could. In the Far East and Southeast Asia, most states were too strong or too advanced for the Portuguese to conquer, and for the most part they settled for trade. Still, they took over certain areas. In addition to their West African outposts, they gained control over East African cities like Mombasa and **Zanzibar**, and even the port of **Muscat** (1507), in the Arab state of **Oman**. They also seized the Indian port of Goa (1510), the thriving commercial center of **Melaka** (Malacca, 1511), and the island of Sri Lanka. Portugal opened up ties with China in the 1510s and with Japan in the 1540s, and while the Chinese granted it the port of Macau in 1557, as a reward for fighting pirates, the Portuguese had no hope of actual conquest here. What they built in this part of the world is generally referred to among historians as a **trading-post empire**. In the 1600s, Portugal would lose many of its colonial and commercial assets to the Dutch, English, and Omani Arabs.

In the New World, by contrast, the Portuguese and Spanish founded **maritime empires**, or overseas colonies fully under their control. Portugal moved into Brazil, while Spain built up power in the Caribbean, using islands such as Cuba, Puerto Rico, and Hispaniola (today Haiti and the Dominican Republic) as bases. The mainland fell to the **conquistadors**: generals who brought huge parts of North and

**NOTE**

For the time being, the Pacific world remained relatively unaffected by European colonization. The Spanish placed the Philippines firmly under their control, and the Portuguese—followed by the Dutch, English, and French—anchored themselves in various ports and outposts in South and Southeast Asia, including some of the islands that make up the East Indies. But it was not until the late 1700s or 1800s that European states truly brought places like Australia or the islands of Oceania into their colonial grasp.

South America under Spanish control. Florida fell to Juan Ponce de León in 1513. From 1519 to 1521, **Hernán Cortés** waged an effective and brutal campaign against the Aztecs, and the Aztec capital of Tenochtitlan became the headquarters for all of **New Spain**. Mesoamerica and most of what is now the U.S. Southwest, including California, fell to the Spanish, as did other parts of the Gulf Coast. Farther to the south, in the 1530s, **Francisco Pizarro** destroyed the mighty Incan empire. Such conquests were partly due to the military advantages that **horses** and **gunpowder weapons** gave the Spanish and Portuguese. European arrivals also proved adept at **divide-and-conquer tactics**, whereby they stirred up rivalries among native tribes and allied with some against others. (As noted in Chapter 15, local women sometimes provided invaluable guidance and contacts here, the most notable example being Cortes's mistress **Malinche**.) However, the most important reason for Spain's and Portugal's success in conquering the New World involved disease, the grimmest aspect of the **Columbian Exchange** discussed in Chapter 16. In particular, **smallpox** and **measles** killed indigenous Americans in massive numbers. Anywhere from one-quarter to one-half of the Americas' original population perished—some historians think even more may have died—and the survivors were left all the more vulnerable to European conquest.

The conquistador Cortés famously stated that he had come to the Americas for "God, gold, and glory." Although the conversion of Native Americans to Catholicism was considered important, particularly to offset the loss of European worshippers to Protestant churches, economic exploitation was the highest priority for Spain and Portugal in the New World. The most important activities here were **mining** (especially for **silver** near Mexico City and at **Potosí**, Bolivia's "mountain of silver") and **plantation monoculture**—with **sugarcane** the most prized and most labor-intensive cash crop. At first, the conquistadors governed the territory they conquered, sending one-fifth (*la quinta*) of their profits back to Spain. Starting in 1535, New Spain was placed under government control as a **viceroyalty** ("in place of the king") and all colonial economic activity was run by the **House of Trade** in Seville. By the 1700s, three new viceroyalties—Peru, New Granada (northern South America), and La Plata (southern South America)—had been added. A similar pattern prevailed in Brazil.

As detailed in Chapter 15, a direct economic consequence of Spanish and Portuguese colonization in the New World was **coerced labor**. Initially, the Spanish attempted to enslave American natives by means of the **encomienda system**, but this worked badly and was judged too inhumane by Catholic clergy, and so it was abolished in the 1540s. In the Andes, the Spanish took the **mit'a system**, the form of coerced labor used previously by the Incas, and adapted it for their own purposes. They also opted to rely increasingly on the importation of slaves from Africa, a practice that the Portuguese had begun in the 1400s and had brought to Brazil and the Caribbean by the 1510s. This led to the rapid rise of the **Atlantic slave trade**, which continued well into the 1800s. Over time, Brazil became by far the largest importer of African slaves, and it was the last country in the Americas to outlaw slavery—not until 1888.

## The Northern Wave: The French, Dutch, and English

During the 1500s, other European nations began to explore and colonize, the most important being France, the Dutch Republic, and England. From the start, Spain and Portugal were anxious to lock these "northern wave" countries out of Atlantic exploration. At stake were immense wealth, military power, and, except in the case of France, Catholic-Protestant rivalry.

**NOTE**

As described in Chapter 14, the principal tool used by the French, Dutch, and English to finance exploration and colonization was the joint-stock company. Prominent examples are mentioned throughout the text.

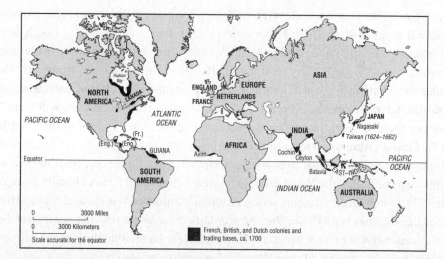

**French, English, and Dutch Colonization by 1700.**

By 1700, France, England, and the Netherlands had gained many imperial footholds in the Americas, the Caribbean, Africa, and Asia.

Initially, the only places open to new exploration were those farther to the north, which the Spanish and Portuguese cared little about. Hoping that a **Northeast Passage** (along Russia's northern coast) or a **Northwest Passage** (through Canada's northern waters) might provide an alternative route to Asia, French, Dutch, and English mariners turned to Arctic and North Atlantic voyaging. They came no closer to Asia as a result of these expeditions, but they did discover rich **fishing** and **whaling grounds**, and they developed an interest in the northern coast of North America. Moreover, by the late 1500s, the French, Dutch, and English had grown strong enough and sufficiently skilled at seafaring to challenge the Spanish and Portuguese for control over Caribbean, Indian Ocean, and Pacific sea routes—and even over actual ports and colonies.

The French colonial presence in North America began in Canada, in the 1530s, when Jacques Cartier charted the St. Lawrence River. It was during the early 1600s that France established its first cities in Canada—among them Quebec, founded by Samuel Champlain in 1608—and it created the **Company of New France** in the 1620s. Later in the 1600s, the French moved southward, claiming the vast Louisiana territory, which included the Great Lakes and the Mississippi basin. Their highest priority in these areas was the **fur trade**, and many French colonists were excellent hunters, trappers, and woodsmen (*voyageurs*). In the south and along the Gulf of Mexico, the French challenged the Spanish, and they seized Caribbean islands such as Martinique and Saint Domingue (today Haiti). Here they grew sugarcane. Also in the 1600s, the French, like the other northern nations, elbowed their way into the Indian Ocean, competing with the Portuguese for trade. The 1700s were less kind to France's colonial efforts. Its principal enemy by this time was England, which took Canada from France as a result of the **French and Indian Wars** (1756–1763), an offshoot of the **Seven Years' War** in Europe. Although the province of Quebec retained its French heritage, French-speaking Acadians were driven out of eastern Canada and forced to resettle in Louisiana—where their descendants are still known as Cajuns. Also during the Seven Years' War, English troops defeated Mughal states allied to the French, ensuring that England, not France, would go on to gain colonial mastery over India.

> **NOTE**
>
> The French were more adept than other Europeans at cooperating with Native Americans (especially the Hurons and Algonquins), learning their ways, and adapting themselves to local customs and environments.

Exploration by the Dutch was closely tied to their long war of independence against Spain, which lasted from 1568 to 1648. Nicknaming themselves "sea beggars," Dutch mariners sought to disrupt Spanish trade and to attack Spanish-controlled ports worldwide, and they did the same to the Portuguese. By 1600, they had begun to seize colonies from both: the port of **Melaka**, the island of Sri Lanka, much of West Africa, and a number of Caribbean islands. They also invaded Indonesia, where they maintained a colonial presence for centuries, running pepper and spice plantations. Dutch operations here were administered by the **Dutch East India Company**, a joint-stock enterprise founded in 1602. In 1621, a Dutch West India Company was established to oversee the Netherlands' Caribbean colonies. For a time, the Dutch also controlled the New York region, which they hired Henry Hudson to explore in 1609. In 1624, Dutch settlers purchased the island of Manhattan from a local Native American tribe, and the city they built there, New Amsterdam, grew into a thriving commercial center under the leadership of Peter Stuyvesant. However, New Amsterdam became New York after 1664, when the English wrested the colony by force from the Dutch.

The English claimed parts of North America as early as the 1490s, thanks to the voyages of John Cabot, who attempted to find a Northwest Passage to Asia through Canada's Arctic waters. In the 1500s, they moved into the New World as part of their commercial rivalry and naval wars with Spain. They established a presence in the Caribbean, particularly on the islands of Barbados and Jamaica, and England's so-called "sea dogs" gained much knowledge about global navigation from their conflicts with the Spanish and Portuguese. Francis Drake, for instance, became the first Englishman to sail around the world (1577–1580), during a voyage whose main purpose was to raid Spanish ships and ports.

In the 1600s, the English established colonies on the North American mainland, from the Carolinas to the Canadian border. The first successful settlement was Jamestown, Virginia, founded in 1607 and led by John Smith. Soon after, religious minorities, especially Puritans and Quakers, came to North America to flee persecution in England. The *Mayflower* Pilgrims landed at Plymouth Rock in 1620, and Puritans also founded the Massachusetts Bay Colony in 1628. Pennsylvania, home to the New World's largest city, Philadelphia, owed its existence to the Quaker William Penn. Economics mattered as well. From the New World, the English took sugarcane, timber, corn, potatoes, and tobacco. They also searched for furs, and the **Hudson's Bay Company**, incorporated in 1670, began to intrude into Canada and other French colonies for that purpose. As in other parts of the New World, **coerced labor** was part of life in English settlements: many colonists paid for their passage by means of **indentured servitude**, and the English gradually came to rely more and more on Africans brought over by the **Atlantic slave trade**.

The English also made incursions into the Indian Ocean basin and South Asia. Their first expedition to the Indies came in 1591. Along with the Dutch, they interfered with Portuguese trade in this region and even forced Portugal to abandon some of its outposts and ports. Shortly afterward, they founded the **British East India Company** (1600) to manage economic—and, later, military—relations with South and Southeast Asia. The English gained a presence in northwestern India by 1608 and would eventually take over more of the subcontinent. They would seize the key port of **Melaka** from the Dutch in 1795.

**NOTE**

Pocahontas proved indispensable in forging relations between the Jamestown colony and the local Native Americans. She saved the life of John Smith from her father, the chief, and she later married one of the colonists. Like Malinche with Cortés in Mexico, she illustrates the vital role that local women often played in the first encounters between Europeans and native populations.

## Russia in Siberia and America

Russia, which established a **land empire** in Siberia during the 1500s and 1600s, also extended its reach to North America. After reaching Siberia's Pacific coast in the 1600s, the Russians set their sights on Alaska and other parts of North America. In the 1730s and 1740s, the **Bering Expedition**, a scientific venture organized by the Russian government, surveyed the waters separating Siberia from North America. Afterward, Russian missionaries and hunters moved into the Aleutian Islands and Alaska. The **fur trade** stimulated Russian settlement of Siberia and North America alike. The Russians established a colony in Alaska in the late 1700s, administered by the **Russian-American Company**. They moved down the Pacific coast, building fortresses as far south as northern California. They sold all their American possessions, Alaska included, to the United States in 1867.

Native Siberians were subjected to the coerced-labor system known as the **yasak**, which required them to pay tribute and hunt fur bearing animals for the Russians. In Alaska, the Russians fought bitter wars against Native Americans and Eskimos. In addition, at least 80 percent of the Aleutians' native population is said to have perished due to Russian colonization, thanks to violence, the spread of disease, and alcoholism.

**NOTE**

What the conquistador Cortés was to the Aztecs, the Cossack leader Yermak was to the native peoples of Siberia. In the mid-1500s, on contract from the merchant family that had been chartered by the tsar to develop the Russo-Siberian frontier, Yermak led the armies which began the long process of conquering all of Siberia.

## MAJOR STATES AND EMPIRES

The world's geopolitical balance was hugely altered in favor of Europe during this era. In the 1400s, Europe was one of many major civilizations, and a relatively weak one compared to places like China, India, or the Middle East. By the late 1700s, it was arguably the world's most powerful region, having outstripped Qing China, Ottoman Turkey, and similar states in terms of military and technological advancement. Its might would only increase in the 1800s, when it truly dominated the world.

## Europe

During this era, most European nations came to resemble **nation-states** in the modern sense of the word: **politically and administratively centralized** political units with fixed borders, a sense of national unity, and mostly (though never completely) homogenous populations in terms of language and ethnicity. Centralization allowed European monarchs to abandon medieval feudalism, with its weak institutions, and to assert their power with more confidence. Frequently this meant competition between monarchs and their noble aristocracies, who were anxious to hold on to the feudal privileges their ancestors had been granted during the Middle Ages.

Between the 1500s and the late 1700s, two major forms of monarchy emerged in Europe: **absolutism** and **parliamentarism**. In the former, the monarch was theoretically all-powerful, with no institutions or legal restrictions limiting his or her authority. (In real life, absolute monarchs were sometimes handicapped by weak personalities, uncooperative nobles, or unreliable armies.) Absolutism in Europe was typically justified by the doctrine of **divine right**, according to which the monarch reigns by the will of God. Europe's archetypal absolute monarch was **Louis XIV** of France, the Sun King who ruled from 1661 to 1715. Louis centralized his bureaucracy and broke the power of stubborn aristocrats by shifting administrative power from traditionally powerful families (nobility of the sword) to civil servants that he himself ennobled, and who therefore owed him loyalty (nobility of the robe). He turned Paris and his palace of **Versailles** into grand, impressive centers of power, and he built the largest army and navy Europe had seen since the fall of Rome. In many ways, Louis illustrates the strengths and weaknesses of absolute monarchy. He was intelligent and capable, but he also persecuted Protestants, even though they had been granted religious freedom in the late 1500s, and he involved France in too many wars, accumulating a national debt that would worsen during the 1700s and eventually help cause the French Revolution. Most other nations in Europe, among them Austria, Prussia, and Russia, were—or attempted to be—absolute monarchies. Noteworthy absolute rulers include **Peter the Great**, who Westernized Russia in the late 1600s and early 1700s, and forced his nobles to serve the state according to a strict Table of Ranks, and **Frederick the Great** of Prussia, an exceptionally skilled general who made his kingdom vastly more efficient during the mid-1700s, but also more autocratic. Censorship and restrictions on social mobility tended to be the rule in absolute monarchies. In Central and Eastern Europe, especially in Russia, **serfdom** remained in place much longer than in Western Europe, where it faded away for the most part during the Renaissance.

A smaller number of European states chose **parliamentarism**, in which the ruler governed in conjunction with some kind of lawmaking body appointed by the aristocracy, elected by some or all of the people, or some combination of both. As they freed themselves from Spanish rule in the late 1500s, the Dutch developed a parliamentary system in which there was not even a king, but an executive official—the *stadholder*—who shared power with a large council called the States General. Several minor powers, including the city-state of Venice, created systems similar to this in place, but the most famous arose in England. Here, monarchs had been compelled to share power with Parliament since the 1200s—even strong-willed ones like **Henry VIII** and his daughter **Elizabeth I** during the 1500s. In the 1600s, the balance of power between the two shifted decisively in favor of Parliament. The English Civil War (1640–1649) led to the execution of the king by Parliamentary forces and also to a temporary assumption of power by the Puritan general and parliamentarian Oliver Cromwell. When the royal family returned in 1660 and resumed the rivalry between monarch and Parliament, the latter overthrew their king once again, in the Glorious Revolution of 1688. Parliament then invited the Dutch leader William of Orange to become their king, but with conditions. William had to agree to the **English Bill of Rights**, which curtailed the powers of the monarch and made Parliament the dominant partner in the English political system. From this point forward, Parliament grew increasingly stronger, while the monarchy steadily weakened.

Nations with parliamentary systems typically enjoyed certain advantages. Both the Dutch and the English, for example, developed strong commercial economies, powerful navies, urbanized societies, and intellectual and cultural outlooks that were relatively open and free from religious persecution. Although poverty and inequality existed in parliamentary systems, social mobility tended to be greater than in absolutist states.

## The Middle East

The unity of the Abbasid caliphate as a single Islamic state, stretching from Spain to India, crumbled during the Middle Ages and vanished in the 1200s. Decades of political confusion followed, as Mongol warriors invaded and the Seljuk and Ottoman Turks rose up as regional powers. Afterward, strong political units emerged in the Middle East: the Ottoman

Empire, centered in present-day Turkey, and the Safavid Empire in Persia. Both were highly centralized, technologically advanced, and militarily powerful. Along with the Mughal Empire in India, the Ottoman and Safavid states are commonly referred to as **gunpowder empires**, because of their mastery of new weaponry and their effective use of it—at least during the 1500s and 1600s—in accumulating regional might.

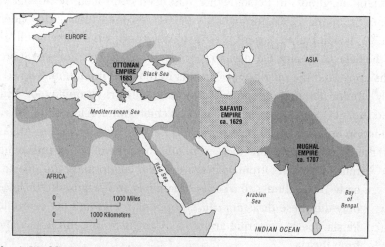

The Islamic World's Gunpowder Empires, ca. 1629–1707.

Nomads from Central Asia, the Ottoman Turks established their own state in the late 1200s. In the late 1300s and 1400s, they gained hegemony over most of the Middle East, restoring central authority to the region. Making effective use of gunpowder artillery, they accomplished the **conquest of Constantinople** in 1453, and a further wave of expansion in the early 1500s, led by **Suleiman the Magnificent**, carried the Ottomans deep into southeastern Europe and across North Africa. The Ottoman presence lingered in both places until the late 1800s and early 1900s.

The Ottoman sultans borrowed many state-building techniques from the past. In the early 1500s, Selim I claimed religious authority as well as political power, equating the Ottomans' right to rule with that of the Arab caliphates of bygone years. The sultans also adopted the **circle of justice** ideology that had existed in the Middle East for centuries. They ruled with the help of an elaborate bureaucracy, headed by the grand vizier and staffed by lesser viziers and provincial governors called pashas and beys. Key institutions in the Ottoman Empire included the **devshirme** system of recruiting civil servants and elite troops—musketeer infantry known as **janissaries**—by enslaving sons from Christian families and placing them in positions of privileged servitude. Also important was the **millet** system, which sorted non-Muslims into religious categories and administered them according to that status. These subjects, known as dhimmi, included Jews and Christians of several denominations and paid the **jizya**, or unbelievers' tax.

The last truly gifted Ottoman sultan was Suleiman the Magnificent (1520–1566), whose talents as a lawmaker and domestic ruler matched his abilities as a general. Many of his successors were mediocre or worse, and the empire entered a long decline after the 1600s. A key turning point came in 1683, when the Turks launched their last major offensive against the European mainland. That year, they drove deep into Austrian territory, and it was feared that their **1683 siege of Vienna** would lead to a general breakthrough and a full-scale invasion of Europe. At the last minute, however, Vienna was saved by a massive Catholic counteroffensive. After this victory, the Austrians pushed the Ottomans far back to the east, and although the Turks were not expelled from Europe, they lost much territory there during the late 1600s and early 1700s. As the rest of the 1700s passed, the Ottomans fought the Europeans—especially the Austrians and Russians—frequently. However, they never again seriously threatened Europe, and their global power weakened during the 1700s and 1800s.

The Ottomans' neighbors in Persia, which had been controlled by various Mongol and Turkic regimes from the 1200s through the 1400s, regained their independence during this era. In 1501, Ismail I, at the age of 15, rose to power, took the ancient title of shah, and proclaimed the Safavid Empire. Devoted to the messianic "twelver" form of Shiite Islam, the Safavid shahs converted the majority of Persians to that denomination. Safavid Persia was economically vibrant (although it competed bitterly with the Ottomans for influence over Silk Road and Indian Ocean trade), and Isfahan, its chief commercial center, was a great hub for the production and sale of silk, ceramics, and Persian rugs. Thanks to Abbas the Great (1587–1628), the Safavids made effective use of gunpowder weaponry and military slavery, much like their Ottoman rivals. Unlike the Ottomans, the Safavids fell in the early 1700s, thanks to a series of famines and plagues in the late 1600s. Not only did these disasters cause population loss and tax shortfalls, they left Persia open to external attacks by Uzbeks from Central Asia and Cossacks from Russia.

**NOTE**

Existing on the periphery between Russia and the Middle East and Central Asia were Cossack hosts, made up of Russians and Ukrainians living semi-autonomously on the frontier—free from serfdom—and intermarrying with local populations. Skilled cavalry warriors, they clashed often with Turks and Persians, sometimes on their own behalf, sometimes in alliance with the Russian state. Although several large Cossack revolts troubled Russia in the 1600s and 1700s, their hosts came firmly under Russian control during the 1800s, when many of them served the tsar as his most loyal troops.

## Africa

While North Africa came to be ruled by the Ottomans in the 1500s, the rest of the continent was governed in a variety of ways. The biggest changes experienced by the region during this era were the establishment of a long-term European presence along Africa's coasts, and also the ravages caused by the horrific **Atlantic slave trade**.

Africa's most powerful states arose in the west. As the previously dominant empire of Mali faded, the Muslim kingdom of **Songhai** took its place in the mid-1400s, asserting control over the city of **Timbuktu** and the region's key trade routes. Songhai's most famous ruler was **Askia Mohammed**, who came to the throne by overthrowing the previous monarch (*askia*, his adopted name, means "usurper"). A skilled general who governed from 1493 to 1528, Askia expanded Songhai's boundaries, centralized his power by creating a complex bureaucracy, and sponsored art, scholarship, and the building of many mosques. He expanded trade, and Songhai's growing merchant class generated wealth by exchanging salt for gold. A fictional account of his reign, *The Epic of Askia Mohammed*, is one of the classics of the West African oral tradition, performed by **griot** storytellers since the 1500s. Songhai prospered until civil war and invasion by Moroccan forces destroyed it in the 1590s.

From the 1400s onward, the arrival of the Portuguese and other Europeans profoundly shaped the development of West African states, several of whom attained or maintained power by cooperating with the outsiders at the expense of their neighbors. One example is that of **Kongo**, a Bantu state that took shape around 1400 between the Atlantic coast and the western edge of what is now the modern state of Congo. In 1483, the Portuguese arrived in force, and though they did not conquer Kongo outright, they took hostages and compelled it to enter a long and coercive partnership. Kongo's monarchs converted to Catholicism, took European names, and gave Portugal favorable trade terms and the right to use their ports.

Kongo had little choice in the matter, but in many ways, its ties with Portugal enriched and strengthened it. Kongo acquired gunpowder weapons from the Portuguese and enlarged its army. With that army, it defeated its fellow Africans and captured thousands of them as prisoners of war—who were promptly sold to the Portuguese as slaves. During most of the 1500s, Kongo expanded and centralized, but internal disputes then weakened it in the late 1500s and early 1600s. Despite its difficulties, it expelled the Portuguese, with help from the Dutch, between the 1620s and the 1670s. It went through various phases of unity and disunity during the 1700s and 1800s, and then was fully colonized in the 1870s and 1880s. In the 1600s and 1700s, Kongo's example was followed by other West African societies that warred on and imprisoned other African tribes, then sold the captives to European slavers. In particular, the **Ashanti** (Asante) **kingdom**, founded by Osei Tutu in 1680, became immensely powerful because its leaders sold gold and slaves to Europeans in exchange for muskets and gunpowder.

**NOTE**

One West African leader who resisted European encroachment during the 1600s was Nzinga, queen of the Mbundu peoples in what is now Angola. Although she converted to Christianity and eventually signed treaties that gave Portugal control over Angola, she spent years fighting the Portuguese, occasionally leading troops into battle herself.

**Sketch of Queen Nzinga (1582–1663)**
Ruler of Angola's Mbundu people, Nzinga eventually signed treaties that allowed Portugal access to her country. Before that, however, she stoutly resisted Portuguese domination, accepting aid from Portugal's Dutch enemies and occasionally commanding forces in the field.

In South and East Africa, just as in the west, it was Portugal that had established itself as a colonial and trading-post power. This changed significantly in the mid-1600s. Control of South Africa passed to the Dutch, who began to settle the region with colonists known as **Boers**. Also known as Afrikaners, the Boers enslaved the African herding tribes nearest them, including the peaceful Xhosa, and then encountered a stronger and more warlike group, the **Zulu**. Many wars broke out between the Zulu and the Boers, and later the English, who arrived on the scene somewhat later. Portuguese power in East Africa was broken during the 1600s and 1700s, both by other Europeans—particularly the Dutch and the English—and **Omani Arabs** who rose up against Portuguese rule in the 1650s. After expelling the Portuguese from their home port of Muscat, the Omanis proceeded down the East African coast, starting in the 1690s and continuing into the early 1700s, pushing the Portuguese out of a number of cities, including Zanzibar and Mombasa. Despite this, Portugal maintained a colonial presence in certain parts of East Africa for a long time to come.

## East Asia

Up through the early 1400s, Ming China had been politically dynamic and militarily active. Thanks to the voyages of **Zheng He**, the Chinese also had an opportunity to engage in their own campaign of global exploration. But although the Ming kept up their tradition of cultural brilliance, and although economic prosperity continued for a time, China grew militarily softer and politically stagnant in the late 1500s and early 1600s. The Ming also opened up China to the European traders and Christian—especially Jesuit—missionaries who began arriving in the 1500s: first the Portuguese (who received the port of Macau as a gift for driving away local pirates), and then the Spanish and Dutch.

For the Ming, the 1600s were a time of rapid decline. The government decentralized and unraveled. The massive **influx of silver** with which the Portuguese and Spanish paid for trade goods triggered inflation and then economic breakdown. At the same time, agricultural yields shrank, whether because of worsening soil quality or a general cooling caused by the **Little Ice Age**. The population grew more rapidly than the land's ability to support it, and famines recurred regularly.

Finally, in the 1630s and early 1640s, **Li Zicheng's peasant revolt** toppled the Ming dynasty, whose last emperor committed suicide. This opened the door for an external conquest of northern China by the **Manchus**, an ethnically related but distinct people living to China's northeast. Their new dynasty was called the **Qing** ("pure") and lasted from 1644 to 1912. Skilled warlords, the early Qing rulers spent the last half of the 1600s consolidating their rule over southern China and expanding it to the island of Formosa (now Taiwan). They also gained control over Mongolia, Tibet, and much of Central Asia, and they forced many neighboring areas into their **tributary system**. For many years, the Manchus—who made up less than 5 percent of the population—subjugated their Chinese subjects by enforcing the ethnically based system of social stratification mentioned in Chapter 15.

Starting in the 1690s, the Qing traded with European nations, but regulated commerce tightly and limited foreign contacts as much as possible. Christianity was banned in 1724, and by the middle of the 1700s, foreign trade was funneled through a handful of ports and border cities, the most important of which was **Canton**, on the Pacific coast. While Qing China sold a high volume of **tea**, **silk**, and **porcelain**, it allowed few imports. This policy of **trade protectionism** made China wealthy, but also angered its European trading partners—a growing problem whose consequences were felt in the 1800s.

During the late 1600s and early 1700s, the Qing emperors were capable rulers, good administrators, and strong centralizers. **Kangxi** (1662–1722) is widely considered one of China's greatest rulers: an adept general, a just lawgiver, and a sponsor of culture of learning. He bolstered Qing authority by claiming to have the **mandate of heaven**, and also by patronizing Confucianism, with its emphasis on respect for authority. Unlike many of the rulers who followed him, he appreciated the importance of the West's growing technological aptitude. In the late 1700s and afterward, Qing rulers grew more complacent, and China began slipping backward in terms of scientific and technological advancement—leaving the country increasingly open to foreign domination in the 1800s.

Japan had been ruled since the end of the 1100s by **shoguns**, military rulers who wielded power on behalf of the symbolically important, but politically impotent, emperor. A feudal system from the beginning, in which the shoguns shared power with landholding **daimyo** of the **samurai** class, the regime grew increasingly decentralized during the 1300s and 1400s, to the point that civil war, banditry, and economic breakdown became the norm during the late 1400s and 1500s. This disunity left Japan open to European commercial and religious influence when the Portuguese arrived in the 1540s, followed by Spanish and Dutch traders and missionaries from several countries. The Europeans also introduced gunpowder weaponry into Japan.

The **reunification of Japan**, which lasted from 1560 to 1615, involved the military and diplomatic efforts of three warlords. The first two harnessed the power of gunpowder weapons and relied on an increasingly harsh system of social stratification to defeat their rivals and restore civic order. The general who completed the process was **Tokugawa Ieyasu**, a brilliant, ruthless commander who declared himself shogun in 1603 and brought the entire country under his control by 1615. The shogunate he founded lasted until 1868, and the Tokugawa era is often referred to as the "great peace." Peace, however, came at the price of increased autocracy and social stratification. Ieyasu moved Japan's capital to the city of Edo (modern-day Tokyo), but the emperor remained a figurehead as before. Japan's **caste system**—samurai, peasants, artisans, and merchants, with *eta* "untouchables" at the bottom—was still justified by **Confucian ideology**, but it became more rigid than before, and until after the mid-1700s, it was virtually impossible to move from one class to another. Although samurai retained the privilege of owning swords, ordinary citizens were forbidden to own weapons or serve as soldiers, and the Tokugawa regime maintained a strict monopoly on gunpowder technology. **Salaried samurai**, now that their warrior function was no longer needed, served the Tokugawa regime as bureaucrats and civil servants.

Another feature of Tokugawa policy was **isolationism**, a trend that had begun even in the late 1500s. Japan's authorities feared the influence of foreign ideas and European Christianity, and also the importation of gunpowder weapons. Ieyasu's predecessors began the process of restricting foreign access and persecuting Christians, and the Tokugawa shoguns formalized these practices. Christianity was officially discouraged, and the **national seclusion policy**, instituted in the 1630s, allowed foreign traders access to only one city, the port of **Nagasaki**. Despite such restrictions on trade, Japan's economy flourished under the Tokugawa shoguns. The population grew rapidly. Rice production more than doubled between 1600 and 1720. Tokugawa Japan became highly urbanized, and the government built an elaborate network of roads and canals. During this era, the Japanese became great producers of lacquerware, pottery, and steel. The merchant class gained a great deal of economic and social clout in the 1600s and 1700s, despite the very low status they occupied in the Japanese caste system.

## South Asia

In the late 1400s, India was still ruled by the Delhi Sultanate, although it had been weakening for decades. In 1520, the Mongol warlord **Babur the Tiger** invaded the Delhi Sultanate from the north and shattered it at the battle of Panipat, in 1526. This led to the establishment of the **Mughal Empire**, which eventually conquered the rest of India and ruled there for the next several centuries. (Its name comes from the Persian word for "Mongol," and its alternative spelling, "mogul," is still used to describe a rich or powerful individual.)

Like the Delhi sultans, the Mughals were Muslims and turned their state into one of the Islamic world's three **gunpowder empires**. They centralized India and turned the previously autonomous landowning **zamindar** class into regional governors and bureaucrats. The economy thrived, thanks to a boom in India's **cotton trade**. Mughal rule reached its peak under **Akbar the Great** (1556–1605), who used gunpowder weaponry to complete the conquest of India. Not only did he carry out the centralization described above, and also reform taxes and the law code, he gained fame for his religious tolerance. He abolished the **jizya** tax paid by non-Muslims, and encouraged friendly relations among Muslims, Buddhists, Hindus, and Sikhs. He ensured that a minimum percentage of government officials were Hindu, and he married a Hindu princess. He even attempted, but without success, to outlaw the Hindu funeral custom of **sati**. Akbar's grandson, **Shah Jahan**, was also a benevolent ruler, and left behind a great architectural legacy that includes the beloved **Taj Mahal**.

The Mughals' fortunes took a downward turn under Akbar's great-grandson, **Aurangzeb** (1658–1707), a militant Muslim who abandoned the early Mughals' policy of religious flexibility, reimposed the jizya tax, and began to force non-Muslims to live under **Sharia law** and Muslim dietary restrictions. Aurangzeb's intolerance stirred up civil strife and violence and also affected the economy adversely. He militarized India's Sikhs by putting their leader, or guru, to death in 1675, and he provoked the secession of the **Maratha Empire**, a Hindu state founded by the warrior-sovereign Shivaji in west-central India.

The Mughal state declined during the 1700s, as religious struggles continued, and as many provinces joined the Sikh and Maratha states in declaring independence. European interference in India's affairs also increased. During the 1500s and early 1600s, Mughal India was militarily and technologically advanced enough to keep European traders in their place, as the Portuguese and Spanish, followed by the French, the Dutch, and the English, came to South Asia. In the 1600s, however, the balance of power shifted. The English built textile factories at Fort William near Calcutta, in the northeast, and Madras. The western gateway port of Bombay (now Mumbai) was ceded to the **British East India Company** in 1661. The Dutch East India Company—also the master of Indonesia—established bases in Ceylon (now Sri Lanka), and the French created a great garrison and trading center at Pondicherry, on the east coast. During the 1700s, European control over India increased. In the early decades, the European presence was concentrated mainly on the coastline, but by the 1740s, large numbers of French and British troops were clashing for the "right" to colonize more of the interior. In the 1750s, during the **Seven Years' War**, the English defeated key Indian allies of the French, after which they turned to the domination of India itself. They easily triumphed over Mughal rulers, although they kept many Mughal states in place as puppets. In a short time, one of the world's mightiest empires would be transformed into a weak colonial possession.

## The Americas

As described in the section above, most of Mesoamerica and South America, and a vast portion of North America, fell under European colonial control in the 1500s. Once-mighty states like the Aztec and Incan empires quickly collapsed due to a combination of European-borne diseases and European military and technological advantages. Various colonial regimes and joint-stock companies came to exert power over both continents.

## War and State Rivalries

A number of Eurasian states during this era experienced what many historians refer to as the **military revolution**: the process by which nations fully incorporated gunpowder weaponry into their way of war, roughly between 1500 and 1700. This did not mean simply adopting cannon and muskets, but completely readjusting one's military methods. It also meant replacing medieval castles with gunpowder fortresses and learning how to safely install cannon on ships. Just as important, it entailed the development of bureaucracies capable of conscripting larger numbers of soldiers, training them, and supplying them with uniforms, gear, and food. Ironically, China, which invented gunpowder, was slowest to undergo this process and only did so partially. The **gunpowder empires** of Ottoman Turkey, Safavid Persia, and Mughal India started off strong in the 1500s, but stagnated in the 1600s and 1700s. It was Europe where military modernization played out most thoroughly and most efficiently—a major cause of its rise to global dominance in the 1700s and 1800s.

Major conflicts of the era erupted over several issues: religious disputes, competition over trade routes, and longstanding territorial rivalries. Franco-Habsburg hostilities divided Europe in the 1500s and early 1600s, as did the **Catholic-Protestant religious wars**, which culminated in the **Thirty Years' War**, from 1618 to 1648. These wars weakened Spain and Austria, but strengthened France, which now engaged in an **Anglo-French rivalry** that lasted from the late 1600s to the early 1800s. The global ramifications of this rivalry were profound: the **Seven Years' War** (1756–1763) raged not only in Europe, but across the globe. A true "world war," it shifted control of Canada and India to Great Britain but also set into motion the chain of events that led to the American Revolution by increasing the costs of defending the American colonies. Other major rivalries include the **Ottoman-European conflict** that played out in southeastern Europe and in the Mediterranean. The advantage here belonged to the Turks during the **1453 conquest of Constantinople** and the campaigns of **Suleiman the Great** in the 1520s. However, the balance tipped permanently in the other direction after the Ottomans' failed **1683 siege of Vienna**. The Indian Ocean basin was the scene of an **Ottoman-Safavid rivalry** over trade and religious differences (Sunni Islam vs. Shiite Islam), as well as the **Omani-European rivalry** for influence over the East African coast. European powers competed with each other over trade routes worldwide. This involved **piracy in the Caribbean**, as well as French, Dutch, and English sparring with the Portuguese and Spanish (and with each other) in many parts of the globe.

# Culture, Science, and Technology, 1450–1750

**13**

→ THE PRINTING PRESS (MOVABLE TYPE, RISING LITERACY)

→ GUNPOWDER AND THE "MILITARY REVOLUTION"

→ MARINE AND NAVIGATIONAL TECHNOLOGY (INCLUDING THE COMPASS AND CARAVEL)

→ THE HELIOCENTRIC THEORY AND THE SCIENTIFIC REVOLUTION

→ WIDENING OF THE SUNNI-SHIITE SPLIT

→ THE PROTESTANT REFORMATION

→ MISSIONARY ACTIVITY AND THE GLOBAL SPREAD OF CHRISTIANITY

→ RELIGIOUS SYNCRETISM (VODUN, LATIN AMERICA'S CULT OF SAINTS, SIKHISM)

→ POLITICAL USES OF ART AND ARCHITECTURE

→ THE RENAISSANCE AND THE ENLIGHTENMENT

→ ISLAMIC MINIATURE PAINTING AND JAPANESE UKIYO-E PRINTS

→ GRIOT STORYTELLERS AND THE *SUNDIATA* EPIC

→ WU CHENGEN, *JOURNEY TO THE WEST*

→ KABUKI THEATER

→ THE TAJ MAHAL

→ CREOLE AND MESTIZO TRADITIONS

→ MESOAMERICAN CODICES

Even more so than during the previous era, cultural sophistication rose worldwide during these years. Virtually everywhere, scientific knowledge and technological expertise improved—although Europe in particular underwent huge changes in this sphere. Artistic and literary traditions took deeper root in their respective states and regions, in some cases building on older traditions and, in other instances, taking advantage of new styles and innovations.

Other—and less gradual—departures from the previous era include the colossal effects of the encounter between Eurasia and the Americas: especially in the Atlantic, between Europe and the New World, new interactions led to a profound fusing and mixing of cultures. Also, significant religious changes occurred in several parts of the world, involving either the appearance of new syncretic faiths or major schisms and conflicts within established ones. Finally, the widening impact of the printing press and a corresponding growth in the infrastructure by which knowledge was spread (publication of books and newspapers, schools and other educational institutions, and so on) meant that general levels of literacy rose, and also that art and ideas exercised much greater influence over a greater number of people than ever before.

# SCIENTIFIC AND TECHNOLOGICAL INNOVATION

## The Impact of the Printing Press

One of the most transformative technologies of this era, if not of all time, was the **printing press**, a feasible, movable-type version of which was invented by Johannes Gutenberg in the 1430s.

Starting in Europe and eventually winning a place for itself throughout Eurasia and even in the Americas, the printing press exerted a steadily growing influence over the way information was disseminated over great distances and to large audiences. Thanks to the printing press, literary works, scientific theories and discoveries, religious debates, and new ideas in general spread more rapidly and more widely than had ever been possible in previous centuries. By creating more materials to read, and more incentive to read, the printing press helped to elevate literacy rates—quickly among the upper and middle classes, but gradually among the lower classes as well. The press's spinoff effects, which typically included the expansion of a given society's network of libraries, publishers, schools, universities, and museums, further boosted the power of ideas and new knowledge to affect historical events.

## Gunpowder and Marine/Navigational Technology

Aside from printing, the technologies with the biggest global impact during this era were gunpowder weaponry and advances in marine and navigational technology. Although **gunpowder weaponry** had originated in China during the 1100s and spread to the Middle East and Europe during the 1200s and 1300s, it was not until the 1400s and afterward that it fundamentally changed warfare. Several parts of Eurasia—most notably Europe, but also the so-called gunpowder empires in Turkey, Persia, and India—experienced what some historians refer to as a **gunpowder revolution**, in which states learned to deploy cannon and hand-held weapons like muskets in sieges and battles, to build new fortresses better able than medieval castles to withstand cannon attacks, and, in the case of Europe, to create oceangoing ships capable of traveling vast distances and carrying gunpowder weapons. The incorporation of gunpowder weaponry led to the formation of huge armies consisting of infantry soldiers (as opposed to more expensive and increasingly old-fashioned cavalry), thereby increasing the social and economic burdens of war, and the enormous costs involved with converting to the new style of warfare—not to mention conscripting and supplying ever-larger armies—provided many states with the crucial incentive they needed to centralize their political systems and to modernize their bureaucracies and tax-gathering systems.

With respect to **marine and navigational technology**, the most dramatic changes were felt in Europe. Here, homegrown innovations combined with others that had arrived from China via the Middle East, all of them joining together to launch the **European age of exploration** described in Chapter 12. From the east had already come the **astrolabe**, which measured latitude, and the magnetic **compass** for determining direction. During the Renaissance, the Europeans improved their knowledge of cartography and astronomy: **better maps** and more precise understanding of the stars' movements further advanced their navigational skills. Finally—after centuries of relying on oared galleys in the Mediterranean and on sailing ships that were clumsy and incapable of venturing far from shore—the Europeans learned to build sturdy and maneuverable **sailing ships** that could travel far out into the open ocean. These vessels had deeper keels for greater stability, **sternpost rudders** (a highly effective steering system first used in China), and **lateen sails** on several masts with complex systems of rigging (unlike square sails on a single mast, these allowed boats to sail in the direction they needed to even in unfavorable winds). Of the new models that appeared in the 1400s and 1500s, the one that first enabled true oceanic exploration was the **caravel**, largely invented by the Portuguese, who combined square sails with lateen sails for better control over direction. Larger ships like the carrack and galleon quickly followed, and all of them were used for purposes of trade and war alike.

## Europe's Scientific Revolution

Relative to other civilizations during this era, Europe enjoyed the most explosive increase in scientific and technological aptitude. Already during the Renaissance, certain scholars were moving away from the intellectual orthodoxy of the Middle Ages, in which a fixed set of ideas taken from certain ancient Greek and Roman thinkers were combined with Catholic doctrine.

During the mid-1500s, despite the Catholic Church's continued control over European intellectual life, individuals such as the Polish astronomer **Nicolaus Copernicus** began to cross important scientific boundaries. Copernicus provided mathematical proof for the **heliocentric theory**, according to which the earth and other planets revolve around the sun. This ran counter to the standard wisdom, in which the earth sat at the center of the universe. Handed down by the Greek scientist Ptolemy, this geocentric theory found favor with religious authorities in Europe, especially the Catholic papacy, because it placed human beings—God's greatest creation, in the Christian view—at the heart of all existence. It took more than another century after Copernicus published his findings for the heliocentric theory to be accepted as fact throughout Europe.

The pace of scientific discovery accelerated during the 1600s and early 1700s, which are commonly spoken of as a time of **Scientific Revolution**. Early in the 1600s, thinkers such as René Descartes of France and Roger Bacon of England laid the groundwork for formal logic and the modern **scientific method**, in which observation and experimentation are used to prove theoretical hypotheses. In a way, this revived the mode of scientific thinking that had arisen among the ancient Greeks, but it was more systematic and rigorous.

Also in the 1600s, the German astronomer Johannes Kepler and the Italian physicist **Galileo** confirmed and popularized Copernicus's theories. In doing so, they ran afoul of the Catholic Church. Galileo was tried by the Inquisition and forced to reject his own scientific conclusions in public; his scientific writings remained on the Church's index of forbidden books for centuries. Although some Protestant clergy rejected the new science, Protestant nations such as England and the Dutch Republic were still safer havens for scientific pioneers. Only in the 1700s did it become less risky for those in Catholic countries to challenge church doctrine.

Many of the ideas behind the modern understanding of science were discovered or proven during the Scientific Revolution. They include the states of matter (liquid, gas, or solid), the question of whether light consists of waves or particles, the fact that living creatures are made of cells, the concept of the vacuum, and the science of statistics. Zoological and botanical taxonomy—the modern system of classifying animals and plants—began during the early 1700s. Among the scientific instruments invented or perfected during the 1600s and 1700s were the telescope, the microscope, the pendulum clock, the thermometer, and the barometer.

**NOTE**

Europe was not alone in clinging to a geocentric understanding of astronomy. Ptolemy, geocentrism's originator, was just as respected in the Muslim world as he was in pre-Copernican Europe. Astronomers in other parts of the world, including China and India, concluded that the sun, stars, and planets revolved around the earth. Apart from the handful of ancient Greeks who opposed Ptolemy's geocentric views, no one prior to Copernicus, either in Europe or elsewhere, appears to have considered heliocentrism a real scientific possibility.

**Isaac Newton** (1642–1727) of England represents the Scientific Revolution at its peak. Newton is famous for the laws of motion, his thoughts on the concept of gravity, and as one of the two mathematicians who invented the system of calculus. Just as important is the fact that Newton, more than any other figure of the Scientific Revolution, understood scientific thought as a totality. He took the discoveries of his day and tied them together into a single system of thought—Newtonian physics—backed up by mathematical proof. Newton's book *Principia* (1687) is considered to be among the most influential scholarly treatises ever written, and not until Einstein's theory of relativity in the early 1900s would his fundamental principles be seriously challenged or altered.

Globally speaking, the Renaissance, the Scientific Revolution, and the Enlightenment (see below) furthered the intellectual growth of Europe to the point that, by the 1700s, it was overtaking civilizations that had been more advanced at the beginning of this era, such as China, Persia, and Ottoman Turkey—not just in a scholarly sense, but in terms of technology and global power.

## RELIGIOUS DEVELOPMENTS

Although religious beliefs and practices diversified in many ways during this period—even to the point of including publicly declared atheism in certain places—religion remained central to the lives of most people. As noted further in Chapter 12, religion served as the cause of numerous wars and other conflicts, and it continued to be used for political purposes, mainly to justify regimes and rulers.

### Divisions: New Sects and Denominations

Within established religions, several major schisms appeared or widened. As Buddhism spread throughout Asia, for example, the rift grew wider between older **Theravada**, or Hinayana, schools of thought, which emphasized simplicity and meditation and were more popular in South Asia, and newer **Mahayana** denominations, which predominated in East Asia and put more of a premium on rituals, deities, and concepts of an afterlife. And even among Mahayana traditions, approaches like **Zen** (Ch'an in China) differed greatly from sects like Pure Land.

In the Muslim world as well, existing divisions deepened. Sufism, the mystical strain within Islam, continued to flourish after taking root between the 900s and the 1300s, emphasizing communion with Allah over doctrinal strictness. Far more disruptive than that was the hardening of the **Sunni-Shiite split**, which, since the mid-600s, had divided most Muslims from the minority who viewed Mohammed's son-in-law Ali, not the Umayyad caliphs, as Mohammed's rightful successor. Largely due to the way it took hold in Safavid Persia, Shiism's differences from the Sunni majority became even more pronounced than before. Shiite Muslims, who form a majority in what is now Iran, and a sizable minority in many other places, believe that correct interpretations of Islamic doctrine and Sharia law flow from the teachings of 12 religious authorities called **imams** (a term also used by Sunnis, but in a different sense), and this now-standard version of Shiism is often referred to as "Twelver Shiism." The imams include Ali and the 11 leaders who followed him until the mid-800s. The Twelfth Imam is considered by Shiites not to have died, but to have entered a hidden spiritual state—from which he is someday supposed to return as a messiah figure known as the Mahdi. Tensions between Sunnis and Shiites persisted throughout this era, paralleling in many respects the ongoing conflict between the Ottoman Empire, a Sunni state, and Safavid Persia.

Europe experienced its own religious earthquake during this era: the **Protestant Reformation**, which affected not just matters of faith, but culture, politics, and the way Europeans spread Christianity to other parts of the world. Prior to the 1500s, two established denominations wielded religious authority over Europe: Eastern Orthodoxy, which prevailed in and around Byzantium, and Roman Catholicism, which dominated the larger central and western parts of the continent. During the 1300s and 1400s, both churches suffered a series of grave crises. In the east, Byzantium's gradual weakening, followed by its destruction in 1453, left Orthodoxy politically weakened and confined mainly to Europe's Slavic and Balkan periphery. In Catholic Europe, the power and prestige of the papacy waned, thanks first to its forced transfer from Rome to the French city of Avignon for most of the 1300s, and then to several decades of confusing and painful rivalry between two papacies, each of which claimed allegiance from all Catholics. Even after the restoration of a single pope to Rome, the situation worsened during the 1400s, this time due to growing corruption within the Catholic hierarchy. Church offices were sold, not earned by merit, and certificates of forgiveness for sins (indulgences) were granted in exchange for money. All this caused many people to view the church as hypocritical and overly concerned with wealth and power. Much of this growing willingness to address problems with the Church had to do with the questioning spirit of the **Renaissance**. Until the early 1500s, however, Catholic authorities were able to crush any opposition.

This changed in 1517, when a German monk, **Martin Luther**, protested the sale of indulgences in his hometown. In his Ninety-Five Theses, Luther launched a general attack against church abuses and certain parts of Catholic doctrine. When he refused the pope's order to retract his criticisms, he was excommunicated and threatened with arrest and death. Now a fugitive, Luther took shelter with sympathetic political figures and, in the 1520s, founded a new church: Lutheranism, the first of Europe's major Protestant denominations.

With the **Protestant Reformation** under way, other movements soon emerged, with the **printing press** playing a key role in spreading new religious ideas across Europe. The French scholar **John Calvin** established a theocratic community in the Swiss city of Geneva and preached an even stricter form of Protestantism. Calvinist denominations caught on in France (the Huguenots, an oppressed minority), the Dutch Republic (the Reformed Church), parts of England (the Puritans), and Scotland (the Presbyterians). In England, Henry VIII formed the Protestant **Church of England**, also known as the **Anglican Church**. Many beliefs and practices separated Protestants from Catholics. The former favored institutional simplicity, in contrast to the bureaucracy of the Catholic Church, and sacraments were less important to them as well. Protestants did not venerate the saints or the Virgin Mary the way Catholics did, and they allowed their clergy to marry. Most important was the concept of **salvation by grace**, the belief that only God's forgiveness—not good works, observance of rituals, or the power of the pope—could bring a worshipper to heaven. (Calvin's doctrine of predestination took this idea further, arguing that whether a person would be saved or not was known to God from the beginning of time.) Protestants conducted their services in their own languages, as opposed to Latin, and—unlike Catholics—they were encouraged to read scripture for themselves. This resulted in the translation of the Bible into numerous languages, and it made education and literacy a particular priority among many Protestant populations.

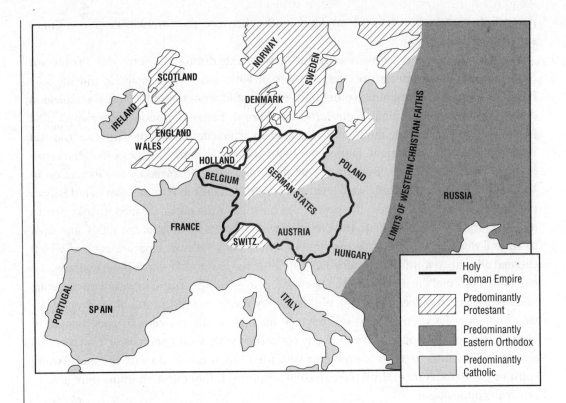

**Religious Divisions in Europe, ca. 1600.**
For centuries, Christianity had been divided into two large denominations, Eastern Orthodoxy and Roman Catholicism. In most of Europe, the latter had predominated. Starting with the Protestant Reformation in 1517, new religious rifts began to appear. By the end of the 1500s, western and northern Europe were divided into Catholic and Protestant camps, as shown in this map.

In the mid-1500s, in response to the Protestant Reformation, the Catholic Church subjected itself to a process of change called the **Catholic Counter-Reformation**. On one hand, it eliminated the worst of its corruption. On the other, it reaffirmed the authority of the pope, gave new powers to the Holy Inquisition, and created an Index of Forbidden Books that remained in place until the 1960s. As described in Chapter 12, Europe suffered a series of **religious wars** between the 1520s and the 1640s, as Catholic monarchs tried in vain to stem, and even reverse, the spread of Protestantism.

## Missionary Activity and Syncretism

In conjunction with trade and colonization, **missionary activity** did much during these years to spread certain faiths over wide distances. Throughout Asia, this was a time of especially active proselytization of Buddhism, and other religions extended their reach in this manner as well.

Christianity experienced the era's most massive growth. The **global spread of Christianity** went hand-in-hand with Europe's campaign of worldwide exploration and colonization, starting in the late 1400s and continuing throughout the rest of this period. Not long after the Portuguese and Spanish reached South and East Asia, Catholic priests—including the Jesuit **Francis Xavier**—brought Christianity to both regions. Christian missionaries won a surprising number of converts in Asia, even though in some cases, political leaders reacted to the new religion with hostility, either immediately or eventually. Even more dramatic was the extent to which Christianity was imported to North and South America, first by the Catholic Spanish and Portuguese, then also by French Catholics and Protestant English and Dutch. Christianity's presence on both hemispheres represented a truly remarkable change in the history of religions. The almost monolithic **Catholicization of Latin America** remains as a particular testament to the power of this change.

Another prominent trend of the time was the development of new **syncretic religions**, or faiths that emerged from the blending of two or more religions' traditions. Many of these arose from Europe's colonization of the New World, as well as the forcible transfer of African slaves there. One example is **vodun** (popularly known as "voodoo"), which developed among African-descended populations throughout the Caribbean and the Gulf of Mexico, due to the mixing of animistic spirit worship from West Africa not just with animistic practices native to the Americas, but also with elements drawn from Christianity. Similarly, native traditions in Latin America combined with Catholicism to create a **cult of saints**, in which indigenous worshippers came to identify their own polytheistic gods and goddesses with the large array of saints venerated by Catholics. Encouraging, or at least tolerating, this logic made it easier for Spanish and Portuguese missionaries to win converts in the Americas. In Mexico, for example, Aztecs and other Nahuatl-speaking natives equated Mary, the mother of Jesus, with their own mother goddess, giving rise in the 1500s and 1600s to stories and icons of the **Virgin of Guadalupe**—a much-loved depiction of Mary as a native girl and even today a symbol of central importance in Mexican Catholicism.

**NOTE**

In Asia, the spread of Christianity sometimes provoked official backlashes. During the late 1500s and early 1600s, Japan's rulers occasionally persecuted or even executed Christians, and essentially shut the religion out after imposing their national seclusion policy in the 1630s. China's emperors tolerated Christianity until 1724, when they banned it officially. By contrast, in places like the Philippines, which was colonized by the Spanish between the 1520s and the 1890s, large segments of the population became devout Christians.

**The Virgin of Guadalupe**
As Catholicism came to Mexico, tales arose in the 1500s and 1600s of a peasant boy who had a vision of the Virgin Mary in the form of a young girl who spoke Nahuatl—the indigenous language—and had native features. The location of her sighting happened to be a key place of worship for the Nahuatl mother goddess, and the emergence of a distinctly New World version of an Old World Catholic figure is a classic instance of religious syncretism.

While many consider **Sikhism** to have emerged as an independent tradition, it is categorized by others as a syncretic faith, joining certain aspects of Hindu theology with the monotheism associated with Islam. Whatever label one gives it, Sikhism was founded in the late 1400s, in the Punjab region of India, by **Guru Nanak**. The ten Sikh gurus, who led the religion until the death of the tenth guru in 1708, taught that meditation and virtuous behavior would help worshippers penetrate the veil of maya, or worldly illusion, and thereby come to know Waheguru, or the one true god. Originally a relatively pacifistic faith, Sikhism embraced a warrior culture during the seventeenth century because of growing persecution, particularly during the late 1600s, when the emperor killed the guru and provoked the creation of a powerful Sikh army called the Khalsa. Over time, Sikhism has grown into one of the world's largest organized religions, with almost 30 million followers.

## TRENDS IN ART, LITERATURE, AND ARCHITECTURE

### General Developments

By this point in time, major societies worldwide had well-defined artistic and literary (or oral) traditions. Increased technological aptitude enabled the production of arts and crafts of high quality. In areas where the printing press was adopted, the availability of written works expanded considerably.

**Cultural interaction** continued as it had in previous centuries but received an extra boost during these years from Europe's campaigns of exploration, and especially from the movement of Europeans and Africans to North and South America. The arrival of European merchants and colonizers in Africa and Asia affected local cultures, and Europeans in turn were influenced by the arts and crafts brought back from these far-off places. Even more dramatic, however, was the **transatlantic impact on the Americas**, whose languages, religions, artistic traditions, and music were all profoundly reshaped by the importation of European and African culture. As described in Chapters 15 and 16, even the very ethnicity of the Americas was changed, with **mixed populations** of various types appearing over time.

The **political use of art and architecture** likewise continued. Impressive artworks and buildings showed off the power and grandeur of various rulers and regimes, and helped to legitimate them as well. Cultural patronage, the organizing of elaborate court dances, and the staging of musical or dramatic performances all contributed to the same goals. Key examples from this era of how architectural masterpieces served political purposes include the French palace of **Versailles** (built by Louis XIV to demonstrate his power as an absolute monarch and avidly imitated by other European rulers), China's **Summer Palace** (an exquisite garden complex constructed near Beijing by the Qing emperors), and the **Red Fort** in Delhi (the residence of the Mughal emperors, erected by Shah Jahan, who also commissioned the Taj Mahal).

Particularly in Afro-Eurasia, the **availability of culture** steadily widened. Not just elite members of society, but merchant and middle classes—and in some cases the lower classes—enjoyed greater access to art, literature, and musical and dramatic performances. As merchants earned bigger profits, and as states improved their tax-collecting capabilities, more money was there to be spent on art, expanding the cultural marketplace. As print technology became more commonplace, written works became easier and cheaper to produce, and literacy increased as a result. With the passage of time, genres of art and literature specifically targeted toward popular audiences began to appear.

Further examples of all these trends are included in the following section.

**Palace of Versailles, ca. 1688**
Built by Louis XIV of France, the stunning palace of Versailles, with acres of gardens and its famous Hall of Mirrors, communicated wealth and majesty to all onlookers. Intended by Louis to serve as an architectural embodiment of his political might, Versailles served as a model for other European monarchs of the era, who sought to build their own palaces to convey the same message.

## Cultural Innovations by Region

In Europe, the **Renaissance**, which had begun in Italy during the late 1200s and early 1300s (as described in Chapter 8), spread to the rest of Europe and continued until the early 1600s. By the late 1400s and early 1500s, Italy was in the midst of the High Renaissance—the era of Michelangelo and Leonardo da Vinci—while the **northern Renaissance** featured the Dutch philosopher Erasmus (known for his religious debates with Luther, as well as his satirical novel *In Praise of Folly*), the English scholar Thomas More (who invented the term *utopia* in his book of the same name and lost his life to Henry VIII by remaining Catholic in the face of the king's Anglicanism), the Spanish novelist **Miguel de Cervantes** (author of *Don Quixote*, the tale of an aged knight bewildered by the changes caused by Europe's transition away from the medieval period), and the English poet and playwright **William Shakespeare**. Novels like Cervantes's and theatrical productions like Shakespeare's are prominent examples of art forms that catered to all classes, not just the elite. So are the paintings and other artworks commissioned by increasingly prosperous **merchant and middle-class patrons**, both during the Renaissance and the eras that followed.

The cultural style that followed the Renaissance was the **baroque**, which dominated European painting, architecture, and music from the early 1600s through the early to mid-1700s. Baroque culture emphasized the bold, the dynamic, and the colorful, and was often used by political and religious elites to impress the public and to legitimize their policies. During the 1700s, Europe, as well as its colonies in the Americas, experienced what came to be known as the **Enlightenment**: a philosophical and intellectual movement that put full confidence in the power of rational thought to solve social and political problems and to understand the wider world. Inspired by the Scientific Revolution and by certain philosophers from the late 1600s—particularly **John Locke** of England—Enlightenment thinkers prided themselves on logic and progressive ideas, and they provided much of the intellectual justification for the American and French revolutions in the late 1700s. The Enlightenment is discussed further in Chapter 18.

Although the leading states of the Middle East—Ottoman Turkey and Safavid Persia— allowed their technological and scientific edge over Europe to slip away by the end of this era, they both displayed cultural brilliance throughout. During this period, Islamic culture as a whole was dominated by a synthesis of Arabic, Turkish, and Persian elements, with the last proving especially influential. Ottoman architectural innovation reached its peak during the 1500s and early 1600s, due mainly to Mimar Sinan, who designed more than eighty mosques with large domes and tall, thin minarets. (It was one of Sinan's students who built the renowned **Blue Mosque** in Istanbul.) Both in Turkey and Persia, **carpet-weaving** stood out as a key art form and also as a profitable enterprise that generated a high volume of foreign trade. Most distinctive, however, was the tradition of **miniature painting**, which arose in Persia during the 1300s and 1400s, then spread to the Ottoman Empire and Mughal India in the early 1500s. These vibrantly colored illustrations, collected in albums called *muraqqas*, featured many subjects, including portraits, because the traditional disapproval of depicting human subjects had always been weaker in Persia than in Arabia and the areas neighboring it. Despite their exceptional skill, Ottoman and Persian miniaturists did not strive for the same level of exact realism as Renaissance artists in Europe did, or apply the laws of perspective as rigorously as they did. This was largely due to their religious-philosophical conviction that the physical world was imperfect, and that art should present a more idealized (and thus slightly non-realistic) version of reality. The most famous miniatures were produced at the Herat and Tabriz workshops in Persia, and in the Topkapi Palace in Istanbul. The best-remembered Ottoman painters are Nakkas Osman (late 1500s) and Levni (early 1700s).

**The Blue Mosque, Istanbul, Turkey.**
Officially the Sultan Ahmed Mosque, this seventeenth-century masterpiece is popularly known as the Blue Mosque. One of the great landmarks of Istanbul, the Blue Mosque is unusual in having six minarets, rather than the usual four.

The diversity of traditions in Africa makes it difficult to generalize about art and culture there, but **sculpture** and **carving** remained dominant during this era, as they had in earlier years. Many materials were used, including wood, metal, and **ivory**. Much of this art was **abstract**—deliberately avoiding the replication of visual reality—long before the concept of abstraction gained popularity among artists in places like Europe. **Textile arts** and **basketry** were also prominent during these years, often featuring highly complex geometric patterns. African architecture came to be gradually influenced by Arabs and European colonists, who built fortresses and residences along the coasts of East and West Africa. Where tales, songs, and poems were concerned, the **oral tradition** far overshadowed written works, which were rare. As noted in Chapter 8, professional storytellers—known in West Africa as **griots** or djeli (and elsewhere by other titles)—acted as entertainers, historians, musicians, and, in some cases, advisers to kings and rulers. As before, the most famous African saga during these years was the ***Sundiata*** epic, a fictionalized account of the adventures and accomplishments of the chieftain who, in real life, founded the Mali empire in the 1200s. Sundiata's tale took shape during the 1300s and remained popular for centuries afterward.

In East Asia, the artistic and cultural dynamism of China's Ming dynasty (1368–1644) continued. As described in Chapter 8, the Ming were famous for their fine **porcelain**, as well as literary masterpieces like Wu Chengen's ***Journey to the West***. This highly successful novel, published in the late 1500s, narrates the travels of the seventh-century monk Xuanzang to India, but in the form of an adventure fantasy starring the half-beast Monkey King as Xuanzang's companion. Part of *Journey*'s appeal was that its author, rather than imitating old-fashioned prose from earlier dynasties, wrote in a style that matched how people in his own time spoke. This made *Journey* accessible to the middle classes, not just elite audiences. As China moved into the Qing era, its cultural attainments included the construction in the mid-1700s of the beautiful **Summer Palace** outside Beijing. Also in East Asia, Japan's transition from civil war in the 1400s and 1500s to unification under the Tokugawa shogunate (1603–1868) brought about certain cultural changes. On one hand, Japan's samurai class maintained many of the traditions and styles mentioned in Chapter 8. On the other, new art forms arose in response to the growing wealth of merchants and the urban classes in general. Especially popular was **kabuki theater**, which featured acrobatics, swordplay, and scenes of city life—and contrasted greatly with the older, more elegant Noh drama favored by the upper classes. Thanks to woodblock printing, **ukiyo-e** painting became affordable and, like kabuki, was driven largely by urban, middle-class tastes.

The highlight of South Asian culture during these years was the fusion of Indian traditions and Persian influences that took place under the Islamic Mughal emperors who ruled from Agra and Delhi, beginning in the early 1500s. As in Ottoman Turkey and Safavid Persia, **miniature painting** caught on here as a dominant art form. The 1600s were also an age of architectural magnificence in South Asia, as illustrated by India's most famous landmark, the **Taj Mahal**, the white marble mausoleum built in Agra by Shah Jahan in memory of his wife. It was also on Shah Jahan's initiative that the mammoth **Red Fort** was constructed as a royal residence in Delhi.

**Ukiyo-e print of an actor, by Kiyotada (early 1700s)**
Literally meaning "pictures of the floating world," ukiyo-e woodblock prints were easily mass-produced and increasingly affordable to middle-class and urban audiences. They featured portraits of actors and geisha courtesans, scenes of city life, landscapes, and similar subjects.

In countless ways, the arrival of European conquerors and colonists—and the slaves they brought from Africa—affected cultural life in the Americas. This blending of European, African, and indigenous elements gave rise to **creole and mestizo traditions**, along with other "mixed" cultures, with a powerful impact on language, religion, music, and art. In addition, the Europeans' arrival caused literature and writing to assume widespread importance for the first time in a region where written scripts had been extremely rare over the course of many centuries. An interesting example of the interchange between native and European literary practices can be found in the **Mesoamerican codices** written in the Aztec lands during the 1500s, after the Spanish conquest. Approximately five hundred of these texts survive, written by Aztec converts to Catholicism, partly in Nahuatl, partly in Spanish, and partly in Latin. They combine the pre-Columbian tradition of codex-painting and the European emphasis on writing, and they address many subjects, including translations of Aztec pictograms, explanations of Aztec beliefs and customs (religious practices, folk medicine, the calendar system), and occasionally complaints about Spanish abuses.

# Economic Systems, 1450–1750

14

→ **THE IMPACT OF EUROPE'S AGE OF EXPLORATION ON EXISTING TRADE ROUTES**

→ **THE INDIAN OCEAN BASIN AND ASIAN TRADE**

→ **ECONOMIC EFFECTS OF THE COLUMBIAN EXCHANGE**

→ **EMERGENCE OF THE ATLANTIC SYSTEM (TRIANGULAR TRADE)**

→ **INFLUX OF PRECIOUS METALS (SILVER) FROM THE AMERICAS INTO THE WORLD ECONOMY**

→ **FISHING, WHALING, SEA-MAMMAL HUNTING, FUR HUNTING**

→ **MONOPOLY CHARTERS AND JOINT-STOCK COMPANIES (DUTCH EAST INDIA COMPANY, BRITISH EAST INDIA COMPANY, HUDSON'S BAY COMPANY)**

→ **PIRACY AND STATE COMPETITION OVER TRADE (CARIBBEAN PIRACY, OTTOMAN-PERSIAN COMPETITION, OMANI-EUROPEAN RIVALRY)**

→ **INCREASED AGRICULTURAL PRODUCTION**

→ **THE RISE OF MANUFACTURING AND PROTO-INDUSTRIALIZATION**

→ **MERCANTILISM VS. CAPITALISM**

→ **ECONOMIC RELIANCE ON COERCED LABOR**

The incorporation of the Americas into Afro-Eurasia's existing networks of exchange led to the emergence, for the first time in history, of a truly global economic system. Raw materials and finished products now circulated globally, and the worldwide demand for both grew steadily.

Modes of production also changed during this period. Among the world's settled societies, the vast majority of people worked as agriculturalists and lived in rural settings. This continued to be the case until well into the industrial era, and agricultural production increased throughout these years. At the same time, though, other sectors of the economy expanded. Trade, banking, and manufacturing became more important during these years, generating a great deal of wealth and encouraging significant growth among urban populations.

Interregional trade and agricultural production were both affected during these years by the global cooling that caused the Little Ice Age.

## THE EARLY GLOBALIZATION OF ECONOMICS

By extending Europe's physical and commercial reach directly to Africa and Asia, and also by bringing Afro-Eurasia into permanent contact with the Americas, the **European age of exploration** exerted a profound impact on the world economy—making it possible to speak of an early stage of economic globalization.

## Changing Trade Routes and New Trade Goods

Europe's encounter with the Americas, combined with its newfound ability to voyage to Asia and the Indian Ocean basin, dramatically reshaped existing patterns of interregional trade. Certain trade routes became less relevant. The most notable example was the **Silk Road**, which never fell into complete disuse, but, because of the relative slowness and expense of overland transport compared to overseas transport, declined in importance after the 1500s.

Seaborne trade in the **Indian Ocean basin** (and the Pacific regions closest to it) increased in volume, and was also altered by the Europeans' arrival in the 1400s and 1500s. The Portuguese came first, establishing a **trading-post empire** that consisted of ports along the African coast and wherever in Asia they were strong enough to conquer or persuasive enough to negotiate territorial concessions. Key possessions included **Oman** on the Arabian peninsula; **Zanzibar** and Mombasa in East Africa; Goa in India; **Melaka** (Malacca) on the Malay peninsula; and Macau in China. Following the Portuguese in the late 1500s and 1600s—and in some cases replacing them—were the Dutch, English, and French, all of whom were firmly entrenched in the Indian Ocean, and in Asia generally, by the early 1700s. Europe's colonial presence in Asia was still quite small, and for the most part, its economic role involved moving goods from one Asian market to another, or of pumping silver into Asian economies in exchange for goods to sell back home. These activities—especially the **influx of silver**—had a noticeable impact on the region, but just as important was the precedent set by the Europeans as, early on, they worked to gain thorough and widespread control of Indian Ocean sea lanes—at first to combat piracy, and then to compete against one another, as well as against Muslim fleets. No state had ever attempted this before, and naval escalation of this sort paved the way for a larger European military presence in Asia, and eventually for full-scale colonization there.

Although the Europeans learned how to cross the Pacific in the early 1500s, their direct impact on it remained comparatively light for the time being, and the ocean itself was too big for a true trans-Pacific economy to form during this period. By contrast, a full-fledged **Atlantic system of trade** quickly sprang into being. The **Columbian Exchange**, whose environmental impact is described in Chapter 16, introduced a large assortment of trade goods to the global economy—whether they were extracted from the New World or transplanted to it. Aside from staple foodstuffs taken from the Americas (like **manioc**, **corn**, and **potatoes**), cacao and tobacco became desirable luxury goods. Of the crops introduced by Europeans to the Americas, several had a mammoth impact on world trade: the arrival of coffee in the 1700s was noteworthy, but most important were **cotton** and **sugarcane**. Immensely profitable, both crops required backbreaking labor to cultivate, and the lightning rise and expansion of the Atlantic slave trade was due primarily to growing demand for each of these goods.

Two other aspects of Atlantic trade had global consequences. First, during the 1500s and 1600s, Spanish and Portuguese extraction of precious metals—especially silver—from the Americas affected economies around the world. The huge and sudden influx of silver and gold bullion into so many places at once created a harmful glut of precious metals throughout Afro-Eurasia. Severe inflation resulted not just in Europe, but in places as diverse as North Africa and China.

Second, during the 1600s and 1700s, the expansion of European wealth became increasingly dependent on the Atlantic commercial network known as the **triangular trade system**. Here, European manufactured goods (metalware, cotton textiles, firearms, and processed alcohol such as gin and rum) would be brought to Africa's west coast and exchanged for gold, ivory, and slaves. The voyage would continue to the Americas, where the slaves were sold in exchange for sugar, tobacco, furs, cotton, and other raw materials. These, along with the gold and ivory from Africa, would be shipped back to Europe. The centrality of the Atlantic slave trade to this system—and of coerced labor to this era's economic growth in general—should be noted.

Another economic byproduct of European exploration was a tremendous rise in the harvesting of animal products over vast distances. **Fishing** and **whaling** led European ships to venture throughout the Atlantic, and into Arctic waters where possible. **Sea mammal hunting**—for walrus ivory and for the oil and pelts of seals—escalated sharply, as did **fur hunting**, which played an enormous role in the settlement of remote regions like Canada and Siberia.

## Controlling Trade: Companies and Competition

The exploration and exploitation of newfound lands was expensive and represented an extremely risky investment. It was therefore rarely paid for by governments, at least not directly.

Instead, mariners, merchants, explorers, and investors tended to operate under **monopoly charters** awarded by the state. Those given the charter assumed the costs and risks of exploration or of trade that required long voyaging. In return, they enjoyed exclusive rights to profit from new territories or markets—although all new discoveries were considered to belong to the nation granting the charter, and a share of earnings might be owed to the government. For example, early Spanish conquistadors handed over to the state a portion of the wealth they gained in the New World, and all trade and resources extracted from the Spanish Americas had to pass through the state-run **Board of Trade** in Seville. In Russia, the mapping and settlement of Siberia was begun by merchant clans authorized by the tsars to search eastward for precious metals and fur-bearing animals.

Elsewhere in Europe, a common way to share the expenses and the risks involved with exploration and overseas trade was to form **joint-stock companies**: early forerunners of the modern corporation, in which investors pooled their funds and received a share of the profit based on the size of their investment. Among the first of these was the Muscovy Company, founded in England during the mid-1500s to carry out trade with Russia via the Arctic port of Arkhangelsk. During the 1600s, nations such as Britain, the Netherlands, and France founded numerous joint-stock companies to oversee commercial and colonial interests in the West Indies, in North America, and in the East Indies. Among the most famous and influential were the **British East India Company** (1600), the Dutch East India Company (1602), the Company of New France (1664), and the **Hudson's Bay Company** (1670). Not only were such entities in the business of making money, they often became chiefly or even solely responsible for carrying out their home nation's political and strategic will in overseas regions.

Competition over trade routes led to tension and even armed conflict, both among European powers and between Europeans and non-Europeans. **Piracy** was common, especially in the Caribbean, the Indian Ocean, and the waters of Southeast Asia, and also along Asia's Pacific coast. As they competed against each other, particularly in the Atlantic and the Caribbean, European states relied not just on their navies, but also on the practice of **privateering**, or the licensing of captains who owned their vessels privately to capture enemy ships or raid enemy ports and outposts. (The line between piracy and privateering was typically very thin.) In Asian waters, Malay and Japanese pirates were a particular concern, and when the Chinese government allowed the Portuguese to establish themselves in Macau, it was principally to reward them for their role in suppressing piracy in the region.

There are several important trade- and colony-related rivalries to be aware of. One is the Anglo-Dutch and Anglo-French competition over parts of North America—the New York area in the case of the former, Canada in the case of the latter—both won by the English in the 1600s and 1700s. Also, most European powers quarreled over island colonies and shipping lanes in the Caribbean, or "West Indies." Southeast Asia and the Indian subcontinent became an arena of competition during the late 1500s and 1600s, as the Spanish and especially the Portuguese, who had inserted themselves into these economies earlier in the 1500s, were now elbowed aside by the Dutch, French, and English. As more time passed, the Dutch cemented their presence in the "Spice Islands" (in and around present-day Indonesia), while the English, during the 1700s, managed to enlarge their presence in India at the expense of the French.

The Indian Ocean as a whole witnessed a great deal of trade-related rivalry during the 1600s and 1700s. Aside from their concern about European encroachments into the region, the Ottoman Empire and Safavid Persia dueled for economic influence over this region. Also important was the **Omani-European rivalry** that erupted in the mid-1600s, as the Arab state of Oman rebelled against Portuguese colonial rule. Not only did the Omanis expel the Portuguese from their own territory, they pushed the Portuguese out of Swahili ports such as Zanzibar and ruled them as their own for many decades. Also for a time, the Omani empire competed with the British East India Company and other European commercial entities attempting to break into Indian Ocean markets during the 1600s and 1700s.

## FROM MERCANTILISM TO CAPITALISM AND PROTO-INDUSTRIALIZATION

Agriculture remained the world's dominant mode of economic production during these years. Even so, this era witnessed many profound changes with respect to how crops were grown and goods produced.

In the agricultural sphere, production vastly increased during these years, even though much of the world, especially in the northern hemisphere, was affected by the Little Ice Age. Many factors caused this rise in production. Crops transplanted as a result of the **Columbian Exchange** tended to flourish in their new homes, especially in the case of **corn**, **potatoes**, and **manioc** brought to Afro-Eurasia from the Americas. More land was brought under cultivation during this period, especially in those parts of the Americas colonized by Europeans. The **improvement of agricultural methods** also played a role: better fertilizers came into wider use, and the scientific rotation of crops and fields—which kept soil from becoming depleted too quickly or easily—was practiced more commonly.

Growth was just as dramatic in other sectors of the economy. **Trade** and **banking** became more important than ever before, with **merchant classes** earning great wealth and rising to positions of social, cultural, and political prominence. **Manufacturing** expanded as well, with artisan and craftsman classes growing in size and importance. Worldwide, most manufacturing continued to be done by hand and on a small scale. Still, by the 1600s and especially the 1700s, there was a noticeable rise in machine-assisted production, cottage industry, and other forms of manufacturing that can be considered proto-industrial. This **proto-industrialization**—most prominent in Europe, but also present elsewhere—helped to lay the groundwork for actual industrialization in the late 1700s and 1800s.

Whether or not they used the term, the dominant economic philosophy in most advanced societies, particularly in Europe, tended to be **mercantilism**. Mercantilist states viewed all other nations as rivals and aimed to be self-sufficient. They believed that state control over all economic activity was desirable, and if they possessed colonies, they viewed them as economic extensions of the homeland: as a source of raw materials, and as a market for manufactured goods. By contrast, a new economic concept was beginning to catch on by the second half of the 1700s, at least in Europe. This was **capitalism**, which emphasized free trade and argued for less state control over the economy. Hand in hand with industrialization, capitalism would soon revolutionize economic life worldwide.

## ECONOMIC BUBBLES

The boom-and-bust nature of commercial economies was already becoming apparent during the 1600s and 1700s, when several financial disasters resulted in optimistic overinvestment in corporate schemes whose potential profitability turned out to be wildly overvalued. Many of these bubbles involved investment in foreign trade or exploitation of colonies. Most infamous during this era were the tulipmania of the early 1600s, when Dutch merchants purchased huge quantities of tulips from Ottoman Turkey, causing a terrible crash of the tulip market in 1637; the Mississippi bubble of 1720, which involved overvalued shares in the Mississippi Company, meant to reap profits from France's New World colonies; and Great Britain's South Sea Bubble, also in 1720, and due to similar overinvestment in Pacific territories.

Unfortunately, the global rise in productivity and wealth rested on a foundation of **coerced labor**, which took many forms. The **Atlantic slave trade** was extensive (and formed the heart of the Atlantic world's **triangular trade**), and so were the Arab slave trade and the market for slaves in Southeast Asia. **Serfdom** was common in Europe, especially in eastern regions like Russia. In the Americas, **plantation** and **cash-crop agriculture**—particularly the cultivation of **sugarcane**, **cotton**, and **coffee**—was based on unfree (or badly treated and poorly paid) labor.

# Social Structures, 1450–1750

15

→ **INCREASED AGRICULTURAL PRODUCTION AND HEAVIER BURDENS ON PEASANT POPULATIONS (TAXATION, CONSCRIPTION)**

→ **PLANTATION MONOCULTURE + EFFECTS ON LABOR AND SLAVERY**

→ **FOOD RIOTS AND PEASANT UPRISINGS**

→ **URBANIZATION AND CLASS DIVERSIFICATION (MIDDLE AND MERCHANT CLASSES**

→ **ADJUSTMENTS MADE BY ELITE CLASSES TO POLITICAL CENTRALIZATION AND ECONOMIC CHANGES (EUROPEAN NOBLES, JAPANESE DAIMYO, INDIAN ZAMINDARS)**

→ **TRADITIONAL ARISTOCRACIES VS. NEW BUREAUCRATIC ELITES**

→ **FORMS OF COERCED LABOR (SERFDOM, DEVSHIRME, ENCOMIENDA, SPANISH ADAPTATION OF MIT'A, INDENTURED SERVITUDE)**

→ **CHATTEL SLAVERY (ARAB SLAVE TRADE, ATLANTIC SLAVE TRADE)**

→ **PROTESTANT-CATHOLIC RELIGIOUS TENSIONS**

→ **EUROPEAN ANTI-SEMITISM**

→ **MUDARRA, THE MILLET, AND THE JIZYA TAX**

→ **HINDU-MUSLIM-SIKH TENSION IN INDIA**

→ **CREOLE AND MIXED POPULATIONS + RACE-BASED HIERARCHIES IN THE AMERICAS**

→ **PATRIARCHY AND GENDER INEQUALITY**

→ **FORMS OF GENDER DISCRIMINATION (WITCH HUNTS, SECLUSION, HAREMS, SATI, FOOT BINDING)**

→ **ROLE OF LOCAL WOMEN IN ENCOUNTERS BETWEEN EUROPEAN TRADERS AND EXPLORERS AND LOCAL POPULATIONS**

**M**any of the main social trends from the previous era continued during this one. These included a high degree of **social stratification**, a steady move toward greater **urbanization**, continued reliance on **coerced labor**, and the perpetuation of a **secondary status for women**.

At the same time, certain changes were afoot as well. The new economic complexities described in Chapter 14 led to greater **class diversification** and, along with a general tendency toward political centralization, forced **elite classes** to adapt to new realities or risk losing their power. **Literacy rates** tended to improve, especially in urban settings, as did greater accessibility to art and culture. Unfortunately, more varieties of coerced labor appeared during this period, and the number of people forced into it increased significantly.

## SOCIAL CLASSES IN FLUX

### Agriculture

Agriculture remained the dominant form of labor worldwide, and most people continued to live in rural settings.

Nonetheless, changes came to the countryside. For one, new forms of peasant labor arose to take their place alongside traditional methods. **Plantation agriculture** and **cash-crop monoculture**, which prevailed especially in Europe's overseas colonies, were extremely labor-intensive. They placed immense strain on peasant populations and typically involved **coerced labor**, if not outright **slavery**. Peasant labor intensified in other places and other ways as well. Examples include the expansion and greater systemization of **cotton production in India**, as well as the similar enlargement of **silk production in China**. Also falling in this category is the imposition or continuation of **serfdom** in certain places. Most notably, serfdom arose in Russia during the 1400s and 1500s—and was exported to the Siberian frontier in the 1600s and 1700s—just as most parts of Europe were abandoning the practice or relying less heavily on it. Serfdom also became increasingly important in Japan during this period.

Another source of pressure was the expansion of state power in most parts of the world. As governments centralized, their power to affect peasant communities grew. Along with the imposition of **serfdom** described above, the most common ways for states to intrude into peasants' lives were **taxation** (which grew more efficient during these years, and therefore more burdensome) and **conscription** (meaning that more serfs and peasants were drafted into armies that were growing larger as states centralized). Sometimes states proved unable or unwilling to assist rural populations when floods or bad harvests caused **food shortages**.

Increasingly often, conditions in the countryside caused enough frustration and desperation to trigger **food riots** and **peasant uprisings**. The largest social disturbance in Europe prior to the French Revolution was the **German Peasants' War** of the 1520s, in which 300,000 rebelled against landowners and aristocrats in central Europe. Japan was rocked from the late 1400s through the mid-1500s by the Ikko-ikki revolts, and again in the 1630s by the Shimabara rebellion. Both pitted peasants against samurai landowners and high taxes. Russia experienced numerous **Cossack and serf uprisings** in the 1600s and 1700s, including that of Stenka Razin—popularly remembered as a Robin Hood-style figure—in 1670 and the Pugachev revolt in the 1770s, which shook the regime of Catherine the Great to its foundations. In China, the Ming dynasty was brought down by a peasant war launched in the 1630s by the shepherd and ironworker **Li Zicheng**, who called for the abolition of grain taxes and the redistribution of land from the upper classes to the farmers. He ruled briefly as China's "Dashing King" until the Manchus toppled him in 1644 and established the Qing dynasty.

### Urban and Merchant Classes

In most parts of the world during this era, **urbanization** continued. In many cases, this encouraged greater **social mobility**, and it nearly always resulted in greater **class diversification**.

The growing importance of artisanry, manufacturing, shopkeeping, unskilled labor, and domestic servitude to middle- and upper-class households led to the enlargement of **urban working classes** and servant classes. Like peasants, they tended to be near the bottom of the hierarchy in most societies, and many of them suffered poverty and related hardships.

It was also mainly in urban settings that the percentage of people belonging to what later came to be known as the **middle classes** rose. These included highly skilled artisans, professionals such as lawyers and physicians, and, most important in terms of economic clout, **merchants** and **bankers**. The middle classes placed a high premium on initiative, hard work, and education. Where they stood in a given social hierarchy depended on which part of the world they were from. (As a reminder of this, consult the table "Social Hierarchies: A Comparison," in Chapter 10.)

Frequently, the middle classes, especially merchants, found themselves in a highly ambiguous situation. On one hand, the economic importance of merchants increased by leaps and bounds during this era, and they often commanded as much wealth—and sometimes as much informal power—as members of the elite classes. On the other hand, in most societies, elite classes looked down at merchants, scorning trade and the earning of money as somehow beneath them. Also, in most places, merchants were categorized as commoners, meaning that no matter how hard they worked or how much wealth they amassed, they found it difficult or impossible to gain the prestige that many elites simply inherited. Also, in societies where commoners paid taxes and elites did not, merchants ended up making valuable contributions to society without ever gaining society's full respect.

Merchants fared best in places with a high degree of social mobility. They played hugely influential social and political roles—and sometimes moved into the elite classes—in England, the Netherlands, the Italian city-states (especially Florence and Venice), and the Swahili city-states. In much of Europe, they experienced difficulty entering the top levels of society. In many parts of Asia, their status remained low, and where Confucianism prevailed—as in China and Japan—they ranked below artisans and peasants, at least in theory.

Middle-class frustrations with existing social orders increased throughout this period. While they remained bottled up for the most part during these years, they would prove to be an enormous force for change in the late 1700s and 1800s.

**NOTE**

In medieval and Renaissance Europe, merchants and other prosperous city dwellers were typically known as burghers, a Dutch and German term whose French equivalent— the bourgeoisie—became famous during the industrial era, when Karl Marx adopted it as a label to describe businessmen, factory owners, bankers, and others belonging to the higher levels of the middle class.

## Elite Classes

Most elite classes continued to hold onto their power and privileges, although political centralization and changing economic circumstances forced them to make various adjustments. In addition, new elites arose in many societies to coexist alongside traditional elites, and in some cases replaced them or threatened to do so.

**Political centralization** deeply affected aristocrats and nobles whose authority depended on inherited status and landownership. Traditionally, these elites had provided military leadership and local governance in decentralized or feudal systems. This meant that, while they were theoretically subject to their monarchs, they in fact wielded a great deal of power in their own lands. They could not always be dictated to by the monarch, and there were often clashes between the will of the monarch and that of the nobility.

Centralization altered this equation in several ways. First of all, power shifted decisively to the monarch in many places. Second, nobles and aristocrats often found themselves compelled by monarchs to serve their state more actively. During and after the Renaissance, **European nobles**, due to pressure from their monarchs, served as officers in their nations' rapidly expanding armies and navies, and as civil servants in their governments' growing bureaucracies. As the Mughal empire strengthened its hold over India, landowning **zamindars**, who had previously enjoyed much local autonomy, were increasingly incorporated into the Mughal system as local officials and regional governors. Similarly, the **daimyo**, Japan's samurai landowning nobility, tended to be masters of their own domains during the feudal disunity of the 1400s and 1500s but were forced into loyalty and service by Japan's unifiers in the late 1500s and early 1600s, and especially by the Tokugawa shogunate in the 1600s and 1700s.

Another political reality for traditional elites to cope with was the tendency of modernizing and centralizing states to create or elevate new **bureaucratic elites** and **military professionals**, sometimes based on skill or merit instead of hereditary status. There was already a long history of this in China, where the **Confucian examination system** continued to produce a **mandarin class** of bureaucrats who served the government regardless of what dynasty happened to be in charge. Also in Asia, **salaried samurai** took up administrative and bureaucratic posts in a Japan that had been made more peaceful by unification after about 1600 and no longer required their traditional warrior skills. The Ottoman **devshirme system**, which recruited boys from the empire's Christian populations, provided the sultan and his government not just with **janissary gunpowder troops**, but also **civil servants**, and while both groups remained slaves, they converted to Islam and enjoyed elite status and many privileges. In Europe during the 1600s, as a deliberate way to centralize at the expense of his powerful traditional aristocrats—known as "nobles of the sword," in honor of the military roles they had played since the middle ages—Louis XIV of France transferred many of his state's increasingly important (but less glamorous) bureaucratic jobs to **nobles of the robe**: civil servants and administrators who were promoted to the nobility by Louis himself and who therefore owed their aristocratic status to the king rather than to their own distinguished family tree. This ensured their loyalty to, and continued dependence on, the goodwill of the king.

> **NOTE**
>
> **An extreme example of how European nobles were pressed into service by centralizing monarchs was Russia's Table of Ranks. This was created shortly after 1700 by Peter the Great, who required all Russian nobles to take positions in the army, the navy, or the civil service if they wished to retain their rights and privileges.**

Traditional elites also faced economic challenges during this era. Because their wealth depended so much on landownership and profits derived from agricultural production, the rising importance of trade and commerce—which they tended to disdain in many places— did not work in their favor. In an era where merchants, bankers, and urban entrepreneurs were generating more and more wealth, and gaining more social and even political influence (at least unofficially), traditional elites would have to work harder and display a certain amount of adaptability if they wished to remain relevant. Those who failed to do so would fall behind or suffer serious consequences—if not during the 1700s, then in the 1800s or later.

## SLAVERY AND COERCED LABOR

Forms of **coerced labor** increased in variety during this era, as did the number of people who fell under its yoke.

### Miscellaneous Forms of Coerced Labor

**Serfdom**, or the binding of peasant laborers to the land in a way that left them unfree, although not technically enslaved, had been practiced in medieval Europe and elsewhere, mainly in centralized, feudal conditions. In many areas, it now faded away, but it remained important in places like Japan and the eastern half of Europe—especially in Russia, where serfdom formed the bedrock of social and economic life until after the mid-1800s.

Other forms of coerced labor that continued from the previous era were the Ottoman empire's **devshirme system** (which, as described above and in Chapters 10 and 12, recruited scribes, civil servants, and **janissary gunpowder troops** from non-Muslim communities, converted them to Islam, and placed them in conditions of privileged slavery) and the **Arab slave trade** (which exported African captives throughout the Middle East and the Indian Ocean basin). As the Russians expanded into Siberia between the 1500s and 1700s, they forced native populations to work for them and also to provide them with a yearly quota of fur pelts and other goods. This combination of labor obligations and tribute payments was called the **yasak**.

Change was most apparent in the Atlantic and in the Americas, where European colonization radically altered economic production and labor conditions. During the late 1400s and early 1500s, Spain exploited its New World possessions by means of the **encomienda system**, which declared all American natives to be Spanish subjects and used many of them as slaves in mines, on sugarcane farms, and elsewhere. However, not only did indigenous Americans prove unable and unwilling to work as slaves, but Catholic clergymen protested the cruelty caused by the encomienda system. The book *Tears of the Indians*, by the monk Bartolomé de las Casas, did much to sway Spanish opinion about the plight of American natives, and the encomienda was abolished in 1543.

Unfortunately, this did not end coerced labor in the Americas. In South America, the Spanish adapted the **mit'a system** that Inca rulers had previously used in the Andes to harness labor in a manner similar to serfdom. The rise of **plantation monoculture**, both in Spain's New World colonies and in Portuguese Brazil, involved the intensive cultivation of a single crop on large estates, known variously as **haciendas**, estancias, and latifundias. Along with **mining**, this sort of agriculture required an immense amount of labor and encouraged the employment of native workers on harsh terms and for little pay. Even more ominously, it persuaded the Spanish and Portuguese to rely heavily on **slave labor from Africa**. Plantation monoculture spread to North America, where French and especially English colonists practiced it and also resorted to slave labor as a result. The crops most directly connected with this trend were **sugarcane** in the Caribbean and South America, and **cotton** in North America.

## The Atlantic Slave Trade

Once started, the **Atlantic slave trade** became a central part of the European economy and a primary factor in Europe's ability to generate such great wealth from the 1500s onward. By the 1440s, the Portuguese had begun to enslave Africans, taking them to Portugal and selling them in Europe. The number of slaves brought directly to Europe was relatively small, and household service, not manual labor, was the rule. But when the Portuguese and Spanish started to ship slaves to the Americas and the Caribbean in the 1500s—because of the encomienda's abolition and because of the labor requirements of mining and plantation monoculture (especially sugarcane production)—the numbers grew, and conditions became harsher.

Europeans took roughly 1,000 slaves per year from Africa in the late 1400s, and more than 2,000 per year in the 1500s, for an estimated sum of 325,000 during these two centuries. During the 1600s and 1700s, the Atlantic slave trade mushroomed far beyond this: more than a million slaves were transported from Africa in the 1600s, and at least 6 million in the 1700s.

**Although the Arab and Atlantic slave trades are the most famous examples, chattel slavery—the outright ownership of human beings as personal property—was commonly practiced around the world during this era.**

**One institution that brought labor to North America, especially to the English colonies, was a form of debt-bondage called indentured servitude. In this system, would-be colonists who could not afford passage across the Atlantic agreed to work for a period of time for the families who paid their way. In addition, English criminals were often punished by transportation, or exile, to the Americas.**

It is thought that, in total, no fewer than 12 million Africans became slaves in the New World between the mid-1400s and the late 1800s. Thirty-seven percent went to Brazil (the largest slaveholding country), 15 percent to Spanish America, 41 percent to non-Spanish parts of the Caribbean, and 5 percent to the southern colonies of British North America, where they grew crops such as cotton and tobacco.

Slaves were captured and shipped to the Americas under notoriously appalling conditions. Many were captives or prisoners of war, conveyed to Africa's west coast and sold to European slavers by Africans from enemy tribes, and many were separated from families or mixed in with other tribes with unfamiliar languages and customs. They were then loaded onto ships to make the infamous **Middle Passage** across the Atlantic. The more slaves a ship could carry, the greater the profit, so slaves were packed into boats as tightly as possible. Chained, lying on their backs, surrounded by hundreds of other bodies, all in darkness, slaves endured a nightmarishly claustrophobic sea journey that lasted for weeks. Upon arrival, they would be taken to slave markets and sold. In the early years, up to 25 percent of slaves perished during the Middle Passage. During the 1700s and 1800s, slavers cut the average death rate to 10 percent or less—not for humane reasons but because each dead slave was a financial loss. The shipment of slaves via the Middle Passage was an integral part of the **triangular trade** that made Europe so rich during this era.

## GENDER AND ETHNICITY

### Religious and Ethnic Differences

Ethnic and religious minorities—or, on occasion, populations governed by an ethnic or religious minority—were treated differently in various parts of the world. In some cases, they enjoyed freedom and equal status. More often, though, they were persecuted, treated as second-class citizens, or restricted in various ways.

In Europe, **Protestants and Catholics** regularly persecuted each other, and **anti-Semitism** was rampant throughout the continent. Jews were stereotyped by European Christians as greedy because of their success since the Middle Ages in fields like banking and commerce, and they were further resented because of the popular but misguided belief that they bore responsibility from Biblical times for the death of Jesus. Due to tensions stirred up by the Spanish Reconquista and the Ottoman Empire's campaigns against Constantinople and the Balkans, **anti-Islamic tendencies** prevailed among European Christians as well.

Middle Eastern states imposed their own restrictions on non-Muslims. Although violence and persecution were not unknown, both Ottoman Turkey and Safavid Persia officially operated according to a policy of relative religious tolerance, referred to among the Ottomans as **mudarra**, or "moderation." As under the caliphates in earlier times, non-Muslims were allowed to convert to Islam if they wished, but were not forced to do so. Dhimmis, or non-believers, did not have equal rights: they could not serve in the military, their testimony in trials was given less weight than that of Muslims, and, as they had under the caliphs, they paid a special tax called the **jizya**. The **devshirme** system of taking boys from Christian families to serve the Ottoman regime as privileged slaves was generally disliked—although some families saw this as an opportunity for their sons to rise up in the world. To administer its non-Muslim subjects, the Ottoman empire organized each religious minority into a unit called a **millet** ("nation"). Three millets existed before the 1700s: one for Jews, one for Armenian Christians, and one for Greek Orthodox Christians. Treatment of non-Muslims tended to remain relatively mild until the 1800s, when nationalist aspirations among the Ottomans' subject peoples began to heighten tensions.

In Mughal India, where a Muslim minority ruled a Hindu majority, as well as a growing population of Sikhs, religious policy varied widely. It ranged from the tolerant benevolence of **Akbar the Great**, who abolished the jizya tax for Hindus in the late 1500s and encouraged friendly relations among those of all faiths, to the Islamic militancy of **Aurangzeb**, who imposed Sharia law on India's Hindus in the late 1600s, and whose persecution of the Sikhs caused them to revolt and to establish their own state in the Punjab.

Colonization and conquest led to the formation of new **race-based hierarchies** in various places. For many years after the 1644 establishment of the Qing dynasty in China, the ruling Manchus, who comprised less than 5 percent of the population, stratified society according to race. They forced their Chinese subjects to wear certain clothes and to braid their hair into long queues. Males had to shave their foreheads, as reflected in the classic proverb, "lose your hair or lose your head." In the Americas, colonization created **mixed populations**, as Europeans had children with Native Americans or transplanted Africans, or as Africans had children with Native Americans. **Mestizos** and **métis** (Spanish and French for "mixed") were the most common names for the offspring of Europeans and American natives. Those of European and African descent were known as **mulattos**, while **zambo** described someone of mixed African and Native American heritage. The word **creole**—the French equivalent of the Spanish *criollo*— eventually came to mean someone of mixed descent, but it originated from the Portuguese term *crioulo* (from the verb *criar*, or "to raise") as a way to describe a person of European descent who happened to be born in the colonies.

> **NOTE**
>
> As before, but now on a greater scale, due to the expansion of interregional and global trade, diasporic communities and foreign enclaves formed in many towns and ports. The desire for profits often trumped ethnic or religious prejudice, or at least blunted it. Not always, though: in some cases, the presence of foreign traders was highly restricted, as in China and Japan, where, by the 1600s and 1700s, outsiders were confined to specific port cities, such as Canton and Nagasaki, and forbidden entry elsewhere.

In the long run, the emergence of creole cultures and mixed populations hugely enriched the cultures of the New World, especially in Latin America and the Caribbean. Unfortunately, during the centuries of Portuguese and especially Spanish rule, these groups were organized into a rigid social hierarchy. Pure-bred Spanish who settled in the New World were known as *peninsulares* and remained at the top, with *criollos* (creoles according to the original definition of the word) alongside them, enjoying elite status. Those of mixed blood and native ancestry were nearer the bottom, and slaves, not surprisingly, were on the lowest rung of the social ladder. For a time, Spanish colonial authorities tried to set natives apart by forming a **República de Indios**, an administrative unit that resembled the Ottoman millet in that it kept natives under Spanish jurisdiction (and harnessed their labor and taxes) but allowed a certain degree of social and cultural autonomy.

## Gender Questions

In most parts of the world, women continued to occupy a secondary status in terms of social roles, economic opportunities, and political influence. In certain places and in some ways, conditions for women improved. Individual women from small but important segments of society—such as the aristocracy and the emerging middle class—gained educations, became active in business, and became artists and writers. Improvements were limited, though, and not all changes were positive.

In Europe, women of the upper classes enjoyed more access to education and took a more active role in intellectual life. Many in the middle classes also became more educated and assumed a greater economic role as operators of businesses or partners in them. Those of all classes gained more control over when and whom they married, as well as over issues like divorce, childbirth, and inheritance. Particularly in urban settings, where the labor of children was needed less than on a farm, women opted to have fewer children, causing a decline in the average size of European families. Progress in cultural life was significant as well. Many Catholic nuns achieved a high level of education, and Protestantism's emphasis on literacy led upper- and middle-class women to attain at least some learning. A number of prominent baroque and eighteenth-century painters were women, and women also turned to writing, philosophy, and scientific research—although they were not allowed to become university faculty. Some of the most important monarchs of this period of European history were women, including Isabella of Castile, Elizabeth I of England, Maria Theresa of Austria, and, in the late 1700s, Catherine the Great of Russia.

In no sense, however, were women in Europe treated as equal to men. Legally and economically, they remained subservient. Rates of death during childbirth were still high. Women made up approximately 75 percent of the victims of the witch hunts of the 1500s and 1600s, and both Catholicism and the new Protestant faiths used scripture to justify the view that women were inferior to, and more sinful than, men. Even during the Enlightenment of the 1700s (see Chapter 18), very few among Europe's otherwise more liberal thinkers were willing to entertain the notion of women's equality—despite the crucial role that women played in shaping Enlightenment culture.

A similar ambiguity prevailed in the Muslim world, whether in the Middle East or South Asia. Among the elite classes, women played informal but influential roles. In Ottoman Turkey, the sultan's mother ran the household, controlled marriage alliances, and sometimes conducted diplomacy. Both among the Ottomans and the Persian Safavids, the **harem** was not simply a collection of concubines for the ruler's pleasure, as is popularly thought. Instead, it was a complex social network that included most female members of the imperial family—relatively few of whom were used for any sexual purpose—and involved itself with the raising of children and pursuit of the arts. **Polygamy** was also much rarer in the Muslim world than is generally believed. On the other hand, the **seclusion of women** was practiced consistently throughout the Muslim world and among most classes. And while Muslim women had certain rights with respect to owning and inheriting property, they had few rights within marriage or when it came to divorce. Although they could testify in court, their testimony was not counted as equal to a man's.

In India, the impact of Mughal rule on women was mixed. By and large, Muslim women had more rights than their Hindu counterparts, who remained subject to the **caste system** and, depending on their status, the funeral practice of **sati**, or ritual burning. On the other

## WOMEN IN POWER

Many women throughout history have held political power on an individual basis. Examples include Cleopatra, Elizabeth I, Catherine the Great, Nzinga, Cixi, Golda Meir, Indira Gandhi, and Margaret Thatcher. Matrilineal societies, like those found in parts of West Africa, often afforded women more respect and authority than elsewhere. An interesting question, however, is whether this means that women were treated *equally*. Many queens and empresses came to power only because male alternatives were not available, and it did not necessarily follow that they could (or even wanted to) use their position to improve the overall condition of women. Even in modern democracies, women tend to be underrepresented as elected officials. In discussing how women have influenced historical developments, be sure not to overgeneralize from the often atypical experiences of powerful individuals. Until very recently, sexism and inequality have been the norms in most times and places.

hand, the **seclusion of women** applied both to Muslim women and Hindu women of high caste, and when Mughal rulers chose in the 1600s to impose **Sharia law** on non-Muslims, these restrictions fell on Hindu women, not just Muslims. In China, **foot binding** became more widespread, and Confucian doctrine continued to justify a secondary status for women. The stratification of Japanese society by the Tokugawa shogunate placed heavier restrictions on the behavior of women, especially if they belonged to the samurai class. Obliged to obey their husbands or face death, women in Tokugawa-era Japan had little authority over property and received less education than men, even if artistic and cultural pursuits were encouraged among elite women. Both in China and Japan, girl children, as in earlier eras, were less valued and sometimes put to death or sold into prostitution or servitude. In Japan, some women gained status and fame as **geishas**, special courtesans valued not just as sex objects but for their musical, artistic, and conversational skills.

As before, several African societies, especially in the west, were **matrilineal** and relatively willing to accept female leadership, as in the famous case of **Queen Nzinga** of Angola during the late 1500s and early 1600s. Throughout the continent, gender and family relations were affected by Islam's deepening presence, which led to more veiling and seclusion, and also by the arrival of Europeans and Arabs along the coasts. The escalation of the Arab and Atlantic slave trades had the effect of breaking apart many families, even in the interior, beyond the direct reach of foreigners.

As European colonizers and traders spread their influence to Africa, Asia, and the Americas, **local women** often played crucial roles during the economic and political encounters that unfolded between the outsiders and their own people. For instance, the Portuguese and other Europeans who arrived in Southeast Asia found themselves heavily dependent—for cultural orientation and social connections—on the local women they took as mistresses or wives. In the Americas, Hernán Cortés's success in conquering the Aztecs was due at least in part to the guidance and diplomatic skills provided by his native mistress **Malinche**. The story of **Pocahontas** and her helpful interactions during the early 1600s with English colonists in Virginia—saving the life of John Smith from her own people and later marrying John Rolfe—is perhaps the most famous illustration of this trend.

# Humans and the Environment, 1450–1750    16

→ THE LITTLE ICE AGE

→ THE COLUMBIAN EXCHANGE

→ AFRO-EURASIAN ANIMALS TO THE AMERICAS (HORSES, PIGS, CATTLE)

→ AFRO-EURASIAN CROPS TO THE AMERICAS (SUGARCANE, COTTON, OKRA, RICE, COFFEE)

→ AMERICAN CROPS TO EURASIA (MANIOC, CORN/MAIZE, POTATOES)

→ THE IMPACT OF AFRO-EURASIAN DISEASES ON INDIGENOUS AMERICAN POPULATIONS

→ PLANTATION AND MONOCULTURE AGRICULTURE

→ MINING AND MANUFACTURING

→ FUR HUNTING, FISHING, AND WHALING

Because of technological advances and the worldwide expansion of trade, **human impact on the environment** increased substantially during this era. Reinforcing this trend was the intensification of certain economic activities, including new forms of agricultural production, the rise of manufacturing, and resource extraction on a greater scale than ever before. Worldwide population growth added to this impact.

Even more dramatically, the ecosystems of Afro-Eurasia and the Americas were brought into contact with each other at the end of the 1400s by the European campaigns of exploration that continued into the 1500s and 1600s. The environmental impact of this encounter on both hemispheres was monumental, and the resulting two-way transmission of foodstuffs, animal species, disease pathogens, and human populations is known as the **Columbian Exchange**.

With respect to climate, the **Little Ice Age**—after a gradual cooling during the 1300s and 1400s—hit its peak between the early 1500s and the mid-1800s. This affected agricultural practices, trade routes, and patterns of animal migration and human settlement, especially in the northern hemisphere.

> **NOTE**
>
> Thanks in large measure to the arrival of new foodstuffs from the Americas, the populations of Europe, Africa, and Asia underwent significant growth from the 1500s onward.

## THE COLUMBIAN EXCHANGE

Europe's encounter with the Americas—truly a "New World" from the perspective of the European arrivals—led to one of the greatest ecological and demographic transformations in world history, known commonly as the **Columbian Exchange**.

The exchange of animals, plants, and foods shaped the environments of Old World and New World alike. From Afro-Eurasia came sheep, goats, cattle, and pigs, which increased the meat and milk supply in the Americas. The Europeans also brought the **horse**, which provided labor and transport and radically changed the lifestyle of Native Americans who lived and hunted on plains and grasslands.

Columbus himself introduced **sugarcane** to the Americas, where it would eventually be produced in massive quantities—a crucial factor in the emergence of the Atlantic slave trade. The southeastern part of North America joined Egypt and India as one of the world's great sources of **cotton**, yet another development that encouraged the use of slaves in the Americas. **Okra** and **rice** from Africa, along with wheat, olives, grapevines, citrus, and other fruits, were brought to the Americas as well. Later, during the 1700s, **coffee** (which had originated in northeast Africa and spread to the Middle East and Europe between the 1400s and 1600s) was found to flourish in the Caribbean and South America.

From the Americas came crops that were eventually adopted as staple foods by populations throughout Afro-Eurasia. **Manioc** and **corn** (maize) displaced many traditional foods in Africa, while **potatoes** and **corn** (maize) had the biggest impact on Europe and Asia. All three were relatively easy to grow and yielded many calories per acre. They sparked a general growth in Afro-Eurasian populations, and they also helped to offset the negative effects that the Little Ice Age had on agricultural production in many parts of the northern hemisphere. Other plants that traveled from the Americas to Afro-Eurasia included squash, sweet potatoes, chili peppers, beans, peanuts, and vitamin-rich tomatoes. Tobacco and cacao (for making chocolate) became eagerly sought luxury goods in Europe.

**NOTE**

**The arrival of Afro-Eurasian diseases in the Americas is the most attention-getting medical story of this era. Even so, remember that, in Afro-Eurasia itself, many diseases— whether well-established or newer—continued to have a recurrent and lethal impact on large numbers of people until the discovery of germ theory and the development and widespread distribution of vaccines. Bubonic plague flared up periodically until the late 1700s and early 1800s, and smallpox, influenza, and measles remained deadly killers. The growing trend toward urbanization helped certain diseases to spread quickly and widely, especially among the poor. Along with the diseases already listed, these included cholera, typhus, tuberculosis, and polio.**

Tragically, the Columbian Exchange also involved the movement of diseases, and almost exclusively in a one-way direction, from Afro-Eurasia to the Americas. Yellow fever and malaria came from Africa, and even deadlier in their effect were **smallpox**, **measles**, and **influenza**. Because of their centuries-long environmental isolation from Eurasia and Africa, the inhabitants of the Americas had no immunity to these new illnesses. The one disease the Europeans may have brought back from the New World is the sexually transmitted disease syphilis (although scholarly debate continues about the about the origins of this malady).

The death rate caused by the American natives' first encounters with Afro-Eurasian diseases is considered by most historians to have run between 25 and 50 percent of the Americas' pre-Columbian population. Some estimates go even higher, reaching as high as 80 or 90 percent. Here, the principal research difficulty is the scarcity of evidence that would provide a reliable estimate of how many people lived in the Americas prior to European contact. Either way, the Europeans' arrival spelled medical disaster for indigenous Americans.

Another demographic change associated with the Columbian Exchange was the **mass transfer of populations**. Economic and geopolitical traffic back and forth across the Atlantic increased steadily during this period, touching off a huge series of **migrations**, both voluntary and involuntary. Millions of slaves and hundreds of thousands of colonists came from Africa and Europe to the New World. Once in the Americas, their interaction with the indigenous peoples—and with each other—led to rich and complex ethnic and cultural mixing. More on this trend can be found in Chapter 15.

## MONOCULTURE AND RESOURCE EXTRACTION: ECOLOGICAL EFFECTS

Nearly every economic activity pursued by major societies during this period placed a greater burden on the environment. In and of itself, human population growth did the same.

Agriculture remained the dominant form of production in most parts of the world. With greater numbers of people practicing it in more parts of the world, it increased in scale and intensity. Especially striking, and especially harmful to the environment, was the European introduction of **plantation agriculture** and **monoculture**—the use of a sizable territory for the large-scale production of a single crop—to the Americas. Whether in the Americas or elsewhere, overexploitation of the land typically led to **soil depletion** (as nutrients were exhausted) and **deforestation** (as woods were cleared to make room for farms), and it could cause **water shortages** as well. In areas where herding and pastoralism were still practiced, the risk of **overgrazing** was always present.

With the emergence of manufacturing as a larger sector of the economy in places like Europe, the Middle East, and Asia—and with urbanization generally accompanying this trend—other stresses on the environment became more severe. The number of **water mills** and **windmills** grew. For metallurgy and for proto-industrial production, and also to heat a growing number of homes and buildings, the **burning of coal and wood fires** vastly increased in scale. This led to a gradual rise in **pollution** that would only grow worse with the advent of modern industrialization in the late 1700s and early 1800s.

> ### EFFECTS OF CASH-CROP AGRICULTURE
>
> Certain cash crops had a particularly profound impact during this period. These included sugar in the Caribbean and tobacco in the Americas, as well as cotton, the cultivation of which spread to the Americas and was intensified in places like India. Coffee from Ethiopia, which was adopted by Sufi Muslims in southern Arabia during the mid-1400s, spread throughout the Middle East during the 1500s. Over the course of the next century, the Europeans grew fond of coffee, importing it from the Middle East, but also transplanting it to Southeast Asia in the mid- to late 1600s, and then, starting in the early 1700s, to the Caribbean and Brazil. The production of cash crops by means of plantation monoculture placed huge strains on the environment and accelerated the rise of slavery and other forms of coerced labor.

It also heightened the extent of **resource extraction** in all parts of the globe during this period. Wood—needed both for fuel and for the making of houses, furniture, and ships, among other things—was one of the many **raw materials** for which manufacturing created a greater hunger. The growing appetite for metals and minerals—whether for currency, for the production of gunpowder weaponry, or for the manufacture of trade goods—caused **mining** to become more significant and more environmentally damaging than ever before. (The extraction of gold and especially **silver from the Americas** had an especially pronounced impact during these years.) Expansion of the **textiles trade** required larger and larger quantities of cotton and silk.

Other forms of resource extraction similarly intensified during these years, especially as European mariners, merchants, and colonizers extended their reach to the Americas and throughout the Atlantic and Pacific. Large-scale **fishing** became more important, as did the **hunting of whales** for meat and oil, used mainly to light lamps. The quest for **furs**—often referred to as "soft gold"—fundamentally shaped the course of European expansion into places like North America and Siberia, and it drastically reduced the numbers of dozens of animal species, including seals, beavers, otters, sables, and many others. The killing of walruses and elephants for **ivory** ramped up during these years as well.

# UNIT 5

## INDUSTRIALIZATION AND GLOBAL INTEGRATION (1750–1900)

# Unit 5 Short Cut

## GENERAL REMARKS

During the 1750–1900 period, the world entered the modern age. In this, it was led by the nations of the West, consisting of Europe and the United States.

Exactly what defines **modernity** is a question of debate among historians. In popular terms, the word *modern* is used as a synonym for "contemporary" or as a way to describe one's own times. In historical terms, it describes an era characterized by certain features. Different scholars outline modernity's features in different ways, but most agree on the following:

- In politics, there is a move from traditional monarchy toward greater political representation. The end result in most societies is some form of democracy or at least the appearance of democracy.
- In economics, industrialization becomes a driving force. A shift occurs from feudalism and mercantilism to capitalism. Rather than being based primarily on agriculture, economies are based increasingly on industry and commerce.
- In society, there is class transformation and the breakdown of traditional hierarchies, as old aristocracies fade away in favor of new elites whose status derives from wealth. New classes expand or emerge, especially the middle class and industrial working class. As agriculture gives way to industry, societies urbanize. Population growth accelerates, and large-scale migration becomes easier and more prevalent.
- In culture, a scientific, secular worldview becomes dominant. Artistic and literary styles change more rapidly and radically than ever before.

In all these things, Europe, with the United States, moved forward first. Great political upheavals such as the **American Revolution** and the **French Revolution** began the long process of expanding political representation and giving more people a greater voice in politics. It was in Europe that the **Industrial Revolution** began, and it was there that **capitalism** emerged (as well as visions alternative to it, such as **socialism**). These changes transformed the economies of the world. Population growth, class diversification, and urbanization were hallmarks of Western social development during the late 1700s and throughout the 1800s. The foundations for modern culture and intellectual life had been laid in Europe during the 1700s, during the Scientific Revolution and **the Enlightenment**.

To varying degrees, modernization reached the rest of the world in the nineteenth and early twentieth centuries. A few non-Western nations adapted quickly, such as Japan. Some, including the Ottoman Empire, China, and the nations of Latin America, modernized slowly or partially. Other civilizations, most notably in Africa and parts of Asia, lagged farther behind. No matter the pace, however, change came to all these regions. **Coerced** and **semi-**

coerced labor remained common worldwide, although anti-slavery sentiment grew into a steadily more powerful political force.

Another overarching development between 1750 and 1900 was the **rise of the West** as the world's dominant civilization. Not only did industrialization and modernization make the West prosperous and technologically advanced, they made it powerful as well. European and American imperialism resulted in control over a vast percentage of the world's habitable territory. Many areas that had originally been colonized during the Age of Exploration—such as North and South America—became free during the late 1700s and early 1800s. However, a **new imperialism** swept over Asia, the Middle East, the Pacific, and Africa during the 1800s and early 1900s. Seeking markets and raw materials, and armed with industrial-era weaponry, the nations of the West established control over an unprecedented portion of the globe. Never before in history had a single civilization become so powerful. But as impressive as imperialism was as a practical accomplishment, it carried a steep moral and ethical price. Imperialism was inextricably bound up with warfare, racial prejudice, economic rapacity, and slavery. Many of the harmful effects of Western imperialism are still felt to this day.

By the end of the nineteenth century, Europe had reached the peak of its power, but would soon fall from that pinnacle. The young United States was overtaking Europe in economic and military strength. New philosophies, scientific theories, and cultural movements were calling into question the traditional certainties and values of the Western world. Most important, Europe was moving toward war. The conflict resulting from the diplomatic tensions of the late 1800s and early 1900s—World War I—was, to that date, Europe's worst ever. It did much to start and then speed up the process of European decline.

## BROAD TRENDS

| State Building, Expansion, and Conflict, 1750–1900 | |
|---|---|
| **Europe** | French Revolution (1789–1799, Lafayette, Declaration of the Rights of Man and the Citizen) and Napoleonic Wars (1799–1815) |
| | Congress of Vienna (1814–1815) and reactionary politics (1815–1848) |
| | revolutions of 1848 |
| | reform and widening of political representation (1848–1914) |
| | women's suffrage movements |
| | anti-Semitism |
| | wars of Italian and German unification (Franco-Prussian War) |
| | geopolitical conflict (from balance of power to European alliance system; competition over empire) |
| **Middle East** | Tanzimat reforms and the Ottoman constitution of 1876 (vs. janissaries and Islamic traditionalism) |
| | Young Turk movement |
| | Balkan nationalism (Greek War of Independence, Balkan Crisis of 1876–1878) |
| | French colonization of Algeria (1830s–1840s) |
| | Muhammad Ali's revolt (1805) in Egypt and construction of the Suez Canal (1850s–1860s) |
| | geopolitical conflict (Eastern Question, Great Game) |
| | millenarian revolts (the Mahdi) |

| State Building, Expansion, and Conflict, 1750–1900 | |
|---|---|
| **Africa** | continuation and decline of the Atlantic and East African slave trades<br><br>African states (Barbary states, Ashanti and Zulu kingdoms, Zanzibar) vs. European imperialism (Berlin Conference, South Africa, Belgian Congo, Herero Wars)<br><br>geopolitical conflict (Scramble for Africa, Boer War)<br><br>millenarian revolts (Xhosa cattle-killing movement, the Mahdi)<br><br>training of native elites and native troops by imperial powers |
| **East (and Central) Asia** | Qing China's positive balance of trade vs. technological stagnation<br><br>Opium Wars and the "unequal" treaties (economic imperialism and foreign concessions)<br><br>self-strengthening movement vs. Qing conservatism (Cixi)<br><br>Taiping Rebellion (1850–1864) and Boxer Rebellion (1900)<br><br>isolation of Tokugawa shogunate vs. Matthew Perry's "opening" of Japan (1853)<br><br>Meiji Restoration (1868) and the modernization of Japan (Constitution of 1890)<br><br>geopolitical conflict (foreign concessions, Open Door policy, Russo-Japanese War)<br><br>millenarian revolts (Taiping Rebellion) |
| **South (and Southeast) Asia and Oceania** | fracturing of Mughal empire (Marathas, Sikhs)<br><br>British East India Company<br><br>Indian Revolt (1857–1858)<br><br>colonization in Southeast Asia (Dutch Indonesia, Singapore, French Indochina, U.S. annexation of the Philippines)<br><br>modernization in Siam (Mongkut)<br><br>colonization of Australia (Aborigines) and New Zealand (Maori)<br><br>U.S. annexation of Hawaiian kingdom<br><br>geopolitical conflict (battle of Plassey, Great Game)<br><br>training of native elites and native troops by imperial powers (sepoys) |
| **Americas** | American Revolution (1775–1783, Thomas Jefferson, Declaration of Independence)<br><br>U.S. expansion (Louisiana Purchase, "manifest destiny," Mexican-American and Spanish-American wars, Hawaiian kingdom)<br><br>suppression of Native Americans (Cherokee Nation and Trail of Tears, Indian wars, Wounded Knee, reservation system)<br><br>slavery in the Americas (Maroon societies, U.S. Civil War)<br><br>Haitian Rebellion (1791–1804, François Toussaint L'Ouverture)<br><br>Latin American wars of independence (1810–1825, Simón Bolívar, Jamaica Letter)<br><br>failure of constitutional rule in Latin America (caudillos)<br><br>economic imperialism in Latin America<br><br>geopolitical conflict (Monroe Doctrine)<br><br>millenarian revolts (Ghost Dance and Wounded Knee) |

| State Building, Expansion, and Conflict, 1750–1900 | |
| --- | --- |
| **Global and Interregional** | increased prominence of the nation-state <br> global impact of "new" imperialism (white man's burden, *la mission civilisatrice*, social Darwinism) and economic imperialism <br> nationalism and national-liberation impulses (Indian Revolt, Indian National Congress, Boxer Rebellion, José Martí in Cuba, Emiliano Aguinaldo in the Philippines) |

## State Building, Expansion, and Conflict

- With every passing decade, the nation-state emerged as the leading form of political organization in more parts of the world.

- Modern political and economic ideologies—including conservatism, liberalism, nationalism, and socialism—emerged (see also Chapter 18, "Culture, Science, and Technology").

- The hallmark of modern political life is greater popular representation. This trend first got underway in the West, beginning in the late 1700s with the American and French revolutions. During the rest of the era, Western nations followed various paths—revolutionary or reform-oriented, faster or slower—toward greater democratization.

- Other parts of the world were slower to move away from traditional autocracies or monarchies. A few, such as Japan and the Ottoman Empire, did so, developing parliamentary forms of monarchy by the start of the twentieth century. The nations of Latin America developed parliamentary governments in theory, but many slipped into dictatorial or military rule.

- The technological, economic, and military rise of the West—Europe and the United States—completely altered the balance of global power. World affairs were increasingly determined by foreign policy and military developments in Europe, especially in the 1800s.

- The United States broke away from English rule during the late 1700s and became a world power during the 1800s by achieving dominance over the North American continent.

- The Spanish and Portuguese colonies of Latin America freed themselves from European rule during the early 1800s, another large alteration of the global balance of power.

- In North Africa and the eastern Mediterranean, the gradual collapse of the Ottoman Empire presented Europe and the Middle East with a troubling and destabilizing diplomatic issue known as the Eastern Question.

- European and U.S. imperialism—the "new imperialism" of the mid- to late 1800s—gave the nations of the West unprecedented global dominance. In 1815, the nations of the West controlled roughly 35 percent of the world's habitable territory. By 1914, that figure had risen to approximately 85 percent.

- The one non-Western nation that developed a modern colonial empire in the late 1800s and early 1900s was Japan.

- By the end of the 1800s, diplomatic tensions, nationalism, and competition over colonies made it increasingly likely that the nations of Europe would go to war. An alliance system formed, and the level of aggression rose steadily until the outbreak of World War I in 1914.

| Culture, Science, and Technology, 1750–1900 | |
|---|---|
| **Europe** | the Enlightenment (1700s; Locke, Montesquieu, Voltaire, Rousseau)<br>romanticism, realism, and modernism (late 1700s–early 1900s)<br>conservatism (and reaction) vs. liberalism<br>capitalism (Adam Smith) vs. socialism (utopians) and communism (Karl Marx)<br>nationalism (Social Darwinism)<br>Charles Darwin (natural selection)<br>Albert Einstein (relativity)<br>Sigmund Freud (psychoanalysis)<br>Western crisis of faith |
| **Middle East** | cultural Westernization during Tanzimat reforms (mid-1800s)<br>revival of Arabic |
| **Africa** | oral tradition and griot storytelling<br>non-representational art and impact on Western modernism<br>influence of Christian missionaries |
| **East (and Central) Asia** | *Dream of the Red Chamber* (late 1700s)<br>influence of Christian missionaries in China<br>ukiyo-e woodblock painting (Hokusai, early to mid-1800s)<br>"Goodbye Asia" and Japanese ideologies of nationalist-racial superiority (late 1800s) |
| **South (and Southeast) Asia and Oceania** | "Company" style in India<br>Gateway to India arch<br>influence of Christian missionaries<br>early national liberation movements (Indian National Congress) |
| **Americas** | the Enlightenment (1700s; founding fathers)<br>romanticism, realism, and modernism (late 1700s–early 1900s)<br>conservatism (and reaction) vs. liberalism<br>capitalism vs. socialism and communism<br>nationalism (Social Darwinism)<br>Western crisis of faith |
| **Global and Interregional** | rising literacy rates<br>increased Westernization of non-Western cultures<br>nationalism |

## Culture, Science, and Technology

- In eighteenth-century Europe and America, the intellectual trend known as the Enlightenment built on the recent insights of the "scientific revolution" and prompted rational inquiry into the nature of politics and society. By questioning social hierarchies and traditional forms of monarchy, it paved the way for massive political changes—including key revolutions—in Europe and the Americas.
- Starting in the West, a scientific, secular worldview became increasingly paramount, thanks initially to the "scientific revolution" and the Enlightenment, and then additionally to the technological and scientific advancements of the industrial era.

- Greater access to public education became a normal part of life in North America and most parts of Europe throughout the 1800s. Literacy rates rose as a result. The same became true for many other parts of the world during the late 1800s.
- Modern political and economic ideologies—including conservatism, liberalism, nationalism, and socialism—emerged (see also "State Building, Expansion, and Conflict").
- Nationalism became a powerful political and cultural force in Europe and then elsewhere. By the end of the 1800s, nationalist and national-liberation movements became prevalent in non-Western parts of the world dominated by foreign colonial rule.
- Ideologies of racial superiority, in some cases based on pseudo-scientific concepts like social Darwinism, arose in many quarters.
- The non-Western world began to adopt many of the artistic and literary forms of the West, especially print culture and writing styles, as well as architecture. Conversely, styles from Asia, Africa, and the Middle East had an influence on Western culture, particularly in painting, sculpture, and décor.
- In Europe and the Americas, the pace of cultural change sped up. By the end of the 1800s and the beginning of the 1900s, new artistic and literary trends were emerging at a rapid rate. Increasingly, these were about breaking rules and defying conventions.
- Technological change was profound, rapid, and thorough in those parts of the world affected by industrialization. National economies and personal lives alike were influenced by constant and increasingly affordable innovations that involved machine power, fossil-fuel energy sources such as coal and oil, and, near the end of the 1800s, electricity.

| Economic Systems, 1750–1900 | |
|---|---|
| **Europe** | from proto-industrialization to Industrial Revolution (ca. 1780s–1840s; steam engine, coal, iron, textiles) |
| | Second Industrial Revolution (late 1800s; steel, electronics, petroleum) |
| | free-market vs. state-sponsored industrialization |
| | steamships, railroads, telegraph |
| | free-market capitalism (classical economists = Adam Smith, John Stuart Mill) and state capitalism |
| | trade-unionist and socialist (Karl Marx) reactions to capitalism |
| | financial instruments (central banks, stock exchanges, corporations, gold standard) |
| | the Panic of 1873 and the Long Depression (1870s–1890s) |
| | rise of the middle and industrial working classes |
| **Middle East** | state-sponsored and limited industrialization (Muhammad Ali in Egypt, Tanzimat reforms in Ottoman Turkey) |
| | construction of Suez Canal (transnational company = Suez Canal Company) |
| | resources (cotton, petroleum) |
| **Africa** | economic imperialism by Western powers |
| | continued reliance on African slaves by Western economies |
| | construction of railroads by Western powers |
| | resources (gold, diamonds, rubber, ivory) |

| Economic Systems, 1750–1900 | |
|---|---|
| **East (and Central) Asia** | economic imperialism by Western powers in China (Opium Wars, foreign concessions and treaty ports)<br>transnational company = Hong Kong and Shanghai Banking Company<br>state-sponsored and limited industrialization in China (self-strengthening movement)<br>state-sponsored and full industrialization in Japan (Meiji Restoration of 1868, zaibatsu) |
| **South (and Southeast) Asia and Oceania** | economic imperialism by Western powers<br>construction of railroads, telegraphs, and infrastructure by Western powers<br>British industrialization of Indian cotton trade<br>transnational company = British East India Company<br>resources (cotton, coffee, metals, rubber, petroleum) |
| **Americas** | Industrial Revolution (ca. 1780s–1840s) and Second Industrial Revolution (late 1800s) in the United States<br>free-market capitalism in the United States<br>financial instruments (central banks, stock exchanges, corporations, gold standard)<br>rise of middle and industrial working classes<br>state-sponsored industrialization and limited industrialization in Latin America (late 1800s)<br>economic imperialism in Latin America (transnational company = United Fruit Company)<br>resources (metals, petroleum, guano, fruit, coffee, sugar) |
| **Global and Interregional** | widespread proto-industrialization<br>international impact of industrialization (importation by colonial powers, state-sponsored imperialism)<br>economic imperialism by Western powers (raw materials, consumer markets, transnational corporations, "banana republics")<br>population growth and urbanization<br>oceanic whaling and sealing in search of oil |

## Economic Systems

- Economic life was transformed by the phenomenon of industrialization, which displaced agriculture as the most crucial and most influential sector of the economy.

- Industrialization began in England and spread to parts of Europe during the late 1700s and early 1800s—the era of the Industrial Revolution. During the late 1800s, a period often referred to as the Second Industrial Revolution, industrial practices matured and spread further throughout Europe, expanding to include steel, electricity, chemical industries, and petroleum. Gradually and to varying extents, industrialization spread to other parts of the world.

- The non-Western world adopted industrialization at varying speeds and in different ways. Sometimes, European imperial powers introduced it to their colonies. In other cases, rulers of free non-Western nations imposed industrialization from above, or at least attempted to do so.

- The dominant mode of economic organization in the industrial-era West became capitalism, although this sometimes took a form that was more state-directed than the free-market variety of capitalism most familiar in the English-speaking world.
- Reactions to the stresses and strains of early industrialization, and to the more exploitative aspects of early capitalism, included trade-union activism, utopian socialism, Marxism, and anarchy.
- Commerce and banking—the foundations of a money-based economy, as opposed to a land-based one—grew in importance. Banks, stock markets, and other modern financial instruments became more common and more solidly established.
- See "Social Structures" below for the relationship between economic growth during this era and reliance on coerced and semi-coerced forms of labor.

| Social Structures, 1750–1900 | |
|---|---|
| **Europe** | class diversification (impact of revolutions and industrialization; growth of industrial working class, rise of middle class) <br> serfdom in Russia (uprisings, emancipation) <br> Siberian exile and prison labor <br> migration to the Americas (Irish Potato Famine, anti-Jewish pogroms) <br> emergence of modern feminism and suffragette movements (Mary Wollstonecraft, Olympe de Gouges, Emmeline Pankhurst) <br> industrialization and women (domestic sphere, cult of domesticity) |
| **Middle East** | millets <br> Tanzimat reforms and limited social liberalization <br> corvée labor (Suez Canal) |
| **Africa** | racially segregationist policies in Western-controlled colonies (native elites) <br> East African slave trade <br> Atlantic slave trade <br> Indian migration to East and South Africa <br> imperialism's impact on women's roles |
| **East (and Central) Asia** | social stratification and increased tensions in Qing China (opium addiction, Taiping Rebellion) <br> social stratification in Tokugawa Japan <br> Meiji Restoration in Japan: rise of merchants, abolition of samurai status <br> indentured servitude (coolie labor) <br> Chinese migration throughout Southeast Asia <br> missionary efforts against Chinese foot binding |
| **South (and Southeast) Asia and Oceania** | racially segregationist policies in Western-controlled colonies (native elites) <br> British undermining of Hindu caste system <br> indentured servitude (coolie labor) <br> transportation to Australia <br> Indian migration throughout Southeast Asia, East Africa, and South Africa <br> Chinese migration throughout Southeast Asia <br> White Australia Policy <br> British struggle against sati |

| Social Structures, 1750–1900 | |
|---|---|
| **Americas** | class diversification (impact of revolutions and industrialization; growth of industrial working class, rise of middle class) <br> continued reliance on African slavery <br> migration from Europe and Asia (Chinese Exclusion Act) <br> emergence of modern feminism and suffragette movements (Susan B. Anthony, Seneca Falls Convention) <br> industrialization and women (domestic sphere, cult of domesticity) |
| **Global and Interregional** | urbanization <br> expansion of resource extraction and cash-crop monoculture as forms of labor <br> persistence, then gradual fading, of slave systems <br> seasonal and permanent migration (Europe and Asia to the Americas, Chinese and Indians in Indian Ocean basin) <br> anti-immigrant sentiment |

## Social Structures

- During the 1800s, especially after the 1848 revolutions, politics in Europe and the West became increasingly representative, with a few countries becoming democratic by the end of the century (although women could not yet vote). Even in less representative states, bureaucracies and parliamentary bodies became an increasingly important part of government, relative to the will of individual monarchs.

- Hierarchies and caste systems tended to break down or weaken, and if they remained in place, they heightened social discontent. Revolutions and rebellions became increasingly frequent throughout the world.

- Industrialization transformed class structures. Traditional aristocracies, with their status based on land and family prestige, faded. Among the lower classes, the proportion of peasants and farmers shrank. The middle class (bourgeoisie) expanded, gained great wealth, and diversified. A new lower class, the industrial working class (proletariat), was born.

- Industrialization led to urbanization. Cities grew in size, and more of them were established.

- For any society, the first decades of industrialization were typically painful for the lower classes. Working conditions were poor, and wages were low. Over time, industrialization raised the average prosperity of a society's population, and even the lower classes benefited after some time.

- Coerced and semi-coerced forms of labor persisted. Along with slavery, indentured servitude (common in places like India and China) and migrant labor (technically free, but poorly paid) were common. Africa was the primary victim of slave trading. The East African and Atlantic slave trades continued well into the 1800s, as did Russian serfdom.

- There was a tremendous migration of peoples during this period, both permanent and seasonal. In particular massive waves of emigrants moved from Europe and China to the Americas during the 1800s and early 1900s. The United States was the preferred destination, but Canada, Argentina, and Chile took in many immigrants as well, as did Australia. Anti-immigration sentiment was common in these places, both on a popular and official level.

- Diasporic communities and foreign enclaves remained common, thanks to expanding commercial ties or overcrowding at home.
- Although in most societies, the status of women remained secondary, the 1750–1900 period saw great changes in gender relations. In the West, a greater awareness of the unequal treatment of women began to spread, starting around the late 1700s. This was stimulated largely by the theories of Enlightenment philosophy, as well as the active role played by women in the American and French Revolutions.
- The Industrial Revolution profoundly altered the conditions under which families worked. It shifted the workplace away from the farm, where both men and women worked, to mines, factories, and similar places, creating separate domestic and working spheres.
- In Europe and North America, lower-class women entered industrial workplaces during the early 1800s, but left again after the mid-1800s, when wages for industrial workers rose (making such jobs more desirable to men) and new laws restricted the number of hours that women and children could work. A cult of domesticity, stressing that a woman's place was in the home and a man's in the workplace, dominated Western society, especially among the middle and upper classes, during the mid- to late 1800s.
- Strong and vigorous women's movements appeared in Europe, Canada, and the United States. They agitated for suffrage, equal opportunities, and other causes. A handful of places, but not major nations, granted women the right to vote before World War I.
- The move toward women's equality tended to be slower in non-Western societies. In some, however, the educational level of women rose, as did the extent of property rights. As in the West, women worked, especially in certain occupations, such as agricultural labor, domestic service, and nursing. As non-Western parts of the world industrialized, lower-class women tended to enter the workplace.

| Humans and the Environment, 1750–1900 | |
| --- | --- |
| **Europe** | industrial-era pollution (carbon-based and fossil-fuel emissions) industrial-era resource extraction (mining) earth-shaping (major canal systems, road and rail networks) vaccination (late 1700s) and germ theory (mid-1800s) severity of cholera and tuberculosis worsened by industrial-era living conditions resources (coal, metals, timber) |
| **Middle East** | earth-shaping (Suez Canal) resources (cotton, petroleum) |
| **Africa** | industrial-era resource extraction by colonial powers (mining and cash-crop monoculture) treatments for tropical diseases like malaria allow Western penetration of African interior resources (gold, diamonds, ivory, rubber, fruit, palm oil) species endangerment (elephants) |
| **East (and Central) Asia** | industrial-era resource extraction by colonial powers (mining and cash-crop monoculture) species extinction and endangerment (sables, otters) resources (tea, silk, cotton) |

| Humans and the Environment, 1750–1900 | |
|---|---|
| South (and Southeast) Asia and Oceania | industrial-era resource extraction by colonial powers (mining and cash-crop monoculture)<br>treatments for diseases like malaria allow Western penetration of tropical interior<br>resources (cotton, rubber, spices, coffee, metals, petroleum) |
| Americas | industrial-era pollution (carbon-based and fossil-fuel emissions)<br>industrial-era resource extraction (mining and cash-crop monoculture)<br>earth-shaping (Erie and Panama canals, road and rail networks)<br>species extinction and endangerment (passenger pigeon, bison, great auk)<br>treatments for diseases like malaria allow Western penetration of tropical interior<br>coal, metals, petroleum, timber, meat, fruit, sugar, coffee, guano |
| Global and Interregional | Little Ice Age ends (mid-1800s)<br>permanent and seasonal migrations (Eurasia to the Americas; regional movements within Indian Ocean basin)<br>species extinction and endangerment (whales, fur seals, walruses) |

## Humans and the Environment

- Industrialization vastly increased humanity's impact on the environment. Rising levels of pollution were one result. Carbon-based and fossil-fuel emissions began an upward spike that has increased ever since, all the way to the present day.
- The hunger of industrializing economies for natural resources (metals, minerals, guano for fertilizer, oil, rubber, foodstuffs, and cotton) led to extractive practices that hugely strained the environment. Mining and cash-crop monoculture tremendously damaged ecosystems.
- Industrialization permitted major earth-shaping engineering projects such as the Erie Canal and the Suez Canal (and, in the early 1900s, the Panama Canal).
- Human-caused extinction or endangerment of animal species became increasingly common.
- Industrial-era forms of transportation contributed to the widespread distribution of diseases.
- Diseases such as tuberculosis and cholera spread easily amid the overcrowded living conditions created by industrialization and rapid urbanization.
- The development of effective treatments for tropical diseases such as malaria enabled imperial powers like Europe and America to penetrate deeper and more efficiently into Africa and Asia.
- A global wave of migration (discussed in more detail under "Social Structures") caused millions of people to travel vast distances—most famously from Europe and Asia to the Americas, but in other directions and to other places as well.
- The Little Ice Age came to an end during the early to mid-1800s.

# QUESTIONS AND COMPARISONS TO CONSIDER

- What distinguishes the nation-state from other forms of political organization? Why did it become increasingly prevalent during these years?
- What factors contributed to the rise of industrial production, whether in Europe or in the places it gradually spread to?
- What distinguished the initial Industrial Revolution from the second one that is said to have occurred during the late 1800s?
- What role did the exploitation and export of raw materials play in world trade? In international politics? In shaping systems of labor?
- What socioeconomic visions alternative to capitalism appeared during this era? What were their strengths and weaknesses?
- How were gender and family dynamics affected by industrialization (or failure to industrialize), whether in Europe or elsewhere?
- What impact did the Enlightenment of the 1700s have on the political and social changes of the late 1700s and 1800s?
- Compare the nature and content of major political philosophies, including nationalism.
- Compare various acts of resistance against Western imperialism. Examples include Japanese modernization, the Indian Revolt, the Boxer Rebellion, the Filipino war against U.S. occupation, the Xhosa cattle-killing movement, and Wounded Knee.
- Compare two or more of the following revolutions or rebellions: the American Revolution, the Haitian rebellion, the Latin American wars of independence, the Indian Revolt, and the Taiping Rebellion. Be able to compare key revolutionary documents, such as the Declaration of Independence, France's Declaration of the Rights of Man and the Citizen, and the Jamaica Letter.
- Discuss the response of non-Western parts of the world such as China, India, Japan, and the Ottoman Empire to imperial encroachments and foreign pressures (especially from Europe and the United States) during this period.
- What factors caused such widespread migration during the 1800s? Where did it generally take place, and what forms did those migrations take?
- Compare the status of women in the West and that of women in other parts of the world. Compare the roles and conditions of upper- and middle-class women with those of the peasant and working classes.
- Describe the various approaches taken by various Western powers to colonization. Also, what caused the late-nineteenth-century wave of imperialism (the "new" imperialism), and how did this compare to earlier waves of colonization?
- Discuss various ways in which non-Western states attempted to modernize and adopt industrial practices. How important is the question of whether industrialization was imposed on a society from above, by the ruler, or emerged from below?
- Compare Japanese industrialization and European modernization.
- Compare Western intervention in Latin America with Western intervention in Africa during the 1750–1900 period.
- Examine nationalist and anticolonial movements in non-Western parts of the world. Compare and contrast their methods and their successes and/or failures.

# UNIT 5

## SCENIC ROUTE
### (Chapters 17–21)

# State Building, Expansion, and Conflict, 1750–1900

# 17

→ **GROWING PROMINENCE OF THE NATION-STATE**

→ **ATLANTIC REVOLUTIONS + REVOLUTIONARY DOCUMENTS (U.S. DECLARATION OF INDEPENDENCE, DECLARATION OF THE RIGHTS OF MAN AND THE CITIZEN, JAMAICA LETTER)**

→ **"NEW" IMPERIALISM AND WESTERN POWER VS. ACTS OF ANTI-IMPERIAL RESISTANCE**

→ **DOCTRINES OF RACIAL SUPERIORITY (SOCIAL DARWINISM, WHITE MAN'S BURDEN, *LA MISSION CIVILISATRICE*)**

→ **BALANCE OF POWER VS. COMPETITION OVER EMPIRE AND JINGOISTIC NATIONALISM**

→ **GEOPOLITICAL CLASHES (MONROE DOCTRINE, EASTERN QUESTION, GREAT GAME, SCRAMBLE FOR AFRICA, EUROPEAN ALLIANCE SYSTEM)**

→ **REACTION IN EUROPE (CONGRESS OF VIENNA) VS. THE REVOLUTIONS OF 1848**

→ **REACTION, REVOLUTION, AND REFORM IN EUROPE (MALE VS. WOMEN'S SUFFRAGE)**

→ **OTTOMAN DECLINE (TANZIMAT REFORMS, YOUNG TURKS)**

→ **AFRICAN STATES VS. SCRAMBLE FOR AFRICA (BERLIN CONFERENCE)**

→ **OPIUM WARS + QING DECLINE ("UNEQUAL" TREATIES VS. SELF-STRENGTHENING MOVEMENT)**

→ **TOKUGAWA SHOGUNATE VS. MEIJI RESTORATION**

→ **BRITISH EAST INDIA COMPANY (SEPOY TROOPS AND INDIAN REVOLT)**

→ **SPANISH-AMERICAN AND PHILIPPINE-AMERICAN WARS**

→ **"MANIFEST DESTINY" IN THE UNITED STATES**

→ **ECONOMIC IMPERIALISM AND CAUDILLO RULE IN LATIN AMERICA**

During this era, the **nation-state**—a state-level community united at least in theory by a common ethnic, linguistic, religious, and cultural heritage—emerged as the leading form of political organization in more parts of the world, particularly in the West.

As this era progressed, it became clear that the hallmark of modern political life would be greater popular representation. This trend began in the West during the late 1700s, with the **American** and **French revolutions**. Over the course of the next century, Western nations followed various paths—revolutionary or reform-oriented, faster or slower—toward greater democratization. **Industrialization** played a role in driving these changes as well.

Other parts of the world were slower to move away from traditional autocracies or monarchies. A few, such as Japan and the Ottoman Empire, did so, developing parliamentary forms of monarchy by the start of the twentieth century. The nations of Latin America developed parliamentary governments in theory, but many slipped into dictatorial or military rule. **Revolutions** were periodically sparked in these parts of the world, whether because of middle- or lower-class discontent or as a form of protest against Western imperial influence.

The global balance of power changed profoundly during these years, thanks to the technological, economic, and military rise of Europe and the United States. World affairs between the late 1700s and early 1900s were increasingly determined by Western foreign policy. Moreover, the "**new imperialism**" of the mid- to late 1800s gave Europe and North America unprecedented global dominance. In 1815, the nations of the West controlled roughly 35 percent of the world's habitable territory. By 1914, that figure had risen to approximately 85 percent. By that time, however, diplomatic tensions, **nationalism**, and competition over colonies made it increasingly likely that the nations of the West would go to war. The **European alliance system** formed in the late 1800s and the level of aggression rose steadily until the outbreak of World War I in 1914.

## THE ATLANTIC REVOLUTIONS AND THE BIRTH OF MODERN POLITICS

Early in this era, the political order in Europe and the Americas changed dramatically. In the mid-1700s, all of Europe's major powers were monarchies, in which the ruler shared power almost exclusively with aristocratic nobles who, despite their small numbers, controlled most of the country's wealth, owned most of the nation's land, and enjoyed virtually all influence over politics. (Even parliamentary monarchies like Great Britain allowed comparatively little popular representation at this time.) Most of Latin America and the Caribbean, along with much of North America, lived under European colonial authority.

This state of affairs was shaken apart by a wave of **Atlantic revolutions** between the 1770s and the 1810s. These include the **American Revolution**, the **French Revolution**, the **Haitian Rebellion**, and the **Latin American Wars of Independence**. Although not all their goals were met, they dealt a death blow to absolute monarchy in most of Europe, and they ended European colonial rule over most of the Americas. Another legacy of the Atlantic revolutions was that an ever-increasing number of people began to dream of—and fight for—social and political systems that gave them more voice in government. (Another factor that changed ordinary people's social and economic aspirations at this time was the **Industrial Revolution**, which coincided with the Atlantic revolutions and is detailed more fully in Chapter 19.)

### THE CAUSES OF REVOLUTION

Understanding how and why revolutions take place is a daunting task for any historian. Social stress and class differences, economic inequality and poverty, incompetent or oppressive political leadership, and intellectual and cultural forces (religion, nationalism, doctrines, ideologies) are almost always at the root of any major revolution. Studying and comparing revolutions involves trying to figure out which of these is more or less important in any given case. Another important distinction has to do with whether forces causing revolution come *from above* (top-down), *from below* (bottom-up), or, as is often the case, both. Who are the actual revolutionaries? Do they continue to cooperate after the initial seizure of power, or do they disagree and quarrel among themselves, leading to further struggle?

## The American Revolution and the Birth of the United States

During the 1760s and 1770s, several trends combined to spark the **American Revolution** (1775–1783) that swept the 13 British colonies of New England and the mid-Atlantic coast. One was a growing sense of **nationalism**. Another was increased resentment of Britain's economic mastery. The taxes Britain levied to pay for the army it maintained in North America angered many colonists, especially because they lacked representation in Britain's parliament. The spirit of **capitalism** was catching on among colonial merchants and other members of the middle class, many of whom believed that free trade—something not permitted by Britain's **mercantilist policy** (which required the colonies to trade only on British terms)—would create greater wealth. Just as important as these practical causes was the influence of **Enlightenment philosophy**, which Chapter 18 describes in more depth. Most of the leaders who carried out the American Revolution and wrote the Constitution followed the intellectual lead of Enlightenment thinkers such as **John Locke** and the Baron Charles de **Montesquieu** about social contracts and civil liberties guaranteed by natural rights. The **Declaration of Independence** (1776), authored chiefly by Thomas Jefferson, is considered a classic Enlightenment text.

The revolution itself broke out in 1775. At first, the poorly trained and poorly equipped American forces, led by George Washington, struggled against Britain's professional armies and superior navy. In 1777, however, the tide began to turn. Although so-called Tories remained loyal to the British, popular support for the revolution grew. The Americans had the advantage of fighting on their home territory. Also, after their victory at Saratoga, late in the year, France—Britain's mortal enemy—decided to lend them money and military aid. The French fleet's assistance against Britain's Royal Navy was helpful, as was the military training provided by French officers (and other Europeans) at Washington's Valley Forge encampment in 1777–1778. By 1781, the British war effort was failing. When the Americans surrounded the main British force at Yorktown, the war was effectively over, although peace talks dragged on until 1783.

After victory, the next step was to devise a form of government. This process involved much disagreement and lasted until the Constitutional Convention of 1787 and the ratification of the **United States Constitution** in 1789. The resulting system was a democratic republic, in which a federal government shared power with governments in each of the 13 states. It was also the first attempt by a major state to base a political system as thoroughly as possible on the rights-oriented political philosophy of the Enlightenment. To ensure that political authority was not concentrated too much in any one office or body, power at the federal level was shared among three branches—executive (president), legislative (Congress), and judicial (Supreme Court)—according to a concept borrowed from the Enlightenment thinker Montesquieu. Both at the state and federal level, governments were to be elected.

However, democracy in the early American case—as in every case before the twentieth century—was not all-inclusive. Elections were indirect, favoring the upper and middle classes. Women and Native Americans could not vote, and neither could men who failed to fulfill certain property requirements. Free blacks could vote in some states, but not all, and lost many of their voting rights in the early 1800s. Most glaringly, the U.S. Constitution did not outlaw slavery, with vast long-term implications for race relations in America.

Despite its initial flaws, the U.S. Constitution, largely because of the adaptability built into it, has remained one of the most successful political documents in world history. For the purposes of this course, it should also be remembered as both the product and the cause of an international philosophical exchange: just as European Enlightenment ideals inspired the American Revolution, the revolution and the constitutional arrangement that sprang from it went on to inspire political action in Europe during the 1780s and 1790s—including in France. The impact of the American Revolution can also be seen in Haiti and Latin America during the 1790s and early 1800s.

## The French Revolution and the Napoleonic Era

As in America, it took a complex mix of political, social, economic, and intellectual causes to touch off the **French Revolution** (1789–1799).

Long-term factors included the yawning **socio-economic gap** between ordinary citizens (Third Estate) and the country's elite, which consisted of the Catholic clergy (First Estate) and the aristocracy (Second Estate). To make things worse, France's blatantly **unfair tax system** exempted the wealthy First and Second Estates, while members of the middle class—who possessed wealth and education but were barred from social advancement (and forced to pay heavy taxes) because they belonged to the Third Estate—grew increasingly frustrated. Added to this were the political ineptitude of France's kings and the **long-term debt** they had piled up since the early 1700s. (This was made even worse in the 1770s by France's financial support for the American Revolution.) Also, just as it did in the American colonies, **Enlightenment philosophy**, much of which originated in France, inspired a growing number of people with its powerful arguments in favor of fair government, social contracts, and civil liberties guaranteed by natural rights.

The immediate cause of the French Revolution was the impending bankruptcy of the government. Saddled with debt, unable to tax the rich First and Second Estates, and burdened with a wife, Marie Antoinette, who spent lavishly, **Louis XVI** (1774–1792) could not solve France's financial crisis. In 1787–1788, inflation, unemployment, and food shortages were tormenting the entire country. Searching for a solution, Louis XVI summoned the **Estates General**, a national assembly of delegates from each estate, to meet with him at Versailles in May 1789. The delegates elected by the Third Estate—mainly middle-class lawyers— expected to negotiate seriously about changing the tax system and granting equal rights to all classes. By June, however, it was clear that neither Louis XVI nor most delegates from the other Estates were prepared to compromise. This clash of wills set off ten years of revolution.

In late June, the delegates of the Third Estate, with liberal members of the First and Second Estates, formed a new governmental body, the National Assembly, and vowed not to leave Versailles until the king granted them a constitution. In July, climaxing with the **storming of the Bastille**, the people of Paris and other cities rose up in support of the assembly, as did peasants in the countryside. Over the summer, the assembly assumed power in Paris.

During the first three years of the revolution, Louis XVI was allowed to remain king, but with reduced powers. Guided by Enlightenment ideals and the American Declaration of Independence, the assembly guaranteed civil liberties in the **Declaration of the Rights of Man and the Citizen**—the writing of which was overseen by the Marquis de **Lafayette**, a liberal noble who had fought at Washington's side during the American Revolution and now took advice directly from Thomas Jefferson. Future assemblies were to be elected by popular vote. Aristocratic status and privileges, especially the exemption from taxes, were done away with, and church and state were separated. Policy was guided by the motto "Liberty, Fraternity, and Equality."

There were, however, problems. At first, the rights proclaimed by the revolution, including the vote, applied only to white, Catholic, adult males. Only with time did Jews, Protestants, and blacks gain those rights, and women did not until well into the 1900s. Slavery was not ended in France's colonies until 1794. Also, the assembly failed to solve worsening economic problems. Louis XVI, encouraged by Marie Antoinette, secretly plotted **counterrevolution**, as did many former aristocrats. Worst of all, the victorious revolutionaries could not agree on how to change France. Liberal nobles and clergy, with much of the middle class, were satisfied with parliamentary monarchy and moderate change. The rural population, happy to have equal rights and to limit the power of the king, wanted economic relief but not deeper social change. The urban lower classes (known as sans-culottes) and certain middle-class idealists were more radical. They wished to end the monarchy altogether, drive out or persecute former aristocrats (even liberal nobles), change society more thoroughly (some favored abolishing Catholicism), and export their revolution to other countries by force. Resolving all these desires would prove impossible.

From the spring of 1792 through the summer of 1794, the French Revolution took a sharply radical turn. In April 1792, France went to war with Austria and Prussia; other countries, including Britain, joined in, and France would be at war for almost the next quarter century. The economy worsened, and early military failures caused mass hysteria. Remaining aristocrats and political moderates—even heroes from the early years, such as Lafayette—fell under suspicion, as did the royal family. Radical parties became more influential.

In the fall of 1792, a new constitution stripped the king of all powers and proclaimed the French Republic. Elections to a new legislature brought radicals to power, the most important of whom were the **Jacobins**, led by **Maximilien Robespierre**, a fanatically idealistic lawyer. In January 1793, Louis XVI was executed for treason; Marie Antoinette was killed in October. The Jacobins created an executive body, the **Committee of Public Safety**, which assumed dictatorial powers and attempted the radical transformation of French society. It expanded the war effort, mobilized the economy for combat, and carried out modern Europe's first national draft. Civil war erupted in the countryside, as peasants rebelled against conscription and the radicals' efforts to do away with Catholicism.

Between the summer of 1793 and the summer of 1794, Robespierre and the Committee, supported by the urban sans-culottes, carried out a **Reign of Terror**, searching for traitors and counterrevolutionary foes. In this panicked, witch-hunt atmosphere, civil liberties were largely ignored. More than 300,000 people were arrested without warrant and tried without jury or appeal. Between 30,000 and 50,000 were killed, many beheaded by the guillotine. In July 1794, a coup within the committee overthrew and executed Robespierre, ending the Terror.

For five years, a more moderate regime, the Directory presided over the revolution, stabilizing the military situation and attempting to heal the wounds caused by the Terror. However, it proved unpopular, and its 1799 overthrow brought an end to the revolution.

Among those who ousted the Directory was a talented general, **Napoleon Bonaparte**, who quickly seized power for himself. Napoleon claimed to be a man of revolutionary ideals, but in reality he created a new dictatorship, going so far as to crown himself emperor in 1804.

Evaluating Napoleon's reign is difficult. He was arrogant and autocratic, but also charismatic and popular. His wars cost untold amounts of money and killed hundreds of thousands, but—until near the end—made France rich and mighty. He modernized France, creating institutions that still exist today, such as the **Bank of France** and the internationally influential **Civil Law Code** (**Napoleonic Code**), still the foundation for modern law not just in France, but wherever France extended its colonial influence.

Napoleon is best known for his military career. After rising to power, he continued the wars France had begun during the revolution. From 1805 to 1811, his victories made France the most powerful country in Europe; the only major nations not under his direct or indirect control were Britain and Russia. After this, several factors brought about Napoleon's downfall: his inability to counter British naval power, bloody guerrilla resistance to his authority in

Spain, and his famously overambitious invasion of Russia in 1812. He was defeated and exiled in 1814. In 1815, he escaped and had to be beaten again at the battle of **Waterloo**. Peace was restored at the **Congress of Vienna** (1814–1815). Napoleon died in captivity in 1821.

What made the French Revolution so important, especially considering its many failures? For one, it did away with absolute monarchy in Europe. Kings and emperors continued to sit on thrones there (including in France, where the royal family was restored), but in no major country were they all-powerful, and as time passed, monarchs yielded more of their authority to ministries and legislatures. Also, the French Revolution, like the American Revolution before it, inspired future uprisings, as described below. As detailed in Chapter 18, the emergence of modern politics in the West—including the use of the terms "left" and "right" and the formation of **conservatism** and **liberalism** as coherent movements—had much to do with the French Revolution. Finally, the greatest legacy of both the American and French revolutions was to cause people to demand greater popular participation in government and to force nineteenth-century governments to be more attentive to their desires. The story of modern politics is primarily *this* story.

## Haiti and the Latin American Wars of Independence

Revolutionary influence catapulted back across the Atlantic, as the impact of events in France spread far beyond Europe's borders, and especially to Haiti and Latin America.

Prior to independence, the sugar- and coffee-producing colony of Haiti was called Saint Domingue by the French and Santo Domingo by the Spanish, with each country occupying half the island and relying heavily on slave labor imported from Africa. After 1789, revolution in France threw Saint Domingue into turmoil, largely because the "rights of man and the citizen" were not extended to everyone living in French colonies. Revolutionary freedoms went automatically to Frenchmen and Creoles (those of French descent but born in the colonies) but were not extended to free blacks and mulattos until May 1791. And because France's revolutionary government decided at that point not to end slavery, the half-million slaves of Saint Domingue revolted in August. This began the **Haitian Rebellion** (1791–1804), the only large-scale slave revolt to succeed in the New World.

By 1793, **François Toussaint L'Ouverture**, a talented commander known as the "Black Washington," had come to lead the revolt. Although the French government finally abolished slavery in 1794, L'Ouverture's goal was now full independence and the liberation of slaves on the Spanish side of the island, which he invaded in 1798. For several years, France heatedly debated the question of whether to let Haiti go free and establish friendly relations with it (the outcome L'Ouverture hoped for) or to retake it by force. In 1802, Napoleon—who, ironically, as a junior officer in the 1790s, had greatly admired L'Ouverture—sent a large force to end the rebellion. Unfortunately for Napoleon, although L'Ouverture fell into French captivity and died in prison, the French proved unequal to tropical warfare and lost 40,000 soldiers to yellow fever. They went home in disgrace, and the independent nation of Haiti was born in 1804. Not only did the Haitian Rebellion lead quickly to further uprisings in Latin America, it convinced Napoleon that it was strategically wasteful for France to maintain major colonies in the New World. Consequently, he sold the vast Louisiana territory, stretching from the Great Lakes to the Mississippi delta, to the young United States at a bargain price. This **Louisiana Purchase**, secured by Thomas Jefferson in 1803, significantly boosted the United States' chances of eventually mastering the entire continent and can be seen in hindsight as a major shift in global power.

In the meantime, revolutionary impulses were gathering force in Mexico, Central America, and South America, where the **Latin American wars of independence** would rage from 1810 to 1825. Underlying factors here included a growing sense of nationalism and local resentment of Spain's and Portugal's restrictive economic policies. Also important was the frustration that the *criollo* ("creole"), or European-descended, upper and middle classes felt at being barred from upward mobility by the rigid social hierarchy that prevailed in Latin American colonies. And for clear examples of how political action could achieve decisive results, discontented Latin Americans had the American Revolution and the Haitian Rebellion close at hand.

It was Napoleon, between 1807 and 1809, who toppled the colonial order in Latin America by invading Spain and Portugal. With the Spanish king under house arrest and Portugal's royal family forced to flee to Brazil, rebellions sprang up throughout Central and South America.

The most influential of these revolutionaries was **Simón Bolívar** (1783–1830), known as the Liberator. A member of Venezuela's *criollo* upper class, Bolívar was inspired by Enlightenment ideals, frustrated by the inefficiency and injustice of Spanish rule, and personally ambitious. In 1810, he took control of the independence movement sweeping across the northern parts of Spanish South America. Unlike many others of the creole elite, who rebelled against Spain for their own narrow interests, Bolívar realized that no revolt could succeed unless it attracted all classes. In a bold stroke, he promised to fight for the rights of mixed-race Latin Americans and the emancipation of slaves. These principles, elaborated in documents like Bolívar's 1815 **Jamaica Letter**, turned a small and unsuccessful upper- and middle-class rebellion into a mass war of independence. The military turning point of Bolívar's wars came in 1819–1821, when he gained control over present-day Venezuela and Columbia. At this juncture, Bolívar joined forces with another freedom fighter, José de San Martín, a general turned revolutionary. Between 1816 and 1820, San Martín had freed southern areas such as Argentina, Chile, Uruguay, and Paraguay. Despite political differences—San Martín was more conservative—the two decided to cooperate, with Bolívar as leader. By 1825, royalists had been cleared out of Bolivia, Ecuador, and Peru, and Spanish South America was free.

> **NOTE**
>
> In 1820, the king of Portugal went back to Europe to reclaim his throne. He left his son, Prince Pedro, to govern Brazil, but gave him this advice: "My son, if Brazil starts to demand independence, make sure you are the one to proclaim it. Then put the crown on your own head." This is exactly what happened in 1822.

Mexico and Central America liberated themselves as well. The **Mexican War of Independence** (1810–1823) was complicated by the inability of various social classes to cooperate. It began when the priest **Miguel Hidalgo**, unfurling the flag of the Virgin of Guadalupe, called for freedom from Spain. Hidalgo was killed in 1811, but his fight was carried on by another priest, José Maria Morelos. Both fought not just for national independence, but also for constitutional rule, equal rights for Indians and mestizos, and the liberation of slaves. Their platform gained mass support from the lower classes, but angered many upper-class Mexicans, even those who wanted independence. In 1815, Morelos was killed like Hidalgo before him, but by conservative Mexicans, not the Spanish. In the end, Mexico's revolt was completed by the elite, not the lower classes. A right-wing colonel, Agustín Iturbide, overthrew Spanish rule in 1820–1821. He tried to establish himself as a dictator, but was quickly ousted. A Mexican republic was proclaimed in 1923, the same year that the nations immediately to the south established the United Provinces of Central America.

As discussed below, the constitutional arrangements that followed the Latin American Wars of Independence, although based on similar principles, did not prove as successful as the one established in the United States.

## WESTERN IMPERIALISM AND GLOBAL CONFLICT

One of the most astounding facts of the nineteenth century is that, while in 1815, the nations of the West—Europe and North America—controlled 35 percent of the world's habitable territory, they controlled 85 percent by 1914.

Western colonial expansion, pursued since the 1400s, was nothing new. From the mid-1800s to the early 1900s, however, it took on a more aggressive and systematic character, referred to by many as the **new imperialism**. As a practical undertaking, this domination of the world was an impressive military feat, and it brought Europe and America great power and wealth. On the other hand, it was inseparable from bloodshed, racial prejudice, and slavery. As the English-Polish author Joseph Conrad wrote in the novel *Heart of Darkness*—one of the classic literary depictions of European imperialism—"The conquest of the earth, which mostly means taking it away from those who have a different complexion or slightly flatter noses than ourselves, is not a pretty thing when you look into it too much." Moreover, Euro-American imperialism left deep political scars around the globe, many of which have not yet healed in the twenty-first century.

## Causes and Motivations

A variety of factors enabled and motivated the new imperialism. Industrialization made Western economies hungry for **raw materials**—including timber, industrial and precious metals, coal, rubber, and various chemicals—which could be wrested from less powerful societies by force, and for **overseas markets**. Industrial-era weaponry lent Western armies and navies **military superiority**, and because modern ships powered by coal (and then petroleum) required repair bases and refueling depots, Western **sea power** depended on control over islands and ports around the world. Also prompting imperialism was Europe's rapid **population growth**, which caused **migration** not just to the Americas (as described in Chapter 20), but also to **settler colonies** far from the homeland. **Geographical and scientific aptitude** allowed for easier penetration of the African and Asian interior. In particular, medical advances—such as the anti-malarial treatment **quinine**—made it possible for Westerners to establish themselves in tropical zones where illnesses like sleeping sickness, yellow fever, and **malaria** had previously kept them from gaining footholds.

Finally, a complex set of cultural factors motivated empire building. A sense of **racial superiority**, buttressed in many cases by the doctrine of **social Darwinism** discussed in Chapter 18, was widespread among white Europeans and Americans, a large proportion of whom believed they were naturally entitled to conquer and colonize the darker-skinned, less technologically advanced peoples of Africa and Asia. Beyond that, many Westerners became convinced that they had a duty to teach and modernize those peoples. The English poet Rudyard Kipling famously labeled this the **white man's burden**, and the French spoke of their civilizing mission, or *la mission civilisatrice*. This attitude could be well-meaning, and Euro-American missionaries, doctors, scientists, and colonial officials sometimes did useful work. However, they did so at least partly out of condescension, and they often trampled on or eradicated native cultural practices and beliefs.

## Forms of Imperialism

Empires took different forms during this era and were governed with different degrees of severity. Individual empires are dealt with on a region-by-region basis in the following section, but some generalizations are possible here. **Overseas empires** and **settler colonies** were the best-known. By far the largest was Britain's, on which "the sun never set," as expressed in a famous motto of the time. France gradually accumulated the era's second-largest empire, and countries like Spain, Portugal, and the Netherlands, which had been more active during the Columbian age of exploration, continued to hold on to certain overseas possessions. After 1870, new countries such as Germany and Italy began to build overseas empires, in an attempt to catch up with more established imperial powers like Britain and France. **Land-based empires** expanded as well. Austria, not commonly thought of as a colonizing power, maintained one in eastern and southeastern Europe, colliding with the empire ruled by the Ottoman Turks. Russia conquered Siberia, much of Central Asia, and for a time, parts of North America. At the end of the century, Japan extended its imperial reach to the Asian mainland, a short distance away.

When Japan emerged as an imperial power, social Darwinism and ideologies of racial exceptionalism became increasingly popular there. The influential 1885 essay "Goodbye Asia" (discussed at greater length in Chapter 18) shows how many Japanese were coming to believe that their rapid modernization made them inherently superior to other Asians.

**Economic imperialism**, which typically involved pressuring weaker nations to offer favorable trade terms, rather than outright colonization, was practiced as well. Prominent targets during this century included Latin America and Qing China, and arguably Egypt during and after the construction of the **Suez Canal**.

## Geopolitical Tensions and Rising Conflict

Wherever imperial expansion was pursued, it caused a steady rise in global conflict as the century passed. Campaigns of conquest were violent in their own right, and Euro-American **competition over empire** became increasingly bitter in the late 1800s, with fewer desirable territories left to be claimed. Tensions were heightened even further by specific geopolitical conflicts, including the **Eastern Question** (how to fill the power vacuum caused in the Balkans and the eastern Mediterranean by the Ottoman Empire's steady decline), the **Great Game** (the collision of British and Russian spheres of influence in Central Asia), and the **Scramble for Africa** (the rush to subjugate the entire continent between the 1880s and the 1910s). The growing intensity of **nationalism** in Western nations added to the problem.

All this made it increasingly harder for Western states to maintain their **balance of power**. Between Napoleon's defeat in 1815 and the outbreak of the Crimean War (1853–1856), the settlement devised at the **Congress of Vienna** (1814–1815) preserved peace among the European powers. After mid-century, wars involving Western states became more common—including the **Franco-Prussian War** (1870–1871), which created the modern German state and completed the process of Italian unification—and although these tended to be relatively short and

### NATIVE ELITES

One technique commonly used by imperial powers was the Western-style training of native elites to serve as officials and bureaucrats, and of native troops—such as sepoys in India and askaris in Africa—to fill the ranks of overseas forces. The aims here were to economize on labor and to ensure loyalty. The educational system in British India, in the words of one of its architects, was to create elites who were "Indian in blood and color, but English in taste, in opinion, in morals, and in intellect." Likewise, the reasoning behind America's sponsorship of the pro-U.S. Federalista Party in the newly acquired Philippines was that "these picked Filipinos will be of infinite value as the chief agents in securing their people's obedience." In the economic sphere, compradors were native merchants, particularly in East and South Asia, who cooperated with Western colonists and corporations as commercial agents and middlemen.

limited in scope, they encouraged a growing spirit of belligerent patriotism (nicknamed **jingoism** by the British press at this time). On the surface, relative stability among the Western powers was maintained between 1871 and 1914, a period in European history

**NOTE**

Southeastern Europe—the Balkans—became one of the world's most unstable regions during the late 1800s and early 1900s. The imperial ambitions of Russia, Austria, Italy, and the Ottoman Empire all centered on it. Many of the states there, most famously Serbia, were newly independent and fiercely nationalistic. The Balkans earned the label "powderkeg of Europe" during the turn of the century, as several short wars broke out there, even before the events that triggered World War I.

known as the Long Peace. Underneath, however, the potential for a major conflict grew with every passing year, especially after 1890, when the German chancellor **Otto von Bismarck**—a cautious diplomat and a key architect of the European balance of power—was dismissed by the rash and impatient emperor, Wilhelm II.

During the 1890s and the early 1900s, the **European alliance system** divided the great powers into two armed camps. Germany and Austria were already aligned with Italy in the Triple Alliance (formed in 1881, although Italy would drop out in 1914). In the mid-1890s, France, bitter about defeat in the Franco-Prussian War, allied with Russia, which viewed Austria as a threat in the Balkans, which both countries viewed as their rightful sphere of influence. Geographically, France and Russia had their rivals surrounded. As long as possible, Britain remained uncommitted: thanks to the Great Game in Central Asia, it viewed Russia as an enemy, and it had little affection for France. But after 1900, Britain grew increasingly alarmed by Germany's aggressive empire building, especially in Africa, and its rapid naval expansion, which threatened Britain's sea power, the root of its global might. In 1907, Britain informally partnered with the Franco-Russian alliance, forming the Triple Entente ("understanding"). From this point forward, any crisis between two countries could potentially involve all of Europe's major powers—significantly increasing the likelihood of a major war.

## POLITICAL DEVELOPMENTS BY REGION

### Europe

In the years following the French Revolution, and as the Industrial Revolution progressed, European governments had to decide how to respond to the shock waves caused by both events. The political philosophies and ideologies discussed in Chapter 18 were a product of those decisions.

Between 1815 and 1848, most governments, convinced that even the slightest liberalism would lead to renewed political chaos, attempted to minimize change or even undo what had transpired during the revolutionary and Napoleonic years. This arch-conservative stance, known as **reaction**, was the guiding principle of the **Congress of Vienna** (1814–1815), which not only ended the Napoleonic wars, but forged a long-lasting if informal agreement among Europe's major regimes to work together to preserve order and prevent change. Monarchies were no longer absolute, but royal families were restored wherever possible, including in France. In addition, civil liberties were restricted, censorship was heavy, and secret police forces were common. Trade unions were illegal, as were political parties in many countries. Repression lightened somewhat in parliamentary states like Britain—where the 1832 Reform Act slightly expanded the vote, and where the worst industrial-era working conditions began to attract Parliament's attention—and France, where the 1830 revolution further limited the power of the monarch. In Central and Eastern Europe, the level of repression was much greater: if voting systems existed at all, they were limited, and Russia not only remained an absolute monarchy, but still continued the practice of **serfdom**.

A key turning point came with the **revolution of 1848**, whose underlying causes included popular impatience with reactionary rule, socioeconomic stress caused by industrialization, and a series of bad harvests (like the Irish Potato Famine) that caused the decade to be known as the "hungry forties." The revolution began in France, where the king was deposed and Napoleon's nephew appointed president. Uprisings then spread to much of the rest of Europe, although they spared Britain and Russia. They were all crushed by the summer of 1849, but had lasting effects nonetheless. They compelled Austria and German states like Prussia to grant constitutions, and since many of them had involved ethnic revolts against Austrian rule, they demonstrated the growing political importance of **nationalism**. They inspired **Karl Marx** and Friedrich Engels to write *The Communist Manifesto*. Most of all, they hammered home for good the lesson of the French Revolution: that the demands of ordinary people had to be taken seriously.

Therefore, during the second half of the century, most European governments expanded **political representation** and legislated the **improvement of working conditions**, although whether they did so by means of **reform** or **revolution** varied. Even in less representative regimes, political power spread outward to larger numbers of governmental ministries and agencies.

In Victorian Britain, the Parliament gradually extended the vote to middle- and lower-class males by means of the **Second** (1867) and **Third** (1885) **Reform Acts**, and also granted economic concessions and fairer labor laws to the lower classes. Britain by the late 1800s possessed the world's largest empire and was extremely prosperous. It wrestled, however, with the questions of **women's suffrage** and Irish nationalism. France's progress toward democracy was less gentle. After 1848, all adult males could vote in France, but in 1851, the president, Louis Napoleon, staged a coup and crowned himself Napoleon III. He was not an absolute dictator, and he helped to modernize Paris and industrialize the country, but his humiliating defeat during the **Franco-Prussian War** (1870–1871) caused his abdication. After a short but bloody revolution, a new democratic republic arose in 1871 and lasted until 1940. Unfortunately, democracy did not solve all of France's problems. Corruption, financial scandals, and party rivalries rocked France, and worst of all was the **Dreyfus Affair** (1894–1906), in which the army and government falsely blamed a Jewish officer for the leaking of military secrets to Germany. The controversy divided the left (which maintained Dreyfus's innocence) from the right (which was convinced of his guilt) and exposed the ugly streak of **anti-Semitism** in modern European society.

**Nationalism** profoundly affected politics in Italy, Germany, and Austria. The **unification of Italy** as a parliamentary monarchy took place in the 1860s and was finished in 1870. The **unification of Germany** was spearheaded by Prussia in a series of three short conflicts, culminating in the **Franco-Prussian War** of 1870–1871. The new German emperor shared power with a legislature called the Reichstag, and all adult males technically had the vote—although the electoral system was heavily stacked in favor of the upper classes. With **Otto von Bismarck** serving the emperor as chancellor (and also as Europe's most skilled diplomat), Germany rapidly modernized, thanks to a policy of **state-directed industrialization**. Despite his staunch conservatism, Bismarck craftily offered the lower classes substantial economic concessions—the most generous in Europe at the time—to keep them from becoming attracted to trade unions or socialism. In Austria, post-1848 liberalization led to the creation of a parliament in 1861 and various concessions to the empire's many minority populations, whose nationalist aspirations were rising. Most strikingly, the **Ausgleich** ("compromise") of 1867 granted equal status to Austria's largest minority, the Hungarians, and the state was renamed the Austro-Hungarian Empire. As in other parts of Europe, **anti-Semitism** became a major part of political life here.

**NOTE**

Economic concessions desired by the working class in any given country generally included all or most of the following: higher wages, shorter workdays and work weeks, safer working conditions, insurance in case of injury, and pensions for retirement. The right to form trade unions and go on strike was considered crucial as well.

Even autocratic Russia was forced to change. Shaken by his country's embarrassing loss in the Crimean War (1853–1856), the moderately liberal Alexander II modernized Russia with a series of "great reforms," the most important of which was his 1861 **emancipation of the serfs**. However, Alexander was assassinated by radical terrorists who believed he had not gone far enough, and the conservative tsars who succeeded him undid many of his changes. Nicholas II, who met with a terrible defeat during the **Russo-Japanese War** (1904–1905), almost lost his throne during the 1905 Revolution. This compelled him to share power with a new and popularly-elected legislature, the Duma—but once the danger passed, Nicholas weakened the Duma and avoided cooperating with it. Anti-Semitic persecution escalated in late tsarist Russia, and **pogroms**, or anti-Jewish raids, became distressingly common.

## The Middle East and Central Asia

This was a time of decline for the Middle East, as the glory days of the once-mighty "gunpowder empires" faded away. Safavid Persia had disappeared in the early 1700s, and although the Ottoman Empire survived into the early 1900s, it lost territory at an alarming rate during the 1800s and came to be derided as the "sick man of Europe."

Not only did the Ottoman Empire lose a number of wars—and much land—to Austria and Russia during the 1700s, internal troubles plagued it. The chief dilemma was that sultans and reformers who wished to modernize met with resistance from Islamic traditionalists or influential groups with a vested interest in preserving old ways. A key example involved the armed forces, where the once-innovative **janissaries**, now privileged but woefully outdated, blocked any attempt to improve the military, to the point of assassinating the sultan in 1807.

Reformers had better luck between the 1820s and the 1870s, although not enough in the long run. Janissary power was broken in the 1820s, and the army and navy were upgraded and Westernized. From 1839 to 1876, in a series of changes known as the **Tanzimat reforms**, the government promoted greater religious tolerance for non-Muslims; introduced Western science and technology into the educational system; boosted industrialization and built railroads and telegraphs; and liberalized and secularized the legal system, at least to a degree. Sultan **Abdul Hamid II** even proclaimed the **constitution of 1876** and agreed to share power with an elected legislature.

**NOTE**

Technically governed by the Qajar dynasty between 1794 and 1925, Persia suffered a fate similar to that of Qing China. It was dominated by foreign powers in the 1800s without being formally colonized. Although they kept the Qajar rulers in place, Russia and Britain cynically divided the country into northern and southern spheres of influence—an arrangement that lasted until after World War II.

Unfortunately, in 1878, the sultan suspended the constitution for 20 years, and the Tanzimat effort fizzled. Internally, Abdul Hamid was caught between traditionalists who opposed any changes at all and a growing number of modernizing politicians and military officers—the so-called **Young Turks**—who wanted more change than he was willing to deliver. By the early 1900s, the Young Turks would play a decisive role in ending his rule.

In the meantime, the Tanzimat effort, and Ottoman domestic policy in general, was handicapped further by a cascade of rebellions and wars that threatened the empire with disintegration. The **Greek War of Independence** (1821–1832) inspired future nationalist uprisings among other Balkan Christians, and by persuading Britain and Russia to intervene out of sympathy for the Greeks, it stoked a decades-long anti-Turkish prejudice in Europe. At the same time, the rebellion of **Muhammad Ali** (who transformed Egypt into an autonomous principality in 1805), along with the **French colonization of Algeria** (taken from the Turks in 1830 and brutally pacified by the end of the 1840s), vividly demonstrated the Ottoman state's structural vulnerability. Before Ali's death in 1839, he created a Western-style military, recruited European professionals and advisors, and industrialized the production of Egyptian cotton. Visionary in certain ways, he governed autocratically as khedive (hereditary prince) and subjected cotton growers and textile workers to oppressive labor conditions.

The Ottomans' external problems worsened after mid-century. Russia's sudden annexation of Ottoman provinces on the Danube provoked the Crimean War (1853–1856), in which Britain and France stepped in to aid the Turks against Russia. Balkan nationalism intensified, as illustrated by the **Balkan Crisis** of 1876–1878, when Bulgarians, Montenegrins, Serbs, and Romanians revolted against economically harsh policies. In lashing back, Ottoman troops committed terrible anti-Christian atrocities, undermining the Tanzimat reforms' modernizing spirit and triggering widespread anti-Turkish revulsion in Europe. Russia warred against the Ottomans on the rebels' behalf and imposed a punitive treaty. Although other European powers, not wishing the Ottomans to be fatally destabilized by their defeat, negotiated a more lenient treaty, the rebel nations went free, and the empire's grip on the Balkans continued to loosen.

The Ottoman Empire's seemingly unavoidable collapse presented Europe with the geopolitical challenge known as the Eastern Question. Although Europe had viewed the Turks as enemies since the 1300s, the Ottomans were predictable and held together many volatile parts of the eastern Mediterranean. If they fell, chaos or a stronger foe might arise in their place. Also, if European nations let themselves be tempted into seizing too much of the crumbling empire at one time, it might upset Europe's fragile balance of power. They therefore agreed to manage the empire's decline slowly and carefully, and even to prop it up if it seemed in danger of immediate collapse.

Ottoman control over North Africa likewise weakened. Egypt remained outside the Ottoman orbit, ruled by the khedives (Muhammad Ali's descendants) and then, after the 1850s, falling increasingly under European influence. The 1854–1869 construction of the **Suez Canal**, financed by the French-dominated **Suez Canal Company** and overseen by the French engineer Ferdinand de Lesseps, gave France huge economic leverage over the khedive. That leverage passed in the 1870s and 1880s to Britain, which purchased shares in the canal and then stepped in militarily to save the khedive from an 1881 revolt. That same year, the British established a protectorate called the Anglo-Egyptian Administration, which left the khedive on the throne but placed real control in British hands. To the west of Egypt, the Ottomans had already lost Algeria to the French. They now watched helplessly as Tunisia fell to France, Morocco to the French and Spanish, and Libya to Italy.

As the new century began, the sultan's days were numbered, thanks to the pro-Western **Young Turks** who had coalesced in the late 1800s around an agenda of rapid modernization. Led by the army officer **Enver Pasha**, the Young Turks deposed Abdul Hamid II in 1908–1909, installing a figurehead sultan and restoring the **constitution of 1876**. The Young Turks pursued a program of industrialization, secularization, and socioeconomic reform. However, they continued to lose territory in North Africa and the Balkans, and their decision to forge close ties with Germany led them to support the losing side in World War I—the final step in the empire's ultimate demise.

As for Islamic Central Asia, home to the Silk Road khanates, Russia waged long wars of imperial conquest here throughout the 1800s. The Russians fought to gain natural resources (Central Asia is a great cotton-producing center), to secure their open southern frontier (a longstanding strategic concern), and to further their dream—never realized—of winning warm-water ports on the Indian Ocean coast. As noted above, Russia's ambitions in this region brought it into diplomatic conflict with the British, who feared any possible interference with their lines of communication to India. The resulting **Great Game** caused bitter Anglo-Russian rivalry until the early 1900s.

## Africa

Paradoxically, Africa, which had been victimized by foreign colonists and slave-traders for hundreds of years, remained comparatively free of direct outside influence until well into the 1800s. The Ottoman Empire controlled North Africa (although its authority was slipping), Omani Arabs ruled most of the East African shore and Swahili ports (after displacing the Portuguese who had dominated there before), and the European presence on the continent was restricted to selected spots on the coast.

**As described in Chapter 20, the Atlantic slave trade continued to ravage Africa—approximately two million Africans were forcibly taken to the Americas during the 1800s—but it was made illegal and eventually shut down. The East African slave trade ended as well during the late 1800s.**

In other words, many African states and societies were strong enough in the late 1700s and early 1800s to resist foreign domination. Others were cooperative enough that Europeans, who were arriving in greater numbers, found it useful to work with them rather than fight them. Many of these states, such as Benin, Dahomey, Kongo, and the Ashanti (Asante) kingdoms, played significant roles in the Atlantic slave trade; in exchange for gold and guns, they took prisoners from enemy states and tribes and sold them to Euro-American slavers. Among this era's most powerful and unified African states were:

- The **Barbary states** of Islamic North Africa (present-day Morocco, Algeria, Tunisia, and Libya), which were technically ruled by the Ottomans but increasingly autonomous. Piratical **corsairs** from these states threatened European and American shipping and enslaved captives as galley oarsmen. Their raids embroiled the young United States in some of its earliest military conflicts (the Barbary Wars, commemorated in the line from the U.S. Marine hymn, "to the shores of Tripoli"), and partly provoked the **French colonization of Algeria**, starting in 1830.
- The **Ashanti** (Asante) **kingdom** in West Africa's Gold Coast (present-day Ghana), which engaged in a dramatic military buildup during the late 1700s, financed by its participation in the Atlantic slave trade. The Ashanti threatened European outposts and trade routes along the Gold Coast and resisted Euro-American attempts to destroy the slave trade. Starting in 1823, Britain found itself locked in a long series of wars with the Ashanti, who kept up their fight for independence until 1902.
- The **Zulu kingdom**, which existed on the edge of Dutch and British possessions in South Africa. Before 1800, the Bantu-speaking Zulu were organized into small, relatively peaceful clans. Around 1816, though, a new chieftain, **Shaka**, united them into a single tribe and used his military talents to conquer neighbor after neighbor. The Zulus' warlike expansion caused a large wave of tribal migration throughout the southern part of the continent, and they also clashed with Dutch Boers and British settlers. Only after several conflicts, especially the **Zulu War of 1879**, were they pacified.
- **Zanzibar**, which was a producer of spices, sugar, and cloves for the Indian Ocean trade network and a key hub for the **East African slave trade**. Ruled by the Arab sultanate of Oman after 1698, it became the Omani capital in 1840 and was promoted to the status of sultanate in 1861. It controlled the Zanj, a large portion of the East African coast.

■ **Ethiopia**, which remained Coptic Christian in predominantly Muslim East Africa. Ethiopia existed largely in isolation between the mid-1600s, when it expelled the Portuguese, and the mid-1800s, when Theodore II, a pro-Western but mentally erratic king, began a process of military modernization. This policy, continued by his successors, allowed Ethiopia to ward off European invasion. Its 1896 victory over Italian forces at Adowa ranks as one of the most embarrassing setbacks suffered by a nineteenth-century European power.

As the century progressed, nearly every part of Africa lost its freedom to European states. The coastal areas, easiest to reach, were the first to fall. **South Africa**, which had been colonized by Dutch **Boers** (also known as Afrikaners) as early as the mid-1600s, saw an influx of new settlers after the Napoleonic Wars, when the British assumed control over the region. Displaced by the British, the Boers made a **Great Trek** to the north and east during the 1830s and soon founded their own states (the Orange Free State and Transvaal) on the border of British South Africa. The Boers and British periodically clashed with each other, and more regularly with the local Xhosa and Zulu until the capitulation of the latter in the **Zulu War of 1879**. The discovery of **South African gold mines** and **diamond fields** heightened military tensions here and led to the cruel exploitation of African laborers. Also on the coast, but far to the north, the **French colonization of Algeria** was carried out during the 1830s and 1840s with scorched-earth devastation and frightful violence against local civilians. The French became particularly attached to Algeria, viewing it as their most important possession in the way Britain regarded India. The economic and political domination of Egypt from the 1850s onward, thanks to the construction of the **Suez Canal**, is described above.

Despite all this, only about 10 percent of African territory fell under European control before 1880. At that point, the so-called **Scramble for Africa** began, lasting until the eve of World War I and subjugating virtually the entire continent with astonishing rapidity. Thanks to geographical knowledge gained by explorers between the late 1700s and the mid-1800s, and also to industrial-era weaponry and effective medical treatments for tropical diseases, Westerners were now able to press fully into the African interior. Civil and intertribal conflict made numerous parts of Africa vulnerable to European takeover, and African states that had benefited from the slave trades found themselves economically weakened when that commerce came to an end. The Europeans themselves were motivated by a combination of greed (**gold**, **diamonds**, **ivory**, and **rubber** were just a few of the resources they coveted), belief in their own racial superiority (reinforced by the doctrine of **social Darwinism**), and their condescending **white man's burden** conviction that they had a duty to "civilize" what they thought of as "the dark continent." Moreover, the century's long antislavery campaigns accustomed Westerners not just to taking military action in Africa, but to thinking of intervention there as morally justified.

**NOTE**

In 1856–1857, British settlement in South Africa touched off the Xhosa cattle-killing movement, an example of the many millenarian rebellions, or religiously inspired episodes of resistance, that occurred during the era of new imperialism. Here, the Xhosa came to believe that, if they killed their own livestock, who were already falling ill, the spirits would expel the British from their lands.

A pivotal moment in the Scramble for Africa was the **Berlin Conference** (1884–1885), convened by the German statesman **Otto von Bismarck** to defuse diplomatic tensions stirred up by the Europeans' headlong rush to carve up Africa. Boundaries were agreed upon, as were guidelines for further expansion, but long-term harm was done to Africa by the fact that the lines drawn on the map during and after Berlin reflected only European desires. They bore no relation at all to the traditional territorial demarcations used by Africans themselves, and even today many African ethnic groups remain divided by European-drawn borders, or are forced by those borderlines into close proximity with their enemies.

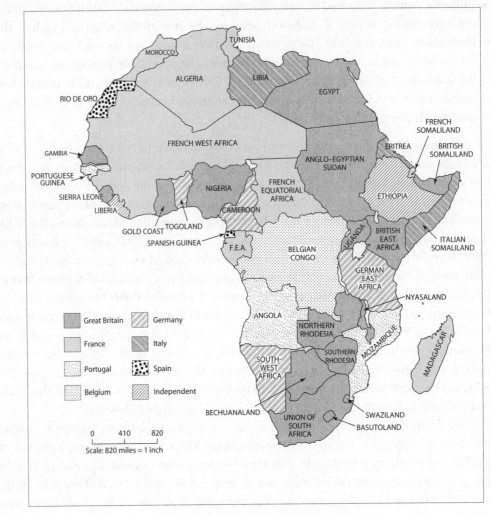

**European Imperialism in Africa, 1914.**

Europe's colonial experiences and policies varied widely in Africa. Britain controlled several colonies in the west, including the Gold Coast (home to the Ashanti), but even more extensive was the nearly unbroken chain of possessions it gained in the east, largely at the expense of the Omani Arabs. This ran from South Africa to Egypt (where its Anglo-Egyptian Administration established a protectorate in 1881 and went on to conquer the Sudan in the 1880s and 1890s). The British dreamed of building a railroad stretching the entire length of the continent—"from **Cape to Cairo**," as the imperialist Cecil Rhodes put it—but were blocked by Germany's acquisition of territory on the eastern coast. As in India, the British governed with a blend of exploitative selfishness, racist sentiment, and well-meaning condescension. They trained native elites and native troops in the Western style, and brought new science, medicine, and industrial technology to Africa. Much the same can be said of France, which (after its initial brutality in Algeria) acted mainly in accordance with its *mission civilisatrice*. France dominated the Saharan north and large portions of the west, in addition to the island of Madagascar.

By contrast, Portuguese rule in colonies like Angola and Mozambique was quite harsh. Even worse were the Belgians and Germans. Starting in the 1870s, **Leopold II**, the Belgian king, established a private company (later bequeathed to the Belgian nation) for the economic development of the **Congo**, and its claim to the colony was recognized at the Berlin Conference of 1884–1885. Belgian-owned **rubber plantations** brutally forced Congolese villagers to meet production quotas, often allowing overseers to chop off the right hands of harvesters who fell short, and sometimes massacring workers as punishment. Before the Belgians' arrival, Congo had a population of around 20 million, but that number fell to 8.5 million by 1911. Germany, a new country anxious to build an empire on par with those of Britain and France, moved aggressively into Tanganyika, near Zanzibar in the east, and several small areas in the east. However, these were unprofitable leftovers, and the Germans also faced several costly uprisings. Their infamous **Herero Wars** (1904–1907) involved the use of **concentration camps** against civilians and killed nearly 80 percent of Southwest Africa's Herero natives. They are considered by some scholars to have been an early instance of twentieth-century genocide.

**NOTE**

In the Sudan, the British were opposed by a millenarian rebellion led by the Mahdi—Arabic for "one who is rightly guided," and the title of the messianic figure foretold in Islamic prophecy. In 1885, the Mahdi's army, driven by religious fervor and anti-colonial fury, massacred a British force at Khartoum, one of Britain's most stunning imperial defeats. Not until 1898 did the British gain revenge, crushing the Mahdi at Omdurman.

Within three decades, all of Africa—except for Liberia and Ethiopia—had been brought under Europe's imperial sway. However, the Scramble for Africa backfired on the Europeans by rousing their combative passions and contributing to the diplomatic tensions that helped cause World War I. In 1896, France and Britain almost came to blows because of the Fashoda Incident, in which French troops moving eastward into the Nile Valley encountered British forces who regarded the region as theirs. German interference with French and Spanish plans for northwestern Africa led to a Morocco Crisis in 1906 and another in 1911.

Even worse was Germany's public support of the Dutch Afrikaners in their **Boer War** (1899–1902) against Britain. Although the British had a more powerful army, the Boers were skilled guerrilla sharpshooters fighting on their home territory. The war grew painfully vicious, with the British using concentration camps to keep 120,000 civilians—over 20,000 of whom died—from supporting the Boer guerrillas. Germany's open sympathy for the Boers worsened Anglo-German relations (already strained by the two countries' naval race), with profound implications for the **European alliance system** that took shape in the years prior to World War I.

## East Asia

Largely isolated from the wider world during the late 1700s and early 1800s, and highly self-satisfied with the cultural splendor of bygone days, both China and Japan were confronted by Western imperial pressures in the mid-1800s. To China's loss and Japan's gain, they reacted in diametrically opposed ways.

Qing China in the late 1700s still enjoyed immense wealth, artistic and intellectual grandeur, and firm political and military sway over the states in its **tributary system**, and over most of the neighboring region. The emperor **Qianlong** (1763–1795) is remembered as the Qing dynasty's last truly capable ruler. Unfortunately, even during Qianlong's reign, and more so afterward, **Confucian-based social stratification** remained rigid, and the cost of defending China's northern and western frontiers—combined with too-rapid population growth (from 300 million in 1799 to 400 million a century later)—terribly burdened the economy. Popular discontent erupted in violent uprisings like the **White Lotus Rebellion** (1796–1804), and the government grew even more corrupt and incompetent after Qianlong's death.

At the same time, the Qing badly mishandled relations with the West. In the late 1700s and early 1800s, Europeans and Americans were allowed to trade with China only in a handful of designated cities (most famously **Canton** on the southern coast). Also, while the Chinese were happy to sell silk, porcelain, and increasingly large quantities of **tea** to Western nations, they accepted only silver bullion in exchange, refusing to allow any more than a tiny selection of Western goods to be sold in their country. For many years, this lopsided balance of trade angered Westerners, but when the **Macartney mission** petitioned Qianlong in 1793 for permission to open a British embassy in China and to sell British goods there, the emperor replied dismissively that "your country has nothing we need." Similar European requests met with similar responses, and while this refusal to bargain was partly tough business sense, it also reflected an imprudent sense of superiority. Based on past glories, the Qing continued to believe that China was the **Middle Kingdom** and that all outsiders were barbarians. What they failed to recognize was that, already by the end of the 1700s, China had fallen far behind the West when it came to science and technology, and that it could not hope to match the stronger navies, better weapons, and more effective armies that would be pitted against them in the 1800s.

**Tea Harvesting in China.**
For hundreds of years, silk, then porcelain, had been China's chief trade commodities. During the 1600s and 1700s, however, tea overtook both in importance. The tea trade played a great role in global economics during the 1700s and 1800s. During those centuries, "all the tea in China" became the most popular slang phrase to describe unimaginable wealth.

In the meantime, the British, followed by other Westerners, including from the United States, embarked on a campaign of **economic imperialism** by flooding China with a highly potent variety of opium from British India. With lightning speed, this new substance became the drug of choice among Chinese of all classes, and the **opium trade** overwhelmingly reversed the economic balance of power: instead of flowing into China, silver bullion now flowed out at an alarming rate. Also to the authorities' dismay, opium addiction became so widespread during the early 1800s that on any given day, millions of farmers and workers were too incapacitated to work. In 1839, the Qing trade commissioner **Lin Zexu** protested to the British, begging Queen Victoria herself to end the trade. He then confiscated a huge quantity of opium from British warehouses in Canton and cast it into the ocean—a stunning financial blow that incensed British merchants and sparked the **First Opium War** (1839–1842). The fighting, easily won by the technologically advanced British, ended with the

Treaty of Nanking, the first of the many "**unequal treaties**" forced on nineteenth-century China by the Western powers. The Qing government had to open more ports to foreign trade, lower tariffs on British goods, and surrendered **Hong Kong** to Britain. Further trade conflicts in the 1850s and 1860s, including the Second Opium War and a Franco-British assault on Beijing, resulted in more unequal treaties, which legalized the opium trade, opened even more ports to outsiders, and allowed Americans and Europeans to set up **foreign concessions**—large coastal districts where Western, not Chinese, law prevailed. By 1898, foreign vessels were allowed to sail as far up Chinese rivers as they pleased.

**NOTE**

The unequal treaties also compelled China to readmit Western missionaries—both Protestant and Catholic—who had been banned since the early 1700s. Missionaries undermined traditional Chinese culture, but also brought the benefits of modern medical treatment and worked to eliminate practices like female foot binding.

### MILLENARIAN REBELLIONS

A number of millenarian rebellions during the 1800s were motivated in part by religious and apocalyptic thought. In addition to the Taiping Rebellion discussed here and the revolt of the Mahdi described previously, examples include the Xhosa Cattle-Killing Movement of the mid-1850s and the Ghost Dance frenzy that led to an 1890 massacre of Sioux. In the former, a female prophet foretold in 1856 that, if the Xhosa of South Africa slaughtered their cattle, spirits would wipe out the British settlers. With many of their animals already dying from a sickness probably brought to Africa by European cattle, the Xhosa began killing their cattle in early 1857, leading to a vast famine. In the case of the Ghost Dance, the Paiute visionary Wovoka—ironically a preacher of peace—popularized the ritual among many western Native Americans. It became a rallying point for the Sioux, many of whom were killed by U.S. forces at Wounded Knee.

Internal crises dogged the Qing at the same time. Worst was the **Taiping Rebellion** (1850–1864), which claimed between 20 million and 30 million lives, making it possibly the second deadliest war in history, next to World War II. The uprising was led by Hong Xiuquan, a Cantonese clerk educated partly by Protestant missionaries. Shocked by failing his civil service examination, Hong began having visions that convinced him that he was Jesus Christ's younger brother, destined to establish a "heavenly kingdom of supreme peace"— the meaning of *taiping*—in China. An extraordinarily magnetic leader, Hong organized an effective modern army and appealed to millions of ordinary Chinese who resented the Qing's high taxes and oppressive rule. The rebels also opposed practices like the binding of women's feet. At their peak, the Taiping movement controlled a third of China, but Qing forces, assisted by foreign military units, recovered by the early 1860s. Hong committed suicide in 1864, and the rebellion soon collapsed.

In reaction to the chaos caused by the Taiping Rebellion, elements within the Qing government attempted a reform campaign, the **self-strengthening movement**, starting in the 1860s and pursued sporadically over the next few decades. It was of limited impact, though, because it confined itself to economic and military modernization without meaningful social change. It was also opposed by the leading figure in Chinese politics, the dowager empress **Cixi**, who governed as regent for her nephew Guangxu, beginning in 1878, and controlled him even after he grew to adulthood. Conservative and oppressive, Cixi resisted all change and even placed Guangxu under arrest when he launched a short-lived "Hundred Days' Reform" in 1898. (Guangxu's reformist advisors were executed.)

The price of Cixi's stubbornness was internal decay and economic decline at home, and continued humiliation on the military and diplomatic front. Outlying possessions and countries formerly in China's tributary system gained autonomy or fell into foreign hands. France seized Indochina, for example, after a short conflict with China in 1883. Even more embarrassingly, tiny Japan thrashed China in the **Sino-Japanese War** (1894–1895), occupying Korea and Taiwan as a result. In 1899, the United States' **Open Door Policy** arranged equal access to Chinese markets for all Western nations, further increasing foreign intrusion.

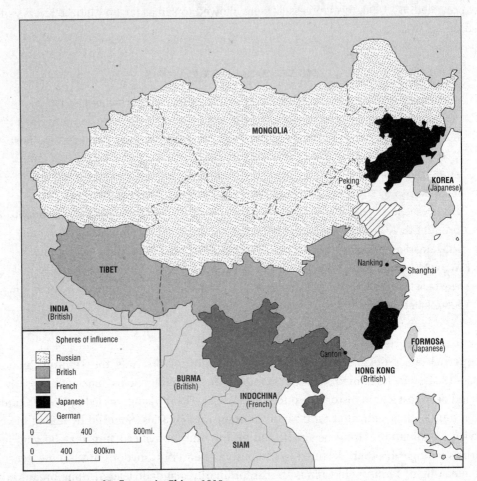

**Western Spheres of Influence in China, 1910.**
Starting in the early-to-mid-1800s, Great Britain, then other Western nations, pressured China into opening its markets and yielding up economic and political control over much of its coast. These concessions grew in size and number during the 1800s and early 1900s, reaching their peak just before the Qing dynasty's collapse in 1911.

In 1900, Chinese anger at foreign influence burst out of control. Making things worse were a severe drought and unusually high unemployment. What followed during the summer was the **Boxer Rebellion**, so called because many of the rebels were martial artists. The Boxers' rage, encouraged by Cixi, was unleashed against Westerners in major cities, especially Beijing, but put down after weeks of violence by foreign troops. In revenge, the Western powers burned a number of Chinese temples and forced the Qing to pay heavy reparations. Even Cixi now recognized the need for change and formed a committee to investigate the possibility of writing a constitution. She and Guangxu both died in 1908, leaving Henry Puyi, China's last emperor, to take up the reform effort. Unfortunately for him, revolution destroyed the Qing regime in 1911–1912, as described in Chapter 22, leading to the rise of the Chinese Republic.

As for Japan, the **Tokugawa shogunate** tried in the late 1700s and early 1800s to enjoy the fruits of urbanization and proto-industrialization, all while keeping in place its dictatorial rule and its rigid social stratification, which favored the **samurai** elite. It had also sealed itself off from the wider world: Christianity had been banned since the 1600s, and only through the port of **Nagasaki** did the regime allow a trickle of foreign trade.

All this changed with the appearance in 1853 of American gunships captained by **Commodore Matthew Perry**. With the threat of force behind his friendly words, Perry asked the Japanese to open up to trade, and once the shogun agreed to end his country's long isolation, other Western fleets appeared with similar demands. For a time, it appeared that Japan might suffer the same fate as China, and so in 1867–1868, a coalition of samurai clans, angered by the shogun's unwillingness to stand up to foreign intimidation, abolished the shogunate and restored the emperor—a symbolic figurehead since the 1200s—to a position of full authority. The **Meiji Restoration** of 1868, named after the new emperor, began Japan's modern age. In a revolution from above, Meiji, who ruled until 1912, rapidly industrialized Japan's economy and thoroughly modernized political and social life in his country. Japan even emerged as an imperial power in its own right, making this the non-Western world's most successful adaptation to the industrial era.

Meiji decisively swept away the feudal social hierarchy of the Tokugawa era. In the 1870s, the samurai lost their hereditary privileges, including immunity from taxation, the annual subsidies paid to them by the government, and their right to wear swords, their traditional symbols of authority, in public. Access to political positions became increasingly dependent on merit and civil service examinations. As it did in the West, industrialization increased the size and influence of the merchant and middle classes, and the feudal prejudice against trade and artisanship faded away. The lower classes gained access to public education and were now allowed to serve in the military, after centuries of not being allowed to handle weapons of any kind. Meiji's **Constitution of 1890** created an elected parliament, the Diet, and the Civil Code of 1898 updated Japan's legal system.

Liberalization only went so far, however. Taxes increased for farmers, and as described in Chapter 19, working conditions for the industrial lower classes resembled the ghastly ones that had characterized the early Industrial Revolution in Europe. Owing to property qualifications and other restrictions, only about 5 percent of the population could vote for the Diet, and the emperor exercised a great deal of control over it. The civil code also made little room for the rights of women, who were largely confined to a secondary status. In effect, Meiji created an oligarchy that was less repressive than the Tokugawa regime, but hardly representative.

The Meiji regime excelled at Westernization, economic efficiency, and militarization. The new tax system of 1872 funded a national educational system, and Japan imported Western science and technical know-how at an astonishing rate. The elite and middle classes adopted Western dress and manners, the Western calendar, and the metric system. From Britain and Germany, the Japanese navy and army adopted not just industrial-era technology, but also Western tactics and organizational methods.

**NOTE**

To build popular allegiance, Meiji and his successors turned to Japan's ancient indigenous faith, creating an Office of Shinto Worship in 1872. All priests became state employees and emphasized the veneration of the emperor as a descendant of the gods. By the 1930s and 1940s, this form of "State Shinto" was used to justify a sense of Japanese racial superiority and blind obedience to government.

With this new military machine, Japan began to expand in the 1870s. A resource-poor island, Japan needed raw materials to feed its industrial growth, and nationalist sentiment swelled there as the century wore on. From China in 1879, it took the Ryukyu Islands, which include Okinawa, the most cherished of Japan's possessions. It joined the Western powers in forcing China to grant it **foreign concessions** in China, and more success followed in the **Sino-Japanese War** (1894–1895), which resulted in Japan's occupation of Taiwan and Korea. Even more impressive was the **Russo-Japanese War** (1904–1905), the first large-scale conflict of the modern era in which a non-Western state defeated a European power. Russia's imperial and railroad-building ambitions in eastern Siberia, Mongolia, and Manchuria collided with Japan's plans for expansion. Instead of negotiating spheres of influence with the Japanese, the tsar pushed ahead with aggression and foolish overconfidence. Equipped just as well as the Russians were, and fighting close to home—while the Russians struggled to supply their war via the Trans-Siberian Railway, several thousand miles long—the Japanese shocked their foes. Victory gave them title to the Kurile Islands and southern Sakhalin, and Japan strengthened its position in Korea and mainland China. It entered the new century as an empire on the rise, and as a regional power to be respected. Unfortunately, its militaristic streak would continue to widen and its imperial ambitions would eventually spin out of control.

## South Asia, Southeast Asia, and Oceania

In eighteenth-century India, the centralizing authority of the once-mighty **Mughal Empire** fractured. During the late 1600s, the Islamic militancy of the emperor Aurangzeb had provoked the creation of a **Sikh** state in the Punjab and the breakaway of the Hindu **Maratha Empire**. Muslim states like Mysore won their freedom as well. The Maratha princes, who belonged to the warrior caste and demonstrated a willingness to innovate with gunpowder weaponry, were formidable leaders.

Another threat was the steadily growing European presence in South Asia: first the Portuguese and Dutch, and then the French and British, who emerged as the main competitors for influence over India. Britain's victory over France during the **Seven Years' War** (1756–1763)—particularly its 1757 defeat of France's Mughal allies at the battle of **Plassey**, in Bengal—ensured British superiority on the subcontinent and confined France's colonial presence to the southeastern port of Pondicherry.

Until the mid-1800s, the **British East India Company** carried out the colonization of India. In 1800, it controlled only a small part of the country, mainly around Bombay (now Mumbai, the gateway port of the west coast), Madras (a textile-producing center on the southeast shore), and Calcutta (in the Bengal northeast). The company's initial interest was the **cotton industry**, although it traded in tea, spices, and opium as well. During the first half of the 1800s, it expanded through a combination of diplomacy, warfare, and the training of **native elites**. The rulers of many Mughal states surrendered administrative and tax-gathering authority to the British in exchange for being allowed to keep their thrones. Company armies gradually defeated the Mysore sultanate, the mighty Maratha princes, and the Sikhs, extending British authority in several directions: into the interior, along the vital Ganges River valley, and up to the northwest frontier. To save on humanpower, the company relied as much as possible on native personnel. For administration and tax-gathering, the British turned to native officials and **zamindar** landowners. (This backfired at first, during the late 1700s, when many zamindars overtaxed their countrymen and seized land from peasants who could not pay.

Famines then killed approximately one-third of the rural population under British control, after which the company reformed its tax-gathering system.) The most famous native personnel were the **sepoys,** or Indian soldiers trained and equipped in Western style. This practice, begun by the French in the mid-1700s, was used on a huge scale by the British, who stationed a surprisingly small number of their own officers and soldiers in India.

After their missteps in the 1700s, the British came to administer India more efficiently, and with the combination of self-interest and well-meaning but condescending "**white man's burden**" thinking that typified their approach to imperial rule. They made no secret about their feelings of racial superiority or their hunger for profits. And when they built schools, railroads, and telegraphs, or when they improved the food-distribution network to prevent famines, it was more for their own benefit than for that of native Indians. Still, there were enough positive aspects to British rule in India that it can be difficult to evaluate. Although it was mainly to keep order, the English reduced the level of religious strife between Muslims and Hindus. British authorities officially discouraged the conversion of Indians to Christianity and generally strove to respect local religious and cultural practices. Yet they also combatted customs they felt were inhumane, including **sati** (the Hindu funeral practice of burning widows with their dead husbands), **thuggee** (ritual assassination in the name of the Hindu goddess Kali), and the **caste system**'s harsh treatment of so-called untouchables.

A key change in Britain's handling of India came in 1857–1858, with the **Indian Revolt** (also known as the Sepoy Mutiny), one of the most traumatic events in modern British and Indian history. Here, underlying resentment of British rule exploded into open violence, owing to false rumors that British officers were deliberately trying to undermine Hindu and Muslim beliefs. With lightning speed, the initial disturbances grew into a massive wave of nationwide revolt, and sepoy units in Delhi proclaimed the aged and impotent Mughal sultan the new emperor of India. Savage massacres of British civilians, especially at Cawnpore (where the butchered remains of women and children were cast into a dry well to rot), inflamed the British, who responded with devastating reprisals and mass executions. With their Western training and anti-colonial zeal, the sepoys gravely threatened British rule in India, but they had no clear plan or single leader, and Muslim and Hindu rebels often failed to cooperate. In 1858, the British, along with native troops who remained loyal, put down the rebellion and declared a formal end to the Mughal dynasty. Several hundred thousand, most of them Indian, perished.

After the Indian Revolt, the British crown took over from the British East India Company as India's colonizing authority. Order was restored, and for the next 90 years, the government directly oversaw politics, ran the army, and supervised the economy. In 1877, Victoria, queen of England, titled herself empress of India as well. India became the British Empire's proverbial "jewel in the crown"—by the late 1800s, one-quarter of the wealth generated by the empire came from there, making it an indispensable strategic and economic asset.

Southeast Asia—rich in rubber, petroleum, and metals like copper, tin, chrome, and aluminum ore (bauxite)—also came under Western dominance during these years. The Dutch East Indies, known today as Indonesia, had been administered by the **Dutch East India Company** since the 1600s, although the Dutch government itself had to step in after 1798, when the company went bankrupt. The British, as they tightened their grip on India, made parallel advances into Southeast Asia, negotiating permission from the Dutch to move into the

> **NOTE**
>
> In the late 1800s and early 1900s, Britain's strategy of educating native elites began to backfire. Many of them were exposed to liberal or radical ideas and concluded that the British, with their long tradition of civil rights, were treating their non-white subjects hypocritically. Many became attracted to national-liberation movements, including the Indian National Congress, which formed in 1885.

Malay Peninsula. In 1819, the British established the outpost on **Singapore**, an island at the peninsula's tip. A strategically placed stronghold and trading center, Singapore quickly became a key naval base and one of Britain's most prized possessions in Asia. The British colonized nearby Burma in 1826. The French developed their own interest in Southeast Asia, gradually pressuring **Indochina**—the region that consists of Vietnam, Cambodia, and Laos—into granting them favorable trade terms and accepting their political influence. China, which regarded Indochina as part of its tributary system, was helpless to halt the French advance after a Sino-French conflict in 1883, and Indochina was fully colonized in the 1880s and 1890s. Much more so than the British, the French placed heavy emphasis on religious conversion, and so their native elites were almost exclusively Catholic. In most other respects, the French imperial model was similar to that of Britain's.

The one mainland state in Southeast Asia to avoid European colonization in the 1800s was Siam, or Thailand, due to good leadership and good luck. Like Meiji in Japan, King Mongkut, who ruled from 1851 to 1868, and his son Chulalongkorn, who ruled until 1910, saw modernization as the key to continued freedom. Both introduced industrialization and Western-style reforms. Siam's geographic setting was also fortunate: it served as a convenient buffer zone between British-controlled Burma and French Indochina. Both rulers are remembered in the West because of the (grossly inaccurate) literary and movie adaptations of the memoirs of Anna Leonowens, the English educator and anti-slavery activist hired in the 1860s to tutor Mongkut's children.

The last major acquisition in Southeast Asia was the **U.S. annexation of the Philippines**, a Spanish colony since the early 1500s, but forfeited to the United States in 1898 after the **Spanish-American War**. The Filipinos, whose **Katipunan** national-liberation society had long been struggling against Spanish rule, initially welcomed the Americans as liberators. But then the United States, fearing that the Philippines would fall into Japanese hands (and realizing what a superb naval base the islands would make), proclaimed a policy of "benevolent assimilation" and took possession of them in 1899. Tragically, this led to a three-year **Philippine-American War** of occupation, in which a guerrilla force led by the Katipunan rebel **Emilio Aguinaldo** resisted the U.S. takeover until 1902. Over 200,000 Filipinos are thought to have died during this conflict.

Thanks to the work of explorers like Britain's **James Cook**, the Pacific became increasingly familiar to Europeans, and increasingly subject to their colonial authority. Cook, charting Australia's east coast in 1770, claimed the continent for his country, and the nearby islands of New Zealand, home to the Polynesian **Maori**, came under English control as well. Full-scale settlement of Australia began in 1788. For years, the population consisted mainly of soldiers, colonial officials, and criminals **transported** to the colony as punishment. (During the 1700s, New England and the Caribbean had been the most common destinations for those "transported" by the British.) In 1830, Britain formally extended its authority to all of Australia, and the rate of free settlement increased, bringing miners and **sheep farmers** to the colony—and into the interior—in large numbers. Often with violence, Australia's **Aborigines**, who had lived there for tens of thousands of years, were dispossessed and driven into the bush. During the "musket wars" of the early 1800s, New Zealand's Maori gained access to gunpowder weapons, and it took another series of wars, the Land Wars of 1845–1872, for the British to bring them fully under control.

The United States hugely expanded its Pacific presence in 1867, by purchasing the Russian colony of Alaska. It also extended its reach to the **Hawaiian kingdom**, which had been founded in 1795, when Kamehameha I used Western weaponry to conquer the Hawaiian islands and forge them into a European-style absolute monarchy. Hawaii adopted constitutional monarchy and became a noteworthy producer of fruits and sugar (many immigrants from China and Japan arrived to work in these industries). However, it was attacked several times by powers like France and, in the 1840s, sought protection from the United States. Although they recognized Hawaii as an independent nation, the Americans gained much influence over its affairs in the late 1800s—and in 1893, when Queen Liliuokalani proposed to amend the constitution in ways contrary to U.S. interests, she was overthrown. With the monarchy ended, the United States annexed Hawaii in 1898, just prior to its occupation of the Philippines.

## The Americas

The domestic history of the United States is largely beyond the scope of the AP World History exam. A few comparative notes, however, as well as some points about the United States' effect on global affairs, should be made:

- *Inspiring freedom*: Democratic government and respect for civil liberties (despite racial and gender inequality) made America an example during the 1800s for those in other countries who wished to bring about similar changes.
- *Sphere of influence*: The **Monroe Doctrine** (1823), in which the U.S. government warned Europe against intervening in the western hemisphere's political affairs, was the first step in creating a sphere of influence. The United States quickly became the dominant power in the Americas, practicing **economic imperialism** in much of Latin America and gaining ownership of or protection over Caribbean (and Philippine) territories after the **Spanish-American War** (1898).
- *Expansion*: The United States' rapid growth, which greatly altered the balance of world power, began with the **Louisiana Purchase** (1803) and continued with the **Mexican-American War** (1846–1848), numerous "**Indian wars**," the 1867 purchase of Alaska, and the above-mentioned annexation of the **Hawaiian kingdom** in the 1890s. This growth was motivated by the ideology of **manifest destiny**, the belief that America was naturally entitled to expand territorially.
- *Native American policy*: U.S. handling of Native Americans vacillated between assimilationist attempts to "civilize" them and military campaigns of expulsion or pacification—the so-called **Indian wars**. A key step in this process was Andrew Jackson's **Indian Removal Act** of 1830, which pushed many tribes west of the Mississippi. Treaties typically arranged for Native American tribes to be placed on **reservations** with some degree of autonomy, but even when the U.S. government negotiated in good faith, farmers, ranchers, and miners often broke the peace, leading to more forced resettlement. For example, the **Ghost Dance** resistance which

### THE CHEROKEE NATION

Even "civilizing" along American lines was not enough to save the Cherokee Nation, which formed in the late 1700s as a confederation of related tribes in Georgia and its environs, from abuse. Early adopters of new technology and farming techniques from the Americans, the Cherokee also devised their own written script—Sequoyah's alphabet—and a sophisticated political system, later adapted to U.S. constitutional norms (including the right to own slaves, which many Cherokee did). In 1820, the U.S. government asked the Cherokee to move west to Arkansas and Oklahoma on a voluntary basis, but this became mandatory with the passage of the 1830 Indian Removal Act, and thousands died of starvation and disease on the Trail of Tears that led to their new homes. The Cherokee Nation continued to exist as a sovereign entity on the periphery of the United States until 1906, when the U.S. government dismantled it.

led to the 1890 massacre of Sioux at **Wounded Knee** was precipitated by American desire for the gold discovered in the Black Hills territory sacred to the Sioux.

- *Slavery*: The persistence of **slavery in the American South** was a key factor in allowing the Atlantic slave trade to continue for so long. It was the underlying cause of the **U.S. Civil War** (1861–1865), and race relations are still affected by its legacy today. Prior to the Civil War, several slave revolts were attempted—most famously by **Nat Turner** in 1831 and **John Brown** at Harpers Ferry in 1859.

- *Industrial and commercial growth*: During the last two-thirds of the 1800s, the United States equaled, and then surpassed, Europe as an industrial power. Many of the era's key innovations came from here. In addition, New York joined London as one of the world's most important hubs for banking and commerce.

- *Immigration*: Political freedom and economic opportunity drew huge quantities of **immigrants**—an estimated 17 million between the 1830s and the 1890s—from Europe and Asia. As described in Chapter 20, **anti-immigration sentiment** was common, especially against non-whites.

As for Latin America, Simón Bolívar drafted constitutions for more than a dozen nations after the wars of independence, influenced by the Napoleonic law code and the ideals of the American and French revolutions. But good constitutions did not by themselves bring about good government, social justice, or healthy economies, and even Bolívar, before his death in 1830, mourned that "we have achieved our independence . . . at the expense of everything else." Latin American democracy was frequently subverted by political strongmen known as **caudillos**, who ruled by means of personal charisma, military force, or oppression.

An important exception to caudillo rule in Latin America was Mexico's president **Benito Juárez**, descended from Zapotec natives and a determined proponent of land reform, separation of church and state, and equal treatment for all races. A member of the Liberal Party, Juárez served as president several times between 1858 and 1872. His first election, however, took place during an armed conflict with Mexico's Conservatives—the Reform War (1857–1861)—and he also led the war of resistance against France's attempt to install Maximilian of Austria as Mexico's emperor. Juárez's onetime ally, the general **Porfirio Díaz**, reverted to the caudillo mode, securing his hold over the presidency between 1876 and 1911, when the **Mexican Revolution** (1910–1920) forced him out of office.

Also problematic was the persistence of **racial inequality** in Latin America. Although constitutions theoretically did away with rigid colonial-era hierarchies, Indians, blacks, and those of mixed race still experienced much prejudice. As in the United States and Canada, **Indian wars** and guerrilla uprisings were common throughout Latin America, particularly in Mexico's Yucatán Peninsula, the Argentinian pampas, and Brazil's Amazon basin. During the late 1700s and much of the 1800s, the **Atlantic slave trade** continued to bring Africans against their will to Latin America and the Caribbean, and **slavery** remained legal in Cuba and Brazil until the 1880s.

Moreover, Latin America contended with **economic backwardness**. Centuries of colonial rule had geared Latin American economies toward an overreliance on **resource extraction** (guano for fertilizer, various precious metals) and **plantation monoculture** (sugar, coffee, fruits), both of which damaged the environment and hindered economic development. It is no surprise that, until late in the 1800s, the pace of industrialization remained slow in most of Latin America. These practices, which depended on slaves

**NOTE**

Resistance to slavery took an interesting form in the Caribbean and the Gulf of Mexico, as runaways called Maroons (from the Spanish *cimarrón*, a colloquial term for "fugitive") formed communities on islands or coastlines on the periphery of larger states. They preserved not just their independence, but also their African heritage.

or poorly-paid peasants and migrant laborers, also fostered **social inequality**. Profits went overwhelmingly to the elite classes (and the foreign investors practicing "**dollar diplomacy**," or **economic imperialism**, in partnership with them). This left a wide gap between rich and poor, and only a narrow middle class between them. A certain measure of industrialization and modernization occurred in some parts of the region by the late 1800s, with countries like Mexico and Argentina leading the way.

**Slavery in Brazil.**
From the mid-1500s to the end of the 1800s, Brazil was the largest single importer of slaves from Africa. In particular, the sugar industry depended on slave labor. Not until the 1800s did Brazil's government make slavery illegal. Shown here are scenes of the work and punishment of slaves in Brazil.

Foreign influence over Latin America remained heavy even after independence. The United States seized vast amounts of territory from Mexico during the Texas rebellion of the 1830s and the **Mexican-American War** (1846–1848), and then France under Napoleon III sponsored the ill-fated attempt in 1864–1867 to install the Habsburg prince Maximilian as emperor of Mexico. British and American **economic imperialism**—exemplified by the actions of the **United Fruit Company**—became more rampant. Spain maintained a presence in islands like Cuba and Puerto Rico, which received harsh treatment. A **national-liberation** movement led by the Cuban **José Martí** sparked a war of independence, during which opponents of Spanish rule were placed in **concentration camps**, the modern world's first such prisons (soon to be borrowed by the British during the Boer War and the Germans during their campaign against the Hereros of Southwest Africa). Events in Cuba led directly to the **Spanish-American War** (1898), which ended Spain's influence in the Caribbean, but handed dominance over to America, which annexed Puerto Rico and established a protectorate over Cuba. The United States soon went on to build the **Panama Canal** in the early 1900s, another sign of its regional influence.

**NOTE**

When the Pan-American Union formed in 1889 to promote cooperation among Latin American nations, cynics referred to it as the "Colonial Division of the U.S. State Department."

# Culture, Science, and Technology, 1750–1900

18

- → THE ENLIGHTENMENT (JOHN LOCKE, MONTESQUIEU, VOLTAIRE, JEAN-JACQUES ROUSSEAU)
- → SOCIAL CONTRACT, NATURAL RIGHTS, AND THE SEPARATION OF CHURCH AND STATE
- → ROMANTICISM, REALISM, AND MODERNISM
- → DEGREES OF WESTERNIZATION IN NON-WESTERN CULTURES
- → CONSERVATISM (AND REACTION) VS. LIBERALISM
- → CAPITALISM (ADAM SMITH) VS. SOCIALISM (UTOPIANS) AND COMMUNISM (KARL MARX)
- → NATIONALISM (SOCIAL DARWINISM)
- → NATIONAL LIBERATION MOVEMENTS
- → CHARLES DARWIN (NATURAL SELECTION)
- → ALBERT EINSTEIN (RELATIVITY) AND SIGMUND FREUD (PSYCHOANALYSIS)
- → THE WESTERN CRISIS OF FAITH

In Europe and America during these years, the pace of cultural change sped up. In contrast to long-lasting cultural and intellectual movements like the Renaissance and even the Enlightenment, with which the modern period began, trends and styles in the 1800s and 1900s changed constantly. Such rapid evolution has been a hallmark of modern Western culture. Also characteristic of Western culture during these years were increased literacy and greater access to culture, a more scientific and secular worldview, and the formation of modern political philosophies, which remain influential even today.

Elsewhere, the non-Western world began to adopt many of the artistic and literary forms of the West, especially print culture and writing styles, as well as architecture. Conversely, styles from Asia, Africa, and the Middle East had an influence on Western culture, particularly in painting, sculpture, and décor.

## ART AND CULTURE IN THE MODERN ERA

In the Western world, cultural modernization is considered to have begun with the **Enlightenment** of the 1700s, also commonly referred to as the Age of Reason, the name given to it by the American revolutionary Thomas Paine.

Enlightenment thinkers put great faith in the power of human logic and in the recent discoveries of the Scientific Revolution. They also pondered how to make society and government more efficient and humane. The sociopolitical philosophies of the Enlightenment—as articulated by individuals like **John Locke**, the Baron Charles de **Montesquieu**, **Voltaire**, and **Jean-Jacques Rousseau**—are detailed further in the next section, but generally opposed tyranny, or arbitrary exercise of

**NOTE**

Immanuel Kant, the principal spokesman of the German Enlightenment, described the 1700s as the time when humanity had grown out of its "self-imposed immaturity" and proclaimed that the motto of the century was "Dare to Know!"

monarchical power, and favored greater respect for individual rights. Freedom of opinion and religion were also important to Enlightenment thinkers, some of whom remained devoutly Christian, some of whom adopted vaguer religious stances like **deism** (belief in a divine being but not the literal truth of a specific doctrine), and some of whom became atheistic. Enlightenment circles and salons appeared throughout the Western world during the 1700s and helped to inspire the **American and French revolutions**. Women shaped Enlightenment culture in many ways, either by organizing the salons at which philosophical debate took place or—like **Mary Wollstonecraft** of England and Russia's **Catherine the Great**—by participating directly as authors, activists, and political actors.

Moving from the late 1700s into the early 1800s, the principal cultural movement in the West was **romanticism**. A backlash against the rational Enlightenment, romanticism emphasized emotion, heroism, individuality, and the imagination. As summed up by the English poet Samuel Taylor Coleridge, romantics considered the "creative faculty" to be superior to the "calculating faculty." Around the 1840s, romanticism, while it did not die away, yielded its place of prominence to **realism**. Realists were concerned with everyday life, social problems, and the psychology of their characters.

Both romanticism and realism reacted strongly to the process of industrialization in Europe and America. As illustrated by William Blake's poetic contrast of England's "green and pleasant land" with the "dark Satanic mills" of industry, romantics tended to idealize nature and view industrialization as a blight upon it. In their best-known novels, authors like Victor Hugo and Charles Darwin disapprovingly portrayed the social miseries of the industrial era. Realist painters and writers regularly addressed themes such as poverty and inequality.

**Romanticism and Nature**
*The Wanderer above the Mists* (ca. 1818), by the German painter Caspar David Friedrich, exemplifies the trend among romantic artists and writers to portray the natural world not just as picturesque, but as embodying sublime qualities.

The culture of the late 1800s and early 1900s was characterized by diversity and innovation. Turning away from realism in the 1870s, **modernist** artists and writers (including Vincent van Gogh and a young Pablo Picasso) broke the rules of traditional culture and experimented with a dazzling array of new styles: impressionism, post-impressionism, cubism, and abstraction. Asian and African art powerfully influenced this generation of artists.

*Aristide Bruant at Les Ambassadeurs* (1892), by Henri de Toulouse-Lautrec. *
French painter and poster artist Henri de Toulouse-Lautrec (1864–1901) was one of many artists who, during the late 1800s, departed from the strictly realist styles of the early and middle nineteenth century. Like many of France's impressionist and post-impressionist painters, Toulouse-Lautrec was influenced by foreign art, most particularly Japanese prints.

In other parts of the world, Western forms of art and writing often blended with indigenous styles, whether because of voluntary adoption or because they were imposed by colonial masters as they built empires in non-Western regions and trained **native elites** according to Western norms. In the Middle East, for example, especially during the **Tanzimat reforms** of the mid-1800s, Ottoman authors adopted European styles like romanticism and realism. At the same time, and partly in opposition to Westernizing trends, a resurgence of Arabic culture—which had long been overshadowed by Turkish and Persian art and literature—began to make itself felt throughout the region.

In Africa, the **oral tradition** remained dominant, as witnessed by the continued popularity of **griot storytelling** and other forms of poetic and epic recitation. As more of the continent fell under imperial control after the mid-1800s, foreign colonists and Christian missionaries imported Western culture on a much larger scale than before. In turn, Western artists who were tiring of traditional realism found themselves energized by Africa's **non-representational art**, which inspired innovative **modernist** styles, such as primitivism and abstraction, in Europe and America.

East Asia continued its tradition of cultural grandeur during these years. One of the greatest novels in Chinese literature appeared during the late 1700s: Cao Xueqin's ***Dream of the Red Chamber***, which narrates the tragedy of two young lovers caught up in the decline of a wealthy and powerful clan. In Japan, the **ukiyo-e** style of woodblock painting reached its highest peak of development during the first half of the 1800s, thanks to artists like **Hokusai** and Hiroshige, both of whom gained international reputations and influenced impressionist and post-impressionist painting in Europe. Throughout the region, though, Westernizing tendencies were increasingly evident.

***The Great Wave off the Coast of Kanagawa*** (ca. 1831)
Arguably the most internationally recognized painting to come out of Asia, this scene—part of Katsushika Hokusai's "Thirty-Six Views of Mount Fuji"—illustrates the delicacy and refinement of Japan's ukiyo-e style, as well as the blend of realistic and non-representational elements that made Asian painting so fascinating to Westerners in the late 1800s.

South and Southeast Asia experienced an even higher level of Westernization, thanks to the influx of missionaries and colonial authorities. In India, for instance, Mughal culture did not fade away completely, but yielded much of its preeminence to what came to be known as the "**Company style**": art and architecture heavily conditioned by admixtures brought to the subcontinent by the British East India Company. Such cultural fusion can be seen in later monuments like the **Gateway to India** arch, built in early-twentieth-century Bombay (Mumbai) to celebrate British imperial control over India. Catholicism and the French language were imported into Indochina during the late 1800s, and Siam (modern-day Thailand)—much like Japan under the Emperor Meiji—decided to Westernize thoroughly as a way to avoid foreign conquest and colonization.

**The Gateway to India**
Erected between 1911 and 1924 by the British government to welcome visitors to the port of Bombay (now Mumbai), the "Gateway to India" arch symbolizes British colonial authority. It also demonstrates vividly the fusion of Western and South Asian architectural styles during the era of "new" imperialism.

# POLITICAL THOUGHT: NEW PHILOSOPHIES AND IDEOLOGIES

## The Enlightenment

In eighteenth-century Europe and America, the **Enlightenment** prompted rational inquiry into the nature of politics and society. As described in Chapter 17, Enlightenment thinkers, by questioning social hierarchies and traditional forms of monarchy, paved the way for massive political changes—including key revolutions—in Europe and the Americas.

Among the earliest Enlightenment thinkers was **John Locke** of England, who argued during the late 1600s and early 1700s that the government's power to govern should depend above all on the consent of the governed. He also favored freedom of religion and opinion and the protection of private property. Owing largely to Locke, the concepts of **natural rights**, the **social contract** (the mutual obligations owed to each other by governments and their people), and the **separation of church and state** became cornerstones of Enlightenment social and political thought. Other influential Enlightenment figures include

- Baron Charles de **Montesquieu**: Author of *The Spirit of Laws* (1748), which proposed the **separation of powers** (executive, legislative, and judicial) as a way to avoid tyranny
- **Voltaire**: Versatile playwright, novelist, and philosopher best remembered as a champion of **freedom of expression**, and also as a fierce enemy of organized religion, which he viewed as corrupt and hypocritical
- Jean-Jacques **Rousseau**: Philosopher who felt more strongly than many of his fellow cohorts that ordinary people deserved more political power, as expressed in his 1762 book *The Social Contract*, a forceful continuation of Locke's thinking on the subject
- America's **founding fathers**: Thomas Jefferson, George Washington, Benjamin Franklin, Thomas Paine (who coined the term "Age of Reason"), and others who led the American Revolution and designed the U.S. Constitution and were the first to establish an entire political system (however imperfectly) on Enlightenment principles

As noted in Chapter 17, revolutionary documents on both sides of the Atlantic, including the **Declaration of Independence**, France's **Declaration of the Rights of Man and the Citizen**, and Simón Bolívar's "**Jamaica Letter**," belong squarely within the Enlightenment tradition.

## New Ideologies: Reacting to Revolution and Industrialization

Most modern forms of political thought were born in the West, either during the Atlantic and industrial revolutions, or in reaction to them.

**Conservatism** regarded the changes brought about by the Atlantic revolutions as completely undesirable or as having taken place too quickly and with too much violence, and it feared many of the social and political effects of industrialization. The more uncompromising form of conservatism is known as **reaction** and was typified by leaders at the **Congress of Vienna** like Austria's Klemens von Metternich. A more moderate form of conservatism, which argued for gradual reform rather than sudden change, is associated with thinkers like the Anglo-Irish philosopher **Edmund Burke**. Political **liberalism** favored the extension of political privileges and individual freedoms, at least to the middle class, but not always to the lower classes or to women. It also tended to favor the **free-market capitalism** preached

**NOTE**

Even the use of "left" and "right" as political terms emerged during the early days of the French Revolution, when radical members of the National Assembly sat on the left-hand side of the building and conservative opponents of the revolution took places on the right.

by **Adam Smith** and other **classical economists** (see Chapter 19). The century's most famous liberal philosopher is **John Stuart Mill** of England.

Liberal optimism about industrialization and capitalism was not uniformly shared by members of the industrial working class or by certain thinkers who came to see capitalism as unfair and exploitative. Especially after the **1848 revolutions** in Europe, it became clear that pure capitalism, in its original dog-eat-dog form, could not remain as it was without causing severe, if not unbearable, socioeconomic stress. But how should it be changed? Liberals and reformers, along with conservatives who felt there was no choice, worked to keep capitalism in place by gradually eliminating the worst of its abuses and sharing its benefits more fairly. From the other end, many members of the working class turned to **trade-union activism** to gain concessions like pensions, better hours, and higher wages, and thereby improve their lot.

Other alternatives arose as well. Perhaps most extreme was **anarchism**, which rejected all forms of government. More widespread was **socialism**, which appeared in many forms during the 1800s, all sharing the belief that economic competition is inherently unfair and eventually leads to injustice and inequality. The **utopian socialists** of the early 1800s believed that governments and business owners should forego maximum profits to pay workers better and care for them more properly. Many of their demands and suggestions became standard policy during the late 1800s and early 1900s. The most practical of the utopian socialists, the Welsh businessman **Robert Owen**, founded a number of factory-based communities along these cooperativist lines, both in the British Isles and the United States.

The most radical and most influential form of socialism was **communism**, originated by the German philosophers **Karl Marx** and Friedrich Engels and most famously outlined in *The Communist Manifesto* (1848) and *Das Kapital* (1867–1894). Marx and Engels argued that all historical development was driven by a **class struggle** between the upper class (which controls capital, or the means of economic production) and the lower class (which is forced to labor for the upper class). They predicted that the age of industrial capitalism, with its struggle between the bourgeoisie and the working-class proletariat, was the final stage of human history before the realization of socialism. Society would then move on to communism, which Marx and Engels described as an economic state of perfect justice, equality, and prosperity. To achieve socialism, however, Marx and Engels believed that **revolution** would most likely be needed, so they advocated force as a possibly necessary means to overthrow capitalism.

**NOTE**

Even the Catholic Church stepped into the debate about workers' treatment under capitalism. In 1891, Pope Leo XIII issued the decree Rerum Novarum (also known as "The Rights and Duties of Capital and Labor"). While Leo condemned communism, he called for legalizing trade unions and criticized unfettered capitalism for causing "misery and wretchedness."

The boldness with which Marx proclaimed the impossibility of fixing capitalism and the inevitability of socialist revolution made communism appealing to many—more so than most other varieties of socialism. His confidence, however, turned out to be misplaced (or at least premature), and already during the late 1800s, many who agreed with Marx's critique of capitalism began to question whether violent revolution was desirable or even necessary as a way to achieve Marxism's goals. These **revisionists** and their allies began to seek legal ways to bring about socialism, such as trade-union activism and parliamentary politics. They founded **social democratic parties**, which gained large followings in countries like France and Germany before World War I and which sometimes opposed communists who remained more radical. The quarrel between Russia's Mensheviks (communists who favored gradual change and working within the system) and Lenin's Bolsheviks (communists who favored faster change and revolutionary action) is typical of this split.

**International Socialism vs. Capitalism**

The attempt to coordinate socialist and communist movements throughout Europe can be seen in these nearly identical propaganda posters, dating from the turn of the century. Both portray rigidly stratified social orders, with the industrial working class at the bottom, their labor enriching the prosperous middle class, an army that serves as a tool of oppression, a clergy that deceives ordinary people into being content with their situation (inspired by the Marxist dictum that "religion is the opiate of the masses"), and a ruling class at the top of the pyramid. The poster on the left was distributed in Russia, while the one on the right is from England.

## Nationalist Strains of Thought

Although patriotism had not been absent from Western political life in earlier eras, it was not as prominent or as powerful as it became in the modern era. The late 1700s and early 1800s witnessed the advent of **nationalism** as a political force in Europe and the Americas.

Much of this had to do with the rise of the **nation-state**—which increasingly equated citizenship with belonging to a distinct ethnic and/or linguistic group—as the dominant form of political organization in the West. In addition, the Enlightenment ideal of the **social contract**, which was put into political action during the **American and French revolutions**, fostered the growing sentiment that, just as an individual owed certain obligations (such as obedience, taxes, and military service) to his or her nation, the individual was owed certain things in return *by* his or her nation—making the nation something worth belonging to and worth feeling pride in. Not only was nationalism felt more strongly in existing states, it burned with great intensity among groups that did not have a nation of their own, but were divided or ruled by others. Therefore, nationalism flared up especially among the Germans and Italians (each of whom would unify during the 1800s), the Irish, the Polish, and the various East European and Balkan peoples who lived under Austro-Hungarian or Ottoman rule.

Properly channeled, nationalism manifested itself as healthy patriotism and no more. Unfortunately, as the nineteenth century progressed, nationalism frequently encouraged aggressive **militarism** and can be seen as a contributing factor to Europe's armed conflicts of the late 1800s—especially the wars of Italian and German unification—and to its overseas campaigns of imperial conquest. It also aroused feelings of **ethnic and racial superiority**, which were further reinforced by pseudo-scientific notions regarding racial difference and the interaction of peoples. The most famous of these was **social Darwinism**, a misguided interpretation of Darwin's insight that, in nature, the better-adapted are better able to compete for scarce resources. This application of survival-of-the-fittest thinking to human relations was popularized by the English social scientist Herbert Spencer; Darwin himself strenuously objected to it. Based on the false premise that white races had progressed farther along the evolutionary scale than non-white ones, social Darwinism and similar strains of thought were used to justify numerous forms of inequality, including ethnic prejudice and colonial domination. At home, most social Darwinists regarded women as the provably "weaker sex" and felt that the poverty of the lower classes was a "natural" product of human competition.

By the late 1800s, nationalist tendencies were spreading to non-Western parts of the world. The modernizing **Young Turks** in the Ottoman Empire were ardent nationalists trying to keep their country on a technological par with Europe. Where foreign colonists ruled, **national-liberation movements**—which would grow increasingly potent in the twentieth century—began to emerge as a way to protest imperialism's abuses or even to overturn it altogether. Before his death in battle, the poet-philosopher José Martí used his eloquence to awaken Cuba's nationalist movement against Spain and to launch its 1895–1898 war of independence. The **Katipunan**, the Filipino national-liberation society, fought against Spanish colonization in the 1890s, only to face U.S. occupiers after Spain relinquished control over the Philippines in 1898. The **Indian National Congress**, consisting mainly of British-educated native elites, formed in 1885 to gain more rights for natives in British India, and eventually to end colonial rule there. China's **Boxer Rebellion** in 1900 can be seen as a national-liberationist backlash against the West's growing domination of Chinese ports and coastal territories.

The non-Western country that came closest to adopting Western-style nationalism, complete with a Social Darwinist outlook, was Japan after 1868. As Japan industrialized, militarized, and defeated neighbors like Korea and China—not to mention Russia in 1904–1905—many Japanese became convinced that they were not just more technologically advanced than their fellow Asians, but innately superior to them. This sentiment is clearly communicated in the influential 1885 essay "**Goodbye Asia**," which foreshadowed the "master race" thinking Japan would later adopt by proclaiming that "We do not have time to wait for the enlightenment of our neighbors. . . . It is better for us to leave the ranks of Asian nations and cast our lot with the civilized nations of the West. . . . [We are] no different from the righteous man living in a town known for foolishness and lawlessness."

## SCIENCE AND SECULARISM IN THE INDUSTRIAL ERA

Greater access to **public education** became a normal part of life in North America and most parts of Europe throughout the 1800s. **Literacy rates** rose as a result. The same became true for many other parts of the world during the late 1800s.

As described in Chapter 19, **technological change** was profound, rapid, and thorough in those parts of the world affected by industrialization. National economies, transportation networks, and personal lives were all influenced by constant and increasingly affordable innovations that involved machine power, fossil-fuel energy sources such as coal and oil, and, near the end of the 1800s, electricity.

Also during this era, a **scientific, secular worldview** became increasingly paramount, at least in the Western world. This did not mean that religions lost their political and social importance, or that people ceased to follow them. However, in a growing number of countries, **separation of church and state** became the norm, and less risk and scandal was attached to openly professing unconventional beliefs like **deism** or **atheism**. In the public sphere, religion became less convincing to many as a justification for keeping certain rulers in power or maintaining social or gender-based hierarchies.

Numerous discoveries in the late 1700s and early 1800s accelerated the rise of science relative to religion in the West. Archaeological and linguistic research in the Middle East and Asia (including the use of the **Rosetta Stone**, unearthed by Napoleon's armies in Egypt, to decipher hieroglyphs) revealed that certain cultures and ancient languages, such as Sanskrit, predated even the oldest described in the Judeo-Christian Bible. The discovery of fossils and the findings of the renowned geologist **Charles Lyell** indicated that the world was orders of magnitude older than the 10,000 years or less accounted for in the Bible. The theory of **evolution** came to be widely accepted among most scientists during the early 1800s, although explaining *how* evolution worked remained a formidable challenge.

Answering that challenge was the English naturalist **Charles Darwin**, who explained the process of evolution with his **theory of natural selection**. In *On the Origin of Species* (1859), Darwin caused a scientific and cultural storm by arguing that evolution is a random process in which physical changes that increase an animal's chance for survival are passed on to that animal's offspring. In *The Descent of Man* (1871), he applied the principles of natural selection to human beings and postulated that humans and apes share a common evolutionary ancestry. Darwin's ideas, along with discoveries in other sciences, including geology and archaeology, did much to erode faith in traditional religion and encouraged a more secular worldview in the West.

Western feelings about the century's scientific and technological developments were mixed. On one hand, scientific and technological progress (and the rising economic prosperity that accompanied it) infused Western culture with excitement and confidence, and for the most part—especially among the general public—this sense of optimism continued until the eve of World War I. On the other hand, particularly among intellectuals and artists, this was a time of growing uncertainty and anxiety. As scientific insights like Darwin's made it harder to sustain a literal belief in the Christian Bible, a **crisis of faith** shook the Western mindset during the late 1800s and early 1900s. Most famously, German philosopher Friedrich Nietzsche proclaimed famously that "God is dead," and argued that all systems of morality were valueless in the materialistic modern age. Quantum theory and **Albert Einstein's theory of relativity**, elaborated in 1905, opened up new and mathematically unsettling questions in the fields of physics for the first time since the days of Isaac Newton. The early theories of the Austrian doctor **Sigmund Freud** about dreams and the subconscious advanced the new science of psychology, but his insights into how poorly most individuals understand themselves—much less the world around them—made many people uneasy, both before and after World War I.

# Economic Systems, 1750–1900

## 19

- → PROTO-INDUSTRIALIZATION VS. TRADITIONAL ARTISANRY
- → INDUSTRIALIZATION AND THE INDUSTRIAL REVOLUTION
- → THE STEAM ENGINE AND THE MINING AND TEXTILE INDUSTRIES
- → STEAMSHIPS, RAILROADS, AND THE TELEGRAPH
- → SECOND INDUSTRIAL REVOLUTION (STEEL, ELECTRICITY, AND PETROLEUM)
- → THE FACTORY SYSTEM AND INTERCHANGEABLE PARTS
- → FREE-MARKET VS. STATE-SPONSORED INDUSTRIALIZATION
- → RISE OF THE MIDDLE AND INDUSTRIAL WORKING CLASSES
- → POPULATION GROWTH AND URBANIZATION
- → CAPITALISM (ADAM SMITH, JOHN STUART MILL), TRADE UNIONISM, AND SOCIALISM (UTOPIAN SOCIALISTS, KARL MARX)
- → FINANCIAL INSTRUMENTS (STOCK EXCHANGES, CORPORATIONS, THE GOLD STANDARD)
- → TRANSNATIONAL BUSINESSES (HSBC, UNITED FRUIT COMPANY, SUEZ CANAL COMPANY)
- → INTERNATIONAL EFFECTS OF INDUSTRIALIZATION (RELATIONSHIP WITH WESTERN IMPERIALISM)
- → TANZIMAT REFORM AND QING "SELF-STRENGTHENING" VS. MEIJI INDUSTRIALIZATION

Until the end of the 1700s, the economies of the world's major civilizations were principally agricultural, and their societies rural. Over the centuries, trade and commerce, as well as arts and crafts, had become increasingly important but, compared with agriculture, remained relatively minor.

In Europe and North America, this state of affairs changed dramatically in the late 1700s and early 1800s. The mass production of goods by means of machine power—**industrialization**—became a key part of Western economies. The importance of trade and commerce skyrocketed, and a growing number of people moved from rural areas to the city. **Capitalism** became the dominant economic system. Taken together, these changes form what is commonly known as the **Industrial Revolution**, whose first stage coincided roughly with the political revolutions taking place in America, France, and the Atlantic world. Although industrialization was a "revolution" only in a metaphorical sense—it lasted decades and had no clear-cut beginning or end—it changed life in Europe and the rest of the world as thoroughly as its political counterparts. It placed new machines and inventions at the disposal of ordinary people. It affected old social classes and created new ones. It changed the way millions worked, where they lived, and how they understood political problems. By

1900, the United States and northern and western Europe had industrialized and urbanized. Many other parts of the world were starting to follow suit.

## INDUSTRIAL REVOLUTIONS IN THE WEST

### Background to Industrialization

The Industrial Revolution is considered to have begun in England in the 1770s and 1780s with the successul application of the **steam engine** to two sectors of the economy: **mining** and **textiles**.

Many things combined to spark industrialization in the British Isles. Already from the 1600s, **proto-industrial practices**, methods more productive than traditional artisanry and craftsmanship, had been in place. Machines such as the flying shuttle and the spinning jenny, which sped up the manufacture of cotton, were invented as early as 1733 and 1764. England was already relatively urbanized, and a set of harsh agricultural laws, the **Enclosure Acts**—which, in favor of wealthy landowners, fenced off large pieces of farmland that had once been common property—impoverished many farmers and forced them to relocate to the cities, creating a large pool of available labor. Environmental change played a role as well: the depletion of forests in England and Ireland (timber was used both for fuel and to build ships for the Royal Navy) increased dependency on coal, and efficient coal mining required machine power, especially to pump water out of mine shafts. Other factors working in Britain's favor were its location in the Atlantic, an excellent system of **roads** and **canals**, large supplies of **iron** and **coal**, and a strong tradition of trade and commerce, which allowed investors to accumulate capital.

**NOTE**

One global effect of early industrialization involves the 1793 invention of the cotton gin by American Eli Whitney. This, the final step in fully mechanizing the textile industry, phenomenally boosted the international demand for raw cotton, especially in England. Along with Egypt and India, a key source of cotton was the U.S. South, where the crop was grown and harvested by slaves. Slavery at this time was becoming less profitable in the U.S. and might have died away relatively easily, but most historians agree that the invention revived and prolonged it for decades.

### Steam Power and Beyond: The Industrial Era Begins and Matures

What was needed by the end of the 1700s was a power source greater and more reliable than wind, water, or muscle to drive new machines in factories and mines. In 1782, the Scottish inventor **James Watt** patented a steam engine that was both powerful and cost-effective. The first stage of the Industrial Revolution involved the integration of Watt's steam engine into the textile and coal-mining industries.

The next stage of the Industrial Revolution, which lasted roughly until the middle of the 1800s, involved the universal application of steam power—and, more slowly, electricity—to all areas of economic activity. Industrialization spread to other parts of Europe, as well as to North America. Key trends include

- The modernization of transport, thanks to **steamships** (1807) and **railroads** (the 1820s)
- The modernization of communications, beginning with the **telegraph** (1837)
- The **factory system**, which systematized, mechanized, and increased the scale of production
- The concept of **interchangeable parts**, pioneered by two Americans, the inventor Eli Whitney and the gunsmith Samuel Colt

Although the Industrial Revolution is generally considered to have ended around the mid-1800s, the **industrial era** continued throughout the rest of the century and gave birth to a huge wave of invention. Crucial innovations during the second half of the 1800s—often referred to as the **Second Industrial Revolution**—include the **Bessemer process** (1850s), which made **steel** production cheaper and easier; concrete-and-steel **construction**, which enabled the building of skyscrapers (pioneered by Chicago in the 1880s) and engineering projects like the Suez and Panama canals; the wider use of **electricity** (Thomas Edison's light bulb came in 1879); the commercial use of **petroleum** (starting in 1859); the birth of chemical industries and the increased use of **rubber**; the **internal combustion engine** (1866–1885), which led to the automobile; the **telephone** (1876–1879); the **radio** (1895–1901); and the **airplane** (1903). Warfare industrialized as well, with modern rifles, better artillery, and the machine gun. In the countryside, the **tractor** helped cause an agriculture boom.

Industrialization occurred first and most thoroughly in Western Europe (especially Britain, the Low Countries, France, and Germany), as well as in the United States. Southern and Eastern Europe lagged behind. Britain led the world in industrial production for most of the 1800s, as measured by key indices like railroad building and output of iron, steel, coal, and textiles. By the end of the century, Germany and the United States were catching up to, then surpassing, Britain.

As industrialization spread, two models took hold. One was the **free-market industrialization** that arose in Britain and dominated in most of Western Europe and North America. The fundamental assumption here was the *laissez-faire* principle that government involvement in, and regulation of, industrialization should be kept to a minimum. In several parts of Europe, though, **state-sponsored industrialization** prevailed. Here, governments either directed industrialization from above or, following an approach sometimes described as **state capitalism**, set nationwide economic and industrial priorities and then contracted with certain favored private firms to achieve those goals. In Europe, Germany was the most successful proponent of this approach, and as it spread elsewhere, the Japanese made it work most effectively.

**NOTE**

On the impact of industrialization on women and family life in the West, see Chapter 20. For environmental effects, see Chapter 21.

## The Social Impact of Industrialization

The Industrial Revolution and its aftermath vastly transformed Western society. Especially for the lower classes, the industrial era's birth pangs, suffered between the 1780s and 1840s, were as traumatic as they were important.

The economic clout of the traditional aristocracy, whose wealth had been based primarily on land, was diminished by industrialization. The class that benefited most was the **middle class**, particularly the bankers, merchants, and factory owners who came to be known as the bourgeoisie.

The Industrial Revolution astronomically expanded the size of the **working class**, or proletariat. During the first decades of industrialization, this class bore the heaviest economic burden. Their labor allowed the Industrial Revolution to move forward, but until the second half of the 1800s, they were badly treated and barely compensated. Workers received low wages, lived in squalid and crowded housing, worked long shifts (14 hours a day, six days a week, was not unusual), coped with unsafe working conditions (risk of fire, dangerous machines, exposure to poisonous or harmful substances), and had no pensions, safety laws, or insurance. Child labor was common.

During the industrial era, as machines came to play a larger role in production, workers used to traditional forms of labor sometimes reacted with extreme technophobia. Most famous were the **Luddites**: English textile artisans who, during the 1810s, rioted and wrecked power looms and other industrial devices they felt were destroying their livelihood. Their name now describes anyone who reflexively fears new technology.

In the countryside, industrialization caused new social divisions. More land came to be owned by well-off farmers and homesteaders who were essentially middle class. Under them were poor agricultural laborers who formed a rural working class of sorts.

Only after the 1840s is industrialization considered to have brought about meaningful improvements for large numbers of Americans and Europeans. Especially after the **1848 revolutions** (caused partly by the socioeconomic stress of early industrialization), various laws and measures began to give relief to the working class—although completely fair treatment and full political equality were still distant goals, achieved only after hard effort and not until the late 1800s or early 1900s. The overall standard of living rose during the second half of the 1800s, even for the lower classes. At least in major cities, many features of modern life became available after mid-century, including bus service, streetlights (gas, then electric), citywide sewage systems, icebox refrigeration, indoor plumbing, steam heating, canned food, and medical advances (vaccination, antiseptic surgery, anesthesia).

Related social trends are massive population growth and urbanization. Europe's population grew from an estimated total of 175–187 million in 1800 to 266 million in 1850 and 423 million in 1900. Similar growth took place in the United States. European cities that existed grew larger; in 1800, London reached the 1 million mark, as did Paris in the 1830s. Many new cities sprang up, such as Liverpool and Manchester, precisely because of the Industrial Revolution. By the mid-1800s, England and Wales were urban societies, meaning that 50 percent or more of the population lived in cities. At the time, the level of urbanization reached 25 percent in France and the German states, and it continued to grow, as it also did in the Low Countries and the United States. Urbanization is generally associated with social advancement, but it had its seamier side during the industrial era. Cities were typically polluted and crowded, and the lower classes lived in slums or shantytowns where sewage was primitive or nonexistent. Diseases such as **cholera**, **tuberculosis**, and typhoid ran rampant in such conditions.

Industrialization went hand in hand with the rise of **capitalism** as an economic philosophy. For more on this, as well as **socialism** as a reaction to it, see Chapter 18 and the section directly below. Other reactions to the initially harsh conditions that arose during capitalism's early decades included the fairer labor laws and social welfare measures passed by various governments, mainly by liberals and reformers, in the mid- to late 1800s. For workers, a more radical option (by the standards of the day) was the **trade union** movement. In the early 1800s, unions were illegal in Europe and the United States, and workers risked injury and arrest if they joined unions or went on strike. Still, the union movement gave them a way to struggle for political rights and better treatment in the workplace (higher wages, five-day work week, shorter hours, safety regulations, pensions, and employee insurance). In the late 1800s and early 1900s, unions earned legal status in most countries and gained greater economic and political strength. Political parties dedicated more specifically to workers' needs and interests, such as Britain's Labour, France's Radicals, and Germany's Social Democratic Party, formed.

## CAPITALISM AND COMMERCE

### Capitalism and the Classical Economists

**Adam Smith's** *The Wealth of Nations* appeared in 1776, just as the Industrial Revolution began. Smith's brand of economic thinking, later associated with **free-market capitalism** (also called *laissez-faire* capitalism, or "let it alone"), encouraged free trade and political liberalism, at least for the middle classes. In the long term, as with industrialization, capitalism led to the creation of great wealth in the Western world. On the other hand, it was based on competition and, left unregulated, could be cruel to those on the losing end—such as the working class in the early 1800s.

Smith and the other **classical economists** who favored capitalism argued that the laws of supply and demand—the "**invisible hand**," to use Smith's metaphor—should operate freely, with minimal government intervention. (As noted above, the more **state-directed capitalism** pursued in certain nations yielded their own successes, especially in Germany and Japan, which became economic powerhouses.)

Although Smith himself insisted that governments should take measures to fight extreme poverty—a point often forgotten today—other classical economists maintained that little could be done for the poor. Thomas Malthus of England wrote in his influential *Essay on Population* (1799) that poverty was one of the inevitable consequences of population growth. David Ricardo's "**iron law of wages**" was just as pessimistic. Employers, he said, will naturally pay workers no more than what is needed to allow them to survive. To force them to pay higher wages, Ricardo predicted, would cause them to fire workers, who would then starve. Such theories caused economics to be nicknamed the "dismal science" and were used for a long time by middle- and upper-class industrialists to justify oppressive labor practices.

Somewhat later, in the mid-1800s, the English liberal thinker and economic theorist **John Stuart Mill** continued to favor free-market capitalism. However, Mill—having observed many of the abuses of early industrialization, and sensitive to political disturbances like the **1848 revolutions**—was more inclined than other classical economists to favor at least some government regulation of capitalist and industrial practices. Also by this time, alternative visions to capitalism were emerging in reaction to the severe socioeconomic strains caused by it. Among these were various forms of **socialism**, including **communism** as preached by **Karl Marx**, and they are detailed in Chapter 18.

## Commerce and Banking

The rise of capitalism and industrialization coincided with an equally steep rise in the global importance of **commerce** and **banking**. Having already contributed to European growth during the 1450–1750 period, these sectors now became economically crucial throughout the Western world—and wherever else in the world the Europeans and Americans extended their commercial and imperial reach.

To protect and expand the growing wealth of merchants and investors, new financial instruments appeared or became more sophisticated than before. Governments formed **central banks** to house national reserves of precious metals to back their currencies, and to determine economic policy. (The Bank of England had been in existence since the 1690s, but it was in the 1800s, starting with Napoleon's establishment of the Bank of France, that most other Western nations followed suit.) Limited liability **corporations** grew in number and size and became more legally formalized. Not only did this allow investors to pool their resources as in the past, it allowed them to further minimize risk by separating their personal assets—which could not be touched in case of disaster or bankruptcy—from the assets they invested in the corporation. **Stock exchanges**, also called bourses, appeared to regularize the buying and selling of corporate shares. The century's most dominant were the London Stock Exchange, founded in 1801 after decades of less formal trading, and the New York Stock Exchange, established in 1817. Most European capitals, from Paris and Berlin to Vienna and St. Petersburg, operated major exchanges. Also during the 1800s, **insurance** became more common as a way to protect personal property, corporate assets, and even one's life and health. (Lloyd's of London, perhaps the world's most famous insurance company, took shape in the 1770s and formally incorporated during the 1800s.)

A key economic debate during the 1800s involved the question of whether or not governments should adopt the **gold standard**: the practice of tying the value of a country's currency (and its rate of exchange with other currencies) to gold rather than the more traditional silver. Britain moved in this direction in the 1810s, but other countries stayed with silver or attempted bimetallism (working with both silver and gold) until late in the century. A major shift occurred after the Franco-Prussian War of 1870–1871, when the newly united Germany moved from silver to gold, vastly debasing the value of silver. Other European nations made the transition as well. The United States adopted the gold standard in 1900 after a bitter debate during the 1890s that featured one of the most famous speeches in American political history, the "cross of gold" address ("you shall not crucify mankind upon a cross of gold") by Democratic presidential candidate and silver advocate William Jennings Bryan.

The crisis that shocked Western economies the most during the 1800s was the **Panic of 1873**, caused by many factors, but mainly by Germany's conversion to the gold standard after its 1871 unification. The sudden drop in silver's value profoundly affected mining enterprises, railroad building, and a myriad of industrial efforts worldwide. This caused a global slump, the **Long Depression**, lasting from 1873 to the mid-1890s.

**NOTE**

*The Wizard of Oz*, which appeared in book form in 1900, is thought by many to have been an allegory of the gold-standard crisis, with the yellow brick road and the name Oz (the abbreviation for "ounce") signifying gold. Here, the Cowardly Lion represents Bryan, with the Wizard symbolizing the chair of the Republican Party, which favored the gold standard. In the book, as opposed to the movie, Dorothy returns to Kansas thanks to her *silver* slippers.

## Transnational Businesses

Also during these years, especially with the spread of the West's "new" imperialism, **transnational businesses** came to dominate the economic landscape. Some of the **joint-stock companies** from the previous period survived and modernized their operations during the 1800s, such as the Hudson's Bay Company and the British East India Company. Some of the century's new companies came into being to fund major construction projects in far-off regions. Among these were the Russo-Chinese (later the Russo-Asiatic) Bank, created in 1895 by French and Russian investors to finance the Chinese Eastern Railway, and France's **Suez Canal Company**, opened in 1858 to oversee the construction of the Suez Canal. After the canal's 1869 completion, the company remained in Egypt to oversee its operation. However, while the French owned a majority of shares, their influence waned in 1873, when the Egyptian government sold its shares to Britain, and was lost altogether in 1888, when Egypt's ruler placed the canal under Britain's protection in exchange for military aid against internal rebellion.

One particularly successful transnational—it still thrives today—was the **Hong Kong and Shanghai Banking Company** (HSBC), opened in 1865 by British merchants who received special privileges and permissions in exchange for consolidating British commercial interests in Hong Kong (a British colony after the Opium Wars) and Shanghai (where Britain enjoyed economic concessions). The HSBC assumed responsibility for issuing banknotes—official currency—in British possessions like Hong Kong and Singapore, and it was commissioned to do the same even in independent states like Thailand. It quickly established branches in Japan and throughout Southeast Asia, and its widespread presence gave Britain a great deal of informal economic influence over much of East and Southeast Asia.

A similar influence was exercised over large parts of Latin America by the **United Fruit Company**, a U.S. corporation that formed in 1899 by merging smaller outfits that had been operating in Central America since the 1870s. Starting in Costa Rica, then spreading throughout Central America, Ecuador, Colombia, and the Caribbean, United Fruit came to monopolize the **cash-crop monoculture** of many fruits, with a special emphasis on **bananas**. It also involved itself in large infrastructure projects, such as railroad building and the expansion of shipping. United Fruit used mutually profitable relationships with local business and political elites to gain a tremendous amount of influence over Latin American economies and governments—to such an extent that historians consider its actions (and the actions of corporations like it) to have been *economic* imperialism.

## INDUSTRIALIZATION AND CAPITALISM IN GLOBAL PERSPECTIVE

**NOTE**

In the tropics, the derisive slang term for countries with monoculture-based economies is "banana republic"—a term that first arose to describe the Latin American nations which fell under United Fruit's influence.

Few places outside Europe and North America industrialized during the 1800s to the same extent as those two regions did, and capitalist economies were rare outside the West. Still, the effects of both trends were felt worldwide, thanks to the expansion of global trade and the growing imperial influence of Western nations over non-Western parts of the world. As during the age of mercantilist colonization, but even more intensely during the industrial era, Western economic growth depended heavily on both the acquisition of **raw materials** from non-Western regions and the transformation of those non-Western regions into new **consumer markets** for the goods they produced.

By placing new weapons—gunboats, machine guns, faster and more accurate rifles and artillery—in the hands of Westerners, industrialization made it easier for them to acquire new imperial conquests at the expense of primitively-armed Asians and Africans. Also, the growing importance of industrial-era warships, powered by coal and petroleum, required Western nations to maintain naval bases around the world, a key way in which industrialization motivated imperialism in addition to making it more feasible.

Even in parts of the world that Europe and America did not conquer or colonize, industrialization and industrial-era capitalism had a profound effect. In Africa, Asia, and Latin America, Western businessmen and industrialists—often on behalf of **transnational businesses** like the ones described above—struck deals with aristocrats or the political elite to exploit or extract **cash crops** or **natural resources**. Such practices tended to retard the development of a healthy, diverse economy. They also exploited native workers in non-Western nations: foreign payments or investments ended up in the pockets of a small number of local elites, rather than adding to the national well-being, and the workers themselves typically labored under harsh or **(semi-)coerced conditions**. The extraction of gold, diamonds, ivory, rubber, and foodstuffs from Africa was a classic example of direct exploitation, as was the extraction of rubber, tin, aluminum ore (bauxite), oil, and cotton from Southeast Asia, Indonesia, and India by the Dutch, French, and British. The industrialized West's relations with Latin American nations and Qing China—which were technically free but dealt with on economically unequal terms—was more indirectly exploitative.

In the long term, most non-Western parts of the world came to imitate industrial methods of production. Western colonizing powers exported industrial practices to their imperial possessions or created industrial-era infrastructures there, in the form of railroads, canals, and telegraph systems. In one prominent example, Britain brought industrial methods to India, although with varying motives and results. To make their own lives in India more comfortable and to maximize profits, and also because they thought it would be better for native Indians, British colonizers modernized the country in many ways. They created roads and railways (which reduced the number of famines by improving food distribution), a telegraph network, and a postal service. On the other hand, the profits generated by Indian raw materials went to Britain, rather than benefiting the local economy. In addition, the size and efficiency of British-built textile mills drove local textile enterprises, often run by women, out of business.

Also spreading industrialization to the non-Western world were political leaders in free nations there, who in some cases came to see industrialization as a way to gain wealth and power. Here, industrialization was typically imposed from above by the ruler and/or encouraged by members of the elite. In Latin America, mining for copper and guano, along with the railroad building and shipping expansion that supported not just those industries, but also the cash-crop monoculture of fruits and coffee, was generally carried out by local elites in conjunction with transnational businesses like the **United Fruit Company**. Near the end of the 1800s, countries like Mexico and Argentina, largely thanks to impetus from above, were starting to industrialize more sectors of their own economies.

In the Middle East, the initiative for industrializing came overwhelmingly from above. Muhammad Ali, the breakaway ruler of Egypt, encouraged industrialization, especially in the textile trade. The **Tanzimat reforms** attempted by the Ottoman Empire between the 1830s and the 1870s involved a concerted effort to import industrial methods, but these depended on the determination and foresightedness of the sultans, who gave up on the reforms prematurely. Also, the Tanzimat program was bitterly opposed by Islamic traditionalists, who resisted modernization. A similar pattern unfolded in Qing China, where the **self-strengthening movement** of the late 1800s brought about only limited industrialization and also aroused the wrath of traditional-minded foes who undermined its effectiveness.

The one place in the non-Western world to fully industrialize was Japan after the **Meiji Restoration** of 1868. Here, too, the impetus for change came from above, although the level of success was much greater than in China or the Ottoman Empire. Meiji and the emperors who followed him altered the economy beyond recognition. Young members of the upper class were sent to visit or study in Europe and America, to learn engineering, economics, and military science. Meiji created a ministry of industry in 1870 as well as state banks to finance his industrial campaign. New railroads, steamships, ports, and canals were constructed. Huge corporations called **zaibatsu**, sponsored largely by the state, carried out large-scale industrial efforts, but the government also encouraged private enterprise, spurring the growth of a larger middle class. At the same time, Japan's lower classes experienced many of the same travails that Europe's workers had gone through in the early 1800s. Sweatshop environments, low wages, and unsafe labor practices prevailed, especially in textile mills and coal mines. In one mine near Nagasaki, workers toiled in temperatures of up to 130 degrees Fahrenheit, and were shot if they tried to escape. Unions of any type were forbidden.

In the twentieth century, industrialization was adopted on a much greater scale worldwide. This process continued throughout the century and is still ongoing to this day.

# Social Structures, 1750–1900

20

→ **URBANIZATION AND CLASS DIVERSIFICATION IN THE WEST (MIDDLE AND INDUSTRIAL WORKING CLASSES)**

→ **NON-WESTERN CHANGES IN SOCIAL CLASSES (TANZIMAT LIBERALIZATION, MEIJI ABOLITION OF SAMURAI STATUS, BRITISH UNDERMINING OF INDIAN CASTE SYSTEM)**

→ **RACIALLY SEGREGATIONIST POLICIES IN WESTERN-CONTROLLED COLONIES (NATIVE ELITES)**

→ **INDENTURED SERVITUDE, COOLIE LABOR, AND SERFDOM (EMANCIPATION IN RUSSIA)**

→ **THE EAST AFRICAN AND ATLANTIC SLAVE TRADES**

→ **SEASONAL AND PERMANENT MIGRATION (EUROPE AND ASIA TO THE AMERICAS, CHINESE AND INDIANS IN INDIAN OCEAN BASIN)**

→ **ANTI-IMMIGRATION SENTIMENT**

→ **EARLY FEMINIST WRITERS**

→ **WESTERN SUFFRAGETTE MOVEMENTS**

The 1750–1900 era witnessed tremendous change in how societies worldwide were composed and organized. These changes resulted from a combination of political transformation and economic industrialization. Such trends were most pronounced in the West, but to one degree or another, their influence spread to most parts of the globe.

On the political front, revolutions and rebellions strove to make governments more representative and more responsive to people's needs, and in a number of cases they succeeded. Industrialization and urbanization transformed class structures, and while systems of coerced and semi-coerced labor did not disappear, the most extreme forms of slavery were gradually done away with. In general, hierarchies and caste systems tended to break down or weaken, and if they remained in place, they heightened social discontent.

Migration took place on an epic scale during these years, both for economic and political reasons. The best-known examples of migration are the mass movements from Europe and China to the Americas, but it occurred in other areas as well. The roles of women changed in most societies as well, although most notably in Europe and the Americas.

## THE TRANSFORMATION OF SOCIAL CLASSES

### Class Diversification in Europe

One of the modern era's hallmark social developments is **class diversification**. This was evident in many places, but was most striking in Europe and North America. Here, in the late 1700s, as shown in Chapters 17 and 18, Enlightenment philosophy and the Atlantic revolutions—followed in the 1800s by the gradual expansion of political representation—called into question the fairness and efficiency of old social hierarchies. At the same time, industrialization and **urbanization** exerted their own influence on social relations.

Consequently, in most of the Western world, traditional aristocracies, with their status based on land and hereditary noble status, saw their political power and social clout weaken, if not fade altogether (in the most extreme cases, as in revolutionary France, noble privileges were formally abolished). In those parts of Europe and the Americas that industrialized fastest, urbanization and increased agricultural efficiency meant that rural populations decreased. There were also new social divisions in the countryside: more land came to be owned by well-off farmers and homesteaders who were essentially middle class. Under them were poor agricultural laborers, renters, and sharecroppers who formed a rural working class of sorts.

If the proportion of peasants and farmers among the lower classes shrank, this was more than made up for by the mammoth expansion of the **industrial working class** (or **proletariat**, in the term popularized by Karl Marx). This newer working class included not just factory workers, miners, and so on, but most wage laborers of any sort, skilled or unskilled, in urban and industrial settings. As described in Chapter 19, it was this working class that shouldered most of the burden of early industrialization, without enjoying many of its benefits until several decades into the process. It was also this class which endured the harsh living and working conditions, and the low wages, associated with the first stages of industrial growth. It spent most of this period struggling for greater political representation, better working conditions, and the right to form unions.

An equally dramatic change in modernizing societies involved the rising prosperity and prominence of the **middle class**. This class expanded and greatly diversified, including in its ranks landowners, well-off farmers, master artisans and craftsmen, professionals such as doctors and lawyers, and many others. The most socially and economically influential members of the middle class were the bankers, merchants, and factory owners who increasingly controlled the means of generating wealth during this era and drew direct profits from industrial and commercial growth (the term popularized by Marx for this segment of the middle class was the **bourgeoisie**). The middle class stood out for its industriousness, its commitment to education and literacy, and its generally liberal outlook, which favored the expansion of political participation, civil rights, and economic opportunity—at least for itself. When it came to the plight of the lower classes, or to issues such as slavery and women's rights, the liberalism of the middle classes sometimes went so far as to sympathize with them, but surprisingly often, it did not. The political role of Europe's and North America's middle classes—in leading revolutions and in helping to widen political representation, whether through revolt or reform—proved immense during this era.

There were, of course, variations on this pattern and exceptions to it. Even in Europe, noble and aristocratic privilege lessened at a faster or slower pace depending on the place, and societies tended to remain more agrarian, and to have smaller middle classes, the further east and south they were, especially in Russia.

## Social Classes in Non-Western Societies

In non-Western parts of the world, class diversification came more slowly, if at all. Throughout Latin America, middle-class ambitions did much to motivate the wars of independence of the early 1800s, and the frustrations and desires of the lower classes, especially those of mixed, black, or indigenous background turned those wars into mass movements. However, even though Spanish and Portuguese colonial hierarchies were overthrown, and new constitutions written, inequality persisted. Indians, blacks, and those of mixed race still suffered official prejudice, and the economic gap between a small, wealthy landowning and business elite on one hand, and the lower-class masses on the other, not only continued, but grew wider during the 1800s. In the Ottoman-dominated Middle East, the **Tanzimat reforms** of the mid-1800s ushered in a degree of liberalization and secularization and also emphasized greater religious toleration for non-Muslim **millets** (administrative units categorized by religion). Still, these changes were limited, and the reforming impulse died away after the 1870s.

Africa, the region least touched by industrialization, underwent little of this class diversification. As the continent fell steadily under colonial domination, social dynamics there were shaped more and more by foreign imperial powers, most of which enacted **racially segregationist policies** of varying severity. The record in Asia was mixed when it came to social change. Social stratification in Qing China remained rigid, with increasingly heavy taxes levied on the impoverished masses—a prime reason for the popularity of uprisings like the White Lotus Rebellion (1796–1804) and the **Taiping Rebellion** (1850–1864). Another social crisis for China during these years was widespread **opium addiction**, which one Qing official despairingly described as "a disease which will dry up our bones, a worm that gnaws at our hearts, and a ruin to our families and persons." As in Africa, South Asia experienced **racially segregationist policies** in those places where Western imperial powers came to rule. Interestingly, in some cases, imperial rule brought about a measure of social modernization, as colonizing powers like Britain in India and France in Indochina imported industrial practices and technologies and educated **native elites** according to Western norms. In India, the British authorities also strove to undermine the most abusive aspects of the **Hindu caste system**, as well as to reduce **Hindu-Muslim religious strife**.

The one non-Western part of the world that came closest to following the Western model of social diversification was Japan after the mid-1800s. Prior to the Meiji Restoration of 1868, the Tokugawa shogunate did its best to preserve its **samurai**-dominated system of **social stratification**, with low social mobility for the lower orders. However, partial modernization during the late 1700s and early 1800s placed the shogun and the samurai classes in a dilemma: although it added to Japan's prosperity, it undermined the power and land-based wealth of the traditional aristocracy by encouraging urbanization and lending more influence to the **merchant class**—which technically occupied one of the lowest spots in the **Japanese caste system**, but was emerging as an increasingly important middle class. During the 1870s, the Meiji emperor took things even farther with the **abolition of samurai status** and hereditary privileges (including the exclusive right to wear swords), a major step in ending the Tokugawa regime's rigid social hierarchy. The feudal prejudice against trade and artisanship died away, and an increasingly **Westernized middle class** appeared and expanded in Meiji Japan. As in Europe, the farming population decreased relative to a new industrial working class. Also as in Europe, working-class conditions during Japan's early decades of industrialization remained quite harsh. Commoners of all types received better, nationally funded educations and were now eligible to serve in the military, whereas during the Tokugawa years they had been forbidden to handle weapons of any kind under any circumstance.

## LABOR AND MIGRATION

The prevailing trend with respect to labor during these years, particularly in Europe and North America, was the steadily rising impact of **industrialization** on the ways people worked. In addition to factory work and other forms of **manufacturing**, various forms of **resource extraction**, especially **mining**, were made increasingly important by industrialization. Also prominent during this period was **cash-crop monoculture**.

In all these fields, even **free laborers** experienced oppressive conditions, until the advent of **labor laws** and **trade unions**, which came into effect at different points during the 1800s and early 1900s, depending on the country in question. Harshest of all, though, was the long persistence of **coerced** and **semi-coerced forms of labor** in many parts of the globe, even as popular sentiment against them was growing.

### Indentured Servitude and Serfdom

In Asia, an oppressive form of **indentured servitude** arose during the late 1700s and 1800s, popularly known as **coolie labor** (from the Hindi word *kuli*, later adopted in China as well). To pay off debts or because they were deceived into thinking that good jobs awaited them, large numbers of Asian workers—particularly from India and especially China—signed labor contracts that placed them under the near-complete control of their employers. This often involved being shipped abroad over great distances, to the Pacific islands, to the Americas, or to the Caribbean, where they were exploited as cheap labor on plantations, in mines, and on construction projects. They planted and harvested sugar, collected guano in South America, and worked on some of America's and Canada's most important western railroads.

In parts of Central and Eastern Europe, the system of **serfdom** lasted into the late 1700s. In most places, it was done away with by the end of the century, thanks to Enlightenment-era reform (as in Austria) or to the influence of the French Revolution and Napoleon's conquests (as in Prussia and other German states). However, **Russian serfdom** not only continued, but remained central to economic and social life. Even with the number of **serf uprisings** growing yearly during the early 1800s, noble landowners were reluctant to surrender what was a near-limitless supply of cheap labor. Finally, in the mid-1850s, Russia's defeat in the Crimean War made it abundantly clear that serfdom was holding back economic and industrial modernization—to the point of jeopardizing Russia's military security—and the system was discarded. Alexander II presided over the **emancipation of Russia's serfs** in 1861.

**NOTE**

Other forms of coerced labor prevailed. In many non-Western parts of the world, corvée labor—the forcing of people to work on large-scale projects against their will—was still practiced. Egypt's Suez Canal was built largely in this fashion between 1859 and 1869. Prison labor was equally common: Russia sentenced serf rebels and political dissidents to hard labor in Siberia and Britain relied on transportation—banishment to under-populated colonies like Australia—to get rid of unwanted criminals.

### African Slave Trades

Ending the **East African** and **Atlantic slave trades**, which were as profitable as they were notorious, proved much more complicated and required long international efforts. The former, run largely by Arabs and headquartered in market cities like **Zanzibar**, flourished throughout most of the 1800s, fueled by a steadily growing demand for spices and sugar produced by plantation agriculture in East Africa. By the 1870s and 1880s, just before the slave trade was shut down there, it is estimated that over 40 percent of the population in the East African plantation zone was made up of slaves. Abolition here took decades, and came about as a result of popular outrage in the West, military action on the part of

Western governments, and missionary activity (a key figure was the Scottish explorer and humanitarian **David Livingstone**). A major step in the process was the closing of the great slave market in the center of Zanzibar.

Western nations benefited even more directly from the **Atlantic slave trade**, and they took a long time to stop it. During the late 1700s and early 1800s, mining, **sugar cultivation**, and plantation agriculture in Latin America and the Caribbean all depended heavily on African slave labor. Slaves were also used extensively in the southern United States as domestic servants and agricultural laborers, especially for **cotton production**, which the Industrial Revolution made centrally important to the global economy. At least 12 million Africans were victimized by the Atlantic slave trade between the mid-1400s and the late 1800s. It has been calculated that approximately 2 million of them were transported to the Americas during the nineteenth century, with most of them going to Brazil, Cuba, and the Caribbean, and a comparatively small number being smuggled into the United States.

In other words, the scale of the Atlantic slave trade declined during the 1800s, but it also lasted a regrettably long time. Its gradual demise resulted partly from practical economic considerations: as the century progressed, it became more difficult and therefore more expensive to obtain slaves. The **Haitian Revolution** (1791–1804), the first successful uprising of African slaves in the modern era, set a monumental precedent for possible rebellions in the future. Equally important was the growing political, religious, and ethical revulsion for slavery that arose among Western populations in the wake of the Enlightenment and the American and French revolutions. In the 1790s and the first decade of the 1800s, countries like revolutionary France, the Netherlands, and Denmark began to make slavery illegal.

A major turning point came in 1808, when Great Britain made the slave trade illegal (slavery itself was banned in all parts of the British Empire by 1834). During the peace talks that settled the Napoleonic wars, Britain convinced nearly all of Europe and the Americas to outlaw the slave trade. With the exception of Spain and Portugal (and Russia with its system of serfdom), Europe agreed, and the Americas went along as well—for the most part. Canada, still part of the British Empire, and most of Latin America outlawed slavery. The longest holdouts were Cuba and Brazil, which did not end slavery until 1883 and 1888. The United States, split between the slaveholding South and the nonslave North, agreed to make the international slave trade—but not slavery itself—illegal, and the federal government also worked to restrict the spread of slavery within the United States as the country expanded. Not until after the U.S. Civil War (1861–1865) was slavery made illegal throughout the country.

The continued survival of slavery in the Americas meant that the Atlantic slave trade, illegal or not, continued as well. The fact that a number of West African states, as described in Chapter 17, enriched and empowered themselves by cooperating with the Atlantic slave trade, helped to keep it going. Foreign pressure against the slave trade included not just official legislation, but also the efforts of **abolition movements**, especially in Britain and the northern United States. Canada served as a haven for slaves escaping from the southern United States. European and American **missionaries** serving in Africa often campaigned against slave raids and slave markets, both on the Atlantic coast and in East Africa. Starting in the early 1800s, the British government dispatched the Royal Navy to blockade the West African shoreline, hunt down slave ships, and bombard the coastal forts of West African kingdoms that supported the slave trade. Less enthusiastically, France and the United States joined in these expeditions.

Not surprisingly, both slave trades took an immense toll on Africa. Obvious effects included human suffering, population loss, the stirring up of tribal warfare, and the disruption of traditional trade networks and economic practices. It is equally obvious how the ending of the slave trades benefited Africa. However, especially in the case of the Atlantic slave trade, there were unforeseen, less positive consequences. One was a sharp financial slump suffered by those African states that had profited from slavery—and now, having lost their ill-gotten gains, were left more vulnerable to foreign takeover by their economic weakness. Moreover, the antislavery interventions carried out by Britain and other nations, however well-intentioned, gave Europeans a pretext for involving themselves in Africa's affairs and thinking of military action there as legitimate. This helped pave the way for the rush to conquer all of Africa near the end of the century.

## Migration and Immigrant Communities

Another great trend of the era was a tremendous **migration of peoples**, both permanent and seasonal, that began during the 1800s and never truly ceased. If one excludes the involuntary relocation of slaves across the Atlantic or coolie laborers across the Pacific, nineteenth-century migration was in most cases driven by a combination of overcrowding at home and economic opportunity abroad. In other instances, political persecution or violent unrest at home provided people with an incentive to emigrate. Another key reason for migration during this period was Western imperialism, as colonial officials, settlers, and others seeking opportunity or adventure traveled far from home to new places. As they grew more commonplace and more easily affordable, industrial-era modes of transport, such as railroads and steamships, made migration more feasible than ever before.

Most famously, huge numbers of Europeans and Asians relocated to the Americas during the 1800s. The United States' reputation as a land of freedom and economic opportunity drew millions of immigrants from Europe and Asia during the 1800s. Between the 1830s and 1890s, an estimated 17 million people came to settle in the United States, and immigrants continued to arrive in large numbers during the 1900s. Canada, Argentina, and Chile also took in many immigrants, both from Europe and Asia. Migration throughout Southeast Asia and the Indian Ocean basin was common as well, with Chinese merchants and laborers spreading throughout Malaysia and elsewhere, and with large numbers of Indians traveling to East and South Africa because of commercial ties there. Australia also received a number of immigrants from Asia.

In some cases, these migrations were permanent. In others, they were temporary or seasonal, as migrants relocated for work and either returned home or sent wages back to their families. This sort of work tended to involve agricultural labor and typically meant that it was men who migrated and women who assumed new burdens and leadership roles at home and in the family.

Among the diasporic communities and foreign enclaves to be aware of from this era are Asians in Australia; Japanese agricultural laborers throughout the Pacific (with a large concentration in Hawaii and the west coasts of America and Canada, as well as along South America's Pacific coastline); Lebanese merchants in the Americas; the large population of Italians who settled in Argentina; the Chinese diaspora throughout Southeast Asia; and the large presence of Indians in East Africa and South Africa, and even as far away as the Caribbean.

**NOTE**

Three examples of mass emigration illustrate the variety of factors that caused it. The Irish potato famine of the 1840s precipitated the movement of hundreds of thousands of Irish to the United States. In the Russian Empire, the persecution of religious minorities—including anti-Jewish pogroms and the harassment of non-Orthodox Christians like Mennonites—led to a massive outmigration of Jews to the United States and elsewhere, and many Ukrainians to central Canada. In China, the economic ruin and violence caused by the Taiping Rebellion convinced large numbers of Chinese to move to North and South America, often as coolie laborers in mines, on plantations, and on railroads.

**Anti-immigration sentiment** was common, both on a popular and official level. It arose for several reasons, including straightforward ethnic or religious prejudice and the alarmist tendency to view new arrivals as potential economic competitors. Jews and non-whites were rarely well-received in their new societies, but neither were groups like the Irish when they first landed on new shores. Countries hosting large numbers of immigrants typically imposed **quota systems**, limiting the quantity of people they would let in per year from a given country. Other regulations were common as well. Among the most famous was the **Chinese Exclusion Act** in the United States, which suspended Chinese immigration for ten years, starting in 1882, but continued to renew anti-Chinese restrictions beyond 1892, well into the 1900s. Feverish racial fears about a rising "yellow peril," combined with concern about the availability of jobs for white Americans, motivated the passage of this law. A similar logic prevailed in the case of the **White Australia Policy**, enshrined in a number of official measures, including the Immigration Restriction Act of 1901. These laws were intended to give every possible advantage to white immigrants from Great Britain, as opposed to potential arrivals from China, the Pacific islands, and continental Europe, all seeking jobs in Australian mines or on sugar plantations.

**Anti-Immigration Sentiment during the 1800s and Early 1900s**

On the left, a message that all too often confronted Irish immigrants in the United States after the 1840s, when they began arriving in large numbers due to the Irish potato famine. On the right, a poster unabashedly praising the White Australia Policy that discouraged non-British migration to the island in the late 1800s and early 1900s.

## GENDER AND FAMILY ISSUES

## Women's Rights Movements Emerge in Europe and North America

Although in most societies, the status of women remained secondary, the 1750–1900 period saw great changes in gender relations. In the West, a greater awareness of the unequal treatment of women began to spread, starting around the late 1700s. This was stimulated largely by the theories of Enlightenment philosophy, as well as the active role played by women in the American and French revolutions.

The English author **Mary Wollstonecraft** is considered one of the founders of modern feminism. Her 1792 treatise, *A Vindication of the Rights of Women*, insisted that women, like men, possessed reason and were therefore entitled to equal rights. During the French Revolution, the playwright **Olympe de Gouges** argued in her "Declaration of the Rights of Woman and the Citizeness" that women should have the same rights granted to men by the "Declaration of the Rights of Man and the Citizen." The government dismissed her proposal, and she died during the Reign of Terror.

Larger women's rights movements emerged in the 1830s in Europe and North America. Early on, they focused on reforming laws to allow women to own property and file for divorce. This initial effort did not reap quick results, as women did not gain full property rights in Britain until 1870, Germany until 1900, and France until 1907.

Soon, feminists were seeking better access to higher education and jobs, as well as equal pay. The first professions open to women, beyond domestic servitude, were teaching and nursing. Women also led the way in campaigning for temperance, the abolition of slavery, and aid for orphans and the poor.

**NOTE**

During the late 1800s and early 1900s, women engaged in activities even more radical than the struggle for votes. The campaign for birth control and reproductive rights, which featured the American nurse Margaret Sanger, proved extremely difficult. Also, in countries like Russia, where few chances for within-the-system political action existed, many female activists turned to the far left in order to advance feminist agendas.

By the middle of the nineteenth century, women began to seek political rights, most notably suffrage, or the right to vote. As a rule, European and North American **suffragette movements** were led by women of the middle and upper classes. The most vocal women's movement was Britain's, led by Emmeline Pankhurst. Major figures in the U.S. movement were Susan B. Anthony and Elizabeth Cady Stanton. American and Canadian women not only called for the right to vote at the **1848 Seneca Falls Convention**—which based its "Declaration of Sentiments" on the U.S. Declaration of Independence—they agitated for better working conditions for women, child welfare, and temperance. Almost no countries gave women the vote until late in World War I or afterward. Exceptions include Norway, Finland, and a handful of U.S. states.

**Marching toward Women's Rights**

On the left, Nikolai Yaroshenko's *Female Student* (1880) depicts the awakening of a feminist spirit in tsarist Russia, connecting it with the power of education. The "Women Are Persons" Monument on Ottawa's Parliament Hill, on the right, celebrates a court decision that carried the suffragette impulse to its logical conclusion. Although Canadian women had received federal voting rights in 1918 and could serve in many political offices, it was not decided until 1929 that they were "persons" legally able to serve in Canada's senate. Here suffragette and politician Nellie McClung displays the proclamation declaring them eligible to do so.

## Women and Industrialization

During the late 1700s and early 1800s, the Industrial Revolution profoundly altered the conditions under which women and families worked.

Industrialization shifted the workplace away from the farm—where both men and women worked—to mines, factories, and other places away from the home. This shift created a **domestic sphere** and a separate working sphere. In Europe and the United States, women of the lower classes were generally compelled to enter the workplace, most frequently in textile factories—where women made up 50 percent of the workforce until 1870. These women also bore the double burden of serving as the primary homemakers and caregivers for their families.

After the mid-1800s, the number of working women in Europe and North America declined. Women of the middle and upper classes had rarely worked to begin with. As wages for industrial workers rose, making such jobs more desirable to men, and as new laws restricted the number of hours women and children could work, the number of lower-class working women fell. A **cult of domesticity**, stressing that a woman's place was in the home and a man's in the workplace, dominated Western culture—especially among the middle and upper classes—during the mid- to late nineteenth century. Certain occupations were open to women, such as child care (governesses), teaching, domestic household work (servants and maids), nursing, and artisanry.

## Non-Western Developments

The move toward women's equality tended to be slower in non-Western societies.

In some places, however, the educational level of women rose, as did the extent of property rights. As in the West, women worked, especially in certain occupations, such as agricultural labor, domestic service, and nursing. As non-Western parts of the world industrialized, lower-class women tended to enter the workplace, as in the industrial West. It should also be noted that the arrival of Western colonists often affected gender roles and family relations in areas that fell under the influence of European and American imperialism.

In the Middle East, one effect of the Tanzimat reforms was to give women greater access to education. Public schools were founded for women, and more women, although still a small number, began to enter public life in the late 1800s. Countering this trend was a strict form of Islamic traditionalism that opposed modernization in general.

As Africa came increasingly under colonial control, many African families were broken up. Husbands worked in mines or on plantations, or served in native military units, while wives stayed behind in villages to grow food and care for children. When Western commercial employers and colonial officials gave out jobs and introduced new property laws, they tended to favor male heads of household. This left women with fewer economic opportunities and, in many ways, undercut matrilineal authority in those parts of Africa where it had prevailed.

In Qing China, Confucian traditionalism continued to place women in a secondary social position. **Foot binding** continued, although this was increasingly opposed by foreign missionaries, as well as by the Taiping rebels who threatened the Qing regime during the mid-1800s. In Japan, the Meiji Restoration ended the Tokugawa regime's strict social stratification, but even the 1890 Constitution made little room for the rights of women, who remained largely confined to a secondary status. Industrialization in Japan created jobs for lower-class women, but these were low-paying, low-prestige positions. The **Hindu**

**caste system**, complete with its traditional patriarchalism, remained in place in South Asia, although in British India, colonial authorities combatted many of its excesses, including the **sati ritual**.

Most Latin American nations based their legal systems on the **Napoleonic civil code**, which concerned itself even less with women's rights than the constitutional arrangements in North America. Also, industrialization progressed more slowly in Latin America than in the north, so non-agricultural working opportunities were scantier. Over time, however, countries such as Argentina, Uruguay, and Chile made it possible for women to gain educations; in Chile, they could earn degrees in high-status professions such as law and medicine. In general, greater rights were extended to women in these nations.

# Humans and the Environment, 1750–1900

# 21

→ END OF THE LITTLE ICE AGE

→ IMPACT OF URBANIZATION AND POPULATION GROWTH

→ EARTH-SHAPING CAPACITY (DEFORESTATION, ROADS, RAILROADS, CANALS)

→ CASH-CROP MONOCULTURE (COTTON, SUGAR, COFFEE, TEA, RUBBER)

→ MINING AND FOSSIL-FUEL EXTRACTION (COAL, METALS, PETROLEUM)

→ POLLUTION AND CARBON-BASED EMISSIONS (EARLY CLIMATE CHANGE)

→ SPECIES ENDANGERMENT AND EXTINCTION

→ VACCINATION AND GERM THEORY

→ CURES AND TREATMENTS FOR TROPICAL DISEASES (MALARIA)

→ DISEASE AND INDUSTRIAL-ERA LIVING CONDITIONS (CHOLERA, TUBERCULOSIS)

Arguably, the 1750–1900 period can be described as the era when human beings consistently began to influence their environment more than they were influenced by it. Whatever the truth of that, there is no doubting the fact that economic industrialization and rapid technological advancement exponentially increased human impact on the environment. This trend, moreover, continued into the twentieth century and has shown no signs of stopping in the twenty-first.

In a macroscopic development that affected agriculture, patterns of human settlement, and the ability to explore and exploit the polar regions, the **Little Ice Age**, which had persisted since around 1500 (with steady cooling even before that), finally ended during the mid-1800s.

## INDUSTRIALIZATION AND THE ENVIRONMENT

Industrialization provided societies not just with new abilities to affect the environment, but with new incentives to do so.

**Population growth** and **urbanization**, each of which went hand in hand with industrialization, placed greater strains on local ecosystems. Without proper planning, the higher concentration of human beings in a given area leads to greater resource consumption and worsening environmental stress. Mass **deforestation** arose as a growing problem in many parts of the world during this era. Not only were forests cleared to make room for farms, factories, and settlements, but timber became a much-needed commodity for fuel, construction, and the manufacture of paper.

Technology hugely multiplied the **earth-shaping capacity** of industrialized societies, allowing them to leave deeper and more noticeable marks on the environment. **Road networks** and **railroads** quickly expanded over great distances during the industrial era. New and growing cities, along with the ever-larger buildings that appeared in them—such as factories and skyscrapers—spread across more of the landscape. **Large-scale agricultural enterprises**, in the form of plantations and similarly sized farming units, also allowed major manipulations of the environment. Perhaps the most visible and most celebrated earth-shaping endeavors of this era involved the construction of dams and **canals** by industrializing nations that wished to facilitate shipping and transport. Most famous during the 1800s were the **Erie Canal** (1825) in the United States and the strategically and economically vital **Suez Canal** (1869) in Egypt, which linked the Mediterranean with the Indian Ocean basin via the Red Sea. In 1914, the **Panama Canal**, a project pursued by several nations since the late 1800s, was completed by the United States and revolutionized global shipping by connecting the Atlantic and Pacific oceans.

Resource extraction dramatically increased during the industrial era, severely depleting resources and causing higher levels of environmental damage than ever before. **Cash-crop monoculture** intensified, both in colonies governed by Western nations and in countries where Western nations and corporations invested heavily. As textile industries expanded during the era, so too did the growing and harvesting of **cotton** in places like the U.S. South, Egypt, Central Asia, and India. Other crops grown in monocultural fashion during these years included **silk** (China), **coffee** (Latin America, Africa, South Asia), **tea** (China and India), **fruit** (Africa and Latin America), and **rubber** (extracted from trees in Africa and Southeast Asia). Aside from its environmentally harmful nature, cash-crop and plantation monoculture readily lent itself to **coerced** and **semi-coerced labor practices**, including the worst forms of **slavery**. Also increasing the environmental impact of the industrial era was the escalation of **mining** and **fossil-fuel extraction**. Industrializing nations developed a voracious appetite for **coal** and **iron**, and a host of other metals besides iron became crucial as well. **Gold** and **diamonds** were considered precious for luxury purposes, but also because of their industrial uses, and they were avidly sought wherever possible, from Africa to Arctic regions like the Yukon, Alaska, and northeastern Siberia. Already in the late 1800s, and definitely after 1900, the quest for **petroleum** began, both as a manufacturing lubricant and increasingly as a source of energy—with deposits discovered initially in the Americas and in the Middle East, and also in parts of Southeast Asia.

Two forms of environmental damage made themselves particularly obvious. One was the **pollution** of the skies and waters, which reached unprecedented levels. Unlike today, there were few laws to combat pollution, and the first stages of **human-caused climate change**, or global warming, are thought by most scientists to have begun with the carbon-based, fossil-fuel emissions of the early industrial era. Also becoming unavoidably apparent was the **endangerment** or **extinction of species**, as overhunting and the destruction of habitats became more common. The population of fur-bearing creatures like sables, otters, and fur seals dwindled dangerously, as did North America's once-massive herds of bison. Oil from whales and certain species of seals served as lamp fuel and as lubricants for industrial production until the shift to petroleum, and they hovered perilously close to extinction, as did walruses who were hunted for ivory. Notorious extinctions of the era included those of the great auk, the Carolina parakeet, the passenger pigeon, and, in the North Pacific, the Steller's sea cow.

**NOTE**

One of the earliest examples of modern extinction, and perhaps the most famous, is that of the dodo, whose very name is a synonym of the process. Indigenous to the island of Mauritius (east of Madagascar in the Indian Ocean), the dodo came to the notice of Dutch travelers in the late 1500s—and it took only till the mid-1600s for overhunting by foreign sailors to drive it to extinction. This grimly foreshadowed the greater waves of human-caused species depletion to come in the 1800s and beyond.

As noted in Chapters 17 and 20, imperialism and industrialization both spurred extraordinarily large waves of **migration**, both permanent and seasonal. Aside from redistributing human populations over great distances on the order of millions, these migrations had the long-term environmental effect of transferring large numbers of people to regions that had previously been sparsely populated. In addition, new arrivals typically brought with them industrial-era economic practices that burdened local ecosystems far more heavily than the pre-industrial modes of production pursued by indigenous peoples.

## DISEASE IN THE MODERN ERA

For the first time in history, a truly scientific understanding of diseases—and how to combat them—emerged. Experiments with **vaccination** during the late 1700s proved effective in the treatment and prevention of smallpox, one of the deadliest killers in medical history. The practice spread during the 1800s and 1900s, slowly but eventually leading to the complete eradication of many diseases. Also helpful was a proper understanding of **germ theory** and **medical sterilization**, which was achieved in Europe and North America during the mid- to late 1800s. This aided not just medical procedure but, thanks to scientists like Louis Pasteur, the handling and processing of food. This entailed a new level of human mastery over the environment, and it also contributed directly to **population growth**.

Also by the mid-1800s, Europeans and Americans grew adept at developing cures (or at least symptom-relieving treatments) for **tropical diseases** like **malaria**, yellow fever, and sleeping sickness. Medical innovations of this sort played a significant role in enabling the exploration and colonization of previously difficult-to-access parts of Africa and Asia.

On the other hand, disease was not yet entirely conquered. Certain illnesses proved resistant to vaccines or adaptable to them. Also, where treatment was lacking or too expensive to afford, diseases continued to kill large numbers of people. Paradoxically, while industrial-era science played a role in the nineteenth century's medical breakthroughs, industrial-era living conditions—which included overcrowding, air pollution, and unprotected water supplies—helped to worsen the severity of certain diseases. Smallpox, where untreated, remained deadly, but the most infamous of the industrial-era maladies were **cholera** and **tuberculosis**.

# UNIT 6

## ACCELERATING GLOBAL CHANGE AND REALIGNMENTS
### (1900 to Present)

# Unit 6 Short Cut

## GENERAL REMARKS

The twentieth century ranks as one of the most tumultuous eras ever. It was a time of paradox and contradiction, leading the eminent historian Eric Hobsbawm to label it the "age of extremes." Democratic forms of government were adopted more widely than ever before (and women gained the vote in large parts of the world), but history's most oppressive dictatorships appeared as well. The 1900s were a time of unprecedented prosperity, but also of striking socioeconomic polarity, as the gap between rich and poor widened. There were tremendous cultural and scientific advancements, but also the worst wars—including the modern form of violence known as **genocide**—and the greatest arms buildups in human history.

The first half of the century was dominated by two mammoth military conflicts: **World War I** and **World War II**, "total" wars characterized by improved military technology and new tactics, comprehensive mobilization of resources, and immense devastation. World War I destroyed several of the nineteenth century's great empires and sapped Europe's strength. World War II, the bloodiest conflict humanity has ever experienced—especially in combination with **the Holocaust**—completed the dislodging of Europe from its position of global mastery.

The interwar years were marked by economic crisis, culminating in the **Great Depression**, which emanated outward from the United States. This period also saw the rise of powerful dictatorships, such as Soviet Russia, fascist Italy, and Nazi Germany, and it appeared for a time that **totalitarianism**, not democracy, might be the wave of the future. Starting with the establishment of the Soviet state, **communism** became an influential—although, in the end, seemingly unworkable—alternative to **capitalism** as a form of economic organization.

During the century's second half, sweeping trends affected the entire world. One, following the collapse of Europe's global dominance, was **decolonization**. From the 1940s through the 1970s, parts of Africa, Asia, and the Pacific that had been under European (and U.S.) imperial control became free. This wave of **national liberation** created dozens of new nations. In some cases, decolonization proceeded peacefully. In others, it was attained by force or disintegrated into political chaos.

Another effect of World War II was a new geopolitical alignment, the **Cold War**. In the previous century and a half, world affairs had been determined by the workings of the European balance of power, but political and economic might was now concentrated in the hands of two evenly matched **superpowers**: the United States and the Soviet Union. This bipolar equilibrium persisted for four and a half decades, dividing most of the globe into two hostile camps—although the rise of China as a communist power opposed to the USSR, and the attempt of certain nations to form a **non-aligned movement**, provided diplomatic alternatives.

The twentieth century was an era of rapid modernization. Societies already industrialized when the 1900s began—North America, Europe, and Japan—became even more adept at scientific and technological innovation, and shifted toward **postindustrial** (or **service**) economies during the post-World War II era. Such societies are generally referred to as belonging to the **developed world**. A number of other countries, especially in Asia, have similarly modernized. The **developing** or **nondeveloped world** (or, in Cold War terms, the **Third World**) includes most other regions, which remain in a less-advanced stage of economic and technological progress. In global terms, the gap between prosperity and poverty—the **north-south split** between richer societies above the equator and poorer ones below it—is arguably wider today than at any other time in history.

> ### POSTMODERN ERA
>
> With respect to historical labels, it is common to speak of the modern period (ca. 1800–1945) as ending after World War II, at least in the developed West. The years following are generally referred to by historians as the contemporary or postmodern era, characterized by postindustrial and global forms of economic organization, multiculturalism, the blurring of national lines, and extreme individualism. To what degree this label fits less-developed societies in Africa, Asia, and elsewhere is a matter of debate.

The 1980s and 1990s saw the collapse of communism in Europe and the USSR, and with that, the end of the Cold War. The same decades witnessed a wave of democratization in many parts of the world, as well as the increased **globalization** of the world economy. The greater ease with which ethnicities and traditions mix has stimulated a high degree of **multiculturalism**, and mass communications and transport have made the world, metaphorically speaking, a much smaller and more connected place. This is especially due to the proliferation of computer technology, which has caused an **information** (or **digital**) **revolution**. Entities other than **nation-states**—such as **multinational corporations**, **nongovernmental organizations**, and **regional trade alliances**—have had an increasingly large impact on world affairs.

The world's general direction in the early twenty-first century remains unclear. Many trends, such as the end of the nuclear arms race, economic globalization, and the spread of popular culture, mass communications, and computer technology, seem to be drawing the world closer together. On the other hand, ethnic violence and genocide, extreme forms of **nationalism**, **religious fundamentalism**, proliferation of **weapons of mass destruction**, potential tensions between China and the West, and ongoing tensions between the West and Islamic states all threaten to pull the world farther apart. The same is true of **terrorism**, most notably in the aftermath of the terrorist attacks of September 11, 2001. On the planetary level, all modern societies, developed or undeveloped, have had an immensely greater impact on the environment. The most noticeable effect today is **climate change**, popularly known as global warming.

# BROAD TRENDS

| State Building, Expansion, and Conflict, 1900 to the Present | |
|---|---|
| **Europe** | World War I (1914–1918, trench warfare) and Paris Peace Conference (1919, Treaty of Versailles)<br><br>Russia's October Revolution (1917, Vladimir Lenin)<br><br>weakness of interwar democracies (effects of Great Depression) vs. rise of totalitarian dictatorships (Soviet Russia, Fascist Italy, Nazi Germany)<br><br>civilian involvement in war (Guernica, Battle of Britain, strategic bombing and Dresden)<br><br>collective security vs. appeasement in 1930s diplomacy (Munich Agreement)<br><br>World War II (1939–1945, blitzkrieg, aerial warfare)<br><br>genocide (Holocaust, ethnic cleansing in Yugoslav wars)<br><br>Cold War rivalry (arms race and MAD, containment and domino principle, détente, fall of Berlin Wall)<br><br>"iron curtain" division of Europe (NATO vs. Warsaw Pact, Berlin Wall)<br><br>social welfare systems and economic union in Western Europe (EU)<br><br>East European dissidents (Solidarity) and Gorbachev's *perestroika* in USSR<br><br>collapse of European communism (1989–1991) and post-communist "shock therapy" (1990s) |
| **Middle East** | World War I (1914–1918, Gallipoli)<br><br>genocide (Armenians in Ottoman Empire)<br><br>Paris Peace Conference and the mandate system<br><br>interwar modernization under Mustafa Kemal Ataturk and Reza Shah Pahlavi<br><br>Arab-Israeli conflict (Balfour Declaration, partition of Palestine, Arab-Israeli wars, PLO and Hamas, Camp David and Oslo accords, First and Second Intifadas)<br><br>OPEC and the geopolitical importance of Middle Eastern oil<br><br>Gamal Nasser (pan-Arabism) and nationalization of Suez Canal<br><br>Iranian Revolution (1979, Shah of Iran vs. Ayatollah Khomeini)<br><br>Iran-Iraq War and Gulf War (Desert Storm)<br><br>al-Qaeda attacks of 9/11/2001 and U.S.-led "war on terror" (Iraq, Afghanistan)<br><br>the Arab Spring |
| **Africa** | civilian involvement in war (Italian terror-bombing of Ethiopia, child soldiers)<br><br>negotiated vs. violent decolonization in Africa (Ghana vs. Algeria, Congo, and Biafra)<br><br>Kwame Nkrumah and pan-Africanism (Organization of African Unity)<br><br>authoritarianism in Africa (Joseph Mobutu, Idi Amin, Muammar Gaddafi)<br><br>apartheid in South Africa (African National Congress, Nelson Mandela)<br><br>genocide (Rwanda, Darfur)<br><br>impact of HIV/AIDS on society and politics |

## State Building, Expansion, and Conflict, 1900 to the Present

| | |
|---|---|
| **East (and Central) Asia** | Chinese Revolution (1911–1912, Sun Yat-sen, Chiang Kai-shek, and KMT) <br> Japanese invasion of China (1931+) and World War II (1939–1945, East Asian Co-Prosperity Sphere) <br> civilian involvement in war (Nanjing, Tokyo fire bombing, Hiroshima) <br> Japan's economic resurgence and Asia's "little tigers" <br> Mao Tse-tung and People's Republic of China (1949+, Great Leap Forward, Cultural Revolution) <br> Korean War (1950–1953) <br> Deng Xiaoping (economic reform in China, quashing of 1989 Tiananmen Square protests) <br> economic growth and potential superpower status for Communist China <br> nuclear weapons in North Korea |
| **South (and Southeast) Asia and Oceania** | national liberation in India (Indian National Congress, Mohandas Gandhi and nonviolence) <br> World War II (1939–1945, East Asian Co-Prosperity Sphere) <br> Indochina and Vietnam wars (1945–1975, Ho Chi Minh) <br> Indian and Pakistani independence (1947, Jawaharlal Nehru) <br> genocide (Khmer Rouge in Cambodia) <br> Indo-Pakistani rivalry and nuclear weapons |
| **Americas** | U.S. sphere of influence in Latin America <br> Mexican Revolution (1910–1920, PRI) <br> Cold War rivalry (arms race and MAD, containment and domino principle, détente, fall of Berlin Wall) <br> authoritarianism in Latin America (Juan Perón, Augusto Pinochet, death squads) <br> genocide (Mayans in Guatemala) <br> Cuban Revolution (1959, Fidel Castro, Bay of Pigs, Cuban Missile Crisis) <br> Nicaraguan Revolution (1979, Sandinistas vs. Contras) |
| **Global and Interregional** | international organizations (League of Nations, United Nations, GATT/WTO, International Criminal Court) <br> total wars (civilian casualties, economic mobilization, conscription, restrictions on civil liberties) <br> ethnic violence and genocide <br> World Wars I and II <br> global impact of Cold War (proxy wars and brushfire conflicts) <br> decolonization and national liberation <br> rise of terrorism (Black Hand, PLO, IRA, FLQ, Weather Underground, Hamas, al-Qaeda) <br> asymmetrical warfare (WMDs and RMA vs. low-intensity and guerrilla wars) <br> nuclear proliferation ("nuclear club" vs. Israel, India, Pakistan, North Korea, Iran) |

# State Building, Expansion, and Conflict

- During the first half of the 1900s, two world wars profoundly reshaped global affairs. After 1914, Europe's position of world dominance was weakened by World War I, and the United States became the world's richest and most powerful nation. World War II completed the dismantling of Europe's global dominance. Both were total wars that required near-complete mobilization of human and economic resources.

- For four and a half decades after World War II, most of the world was divided into hostile camps, led by two superpowers, the United States and the USSR, in a geopolitical struggle known as the Cold War. This involved a nuclear arms race, the largest weapons buildup in world history, and the creation of huge military-industrial complexes.

- From the 1940s through the 1970s, a mass wave of decolonization deprived the European powers of their empires. Sometimes through peaceful negotiation, sometimes through violent separation, former colonies in Asia, Africa, the Pacific, and elsewhere became free. Dozens of new nations were formed.

- Countries that were neither Western nor Soviet-bloc came to be seen as belonging to the so-called Third World. These nations, many of them recently decolonized, and most of them relatively backward in terms of economic and technological development, experimented with a variety of political and economic systems. During the Cold War, some sided with the United States or the USSR, while others attempted to remain neutral or even to join together in a non-aligned movement. Some were attracted to the leadership of Communist China, whose emerging rivalry with the USSR complicated the bipolarity of the Cold War.

- During the late 1980s and 1990s, communism in Eastern Europe and the USSR collapsed, ending the Cold War. The only remaining superpower since has been the United States, with China—which remained communist—as a rising power.

- The terrorist attacks of September 11, 2001, by al-Qaeda began a new global struggle, the U.S.-led war on terror. This sharpened tensions between the West and the Islamic world, and sparked wars in Iraq and Afghanistan. Terrorism in general (carried out by groups such as the ETA, the IRA, the PLO, Hamas, and others) has played a significant role in international politics in the 1900s and 2000s.

- New weapons and tactics were constantly developed throughout this period. Wars became increasingly destructive and caused greater numbers of casualties, especially among civilian populations. They also created larger numbers of displaced persons and refugees.

- Warfare during this era became increasingly connected with racial hatred and campaigns of ethnic violence such as the Holocaust. The term "genocide" was coined during World War II to describe such crises. Conversely, and largely because of these developments, a greater concern for human rights, and wider recognition of the need to safeguard them, arose.

- By the 1990s and early 2000s, the gap between high-tech and low-level warfare had grown wider than ever before in history. The most advanced armed forces possess weapons of mass destruction, precision-guided ("smart") weapons, and—thanks to what strategists call the "revolution in military affairs"—digitally integrated systems. Much of the rest of the world fights low-intensity or guerrilla wars, using only small arms and hand-to-hand weapons.

- Domestically, the level of popular representation in national governments grew in many countries, especially the Western democracies. Women gained the vote in most Western nations in the early twentieth century, and later in most others.
- Between the world wars, democracies tended to be politically weak and economically depressed. The most dynamic governments of the interwar period were dictatorships, including totalitarian regimes that aimed to control as many aspects of their subjects' lives as possible.
- After World War II, the primary form of political and economic organization in the West (Canada, the United States, and Western Europe) was the democratic state with a capitalist system, although capitalism was modified to varying degrees by social welfare systems.
- A number of regimes, led by the Soviet Union and China, adopted communist economic systems. Their political systems tended to be dictatorial.
- Military and authoritarian dictatorships proliferated throughout the Third World during the Cold War, some of them pro-Soviet, some of them pro-U.S., some of them neutral. Many have democratized during the 1990s and early 2000s, although with varying degrees of success.
- Entities other than nation-states, including regional trade organizations (such as the European Union and NAFTA), non-governmental organizations (such as Amnesty International and the Red Cross), and multinational corporations (such as Coca-Cola, Shell Oil, and McDonalds), began to exert greater influence over world affairs.
- Unofficial actors, including anti-war protesters, civil-rights and freedom activists, and proponents of nonviolent resistance (most famously Mohandas Gandhi and Martin Luther King, Jr.), profoundly affected political events on numerous occasions.

| Culture, Science, and Technology, 1900 to the Present | |
|---|---|
| Europe | uncertainty and anxiety in high culture (impact of world wars, Freudian thought) <br> mass media (high culture, entertainment, propaganda) <br> sports professionalized and politicized <br> existentialism <br> synthetic spirituality (new age, Hare Krishna) <br> rapid progress in new scientific fields |
| Middle East | adoption and adaptation of Western high culture <br> mass media (high culture, entertainment, propaganda) <br> sports professionalized and politicized <br> Americanization and Westernization of global culture ("coca-colonization") <br> religious fundamentalism |
| Africa | adoption and adaptation of Western high culture <br> mass media (high culture, entertainment, propaganda) <br> sports professionalized and politicized <br> Americanization and Westernization of global culture ("coca-colonization") |

| Culture, Science, and Technology, 1900 to the Present | |
| --- | --- |
| **East (and Central) Asia** | adoption and adaptation of Western high culture<br>mass media (high culture, entertainment, propaganda)<br>sports professionalized and politicized<br>Americanization and Westernization of global culture ("coca-colonization")<br>synthetic spirituality (Falun Gong)<br>significant progress in new scientific fields |
| **South (and Southeast) Asia and Oceania** | adoption and adaptation of Western high culture<br>mass media (high culture, entertainment, propaganda)<br>sports professionalized and politicized<br>Americanization and Westernization of global culture ("coca-colonization")<br>religious fundamentalism |
| **Americas** | uncertainty and anxiety in high culture (impact of world wars, Freudian thought)<br>mass media (high culture, entertainment, propaganda)<br>sports professionalized and politicized<br>existentialism<br>Americanization and Westernization of Latin American culture ("coca-colonization")<br>rapid progress in new scientific fields<br>synthetic spirituality (new age, Hare Krishna)<br>religious fundamentalism<br>liberation theology |
| **Global and Interregional** | modernity vs. postmodernity<br>multiculturalism (Marshall McLuhan's "global village," Bollywood, manga)<br>impact of global conflict on mass culture (James Bond, video games)<br>sports professionalized and politicized (modern Olympics)<br>theoretical physics<br>aviation, rocketry, space science<br>medical advances and genetics<br>computers and the digital (information) revolution |

## Culture, Science, and Technology

- Mass media and mass communications technology transformed the cultural sphere. Cinema, radio, television, and other electronic media have been used to create high art.
- Mass media have also been used to create popular (or mass) culture: music, literature, and so forth aimed at a popular audience for purposes of entertainment.
- The art of the twentieth century was characterized by bold experimentation and the distortion, even abandonment, of traditional norms and conventions.
- During the first two-thirds of the 1900s, largely because of the demoralizing effects of Europe's decline, Freudian thought, and the two world wars, Western high art tended to be marked by uncertainty and pessimism—in contrast to the exuberance and energy of popular, or mass, culture.

- Scientific and technological advancement proceeded at a breathtaking pace and scale. Especially innovative fields were physics, biotechnology and genetics, aviation and rocketry, electronics, and computers.
- After World War II, Western culture began to move beyond the "modern" period into a newer "postmodern" era.
- Global cultures have mixed, interacted, and blended to an unprecedented degree. This celebration and acknowledgment of different traditions and styles is generally referred to as multiculturalism.
- Since the 1990s, the proliferation of personal computer technology, particularly access to the Internet, has led to an information (or digital) revolution.
- New forms of spirituality, many of them synthetically combining elements of old religions with new beliefs, appeared. Old or new, religious beliefs were in many cases used to advance political agendas. Religious fundamentalism has proven influential in many places throughout this period.

| Economic Systems, 1900 to the Present | |
|---|---|
| Europe | impact of Great Depression (low exports, mass unemployment)<br>economic intervention: Soviet nationalization (five-year plans), state capitalism (syndicalism) in fascist nations, democracies' relief-and-welfare programs (Keynesian theory)<br>Bretton Woods system (World Bank, IMF, GATT)<br>Marshall Plan<br>economic union (European Coal and Steel, European Economic Community, European Union)<br>1970s economic crisis (gold standard, oil embargo, stagflation)<br>1980s free-market reform and economic liberalization (Margaret Thatcher and theories of Milton Friedman; Mikhail Gorbachev and *perestroika*)<br>globalization in 1990s and 2000s<br>G-7/G-8<br>the EU and the euro<br>2007 economic crisis |
| Middle East | Bretton Woods system (World Bank, IMF, GATT)<br>state intervention: Nasser's nationalization of the Suez Canal<br>OPEC<br>1970s economic crisis (gold standard, oil embargo, stagflation)<br>globalization in 1990s and 2000s<br>north-south split<br>2007 economic crisis |
| Africa | Bretton Woods system (World Bank, IMF, GATT)<br>1970s economic crisis (gold standard, oil embargo, stagflation)<br>globalization in 1990s and 2000s<br>African Free Trade Zone<br>north-south split<br>2007 economic crisis |

| Economic Systems, 1900 to the Present | |
|---|---|
| **East (and Central) Asia** | economic intervention: state capitalism (zaibatsu) in imperial Japan<br>impact of Great Depression (low exports, mass unemployment)<br>Bretton Woods system (World Bank, IMF, GATT)<br>1970s economic crisis (gold standard, oil embargo, stagflation)<br>G-7/G-8 (Japan)<br>economic intervention: Mao's Great Leap Forward<br>1980s free-market reform and economic liberalization (Deng Xiaoping's limited capitalism in China)<br>Asia-Pacific Economic Cooperation group<br>globalization in 1990s and 2000s<br>some nations afflicted by north-south split<br>2007 economic crisis |
| **South (and Southeast) Asia and Oceania** | Bretton Woods system (World Bank, IMF, GATT)<br>1970s economic crisis (gold standard, oil embargo, stagflation)<br>globalization in 1990s and 2000s<br>north-south split<br>2007 economic crisis |
| **Americas** | U.S. origins of Great Depression (Smoot-Hawley Tariff Act)<br>economic intervention: New Deal (Keynesian theory), Cárdenas's nationalization of Mexico's oil industry<br>impact of Great Depression on Latin America (low exports, mass unemployment)<br>Bretton Woods system (World Bank, IMF, GATT)<br>1970s economic crisis (gold standard, oil embargo, stagflation)<br>G-7/G-8<br>1980s free-market reform and economic liberalization (Ronald Reagan, Augusto Pinochet, and theories of Milton Friedman)<br>globalization in 1990s and 2000s<br>NAFTA<br>Mercosur<br>2007 economic crisis |
| **Global and Interregional** | partial or widespread industrialization of nondeveloped and developing world<br>dominance of postindustrial and service economies in developed world<br>observance of Bretton Woods system by majority of non-communist world<br>growing importance of multinational corporations<br>rise of regional economic associations and free-trade zones<br>transition from GATT to WTO |

## Economic Systems

- During the first half of the twentieth century, the West (Europe, Canada, and the United States) fully industrialized. Certain other parts of the world achieved significant degrees of modernization and industrialization (such as Japan, parts of Latin America, and China).

- During the 1930s, the Great Depression, emanating from the United States, negatively affected the economies of most of Europe and Latin America, as well as Asia and Africa.

- Fascist and authoritarian regimes typically relied on state-directed forms of capitalism to regulate their economies, with varying degrees of heavy-handedness.

- A number of countries experimented with communist economies (the Soviet Union, Eastern Europe, China, North Korea, Cuba, Vietnam, and others).

- After World War II, the primary form of political and economic organization in the West (Canada, the United States, and Western Europe) was the democratic state with a capitalist system, although capitalism was modified to varying degrees by social welfare systems. During the Cold War, a wide split separated these economic systems from those of the communist blocs led by the Soviet Union and China.

- A different split emerged between the developed world, whose prosperity steadily grew (with a few minor regressions, as during the 1970s), and the nondeveloped or developing (or Third) world, which lagged behind. Because so many nondeveloped and developing nations are located near or south of the equator, this disparity is sometimes referred to as the north-south split.

- Also after World War II, an elaborate system of international economic organizations appeared, influential mainly in the West and in the Third World (at least during the Cold War), including the General Agreement on Trade and Tariffs (GATT), the World Bank, and the International Monetary Fund (IMF).

- After the 1950s and 1960s, Western economies began to move from industrial production to postindustrial production, based less on manufacturing and more on service, high-tech fields, and computers. This trend continues.

- During the 1970s, a general economic crisis, characterized by oil shortages, recession, and unemployment, struck the capitalist West. A general rise in prosperity—associated with an emphasis on free-market economics, but not necessarily equitably distributed throughout society—took place in Western economies during the 1980s and 1990s. The same was true in China. The Soviet bloc experienced a severe economic downturn.

- The 1980s and 1990s were an era of greater economic globalization, as international trade, economic regionalization (as typified by NAFTA and the European Union), and the clout of multinational corporations became increasingly important. This trend continues.

- A worldwide financial crisis, arguably the worst since the Great Depression, struck in 2007. Its effects still linger.

| Social Structures, 1900 to the Present | |
| --- | --- |
| **Europe** | features of Western and developed societies (transition to postindustrial and service-oriented lifestyles) <br> rise of BRIC nations <br> social activism: 1968 global protests, Solidarity and East European anti-communist protests <br> ethnic violence and anti-immigration sentiment (anti-Semitism and the Holocaust, persecution of Roma, former Yugoslavia, animosity toward "guest workers") <br> migration from former colonies and spheres of influence (India, Pakistan, Caribbean, Indonesia, Africa) <br> extension of vote to women (near-total) <br> feminism and significant progress toward gender equality (Simone de Beauvoir) <br> emerging gay and lesbian rights |
| **Middle East** | partial transition to industrial or postindustrial lifestyles <br> ethnic violence and anti-immigration sentiment (Turkish massacre of Armenians, Arab-Israeli conflict) <br> extension of vote to women (limited to partial) <br> limitations on gender |
| **Africa** | partial transition to industrial or postindustrial lifestyles <br> social activism: anti-apartheid movement in South Africa <br> ethnic violence and anti-immigration sentiment (Rwanda, Darfur) <br> extension of vote to women (partial) <br> limitations on gender equality |
| **East (and Central) Asia** | partial transition to postindustrial and service-oriented lifestyles <br> rise of BRIC nations <br> social activism: Tiananmen Square protests <br> extension of vote to women (widespread) <br> most limitations to gender equality removed |
| **South (and Southeast) Asia and Oceania** | partial transition to postindustrial and service-oriented lifestyles <br> rise of BRIC nations <br> ethnic violence and anti-immigration sentiment (Indo-Pakistani violence) <br> end of White Australia policy <br> social activism: self-immolation of Thich Quang Duc <br> extension of vote to women (widespread) <br> some limitations on gender equality |

| Social Structures, 1900 to the Present | |
|---|---|
| **Americas** | features of Western and developed societies (transition to postindustrial and service-oriented lifestyles; full in North America, partial in Latin America) |
| | rise of BRIC nations |
| | social activism: Jim Crow laws vs. civil rights movement in United States, 1968 global protests |
| | ethnic violence and anti-immigration sentiment (Mayans in Guatemala, U.S. "melting pot" ideal vs. nativist impulses) |
| | migration from former colonies and spheres of influence (Puerto Rico, Philippines) |
| | extension of vote to women (near-total) |
| | feminism and significant progress toward gender equality (Gloria Steinem, Betty Friedan, NOW) |
| | emerging gay and lesbian rights |
| **Global and Interregional** | rapid population growth |
| | social equality vs. hierarchy |
| | urbanization and suburbanization |
| | undeveloped vs. industrial vs. postindustrial lifestyles (the north-south split) |
| | growing importance of social activism (national liberation, civil rights and racial equality, opposition to war, 1968 global protests, feminism) |
| | ethnic violence and anti-immigration sentiment |
| | extension of vote to women (widespread) |
| | uneven progress toward gender equality |

## Social Structures

- In the West, labor unions grew in power during the first half of the century. During the 1920s and especially during the Great Depression of the 1930s, many capitalist societies adopted social welfare policies (the British "dole," the U.S. New Deal, Scandinavia's "third way") to provide a social safety net.
- The middle class became the dominant and most numerous class in most developed societies by World War II, and this trend deepened during the postwar era. In the communist societies, class divisions were minimized, at least in theory. In the developing world, class divisions between the elite and the rest of society were very wide.
- Gender equality made great strides during the twentieth century in the developed world. Most women in these countries received the right to vote after World War I. Job opportunities increased, partly due to the world wars, and especially World War II.
- The postwar development of reliable contraception, especially birth-control pills, gave women unprecedented control over pregnancy and sexuality. The gradual legalization of abortion, while controversial, did the same.
- During the 1960s and 1970s, a powerful feminist movement, agitating for women's liberation and equal rights, swept Canada, the United States, and most of Europe. Since then, women's movements have sought to achieve more than simple legal equality and the right to vote. Their goals have been full cultural and economic equality, and deeper changes in social norms and behaviors.

- Progress toward equal treatment of women has been uneven in other parts of the world.
- Migration has remained as much a global reality in this era as during the 1800s. Work opportunities continue to motivate migration, but refugees and displaced persons have migrated in huge numbers because of war. In addition, many Western nations have allowed significant levels of migration from their former colonies. Anti-immigrant sentiment remains common.
- Racial tensions divided many communities and nations. Racial segregation and ethnic violence—official and unofficial—plagued (and continue to plague) societies throughout this era.
- The collapse of communism in Eastern Europe and the USSR forced a number of countries to make a painful social and economic transition from communism to free-market capitalism. Most of these places continue to wrestle with this transition in the twenty-first century.
- Many parts of the West, including the United States, experienced a general rise in prosperity from the 1980s up through the financial collapse of 2007. However, this was accompanied by a growing split between rich and poor, and increased burdens on the middle class.
- Globally, the world still struggles with a north-south split, meaning that economic prosperity and access to cutting-edge technology, medical care, and social stability tend to be concentrated in the developed world, with many parts of the developing world lagging behind and still impoverished.

| Humans and the Environment, 1900 to the Present | |
|---|---|
| Europe | comprehensive vaccination (eradication of polio and smallpox)<br>diseases associated with lifestyle and longevity (diabetes, Alzheimer's)<br>famine in Stalin's USSR<br>modern environmentalism (recycling, NGOs, green parties)<br>strongest environmental regulations<br>environmental disasters (Chernobyl) |
| Middle East | oil industry and environmental impact of fossil fuels<br>agricultural impact of Green Revolution<br>Aswan High Dam |
| Africa | Ebola<br>HIV/AIDS (origination and particular severity)<br>famine in Ethiopia and elsewhere<br>Green Belt movement |
| East (and Central) Asia | diseases associated with lifestyle and longevity (diabetes, Alzheimer's)<br>famine in Mao's China<br>agricultural impact of Green Revolution<br>Three Gorges Dam<br>environmental disasters (Fukushima) |
| South (and Southeast) Asia and Oceania | Spanish flu pandemic (particular severity?)<br>famine in India<br>agricultural impact of Green Revolution<br>environmental disasters (Bhopal incident, Southeast Asian tsunami) |

| Humans and the Environment, 1900 to the Present | |
|---|---|
| **Americas** | comprehensive vaccination in North America (eradication of polio and smallpox)<br><br>diseases associated with lifestyle and longevity (diabetes, Alzheimer's)<br><br>"dust bowl" crisis in United States and Canada<br><br>agricultural impact of Green Revolution (Latin America)<br><br>modern environmentalism (John Muir, Rachel Carson, Earth Day, Greenpeace, recycling)<br><br>strongest environmental regulations (North America)<br><br>environmental disasters (dust bowl crisis, Three Mile Island, *Exxon Valdez*, Hurricane Katrina, Deepwater, Superstorm Sandy) |
| **Global and Interregional** | vaccination campaigns<br><br>Spanish flu pandemic<br><br>HIV/AIDS pandemic<br><br>rapid population growth (fastest in nondeveloped and developing worlds)<br><br>pollution and ecosystem destruction<br><br>species endangerment<br><br>ozone depletion<br><br>climate change and global warming (Kyoto Protocol vs. climate change denial) |

# Humans and the Environment

- Population growth, caused above all by improvements in medicine and public health, reached unprecedented levels and continues to accelerate.
- Escalating industrialization, increased energy and resource consumption, massive engineering projects, and the production of toxic, chemical, and nuclear waste have exponentially increased humanity's impact on the environment.
- Diseases associated with poverty, such as malaria, tuberculosis, and cholera, persisted in many parts of the world.
- Better and faster transportation hastened the global spread of new epidemic diseases, such as Ebola and HIV/AIDS, and many new strains of influenza, starting with the "Spanish flu," which killed millions at the end of World War I.
- Diseases associated with sedentary lifestyles and new dietary habits, such as heart disease, diabetes, and obesity, became more common. Extension of longevity placed larger numbers of people at risk of diseases associated with old age, such as Alzheimer's.
- Periodic famines, both natural and human-caused, struck various parts of the world, including the USSR in the 1930s (caused by Stalin's collectivization of agriculture), India in the mid-1940s, China during the 1950s (caused by Mao's Great Leap Forward), and Ethiopia in the 1980s.
- In Canada and the United States during the 1930s, the "dust bowl" crisis—which caused thousands of square miles of fertile soil to be lost to aridity and giant windstorms—severely affected agriculture and added to the stress of the Great Depression.
- Between the late 1940s and the 1970s, a Green Revolution spread advanced agricultural techniques around the world, leading to a huge rise in the production of food. Mexico, where it is considered to have originated, played a key role in this development, and its

impact spread not just through Latin America, but to India, China, and other regions that had previously suffered damaging famines. However, the environmental impact of agriculture increased as a result of the Green Revolution, thanks to greater water consumption, the clearing of more land, and the extensive use of pesticides.

- Habitats like wetlands, rain forests, and polar ecosystems have been badly threatened during this era. Large numbers of species in these and other ecozones faced extinction or endangerment.
- Environmental awareness in the West grew steadily but slowly during the early 1900s, and then expanded after World War II. Green movements and non-governmental organizations (NGOs) devoted to environmental issues have grown in size and influence.
- Climate change, or global warming, dramatically increased throughout the twentieth century and is thought by most scientists to have been caused by the human-produced emission of greenhouse gases (especially carbon dioxide). It reached unprecedented levels in the 1990s and early 2000s. The best known international effort to reverse this trend is the Kyoto Protocol (1997).
- Warfare in the twentieth and twenty-first centuries has had a growing impact on the environment. Examples include radiation from nuclear-weapons testing, biological and chemical warfare between Iran and Iraq during the 1970s, the napalming of forests during the Vietnam War, and the destruction of oil wells during times of armed conflict.
- Natural disasters (Hurricane Katrina, the Southeast Asian tsunami, Superstorm Sandy) and energy-related crises (Chernobyl, Three Mile Island, the Bhopal incident, *Exxon Valdez*, the Fukushima nuclear disaster, the Gulf of Mexico oil spill, the melting of Arctic ice) demonstrate how contemporary societies can still be affected by the environment, and how technology now allows them to affect the environment more deeply than before.

## QUESTIONS AND COMPARISONS TO CONSIDER

- Discuss the ways different nations and regions modernized during the twentieth century. Were they industrialized before the 1900s? Did modernization efforts come from the population at large, or were they instituted by the government? Did they have to be put into place by force? Has modernization by force proven effective?
- In what ways did war evolve during this period? Consider tactics, weapons, and impact on population.
- What impact did the world wars have on the non-Western world? Compare different regions, such as Africa and Asia. How did the wars affect women?
- Compare two or more of the twentieth century's major revolutions, such as the Russian, Chinese, Mexican, Cuban, or Iranian. Alternatively, compare one or more of these with revolutions in previous centuries. Compare how each affected women and/or ethnic minorities.
- Examine the process of decolonization as it played out in various parts of the world. Be sure to address cases that involved negotiation (India, the Gold Coast) and those that involved violent separation (Vietnam, Algeria, Angola).
- Focus on specific national-liberation, civil-rights, anti-segregation, and anti-war movements. How did they achieve their goals? To what degree did they rely on force (or the threat of force) or nonviolent resistance?

- How has the legacy of colonialism affected cultural identity and patterns of economic development in Africa, Asia, and Latin America?
- How has nationalism in Europe differed from nationalism in decolonizing and decolonized parts of the world, both in character and in its political effects? Be sure to consider xenophobia, anti-immigration sentiment, and Christian-Muslim tension since 9/11.
- How has the rise of Western consumerism and economic globalism affected different societies outside the West?
- How have twentieth- and twenty-first-century technologies and agricultural techniques affected social structures? The environment?
- How have epidemics and other medical crises affected states and societies during this era?
- How does ethnic violence in the 1990s and early 2000s compare with the Holocaust?
- What effects have major scientific breakthroughs (genetics, quantum physics, the digital revolution) had on society, politics, and culture during this era? How have certain scientific programs (the space race, for example) interacted with global political and military affairs?

# UNIT 6

## SCENIC ROUTE
### (Chapters 22–27)

# State Building, Expansion, and Conflict (Part I), 1900–1945

# 22

→ **TOTAL WARS (INCREASED CIVILIAN CASUALTIES)**

→ **GENOCIDE (ARMENIAN MASSACRES)**

→ **WORLD WAR I (ALLIES VS. CENTRAL POWERS, TRENCH WARFARE)**

→ **PARIS PEACE CONFERENCE (FOURTEEN POINTS, TREATY OF VERSAILLES)**

→ **LEAGUE OF NATIONS**

→ **THE GREAT DEPRESSION AND INTERNATIONAL REPERCUSSIONS**

→ **DEMOCRATIC WEAKNESS IN EUROPE AND TOTALITARIAN STATES**

→ **THE MANDATE SYSTEM AND BALFOUR DECLARATION**

→ **MIDDLE EASTERN MODERNIZERS (MUSTAFA KEMAL ATATURK, REZA SHAH PAHLAVI)**

→ **THE CHINESE REVOLUTION (SUN YAT-SEN)**

→ **MAO TSE-TUNG AND THE CCP**

→ **ZAIBATSU INDUSTRIALIZATION AND MILITARISM IN JAPAN (RAPE OF NANJING)**

→ **INDIAN NATIONAL CONGRESS (MOHANDAS GANDHI)**

→ **U.S. SPHERE OF INFLUENCE IN LATIN AMERICA**

→ **THE MEXICAN REVOLUTION AND THE PRI**

→ **COLLECTIVE SECURITY VS. APPEASEMENT IN 1930s FOREIGN POLICY**

→ **WORLD WAR II (ALLIES VS. AXIS POWERS)**

→ **OFFENSIVE CAPABILITIES IN WORLD WAR II (BLITZKRIEG, STRATEGIC BOMBING, HIROSHIMA)**

→ **WAR CRIMES, GENOCIDE, AND THE HOLOCAUST**

→ **NUREMBERG AND TOKYO TRIALS (CRIMES AGAINST HUMANITY)**

Dramatic political changes have characterized the 1900s and 2000s. During the first half of the 1900s, two **world wars** profoundly reshaped global affairs, weakening Europe's position of global dominance after 1914 and dismantling it altogether after 1945. Both conflicts were **total wars** that required near-complete mobilization of human and economic resources. Also during the first half of the century, the future of democracy seemed doubtful with the seemingly inexorable rise of dictatorships, including **totalitarian regimes** like Soviet Russia and Nazi Germany, during the interwar years.

Throughout the twentieth century, new weapons and tactics made warfare steadily more destructive and increased its impact on civilian populations. It also gave rise to new categories of violence, such as **genocide**. Consider the following factors as underlying sources of conflict during the first half of the 1900s: (1) aggressive expansion of empires by Europe and Japan; (2) Anglo-German geopolitical rivalry; (3) ethnic tensions and racial hatred; (4) nationalism; (5) competition for resources; and (6) international economic stress caused by the **Great Depression**.

# WORLD WAR I AND THE PARIS PEACE CONFERENCE

**World War I** began in the summer of 1914 and, despite general expectations that it would be over quickly, lasted until the fall of 1918. It killed approximately 10 million soldiers, killed another 2 to 5 million civilians, and wounded or disabled 28 to 30 million. It destroyed four great empires—the German Reich, Russia's tsarist regime, Austria-Hungary's Habsburg dynasty, and, after a short delay, Ottoman Turkey—and bankrupted and demoralized even victorious nations like Great Britain and France. It began the process of toppling Europe from its position of global preeminence, and it exposed Westerners' optimistic faith in themselves as models of civilized behavior and cultural superiority as a foolish illusion. It also unleashed or sped up far-reaching social changes. For all these reasons, many consider World War I, rather than the calendar year 1900, to be the true beginning of the twentieth century.

## Background and Combat

The long-term causes of World War I include a potent cocktail of **nationalism, competition over empire**, and an unstable **European alliance system** (France and Russia, informally aligned with Britain against Germany, Austria, and Italy) that had the potential to draw all the continent's powers into conflict in the event of a crisis.

That crisis came in the Balkans, in Sarajevo, the capital of Bosnia: a Slavic province under Austrian authority but with a large Serb population and coveted by the intensely nationalistic state of Serbia. On June 28, 1914, Bosnian Serbs affiliated with the **Black Hand**, a terror group supported informally by influential parties in Serbia, carried out the **assassination of Franz Ferdinand**, heir to the Austrian throne. The Austrian government was genuinely outraged, but also decided cynically to use the event as a pretext to humble its troublesome neighbor—even though its own police concluded that Serbia's government was not to blame. During the **July crisis**, Austria issued a list of humiliating demands and threatened war if Serbia did not accept this ultimatum. Russia, Austria's rival in the Balkans, backed Serbia, but Germany persuaded Austria not to back down—the infamous **blank check**—even if Russia intervened militarily. When Austria declared war on Serbia on July 28, the alliance system began to operate: Russia and Germany mobilized in the east, and because Germany's strategy for avoiding a long two-front war—the Schlieffen Plan, described below—required lightning speed, the Germans moved quickly against France and neutral Belgium. Britain supported its French and Russian partners. Except for Italy, which remained neutral for the moment, Europe's major powers were all at war by August 4.

Germany opened with the **Schlieffen Plan**, a daring gamble which sent 75 percent of its army into France, with the aim of taking Paris in six weeks. The other 25 percent, with Austrian help, would defend against Russia, on which the Germans intended to focus after France's defeat. To catch France off guard, the Germans moved their main attack force through neutral Belgium, an illegal action that killed numerous civilians and enabled Allied propaganda to convincingly depict the Central Powers as villains and aggressors. The Germans drove into northern France as expected and came within reach of Paris. However, during the first week of September, the Allies' determined stand at the **First Battle of the Marne** foiled the Schlieffen Plan and dashed any hope of a quick end to the war.

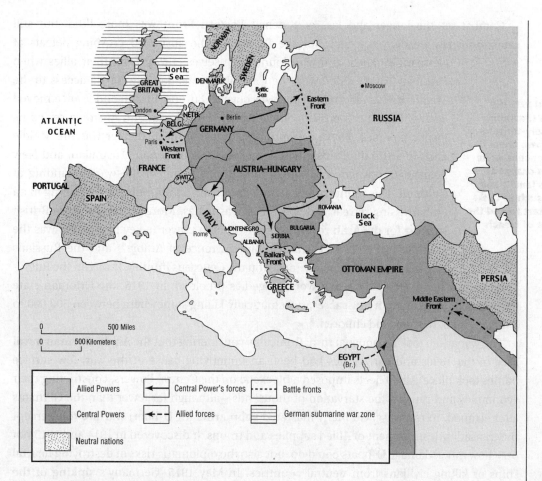

**World War I in Europe, 1914–1918.**
In Western Europe, the basic dynamic of the conflict was determined quite early. Then, thanks
to the stalemate of trench warfare, it changed very little until the last months of war. In the east,
fighting conditions were much more fluid.

The principal reason for the war's surprisingly protracted length was the tactical stalemate
that resulted when evenly matched sides deployed the latest in industrial-era technology
against each other—instead of against the comparatively backward forces they had defeated
in Asia and Africa during their wars of imperial conquest. Modern artillery and rifles,
along with machine guns, made the battlefield so deadly that traditional tactics, which
had climaxed in mass charges against the enemy, were no longer feasible. With military
technology disproportionately favoring the defensive, **trench warfare**, one of history's most
horrific styles of combat, resulted in three years of bloody deadlock—especially on the
**Western Front**, the 500-mile chain of trenches, bunkers, and barbed wire that stretched from
the English Channel to the Swiss border. Here, until late in the war, combat operations such
as the **Verdun Offensive** and the **Battle of the Somme**, both in 1916, brought about no useful
outcome, and virtually no movement, despite costing hundreds of thousands of casualties.
This futility, combined with the horrors of **poison gas** and the ever-present miseries of mud,
filth, and vermin, made the trench-warfare experience maddeningly terrible—as attested to
in the Erich Maria Remarque novel ***All Quiet on the Western Front*** and other works of anti-
war art described in Chapter 24. Trench warfare was also the norm in the south, where the
Italians clashed with their Austrian foes.

**NOTE**

Not until 1917 and 1918 did improved tactics (including the use of precisely-targeted artillery to pin down enemy forces in their trenches while one's own troops charged across "no man's land") and new weaponry—such as tanks and airplanes—start to end the painful stalemate of trench warfare.

Combat on the longer and less entrenched **Eastern Front** was more fluid, but still catastrophically deadly—especially for the Russians, who sustained crushing defeats at Germany's hands, and who found themselves cut off from their allies when Ottoman Turkey sided with the Central Powers, denying Russia access to the Mediterranean. Fighting spread far beyond Europe. Britain and France moved against Germany's possessions in Africa, while Japan and Australia seized its Pacific colonies. The most important non-European theater was the Middle East. In 1915, the British, with large numbers of Indian, Australian, and New Zealand troops, tried to knock the Ottomans out of the war by landing at **Gallipoli**. This months-long campaign proved an utter disaster, resulting in an embarrassing retreat and 50 percent casualties. More successful were British support for the **Arab revolt** against Ottoman power (a key figure here was the guerrilla leader T. E. Lawrence, or "Lawrence of Arabia") and the Russians thrust through Ottoman defenses on the Caucasus frontier. It was on the Russo-Turkish front that one of the war's worst tragedies unfolded: in 1915, the Ottoman state perpetrated the **Armenian massacres**, systematically killing somewhere between 500,000 to 2 million men, women, and children.

The war at sea took an unusual turn. Ironically, considering that the **Anglo-German naval race** of the 1890s and early 1900s had been an underlying cause of the war, few surface battles took place. Allied fleets imposed a blockade on the Central Powers, constricting their economies and causing the starvation of thousands—although far fewer than the Germans later claimed. In response, Germany mastered **submarine** (or **U-boat**) **warfare** to intercept the transatlantic movement of Allied supplies and troops. It discovered in 1914 and 1915 not only how much damage U-boats could do, but also the diplomatic risks of destroying neutral ships or killing civilians from neutral countries. In May 1915, Germany's **sinking of the Lusitania**, a British ship carrying more than a hundred American passengers, nearly brought an angry United States into the war. For the next year and half, Germany sharply curtailed its U-boat campaign—but with great reluctance.

Nineteen seventeen was a year of exhaustion and turning points. Frustrated by the stalemate at sea, the German navy resumed unrestricted submarine warfare, hoping to starve Britain out of the war. This reduced Britain to a six-week food supply by the spring, but also provoked the **U.S. entry into the war** in April. At the same time, Russia was collapsing. The tsarist regime fell in February and March, and while the new government tried to continue the war, the army suffered mass desertions and major defeats. Communists seized power in the **October Revolution** and took immediate steps to pull Russia out of the war, freeing large numbers of German troops for service on the Western Front, where the balance of force was razor-thin.

In the spring of 1918, the Germans, faced with the arrival of hundreds of thousands of Americans and a severe disadvantage in tanks and airplanes, staked everything on the **Spring Offensive**, an all-out assault on Paris. Halted at the **Second Battle of the Marne**, the Germans were forced into full retreat by August. Strikes and mutinies in the fall compelled the Ottomans, the Austro-Hungarians, and the Germans to cease fighting in October and November. World War I ended on November 11, 1918.

## Home Front and Mobilization

World War I was a **total war**, requiring the near-complete mobilization of populations and resources. The **home front** became a crucial part of every combatant nation's war effort, as entire economies were geared for war. The procurement of raw materials—steel, coal, petroleum, rubber, cloth, and more—was centralized, as was agricultural production and the manufacture of uniforms, weapons, and other military necessities. The **rationing** of food, fuel, and consumer goods became increasingly strict, and painfully so by late 1916 and early 1917, when all European belligerents were suffering terrible material shortages.

Another home-front effect of the war was the **restriction of civil liberties**, even in the democracies. All combatants censored the press and the mail. Special laws allowed anyone suspected of espionage or treason to be arrested and tried without due process. Trade unions and socialist parties were supervised and their activities curtailed. Even pessimism or an insufficient show of patriotism could get one in trouble. Men who sought conscientious objector status were often denied and harassed or ridiculed if they succeeded.

The war required mass **recruitment**, and then **conscription**, or the involuntary drafting of soldiers. Most combatant nations began with armies of 1 to 2 million, but these did not suffice, and eventually 70 million personnel were called up for service. Especially in countries with traditions of all-volunteer armies, like Britain and Canada, the move to conscription caused much social stress, including protests and riots. To help relieve this stress, imperial powers mobilized large numbers of colonial troops. Over 2.5 million Africans fought, mainly on their own continent, although the French brought Moroccan, Algerian, and Senegalese soldiers to the Western Front (in a classic instance of racial stereotyping, the Germans feared the Senegalese as cannibals). Soldiers from French Indochina also served on the Western Front. As for Britain, not only did it rely on major contingents of Canadians, Australians, and New Zealanders, it used almost a million Indian, Sikh, and Nepalese Gurkha troops in theaters ranging from Europe to the Middle East.

Especially striking was the **role of women** in World War I, described further in Chapter 26. Some women served on the lines: a few as uniformed auxiliaries but most as nurses. It was on the home front that they stepped up in huge numbers to take the place of men on farms and in factories. These jobs mostly went back to men when the war ended, but women's wartime contributions played a significant role in their being granted the right to vote in many countries after the war.

> **NOTE**
>
> **Black soldiers who served in Europe as part of the American Expeditionary Force were segregated from their white counterparts and used mainly as labor battalions. When they did fight, it was typically alongside French, not American, troops. The United States and Canada were slow in both world wars when it came to integrating black, Asian, and Native American troops, but eventually did so following World War II.**

## The Paris Peace Conference and Long-Term Consequences

After the war, terms were decided at the **Paris Peace Conference**, which lasted from 1919 to 1920 and drew up treaties for each of the five Central Powers. The most important was the **Treaty of Versailles**, imposed on Germany in June 1919.

The peacemaking was marked by conflict on all sides. The defeated nations were allowed no meaningful role in the negotiations, and they believed (whether sincerely or opportunistically) that all the European powers, not just Germany and Austria-Hungary, were equally to blame for the war. Therefore, not only did they consider the final terms too harsh, Germany in particular saw them as fundamentally illegitimate.

Quarrels also divided the Allied leaders. Decisions at Paris were made mainly by Woodrow Wilson of the United States, David Lloyd George of Britain, and Georges Clemenceau of France. All three held the Central Powers responsible for the war and deserving of punishment. But beyond that, Wilson's idealism differed starkly from Lloyd George's and Clemenceau's emphasis on national self-interest. Arriving with his famous **Fourteen Points**, Wilson hoped to use the peace conference as a way to prevent all war in the future, and he called for freedom of the seas, an end to secret treaties, arms reduction, **decolonization**, the rearrangement of borders according to the "**self-determination**" of national groups, and the establishment of an international dispute-resolution body called the **League of Nations**. By contrast, Lloyd George and Clemenceau (and the Belgians and Italians) were anxious to make the Central Powers pay as much as possible for the wartime damage they had caused. Both also feared a future resurgence of Germany and sought to keep it as militarily weak as possible.

The treaties that resulted were the product of bitter debate and compromise. At the cost of bargaining away several of his Fourteen Points, Wilson brought into being the **League of Nations**. (Ironically, because Congress did not ratify the Treaty of Versailles, the United States never joined the League, weakening the new organization from the start.) Other main points included the **dismantling of Austria-Hungary** into two states; the creation of new nations according to the principle of **self-determination** (Yugoslavia, Czechoslovakia, Poland, Finland, Latvia, Lithuania, and Estonia were all carved out of lands lost by Germany, Austria-Hungary, and Russia); and the establishment of a complex **mandate system** to administer the Central Powers' former imperial possessions. According to the mandate system, former colonies were categorized according to their readiness for independence, and then placed by the League of Nations under long-, medium-, or short-term "supervision" by nations like Britain and France. In theory, supervisory powers were meant to guide their mandates to freedom, but in practice this was colonization under a new name, and in a form that allowed the Europeans to avoid offending Wilson's anti-colonial sensibilities. The mandate system affected Africa and the Pacific but had a particularly heavy impact on the Middle East, where the **Arab lands** once under Ottoman rule became British and French mandates—even though the deeply disappointed Arabs had expected independence in exchange for their military aid against the Ottomans. One of these mandates was Palestine, where the British, in the **Balfour Declaration** of 1917, had agreed to help create a Jewish "national home." Intended to redress a set of grave injustices—the historical dispossession of the Jews and modern anti-Semitism in Europe—this policy, even though it was not acted on right away, set the stage for an equally grave conflict between Jews (both local and returning) and Palestinian Arabs.

What about Germany specifically? As the first and most important of the settlements, the **Treaty of Versailles** set the tone for the rest of the conference. It contained a **war-guilt clause** that laid blame for the war on Germany and its partners (this same clause appeared in all five treaties). Germany suffered **loss of territory** (approximately 13 percent) and **population** (approximately 10 percent), as Alsace and Lorraine—which Germany had seized from France in 1871—were returned, and as other pieces of land went to Belgium, Czechoslovakia, Denmark, and Poland. **Loss of African and Pacific** colonies followed as well. **Disarmament** restricted Germany to a token army of 100,000 and forbade all tanks, military aircraft, warships, and submarines. Most controversially, Germany was required to pay **reparations** of over $32 billion (the other Central Powers ended up owing reparations as well). Initially, Britain, France, and Belgium wanted their foes to reimburse them not just for damage done, but for the entire cost of the war, a vastly higher amount. Wilson, however, insisted on a more limited approach—not that this was appreciated by the Germans, who felt any demands for payment were unjust.

In the end, the Paris Peace Conference produced flawed results. Greed and revenge dictated many of the terms and much of the redrawing of the world map—especially concerning former colonies. Ignorance, particularly in Eastern Europe and the Balkans, left ethnic tensions unresolved and created new regimes that looked democratic on the surface, but were weak and unstable at the core. The League of Nations, especially without the United States to lead it, proved too feeble to keep peace in the future. And while one can debate the fairness or unfairness of the *terms* of the Treaty of Versailles, the high-handed *way* the treaty was foisted on the Germans guaranteed that the overwhelming majority of Germans would *perceive* it as unfair—a significant factor in (although not the *direct cause* of) Hitler's later rise to power.

The grim immediate consequences of World War I were obvious: 9 to 10 million soldiers killed, another 2 to 5 million civilians dead, and 28 to 30 million people wounded. The overall cost of the war was assessed at nearly $200 billion, with more than $30 billion of that to be repaid by Germany. Millions of people, particularly in Eastern Europe, with its constantly shifting borders, were made homeless or stateless. Adding to this pain, a global epidemic of **Spanish flu** struck during the closing months of World War I, lasting until late 1920 and killing at least 25 to 40 million, and perhaps many more.

Long-term consequences are discussed throughout this unit, but also summarized here. Geopolitically, they include the **destruction of four empires** (Germany's Reich, Habsburg Austria, tsarist Russia, and the Ottoman Empire, which collapsed shortly after the war), a **general decline in European global power** (even the victor nations were badly drained, and their overseas empires became increasingly difficult to control), and **instability in Central and Eastern Europe** (where German resentment of Versailles would simmer, where Soviet expansionism threatened, and where political inexperience made new nations vulnerable). Far-reaching social and economic changes resulted from or were sped up by the war, including the **continued decline of hereditary aristocracies**, the **growing clout of the middle and lower classes** (especially "**white-collar**" professionals as rising elites), the granting of **women's suffrage** in most Western nations (although France and Italy held out until the 1940s), and the **fuller industrialization of Western economies**. The war also encouraged a greater **sense of uncertainty and anxiety in European culture**.

## DOMESTIC POLITICS, 1900–1939

Many have argued that the world wars were simply two halves of the same conflict, separated by 20 years of temporary armistice and constant crisis. Whatever the truth of that observation, the peace of the **interwar period** rested on a shaky foundation—both in Europe and throughout the globe—and was destabilized in many ways by the **Great Depression** that began in 1929.

### Fragile Peace and Political Extremism in Europe

Peace prevailed in Europe during the 1920s, but was fragile and incomplete. Political violence and civil war rocked Germany, Soviet Russia, and Eastern Europe until 1922, and even afterward, it was exhaustion, rather than true amity, that preserved peace on the continent. The new and well-meaning **League of Nations** resettled refugees and carried out famine relief, but with few powers of enforcement, it soon proved a woefully inadequate peacekeeper. European economies struggled, even during the comparatively prosperous 1920s, and then plunged into free-fall during the 1930s, as the effects of the **Great Depression** (discussed at greater length in Chapter 25) spread outward from the United States.

Democracy did not flourish in interwar Europe. In 1919, 23 governments there could be considered democratic. By 1939, half of them had become dictatorships of varying

**NOTE**

Germany's indignation at the supposed unfairness of Versailles is worth contrasting with its willingness to force the even harsher treaty of Brest-Litovsk, one of the most punitive settlements in history, on Russia in the spring of 1918. A generation before, after defeating France in 1871, Germany had gleefully stripped away the provinces of Alsace and Lorraine and demanded a fortune in gold. These facts were studiously ignored by most interwar Germans.

degrees of severity, especially Italy, which slipped into fascism as early as 1922, and Germany, driven to Nazism in 1933 by the Depression. Even well-established democracies like Britain and France experienced political weakness and economic sluggishness. Only U.S. investment and German reparations kept the British and French economies afloat during the 1920s, and even then, unemployment, deficits, and strikes were the norm. The Depression made things worse, and both political systems suffered: British elections returned weak-willed coalition governments, whereas the French government lurched from left to right and back again in ludicrously frequent elections. On the foreign-policy front, economic frailty and political indecision made it difficult for Depression-era France and Britain to cope with the growing threat of Nazi Germany. One bright light for the interwar democracies is that most of them—including France and Britain—found some relief by putting into place unemployment relief and various other elements of the **social welfare systems** that most Western states enjoy today.

The general crisis of democracy meant that interwar Europe's most dynamic regimes tended to be the dictatorships, several of which attained **totalitarian** levels of control over their people. The first new dictatorship was the Union of Soviet Socialist Republics (USSR), or the Soviet Union, the communist regime that took power in Russia in the fall of 1917. Russia underwent two revolutions that year, with the tsarist regime collapsing in February due to repeated World War I disasters, the political incompetence of Nicholas II, and dire food shortages. After this **February Revolution**, a liberal Provisional Government attempted to repair the dismal economy and build democracy, all while continuing to fight Germany. Its good intentions, however, did not satisfy the desire of the vast majority of Russians for economic stability, land reform (about 80 percent of the population were peasants), and an end to the war at any cost. As popular discontent grew during the summer and early fall, those who benefited most were the **Bolsheviks**, the most radical of Russia's communists, led by **Vladimir Lenin** and his second-in-command, Leon Trotsky. The **October Revolution** of 1917 brought them to power.

The Bolsheviks struggled for survival between 1917 and 1921, pulling out of World War I and then defeating their anti-communist enemies—the Whites—in the terrible **Russian Civil War**, which resulted in the death of millions from disease, starvation, and persecution, and the emigration of hundreds of thousands more. Lenin quickly created a one-party dictatorship and a **secret police** (originally the Cheka, eventually the KGB), and tried to modernize the country along Marxist lines. His main challenge was that, while Marx had spoken of communism succeeding first in a mature capitalist society with a large industrial working class, economically backward Russia had a huge peasantry, but only a tiny working class. In 1921, Lenin compromised with this reality by instituting the **New Economic Policy** (**NEP**), a more gradual approach to socialist development that allowed for limited private trade. This lasted until 1928, although Lenin died in the meantime, in 1924.

In 1928, after a half-decade succession struggle against Trotsky, **Joseph Stalin** gained control of the Soviet government and became one of the most oppressive dictators of all time. Immediately overturning the NEP, Stalin returned to the revolutionary policy of overnight modernization, with his **Five-Year Plans** (complete centralization of the economy to bring about rapid industrialization) and the **collectivization of agriculture** (the forced transfer of peasants from villages to state-run farms, both to control them more tightly and to confiscate their grain more efficiently, in order to pay for the Five-Year Plans). Although the USSR indeed modernized under Stalin, the price was steep. The Five-Year Plans combined the social and economic trauma of a state-sponsored industrial revolution with ruthless police brutality. Millions of peasants who opposed collectivization were imprisoned or executed, and four to six million more died in the **Great Famine** (1932–1933) caused by Stalin's grain confiscations in southern Russia, Ukraine, and Kazakhstan. In 1936–1938, Stalin used the secret police to carry out a series of mass arrests and show trials, called the **Purges**, executing approximately a million people and exiling millions more to labor camps called **gulags**. Like other modern dictators, Stalin used propaganda to indoctrinate his subjects and glorified himself by means of an extravagant **cult of personality**. His state-directed form of modernization brought the country far more torment than benefit.

In Italy, dictatorship came from the right. After World War I, Italy's constitutional monarchy was undermined by economic downturn and political chaos. The upper and middle classes, fearing social breakdown and communist revolution, sought a strong leader to restore stability, but election after election returned weak governments. In October 1922, the king turned in desperation to **Benito Mussolini**, leader of the Fascist Party, placing him in charge of Italy's government for the next 21 years. **Fascism**, Mussolini's invention, is best described as right-wing radicalism (as opposed to right-wing conservatism, which seeks to prevent change). It is anti-communist but also anti-capitalist and anti-democratic and characterized by **militaristic nationalism**—and in some cases by ethnic bigotry. Mussolini killed and arrested few people compared to Stalin and Hitler, and he modernized Italy with new highways, literacy campaigns, and the industrial development of Italy's more backward regions. He was quite well-regarded, both at home and abroad, during the 1920s. On the other hand, he imposed censorship, used propaganda to create a lavish **cult of personality**, and suppressed trade unions and political parties. His foreign-policy aggression, plus his decision to ally with Hitler, damaged his international reputation during the 1930s, and the Depression undercut his modernizing efforts at home.

Germany's road to dictatorship was longer than Italy's, and the results were infinitely worse. From 1919 to 1933, Germany was governed by the democratic **Weimar Republic**. Dogged during the early 1920s by **hyperinflation** (which caused several years of nightmarish poverty) and political unrest from the left (a communist uprising in 1919) and the right (several assassinations and coup attempts, including one by the fledgling Nazi Party in 1923), the Weimar regime managed to restore economic and political order between 1924 and 1929. In 1930, however, the **Great Depression** ended this temporary calm, causing **mass unemployment**—six million, or nearly 40 percent of the workforce, by 1932—and boosting the popularity of Germany's most extremist movements: the Communists and the **Nazi Party**, led by **Adolf Hitler**, originally from Austria, but a fierce pan-German patriot. A conscious imitator of Italian fascism, Hitler despised communism and democracy in favor of **militaristic nationalism**. He embraced racial hatred of many groups, but especially a virulent form of **anti-Semitism**—all expressed in his infamous memoir from the mid-1920s, *Mein Kampf*.

During the relative stability of the late 1920s, the Nazis enjoyed little political appeal, earning less than 3 percent of the vote in Germany's last pre-Depression elections, in 1928. But when the Weimar regime failed to cope with the Depression, ordinary Germans began heeding Hitler's rhetoric—rekindling their resentment of the Treaty of Versailles and in many cases allowing themselves to believe the Nazis' anti-Semitic conspiracy theories about how Jews had supposedly sold Germany out during World War I, or were enriching themselves while the rest of Germany suffered through the Depression, or were responsible for international communism. During the Weimar electoral crisis of the early 1930s, as vote after vote failed to produce a clear majority, the Nazis emerged as Germany's largest party, but with the communists also gaining in popularity. In January 1933, Germany's president—the conservative war hero Paul von Hindenburg, who had little love for the Nazis but feared the communists even more—appointed Hitler chancellor of Germany.

**NOTE**

Fascist and authoritarian economies typically follow the principles of syndicalism, a form of state capitalism, in which business leaders, rather than practicing free trade, cooperate directly with the government. In exchange for obedience, they receive preferential treatment, and the regime ensures that labor unions pose no challenge to them. This approach prevailed in fascist Italy, Nazi Germany, Japan, and many minor dictatorships.

With blinding speed, Hitler established himself as an absolute dictator. In February 1933, the Reichstag building, seat of the German government, was set ablaze by a communist arsonist, allowing Hitler to declare a state of emergency and to pass the **Enabling Act** in March. This suspended the Weimar constitution and gave Hitler the power to rule by decree. He soon outlawed all political parties, banned trade unions, and turned the press and mass media into instruments of Nazi propaganda (relying on a **cult of personality** similar to Mussolini's and Stalin's). In 1934, he assumed the presidency when Hindenburg suddenly died, and he violently purged remaining rivals within the Nazi Party in the "**night of the long knives.**" To control dissidents and opponents, the Nazis built **concentration camps** like Dachau and created a secret police, the **Gestapo**. Hitler's system of **state capitalism**, similar to Mussolini's, ended German unemployment with a giant program of public works and highway building, coupled with mass **military conscription** and renewed **arms production**—both of which required the renunciation of the Treaty of Versailles. Hitler's highly belligerent foreign policy, of course, was a key reason for the steady erosion of European and global peace during the 1930s.

The Nazis also acted on their notorious obsession with racial purity, believing as they did in the **Aryan myth**: the misguided notion that Germans and other northern Europeans were the "truest" descendants of the earliest Indo-Europeans. Hitler's regime targeted several races as "undesirable," including Slavs, Africans, and Roma (Gypsies)—but from the Nazi perspective, the worst of these "subhumans," and the source of all of Germany's troubles, were the Jews. In this way, the Nazis added extra malevolence to a streak of anti-Semitism that had long existed throughout Europe. Although the Nazis eventually resorted to genocide, their **anti-Semitic policies** before the war emphasized official discrimination and physical harassment. Jewish writings and artworks were banned or burned, Jewish businesses were boycotted, and Jews were forced out of professions like law, medicine, civil service, and university teaching. The **Nuremberg Laws** of 1935 deprived Jews of their civil rights and forbade intermarriage between them and non-Jews. Sporadic violence, including the 1938 pogrom called *Kristallnacht* ("night of broken glass"), ramped up during the late 1930s, as the regime tried to pressure Jews into leaving the country. Most stayed, either because places like Britain, Canada, and the United States refused them entry or because European Jews did not anticipate how much worse Nazi rule would become.

## Nationalism and Modernization in the Middle East

Even before World War I, the Middle East was on the threshold of great change, with modernization finally coming to—and ultimately destroying—the Ottoman Empire and nationalism arising throughout the region.

The Ottoman Empire resumed its path toward reform in 1908 and 1909, when the Westernizing **Young Turks**, led by **Enver Pasha**, replaced Abdul Hamid II with a figurehead sultan and restored the constitution of 1876. But even the Young Turks' program of modernization could not save the empire, especially once the Ottomans entered World War I and shared in the Central Powers' defeat in 1918. Disgraced by its military failures and having lost its imperial possessions to revolt or to the Paris Peace Conference, the Ottoman Empire was threatened after the war with the seizure of even more territory by Greece. Into this crisis stepped **Mustafa Kemal**, a heroic World War I commander who now repelled the Greeks and, forming a new government, negotiated a more favorable treaty with the Allies. In 1923, the last Ottoman sultan vacated the throne, and Kemal proclaimed the Turkish Republic— appointing himself president and taking the name **Ataturk**, or "father of all Turks."

From 1923 to his death in 1938, Ataturk governed as a secularizing modernizer, promoting industrialization, Western dress, Western education, and the use of the Roman alphabet for written Turkish. Church and state were separated, with a European law code replacing Islamic Sharia. Women, no longer required to wear the veil, received the right to vote in 1934 and were encouraged to get educations and jobs. Although he wrote a constitution and kept up a democratic pretense, Ataturk tolerated little opposition and began a long tradition of authoritarian rule in Turkey.

> **WHAT ABOUT INTERWAR AFRICA?**
>
> Most of Africa remained firmly under European colonial control. Exceptions include South Africa, which formed a union of British and Boer provinces in 1910 and gained dominion status within the British Empire in 1931. Liberia, founded in the 1800s by freed slaves from the United States, remained independent. Ethiopia, the only state other than Liberia to escape colonization during the Scramble for Africa, was conquered by fascist Italy in the mid-1930s. Although not yet as potent as in Asia or the Middle East, national liberationist impulses started to awaken in Africa.

A similar change took place in Persia, which became the modern state of Iran in the 1920s. Ruled in theory by the Qajar dynasty since 1794, Persia had in fact been divided into British and Russian spheres of influence during the 1800s. Drawn by its oil reserves, the British increased their presence in Persia after World War I, causing a nationalist backlash. In 1921, an officer named Reza Khan mutinied against the Qajar and expelled the British, gaining control of the entire country by 1925. Taking the name **Reza Shah Pahlavi**, he established a new royal dynasty and became an authoritarian Westernizer like his neighbor Ataturk. Although he was less inclined than Ataturk to put up a show of democracy or to clash as hard with the Muslim clergy, the new shah industrialized Iran, boosted education, and did away with the veil for women.

Egypt and North Africa remained in British, French, and Italian hands, although nationalist sentiment there was growing. The Ottomans retained the Arabian Peninsula, but the other Arab lands once under their rulership were now placed into the **mandate system** and administered by France and Britain under the League of Nations' supervision. This arrangement angered the Arabs, who had believed during World War I that the Allies would grant them complete freedom as a reward for their anti-Ottoman revolt. They were further enraged by the **Balfour Declaration** of 1917, which pledged British support for a Jewish "national home" in Palestine, which was 90 percent Arab before substantial Jewish immigration—faster and larger in scale than the British had intended—began in the 1920s and 1930s.

The one Arab state to achieve full independence during these years was Saudi Arabia, formed in 1932 by the prince **Ibn Saud**, who spent the 1920s driving the Ottomans out of the Arabian Peninsula and then uniting its many tribes. An authoritarian monarchy, the Saudi state remained more traditionally Islamic and modernized little—except to industrialize its huge **oil reserves**, whose discovery in 1938 made it instantly wealthy and strategically vital.

## Militarism and Revolution in Asia

Huge upheavals came to interwar Asia, beginning in China, where the **Chinese Revolution** of 1911–1912 had already swept away the Qing regime. The revolution's leading figure was **Sun Yat-sen**, who spent the 1890s and early 1900s promoting Western-style modernization and constitutional rule based on three "**people's principles**": nationalism (opposition to Manchu rule and Western imperialism), democracy (including universal suffrage for women as well as men), and livelihood (a semi-socialist, but not Marxist, concern for people's welfare). When anti-Qing uprisings broke out in the fall of 1911, Sun was in America, but quickly returned and became president of the new Chinese Republic. His movement renamed itself the **Nationalist Party**, or **Kuomintang** (KMT).

Unfortunately, Sun's political idealism was no match for the civil war and anarchy that immediately followed. In 1912, the authoritarian general Yuan Shikai seized power, which remained in his hands until his death in 1916, and then passed to other right-wing officers until 1928. Opposed to this military regime were warlords and bandits, who established

**FACT**

**The Chinese Republic banned foot binding and began preparations for allowing women to vote. However, when Yuan Shikai took power from Sun Yat-sen he canceled suffrage for women. Only in 1947 did Chinese women receive the right to vote.**

control over vast stretches of China, as well as intellectuals and students, whose Western-oriented progressivism clashed with the regime's attempt to revive traditional Confucian values. The clearest expression of popular discontent with the military government came on May 4, 1919, when thousands of students gathered in **Tiananmen Square**. Although they were there mainly to protest the regime's willingness to allow Japan to annex Shantung Province (a German concession awarded to Japan by the Treaty of Versailles), the other goal of this May Fourth Movement was democratic reform.

Also clashing with the military regime were the Kuomintang, still led by Sun and now running a revolutionary effort in the south, based in Canton, and the **Chinese Communist Party** (CCP), founded in 1921 by radicals at Beijing University. In the mid-1920s, both cooperated to combat unruly warlords and to unseat the military government. In 1925, Sun died of cancer, passing the KMT leadership to **Chiang Kai-shek**, a Western-educated officer who leaned farther to the right than Sun had. By early 1927, the KMT-CCP alliance had won control of all China south of the Yangtze River—and then suddenly, in April, Chiang turned against the communists, murdering thousands of them in Shanghai and driving the rest far to the north. In 1928, Chiang took Beijing and founded

**NOTE**

**Like Lenin in Russia, Mao confronted the awkward fact that Marxism was theoretically poorly suited to non-industrial societies with few if any proletarian workers. He radicalized China's vast and oppressed peasant masses and made communism appealing to them.**

a Kuomintang regime that professed allegiance to Sun's principles and attempted a certain degree of modernization but soon grew corrupt, inefficient, and authoritarian. Chiang governed China until 1949, but faced two deadly threats. First was the CCP, kept alive by **Mao Tse-tung** (**Mao Zedong**), who led the party to its new northern base of Yenan during the arduous **Long March** of 1934–1935 and, from there, continued the anti-KMT struggle. Second was Japanese expansion, which began in 1931, worsened after 1937, and never ceased until the end of World War II.

Japan began the interwar period with democratizing potential but veered in the end toward authoritarian militarism. Up through the late 1920s, the powers of the Diet increased, freedom of the press expanded, and a 1925 bill of rights granted universal male suffrage and other civil liberties. On the other hand, Japan continued the policy of **state-directed industrialization** that it had during the 1800s, with a small number of powerful corporations, or *zaibatsu*, benefiting from government favoritism. Not only did this system concentrate wealth in the hands of a tiny oligarchy of influential industrialists, it kept trade unions weak and did little to improve working conditions. Even before the Depression, strikes and riots were common, and social stress was building to a dangerous level.

In the 1930s, the Great Depression and Japan's foreign-policy aggression derailed further liberalization. The Depression caused Japanese exports to plummet more than 50 percent. The resulting economic stress gave rise to left-wing extremism, including communist agitation, and this was met by conservative backlash. Two prime ministers were assassinated, one in 1930 by leftists, the other in 1932 by radical rightists. A steady political crackdown resulted in military control of the government by 1937, climaxing with the 1941 elevation of **Hideki Tojo**, head of Japan's army, to the prime ministership. At the same time, **militaristic nationalism** skyrocketed, bolstered by the ideology of **State Shinto**, which propagandistically perverted Japan's indigenous faith to foster a sense of racial superiority and unquestioning loyalty to the state. Anti-Western feelings sharpened, and the slogan "Asia for the Asians" called for the expulsion of colonizing powers like Britain and France. Starting in 1931, the Japanese put these feelings into action, seizing Manchuria from China and withdrawing from the League of Nations. They resumed their war against China in 1937, committing dreadful atrocities like the **Rape of Nanjing** that December, when Japanese troops butchered 200,000 to 300,000 noncombatants, including thousands of women who were first sexually assaulted. Before the end of World War II, the Japanese would spread this campaign of xenophobic imperialism throughout much of East and Southeast Asia, euphemistically naming their sphere of influence the **Greater East Asian Co-Prosperity Sphere**.

In South and Southeast Asia, most of which remained under European colonial rule, **national liberation movements** became increasingly influential. Anti-colonial agitation escalated in Indonesia, Burma, Indochina (especially among the Vietnamese), and elsewhere. Such efforts were typically led by Western-educated elites and middle-class intellectuals and students, and they tended to involve uneasy alliances between liberal modernizers and radical communists—much like that between the Nationalists and Communists in China, and most often breaking apart in the same way.

The most successful of these movements appeared in India, spearheaded by the **Indian National Congress**. Because they had supported Britain so loyally during World War I, Indians hoped for greater autonomy, perhaps even dominion status, after the war. Aggrieved by the lack of change, they began staging mass protests, one of which, at **Amritsar** in 1919, resulted in the killing or wounding of more than 1,400 unarmed demonstrators by British troops. During the 1920s, India balanced on a political knife-edge. In 1921, the British passed the Government of India Act, a major concession that allowed five million Indians to vote and created a new parliament with two-thirds Indian membership. But this was no longer enough, and the Congress demanded more. India could easily have erupted into bloody revolution.

That it did not was due mainly to the guidance of **Mohandas Gandhi**, a leading figure in the Congress since 1915, known to his followers as Mahatma, or "great soul." Imprisoned several times by the British, Gandhi combined political activism and Hindu religious principle to devise the policy of **nonviolent resistance**, which he called *satyagraha* ("hold to the truth"). An example of *satyagraha* in action came in 1930, after the British imposed a punitively high tax on salt. Rather than protest violently, Gandhi led 5,000 people on a 200-mile march to the seashore, where they began to make salt illegally by drying out seawater. When the British arrived, Gandhi allowed himself to be arrested peacefully.

Freed in 1931, Gandhi continued to work with the Congress, but as a spiritual leader rather than a political one. That role fell to the lawyer **Jawaharlal Nehru**, a secular modernizer. Gandhi and Nehru now pressed for full independence, and even after Britain granted a constitution in 1935 that promised eventual self-rule, Congress responded in 1937 with its "Quit India" campaign. Britain realized that it would have to accelerate its plans for withdrawal—although these were delayed until 1947 by the advent of World War II.

The Congress, which chiefly represented Hindu interests, was not the only force agitating for Indian freedom. In 1930, Muhammad Ali Jinnah ended many years of cooperation with the Congress and founded the All-India Muslim League, which aimed not just for independence from Britain but also for the creation of a separate Islamic state. The failure of the Muslim League and the Congress to resolve their differences peacefully led to great bloodshed and laid the foundation for decades of ongoing Indo-Pakistani rivalry.

**NOTE**

Influences on Gandhi included *On Civil Disobedience* (1849), by the American Henry David Thoreau, and the Russian novelist Leo Tolstoy, who embraced spiritual pacifism. Gandhi himself shaped the outlook of Martin Luther King, Jr., who adopted nonviolent resistance in the African-American struggle for civil rights.

## Authoritarianism in Latin America

During the interwar years, Latin America coped as before with Western **economic imperialism**—the **United Fruit Company** was merely the best known of the many corporations that influenced politics there—and the diplomatic weakness that came with being part of the **U.S. sphere of influence**. The Cuban-American Treaty of 1903 authorized the United States to intervene in Cuba's foreign policy (and gave it the option, still active, to lease the Guantánamo naval base). The Americans also occupied Haiti in 1915 to protect U.S. sugar companies, established a long-term military presence in Panama after opening the **Panama Canal** in 1914, and invaded northern Mexico in 1916, although this was a response to repeated raids on U.S. soil by the rebel leader Pancho Villa. The only attempt to *reduce* U.S. influence in Latin America was Franklin Roosevelt's **Good Neighbor Policy** (1935), which included the withdrawal of troops from Haiti.

Latin American economies modernized unevenly during these years, largely because it remained advantageous for economic elites and foreign investors to continue **plantation monoculture** and the extraction of a handful of **raw materials**, rather than industrializing or diversifying. Also, after 1929, the **Great Depression** devastated Latin American economies by wiping out international demand for nearly half their exports.

Nor did the region escape its long tradition of authoritarian rule, a trend made worse by the Depression. Three examples—Mexico, Brazil, and Argentina—show the varying degrees to which dictatorship prevailed. Mexico was the mildest, after the convoluted **Mexican Revolution** (1910–1920), which followed a pattern not unlike China's. In 1910–1911, the liberal democrat **Francisco Madero** overthrew **Porfirio Díaz**, a general who had ruled since 1876, modernizing the country but growing corrupt and abusive over time. Like Sun Yat-sen in China, Madero was not destined to govern for long. From the left, he was pressured by rural radicals like **Francisco "Pancho" Villa** and **Emiliano Zapata**, who initially supported him, but led uprisings against him when he did not deliver agrarian reform as rapidly as he had promised. From the right, Madero faced opposition from conservative military officers, who staged a coup in 1913 and executed him. Madero's liberal ally Venustiano Carranza took back power in 1914 and enacted the **Constitution of 1917**, which guaranteed universal suffrage (including for women), the separation of church and state, and the right to strike.

Unfortunately, like Madero before him, Carranza was caught between Zapata's and Villa's radical insurrections on one side and military disloyalty on the other. Although he defeated Zapata in 1919, he was removed in 1920 by the general Álvaro Obregón and soon killed.

**Emiliano Zapata**

Zapata, commander of the "Liberation Army of the South" and famed for his slogan "better to die on your feet than live on your knees," perished in battle in 1919. Like his ally "Pancho" Villa (assassinated in 1923), Zapata was derided by his enemies as a bandit. However, he is widely regarded as a hero in Mexico, and many throughout Latin America revere him as an icon of grass-roots activism and principled popular revolt.

Although violence continued into the early 1930s, Obregón fundamentally restored order in Mexico, and Carranza's death is generally considered the revolution's endpoint. Obregón eliminated Villa in 1923 and instituted a number of land, labor, and educational reforms; he stepped down in 1924, only to be assassinated in 1928. In 1929, Obregón's successors founded the **National Revolutionary Party** (PNR), which renamed itself the **Institutional Revolutionary Party** (PRI) in 1946 and ruled until the late 1980s. Like Napoleon in France, the PNR/PRI claimed to govern in the revolution's name, but in reality it created a durable oligarchy, in which the party chose a president every six years and arranged a "democratic" election that guaranteed victory to its candidate. Under this mild form of authoritarianism, the upper classes prospered and the country modernized. However, the lower classes—workers and peasants—lagged far behind the elite, and the middle class remained small. Conditions improved under **Lázaro Cárdenas**, president from 1934 to 1940, who carried out a popular **land reform** (transferring 40 million acres from the upper classes to the peasantry). Cárdenas also stood up to the United States with his **nationalization of the oil industry**. Because Cárdenas compensated U.S. investors for their losses, Franklin Roosevelt abided by his **Good Neighbor Policy** and did not intervene, allowing Cárdenas to form PEMEX, Mexico's state-run oil enterprise.

More so than Mexico, Brazil descended deep into dictatorship in 1930, when an oligarchy dominated by wealthy landowners gave way to the despotic presidency of the cattleman Getúlio Vargas, who ruled from the far right until 1945. Vargas freed Brazil from its economic overdependence on coffee exports and turned it into Latin America's most industrialized nation. But as an admirer of Mussolini and Hitler, he censored the press and authorized his secret police to torture prisoners. Likewise, Depression-era Argentina became a dictatorship, also in 1930, when the military ousted radical president Hipólito Yrigoyen, who had spent the 1920s antagonizing the army and elite classes with pro-union and pro-worker policies. This "**infamous decade**" of dictatorship lasted until 1943, when another series of coups paved the way for the 1946 rise of another strongman, the charismatic general **Juan Perón**.

## WORLD WAR II AND THE HOLOCAUST

**World War II** (1939–1945) was and remains the largest and deadliest conflict in human history. It involved more than sixty nations (the **Axis Powers** vs. the **Allied Powers**), cost several trillion dollars (a third of the entire planet's economic output was dedicated to the war at its peak), and killed nearly 60 million people. **Civilian deaths** account for half that figure, owing largely to **destructive tactics and technologies** (including **terror bombing** and **strategic bombing**) and even more to campaigns of **genocide**—a new term coined during the war— which included the Nazi **Holocaust**. World War II also shifted the balance of global strength completely, toppling the European powers from their position of geopolitical superiority and ushering in the U.S.-Soviet **Cold War** and a massive wave of postwar **decolonization**.

The war's principal actors included

- The **Axis Powers**: Nazi Germany, fascist Italy (joined the war in June 1940; left in July 1943), and Japan
- Major **Allied Powers**: Great Britain, France (left the war in 1940), Canada, Australia, New Zealand, the USSR (joined the war in June 1941), the United States (joined the war in December 1941), and Nationalist China

### Origins and Interwar Foreign Policy

Compared to the complex origins of World War I, the causes of World War II are straightforward: aggression during the 1930s on the part of Japan, Italy, and Germany went unchecked by a feeble **League of Nations**, and was repeatedly answered by the Western democracies with the policy of **appeasement**—letting a belligerent party have what it wants in the hope that it will ask for no more. Foreign-policy destabilization began in 1931, when Japan invaded the Chinese province of Manchuria and left the League of Nations. In 1933, soon after coming to power, Hitler pulled out of the League; in 1935, he began rearmament and conscription in open violation of the Treaty of Versailles. Fearing Hitler's anti-communist rhetoric and his talk of *Lebensraum* ("living space") expansion in Eastern Europe, the USSR attempted a policy of **collective security** with the West, securing a seemingly reliable alliance with France and Czechoslovakia. Britain, distrusting the Soviets, distanced itself from this partnership.

Several factors explain the democracies' passivity in the face of fascism during the 1930s. U.S. isolationism did not help, and neither did British antipathy for the USSR. The Great Depression kept the democracies economically timid, and the memory of World War I bloodshed made them reluctant to risk a new round of fighting. Also, Britain and France put too much faith in defensive barriers to keep them safe: the English Channel in the case of the former and the Maginot Line, a long chain of fortifications meant to act as the ultimate trench, in the case of the latter.

Events quickly proved the hollowness of collective security. In 1935, Italy brutally invaded Ethiopia, and when the League of Nations tried to sanction it, Italy abandoned the League and drew closer to Germany. In the spring of 1936, Hitler defied France and Britain by sending troops into the Rhineland, which the Treaty of Versailles had demilitarized, and the democracies' failure to respond emboldened him. That summer, Mussolini and Hitler joined forces to intervene in the **Spanish Civil War** (1936–1939), aiding the military rebellion led by the right-wing general Francisco Franco against Spain's recently elected coalition of liberals and leftists. The Soviets sent assistance to the Spanish government—but when the French, who also promised to help, were persuaded by Britain to remain neutral, they disappointed Stalin and undermined collective security. The Germans and Italians tested new tanks, airplanes, and tactics in Spain, and with their help, Franco marched to victory in 1939, ruling as Spain's dictator until his death in 1975. Things only grew worse in 1937, as Japan resumed its war in China—committing the horrific **Rape of Nanjing** that December—and forged friendly ties with Germany and Italy.

**Interwar Conflicts: Laboratories of Destruction**

The conflicts of the interwar period served as a test case for many of the destructive tactics and technologies unleashed more notoriously during World War II. Italy's 1935–1936 conquest of Ethiopia and Japan's war in China both included the use of **poison gas** and **terror bombing**, the deliberate targeting of civilians to demoralize an enemy population. Japan's **Rape of Nanjing** in 1937 foreshadowed worse atrocities to come. In addition to experimenting in Spain with the tank-airplane coordination that made *blitzkrieg* warfare possible, Germany pursued terror bombing. Pablo Picasso's renowned *Guernica*, pictured above, stands as an immortal artistic protest against the Germans' aerial destruction of the Spanish city of the same name.

Collective security's final collapse soon followed. In early 1938, Germany annexed Austria and then threatened war that summer against Czechoslovakia over the **Sudetenland**, a border region that the Treaty of Versailles had given to the Czechs, but that contained a large German-speaking population. Because of France's and the USSR's treaties with Czechoslovakia, war seemed unavoidable. Then, at September's **Munich Agreement**— the century's most woeful example of **appeasement**—the British prime minister, Neville Chamberlain, and the French premier, browbeaten by him, agreed to let Hitler take the Sudetenland in exchange for his promise to expand no further. The Czechs and Soviets, both uninvited, were outraged, and Stalin, already upset about the Spanish Civil War, lost faith in collective security. In the spring of 1939, Hitler exposed Chamberlain's foolishness by invading the rest of Czechoslovakia and staking loud claims to Polish territory. The British and French now determined to stand firm over Poland, but in August, Stalin, no longer trusting the democracies, secretly negotiated a nonaggression treaty with Hitler. This **Nazi-Soviet Pact** kept the USSR neutral and allowed Hitler to invade Poland without worrying about a two-front war. Germany's invasion of Poland on September 1, 1939, began World War II.

## World War II: A Combat Overview

Between 1939 and the end of 1941, the Axis Powers enjoyed great triumphs. New technology and tactics gave armed forces tremendous offensive capacity, making World War II far more mobile and faster-paced than World War I had been—but also far more destructive, especially where civilians were concerned.

Germany immediately exploited this new offensive potential with its innovative *blitzkrieg* ("lightning war"), which used tanks and airplanes to penetrate quickly and deeply into enemy territory. Poland fell to Germany in six weeks in the fall of 1939, and when Hitler turned against Norway, Denmark, Belgium, the Netherlands, and France in the spring of 1940, his forces defeated them all between April and June: a remarkably short time for such a decisive victory. From the summer of 1940 through the spring of 1941, Germany focused its attention on Britain, trying—but failing—to bomb it into submission from the air. The Royal Air Force famously defended England's skies in the **Battle of Britain**, and Britain continued to hold out thanks to control of the seas, the skill of its pilots, its use of radar, and economic aid from Canada and the United States (although the latter was neutral, Franklin Roosevelt sympathized with the Allies and began his **Lend-Lease program** of economic assistance to Britain, and later the USSR, in the spring and summer of 1941).

World War II was so dynamic thanks to a plethora of new or improved technologies. At sea, aircraft carriers appeared alongside battleships to give navies an airborne punch, and long-range submarines extended offensive reach. On the ground, tanks combined the power of artillery with excellent mobility, allowing maneuvers like Germany's nimble sidestepping of France's mammoth but ineffectual Maginot Line. Heavy bomber aircraft dropped unheard-of quantities of explosives on dozens of cities from London and Rotterdam to Dresden and Tokyo. Among the wartime innovations that deeply affected postwar life were radar, jet aircraft, rocketry, atomic bombs, and computers.

The war expanded in 1941 to Africa, where German tank forces drove toward the British-controlled Suez Canal, and also to Eastern Europe, as Hitler began a surprise·invasion of the USSR—a fateful decision, since he had not yet finished off the British. **Operation Barbarossa** began in June, and from this point forward, between 60 to 75 percent of all German forces would fight on this Soviet front. At first, it looked as though *blitzkrieg* would topple the USSR as quickly as it had France: the Germans surrounded Leningrad, the country's second largest city, placing it under the worst siege in modern times, and reached the outskirts of Moscow in October. But a last-ditch defensive effort halted the German advance in December, at which point events in Asia further complicated the war. Earlier in the year, the Japanese, extending their imperial reach from China to Southeast Asia, had occupied French Indochina, a bold move that also threatened Britain's Asian colonies and the U.S.-controlled Philippines. Repeated U.S. trade embargoes heightened diplomatic tensions and convinced the Japanese to launch a massive naval and air assault throughout the Pacific, beginning with the December 7, 1941, surprise attack on **Pearl Harbor**. By the late spring of 1942, the Japanese were masters of the South Pacific and Southeast Asia, having captured Hong Kong, Thailand, Burma, Britain's mighty naval base at Singapore, the Philippines, and Dutch Indonesia. However, Pearl Harbor, while devastating, was not a knockout blow, and by bringing the United States into the war—just as the Soviets stalled the Germans outside

Moscow—Japan had roused a gigantic enemy that neither it nor Germany could come close to matching in terms of industrial production or humanpower reserves. Although they were still winning major victories, the Axis Powers had just made the war far more strategically and economically challenging for themselves.

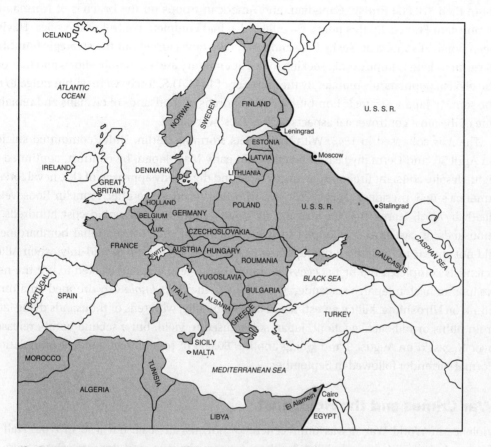

**The European and Mediterranean Theaters of Combat, World War II, 1942.**
From September 1939 until the autumn of 1942, the Axis Powers—Germany, Italy, and Japan— succeeded in seizing the military initiative and keeping it. By the middle of 1942, Nazi Germany had reached the height of its power. The areas shaded in gray mark territory that was controlled directly by Germany before the war, belonged to its allies, or had been conquered by it during the war. Not long after this point, primarily because of defeats at El Alamein and Stalingrad, the tide of war turned against the Germans and their partners.

This fact became clear in the summer and fall of 1942, when three turning-point battles completely reversed the war's tide. Had the Axis won them, their short-term advantages in skill and speed might have forced an end favorable to them before the Allies' long-term economic and population advantages overpowered them. The three battles were **Midway** (June 1942), a Pacific clash in which the U.S. Navy destroyed the bulk of Japan's carrier fleet; **El Alamein** (July–November 1942), where the British turned back the German tanks driving toward the Suez Canal; and **Stalingrad** (August 1942–February 1943), a savage showdown on the Volga, where a huge German force nearly pushed the Soviets across the river and gained access to the USSR's oil reserves but was instead encircled and captured.

In 1943 and 1944, U.S. forces in the Pacific moved west toward Japan in a strategy of **island hopping**, while Allied armies and guerrilla uprisings in China and Southeast Asia pinned down Japanese forces on the mainland. In Europe, the Allies invaded Italy from North Africa in 1943, deposing Mussolini's government. At sea, they neutralized Germany's submarines—the only truly dangerous threat still at Hitler's disposal—in the **Battle of the Atlantic** (1942–spring 1943). From the east, the Soviets pushed the Germans out of the USSR, into Eastern Europe, and toward Berlin. In June 1944, Operation Overlord, or the **D-Day invasion**, landed more than 170,000 British, Canadian, and American troops on the beaches of Normandy, in northern France. By this point, the Allies also had complete control of the skies. Having been bombed so mercilessly in 1940 and 1941, they now carried out the **strategic bombing** of German-held Europe at will, seeking to disrupt military and economic efforts and to break the civilian population's morale. By the summer of 1944, U.S. forces were within range to do the same to Japan. Strategic bombing killed hundreds of thousands of civilians and remains one of the most controversial aspects of the Allies' war effort.

The Axis collapsed in 1945. With the Soviets storming Berlin, Hitler committed suicide on April 30, and Germany ceased hostilities in early May. Japan, by contrast, continued to fight, despite constant firebombing from above and the steady approach of U.S. naval forces. America's new president, Harry Truman, who had taken office after Franklin Roosevelt's death in April, feared that an invasion of Japan's home islands would cost hundreds of thousands of casualties. He hoped to win from the air, but conventional bombardment did not appear to be denting the Japanese leadership's resolve. So in mid-July, when Allied scientists completed the first successful atomic bomb test, Truman elected to use the new weapon to hasten Japan's surrender. On August 6, the B-29 *Enola Gay* dropped an atomic bomb on **Hiroshima**, killing an estimated 80,000 initially, with tens of thousands dying later from burns or radioactive fallout. Japan still refused to yield, but a second bomb, released over Nagasaki on August 9 and killing another 80,000 in total, forced Japan's capitulation. Formal surrender followed in September.

## War Crimes and the Holocaust

Violence in World War II was unprecedented, not just in scale but also in type. Half of the nearly 60 million people killed by the war were civilians, and the **war crimes** were of unprecedented cruelty. It was during World War II that **genocide** came to be formally defined as a crime.

The Allies were not blameless when it came to brutality. The Soviet army raped as many as two million women and girls as it advanced through Germany toward Berlin. The Allies' **strategic bombing** campaign killed over 600,000 in German-held Europe and at least another 500,000 in Japan, and some historians and legal commentators—albeit a minority—have argued that Allied bombing should be considered a war crime. Similarly, the question of whether it was proper or necessary to drop the atomic bombs on Japan, especially the second one, remains a matter of controversy.

Allied bombing proved especially devastating to certain cities, including Hamburg in 1943 and Dresden in early 1945, where firebombing killed approximately 25,000 to 35,000 (this figure was inflated to 200,000 by early but inaccurate German reports that continue to confuse the record today). Dresden remains notorious because it took place when the war was essentially over and because it is debatable whether the city was militarily important enough to warrant targeting. The author Kurt Vonnegut was present in Dresden with a number of other U.S. prisoners of war and portrays the event in his novel *Slaughterhouse Five*. The U.S. firebombing of Tokyo in March 1945 killed approximately 100,000 people—more than either atomic bomb did in its initial blast.

Nonetheless, the Axis committed atrocities more systematically and on a larger scale. Both Japan and Germany killed large numbers of civilians, executed or mistreated prisoners of war, and pressed several million enemy non-combatants into forced labor. Japan plundered its occupied territories, the so-called "Greater East Asian Co-Prosperity Sphere." It used prisoners as human subjects to test biological and chemical weapons, and Japan's army forced thousands of women from mainland Asia to serve as "comfort women," or military prostitutes.

Most heinous were the German campaigns of **genocide**, a crime defined in 1943 by the Polish-Jewish lawyer Rafael Lemkin as the premeditated attempt to annihilate a group based on its ethnic identity. As noted above, Nazi policy singled out several racial groups as "subhumans" who could not be allowed to "contaminate" the Germans' "pure Aryan" blood; these included Slavs, those of African descent, Roma (Gypsies), and especially Jews. Others considered by the Nazis to be "undesirable" were homosexuals, the mentally disabled, and people with venereal or incurable diseases. Before 1939, treatment of these groups—particularly **anti-Semitic persecution**—had grown steadily worse, but the war triggered an escalation of systematic violence, culminating in the mass exterminations popularly known as the **Holocaust**. Nazi officials estimated that there were 11 million Jews in Europe that they would have to expel or eradicate—the so-called "Jewish problem"—and Roma were to be eliminated as well. Slavic peoples were to be conquered with brute force and the survivors enslaved.

In 1939 and 1940, with so much of Europe coming under German control, Nazi authorities began detaining Jews in **concentration camps** and city neighborhoods called **ghettos**. In the spring of 1941, as Germany readied its invasion of the USSR, **special action squads** (*Einsatzgruppen*) were formed to accompany the German army and execute Soviet Jews by shooting. In July, moreover, an order to prepare a "**final solution** of the Jewish problem" was handed down to Nazi security forces, and though it was not signed by Hitler, it came from his chief lieutenant, certainly on Hitler's orders. Firing-squad executions proved too slow for the Nazis' purposes, and by late 1941, they were seeking more efficient means of mass killing. Inspired by how Nazi doctors had been clinically "euthanizing" the mentally and physically ill since 1939, key officials decided in late 1941 and early 1942—principally at the **Wannsee Conference** in January—to use special **extermination camps**, already under construction in German-held Poland, to kill victims on a truly industrial scale. At these camps, which included the infamous **Auschwitz-Birkenau**, victims were gassed, their bodies plundered for hidden loot, and their remains cremated. Also at these camps, numerous victims, especially Jews, Roma, and Soviet prisoners of war, were used for medical and scientific experiments, to the point of mutilation and death.

In the end, the "final solution" killed approximately 6 million Jews out of a total prewar population of 9 to 11 million. Another 5 to 6 million non-Jewish victims—including an estimated 200,000 to 1.5 million Roma—perished as a result of non-military killings carried out by the Germans. It was to punish these atrocities that the Allies organized the **Nuremberg Trials** (1945–1946), where Nazi leaders were prosecuted, and where the concept of **crimes against humanity** was codified. (A similar series of Tokyo Trials followed in 1946–1948.) In 1948, in a collective effort to avoid such barbarities in the future, the United Nations adopted the **Universal Declaration of Human Rights**.

# State Building, Expansion, and Conflict (Part II), 1945 to Present

# 23

→ **THE COLD WAR**

→ **DECOLONIZATION (THIRD WORLD, NON-ALIGNED MOVEMENT)**

→ **"IRON CURTAIN" IN EUROPE AND U.S. CONTAINMENT (BERLIN WALL)**

→ **SOLIDARITY AND EAST EUROPEAN DISSIDENT MOVEMENTS**

→ **SOCIAL WELFARE AND ECONOMIC UNION IN WESTERN EUROPE (EEC/EU)**

→ **1970s ECONOMIC CRISIS AND 1980S FREE-MARKET REFORMS**

→ **THE FALL OF THE BERLIN WALL AND THE COLLAPSE OF THE USSR (PERESTROIKA)**

→ **"SHOCK THERAPY" TRANSITION FROM EAST EUROPEAN COMMUNISM**

→ **OPEC AND GEOPOLITICAL IMPORTANCE OF MIDDLE EASTERN OIL**

→ **THE ARAB-ISRAELI CONFLICT (PLO, INTIFADAS, TWO-STATE PEACE PROCESS)**

→ **GAMAL NASSER, PAN-ARABISM, AND THE SUEZ CANAL**

→ **IRANIAN REVOLUTION (SHAH OF IRAN VS. AYATOLLAH KHOMEINI)**

→ **IRAN-IRAQ WAR, DESERT STORM, THE U.S.-LED "WAR ON TERROR"**

→ **ARAB SPRING**

→ **NEGOTIATED VS. VIOLENT DECOLONIZATION IN AFRICA**

→ **KWAME NKRUMAH AND PAN-AFRICANISM VS. AFRICAN AUTHORITARIANISM**

→ **APARTHEID IN SOUTH AFRICA (ANC, NELSON MANDELA)**

→ **JAPAN'S ECONOMIC RESURGENCE AND ASIA'S "LITTLE TIGERS"**

→ **MAO TSE-TUNG VS. DENG XIAOPING IN COMMUNIST CHINA**

→ **NEGOTIATED VS. VIOLENT DECOLONIZATION IN SOUTH AND SOUTHEAST ASIA (INDIA VS. VIETNAM)**

→ **INDO-PAKISTANI RIVALRY**

→ **KHMER ROUGE AND GENOCIDE IN CAMBODIA (POL POT)**

→ **U.S. SPHERE OF INFLUENCE AND AUTHORITARIANISM IN LATIN AMERICA**

→ **CUBAN AND NICARAGUAN REVOLUTIONS**

→ **POST-COLD WAR GENOCIDES (YUGOSLAVIA, RWANDA, DARFUR)**

→ **AL-QAEDA ATTACKS OF SEPTEMBER 11, 2001, AND THE U.S.-LED "WAR ON TERROR"**

→ **ASYMMETRICAL WARFARE (WMDS, "REVOLUTION IN MILITARY AFFAIRS")**

→ **NUCLEAR PROLIFERATION**

For almost five decades after World War II, most of the world was divided by the **Cold War** into hostile camps, led by the United States and the USSR.

Domestic developments worked themselves out in a myriad of ways during the postwar years. As for the geopolitical struggle that the Cold War became, it resulted in a nuclear arms race and the creation of massive military-industrial complexes that still operate today. Warfare continued to harm large numbers of civilians, and racial hatred continued to motivate **genocide** and "**ethnic cleansing**." Also during the Cold War, a mass wave of **decolonization** deprived the European powers of their empires. Sometimes through peaceful negotiation, sometimes through violent separation, dozens of new nations were formed in Asia, Africa, and the Pacific.

During the late 1980s and 1990s, communism in Eastern Europe and the USSR collapsed, ending the Cold War, and a number of other dictatorships democratized as well. This left the United States as the world's sole superpower, with China—which remained communist—as a rising power. The **al-Qaeda terrorist attack of September 11, 2001**, began a new global struggle, the U.S.-led war on terror, which sparked wars in Iraq and Afghanistan and, more generally, sharpened tensions between the West and the Islamic world. Although the end of the Cold War removed the threat of worldwide, superpower-caused nuclear annihilation, heightened geopolitical instability has prevailed ever since.

## THE UNITED NATIONS AND OTHER INTERNATIONAL ORGANIZATIONS

Compared to the League of Nations, the United Nations has greater powers of enforcement, including a wide variety of sanctions and the ability to call up peacekeeping forces and to intervene in crises and conflicts. The 15-member Security Council, not the larger and more unwieldy General Assembly (which includes all members), theoretically provides streamlined leadership. On the other hand, five permanent members of the Security Council—the United States, Russia, China, Britain, and France—possess automatic veto power, sometimes blocking effective action. Famous branches of the United Nations include UNICEF (children's relief), the World Health Organization, and UNESCO (cultural preservation). Also during the postwar era, but separate from the UN, a variety of non-governmental organizations and humanitarian groups have arisen to promote important causes or carry out relief efforts outside the nation-state framework. Famous examples include the Red Cross and Doctors Without Borders (medical relief), Greenpeace (environmental activism), and Amnesty International (human rights).

## COLD WAR AND DECOLONIZATION: FOREIGN POLICY SHIFTS, 1945–1991

During the final years of World War II, the "Big Three" among the Allies—Britain, America, and the USSR—managed to settle key questions about the postwar peace, including how to occupy German- and Japanese-held territory. Most important, they all supported the creation of a new international body, similar to the defunct League of Nations, to arbitrate disputes and preserve the peace. This **United Nations** (UN) came into being at war's end and was designed to be stronger and more durable than its predecessor. However, tension, not accord, proved the rule after World War II. Disagreements quickly arose between the Soviets and the Anglo-Americans over a host of issues, especially Stalin's intention—abundantly clear at the **Yalta Conference**, a key wartime summit in early 1945—to transform Eastern Europe into a Soviet sphere of influence. The Soviets also refused to take part in the **Bretton Woods system** created by the Anglo-Americans to facilitate free trade after the war (see Chapter 24). The Allies agreed to divide Germany and Austria into occupation zones, with the Soviets in charge of the east. The capitals, Berlin and Vienna, were similarly divided, although this was complicated by the fact that Berlin lay within the Soviet zone. Austria's occupation ended in 1955 but Germany remained divided until 1989. In Asia, the Korean peninsula was likewise split into a pro-communist northern zone and a pro-Western southern one—a state of affairs that persists today.

## The Early Cold War, 1945–1949

Thus began the **Cold War**, the state of rivalry that came to exist between the United States and the USSR—the two **superpowers** that arose after World War II ended Europe's long global hegemony. From 1945 to 1991, the Cold War divided the world into hostile camps, although its bipolar nature was complicated by the eventual breakup of the alliance between Communist China and the USSR. Interrelated with the Cold War was the great wave of postwar **decolonization** because, while some of these newly free nations attempted to preserve neutrality by forming a **non-aligned movement**, many had to choose between allying with one superpower or the other. The Cold War gave birth to the largest **arms race** in history, complete with nuclear arsenals, and while the United States and USSR never went to war with each other, an estimated 50 million people—more than half of them civilian—died in the dozens of small and medium-size conflicts that were fought worldwide during the Cold War.

**The Cold War Division of Europe, 1957.**
From 1945 until 1989, the Cold War divided the nations of Europe—with only a few exceptions—into two camps, one dominated by the Soviet Union, the other led by the United States and its European allies. By the mid-1950s, the so-called Iron Curtain had descended over Europe. A number of Western nations were united by the North Atlantic Treaty Organization, a military alliance, and many also joined in the European Economic Community. The Eastern bloc was held together by the Soviet-imposed military alliance known as the Warsaw Pact, as well as COMECON, an economic union led by the USSR.

The first stage of the Cold War lasted from 1945 to 1949 and mainly involved the division of Europe by what Winston Churchill poetically referred to in 1946 as the "**iron curtain**": the descent of Soviet power over Poland, Czechoslovakia, Hungary, Romania, Bulgaria, Albania (until 1961), and the eastern half of Germany. (Yugoslavia became communist as well, but its stubbornly independent leader, Josip Broz Tito, broke with the Soviets in 1948.) The Soviet bloc also appeared poised to expand into Iran, Turkey, and Greece, which would have brought the USSR closer to the oil fields of the Middle East and the vital waterways of the eastern Mediterranean.

The U.S. responded with **containment**, a strategy devised by the diplomat George Kennan, who predicted that the USSR would expand as far as it could, as long as it did not have to fight—and could therefore be halted not by combat, but by "firm and vigilant" support for countries targeted by the Soviets. In 1947, the United States committed politically to containment with the **Truman Doctrine**, which pledged assistance to Greece and Turkey (and more generally to "any and all countries whose political stability is threatened by communism"), and economically with the **Marshall Plan**, which pumped more than $13 billion of aid and investment into a Europe in dire need of reconstruction. Containment's first major test came during the **Berlin Blockade** of 1948, when the Soviets suddenly cut off highway and rail traffic between West Berlin and the western half of Germany. It was easy for the Soviets to stop ground transport without provoking violence, but when the United States began to fly airplanes through Soviet-controlled airspace to West Berlin, Stalin faced a choice: allow the flights to continue or shoot the airplanes down and start an actual war. The Soviets backed down, seeming to validate the containment strategy. In 1949, the United States committed militarily to the Cold War by forming the **North Atlantic Treaty Organization** (NATO), a strategic alliance that bound America to Canada, Britain, and nine other European states, and whose membership steadily grew over time. (The Soviets created their own military bloc, the **Warsaw Pact**, to oppose NATO.)

## The Cold War Globalizes, 1949–1968

During the next stage of the Cold War, which can be said to have lasted from 1949 to 1968, Europe ceased to be the conflict's only—or even primary—battleground.

The watershed year of 1949 witnessed the **first Soviet atomic-bomb test**, which erased America's edge in military technology, and **communist victory in the People's Republic of China** (PRC), which brought **Mao Tse-tung** to power as a new ally—for now—of the USSR. (China's Nationalist regime fled to Taiwan, which remains non-communist to this day, although the PRC claims it as its own.) Also by this point, the process of postwar **decolonization** and **national liberation** was already underway, shifting much geopolitical focus away from Europe and outward to Asia and Africa. In other words, the Cold War quickly globalized, an early sign of which was the **Korean War** (1950–1953). Encouraged by Mao and supported in a more limited way by Stalin, the communist northern half of Korea attempted to conquer the southern half, which was defended by a United Nations army led by the United States. This was **containment** once again, but for potentially higher stakes than in Berlin. Despite fears that the Korean War might spark a larger superpower conflict, the fighting was confined to the peninsula—although it caused more than a million deaths and left the country divided exactly where it had been before. America's involvement in Korea and Vietnam, as well as its other anxieties about communism's global expansion, were based on the **domino principle**: the belief that if one country in a region "fell" to communism, the rest would too.

This increasing global dimension made the Cold War more complex and stretched U.S. containment to new limits during the 1950s and 1960s. Although a number of the less developed and/or newly decolonized nations in the so-called **Third World** sought to remain neutral or unaligned, most were open to superpower influence, as were national-liberation movements worldwide. As the Soviets and their allies labored to spread communism in these areas, the United States responded with its own interventions. These diplomatic struggles often led to **proxy wars** that could be quite deadly. Unfortunately, America came to choose its Third World allies based principally on how anti-communist they were, not how democratic. It thus supported many dictatorial and authoritarian regimes. After Korea, key Cold War events in the Third World included the **Cuban Revolution** (1959), which heightened tensions by placing a communist regime and Soviet ally less than 100 miles off the U.S. coast. The **Vietnam wars** (1945–1975) began with the liberation of Indochina from French colonization and continued with the division of Vietnam. After France's defeat in 1954, America, prompted by domino-principle logic, attempted to prop up the unpopular southern regime against invasion by the communist north. The U.S. effort took a sharp turn for the worse in 1968 and ended with withdrawal in 1973, opening the way for communist victory in 1975.

As for the superpower duel, it heated and cooled during the 1950s and 1960s. The death of Stalin in 1953 and his replacement by the less hard-line Nikita Khrushchev appeared to create the potential for peace. During the **Suez Crisis** of 1956, when Britain, France, and Israel reacted to Egypt's nationalization of the Suez Canal with a military invasion, the Americans—seeking to avert a wider Middle Eastern war—cooperated with the Soviets against their own allies, forcing them to withdraw from Egypt. Even so, Khrushchev quickly showed the limits of his goodwill. In 1956, when Hungary attempted to reform its communist regime and restore ties with the West, the USSR intervened, sparking a **Hungarian uprising** that Khrushchev brutally suppressed. Encouraged by the Cuban Revolution of 1959 and angered by the flight of American U-2 spy planes over the USSR, Khrushchev pursued an aggressive and unpredictable foreign policy in East Germany and Cuba. The Soviets built the **Berlin Wall**, the most tangible embodiment of the iron curtain, in 1961. A more dangerous showdown came in 1962, when Khrushchev attempted to install nuclear missiles in Cuba, leading to the **Cuban Missile Crisis** in October, when U.S. President John Kennedy successfully countered Khrushchev's move with a naval blockade of Cuba. This was the moment that brought the superpowers closest to nuclear war, and it played a key role in the forced retirement of Khrushchev in 1964 and his replacement by the more authoritarian but less erratic Leonid Brezhnev. In 1968, Brezhnev reaffirmed the Soviet sphere of influence in Europe by sending Warsaw Pact troops into Czechoslovakia to put down the pro-reform **"Prague Spring"** movement. He justified this invasion by asserting the USSR's right to "protect communism" in Eastern Europe, a stance known as the **Brezhnev doctrine**. Of course, proxy struggles in the Third World continued, and the U.S. involvement in Vietnam escalated.

By the end of the 1960s, the superpowers were deeply enmeshed in their **nuclear arms race**. The United States had maintained a sizable edge through the 1950s, but the Soviets achieved **strategic parity** by the mid-1960s: each had roughly the same quantity of weapons, and each had developed the **nuclear triad** (the ability to drop nuclear bombs from airplanes, launch nuclear warheads on intercontinental ballistic missiles, or ICBMs, and fire nuclear missiles from submarines). Nuclear weapons made traditional military thinking obsolete: too destructive to contemplate using except under extreme circumstances, they became known most for their **deterrence**

**NOTE**

Cold War diplomacy grew more complicated with the Sino-Soviet split, which began in the 1960s and continued until the collapse of the USSR.

value. In theory, as long as each side remained convinced that rash action would destroy it as well as its enemy, both sides would avoid doing anything that might trigger a serious crisis. This logic, referred to as **mutually assured destruction** (MAD), was viewed paradoxically (or perversely, depending on one's point of view) by a number of strategists as a way to preserve peace between the superpowers. The economic costs of the arms race were enormous, leading President Dwight Eisenhower to warn of the permanent domination of the U.S. economy by a **military-industrial complex**, and causing Khrushchev in the USSR to complain about weapons as "metal-eaters" devouring resources that could be put to better use. By the 1960s and 1970s, a vigorous **anti-nuclear movement** had formed in Europe and North America, protesting the expense of nuclear weapons, the inherent dangers they posed, and the environmental and human damage caused by nuclear-weapons testing. Major actors here include the Committee for Nuclear Disarmament (CND) and **Greenpeace** (founded as a result of anti-nuclear activism). The *Bulletin of the Atomic Scientists*, while not strictly anti-nuclear, has striven since 1945 to educate the public about the dangers of nuclear weapons, with every issue featuring a "doomsday clock" to show how close to "midnight" (nuclear war) the world is at any given point.

With U.S. assistance, Britain and France built small nuclear arsenals during the 1960s. China developed its own in 1964, without help from the increasingly hostile Soviets. Israel secretly gained nuclear weapons during the Cold War, and South Africa briefly had them, but voluntarily decommissioned them. As for the superpowers, because rocket technology was so tightly connected with the manufacture of nuclear missiles, their arms race was closely paralleled by their space race, which became associated with hyperpatriotic pride and military rivalry. The USSR put the first human-made object into space (1957) and launched the first successful human space flight (1961), but the United States accomplished the first moon landing in 1969.

## The Late Stages of the Cold War, 1969–1991

The late stages of the Cold War encompassed the 1970s and the 1980s, with the final collapse of East European and Soviet communism occurring between 1989 and 1991.

Between 1969 and 1979, the conflict entered a more peaceful phase known as **détente** (French for "relaxation"). The USSR was motivated by fears that America would befriend China—which President Richard Nixon visited in 1972, as part of his skillful exploitation of the **Sino-Soviet split**. The United States was wearied by the Vietnam conflict and weakened by the global recession of the 1970s. Both were therefore eager to scale back hostilities. They cooperated in the enforcement of the **Nuclear Non-Proliferation Treaty** (1968–1969) and signed the Cold War's first substantial arms-control agreements, such as the Strategic Arms Limitations Treaty (1972). They even joined forces in space, during the joint Apollo-Soyuz mission of 1975.

Animosity resumed, however, in 1979. That year, the **Soviet invasion of Afghanistan**, whose purpose was to safeguard against Islamic fundamentalism, but which seemed to threaten the oil supplies of the Middle East, damaged Soviet relations with the West. Another point of tension was the **Sandinista revolution in Nicaragua** (1979), which the Soviets supported. Soviet distress at growing unrest in Eastern Europe—especially the 1980 emergence of the dissident trade union **Solidarity** in Poland—made the USSR more edgy in general, and the election of leaders like **Margaret Thatcher** in Britain (1979) and **Ronald Reagan** in the United States (1980) swung NATO foreign policy to the right. Between 1979 and 1985, the arms race accelerated, Third World brushfire wars worsened, and both superpowers expressed mutual contempt by boycotting each other's Olympic Games (Moscow in 1980, Los Angeles in 1984). Because the weaponry of the 1980s was faster, more accurate, and more powerful than before, the dangers of a civilization-destroying nuclear exchange became higher than at any time since the Cuban Missile Crisis.

The Cold War pendulum started swinging the other way in 1985, with the accession of **Mikhail Gorbachev** as leader of the USSR. A liberal reformer, Gorbachev was unwilling to use force to prop up Eastern Europe's communist regimes, and he realized as well that the inefficient Soviet system could no longer afford to keep up with the arms race or continue fighting in Afghanistan, which had turned into a Vietnam-like quagmire for the Red Army. In 1987, Gorbachev resumed arms talks with his U.S. counterparts. His regime allowed Solidarity and other anti-Soviet movements to arise in Eastern Europe, joking that the USSR was replacing the Brezhnev Doctrine with the "Sinatra Doctrine," letting East Europeans do things "their way." The climactic year was 1989. That summer, Poland held free elections for the first time since the Soviet takeover, giving victory to non-communist candidates backed by Solidarity. Other communist regimes collapsed as well, culminating in the **fall of the Berlin Wall** that November and the reunification of Germany in 1990. In the opinion of most, the fall of the Wall marked the end of the Cold War. It also hastened the end of the USSR. With Gorbachev's economic reforms rapidly failing, and with **anti-Soviet nationalism** surging upward among the USSR's non-Russian ethnic minorities, the Soviet Union itself collapsed in late 1991. Only the United States remained as a true superpower.

## Decolonization: General Patterns

**Decolonization** and **national liberation** deserve to be considered briefly on their own, even though specific cases are discussed in the geographical sections that follow.

Between the 1940s and the 1970s, dozens of new nations came into being, having attained freedom from their imperial masters. This represented an astounding shift in the balance of global power away from Europe and toward the rest of the world, although many of the painful legacies of colonization are still felt. Whether a newly liberated nation succeeded in building a healthy political and socioeconomic system depended largely on the following questions:

- Did it have to fight a war to become free, or did it separate peacefully?
- Had the colonizing power educated a native elite that included trained civil servants and professionals? Did the colonizing power assist actively with the transition to freedom, or did it leave the new country on its own?
- Did serious ethnic, cultural, or religious divisions exist? In some places, the colonizing power had kept such tensions under control. Decolonization sometimes released them, leading to violence.
- Did a country have natural resources to exploit, and did the new government exploit them efficiently and fairly? Many new regimes failed to diversify their economies, and others proved corrupt, hoarding profits for the elites and leaving large gaps between rich and poor.
- Did a newly liberated country take sides in the Cold War? Befriending a superpower could attract technological and economic assistance, but it could also involve a new country in a Cold War proxy conflict. It could also mean superpower intervention in a country's policymaking, or the propping-up of an authoritarian or unpopular leader by a superpower "ally."

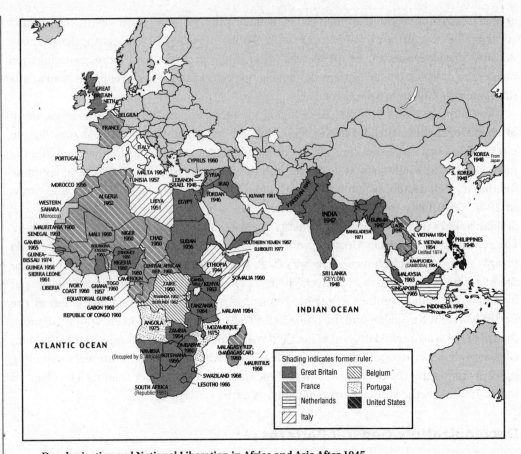

**Decolonization and National Liberation in Africa and Asia After 1945.**
World War II dealt the final blow to Europe's ability to maintain control over colonial empires.
From the 1940s through the 1970s, a great wave of decolonization and national liberation swept
Africa and Asia. Freedom was attained in a variety of ways—sometimes peacefully, sometimes
by force.

In 1955, the **Bandung Conference**, hosted by Indonesia, brought together 29 nations—
most of them recently decolonized—that were interested in staying neutral during the Cold
War and opposing imperialism or neocolonialism of any kind. The conference helped give
birth to the **Non-Aligned Movement** (NAM), which formed in 1961, thanks largely to major
players like Gamal Nasser of Egypt, President Sukarno of Indonesia, India's Jawaharlal
Nehru, and Kwame Nkrumah of Ghana. The NAM eventually came to include 120 states,
although formal cooperation among them was not extensive. Also, many members ended up
aligning with one superpower or another.

## DIVERGENT FORMS OF DOMESTIC DEVELOPMENT, 1945–1991
## Europe

Postwar Europe found itself in a paradoxical situation. On one hand, World War II and global
decolonization ended its global dominance, and the superpowers divided it into a Cold
War battleground. On the other hand, once it repaired its wartime damage, it came to enjoy
unprecedented levels of prosperity and modernization—even in the east, and especially in
the west.

The **sovietization of Eastern Europe** followed quickly after World War II, consisting of the industrialization and nationalization of the economy, the collectivization of agriculture, and the installation of secret police forces and prison camps. Both Eastern Europe and the USSR recovered from the war surprisingly quickly, and the region enjoyed substantial economic growth between the early 1950s and early 1970s. **Social welfare systems** provided education, medical care, pensions, and other basic services to all citizens. However, East European production was characterized by poor quality, and consumer goods were constantly in short supply because of the priority given to the Cold War arms race. Moreover, the environmental damage caused to East European ecosystems by half a century of careless and unregulated industrialization has proven to be nothing short of catastrophic, with the **Chernobyl disaster** of 1986 merely the most famous of countless examples. Politically, the system was maintained by repression. Even though Soviet leader Nikita Khrushchev began **de-Stalinization** with his **"secret speech"** of 1956 (which criticized Stalin's purges), reforms were sporadic and limited, and they were scaled back by Khrushchev's more dictatorial replacement, Leonid Brezhnev. The price of going beyond what the Soviets were willing to allow was demonstrated by the USSR's invasions during the **Hungarian uprising** of 1956 and the **"Prague Spring"** in Czechoslovakia in 1968. In the 1970s, as Western Europe suffered through its own economic crisis, the Soviet bloc entered a steady economic and administrative decline known as the **Brezhnev stagnation**. At the same time, **dissident movements** began to arise throughout the region, but were kept firmly under control for the time being. Only in the 1980s would real change make itself felt.

Recovery was more dramatic in Western Europe, thanks initially to the European Recovery Plan, better known as the **Marshall Plan** (1948). This infusion of more than $13 billion helped to rebuild the war-torn nations of Europe and, by reducing economic desperation, made the spread of communism less likely. Industrial growth and high-tech innovation proved phenomenal during the 1950s and 1960s. With this newfound prosperity, most West European nations put into place **social welfare systems** or improved on the ones created during the interwar era—blending capitalism and elements of socialism in what was frequently referred to as the **"middle"** or **"third way."** At times, this also involved **nationalizing** certain sectors of the economy, typically transport, communications, or utilities.

One way for West Europeans to make up for their loss of global clout was **economic union**, a long process that began with the 1952 birth of the European Coal and Steel Community (Belgium, Luxembourg, the Netherlands, France, and West Germany) and took firm shape in 1957–1958, when the same nations formed the **European Economic Community** (EEC) to eliminate tariffs and allow the freer movement of goods and services. Britain, Ireland, and Denmark joined in 1973, and Greece, Spain, and Portugal were admitted in the 1980s. By the mid-1990s, when the EEC reconstituted itself as the **European Union** (EU), it had 15 members and has even more now. Many members of the EEC/EU also participated in the NATO alliance.

Of course, not all developments were positive. Europe was caught in the crosshairs of the superpowers' nuclear arms race, and **decolonization** was hugely demoralizing, especially when countries fought unsuccessful wars in an attempt to keep their colonies, as France did in Indochina (1945–1954) and Algeria (1954–1962). Generational change, combined with discontent over the Cold War and wars of decolonization, rendered many parts of Europe vulnerable to the global wave of **1968 protests**—with that May's **Paris riots** by students and workers standing alongside the "Prague Spring" as Europe's most famous and most disruptive. Authoritarian rule persisted until after the mid-1970s in countries such as Portugal, Greece, and Spain (where Francisco Franco, dictatorial victor of the Spanish

Civil War, continued to rule). **Terrorism** also arose in the 1960s and 1970s as a persistent problem, sometimes as a manifestation of left-wing extremism (as in Italy's Red Brigades, who kidnapped and killed the prime minister in 1976), sometimes as a strategy pursued by separatist movements (including the Basque ETA, fighting to be rid of Spanish rule, and the **Irish Republican Army**, or IRA, a Catholic paramilitary trying to wrest mostly Protestant Northern Ireland from British rule and unite it with the Republic of Ireland). Thanks to the shock of the U.S. abandonment of the **gold standard** in 1971 and the **OPEC oil embargo** of 1973, Europe suffered the same **global economic crisis of the 1970s** that most of the developed world did, complete with **stagflation** (slow growth combined with inflation). The soaring costs of Europe's social welfare systems became harder to sustain.

To escape the malaise of the 1970s, many West European nations moved economically and politically to the right, with the election of conservatives like **Margaret Thatcher** in Britain and Helmut Kohl in West Germany. Leaders like these pursued **free-market policies**, retreating in part from the social welfare systems of the past, defying labor unions, and **privatizing** many state-run sectors of the economy. Even France's first socialist president, François Mitterand, was compelled to adopt austerity measures of this sort. This approach—paralleled in many ways by Ronald Reagan's in the United States—led to a recovery in terms of overall wealth, but also caused social stress in the form of strikes and layoffs, and its main legacy appears to have been the long-term redistribution of wealth upward from the middle class to the very rich.

Meanwhile, in Eastern Europe, the 1980s led to communism's general collapse. Brezhnev-era stagnation, the rising cost of the arms race (and of the USSR's ill-fated **invasion of Afghanistan**, 1979–1989), the general inefficiency of the system—which led to terrible disasters like the nuclear meltdown at **Chernobyl** in 1986—and the increasingly active **dissident movement** all undermined stability in the Soviet bloc. Unrest was especially apparent in Poland, where the trade union **Solidarity**, led by Lech Walesa, spearheaded a decade-long protest movement that united workers, intellectuals, and Catholic clergy, despite being driven underground after 1981. (Pope **John Paul II**, originally from Poland, did much to support anti-Soviet agitation in Eastern Europe.)

Real change here was impossible until 1985, when **Mikhail Gorbachev**, a younger, reform-minded politician rose to power as the Soviet leader. Keenly aware that the USSR could no longer pay for the Cold War arms race or the maintenance of its East European sphere of influence, Gorbachev launched a twin reform effort: *perestroika* ("restructuring" the economic system and allowing limited capitalism, similar to what Deng Xiaoping was attempting in Communist China) and *glasnost* ("openness," meaning greater freedom of opinion and the media). He ended the war in Afghanistan, entered into arms talks with the United States, and allowed freedom movements, especially Poland's Solidarity, to reemerge in Eastern Europe. As described above, he permitted the **fall of the Berlin Wall** in late 1989, thus helping to end the Cold War. Unfortunately for him, his reforms failed in the USSR—primarily because he did not pursue economic change aggressively enough and because glasnost allowed public discontent to undermine him when things went awry. Also, **anti-Soviet nationalism** spiked among the USSR's non-Russian ethnicities, who wanted the same freedoms that East Europeans had just gained. By 1990 and 1991, Gorbachev found himself isolated between democratizers (who thought he was not changing enough) and communist hard-liners (deeply angry about the limited changes he had already made). He was almost overthrown by a failed coup attempt in the summer of 1991, and then agreed to the disbandment of the USSR that December—ending a long and tumultuous chapter in European history.

**The Fall of the Soviet Union and Formation of the Commonwealth of Independent States, January 1992.**

In late 1991, Mikhail Gorbachev was forced to dissolve the USSR. At that time, leaders of the former republics of the Soviet Union, with the exception of Estonia, Latvia, Lithuania, and Georgia, chose to form the Commonwealth of Independent States as a way to maintain ties and attempt a smooth transition from Soviet rule.

## The Middle East

During the 1950s, Middle Eastern states that were not already free threw off the mandates and protectorates that Europe had established after World War I. (Islamic North Africa decolonized as well.)

Turkey and Iran continued the programs of secularism and modernization that they had begun during the interwar period, and the new state of Israel, founded as a Jewish homeland in 1948, not only did the same but also democratized. As for the region as a whole, developments were dominated by several factors. Foremost was the Middle East's strategic and economic importance as the world's key source of oil: the **Organization of Petroleum Exporting Countries** (OPEC), founded in 1960, consists largely of states from here. Another was the role of **Islamic fundamentalism**, which hindered modernization and democratization, negatively affected the status of women, and increased tensions between Sunni and Shiite Muslims. The seemingly intractable **Arab-Israeli conflict** diplomatically divided the entire region and gave rise to persistent violence and **terrorism**. Domestically, **authoritarian rule** and human rights abuses were prevalent, even in regimes claiming to be democratic.

Independence and oil-based wealth made the states of the Middle East more assertive in the 1950s and 1960s, and their geopolitical importance during the Cold War allowed them to bid for superpower patronage, as the Soviets and Americans competed for their allegiance. The most prominent example of this new Arab nationalism appeared in Egypt, where military officers overthrew the pro-British king in 1952, bringing Colonel **Gamal Nasser** to power in

1954. An authoritarian modernizer, Nasser defied the West by seizing control of foreign-owned industries and businesses, and his boldest step came in 1956 with the **nationalization of the Suez Canal**. This prompted the **Suez Crisis**, in which British, French, and Israeli troops tried to retake the canal, but were forced to withdraw by the United States and USSR—an embarrassing demonstration of how the Cold War had diminished European power. Nasser temporarily strengthened ties with the USSR, whose advisers brought technology and weaponry to Egypt, and also assisted with constructing the monumental **Aswan High Dam**. But when the Soviets became too overbearing in their attempt to control Egyptian politics, Nasser's successors expelled them. Nasser died in 1970. Those ruling after him, Anwar Sadat and Hosni Mubarak, drew closer to the United States and—first among Arab leaders—recognized Israel in 1978. Unfortunately, both men's concerns about rising Islamic fundamentalism persuaded them to continue Nasser's tradition of authoritarian rule.

Certain leaders like Nasser promoted the ideology of pan-Arabism, the notion that Arab identity transcends national boundaries left over from Ottoman and European imperialism, and that Arabs should be united under a single state. Nasser tried to form a "United Arab Republic" with nations like Iraq and Syria, and Muammar Gaddafi of Libya also attempted pan-Arabism, but except in the case of the tiny United Arab Emirates, such schemes have always collapsed. However, many states—currently more than 20—have been joined since 1945 in the Arab League, an influential regional association.

Among the most dramatic developments in the postwar Middle East was the **establishment of the state of Israel** (1948) and the resulting **Arab-Israeli conflict**. The British, who took custody of Palestine after the collapse of Ottoman power there, announced their support for such a plan in the **Balfour Declaration** of 1917 but delayed their decision during the 1920s and 1930s in order to avoid Arab unrest. The horrors of the Holocaust, however, created enough international sympathy for the partition of Palestine to go forward after World War II. When the partition went into effect, Palestinian Arabs refused to comply and, with support from surrounding Arab states, launched a 1948 war to drive the Israelis away. Not only did this fail but it scattered many Palestinians to Jordan, Lebanon, and elsewhere as long-term refugees. Military action on the part of Arab states repeatedly fell short, most notably during the Six-Day War in 1967 and the Yom Kippur War in 1973. Each time, Israel, with superbly trained, highly motivated armed forces and strong backing from the United States, defeated Arab forces, gaining new territories with each conflict. The Palestinians themselves turned to **terrorism**, especially after 1964, when **Yasser Arafat** founded the **Palestinian Liberation Organization** (PLO). PLO attacks increased in frequency; the most infamous was its assassination of Israeli athletes at the Munich Summer Olympics in 1972. Hopes for peace blossomed with the **Camp David accords** of 1978, when Anwar Sadat of Egypt, encouraged by U.S. President Jimmy Carter, agreed to recognize Israel in exchange for the return of the Sinai Peninsula, which Israel had seized in 1967. Other moderate Arab states followed Egypt's lead over the next few years. However, throughout the 1980s, the Palestinian population of Israel staged a continuous uprising called the **(First) Intifada**, protesting what they considered to be apartheid-like discrimination. Not only did intifada demonstrations sometimes result in bloodshed, but the PLO and other terrorist groups—such as the Palestinian radicals in **Hamas** and the Lebanon-based Shiite group Hezbollah—stepped up their attacks. Such violence placed Israel in a difficult position. Despite being a democracy, committed to human rights, Israel felt compelled to use force against civilian agitators in order to avoid a total breakdown of security. The **Oslo accords** of 1993 held out the promise of a **two-state solution**, but foundered in 2000–2001, leading to a **Second Intifada** and continued strife.

The most powerful dictatorships in the Cold War Middle East were those of Iran and Iraq. Since the 1920s, Iran had been ruled by the secular, modernizing Pahlavi shahs. The last of them, **Mohammad Reza Pahlavi**, governed from 1941 to 1979. Like his predecessors, he used oil wealth to industrialize the country, and he opposed Islamic fundamentalism, encouraging Western dress, Western education, the unveiling of women, and the eradication of Sharia law. A staunch U.S. ally, the shah was also ruthlessly authoritarian, relying on torture and secret-police repression to maintain order. Extremely unpopular and in ill health by 1979, he left the country to seek medical treatment and died of cancer in 1980. In the meantime, in 1979, the Shiite cleric **Ayatollah Khomeini**, an Islamic fundamentalist the shah had exiled years before, returned to Iran and took control of the country. This **Iranian Revolution** transformed the country into an anti-Western theocracy in which an elected government came to coexist with authoritarian clerics who held real power and decided ahead of time which candidates could run for office. The new regime stormed the U.S. Embassy, leading to the **Iran hostage crisis** (1979–1981), which damaged American prestige and permanently soured U.S.-Iranian relations. It also became enmeshed in the **Iran-Iraq War** (1980–1988), which caused more than half a million total deaths and devastated both nations. Iraq's ruler at this time was the dictator **Saddam Hussein**, whose Sunni Baath party came to power in 1979. Originally sponsored by the United States because of his opposition to Iran and the USSR, Hussein turned his brutality against his own people and his neighbors. During the Iran-Iraq war, he used poison gas, drafted teenagers for combat, and targeted civilians. He viciously persecuted Iraq's Kurdish minority. In 1990, he also invaded the oil-rich state of Kuwait and appeared ready to move against Saudi Arabia. In the first major conflict of the post-Cold War era, the **Gulf War** (1991), a U.S.-led coalition launched **Operation Desert Storm** to push Hussein out of Kuwait. Between 1991 and Hussein's overthrow in 2003, the international community strove to contain Iraq and prevent its development of weapons of mass destruction.

## Africa

Decolonization began in Africa during the 1950s and 1960s. Transitions to freedom varied wildly, depending on whether the colonial power pulled out peacefully or had to be expelled by force, and also on whether the new state was able to avoid ethnic violence.

The Islamic states of North Africa became free during the 1950s: Egypt and Sudan from Britain, Libya from Italy, and Morocco and Tunisia from France. The **Algerian war of independence** from France (1954–1962) proved agonizingly violent, because the French regarded Algeria as literally part of their country and refused to part with it. Both sides resorted to torture and violence against civilians, and defeat in Algeria led to the fall of the Fourth Republic, which had governed France since the end of World War II. The bloodshed in Algeria notwithstanding, North African states had several advantages over sub-Saharan ones when it came to decolonization. They had existed as meaningful political units before, making the transition to nation-state easier, and they were more homogeneous (although not completely so) in terms of religion, ethnicity, and language. Their colonizing powers also left behind useful industrial, economic, and infrastructural assets.

In sub-Saharan Africa, Britain and, to a lesser extent, France presided over relatively smooth transitions to freedom, training native elites and working to minimize the possibility

**NOTE**

The anti-colonial writer Frantz Fanon who fought for Algerian freedom justified anti-French violence in his 1961 book, *The Wretched of the Earth*, on the grounds that Western imperialism had been inherently brutal and deserved to be opposed by force. His views resembled those of fellow Marxist Che Guevara, a leader of Cuba's revolution, but contrast greatly with those of Gandhi and Martin Luther King, Jr.

of interethnic conflict. The Gold Coast's negotiation of freedom from Britain in 1957, and its transformation into the state of Ghana, was a key success story. The key leader here, **Kwame Nkrumah**, dreamed idealistically of a united Africa, peaceful and prosperous. Unfortunately, such optimism was not justified. All too many decolonization efforts were plagued by violence, much of it against the colonial power. For example, although Jomo Kenyatta pursued nonviolence on the path to Kenyan independence from Britain in 1963, the radical Mau Mau movement killed almost 2,000 people there during the 1950s. Both Angola and Mozambique fought bitter wars of independence from Portugal—a notoriously exploitative imperial master—and both of these struggles (1961–1975 and 1969–1975, respectively) gave way immediately after their conclusion to lengthy civil wars between communist and non-communist forces. In Angola, the U.S.-backed UNITA movement raised more than $3.5 billion for its war effort by selling diamonds, becoming the first to prompt an outcry against the international trade in "conflict diamonds" or "**blood diamonds**." (Diamonds extracted under slavelike conditions in Liberia and Sierra Leone caused even more distress in the 1990s and 2000s.)

Violence or the potential for violence also arose between ethnic groups who fought, or wished to fight, each other once the colonists withdrew (much as Indians and Pakistanis did when Britain left India in 1947). By the time Belgium pulled out of Rwanda in 1962, its divide-and-conquer tactics had artificially exacerbated hatred between two tribes, the **Hutu** and **Tutsi**, and the potential for bloodshed between them simmered. Muslims and Arabs in North Africa suppressed minorities like the desert Berbers and the **Darfurians** of southern Sudan. When Belgium freed the Congo, postindependence violence was so pervasive from 1960 to 1964 that the United Nations had to intervene, and the prime minister, **Patrice Lumumba**, was killed in 1961. A prime example of how new African nations sometimes ended up with "decolonization" problems of their own is the **Biafra secessionist movement**, which began in 1967 as the Igbo people of southeast Nigeria attempted to separate from Nigeria, which had gained its freedom from Britain in 1960. By the time Nigeria reabsorbed Biafra in 1970, over a million people had died in combat or as a result of famine.

White-black tensions persisted longest in **South Africa**, arguably the continent's most unusual state. On one hand the most prosperous, most industrialized, and most technologically advanced country in Africa—and one of the world's richest sources of gold and diamonds—South Africa was also the continent's most deeply racist. In 1948, as an autonomous dominion within the British Commonwealth, South Africa adopted its notorious **apartheid policy**, segregating blacks and "coloureds" (other non-whites, including a sizable Indian minority) and depriving them of the vote. A broad **anti-apartheid movement**—including the Zulu Confederation, the **African National Congress** (ANC), and other groups—arose in the 1950s and called for an end to discrimination in the 1955 Freedom Charter. The killing of almost 70 unarmed protesters during the **Sharpeville massacre** of 1960 further galvanized the movement, and ANC president Albert Luthuli won the Nobel Peace Prize that year. However, the South African government struck back with a series of treason trials, imprisoning leaders like the ANC's **Nelson Mandela**, who remained in jail between 1964 and 1990. In 1961, South African whites voted to withdraw from the British Commonwealth and proclaimed the Republic of South Africa, largely in response to British criticism of their racial policies. Resistance continued, although the ANC and other groups were divided by debates about whether to embrace radicalism and armed struggle or to pursue less violent means.

Major figures included Mandela's spouse Winnie and the Anglican bishop **Desmond Tutu** (another Nobel Peace Prize recipient). Finally, during the 1980s, internal unrest, combined with worldwide revulsion and the threat of economic sanctions and divestment, convinced the white government that apartheid could not be maintained. Nelson Mandela was released in 1990, and the government prepared for free elections—which, in 1994, resulted in ANC victory and Mandela's election as president.

To generalize about postwar Africa is difficult, but it can be said that few nations managed to build democratic regimes, open societies, and equitably prosperous economies. Several key problems hampered modernization efforts in much of Africa during these years:

- **DICTATORSHIP AND CORRUPTION:** Many of Africa's governments degenerated into strongman regimes. Among the most notorious were those of **Joseph Mobutu** in Congo/Zaire (1965–1997) and **Idi Amin**, who ruled Uganda from 1971 to 1979 and killed 300,000 people, many from rival tribes. Dictatorial or not, political elites often milked profits from natural resources like gold, diamonds, and oil for themselves, rather than using them for the betterment of the country. Bribery, nepotism, and tribal favoritism ran rampant.

- **LACK OF CULTURAL AND ETHNOLINGUISTIC UNITY:** Most of Africa's boundary lines were drawn by European colonizers with no regard for tribal or ethnic territorial claims, leaving most African states with a confusing variety of cultures, languages, and religions. This made governance difficult even if groups were not hostile toward each other.

- **ETHNIC VIOLENCE AND CONSTANT ARMED CONFLICT:** Warfare in Africa was near-constant during these years, although most conflicts were fought within national boundaries, not between different countries—a testament to the prevalence of ethnic violence here. Sometimes the Cold War restrained such violence, in places where a strongman supported by one of the superpowers kept order. In other cases, African nations—or rival factions within nations—became pawns in the global chess game between the United States and the USSR. By the end of the Cold War, Africa was awash in the uncontrolled flow of light weapons, and the horrific practice of conscripting thousands of **child soldiers** was well under way.

- **HEALTH-RELATED CRISES:** From the 1980s onward, the **HIV/AIDS** virus, which originated in Africa, has killed millions. Funding for treatment is perennially low, and unprotected sex has caused the virus to spread like wildfire among heterosexual populations as well as homosexual ones. Older diseases like **malaria** and sleeping sickness are still widespread. Moreover, population growth far outstripped economic growth and agricultural production, and **famines** remained common. Among the worst were in Somalia and Ethiopia during the 1980s.

## East Asia

Much like West Germany in Europe, Japan was forced by defeat in World War II to rebuild completely, and therefore emerged as a surprise economic powerhouse. The United States occupied Japan during the 1940s, demilitarizing and democratizing it, although the emperor kept his place on the throne as a symbolic figurehead. Viewing Japan as one of the anchors of its Cold War policy in Asia, America also invested in it heavily and maintained a large military presence on the island of Okinawa. The Japanese Diet, or parliament, came to be dominated by the moderately conservative **Liberal Democratic Party** (LDP), which promoted economic growth by fostering a culture of hard work, discipline, and selfless effort. **Zaibatsu corporations** still played a significant role in Japan. At its peak during the 1980s, Japan's economy—the "**tiger**" of Asia—was the world's third most productive, and its social welfare and educational systems were top-notch. Economic downturn after the early 1990s and a growing spirit of nonconformity among Japanese youth broke the LDP's near-monopoly on power, but even in a weakened state, Japan remains economically important in the post-Cold War era. Joining Japan in prosperity were the so-called "**little tigers**" of Taiwan (home to Chiang Kai-shek's Nationalist regime) and South Korea. Both developed high-tech productive economies, but remained mildly authoritarian until Chiang's death in 1975 and South Korea's liberalization in the 1980s. Both were staunch anti-communist allies of the United States, even after the U.S. government established diplomatic ties with Communist China. Other "little tigers" included Hong Kong (a British colony until its return to mainland China in 1997) and Singapore.

The People's Republic of China (PRC), established in 1949 by **Mao Tse-tung**, has been the most populous communist nation on earth for more than half a century. Appealing to China's vast peasant populace instead of relying solely on proletarian support, Mao easily defeated Chiang Kai-shek after World War II, driving his Nationalist government to Taiwan, which still remains politically separate from the mainland. China was ruled by Mao until his death in 1976. At the start, Mao seemed satisfied with pragmatic social and economic reforms. His New Democracy of the early 1950s was greeted with enthusiasm, as were his initial land reforms. His first Five-Year Plan (1953–1958), which imitated the Soviet model, led to industrial growth. Collectivization of agriculture began in 1955 but was (at first!) carried out more gradually than in Stalin's USSR.

On the other hand, Mao's radical transformation of society, which included persecution of dissenters and so-called class enemies (members of the bourgeoisie or aristocracy), was harsh. Also, at the end of the 1950s, he pressed too quickly for further modernization. In 1958, his **Great Leap Forward** industrialized on a more grandiose scale than the Five-Year Plan, and it intensified the collectivization of agriculture, calling for an unrealistic increase in food production. The stress and confusion caused by the Great Leap Forward led to chaos and breakdown in industry, and agriculture collapsed altogether. The resulting famine killed millions in 1959 and 1960 (the best estimate is 15 to 20 million). Mao halted the Great Leap Forward in 1960, but embarked on another radical program in 1966: the **Great Proletarian Cultural Revolution**, which lasted until 1976. Generally interpreted as a way for Mao and his wife, Jiang Qing, to strike at their political enemies, the Cultural Revolution sought to instill absolute revolutionary purity within Chinese culture. Censorship and indoctrination were crushingly heavy, and young communist activists, known as Red Guards, rampaged through the country, denouncing anyone—professors, managers, journalists, artists—they considered untrue to revolutionary ideals. Victims were harassed, demoted, often sent to labor camps for "reeducation," and sometimes executed. Even members of the communist elite were not immune; among those arrested was Mao's future successor, Deng Xiaoping.

The Cultural Revolution ended with Mao's death in 1976. In 1978, **Deng Xiaoping**, having defeated Mao's widow and her radical allies (the "Gang of Four"), rose to power. Like Mao, Deng was a modernizer, but he was also a pragmatist more concerned with China's well-being than with commitment to abstract Marxist ideals. (He expressed this view in his famous comment that it makes no difference whether a cat is black or white, as long as it catches mice.) In contrast to Mao's strict anti-capitalism, **Deng's economic reforms** returned a measure of collectivized land to the farmers and allowed limited capitalism—

much like Gorbachev's program of perestroika in the USSR, but faster and more permissive. Deng allowed certain levels of private trade and created **special economic zones** where communist regulations did not apply. As a result, China experienced huge economic growth throughout the 1980s, including rising wages and an improved standard of living, and this trend has continued ever since. However, with greater prosperity came the desire for greater freedom, a luxury Deng was not prepared to allow. Unlike his fellow reformer Gorbachev, whose glasnost policy ended censorship and allowed more democracy in the USSR, Deng maintained authoritarian control. The clearest sign of this came in May 1989, when Chinese students gathered at **Tiananmen Square** in Beijing, demanding political freedoms to match their newfound economic ones. Deng refused to grant any concessions and, when the students disobeyed orders to disperse, he crushed the demonstrations by sending in tanks. To this day, China's communist authorities have pursued this same combination of political strictness and economic liberalization.

## South and Southeast Asia

As in Africa, decolonization in these parts of Asia proceeded along two lines: in some cases it was negotiated peacefully, in others it was achieved by means of armed struggle.

Examples of the former approach include **the Philippines**, which had been promised independence by the United States during World War II and received it in 1946. Even more noteworthy was the separation from Britain that led in 1947 to **independence for India and Pakistan**, although bloodshed quickly followed in freedom's wake. During World War II, national-liberationist pressures from the **Indian National Congress** (the party of **Mohandas Gandhi** and **Jawaharlal Nehru**) and the **All-India Muslim League** (led by **Muhammad Ali Jinnah**) made it obvious that the British could no longer hold on to India. Riots and violent clashes between Muslims and Hindus sped up the British timetable for withdrawal, and independence was granted in August 1947. Unfortunately, even though the British did not have to be expelled by force, Hindu-Muslim conflict over the terms of **Indo-Pakistani partition** cost at least a million lives over the next months, created numerous refugees, and resulted in the assassination of Gandhi in 1948—ironically, by a Hindu extremist who opposed his rhetoric of toleration between the two faiths.

Despite their difficult beginnings, both nations survived. Under Jinnah and his successors, Pakistan became a modern Islamic republic and a major regional power. However, it became mired in corruption and military authoritarianism during the Cold War, and it has spent decades locked in a costly and dangerous rivalry with India. (Occasional border wars have broken out over the Kashmir frontier zone, and the development of nuclear-weapons capability by both nations has made this conflict even tenser.) Unlike India, Pakistan decisively chose sides during the Cold War, pursuing a firm alliance with the United States.

As for India, it transformed itself into the world's largest democracy, but also suffered administrative inefficiency, great difficulty in balancing economic growth with population growth, and interethnic and interfaith strife. The dominant political force in free India was the Congress Party, led by **Jawaharlal Nehru**, who served as India's prime minister from 1947 until his death in 1964. Unlike Gandhi, who had favored traditional values and economic simplicity, Nehru worked to secularize, modernize, and industrialize India. Diplomatically, he negotiated a tightrope: neighbor to a hostile China and an even more hostile Pakistan, but not wishing to be a client of the Soviets, the British, or the Americans, Nehru maintained a friendly relationship with the USSR without actually falling into the Soviet camp. Like Nasser in Egypt, Nkrumah in Ghana, and Sukarno in Indonesia, Nehru was a leading figure in the **Non-Aligned Movement**. From 1966 to 1975 and again from 1977 to 1984, Nehru's daughter, **Indira Gandhi**, was prime minister. She continued her father's policies of modernization and diplomatic nonalignment. Religious strife was her downfall: her government's actions against the Sikh minority of Punjab provoked Sikh soldiers to assassinate her. From 1984 to 1991, her son, Rajiv Gandhi, served as prime minister, but he was killed by Sri Lankan separatists. After freeing India, Britain let go of its other colonies in the region. Burma became independent in 1948, Malyasia in 1957, and Singapore in 1965.

Elsewhere, it took violence to end European rule. In the Dutch East Indies, the charismatic leader of the Indonesian Nationalist Party, **Sukarno**, began a war of nationalist liberation in 1945 and, with the Dutch gone, founded the new nation of Indonesia. Although 80 percent Muslim—giving it the world's largest Islamic population—Indonesia is a sprawling archipelago consisting of 18,000 islands, and its bewildering ethnic and linguistic diversity makes it challenging to govern. At first, Sukarno governed democratically, but he grew authoritarian over time. He helped to establish the **Non-Aligned Movement** by hosting the **Bandung Conference** of 1955, and went much farther than Nehru in India or even Nasser in Egypt in calling for the Third World to defy the West. He drew closer to the Indonesian Communist Party until 1965, when the army, allied with conservative Muslims, staged a coup against him that killed as many as half a million people—mainly communists—and forced Sukarno's resignation in 1967. From then until 1998, Indonesia was governed by the military strongman **Suharto**, an anti-communist dictator who promoted economic growth and alliance with the United States, but who also compiled a record of frequent human-rights abuses.

Violence proved even more devastating in **Indochina**, the French colony composed of Vietnam, Laos, and Cambodia. Having lost Indochina to Japanese occupation during World War II, the French hoped to reimpose their authority in 1945, but they were foiled by the national-liberation war launched that September by the Vietnamese communist **Ho Chi Minh**. The French, with U.S. support, tried until 1954 to keep Indochina, but were defeated by Vietnamese expertise in guerrilla warfare and the relative popularity of Ho Chi Minh's policies, which included land reform and appeals to anti-French nationalism. Laos and Cambodia went free in 1953, and Vietnam was temporarily divided into a northern communist zone and a southern non-communist zone.

**NOTE**

In Cambodia during the 1970s, the ultra-radical Khmer Rouge, under Pol Pot, combined Marxism with an ideology of racial superiority and a bizarre notion that "corrupt" city dwellers should be relocated to the countryside. Before Pol Pot was driven from power in 1979, famine and genocide killed approximately two million Cambodians.

Vietnam's two halves were to be united under a single government, chosen by free election as soon as possible. However, Ngo Dinh Diem—the French-educated, Catholic, U.S.-backed leader of South Vietnam—kept delaying the election, fearing that the Buddhist, anti-French peasant masses would vote against him. Tensions and sporadic violence rose steadily, with actual war breaking out by 1959. Throughout the 1960s, the United States, following the **domino-principle** logic of the Cold War, stepped up its military support for South Vietnam, paying insufficient attention to the unpopularity of the regime and of the war effort in general. (One of the clearest signs of opposition to Diem came in 1963, when the Buddhist monk Thich Quang Duc publicly committed suicide by **self-immolation**, or burning himself to death publicly in the capital.) By the end of the decade, anti-war opposition was mounting in the United States and elsewhere and played a significant role in the global wave of **1968 protests**. In 1968, the communists caught the Americans and South Vietnamese badly off guard with their Tet Offensive, and although U.S.

forces withstood that blow, war-weariness caused America to scale back its war effort and withdraw completely in 1973. Communist victory over the entirety of Vietnam followed in April 1975. The severity of communist rule tempered somewhat during the 1980s, especially with the implementation of the **doi moi** ("renovation") **reforms** of 1986, which allowed for limited capitalism along the lines of Deng Xiaoping's reforms in China.

As in other parts of the world, regional associations formed in Southeast Asia. Between 1955 and 1977, Western powers like the United States, Britain, and France allied with Australia, New Zealand, Pakistan, Thailand, and the Philippines in the Southeast Asian Treaty Organization (SEATO), meant as a counterpart to NATO, but in fact much weaker. More important was the **Association of Southeast Asian Nations** (ASEAN), founded in 1967 by Indonesia, Malaysia, Singapore, Thailand, and the Philippines to boost economic and security cooperation. It has since expanded to include other members, including Vietnam.

## The Americas

Despite some temporary progress toward economic modernization and democratization in the late 1940s and early 1950s, many Latin American nations reverted to exploitative economies and dictatorial government from the late 1950s through the early 1980s. By the mid-1970s, only a tiny handful of countries in the region could be considered democratic. During this entire period, the **Organization of American States** (OAS), founded in 1948 and headquartered in Washington, D.C., fostered economic and diplomatic cooperation throughout the region— although cynics were inclined to see it as a tool for enforcing the **U.S. sphere of influence** in the western hemisphere.

Military governments and right-wing dictatorships predominated. Because of their anti-communism, many of these regimes were Cold War allies of the United States, despite their human-rights abuses and their tendency to gear their economies for the benefit of the elite instead of tending to the needs of the population at large. Indigenous natives—Indians, Mayans, Amazon tribes, and so on—were often badly treated. Some selected examples of Latin American governance follow:

> **TIP**
>
> Domestic politics in Canada and the United States will not receive much attention on the AP exam. Focus instead on socioeconomic and cultural issues, including anti-war agitation and the 1968 protests. Note that terrorism played a role in North American politics as well. U.S. radicals like the Weather Underground and the Black Panthers resorted to violence in their opposition to the Vietnam War. In Canada, the separatist group FLQ (Front de libération du Québéc) carried out more than a hundred bombings between 1963 and 1970 in a failed attempt to detach Quebec from Canada.

- **ARGENTINA:** Military rule was established here during World War II. In 1946, the charismatic officer **Juan Perón** came to dominate the government by appealing to the poor. In this, he was aided by his wife, **Eva Perón**, who enjoyed enormous appeal among the lower-class *descamisados* ("shirtless ones"). His modernization program of the 1950s borrowed heavily from Mussolini's brand of fascism and state capitalism. Overthrown by his army in 1955, Perón fled to Spain but returned in 1973, serving as president until his death in 1974. A brutal military regime, calling itself the National Reorganization Process, ruled from 1976 to 1983, ruthlessly purging leftists and dissidents in the "**dirty war**" and causing the deaths of perhaps 30,000, including numerous *desaparecidos*, or "disappeared ones," who were secretly arrested and never seen again.
- **CHILE:** Here, in 1973, General **Augusto Pinochet**—backed by the U.S. Central Intelligence Agency (CIA)—led a coup against Salvador Allende, a Marxist who had been democratically elected in 1970. Like Argentina's military rulers, he arrested thousands

of leftists and suspected opponents, torturing 30,000 and killing or "disappearing" over 3,000. Economically, he instituted a **free-market reform** program (similar to Ronald Reagan's in the United States and Margaret Thatcher's in Britain), on the advice of economists known as the "**Chicago boys**," because of the influence exercised over them by **Milton Friedman** of the University of Chicago. Pinochet stepped down in favor of a democratically elected government in 1990. He left the country but was later arrested; he was on trial for human-rights abuses and corruption when he died in 2006.

- **GUATEMALA:** In 1954, nearly a decade of democratically elected reformist rule came to an end with a CIA-supported coup that brought the general Carlos Castillo Armas to power. A succession of military dictators followed until the mid-1990s, each of them suppressing leftist rebels and ethnic minorities with brute force. In particular, the regime perpetrated an **anti-Mayan genocide** in the 1980s.

- **MEXICO:** An example of mild authoritarian oligarchy, as opposed to extreme dictatorship, Mexico maintained a nominally democratic system that ensured an unbroken string of electoral victories for the paradoxically named **Institutional Revolutionary Party** (PRI). Oil-based wealth during the 1950s and most of the 1960s kept the economy healthy and the population reasonably satisfied. However, by the late 1960s and 1970s, economic downturn, growing awareness of the government's corruption, and anger among Indians and Mayans because of popular and official prejudice all increased general discontent with the regime's less than democratic nature. Mexico City was hit hard by the global wave of **1968 protests**, and emigration to the United States, both legal and illegal, accelerated in the 1970s and 1980s. The PRI regime gradually reformed during the 1980s and 1990s.

Dictatorship also arose as a result of the **Cuban Revolution**, but this time it came from the left. In January 1959, a guerrilla force led by **Fidel Castro** ousted the right-wing dictator Fulgencio Batista. Even the United States was happy to see Batista gone, and Castro initially governed as a non-aligned modernizer, nationalizing industrial sectors of the economy, carrying out land reforms, and combating illiteracy and socioeconomic inequality. But he also regarded the U.S. sphere of influence in Latin America as "yankee imperialism," and under the influence of his Marxist second-in-command, the Argentine doctor and intellectual **Ernesto "Che" Guevara**, Castro declared himself a communist and turned to the USSR for assistance. Because of its proximity to the United States, Cuba's decision to align with the Soviets made it a Cold War hot spot from 1961 onward, as demonstrated by moments like the **Cuban Missile Crisis** of 1962. Cuban troops also supported communist movements throughout Latin America—increasing U.S. anxiety about any sort of leftist activism in the region—and took active part in Cold War brushfire conflicts in Africa. Domestically, the Castro regime's record is mixed. Cuba undeniably modernized and narrowed the gap between rich and poor. However, the government became rigidly dictatorial under Castro, restricting civil liberties and committing human-rights abuses of its own.

Stirring up further Cold War anxieties was the **Nicaraguan Revolution** of 1979, when the Marxist **Sandinista movement** overthrew the Somoza clan that had ruled as right-wing dictators since the mid-1930s. Professing commitment to social democracy instead of dictatorship, the Sandinista regime began with a program of land reform and redistribution of wealth but was quickly distracted by Cold War geopolitics. Nicaragua's new friendliness with the USSR unnerved President Ronald Reagan in the United States, whose détente with the Soviets had just ended over the latter's invasion of Afghanistan. Against the wishes of the

U.S. Congress, Reagan's administration attempted to destabilize the Sandinistas by illegally funding right-wing counterrevolutionary guerrillas known as **the Contras**. This bloody civil conflict persisted until the end of the Cold War.

A wave of **Latin American democratization** occurred in the late 1980s and early 1990s. Much of this was tied to economic improvements, but just as much was due to the cooling down of the Cold War, which reduced the superpowers' anxiety about influence in the region. Pinochet gave up power in 1989–1990, Argentina moved from dictatorship to democracy between 1983 and 1989, and Mexico's PRI loosened its monopoly on power, beginning with the national elections of 1988. Peace and democracy returned to Nicaragua in 1990; an anti-Sandinista candidate, Violeta Chamorro, was elected as the country's first female president, but the Sandinistas have since returned to power via the ballot box. This transition, of course, was not complete. The Castro dictatorship retained power in Cuba, while corruption, resurgent authoritarianism, and dependence on illegal **drug trafficking** have continued elsewhere.

## GLOBALISM IN THE 1990s AND 2000s

In 1990, U.S. President George H. W. Bush proclaimed confidently that the collapse of the Cold War was bringing about a "**new world order**," characterized by greater peacefulness and the foreseeable triumph of democratic capitalism worldwide. The end of the nuclear arms race indeed lowered the risk of nuclear annihilation, and new freedoms improved lives in many parts of the world. However, the superpower conflict had been a predictable diplomatic framework, and it had also kept in check various ethnic and religious tensions around the globe. It soon became clear that the geopolitics of the post-Cold War era would be far more complex than many had expected. As early as 1993, the CIA director pointed out that "we have slain a large dragon, but we now live in a jungle filled with a bewildering variety of poisonous snakes."

One key issue is that **U.S. unilateralism** as the world's remaining superpower has turned out to be limited, not just by the finiteness of its resources, but also by the "**cold peace**" that has arisen between it and former Cold War foes like Russia and China. The former, weakened during the 1990s by **Boris Yeltsin**'s chaotic mishandling of Eastern Europe's "**shock therapy**" transition to democratic capitalism, has entered a more belligerent phase under the "managed democracy" of the authoritarian, nationalistic **Vladimir Putin**. No longer a superpower, Russia has nonetheless regained much of its strength since 2000. It has sought not only to reassert its sphere of influence in the former Soviet Union—as illustrated by the **Chechen wars** of the 1990s and early 2000s—but also to deliberately counter American geopolitical ambitions. As for China, its rise to superpower status seems all but inevitable, an impression it conveyed with its grandiose hosting of the **2008 Beijing Olympics**. With the world's largest population and a huge economy enjoying thunderous growth, China is already in a position to assert military power regionally and will soon be able to do so Pacific-wide, if not globally. Its influence on international trade and finance is already titanic. Key questions related to China are whether its authoritarian communist regime can muster the right combination of strength and flexibility to maintain order in a large, diverse country undergoing the stresses of rapid growth, and whether China will flex its military and diplomatic muscles peacefully or aggressively. China's reabsorption of **Hong Kong** in 1997 (when Britain's colonial lease expired by treaty) went smoothly, but its abuses in **Tibet** are well-documented, and how long it will continue to tolerate the independence of **Taiwan**—which it regards as a renegade province, not an independent nation—remains a matter of grave concern.

Another fact of the present day is that the very nature of war has changed. Thanks to trends that emerged during the Cold War but gained real traction in the 1990s and 2000s, the gap between high-tech forces and low-level military capability has grown wider than ever before. Only a very few states possess meaningful stockpiles of **weapons of mass destruction** (nuclear, biological, and chemical weapons.) The entire post-World War II period has witnessed many **asymmetrical wars**, in which jet aircraft, third-generation tanks, helicopter gunships, aircraft carriers, and global airlift capacity—owned only by the superpowers and the small group of other nations able to afford them—have been pitted against the small arms (assault rifles, grenade launchers, hand-to-hand weapons) that are all most armies and paramilitary groups can afford. After the Cold War, however, computer technology opened this gap even further: during the 1990s and early 2000s, the United States and a handful of other nations underwent the so-called "**revolution in military affairs**," or the full integration of computer technology, satellite communications, and precision-guided ("smart") weapons into military operations. Technological superiority carries with it many advantages, especially in straight-up conventional combat, but it is no guarantee of success (as demonstrated to the superpowers during the Vietnam War and the Soviet invasion of Afghanistan). In particular, **low-intensity** ("brushfire") **conflict** and **guerrilla insurgency** have offered, and continue to offer, many ways for weaker, more poorly equipped forces to frustrate larger, high-tech armies.

Adding further to military instability in the post-Cold War era is the weakening of restraints on the capacity for destruction on a large scale. Of greatest concern is access to **weapons of mass destruction**. Although Russia and the United States have significantly reduced their nuclear arsenals, concern about "**loose nukes**" (actual warheads or weapons-grade radioactive material) disappearing from the former USSR and ending up in the wrong hands has been a persistent worry. Despite the overall success and longevity of the **Nuclear Non-Proliferation Treaty** (1968–1969), **nuclear proliferation** expanded during the 1990s and 2000s, and threatens to worsen in the near future. Moreover, **biological** and **chemical weapons** (infectious pathogens like Ebola and anthrax, gases, toxins, and so on) have become easier to manufacture and weaponize—not just for national governments, but potentially for non-state actors as well—making such weapons much harder to monitor or control. As described below, **terrorism** has remained central to geopolitics in the post-Cold War era and has achieved new levels of destructiveness, as illustrated most infamously by the **al-Qaeda attacks on September 11, 2001**, masterminded by **Osama bin Laden**. At the same time, **genocide** has on many occasions in the 1990s and 2000s proven distressingly easy for even small, crudely armed parties to commit—most notoriously in **Rwanda** and **the former Yugoslavia**, but also elsewhere.

According to the Nuclear Non-Proliferation Treaty, the only legal members of the "nuclear club" are the United States, Russia, China, France, and Britain. Since the late 1960s, Israel has maintained an undeclared nuclear arsenal, and in 1998, India and Pakistan each gained nuclear-weapons capability, making their bitter rivalry more dangerous. Even more disturbing are the successful testing of nuclear weapons by North Korea, from 2006 onward, and Iran's ongoing efforts to build nuclear weapons—a development that would severely destabilize the Middle East.

Looking more broadly at the unpredictable post-Cold War period, it can be seen that centripetal and centrifugal forces have both been acting on the nations of the world, simultaneously keeping them together and pulling them apart. A central question, then, is whether **global integration** has predominated over **global fragmentation**, or vice versa. One trend that has encouraged the former is the expansion and seemingly growing importance of **international organizations** and **regional associations**, both existing and new. The **United Nations**, the **World Trade Organization** (WTO; formed in 1994 from the General Agreement on Trade and Tariffs (GATT) system, and the **International Criminal Court** (ICC, signed into being in 1998 and operating in The Hague since 2002 to prosecute genocide and other crimes against humanity) foster international cooperation and dispute resolution. The **European Union**, which formed in the 1990s as a way for the nations of the European Economic Community to coordinate their economic and policymaking efforts even more closely, expanded immensely after the collapse of East European communism, and most of its states adopted the **euro** as a common currency in 2002. On the other hand, the strength and effectiveness of such organizations is not always evident. Although it has been far more capable than the League of Nations was during the interwar period, the United Nations has often shown impotence and indecision in the face of conflicts and humanitarian crises. Over 150 nations have signed the ICC charter, but not all have ratified it, and major nations like Russia, China, Israel, and the United States have chosen not to fully recognize its authority. How effective the WTO will be in regulating trade in times of crisis remains to be seen.

Likewise, a region-by-region glance makes it difficult to guess whether integration or fragmentation will prevail as the century progresses. Europe's **transition from communism**, for instance, has met with mixed results. The "**shock therapy**" method of moving as quickly as possible to free-market capitalism proved painful even where it worked well (as in East Germany, Poland, the Czech Republic, and the Baltic states) and was disastrous in places like Russia, which suffered hyperinflation and the sudden collapse of once-reliable social welfare systems. The sudden rush of East European nations to join **NATO** (now up to 28 members) and the **EU** (27 members at present, with more hoping to join) deeply angered a Russia that was already smarting from the loss of its superpower status. **Ethnic tensions** in Europe have heightened, even in the most democratic states. **Anti-immigrant sentiment** has been directed at Turkish **guest workers** and other Muslim communities (especially those attempting to retain traditions like Sharia law or the veiling of women), and **anti-Roma** (Gypsy) **prejudice** remains widespread throughout Eastern Europe.

The most terrible manifestations of ethnic violence in Europe came during the **Yugoslav wars** (1991–1995, 1998–1999), when South Slavic tensions, kept under control by the authoritarian Titoist regime, broke loose after the collapse of communism. As the various states that made up the Yugoslav federation declared independence, opportunistic politicians, especially **Slobodan Milosevic** of Serbia—which controlled most of the former Yugoslavia's armed forces—exploited nationalist tensions to seize territory from Croatia and the multiethnic state of Bosnia, home to Orthodox Serbs, Catholic Croats, and Muslim Bosniaks: all Slavs, but now bitterly divided. Serbian forces and Bosnian Serb paramilitaries committed mass rape, massacred civilians (most infamously at Srebrenica, where more than 8,000 Bosniaks were killed in 1995), besieged and shelled the Bosnian capital of Sarajevo for over three years, and carried out forced deportations euphemistically called "**ethnic cleansings**." At least 100,000 were killed, and two million more made refugees, before the UN and NATO overcame their indecisive caution and intervened to impose the **Dayton Accords** in late 1995. Another round of fighting followed in 1998–1999, as Serbia attempted to remove ethnic Albanians from the province of Kosovo, requiring a NATO bombardment of Serbia to end the hostilities.

Latin America has generally stayed on track, although economic inequalities remain in many states, and **illegal drug trafficking** in places like Colombia and the Mexican border can cause enough violence to prove politically destabilizing. Strongman authoritarianism reemerged in certain countries—most notably in oil-rich Venezuela, under the bombastic socialist **Hugo Chávez**, who ruled from 1999 to 2013 by building solid support among the poorer masses, but also by tightly controlling electoral politics and the mass media. Chávez's Venezuela can be seen as part of a "**pink wave**" bloc that includes Nicaragua, Ecuador, and Bolivia, all of which oppose what they see as U.S. imperialism, and support Cuba, which remains communist under the Castro regime.

In Asia, the economic dynamism and high-tech innovation found in places like China, Singapore, and parts of India (such as Bangalore, the Silicon Valley of South Asia) contrasts with the geopolitical perils posed by ongoing Indo-Pakistani border skirmishes, the perpetual instability of Afghanistan, the possibility of clashes between Communist China and Taiwan or Japan, and the increasingly erratic bellicosity of a nuclear-armed North Korea.

Stability has proven even more elusive in Africa. Some areas have made headway with respect to socioeconomic development and open politics, and the **truth and reconciliation process** in South Africa healed a measure of the race-relations damage caused by decades of apartheid. Unfortunately, religious and ethnic differences, combined with competition over resources like oil, gold, and diamonds, have ensured that civil war, mass killings, and the recruitment of **child soldiers** remain depressingly common. In 1994, the **Rwandan genocide** resulted in the deaths of 800,000 members of the **Tutsi** minority at the hands of their **Hutu** rivals. Hatred between the two groups had been fostered by Rwanda's Belgian colonizers but had been kept mainly in check since 1972 by the dictator Juvénal Habyarimana, whose sudden death helped make the genocide possible. Between 1996 and 2003, the **First and Second Congo Wars**, sparked by the crumbling of **Joseph Mobutu**'s repressive regime in Zaire/Congo, sucked nine Central African nations into combat and killed more than five million, if one counts deaths by famine and disease, and the casualties caused by the war's long and violent aftermath. Since 2003, Sudan's persecution of the non-Arab **Darfur minority** in its western provinces has killed more than half a million people and created almost three million refugees.

Most volatile of all has been the Middle East, combined with Islamic North Africa. The **Arab-Israeli conflict** has ebbed and flowed since the end of the Cold War. In 1993, **Yasser Arafat** of the **PLO** signed peace accords with Israel's Yitzhak Rabin, ending the **First Intifada** and creating a Palestinian National Authority as a first step toward a **two-state solution**. U.S. mediation helped preserve a fragile truce until 2000–2001, when extremists on both sides sabotaged negotiations and triggered a **Second Intifada**. Arafat died in 2004, and Rabin was assassinated by an Israeli opponent of the peace process. Since then, Arab and Israeli moderates alike, including the Palestinians' **Fatah** leadership, have struggled with Palestinian terrorists like **Hamas** (which uses violence deliberately to disrupt the peace process), Israeli policymakers who have used Palestinian terror as the pretext to quarantine ordinary Palestinians in apartheid-like conditions (further inflaming Palestinian opinion against Israel), and Israeli religious fundamentalists determined to build **illegal settlements** on Palestinian land (which they regard as the Jews' biblical inheritance).

**Desert Storm**, the U.S.-led response to **Saddam Hussein**'s 1990 invasion of Kuwait, brought war to Iraq in 1991, and then, for the next 12 years, put the United Nations and the West in the position of having to monitor the possibility that Hussein might be amassing a large store of **weapons of mass destruction**. When **Osama bin Laden** and the **al-Qaeda** terrorist group carried out the **September 11, 2001, bombings** against the United States, President George W. Bush used the attacks as the occasion to extend his "**war on**

**terror**" not just against Afghanistan (whose Taliban government, made up of rigid Islamic fundamentalists, had provided al-Qaeda with safe haven) but also against Iraq, which in fact had not been at all involved in the al-Qaeda assault. The American war against Afghanistan began in 2001 and is scheduled for completion in 2014, although Osama bin Laden was killed there in 2011. The war in Iraq began in 2003 and immediately deposed Saddam Hussein (who was captured and killed in 2006), but it plunged the country into political anarchy, and U.S. forces were not able to withdraw until 2011.

Adding recent drama to Middle Eastern affairs are the ongoing **Iranian nuclear effort**, which has not yet yielded a weapon but may well do so in the near future, and the so-called **Arab Spring**, which began in December 2010. The latter politically transformed the region by deposing a number of longtime authoritarian regimes, starting with the Tunisian monarchy and continuing with the strongman government of Hosni Mubarak in Egypt and the dictatorship of Muammar Gaddafi in Libya. The terrible civil war in Syria, between dictator Bashar al-Assad and various rebel forces, began in 2011 as part of this trend. Although it is tempting to view the Arab Spring as a triumph of "people power" against oppression, it remains to be seen whether the outcome will be true democracy, further instability, or the triumph of radical Islamic fundamentalism.

# Culture, Science, and Technology, 1900 to Present

# 24

→ THE MODERN AND POSTMODERN PERIODS

→ HIGH CULTURE VS. MASS (POPULAR) CULTURE

→ UNCERTAINTY AND ANXIETY IN WESTERN HIGH ART (FREUDIAN THOUGHT)

→ EXISTENTIALISM

→ ADAPTATION OF WESTERN HIGH CULTURE (NÉGRITUDE)

→ MASS MEDIA AS HIGH CULTURE

→ MASS MEDIA AS ENTERTAINMENT PROPAGANDA

→ AMERICANIZATION AND WESTERNIZATION OF GLOBAL CULTURE ("COCA-COLONIZATION")

→ MULTICULTURALISM (MARSHALL MCLUHAN'S "GLOBAL VILLAGE," BOLLYWOOD, REGGAE)

→ SYNTHETIC FORMS OF SPIRITUALITY

→ RELIGION AND MODERN POLITICS (RELIGIOUS FUNDAMENTALISM, LIBERATION THEOLOGY)

→ THEORETICAL PHYSICS (ALBERT EINSTEIN, QUANTUM PHYSICS)

→ AVIATION, ROCKETRY, SPACE FLIGHT

→ MEDICAL ADVANCES (POLIO VACCINE, ANTIBIOTICS) AND GENETICS (DNA)

→ COMPUTERS AND THE INFORMATION (DIGITAL) REVOLUTION

The hallmarks of twentieth and twenty-first century thought and culture have been rapid change and incredible diversity. After World War II, high art in the West began its transition from the **modern period** (considered in cultural and intellectual terms to have lasted roughly from the 1870s through the 1940s) to the **contemporary era**, also referred to as the **postmodern era**.

Other major trends, both in the West and beyond, have included **multiculturalism**—the interaction and fusion of the world's various ethnic, artistic, and intellectual traditions—and the effect of **mass media technology** on culture and the arts. Scientific and technological advancement has proceeded at a breathtaking pace and scale. The **information** (or **digital**) **revolution** caused by the computer has vastly altered life in the 1990s and beyond.

## HIGH ART AND CULTURE

High art in the West during this era was characterized by bold experimentation and the distortion, even abandonment, of traditional norms and conventions.

During the first half of the 1900s, Western art tended to be marked by uncertainty and pessimism. Even before World War I, the prevailing faith in progress that had characterized Europe's cultural life during much of the 1800s had been waning (see Chapter 18). Despair caused by World War I brought an even greater sense of anxiety to the cultural forefront. Eloquent accounts of the wartime experience can be found in literary works such as Erich Maria Remarque's novel *All Quiet on the Western Front*, which describes the dehumanizing effects of trench warfare, and the verses of Britain's "war poets" (Siegfried Sassoon, Robert Owen, and others), who questioned traditional patriotism as an adequate justification for the mindless butchery caused by the war. The avant-garde artists of the **Dada movement**, which exhibited in Europe and New York during the war, used shock and absurdism, both to push the boundaries of what should be considered "art" and to highlight the irrationality of World War I, which they opposed. The best-known Dadaist artwork is "Fountain": the bowl of a urinal irreverently turned into a sculpture by Frenchman Marcel Duchamp.

**NOTE**

Alternative literary approaches to World War I included satire (Czech author Jaroslav Hasek's novel *The Good Soldier Svejk*), sentimentality (the poem "In Flanders Fields," by Canadian doctor John McCrae, commemorating soldiers killed by poison gas), and, in a sharp contrast to anti-war works like *All Quiet on the Western Front*, patriotic adventurism (*Storm of Steel* by Germany's Ernst Jünger, who saw World War I as a grand cause and an ennobling experience).

Gloom deepened during the interwar period, due to Europe's political and economic comedown and the unsettling philosophical implications of recent scientific insights, including the theory of relativity, quantum physics, and most of all, the psychological theories of **Sigmund Freud**—all of which called into question whether anything was fully knowable, or whether any objective truths or standards existed. The bestselling nonfiction book in interwar Europe was the philosopher Oswald Spengler's *The Decline of the West*. The prose and poetry of T. S. Eliot and Franz Kafka dealt with dehumanization in an industrialized, bureaucratized era. Experiments with **stream-of-consciousness prose** by Virginia Woolf, Marcel Proust, and James Joyce attempted to capture, almost in Freudian style, the workings of the human mind on the written page. **Abstract painters**, such as Pablo Picasso, distorted reality to demonstrate that things could be seen from a variety of perspectives. **Surrealists** like Salvador Dalí and others placed realistic objects in unrealistic situations to confuse the viewer's sense of reality.

After World War II, the philosophical and literary school of **existentialism** rose to prominence, although it had existed since the interwar years. Championed now by the Irish playwright Samuel Beckett and the French philosophers Albert Camus and Jean-Paul Sartre, existentialists proposed that humanity was not guided by any deity, special destiny, or objective morality. Alone in the universe, the individual must learn to create a worthwhile, ethical existence for himself or herself without the benefit of religion or the hope of any life beyond the earthly one. At the same time, Western culture entered the **postmodern era**, which has been characterized by even more unpredictability, relativism, and unconventionality than before. The notion of an artistic and literary canon—a universally agreed-upon body of "great" works—has been called into doubt by postmodern thinking, in keeping with its rejection of the notion that objective truth exists.

In the non-Western world, the twentieth and twenty-first centuries have seen artistic and literary traditions achieve a status equal to those of the West. In addition to maintaining their own styles, non-Western authors and artists have adopted Western forms of writing, painting, and composing—often modifying them with elements from their own culture.

Prior to World War II, the Indian poet Rabindranath Tagore, the first non-Westerner to win the Nobel prize for literature, dazzled readers worldwide with lyrical verses inspired by Hindu mysticism. China's Lu Xun (Hsun) wrote hard-hitting stories about his country's economic domination by outside powers, and also the government's lack of concern for lower-class commoners. Starting in the 1930s, the **Négritude movement**, inspired by the African-American poets of the Harlem Renaissance and the Marxism percolating in interwar Paris, united African and Caribbean writers from French colonies in their opposition to European imperialism, and in their pride in being black. The Mexican artist **Diego Rivera** created powerful murals expressing the plight of the working poor, as well as that of Mayans and other indigenous peoples. His wife, the painter **Frida Kahlo**, remains famous in her own right for her feminist themes and her bold use of color.

**Frida Kahlo (1907–1954) and Diego Rivera (1886–1957)**
Married, briefly divorced, and married again, Frida Kahlo and Diego Rivera remain Mexico's best-known painters. *The Two Fridas* (1939) shows Kahlo divided between a genteel European identity and a Mexican peasant identity; the twins' exposed hearts are linked by a single artery. Rivera's *The Flower Carrier* (1935) depicts a poor mestizo worker burdened by the flowers that he will attempt to sell as luxuries to the upper classes.

Non-Western voices arose more frequently and outspokenly in the artistic world after World War II. Common themes included the growing pains associated with decolonization, the difficulty of resisting Western (especially U.S.) cultural hegemony, and opposition to politically repressive regimes. **Chinua Achebe** looks backward to the impact of British imperialism and missionary activity on Nigeria's Ibo (Igbo) people in *Things Fall Apart* (1958)—one of the first African novels to gain an international audience—while Anita Desai deals with women's lives in *Cry, the Peacock* (1963). Japan's **Yukio Mishima**, a prolific novelist and traditional nationalist, bitterly opposed what he saw as the destruction of Japan's cultural values. His ritual, samurai-style suicide in 1970 elevated him to cult status. In Latin America, authors such as **Gabriel Garcia Márquez** and Isabel Allende pioneered magical realism, a richly textured style featuring intricately detailed storytelling. In the Islamic world, the novelist Naguib Mahfouz won the Nobel Prize for his *Cairo Trilogy*, a vibrant portrait of postwar Egypt. The Indian-born, English-speaking Salman Rushdie came to world attention in 1988 with *The Satanic Verses*, an irreverent treatment of Islamic orthodoxy. Both Mahfouz and Rushdie fell afoul of Muslim traditionalists. Mahfouz was stabbed by an Islamic extremist in 1984. Rushdie was declared a heretic by Iran's Ayatollah Khomeini, who openly called for his assassination and forced him into hiding for years.

## MASS CULTURE AND MULTICULTURALISM

During the 1900s and 2000s, **mass media** came into their own, vastly transforming the cultural sphere. In many ways, their exuberance and energy contrasted with the anxiety and uncertainty expressed by most high art.

Throughout the twentieth century, radio, film, television, and the inexpensive production of books brought music, drama, literature, and information into the lives of a greater variety of people than ever before. Computer technology and the Internet amplified this trend in the 1990s and 2000s.

The dividing line between **high culture** and **mass** (or **popular**) **culture** has become increasingly difficult to define in the twentieth and twenty-first centuries. All the new media of this era have been used by creative performers, musicians, screenwriters, and filmmakers to create genuinely great artworks that undoubtedly belong in the former category. Film directors such as Russia's Sergei Eisenstein and Fritz Lang dominated **high-art cinema** during the interwar years, and the postwar era has witnessed masterpieces by Sweden's deeply existential Ingmar Bergman, Italy's Federico Fellini, noted for his extravagance and fondness for farce, and Japan's Akira Kurosawa, popularizer of the samurai epic. **Jazz**, which flourished in early twentieth-century America, particularly during the **Harlem Renaissance**, can also be considered to have crossed the line between mass culture and high art. The same is often said of the **cabaret culture** that flourished in Weimar Germany before 1933, featuring jazz music and witty social commentary in musical dramas co-created by Kurt Weill and the Marxist playwright Bertolt Brecht.

On the other hand, mass media have been used mainly to create products aimed at a popular audience for purposes of entertainment, and critics of mass/popular culture have argued that it tends to cheapen or "dumb down" art by catering to the tastes of the lowest common denominator. Whether this is an elitist viewpoint or a valid one, there is no denying the perennial popularity of Disney, Hollywood films, rock-and-roll and popular music, and the press coverage related to popular technologies like aviation and rockets (featuring heroes like Charles Lindbergh and U.S. astronauts or Soviet cosmonauts) and automobiles (car racing, popular on both sides of the Atlantic).

Mass media also gave rise to the international popularity of sporting events. From the beginning, these were intertwined with national pride and political agendas. The **modern Olympic Games**, created in 1896 to foster peace, have been used to make statements of strength (Hitler's Berlin Olympics in 1936, Beijing's summer Olympics in 2008) or to wage symbolic battles (the U.S. and Soviet teams throughout the Cold War). **World Cup soccer** tournaments, active since 1930, galvanize audiences worldwide every four years. Another game exported from Europe to wider parts of the world is **cricket**, played wherever the British established colonies. It is a point of pride for teams from South Asia and the Caribbean that they routinely beat the British in international competition—similar to how Cuban, Puerto Ricans, and other Latin Americans often beat baseball teams from the United States, which taught them the game in the first place.

Another criticism of mass culture is how it has been used for political and corporate purposes. Dictatorships have freely employed mass media as mouthpieces for **propaganda** and indoctrination, or "brainwashing." In Nazi Germany, the brilliant filmmaker Leni

Riefenstahl boosted support for Hitler's regime with visually impressive but thoroughly propagandistic movies like *Triumph of the Will* (1935). Starting in the 1930s, Stalinist Russia used both the artistic community and the mass media to churn out relentlessly optimistic artworks in the style of socialist realism, which featured heroic images of productive peasants, tireless factory workers, and stalwart soldiers and pilots, all toiling happily under Stalin's benevolent leadership. In free societies, critics say, people are "brainwashed" less for political purposes, but for the advertisement of goods and the earning of profits, with mass media functioning as powerful tools in the hands of business interests.

**Propaganda in the Age of Mass Media**
The 78-foot-tall *Worker and Collective Farm Woman* (1937), completed by Vera Mukhina and praised at numerous international exhibitions, is an iconic example of socialist realism, bursting with the heroic grandeur that the Soviet regime wished the style to convey. A similar monumentalism is communicated throughout *Triumph of the Will* (1935), by Leni Riefenstahl, who dedicated her considerable talents to the dubious cause of glorifying the Nazi Third Reich.

Other effects of mass media have included the westernization, even **Americanization**, of global popular culture *and*, somewhat contradictorily, the boosting of a **multiculturalism** that blends cultural traditions from all over the globe and sometimes influences Western and U.S. culture.

With respect to the former, even before World War II, the lure of American jazz and Hollywood movies was immensely seductive. Afterward, when America dominated world markets and mass-media technology, Disney, McDonalds, and Coca-Cola, among others, became economic and cultural symbols recognizable not just in the United States, but almost literally in every part of the globe. Some intellectuals, particularly non-Western ones, have expressed concern about the corporatizing and Americanizing effects of mass culture; the Japanese novelist Yukio Mishima angrily condemned it as "**coca-colonization**." Others, however, have spoken of mass media's potential to draw people closer together. In the 1960s, Canadian sociologist Marshall McLuhan gained fame for his argument that modern communications technology would create a "**global village**"—a prediction that seems to have been partly realized, thanks to the Internet.

**TIP**

Make note of how global conflict has influenced popular culture. At their peak, for example, James Bond films helped to relieve Cold War tensions by turning them into spy-fantasy unreality, and they provide a similar function in the more geopolitically uncertain present. U.S.-Soviet rivalry provided fodder for popular if highly implausible Cold War blockbusters like *Rambo* and *Red Dawn*. Popular video games such as Call of Duty have transformed modern combat in general into entertainment— arguably desensitizing players to the uglier realities of the military experience.

McLuhan's vision also appears to have been fulfilled by the mixing and interaction of global styles and traditions known as multiculturalism. Not only have Western and U.S. influences gone abroad, non-Western influences have mutually affected the West and the United States, especially in the spheres of popular and consumer culture. Examples include **reggae music**, with its Afro-Caribbean roots, the global popularity of **Bollywood films** (produced in India, where Bombay/Mumbai serves as the equivalent to Hollywood), and Japan's manga comics and its anime style of film animation. Global cuisine has long been influenced by multicultural trends, especially with the movement of once-colonized peoples to the countries that formerly ruled them, as described in Chapter 26. Indian, Indonesian, and Georgian dishes, for example, have added extra variety—and spice—to the cuisines of Britain, the Netherlands, and Russia, respectively.

## RELIGION IN THE MODERN ERA

Religion continued to play significant historical roles in the twentieth and twenty-first centuries.

In many ways, religions adapted to what was, overall, an increasingly secular era—when literal belief in traditional scriptures was harder to sustain, and when many dictators, especially in the communist world, sought to ban worship altogether. Numerous **synthetic forms of spirituality** appeared, combining elements of old religions with new beliefs. Examples include the Hare Krishna movement (arising in New York in the mid-1960s and borrowing chants and scriptures from Hinduism), Falun Gong (a meditative and martial-arts oriented practice originating in China in the 1990s and, much to the displeasure of the communist regime, reviving aspects of Daoist and Buddhist worship), and the many varieties of "new age" faiths in the West (alternative spiritualities that incorporate whatever they choose from Buddhism, Hinduism, yoga, shamanism, or paganism).

Old or new, religious beliefs were also used to advance political agendas. **Religious differences** frequently aggravated or contributed to ethnic and political disputes, as in the Turkish massacre of Christian Armenians, the Arab-Israeli conflict, Indo-Pakistani violence, the Catholic-Protestant "troubles" in Northern Ireland, and the Yugoslav wars of the 1990s. **Religious fundamentalism** has proven politically influential in many places during the 1900s and 2000s. Christian fundamentalism in North America has systematically advanced right-wing voting preferences in electoral politics, and in the form of evangelical Protestantism, it has made major inroads into Africa and Latin America, the latter long monopolized religiously by the Catholic Church. Islamic fundamentalism has driven political trends in the Middle East, generally in opposition to Westernization and, at times, to modernization in general. In South Asia, it has caused tensions between Hindus and Muslims, and also between Hindus and Sikhs.

Another instance of how religious belief has been applied to politics involves **liberation theology**, a doctrine that arose during the 1950s and 1960s among Catholic priests in Latin America, although the term was not coined until the early 1970s. Arguing that Christ's teachings mandated a "preferential option for the poor," liberation theologists maintained that it was their duty to support impoverished communities against oppressive governments and elite classes, even if doing so meant opposing the church hierarchy or cooperating with radical or Marxist activists. In the mid-1980s, under the fiercely anti-communist pope **John Paul II**, the Vatican cracked down on liberation theology, but the notion of combining liberal Christianity (of whatever denomination) with social-justice activism remains alive thanks to the movement's influence.

## SCIENCE AND TECHNOLOGY

Scientific and technological advancement during the twentieth and twenty-first centuries has been constant and spectacular. During the first half of the 1900s, the Western world fully industrialized, moving into a world where petroleum and electricity were the primary sources of energy (although coal has remained important as well). Nuclear energy, however controversial, has achieved its own importance in the post-World War II era.

Also in the Western world, great innovation has been made in all fields of science. Progress in certain areas has been most noteworthy. Theoretical physics was revolutionized at the beginning of the 1900s. First, **Albert Einstein** developed the **theory of relativity**, making the first major changes to the system of science and mathematics that had been synthesized by Isaac Newton in the late 1600s and early 1700s. Also in the early 1900s came the birth of **quantum physics**. Major figures here included Max Planck, Niels Bohr, Werner Heisenberg, and Enrico Fermi. The work of Einstein and the quantum physicists completely altered our understanding of astronomy and, on the microscopic level, subatomic particles. It also made atomic weaponry and nuclear energy possible.

**Rocketry** and **space science** emerged in the 1900s, following the birth of **powered flight** in 1903, courtesy of the Wright brothers. Pioneers of rocket science included the American Robert Goddard and Russia's Konstantin Tsiolkovsky. This field matured during World War II, thanks largely to the efforts of German scientists like Wernher von Braun, who went on to work in the United States after the war. The nuclear arms race between the United States and the USSR spurred a parallel **space race**, in which the Soviets became the first to put a human-made object into space (the satellite *Sputnik* in 1957) and the first human being into space (Yuri Gagarin in 1961), while the Americans first succeeded in landing on the moon (1969). The move toward a permanent presence in space was encouraged by the USSR's work in developing orbital laboratories and the United States' development of the space shuttle. Rocket science has also made satellite telecommunications possible.

Great medical advances have been made, including the **polio vaccine** (Jonas Salk, followed by Albert Sabin's oral vaccine, both in the 1950s), the elimination of smallpox, heart transplants (1967, by Christiaan Barnard in South Africa) and artificial hearts (first implanted successfully in 1982), and the development of antibiotics, which began with the 1928 discovery of **penicillin** by Scotland's Alexander Fleming. A related field of special significance is **genetics**, which came into being during the late 1800s, thanks to the work of the Austrian monk Gregor Mendel. The field's great breakthrough came when James Watson and Francis Crick led the deciphering of the **molecular structure of DNA** in 1953. Since then, scientists have gained an unprecedented wealth of knowledge about how living organisms work. Finally, **neurology** in the 2000s has made astounding progress in gaining previously unimaginable insights into the workings of the brain.

**Apollo 15 Mission to the Moon, August 1971.**
To this date, the United States is the only nation that has landed crewed spacecraft on the moon. The first moon landing came on July 20, 1969. The Apollo 15 mission, pictured here, was one of the several landings that followed.

Yet another significant scientific advancement was the invention of the **computer**, during and shortly after World War II, and thanks to the efforts of many individuals, but notably the British mathematician Alan Turing. Beginning in the 1980s, the availability and affordability of the **personal computer**—brought about by innovators like Bill Gates, Steve Wozniak, and Steve Jobs—caused an **information** (or **digital**) **revolution** that altered the way people communicate, transact business, entertain themselves, and work. Key to this development was the invention and expansion of the **Internet**, originally created in the 1960s for U.S. defense purposes. By the end of the 1990s, a World Wide Web had connected millions of users, and it continues to grow, particularly with the rise of **wireless technology** and **mobile communications**, which allows access to the Internet and to **social media** via handheld devices like cellphones. Although a "digital divide" exists between those in the developed world, who have better access to computer technology and reliable cellphone networks, and those in the less developed world, who have less access, the worldwide trend is toward greater access for all.

# Economic Systems, 1900 to Present

## 25

- → BOOM-AND-BUST BUSINESS CYCLE
- → FREE-MARKET CAPITALISM (UNREGULATED VS. REGULATED
- → "MIDDLE" OR "THIRD WAY" ECONOMIES AND SOCIALISM
- → STATE-DIRECTED CAPITALISM (SYNDICALISM, CORPORATISM)
- → NATIONALIZATION OF ECONOMIC ASSETS IN THE DEVELOPING WORLD
- → COMMUNISM AND ECONOMIC CENTRALIZATION (FIVE-YEAR PLANS, GREAT LEAP FORWARD)
- → FREE TRADE VS. PROTECTIONISM
- → THE GREAT DEPRESSION (SMOOT-HAWLEY TARIFF ACT, INTERNATIONAL EFFECTS, NEW DEAL)
- → THE BRETTON WOODS SYSTEM (WORLD BANK, IMF, GATT/WTO) VS. ECONOMIES IN THE COMMUNIST WORLD
- → ORGANIZATION OF PETROLEUM EXPORTING COUNTRIES (OPEC)
- → ECONOMIC CRISIS OF THE 1970S (OPEC EMBARGO, STAGFLATION)
- → FREE-MARKET REFORMS AND RECOVERY IN THE 1980S AND 1990S
- → MULTINATIONAL CORPORATIONS
- → REGIONAL ECONOMIC ASSOCIATIONS (EEC/EU, NAFTA, AND MERCOSUR)
- → ECONOMIC GLOBALIZATION (THE G-7/G-8; WORLD TRADE ORGANIZATION)
- → 2007 GLOBAL ECONOMIC CRISIS

The twentieth and twenty-first centuries have witnessed experiments with widely divergent forms of economic organization, as well as a steady march toward the near-complete **globalization** of economic affairs, a development that has presented both costs and benefits and whose full impact has yet to be measured. Immense wealth has been created in the aggregate during this era—more than the world has ever seen before—but it remains very unevenly distributed, both within societies and between them. Moreover, economies the world over remain vulnerable to **business cycles** of periodic **boom and bust**, and the more integrated they have become, the more they have come to share that vulnerability.

## DIVERGENT APPROACHES TO THE ECONOMY

Throughout this era, while most states attempted economic modernization, they adopted widely different approaches to economic organization.

The primary approach in the West—and gradually in other places—was **capitalism**, typically paired with electoral democracy. Capitalism, however, could be modified to varying degrees. Even **free-market capitalism** could be left mostly **unregulated**, or it could be more heavily **regulated** by means of government intervention. Proponents of minimal regulation favor the *laissez-faire* spirit of the nineteenth-century classical economists, and argue that reliance on the unfettered operation of the **market forces** of **supply and demand** is the surest way to generate wealth for the greatest number of people. Those favoring more regulation counter that even early capitalist thinkers like Adam Smith warned about dangerous levels of poverty and the formation of **monopolies** if governments did not intervene sufficiently. They also maintain that a stronger government hand is necessary to correct downward fluctuations in the market, to provide enough of a **social safety net** to shield citizens from the harshest effects of capitalist competition, and to ensure that a sufficient **infrastructure** exists for the good of the state and the smooth functioning of the economy. The former approach prevailed in most of the West before World War I and in the United States during the 1920s, and it was pursued aggressively in the United States and in much of Europe and elsewhere during the 1980s. The latter is exemplified by the U.S. New Deal of the 1930s, and also by the approach taken by most European democracies, with their highly developed **social welfare systems**, whether during the interwar period or most of the postwar era. The semi-capitalist, semi-socialist "**middle**" or "**third way**" adopted by many regimes at certain junctures can be viewed as either a mild form of socialist centralization or an example of capitalism at its most heavily-regulated.

Modern economic theories regarding capitalism have focused primarily on this question of government intervention. The dominant thinker in favor of regulation is **John Maynard Keynes** of Britain, author of *The General Theory of Employment, Interest and Money* (1936)—the century's classic text on macroeconomics—and an advisor to, or influence on, many governments from the 1920s onward, including Franklin Roosevelt's during the Great Depression. Keynes argued that booms and busts proceed from the waxing and waning of consumer confidence (the "animal spirits," to use his terminology) and that, in times of crisis, governments should invest in public works, relief efforts, and stimulus programs to keep confidence high, even if it means running deficits for a time. In his own time, Keynes was opposed by economists of the **Austrian School**, most famously Friedrich Hayek, who maintained that only market forces properly measure value and allocate resources, and that any state intervention, however minimal, leads to "malinvestment" and fatally distorts the workings of the economy. An even better-known opponent of Keynesian theory (and also a skeptic where the Austrian School is concerned) is the American economist **Milton Friedman**, whose influence on governments in the 1980s and 1990s—especially in Britain, the United States, and Latin America—equaled that of Keynes in earlier decades. An advocate of austerity and privatization, Friedman proposed that governments should intervene as little as possible in the workings of the free market.

More centralized approaches to the economy also prevailed in various places during much of this era. Fascist and authoritarian regimes generally relied on some form or another of **state-directed capitalism** to regulate their economies, with varying degrees of heavy-handedness. Such systems tended to be based on partnerships between political elites and economic elites, whether the latter were landowners, industrialists, or both. Economic elites were allowed to own their enterprises and pursue profits as long as they accepted dictates and priorities set for them by the state. In exchange for obedience, the state refrained from outright nationalization or centralization, and cooperative parties were rewarded with preferential treatment and state contracts. Such regimes also minimized, if not outlawed, trade-union activity and limited workers' rights, an added benefit for economic elites. These

**NOTE**

**Fascist forms of state capitalism are typically referred to as corporatist or syndicalist.**

practices were pursued most famously in Nazi Germany, fascist Italy, and Japan, but also in a host of dictatorial and oligarchic regimes worldwide.

Even more centralized were socialist and communist economies, which emphasized central planning, the nationalization of some or all sectors of the economy, and less concern for—or active hostility toward—private property. The most successful **socialist** or **social democratic** systems have tended to be mild, and to have been put into place by means of electoral politics, and most of them have injected enough elements of capitalism that they can be categorized as "**middle**" or "**third way**" economies. Quasi-socialist or temporarily socialist measures like the nationalization of certain economic assets or certain sectors of the economy have often been carried out by governments in the less-developed world—especially in recently decolonized nations—as a way to encourage development or build wealth quickly. Examples include Lázaro Cárdenas's 1938 formation of the state-owned **PEMEX** conglomerate, following his nationalization of Mexico's oil industry, and Gamal Nasser's **nationalization of the Suez Canal** in 1956.

A number of countries committed more fully to **communism** during the 1900s, including the Soviet Union, most of Eastern Europe, mainland China, North Korea, Cuba, Vietnam, and others. The extent of centralization here is greatest, with communism explicitly aiming—at least in theory—to eradicate the profit motive, to eliminate private property and private trade, and to nationalize the economy as completely as possible. Although communist regimes often claim to be "people's democracies," they nearly always come to power by means of revolution and keep themselves in place by means of dictatorship. They typically pursue ambitious modernization projects, including **state-sponsored industrialization** and the **collectivization of agriculture**. Stalin's **First Five-Year Plan** (1928–1932) and Mao's **Great Leap Forward** (1958–1961) are the most prominent examples, each of them causing astounding levels of social and economic stress, each relying heavily on **prison-camp labor**, and each linked to notorious famines that killed millions. On the other hand, not all communist regimes have pursued such extremist policies, and many have shown themselves capable of effective reform and economic liberalization, such as China under Deng Xiaoping, following Mao's death in 1976, and Vietnam with its *doi moi* ("renovation") reforms in the mid-1980s onward. However, even these reformist regimes remain politically authoritarian.

## BOOM AND BUST: TOWARD THE GREAT DEPRESSION AND BRETTON WOODS

As described in Chapter 19, trade and commerce were highly internationalized before 1900, especially between Europe and North America—London and New York had already emerged as the world's leading centers of banking and commerce—with Western imperialism drawing the rest of the globe into this system as well.

On the eve of the twentieth century, the Western world experienced a bad turn of the **boom-and-bust business cycle**: the **Long Depression** of the early 1870s through the mid-1890s, complete with **protectionist trade policies**. Economic recovery and the resumption of **free trade** caused a rebound between the late 1890s and World War I. As noted in Chapter 22, World War I badly weakened the economies of Europe, but it enriched North America, paving the way for the "**roaring twenties**" in the United States. During and after World War I, all nations in the West industrialized more fully than before, as did Soviet Russia, and certain other areas achieved significant degrees of modernization and industrialization—such as Japan, parts of Latin America, and China. The scope and volume of international trade remained high during the 1920s, but this, along with the world's economic health in general, depended heavily on U.S. investment and U.S. willingness to import goods from abroad.

It was for this reason that the **Great Depression**, caused by the wild overvaluation of stocks in the United States and the resulting crash of the New York Stock Exchange in October 1929, had such an adverse effect on the global economy. (The agricultural downturn caused at the same time by the U.S. and Canadian **dust bowl crisis** added to the country's problems.) The initial reaction of the U.S. government was to institute austerity measures, which depressed consumer confidence, caused runs on banks (as depositors sought to withdraw their money all at once), and led to **mass unemployment** (eventually reaching 25 percent). The Depression also sparked one of the most rashly protectionist measures in U.S. history, the **Smoot-Hawley Tariff Act** of 1930, which attempted to shield U.S. industries and farms by imposing high tariffs on other nations' goods, but almost immediately destroyed the ability of Europe, Latin America, and Asia to export their products—in effect spreading the Depression to these regions as well. Because the USSR's economic connections with the West were so limited, it remained untouched by the Great Depression. Indeed, because Stalin's five-year plans created virtually 100 percent employment, and because propaganda hid their unpleasant realities from public view, many in the West became convinced that Stalinist communism was superior to democratic capitalism.

Political reactions to the Depression are recounted in Chapter 22. Economic reactions generally included some combination of **public works projects** (large-scale construction, dam- or highway-building, electrification, and so on), **social welfare** (soup kitchens, farm relief, unemployment insurance), and, in some cases, **military conscription** and **arms buildup**. Franklin Roosevelt's **New Deal**, begun in 1933, attempted the first two, while Nazi Germany, fascist Italy, and Japan relied mainly on the first and the third. European democracies like Britain and France turned to the second alternative, foreshadowing the even more elaborate **social welfare systems** they would put into place after World War II.

World War II shattered most economies besides those of America and the Soviet Union, and even the latter lost a full third of its economic capacity to the fighting, meaning that the United States took the lead in rebuilding the global economic system during the conflict's waning months. Franklin Roosevelt, guided by the economic principles of John Maynard Keynes and the post-World War I convictions of Woodrow Wilson, believed that free trade was the key not only to economic prosperity, but also to lasting world peace. Therefore, in July 1944, he met with Allied delegates at Bretton Woods, New Hampshire. It was here that the **World Bank** and the **International Monetary Fund** (IMF), whose purpose was to rebuild Europe and lend assistance to countries in Asia, Africa, and Latin America, were created. It was also there that plans were laid for a **General Agreement on Tariffs and Trade** (GATT), which was signed by 23 countries in 1947 and met regularly until 1994, when it became the World Trade Organization. Most currencies measured themselves against the U.S. dollar, which in turn based its value on the **gold standard**. The Soviet Union and its East European bloc refused to join this **Bretton Woods system**, and so their economies would be less integrated with much of the rest of the world's during the Cold War.

## REGIONALIZATION AND GLOBALIZATION AFTER WORLD WAR II

During the 1950s and 1960s, growing prosperity came especially to the United States, but also to Canada, Japan, and the nations of Western Europe. One way Western Europe staged its economic recovery was through **economic union**, forming the precursors to the present-day European Union: the six-nation European Coal and Steel Community in 1952, and then the **European Economic Community**, also known as the **Common Market**, in 1957. Most European nations, along with Canada, began to invest heavily in **social welfare systems** that provided for some combination of universal health care, cheap or free higher education for those who qualified academically, generous pensions, and unemployment insurance, and so on. The reconstruction of war-torn Western Europe, assisted at the outset by the **Marshall Plan** (1948), was nothing short of incredible. The same was true of Japan.

The rest of the world developed unevenly. In Latin America and Africa, many governments still relied on the export of small assortments of natural resources or crops, just as they had done in the 1800s. The Middle East benefited from its dominance of oil production. The **Organization of Petroleum Exporting Countries** (OPEC), formed in 1960 and still one of the most influential cartels in economic history, consists largely of Middle Eastern countries. The economies of the Soviet Union, its East European allies, and Communist China tended to remain largely but not completely isolated from those of the Western world. Certain parts of Asia, such as Japan, the continent's economic "tiger," along with the so-called **"little tigers"** (Taiwan, South Korea, Hong Kong, and Singapore), were quick to adapt to global capitalism and industrialization. Many Asian nations joined together in regional economic associations; the **Association of Southeast Asian Nations** (ASEAN), formed in 1967 to promote regional security, tightened economic ties among its member states.

By the 1970s, Western economies began a long transition from industrial production to **postindustrial production**, based less on manufacturing and more on service, high-tech fields, and computers. At the same time, though, a general economic crisis struck much of the world in the early 1970s and lasted the rest of the decade. In 1971, President Richard Nixon rocked the international community by taking the U.S. dollar off the gold standard. OPEC's 1973 **oil embargo** severely affected the energy-dependent economies of the West. A curious combination of recession and inflation (which generally occurs in times of economic growth) called **stagflation** plagued North America and Western Europe, and those nations with comprehensive and costly social welfare systems found them difficult to maintain. Although the USSR had its own oil reserves and was safe from OPEC's embargo, inefficiency, food shortages, the cost of the arms race, and governmental corruption sapped the economies of the East European bloc.

In the mid-1970s, the countries with the seven largest non-communist economies formed the **Group of Seven** (**G-7**) to coordinate economic policies when mutually beneficial. The original members were Great Britain, West Germany, France, Italy, Japan, and the United States in 1975, with Canada joining soon after.

During the 1980s, most economies outside the Soviet bloc recovered. In the West, the shift from industrial to post-industrial/service modes of production continued. To one degree or another, most governments pursued **free-market reforms**, which involved **privatization** of previously nationalized sectors of the economy (most typically transport and energy), trimming or elimination of social-welfare benefits, and **austerity**, or the reduction of government spending, in general. The economic theories of **Milton Friedman** were particularly influential during these years and followed most eagerly by Ronald Reagan in the United States, Margaret Thatcher in Great Britain, and the dictator Augusto Pinochet in Chile. Such policies seem to have led to an overall rise in economic growth, but also caused great social stress in the form of layoffs and the weakening of unions, and began a 30-year trend of shifting the distribution of wealth upward from the middle class and toward corporate elites.

Debate also continues as to whether free-market policies caused the economic recovery or simply coincided with it.

The 1990s brought about a high tide of **economic globalization**, which has shown no signs of receding in the 2000s. A major factor here was the growing influence of **multinational corporations**, starting in the 1980s and continuing to the present. These large conglomerates, technically "from" a single country, maintain factories and subsidiaries around the world and employ many foreign workers. Examples include Coca-Cola and McDonalds, originally from the United States; Royal Dutch Shell, with fossil-fuel interests worldwide; Nestlé (Swiss-based, the largest food company in the world); and electronics and computer giants such as Sony (originally Japanese) and Microsoft and Apple from the United States. While corporations like these generate massive wealth, critics contend that their profit-seeking weakens societies and challenges state power in many ways. Multinationals engage in **tax-sheltering** (shifting assets out of a home country to places with lower tax rates or no tax at all) and regularly **relocate** or "**outsource**" **jobs** from city to city or country to country—causing sudden layoffs or firings—in their search for the most lenient environmental regulations, the most favorable tax breaks, and, most important, the cheapest labor. The impact of multinationals on the developing world is also mixed: even though they provide jobs and invest in local infrastructure, they often exploit labor (in some cases turning a blind eye to dreadful **sweatshop conditions**), harm local ecosystems, and put homegrown industries and craft production out of business.

The growing extent of globalization is reflected in the increased importance of **international economic organizations** and **regional economic associations**, which foster economic cooperation and, in the case of the latter, provide for freer trade. Throughout the 1990s and 2000s, meetings of the **Group of Seven** (**G-7**), renamed the **Group of Eight** (**G-8**) after Russia's accession in 1997, have become more frequent and more formal. In 1994–1995, the GATT accords were upgraded and strengthened by the formation of the **World Trade Organization** (WTO), whose purpose is to regulate the economic interactions of the more than 100 nations that belong to it. In 1994, the United States, Mexico, and Canada created a zone of free movement of money, goods, services, and labor by means of the **North American Free Trade Agreement** (NAFTA). Other regions have tightened their economic ties as well. In 1989, Pacific Rim nations formed the **Asia-Pacific Economic Cooperation Group** (APEC), which now includes more than 20 members. In 1991, several Latin American nations established the Southern Common Market, or **Mercosur**, consisting of Argentina, Brazil, Paraguay, Uruguay, Venezuela, and Bolivia. A number of free-trade zones formed in Africa during the 1980s and 1990s, all joining together in 2008 to form the **African Free Trade Zone** (AFTZ). By far the boldest experiment in economic integration, however, is Europe's. In 1991, the nations of the **European Union**, or EU (formerly the European Economic Community) signed the Maastricht Treaty, which provided for the creation of the **euro** as a single currency, and also for the free movement of money, goods, and labor. The euro went into circulation in 2002 and was adopted by most EU members (Britain is a major holdout). The EU currently includes 27 member nations. The viability of the euro was seriously called into question in the wake of the **2007 global economic crisis**, but the "eurozone" appears to have survived for the time being.

The costs and benefits of economic globalization are mixed. On one hand, it has generated great wealth, at least in a broad sense and in certain parts of the world. And with some justification, proponents of globalization argue that free trade helps to preserve peace. On the other hand, the above-mentioned practices of multinational corporations may lead to a constant state of economic instability, and agriculture has been greatly affected by globalization, as farmers in one country find themselves competing with cheap food imported from other parts of the world. Also, the fact that so many nations' economies influence each other so strongly means that negative trends in one region—financial crisis in Mexico in 1994 or Asia in 1997, for example, or Russia and Brazil in 1998, never mind the U.S. collapse in 2007—can adversely affect large parts of the world. Finally, it is questionable how far all nations will be willing to subject their individual economic policies to the dictates of the EU, the WTO, or other regional and international bodies.

To this date, globalization has not healed the **north-south split** that continues to divide the developed world from the nondeveloped and developing nations located near or south of the equator. In addition, the effects of the **2007 global economic crisis**, which began in the United States and emanated outward, still linger.

# Social Structures, 1900 to Present

26

→ **GLOBAL POPULATION GROWTH**

→ **SOCIOECONOMIC FEATURES OF THE DEVELOPED WORLD (MIDDLE CLASS, URBANIZATION, SOCIAL WELFARE SYSTEMS) VS. THE COMMUNIST STATES**

→ **INDUSTRIAL VS. POSTINDUSTRIAL (SERVICE AND HIGH-TECH) ECONOMIES**

→ **THE DEVELOPING (THIRD) WORLD AND THE NORTH-SOUTH SPLIT**

→ **SOCIAL ACTIVISM AND PROTEST MOVEMENTS**

→ **ETHNIC VIOLENCE AND GENOCIDE**

→ **ETHNIC PREJUDICE AND SEGREGATION (JIM CROW LAWS, APARTHEID)**

→ **MIGRATION (MIGRANT AND ILLEGAL LABORERS, GUEST WORKERS) AND THE MOVEMENT OF REFUGEES**

→ **ANTI-IMMIGRATION SENTIMENT, NATIVISM, AND XENOPHOBIA**

→ **WOMEN'S SUFFRAGE**

→ **WOMEN'S LIBERATION AND THE FEMINIST MOVEMENT (SIMONE DE BEAUVOIR, BETTY FRIEDAN, GLORIA STEINEM)**

→ **GENDER EQUALITY (EQUAL PAY, REPRODUCTIVE RIGHTS, EQUALITY IN MARRIAGE)**

Different parts of the world have experienced social transformations differently. As a rule, the changes of the 1900s and early 2000s proceeded along four basic tracks:

- In Western Europe, the United States, and Canada—the West—as well as in Australia and New Zealand, movement (although in some cases slow or nonexistent before the end of World War II) was toward stable democratization, social equality and individual rights, economic prosperity, the creation of social welfare systems, the shift from industrial to postindustrial production, and rapid scientific and technological development.

- Prosperous nations in Asia—first Japan, then others like Taiwan, South Korea, Indonesia, and Singapore—made great strides toward economic and technological modernization, especially after World War II. They urbanized, built social welfare systems, and developed postindustrial, high-tech economies. However, they were (and in some cases remain) slower to embrace democracy and to tolerate the individualism that had come to characterize Western societies in the 1800s and 1900s.

- The Soviet Union and Eastern Europe modernized economically. They urbanized and developed social welfare systems, and technological and scientific advancement was considerable. However, political systems were repressive, and not only were the economies here overly centralized, they remained industrial rather than postindustrial, and were cruder in terms of technological finesse than in the West. Even after the collapse of communism, it has been difficult for this region to move toward democracy and prosperity.

- To one degree or another, the developing nations of Asia, Africa, the Middle East, and Latin America are striving to create advanced economies, modern societies, and representative forms of government. Some have made progress, attaining a high level of prosperity or a functioning democracy or both. Others are mired in backwardness, poverty, civil strife, and dictatorship. Most are somewhere in between. Perhaps the most distinctive case is the People's Republic of China, which has the geography, population, and military capacity of a major power, and whose economy has grown considerably since the 1980s. But China's government is still authoritarian, and social and economic progress remains uneven. Some economists use the acronym **BRIC** to refer to Brazil, Russia, India, and China—whose socioeconomic development does not yet match that of the West, but which have been rapidly modernizing and gaining global clout.

## LABOR AND LIFESTYLES

The most dramatic changes in these spheres have been felt in Europe and North America, and to a lesser extent elsewhere.

A cluster of social trends that began in the West during the 1800s sped up significantly in the 1900s and accelerated in many ways by World War I. These included the elimination of legal distinctions between social classes, along with the provision of **equal political rights** and **equal treatment before the law** for all adult citizens, including females and minorities (a slow process, and still ongoing in many places). Aristocratic social elites were replaced by a professional and meritocratic **white-collar class** whose status depended on education, skills, and earned wealth. Developed societies created a large, stable **middle class** and provided access to at least a **minimum standard of living** and an adequate level of well-being, even among the lower classes. Other developments included

**NOTE**

In 1900, the world population was 1.6 billion. By 2000, it had reached 6 billion, and it has since topped 7 billion. Most historians contend that this growth has been caused primarily by improvements in medicine and public health, as opposed to the eradication of hunger.

- The growing power of **trade unions**
- The creation of **universal educational systems**
- The growing availability and affordability of **transportational** and **energy infrastructures**, along with the mobility that came with **mass transit** and the **automobile**
- **Urbanization** throughout the 1900s, with **suburbanization** increasingly common in the postwar era
- The adoption of **social welfare systems**, either as a way to cope with the economic pain of the interwar years and the Great Depression (such as the British "dole" or Franklin Roosevelt's New Deal in the United States) or because of the new possibilities opened up by post-World War II prosperity. These generally included some combination of unemployment insurance, pensions, and health care (at least for the elderly and poor, if not the entire population). In capitalist societies, they required a willingness to place a "safety net" under the workings of the free market or even to blend capitalism with some elements of socialism, as in Scandinavia's "**third way**."

During and after the Cold War, the Western world experienced a gradual transition from industrial economies, still dominant in the 1950s and 1960s, to **postindustrial economies**, more the norm since the 1980s and 1990s. These tend to emphasize **consumerism** and **service industries** rather than manufacturing, and they place a premium on **computerization and cutting-edge technologies**. This change is associated with many innovations and opportunities, but as with the shift from agriculture and craftsmanship to industrialization during the 1800s, it has also caused stress as well as opportunity, with many jobs being made obsolete by new machines or being lost to cheaper labor overseas. Moreover, even the economic boom of the 1980s and 1990s was accompanied by a growing divide between the wealthiest members of Western societies and the less well-off, with increased burdens falling on a noticeably shrinking middle class. The economic crisis caused by the financial collapse of 2007 has only worsened these trends.

In communist Europe, many of these same trends played out during the Cold War, but somewhat differently. Social welfare and universal education were at the heart of the state system, and class divisions were minimized, at least in theory. In reality, a communist elite—comprising about 10 percent of a given society and denounced by the Yugoslav intellectual Milovan Djilas as a corrupt and self-important "**new class**"—enjoyed enormous privileges. For everyone else, the social welfare system provided what cynics referred to as "equality of poverty," or at best "equality of adequacy." Industrial manufacturing was strong, but the production of consumer goods was weak, and high-tech innovation outside the military sphere was nearly nonexistent. When communism finally collapsed in Eastern Europe and the USSR, a wrenching social and economic transition to free-market capitalism followed—and in many places remains incomplete.

In the developing world, social divisions between the elite classes and the rest of society tended to remain very wide, with a very small middle class (if any) separating the very wealthy from very poor masses. Where social and economic modernization did take place, it was generally directed from above—sometimes in opposition to traditional religious outlooks or value systems, as in Turkey and Iran. On a global basis, both during the Cold War and afterward, the world has struggled with a pronounced **north-south split**, meaning that economic prosperity, the availability of food and clean water, and access to cutting-edge technology, medical care, and social stability tend to be concentrated in the developed world, with many parts of the developing world lagging behind and still impoverished.

**Social activism** has been part of modern social life since the days of the American and French revolutions but has brought about particularly tremendous changes during the 1900s and early 2000s. It played a leading role in **national liberation movements** worldwide and in the struggle for **racial equality** in places as diverse as South Africa (the **anti-apartheid movement**) and the United States (the **civil rights movement** versus **Jim Crow laws**). It clashed with existing social and political orders, as during the various **1968 protests** that rocked city streets and college campuses from Paris and Prague to Mexico City and New York, and it gave voice to those who opposed nuclear weapons, Cold War conflicts like Vietnam, and damage to the environment. Social activism advanced the cause of **women's liberation** and **gay rights**, and it has defied dictatorial regimes—unsuccessfully but bravely during the **Tiananmen Square protests** in China in 1989, and with more decisive results during the **Solidarity strikes** against Poland's communist government during the 1980s and the related "people's power" movements that brought down communism in Eastern Europe more widely in 1988 and 1989.

## ETHNICITY AND RACE RELATIONS

Racial tensions divided many communities and nations throughout this era. **Ethnic violence**, **persecution of minorities**, and **segregation**—official and unofficial—plagued societies worldwide and continue to do so.

Ethnic tensions took their most extreme form in the **genocides** and **mass killings** described in Chapters 22 and 23, such as the Armenian massacres of World War I, the extermination of Jews and Roma during World War II, the Guatemalan murder of Mayans in the 1980s, the Rwandan genocide and the Yugoslav ethnic cleansings of the 1990s, and the Arab killing of African Darfurians in Sudan during the early 2000s. There are also certain regions where long-term ethnic tensions—and sporadic violence—persist, such as the Indo-Pakistani animosity in South Asia, the Israeli-Palestinian conflict in the Middle East, intertribal rivalries in Africa, and Greek-Turkish hostility on the island of Cyprus, divided since 1975.

**Segregationist schemes** existed in many places to restrict the rights of unfavored ethnic groups or to keep them apart from those groups favored by the authorities. Certainly in no colony did the imperial power allow natives to mix freely with whites. Prior to the revolutions of 1917, Jews in Russia were not allowed to live outside the **Pale of Settlement**, a special zone in western Russia, Ukraine, and Belarus, without a permit. In the United States, **Jim Crow laws**—enforced by lynching and other forms of legal or semi-legal violence—perpetuated anti-black segregation in a variety of ways, especially in the south, until protests and demonstrations by **civil rights activists** like **Martin Luther King, Jr.**, helped to bring about passage of the **Civil Rights Acts** of 1964 and 1968. Indigenous Americans of all types struggled against secondary status and racial prejudice, whether in the United States and Canada or throughout Latin America. In addition to being forced onto reservations, many people were taken from their families as children, either to be adopted by white families or to be educated in residential schools, where abuse was rampant and native traditions discouraged. One of the most deeply entrenched forms of segregation was the South African system of **apartheid**, instituted in 1948 by white Afrikaners and rigidly enforced until the 1990s. Not only did apartheid earn South Africa decades of world disapproval, it provoked determined opposition on the part of groups like the **African National Congress**, led most famously by **Nelson Mandela**, jailed for his activism between 1964 and 1990. Throughout Eastern Europe, **Roma** (Gypsies) continue to be treated as distinctly second-class.

**Migration** has remained as much a global reality in this era as during the 1800s, and so have **xenophobia** and **anti-immigration sentiment**. Migration continued to be motivated by **work opportunities** (including migrant and illegal labor), but warfare has done its share to prompt it as well, creating **refugees** and **displaced persons** by the millions. The movement of peoples intensified after World War II. During the late 1940s and 1950s, refugees from Eastern Europe, where Nazi genocide and Soviet occupation caused massive population transfers, moved to Western Europe or North America, and in some cases to the recently founded state of Israel. During the entire postwar period, economic opportunity, violence in the developing world, and political repression led millions to leave Asia, Africa, the Middle East, and Latin America for Western Europe and North America. Such migrations increased in scope during and after **decolonization**, as countries that dismantled their empires allowed **former colonial subjects** to live and work in the metropole, or "home" country. Indians, Pakistanis, and Caribbean islanders traveled in large numbers to Britain, Indonesians migrated to the Netherlands, and Algerians and Moroccans came to France. (The migration of Filipinos and Puerto Ricans to the United States can be considered part of this phenomenon as well.) The late Cold War saw an increase in legal and illegal immigration of Latin Americans to the United States and Canada, and also the admission of **guest workers** to Western Europe (there were 15 million of these by the 1980s, many of them Turks living in Germany). More recently, the collapse of communism in the former Soviet bloc and the rise in ethnic conflict in places like the former Yugoslavia has caused new waves of migration.

Migration has typically provided a much-needed labor force (if not always a well-treated one), and it has enriched the cultural diversity of host nations. However, especially when economic times are tight, it has stirred up **anti-immigration sentiments** that involve varying degrees of prejudice and discrimination. At their worst, they involve **race riots** or the formation of **skinhead movements** or **nativist political parties** (such as those founded by Jean-Marie Le Pen in France and Jörg Haider in Austria) which call for an end to immigration.

Wartime can also trigger anti-immigrant sentiment, if a country is home to a large immigrant population originally from a nation it is fighting. Distrust of German-Americans and German-Canadians ran high during World War I, for example. And during World War II, both Canada and the United States took the drastic step of rounding up tens of thousands of Japanese-Canadians and Japanese-Americans without cause and confining them against their will to "relocation centers." The largest and most famous of these was **Manzanar**, near California's Sierra Nevada.

## GENDER ISSUES

One of the most important trends of the twentieth and twenty-first centuries has been the march toward **gender equality**. Progress here came most quickly in the Western world, although other regions moved forward as well, if slowly and partially.

In Europe and North America, the **women's suffrage movements** that had arisen during the late 1800s continued their agitation during the early 1900s. They scored major successes during and after World War I, when large numbers of women—1.35 million in Britain alone—took jobs as farmhands and factory workers, especially in munitions plants. Women also served as nurses and uniformed auxiliaries, and their contributions to their countries' war efforts earned them much respect. It was largely because of this that women got the **right to vote** in many Western nations between 1917 and 1920, with Spain, France, and Italy standing out as noteworthy exceptions.

Mexico's 1917 constitution granted women the right to vote, and much of Latin America did the same in the 1920s and 1930s. Turkey gave women the vote in 1934, but this was a rarity in the Middle East. Japan established universal suffrage in 1945, and India and China did so in 1947. (Although the Chinese Republic was late in giving women the vote, it did outlaw foot binding in 1912.)

Except in the USSR, where rapid industrialization required as large a workforce as possible, the rate of female employment decreased in Europe and North America during the 1920s, as men returned from World War I, and especially in the 1930s, when, during the mass unemployment caused by the Great Depression, it was considered "wrong" for women to have jobs if men were out of work.

The interwar dictatorships differed sharply in their treatment of women. In the USSR, Marxist ideology called for gender equality, and while the Soviets observed this ideal imperfectly (especially under Stalin), women made up a large part of the workforce. By contrast, Italian fascism, German Nazism, and Japanese traditionalism were explicitly hostile to the notion of gender equality. In all three countries, women were expected to be principally mothers and homemakers. Non-Western parts of the world that afforded educational or workplace opportunities to women during the interwar years were rare, although they include Turkey, Iran, and certain parts of Latin America.

Famously, World War II brought women into the workplace in even greater numbers than World War I had. The image of "Rosie the Riveter" became a potent symbol of the role of women in U.S. wartime production. In the Soviet Union, women made up nearly 40 percent of the national workforce. Large numbers of American, Canadian, Australian, New Zealand, and British women served as war nurses and military personnel (although not as combat troops). In the USSR, women served in the military and, in some limited but important cases, saw active duty in combat—mainly as pilots and snipers. Although there was a temporary dip in female employment afterward, World War II served the purpose of permanently cementing a place for women in the working world—at least in North America and Europe. In addition, more countries, including holdouts like France and Italy, gave women the vote after the war.

During the postwar years, women in the developed world assumed an increasingly larger role in the workplace and in public life. Even so, during the late 1940s and 1950s, it was still generally considered that a woman's main roles were that of homemaker and childbearer. Even women who worked were subjected to widespread **gender discrimination**: sexual harassment, unequal wages, and lack of access to positions of leadership (the "**glass ceiling**"). The French philosopher **Simone de Beauvoir** analyzed the place of women in modern society in *The Second Sex* (1949), which investigated the deep-seated cultural and biological reasons for male domination of women.

A great step toward equality was taken by women in the Western world during the 1960s and 1970s, when the modern **feminist movement** began to press for **women's liberation**, which meant not just legal equality and the right to vote, but the elimination of the cultural stereotype of women as the "weaker sex" and the social barriers that still blocked the way toward full equality. Major figures here came from the United States and included **Gloria Steinem**, a founding figure in the **National Organization for Women** (**NOW**), and **Betty Friedan**, whose book *The Feminine Mystique* (1963) joined *The Second Sex* as part of the feminist movement's intellectual foundation. NOW organized a major event, the Women's Strike for Equality, in 1970, although it failed in its goal of passing an Equal Rights Amendment to the U.S. Constitution. Throughout the Western world, achievements of the women's movement include better and more varied career opportunities, higher pay, equal access to higher education, greater respect for women's athletics, a greater role in political life, and the right to equality in marriage and divorce. **Reproductive rights** have also proven crucial. The postwar development of reliable contraception, especially birth-control pills, gave women unprecedented control over pregnancy and sexuality. The gradual legalization of abortion, albeit controversial, did the same.

Progress toward equal treatment of women has been uneven in non-Western parts of the world. In many societies, women are still relegated to traditional and secondary roles. Although it would be an overgeneralization to say that women are not treated equally in *all* parts of Asia, Africa, the Middle East, and Latin America, the fact remains that Islamic fundamentalism, conservative Catholicism, machismo, and old-fashioned views of women as inferior (or of wives as servants or property) constrain women more commonly in these regions than in the West. In sub-Saharan Africa, rates of HIV/AIDS infection among women are unusually high, owing to the reluctance of many African men to engage in safe-sex practices, and one infamous custom, clitoridectomy (female circumcision), is still practiced in certain parts of Africa. On the other hand, the vast majority of societies allow women more rights and legal protections than they once did.

Enormous progress has been made in recent years by **gay and lesbian rights movements** in Europe and North America. In the United States, the contemporary gay rights movement is considered to have begun with the **Stonewall riots** of 1969, in New York's Greenwich Village. But despite Gay Pride parades and protests since the 1970s, and despite growing awareness of gay and lesbian relationships, wider acceptance has been a longer time in coming, with same-sex marriage becoming legal only in the 2000s—in over a dozen countries as of this date, and also in parts of the United States and Mexico.

# Humans and the Environment, 1900 to Present

# 27

→ **POPULATION GROWTH**

→ **PERSISTENCE OF OLDER DISEASES VS. PUBLIC HEALTH (VACCINATION)**

→ **MODERN EPIDEMIC DISEASES (SPANISH FLU, EBOLA, HIV/AIDS)**

→ **DISEASES ASSOCIATED WITH SEDENTARY LIFESTYLES AND EXTENDED LONGEVITY (DIABETES, OBESITY, ALZHEIMER'S)**

→ **EARLY ENVIRONMENTALISTS (JOHN MUIR, RACHEL CARSON)**

→ **ENVIRONMENTAL ACTIVISM AND GREEN MOVEMENTS (EARTH DAY, GREENPEACE, GREEN BELT MOVEMENT)**

→ **RECYCLING, SPECIES PROTECTION, CLEAN AIR AND WATER LEGISLATION**

→ **THE GREEN REVOLUTION (AGRICULTURAL PRODUCTIVITY VS. ECOLOGICAL IMPACT)**

→ **AGRICULTURAL DISASTERS (FAMINES, "DUST BOWL" CRISIS)**

→ **EARTH SHAPING (DAM BUILDING, DIVERSION OF RIVERS, ENVIRONMENTAL IMPACT OF WAR)**

→ **POLLUTION (ENVIRONMENTAL DISASTERS, RELIANCE ON FOSSIL FUELS)**

→ **NUCLEAR ACCIDENTS (CHERNOBYL)**

→ **DEPLETION OF THE OZONE LAYER**

→ **CLIMATE CHANGE AND GLOBAL WARMING (CARBON-BASED GREENHOUSE GASES, KYOTO PROTOCOL)**

At no other point in history has human activity had such an overpowering **environmental impact** as it has had during the twentieth and twenty-first centuries. **Population growth**, due principally to improvements in medicine and public-health programming, has exploded. That, combined with ever-increasing reliance on energy-dependent technology, has led to unprecedented and continually mounting levels of **resource extraction** and **consumption**. **Pollution** and **species extinction** threaten the well-being of the environment as never before, and humanity's **earth-shaping capacity** now operates literally on a planetary scale—with consequences such as widespread flooding, deforestation, desertification, and **climate change** in the form of **global warming**.

## THE ENVIRONMENT

It is common to think of pollution and environmental crisis as modern problems. In fact, societies have affected—and been affected by—the environment from the Stone Age onward. Resource extraction and consumption, as well as pollution, have always been part of the human past. The downfall of civilizations like those of the Indus Valley and Easter Island has been linked directly to environmental disaster or, in the latter case, mismanagement. In countless ways, the industrial era has made humanity's footprint on the environment heavier than ever before: Societies consume more, rely more on machine production and fuel-driven transport, and possess engineering skills that involve the capacity to change the earth in ways unimaginable to preindustrial societies. Currently, climate change (global warming) serves as the clearest demonstration of how profoundly human action has affected the environment.

# DISEASE, HEALTH, AND POPULATION IN THE CONTEMPORARY ERA

Diseases associated with poverty, such as malaria, cholera, and tuberculosis, persisted in many parts of the world. On the other hand, **vaccination campaigns** and other public-health initiatives, both in developed countries and internationally as part of relief efforts, have in many cases reduced or even eliminated certain diseases. **Polio** and **smallpox**, formerly huge killers, are among the illnesses that have been all but eradicated, and treatments for formerly incurable venereal diseases, such as syphilis, have been developed as well.

Also during this era, **new epidemic diseases**, their global spread made easier by better and faster transportation, have emerged—some of them lasting only briefly, others proving to be of greater duration. The era's first, and by far the deadliest, was the influenza outbreak of 1918, popularly known as the "**Spanish flu**," which infected 500 million people between early 1918 and late 1920, and which killed anywhere from 40 million to 100 million. Despite its name, the Spanish flu's origins are unknown (the earliest reports of it came from Spain, where wartime censorship did not apply, but it may have arisen in Asia, where the vast majority of deaths seem to have occurred). The global movement of soldiers and supply shipments during the final months of World War I, not to mention the displacement of peoples and demobilization of troops afterward, helped to spread Spanish flu to all quarters of the globe. Other strains of **influenza** repeatedly threaten to reach pandemic status, such as the H1N1 virus that caused great panic in 2009. Since its identification in the mid-1970s in Africa, the **Ebola virus**, which causes severe internal bleeding and kills a high percentage of its victims, has threatened several times to erupt as a major disease beyond Africa's borders. **HIV/AIDS**, also originating in Africa and identified in 1981, has killed more than 30 million people worldwide. Spread via blood or sexual transmission, HIV/AIDS quickly became a global phenomenon and remained highly fatal until the development of effective treatments in the late 1990s and early 2000s. Still incurable, HIV/AIDS is a chronic disease for those with access to treatment, but deadly to those without. Rates of infection are especially high in Africa, where it is a particular scourge.

The contemporary era has also seen the proliferation of diseases associated with sedentary lifestyles and increased longevity. Diets high in sugar and processed foods—common in North America, but also in other regions where American food habits have caught on—have caused a rapid increase in **diabetes** worldwide. **Heart disease** and **obesity** are more common for the same reason. Paradoxically, medical advances in developed societies and the resulting extension of average human lifespans into the eighties, rather than the sixties or seventies, have placed larger numbers of people at risk of **Alzheimer's disease** and other ailments associated with old age.

Also on the topic of public health, **population growth** during this era has been breathtaking. In 1900, the world population was 1.6 billion. At the century's end, that number had risen to 6 billion, and is estimated to be 7 billion today. Even in the developed world, where birthrates have tended to decline, population has increased. In the developing and less-developed worlds, birthrates are climbing. China and India each have populations of more than one billion. A great concern for the twenty-first century is whether the earth can support continued growth on this scale. **Overconsumption** of food and energy, **overproduction** of waste and pollution, and sheer **overcrowding** are all possible consequences of unchecked growth.

## THE MODERN ENVIRONMENTAL MOVEMENT

Ever since the Industrial Revolution, there has been a spirit of environmentalism, striving to prevent the natural world from overdevelopment or destruction. The Romantic movement's love for nature sparked popular concern about the effects of industrialization on it, and figures such as Henry Thoreau and Ralph Waldo Emerson promoted environmentalist ideals during the 1800s.

Modern conservation efforts date back to the creation of **national parks** (the first in the world being Yellowstone, in 1872) and **national park services** (Canada leading the way in 1911, followed by the United States in 1916). Activism by figures such as the Scottish-American naturalist **John Muir**, co-founder of the Sierra Club, and President Theodore Roosevelt, an avid outdoorsman, were crucial during the turn of the century.

If environmental awareness grew steadily during the first half of the 1900s, it hugely expanded after World War II, with the rise of the contemporary **environmental** (or **green**) **movement**. This arose as it became more evident that pollution, species extinction, and uncontrolled industrialization posed an undeniable threat to the earth's ecological well-being. Under the aegis of the United Nations, the **International Union for Conservation of Nature** (IUCN, founded in 1948), began maintaining a "red list" of **endangered species** and continues to monitor the issue today. Many green groups and organizations took shape in the 1960s and 1970s, both in North America and Western Europe. A major inspiration came with the 1962 publication of *Silent Spring*, by **Rachel Carson**, who warned of the dangers connected with using the insecticide DDT. The first celebration of **Earth Day**—now an annual event on April 22—also popularized the environmental movement.

Non-governmental organizations (**NGOs**) working on behalf of the environment have become globally influential. These include the World Wildlife Fund (1961) and **Greenpeace**, founded in 1969–1972 out of efforts to protect atomic testing in Alaska, and now arguably the most famous eco-activist group in the world—and one of the most interventionist, with its policy of "direct action" to impede industrial, hunting, and fishing efforts of which it disapproves. Also renowned is Kenya's **Green Belt Movement**, established in 1977 by Wangari Maathai, the first African woman to win the Nobel Peace Prize. A prominent example of eco-feminism, the Green Belt Movement trained large numbers of women to fight deforestation by planting trees and engaging in eco-tourism.

In certain countries, especially in Western Europe, **green parties** play an important role in electoral politics. Contemporary environmental efforts are largely focused on the problem of **climate change**.

**Among the environmentalist triumphs of the 1970s and 1980s—at least in the developed world—were the rise of recycling as a common practice, greater protection of endangered species (including a near-complete moratorium on whaling), and stricter laws to ensure clean air and water.**

## POLLUTION, EARTH SHAPING, AND GLOBAL WARMING

The **earth-shaping capacity** of human societies has dramatically increased during this era, thanks to escalating industrialization, greater scientific aptitude, and massive engineering projects. An important example of this trend is the so-called **Green Revolution**: a massive campaign from the 1940s through the 1970s to improve agricultural production, especially in the developing world, by clearing more land, by relying on new scientific techniques, and by using new fertilizers and insecticides. Most consider the Green Revolution to have begun with improvements in corn production in Mexico during the 1940s, and then to have spread throughout Latin America, as well as to places like India, China, and the Middle East, where famine had previously threatened populations on a regular basis. Even though the Green Revolution indeed improved food production—and can be said to have saved many lives—it also had a large and not entirely positive impact on the environment, as it resulted in greater deforestation, increased water consumption, and extensive use of pesticides.

Prior to the Green Revolution, **famine** and other forms of agricultural downturn periodically occurred. Human-caused famines struck the USSR in the 1930s and China in the 1950s, and natural famines blighted India in the 1940s and Ethiopia in the 1980s. In the United States and Canada, the "**dust bowl**" crisis of the 1930s—during which thousands of square miles of fertile soil were lost to a disastrous combination of aridity and huge windstorms—drastically lowered agricultural output and added extra stress to the Great Depression.

**Dam building** and the **diversion of rivers** constitute another form of earth shaping, increasingly frequent during the 1900s and 2000s. Projects like the Hoover Dam in Depression-era America, the Dnieprostroi hydroelectric complex in Stalinist Russia, Egypt's **Aswan High Dam**, and China's mammoth **Three Gorges Dam** have all left gigantic ecological footprints, and sizable bodies of water such as the Aral Sea, between Kazakhstan and Uzbekistan, have dried up or suffered irreversible damage due to the rerouting of rivers. Taken on a large enough scale, the **environmental impact of warfare** can be considered its own form of earth shaping. Examples of how war has affected the environment include radiation from **nuclear-weapons testing** (in the Pacific, off Alaska, in Central Asia, and in the Soviet Arctic, among other places), biological and chemical warfare between Iran and Iraq during the 1970s, the napalming of forests during the Vietnam War, and the destruction of oil wells during times of armed conflict, especially in the Middle East.

**Pollution** has been and remains an ever-present threat, whether on the ground or in the air and water. Both in the developed and developing worlds, communities continue to generate more trash and toxic waste, burn more fossil fuels, and release more emissions into the air and water with every passing year. Habitats like wetlands, rain forests, and polar ecosystems have been especially harmed, and in numerous urban settings—Tokyo, Los Angeles, Mexico City, Delhi, and many cities in China and Russia—air quality reaches noxious levels on a routine basis. Certain **environmental disasters** have proven particularly devastating, including the Bhopal incident of 1984 (when a Union Carbide pesticide factory killed thousands in India with an accidental release of poison gas), the 1989 wreck of the oil tanker *Exxon Valdez* off the Alaskan coast, the 2010 Deepwater oil platform blowout in the Gulf of Mexico, and the nuclear incidents described below. Before the elimination of chlorofluorocarbons (CFCs) in spray form, deep concerns arose during the 1980s and 1990s that the atmosphere's protective **ozone layer** would become dangerously depleted.

A serious failure here has been the inability or unwillingness to develop sources of clean, sustainable energy. Continued **reliance on fossil fuels** such as coal and petroleum leads not only to periodic shortages and economic dilemmas but also to continued pollution. Hydroelectric generation of electric power has its limits, and the dams required for it create huge ecological stresses. Experiments with wind and solar power—potentially the cleanest sources of power possible—have not been adequately supported by governments or corporations. (At times, the latter, whose profits depend on fossil-fuel technologies, have actively opposed such experiments.) The only alternative source of energy that has met with any success is nuclear power. This, however, carries with it serious risks, as **nuclear accidents** at Three Mile Island (1979) in Pennsylvania, **Chernobyl** (1986) in Ukraine, and Fukushima (2011) in Japan have demonstrated.

The most dangerous environmental issue of the present day is **climate change** in the form of **global warming**. This trend has built gradually over the course of the industrial era, caused, in the opinion of a vast scholarly majority, by the human-produced emission of carbon-based **greenhouse gases**. The resulting rise in average temperatures became steadily more noticeable during the 1900s and then spiked upward in the 1980s and 1990s, its effects unmistakably apparent, especially from the catastrophic melting of Arctic, Antarctic, and glacial ice. The combination of a thinner ozone layer, which allows more of the sun's heat to enter the atmosphere, and greater quantities of greenhouse gases, which keep that heat trapped in the atmosphere, has made the problem doubly acute.

**NOTE**

The most damaging non-military nuclear event, the Chernobyl disaster of 1986 exposed the systemic weaknesses of the crumbling Soviet Union. It killed 8,000 in the short term, and thousands more—the number is in dispute—fell ill or died afterward. Fallout spread far beyond the USSR's borders, poisoning fish and reindeer as far away as Scandinavia, and a large exclusion zone in Ukraine and Belarus is still off-limits.

On the whole, international efforts to combat climate change have met with limited success. A prime example is the Kyoto Summit (1997), where more than 150 nations gathered to discuss the dangers of global warming. Although a **Kyoto Protocol** was hammered out, and although subsequent summits have fine-tuned various points, it is still contentious, and many countries, including the United States, have not ratified it. A particular point of conflict is the question of whether industrializing countries in the less-developed world should be compelled to abide by the same clean-air regulations that the richer nations of the developed world do. It is also the case that a wave of **climate-change denial** has arisen during the 2000s, sponsored by corporate and political interests with the goal of convincing the public to disregard the scientific consensus that climate change is indeed an urgent matter for concern.

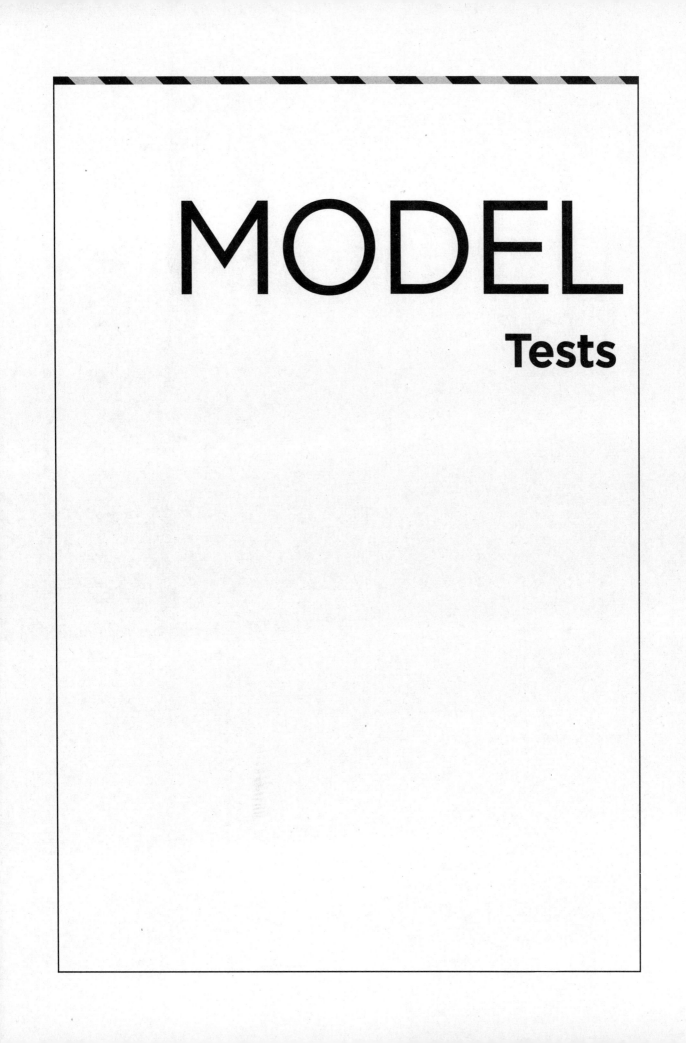

# MODEL

## Tests

# ANSWER SHEET
## Model Test 1

**SECTION 1**

1. Ⓐ Ⓑ Ⓒ Ⓓ
2. Ⓐ Ⓑ Ⓒ Ⓓ
3. Ⓐ Ⓑ Ⓒ Ⓓ
4. Ⓐ Ⓑ Ⓒ Ⓓ
5. Ⓐ Ⓑ Ⓒ Ⓓ
6. Ⓐ Ⓑ Ⓒ Ⓓ
7. Ⓐ Ⓑ Ⓒ Ⓓ
8. Ⓐ Ⓑ Ⓒ Ⓓ
9. Ⓐ Ⓑ Ⓒ Ⓓ
10. Ⓐ Ⓑ Ⓒ Ⓓ
11. Ⓐ Ⓑ Ⓒ Ⓓ
12. Ⓐ Ⓑ Ⓒ Ⓓ
13. Ⓐ Ⓑ Ⓒ Ⓓ
14. Ⓐ Ⓑ Ⓒ Ⓓ
15. Ⓐ Ⓑ Ⓒ Ⓓ
16. Ⓐ Ⓑ Ⓒ Ⓓ
17. Ⓐ Ⓑ Ⓒ Ⓓ
18. Ⓐ Ⓑ Ⓒ Ⓓ
19. Ⓐ Ⓑ Ⓒ Ⓓ
20. Ⓐ Ⓑ Ⓒ Ⓓ
21. Ⓐ Ⓑ Ⓒ Ⓓ
22. Ⓐ Ⓑ Ⓒ Ⓓ
23. Ⓐ Ⓑ Ⓒ Ⓓ
24. Ⓐ Ⓑ Ⓒ Ⓓ
25. Ⓐ Ⓑ Ⓒ Ⓓ

26. Ⓐ Ⓑ Ⓒ Ⓓ
27. Ⓐ Ⓑ Ⓒ Ⓓ
28. Ⓐ Ⓑ Ⓒ Ⓓ
29. Ⓐ Ⓑ Ⓒ Ⓓ
30. Ⓐ Ⓑ Ⓒ Ⓓ
31. Ⓐ Ⓑ Ⓒ Ⓓ
32. Ⓐ Ⓑ Ⓒ Ⓓ
33. Ⓐ Ⓑ Ⓒ Ⓓ
34. Ⓐ Ⓑ Ⓒ Ⓓ
35. Ⓐ Ⓑ Ⓒ Ⓓ
36. Ⓐ Ⓑ Ⓒ Ⓓ
37. Ⓐ Ⓑ Ⓒ Ⓓ
38. Ⓐ Ⓑ Ⓒ Ⓓ
39. Ⓐ Ⓑ Ⓒ Ⓓ
40. Ⓐ Ⓑ Ⓒ Ⓓ
41. Ⓐ Ⓑ Ⓒ Ⓓ
42. Ⓐ Ⓑ Ⓒ Ⓓ
43. Ⓐ Ⓑ Ⓒ Ⓓ
44. Ⓐ Ⓑ Ⓒ Ⓓ
45. Ⓐ Ⓑ Ⓒ Ⓓ
46. Ⓐ Ⓑ Ⓒ Ⓓ
47. Ⓐ Ⓑ Ⓒ Ⓓ
48. Ⓐ Ⓑ Ⓒ Ⓓ
49. Ⓐ Ⓑ Ⓒ Ⓓ
50. Ⓐ Ⓑ Ⓒ Ⓓ

51. Ⓐ Ⓑ Ⓒ Ⓓ
52. Ⓐ Ⓑ Ⓒ Ⓓ
53. Ⓐ Ⓑ Ⓒ Ⓓ
54. Ⓐ Ⓑ Ⓒ Ⓓ
55. Ⓐ Ⓑ Ⓒ Ⓓ
56. Ⓐ Ⓑ Ⓒ Ⓓ
57. Ⓐ Ⓑ Ⓒ Ⓓ
58. Ⓐ Ⓑ Ⓒ Ⓓ
59. Ⓐ Ⓑ Ⓒ Ⓓ
60. Ⓐ Ⓑ Ⓒ Ⓓ
61. Ⓐ Ⓑ Ⓒ Ⓓ
62. Ⓐ Ⓑ Ⓒ Ⓓ
63. Ⓐ Ⓑ Ⓒ Ⓓ
64. Ⓐ Ⓑ Ⓒ Ⓓ
65. Ⓐ Ⓑ Ⓒ Ⓓ
66. Ⓐ Ⓑ Ⓒ Ⓓ
67. Ⓐ Ⓑ Ⓒ Ⓓ
68. Ⓐ Ⓑ Ⓒ Ⓓ
69. Ⓐ Ⓑ Ⓒ Ⓓ
70. Ⓐ Ⓑ Ⓒ Ⓓ

# SECTION I: MULTIPLE-CHOICE QUESTIONS

## Time: 55 Minutes for 70 Questions

> **DIRECTIONS:** Each of the questions or incomplete statements below is followed by four suggested answers or completions. Select the one that is best in each case and then fill in the corresponding oval on the answer sheet.

1. The Sumerian and Olmec civilizations are most alike
   (A) in their creation of long-lasting cultural foundations for later societies.
   (B) because of the way they used horseback warfare to conquer neighboring territories.
   (C) in their early commitment to representative political systems.
   (D) because they each developed monotheistic religions.

2. Historians and archaeologists have designated the earliest period of human prehistory the "Stone Age" because
   (A) most technology from that era was so crudely manufactured.
   (B) the majority of dwellings were carved from that material.
   (C) tools from that material were likeliest to survive as objects for future study.
   (D) societies from that era did not know how to shape tools from other materials.

3. "Know the self to be sitting in the chariot, the body to be the chariot, the intellect the charioteer, and the mind the reins. He who has understanding, who is mindful and always pure, indeed reaches that place from whence he is not born again."

   The excerpt above from the Upanishads reflects which of the following religious propositions?
   (A) Hindus should give up their faith in favor of Buddhism.
   (B) Individual responsibility, not priestly authority, brings about spiritual evolution.
   (C) One lifetime is enough to extinguish one's soul after death.
   (D) The doctrines of karma and reincarnation are heretical.

4. Economic life in Andean societies between 600 B.C.E. and 600 C.E. was characterized by all of the following EXCEPT
   (A) recordkeeping by the tying of knots.
   (B) corvée labor for farming and road building.
   (C) horse-drawn transport.
   (D) trade with peoples of the Amazon basin.

5. Large numbers of Chinese came to live on the Malay Peninsula, starting in the period between 600 B.C.E. and 600 C.E. because
   (A) they were conquered and brought there as slaves.
   (B) transregional trade induced them to form a diasporic community there.
   (C) the missionary efforts of Buddhist monks attracted them southward.
   (D) environmental damage to their homeland forced them to migrate.

6. Which of the following best describes how Buddhism changed as it spread throughout Asia?
   (A) It shed the Buddha's original teachings about a heavenly afterlife.
   (B) It absorbed doctrinal and ritual elements from other Asian religions.
   (C) It rejected the concept of karma in order to appeal to non-Indian worshippers.
   (D) It became more dogmatic as it competed with other faiths.

7. In recent years, many historians have attempted to highlight additional factors in the collapse of the Roman and Han empires beyond the traditional explanation of nomadic invasion. Which of the following would best support such a widening of the common interpretation?
   (A) the epidemic spread of diseases like smallpox in the direction of both empires
   (B) popular revolts sparked among both populations by attempts to suppress religious beliefs
   (C) widespread desertification caused by the intensification of agriculture by both societies
   (D) failure by both governments to develop a system of regional administration

8. The map below indicates that most societies in pre-Columbian Mesoamerica

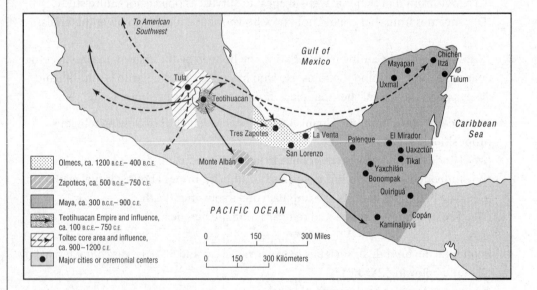

   (A) were governed by a centralized state.
   (B) did not trade extensively.
   (C) were heavily urbanized.
   (D) remained isolated from each other.

**Questions 9–10 are based on the following passage.**

### Gunpowder Weaponry: Europe vs. China

In Western Europe during the 1200s through the 1400s, early cannon, as heavy and as slow to fire as they were, proved useful enough in the protracted sieges that dominated warfare during this period that governments found it sufficiently worthwhile to pay for them and for the experimentation that eventually produced gunpowder weapons that were both more powerful and easier to move. By contrast, China, especially after the mid-1300s, was threatened mainly by highly mobile steppe nomads, against whom early gunpowder weapons, with their unwieldiness, proved of little utility. It therefore devoted its efforts to the improvement of horse archer units who could effectively combat the country's deadliest foe.

9. According to this passage, why did the Chinese, despite inventing gunpowder, fail to lead in the innovation of gunpowder weaponry?
   (A) They were discouraged by Confucian traditionalism from doing so.
   (B) They put too much faith in the numerical strength of their armed forces to feel the need for new weapons.
   (C) They logically decided to develop weapons systems better suited to their immediate military needs.
   (D) They could not afford the initial expense of converting to a new technological system.

10. What traditional view of world history does this passage seem to challenge?
    (A) that China has always been less technologically adept than most other Eurasian civilizations
    (B) that China's rigid form of dictatorial rule suppressed any spirit of innovation in the technological and military spheres
    (C) that China was hindered by religious fundamentalism when it came to modernizing efforts
    (D) that China was surpassed by Europe in global power because it turned a blind eye to the obvious benefits of technological change

---

11. Which of the following foodstuffs began to make their way from Asia to the Mediterranean between 600 C.E. and 1450 C.E.?
    (A) sugar and citrus
    (B) rice and bananas
    (C) beans and maize
    (D) coffee and barley

12. Viking longboats and Polynesian double-hulled canoes have which of the following in common?

(A) The building of both required advanced knowledge of metallurgy.

(B) They both facilitated the effective projection of military force.

(C) Both of them permitted open-water navigation over great distances.

(D) The design of the former was inspired by the latter in a process of cultural diffusion.

13. Which of the following correctly describes differences between China and Europe between 600 C.E. and 1450 C.E.?

(A) China unraveled politically, whereas Europe trended toward unification.

(B) Religious doctrine dominated political affairs in Europe but had little political influence in China.

(C) Most of China was unified during much of this period, whereas Europe was governed by many monarchies.

(D) Chinese law instituted civil rights, whereas European codes preserved the feudal system.

14.
"O ye who believe! Strong drink and games of chance and idols... are
only an infamy of Satan's handiwork. Leave it aside in order that ye
may succeed."

the Qur'an, Sura 5: 89

"When once you hear the roses are in bloom,
Then is the time, my love, to pour the wine."

the *Rubáiyát* of Omar Khayyám

The second passage does not support the first because the second passage

(A) shows a noted Muslim author arguing in favor of gambling.

(B) shows a noted Muslim author favoring a practice discouraged by the Qur'an.

(C) shows a noted Muslim author in violation of the Qur'an's injunction against writing verse.

(D) shows a noted Muslim expressing atheistic sentiments.

15. The fate of Kongo at the hands of foreign powers in the 1500s and 1600s most resembles that of China in the 1800s, in that

(A) large portions of both populations were enslaved.

(B) both nations were politically dominated without being colonized outright.

(C) the rulers of both states were forced to convert to Christianity.

(D) both economies were industrialized by foreign occupiers.

16. Most historians would agree that the factor that made indigenous Americans least able to resist European colonization in the 1500s was

(A) the smallness of their armies compared to the invading forces.

(B) their unfamiliarity with horse warfare.

(C) the politically decentralized nature of their societies.

(D) their vulnerability to Eurasian diseases.

17. Between 1500 and 1700 C.E., the Mughal, Safavid, and Ottoman empires shared which of the following characteristics?
    (A) strong economies based on the cultivation of cotton
    (B) a high degree of political decentralization
    (C) effective and technologically advanced gunpowder armies
    (D) low levels of artistic attainment due to religious austerity

18. Based on the map below, which of the following statements can one most safely conclude to be true?

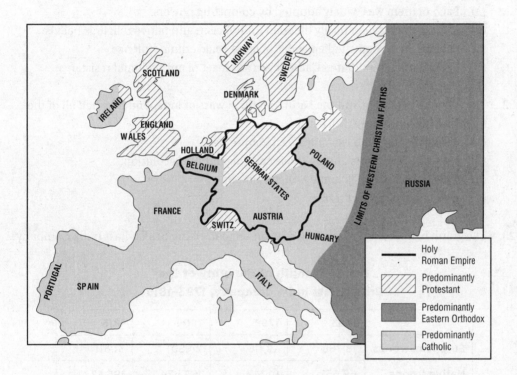

    (A) Jews were all but completely expelled from Europe during the Protestant Reformation.
    (B) The Protestant Reformation brought a high degree of religious unity to the British Isles.
    (C) There were more Protestants than Catholics in Europe by the end of the Reformation.
    (D) The German states experienced the most severe religious divisions in Reformation-era Europe.

19. Russian colonization of Siberia most resembled French colonization of North America in that
    (A) both were motivated largely by the fur trade.
    (B) both made extensive use of indentured servitude to provide a labor force.
    (C) both were carried out by religious minorities who wished to worship as they pleased.
    (D) both were carried out by the deployment of powerful land forces.

20. Which of the following best describes cotton's role in the world economy during the 1450–1750 period?
    (A) Its growing importance increased the U.S. South's dependence on slavery.
    (B) Near the end of this period, India was the leading producer of textiles made from it.
    (C) It was harvested more systematically in response to the Industrial Revolution.
    (D) Compared to wool, it remained economically unimportant during these years.

21. Which of the following best characterizes Vodun and the Latin American cult of saints?
    (A) Each of them was widely adopted by colonizing powers.
    (B) Each of them syncretically blended Catholicism and native religious beliefs.
    (C) Each of them motivated episodes of large-scale ethnic violence.
    (D) Each of them repudiated Catholicism as an act of anti-colonial resistance.

22. The French Revolution and the Latin American wars of independence had all of the following in common EXCEPT
    (A) dissatisfaction with existing social hierarchies.
    (B) class disagreements among those carrying out the revolution.
    (C) a philosophical basis in the Enlightenment.
    (D) a systematic reign of terror.

23. The graph below reflects which priority on the part of the British East India Company?

**Troop strength of the army of the
British East India Company, 1793–1815**

|                 | 1793   | 1798    | 1805    | 1815    |
|-----------------|--------|---------|---------|---------|
| European troops | 18,768 | 22,116  | 24,891  | 31,611  |
| Native troops   | 69,661 | 91,147  | 167,674 | 195,572 |
| TOTAL           | 88,429 | 113,313 | 192,565 | 227,183 |

    (A) to provide training for British troops in an overseas setting
    (B) to instill patriotic pride among Indians by allowing them to serve as soldiers
    (C) to economize on the costs of maintaining imperial authority overseas
    (D) to segregate white Britons from native populations in their colonies

24. Which of the following do the Tanzimat reforms and China's self-strengthening movement have in common?
    (A) They yielded only moderate results because of their limited nature.
    (B) They focused principally on improving the armed forces.
    (C) They provided women with a much greater range of rights and freedoms.
    (D) They emphasized social liberalization at the expense of industrialization.

25. Taken together, the Cherokee Nation, Maroon societies, and Cossack hosts are best understood in which of the following contexts?
    (A) societies consisting of refugees from slave status
    (B) societies practicing a schismatic religion
    (C) societies governed by warrior elites
    (D) societies existing on the periphery of large states

26. Which of the following best describes the impact of industrialization on the lives of European women during the 1800s?
    (A) Women gained steadily greater social and political equality because of the respect they earned in the workplace.
    (B) Growing demand for trained engineers and technicians afforded women easier access to higher education.
    (C) Women in most European nations became only minimally involved with industrial work.
    (D) Women worked for lower wages than men and were still expected to assume primary responsibility for the home.

27. The White Australia Policy most closely resembles which of the following?
    (A) Russia's Pale of Jewish Settlement
    (B) anti-mestizo discrimination in Mexico
    (C) the U.S. Chinese Exclusion Act
    (D) apartheid in South Africa

28. The photograph below most likely illustrates which trend of the late 1800s?

    (A) African hunters pursuing their traditional livelihood
    (B) African hunters exploiting resources under orders from colonial masters
    (C) African hunters engaged in trade with Westerners on equal terms
    (D) African hunters taking charge of ivory harvesting to keep whites from depleting supplies

29. The Bretton Woods system, created after World War II to revive and regulate the global economy, provided for all of the following EXCEPT
   (A) the gold standard as basis for currency exchange.
   (B) the European Union.
   (C) the International Monetary Fund.
   (D) the General Agreement on Trade and Tariffs.

30. "No task is more urgent than that of preserving peace. Without peace our independence means little. The rehabilitation and upbuilding of our countries will have little meaning. Our revolutions will not be allowed to run their course. What can we do? We can do much! We can inject the voice of reason into world affairs. We can mobilize all the spiritual, all the moral, all the political strength of Asia and Africa on the side of peace. Yes, we! We, the peoples of Asia and Africa, 1.4 billion strong."

   The quotation above, from the keynote address given by Indonesian leader Sukarno at the Bandung Conference of 1955, is best seen as a call for
   (A) all nations to pursue complete nuclear disarmament.
   (B) newly decolonized nations to remain non-aligned during the Cold War.
   (C) African and Asian states to join together in a military alliance.
   (D) Third World countries to embrace communism.

31. The poster shown below is most likely meant to communicate

   (A) the Nazi Party's anti-Semitic ideology.
   (B) the Nazi Party's preoccupation with racial purity.
   (C) the Nazi Party's plans for economic recovery.
   (D) the Nazi Party's opposition to communism.

32. Which of the following best explains the global spread of the 1918 influenza pandemic?
    (A) the worldwide movement of soldiers, supplies, and refugees as World War I ended
    (B) the biological weapons program carried out by Germany during World War I
    (C) the failure of governments to attend to public health while distracted by World War I
    (D) the physical weakening caused during World War I by hunger and exhaustion

33. The global popularity of Bollywood movies and manga comics is best seen as an illustration of which of the following trends?
    (A) widening divisions between non-Western and Western forms of mass media
    (B) non-Western cultural appropriation of Western forms of mass media
    (C) rejection by non-Western cultures of Western forms of mass media
    (D) domination of non-Western cultural traditions by Western forms of mass media

**Questions 34–35 are based on the following passage.**

"This has always been a man's world, but what advantage has enabled him to carry out his will? [Historically,] the bondage of reproduction was a terrible handicap for women in the struggle against a hostile world. Pregnancy, childbirth, and menstruation reduced their capacity for work and made them at times wholly dependent upon men for protection and food. As nature failed to provide sterile periods like other mammalian females, closely spaced maternities absorbed most of their strength and their time. With the invention of the tool, maintenance of life became for man an activity and a project, while motherhood left woman riveted to her body like an animal."

Simone de Beauvoir, *The Second Sex*, 1949

34. In de Beauvoir's eyes, what is the root cause of gender inequality?
    (A) innate chauvinism on the part of most human males
    (B) social ramifications of human females' inability to control fertility
    (C) physical weakness of most human females relative to most human males
    (D) greater aptitude for technological innovation among human males

35. In the generation following de Beauvoir's, access to which of the following did most to allow Western women to move past the obstacle she had identified?
    (A) birth control
    (B) higher wages
    (C) political office
    (D) post-secondary education

36. Historians have generally drawn which of the following conclusions from the highly mobile lifestyles pursued by pastoralist societies?
  (A) They favored polytheism less than agriculturalists did.
  (B) Horseback skills caused them to be more warlike than agriculturalists.
  (C) They subjected women to more of a secondary status than agriculturalists did.
  (D) Lack of private property made them less prone than agriculturalists to social stratification.

37. How did the discovery of agriculture affect Neolithic people?
  (A) The need to find new plots of arable land forced a nomadic lifestyle on agriculturalists.
  (B) Permanent settlement added greater importance to the concept of private property.
  (C) The effort involved with agriculture compelled planters to give up animal domestication.
  (D) Labor specialization became less necessary as more people grew food.

38. "Meng Yizi asked about the treatment of parents. The Master said, 'Never disobey!' When Fan Chi was driving his carriage for him, [he asked], 'In what sense did you mean this?' The Master said, 'While they are alive, serve them according to proper ritual. When they die, bury them according to proper ritual, and sacrifice to them according to proper ritual.'"

*The Analects*, Book 2, Chapter 5

The passage above reflects which of the following traditions?
  (A) the Judeo-Christian commandment to respect one's elders
  (B) the Vedic caste system
  (C) the Confucian ideal of filial piety
  (D) the Islamic world's "circle of justice" ideology

39. What role did peoples like the Phoenicians and Sogdians play in ancient Afro-Eurasia?
  (A) Both facilitated trade by settling widely along major networks of exchange.
  (B) Both promoted the spread of Buddhism throughout Asia.
  (C) Both pioneered representative forms of government.
  (D) Both devised systems of writing that influenced a number of cultures.

40. Which of the following played the leading role in the expansion of Indian Ocean trade between 600 B.C.E. and 600 C.E.?
  (A) the sternpost rudder
  (B) the lodestone compass
  (C) the junk
  (D) the lateen sail

41. Persia relied on which of the following state-building techniques to strengthen its imperial power between the 500s and 300s B.C.E.?
    (A) using officials called satraps to provide effective regional administration
    (B) creating a free-trade zone within Persia's economic sphere of influence
    (C) forming a regional military alliance with neighboring peoples like the Greeks
    (D) suppressing all forms of worship besides Zoroastrianism to foster cultural unity

42. "TABLE IX. Concerning Public Law

    Law I. No privileges or statutes shall be enacted in favor of private persons to the injury of others contrary to the law common to all citizens, and which individuals, no matter of what ranks, have a right to make use of.

    Law II. The same rights shall be conferred upon, and the same laws shall be considered to have been enacted for, all the people residing in and beyond Latium, that have been enacted for good and steadfast Roman citizens.

    Law III. When a judge, or an arbiter appointed to hear a case, accepts money or other gifts for the purpose of influencing his decision, he shall suffer the penalty of death."

    The excerpt above from the "Twelve Tables" illustrates which of the following about society in Republican Rome?
    (A) preferential treatment for elite classes
    (B) the patriarchalism inherent in the ancient Roman mindset
    (C) a concern that all citizens enjoy basic equality before the law
    (D) public revulsion for the ownership of slaves

43. "Now if divorce is your wish, I cannot blame you. For the waiting has been long. And I do not know whether the Creator will grant relief immediately so that I can come home, or whether matters will take time, for I cannot come home with nothing. Now the matter is in your hand. If you wish to end our marriage, accept this bill of repudiation, and you are free. May God inspire you with the right decision."

    Letter from a Jewish trader in India to his wife in Cairo, ca. 1200

    Which of the following is the most probable cause of the marital strain evident in this letter?
    (A) the strain placed on merchant families by long periods of separation
    (B) religious disagreements arising from the merchant's exposure to Hinduism
    (C) a decision on the part of the merchant to remain permanently in India
    (D) bankruptcy stranding the merchant far from home

44. Between 600 and 1450 C.E., which of the following was most widespread among Eurasian cultures as a way to treat women?
    (A) seclusion
    (B) sati
    (C) foot binding
    (D) clitoridectomy

45. Which of the following accurately describes an example of technology transfer resulting from the Crusades?
    (A) Europeans gained the formula for gunpowder from the Muslims.
    (B) Muslims acquired knowledge of the movable-type printing press from the Europeans.
    (C) Europeans learned castlebuilding techniques from the Muslims.
    (D) Muslims borrowed the stirrup from the Europeans.

46. Which of the following have most probably proven useful as evidence to historians researching the extent of Great Zimbabwe's role in Afro-Eurasian trade networks between 1200 and 1400 C.E.?
    (A) detailed ledgers compiled by local banking houses
    (B) Chinese ceramics and Persian artworks in the city ruins
    (C) texts left behind by Buddhist missionaries
    (D) Roman coins unearthed in the vicinity by archaeologists

47. A major consequence of Islam's arrival in India was
    (A) some improvement in the status of women where Islam took hold.
    (B) political fragmentation following the destruction of a centralized state.
    (C) the eradication of Hinduism in northern India.
    (D) the nationwide outlawing of the caste system.

48. What factor do most historians consider to have driven the process depicted in the map below?

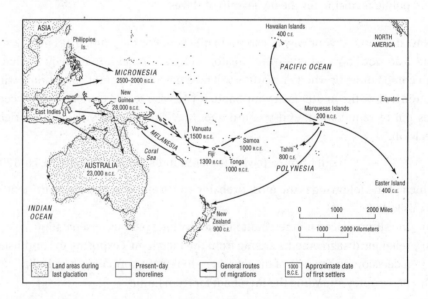

    (A) warfare
    (B) scientific curiosity
    (C) scarcity of resources
    (D) missionary activity

49. What is the principal difficulty facing historians as they assess travel accounts such as Marco Polo's and Ibn Battuta's?
   (A) adjusting for bias caused by political loyalty to their rulers
   (B) deciphering the long-lost languages in which they wrote
   (C) accounting for their religious prejudices
   (D) verifying that they saw everything they claimed to see

50. "What a wonderful and amazing Scheme have we here of the magnificent Vastness of the Universe! So many Suns, so many Earths, and every one of them stock'd with so many Herbs, Trees and Animals, and adorn'd with so many Seas and Mountains! And how must our wonder and admiration be increased when we consider the prodigious distance and multitude of the Stars!"

   Dutch scholar Christiaan Huygens, *Cosmotheros*, Book II, 1695

   The quotation above is most probably associated with which episode in European intellectual history?
   (A) the Renaissance
   (B) the Protestant Reformation
   (C) the scientific revolution
   (D) the Romantic era

51. Which of the following best characterizes Japan's relations with the wider world during the 1600s and 1700s?
   (A) The presence of foreigners was tightly restricted.
   (B) Foreign traders had little interest in Japan.
   (C) Christian missionary activity was actively supported.
   (D) Merchants engaged in free trade with their foreign counterparts.

52. West Africa's coastal states were most likely to avoid European colonization between the 1400s and the 1800s if they
   (A) built their own navies to counter European sea power.
   (B) sold captives from neighboring tribes to European slavers in exchange for guns.
   (C) relied on diseases like malaria and sleeping sickness to ward off European invaders.
   (D) formed regional alliances to repel European forces.

53. In India during the late 1600s, which of the following stemmed largely from Islamic militancy on the part of the Mughal rulers?
   (A) a shift in political allegiance among Hindus to English colonizers
   (B) the formation of breakaway states by the Sikhs and Marathas
   (C) a mass conversion that temporarily made Muslims a religious majority
   (D) the rapid collapse of the Mughal sultanate

54. Which of the following best explains why the early 1500s are treated as a turning point in the historiography of East Africa?
    (A) Sudden desertification made much of the region uninhabitable.
    (B) Abolition of the Arab slave trade liberalized society in the coastal cities.
    (C) European traders and colonists first arrived on the scene.
    (D) Invading Berber warriors converted most of the population to Islam.

55. Plantation agriculture in the Americas between 1450 and 1750 is associated with all of the following EXCEPT
    (A) exploitation of native labor.
    (B) environmental stress.
    (C) the Atlantic slave trade.
    (D) economic diversification.

56. Among Ottoman janissaries and Japanese samurai during the late 1600s and 1700s C.E., which of the following was a common response to socioeconomic and technological change?
    (A) determined opposition to any trends that might weaken their privileged position
    (B) cautious adoption of reforms that seemed militarily useful
    (C) recognition that allowing limited changes might stave off future revolution
    (D) enthusiastic embrace of new fashions, especially from abroad

**Questions 57–58 are based on the following passage.**

"Whether the question be to continue or to discontinue the practice of sati, the decision is equally surrounded by an awful responsibility. To consent to the consignment year after year of hundreds of innocent victims to a cruel and untimely end, when the power exists of preventing it, is a predicament which no conscience can contemplate without horror. But, on the other hand, to put to hazard by a contrary course the very safety of the British Empire in India is an alternative which itself may be considered a still greater evil. When we had powerful neighbours and greater reason to doubt our own security, expediency might recommend a more cautious proceeding, but now that we are supreme my opinion is decidedly in favour of an open and general prohibition."

Governor-General William Bentinck, "On the Suppression of Sati," 1829

57. What appears to have been Bentinck's primary consideration in deciding whether or not to outlaw sati in India?
    (A) imposing Christian values on India's Hindu population
    (B) ensuring the continued solidity of British authority
    (C) progressive concern for women's equality
    (D) racially prejudiced disdain for all Indian customs

58. Bentinck's reflections can be said to undermine which commonly held assumption about Western imperialism?
    (A) that European colonizers sometimes interfered with native religious practices
    (B) that European colonizers concerned themselves deeply with turning profits
    (C) that European colonizers were uniformly eager to impose their cultural norms on native populations
    (D) that European colonizers often resorted to armed force to impose their will on imperial subjects

_____

59. "From this foul drain, the greatest stream of human industry flows out to fertilize the whole world. From this filthy sewer, pure gold flows. Here, humanity attains its most complete development and its most brutish state; here civilization works its miracles, and civilized man is turned almost into a savage."

    This quotation, describing Alexis de Tocqueville's impressions of the English city of Manchester in the 1830s, is best read as
    (A) an expression of modern environmental sensibilities.
    (B) an acknowledgment of industrialization's mixed costs and benefits.
    (C) a full endorsement of rapid technological progress.
    (D) an example of radical opposition to modernization.

60. Which of the following statements best represents an anti-colonial interpretation of the native violence during the Indian Revolt of 1857?
    (A) The dogged defense of isolated outposts by British troops who were far outnumbered by sepoy rebels ranks among the most heroic episodes in modern military history.
    (B) The coercive nature of British power in India, and the popular perception that colonial authorities disrespected Indian ways, brutalized sepoy troops even before the revolt.
    (C) The massacres of British women and children on those occasions when colonial troops surrendered to sepoy forces represent unforgiveable atrocities.
    (D) The irrationality of religious and ethnic hatred drove the sepoy rebels to commit crimes that Western armies considered beyond the bounds of proper military conduct.

61. The cartoon shown below depicts which development of the late 1800s?

(A) Western fears about growing numbers of Asian immigrants
(B) Korean protests against the influx of Christian missionaries
(C) Burmese opposition to the French colonization of Indochina
(D) China's inability to prevent Western encroachments on its sovereignty

62. A transnational bank founded in the late 1800s would have been most likely to interact with non-Western regions by
(A) investing in public works to benefit local populations.
(B) working with local elites to reap profits for foreign investors.
(C) refusing to do business with any native individuals or corporations.
(D) granting microtransactional loans to poor families.

63. Which of the following did State Shintoism and Nazi ideology have in common?
(A) Both called for an end to European imperialism in Asia.
(B) Both called for firmness, but restraint, when dealing with enemies.
(C) Both encouraged a sense of racial superiority.
(D) Both demanded the veneration of the political leader as divine.

64. Which of the following did NOT contribute directly to the establishment of the boundaries depicted in the map below?

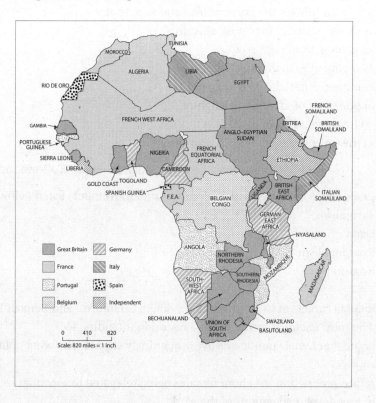

(A) the equipping of Western armies with industrial-era weaponry
(B) the guidelines laid out at the Berlin Conference of 1884–1885
(C) the emergence of effective treatments for malaria
(D) the widespread influence of Muslim merchants and slave traders

65. Cultural historians have traditionally regarded novels like *All Quiet on the Western Front* and the cynical verses of Britain's "war poets" as accurately reflecting a widespread perception of World War I as a pointless and painful experience. Which of the following most directly CHALLENGES this assumption?
(A) awakening public alarm in interwar Europe regarding gas attacks and aerial bombardment
(B) the growing prominence of violent sports such as boxing in interwar mass media
(C) the portrayal of World War I as a grand adventure in interwar fictional works like *Storm of Steel*
(D) popular enthusiasm for long-distance aviation exploits during the interwar years

66. "New York! I say New York, let black blood flow into your blood.
Let it wash the rust from your steel joints, like an oil of life
Let it give your bridges the curve of hips and supple vines...
See your rivers stirring with musk alligators
And sea cows with mirage eyes...
Just open your eyes to the April rainbow
And your eyes, especially your ears, to God
Who in one burst of saxophone laughter
Created heaven and earth in six days,
And on the seventh slept a deep Negro sleep."

from Léopold Sédar Senghor, "To New York," 1956

The verses above belong to which of the cultural movements listed below?
(A) Surrealism
(B) Dada
(C) Existentialism
(D) Négritude

67. The political careers of Corazon Aquino, Violeta Chamorro, and Benazir Bhutto would be most useful as evidence for a historian intending to
(A) argue that female politicians overwhelmingly support left-wing political causes.
(B) refute generalizations about females being relegated to secondary status in less-developed regions of the world.
(C) prove that female political figures began to outnumber male political figures during the 1980s onward.
(D) show that the earning potential of female career women has started to approach that of males in the non-Western world.

68. A key difference between India's national-liberation movement and South Africa's anti-apartheid movement is that
(A) the former embraced communism, whereas the latter leaned toward anarchism.
(B) the former was led by advocates of non-violence, whereas the latter turned more readily to violent action.
(C) the former collaborated with Britain's foes during World War II, whereas the latter remained loyal.
(D) the former wished to remain in the British Empire as a dominion, whereas the latter wanted complete freedom.

69. Which of the following would most historians consider the best explanation for the rapid changes depicted in the chart shown below?

| World Human Population Growth: 1 C.E.–1999 | |
| --- | --- |
| *Year* | *Population* |
| 1 C.E. | 200 million |
| 1650 | 500 million |
| 1850 | 1 billion |
| 1930 | 2 billion |
| 1975 | 4 billion |
| 1999 | 6 billion |

(A) the global movement of peoples, enabled by industrial-era transportation

(B) the eradication of major famines by improvements in agricultural science after 1800

(C) the decreased impact that modern wars have had on civilian populations

(D) the effect of modern medical innovations and increased access to vaccines

70. The image below is best interpreted as an example of

(A) U.S. military domination over the Middle East.

(B) foreign takeover of U.S. corporations.

(C) cultural autonomy on the part of the non-Western world.

(D) the global influence of U.S. mass culture.

STOP

END OF SECTION I

# SECTION II: FREE-RESPONSE QUESTIONS

## Part A: Document-Based Question

**(Suggested planning and writing time—40 minutes)**

**Percent of Section II score—33$\frac{1}{3}$**

**DIRECTIONS:** The following question is based on the accompanying Documents 1–8. (The documents have been edited for the purpose of this exercise.) Write your answer on the lined pages of the Section II free-response booklet.

This question is designed to test your ability to work with and understand historical documents.

Write an essay that

- has a relevant thesis and supports that thesis with evidence from the documents.
- uses all of the documents.
- analyzes the documents by grouping them in as many appropriate ways as possible, and does not simply summarize the documents individually.
- takes into account the sources of the documents and analyzes the authors' points of view.
- identifies and explains the need for at least one additional type of document.

You may refer to relevant historical information not mentioned in the documents.

1. Using the documents, analyze Western and non-Western attitudes toward scientific and technological change from the 1500s onward. Identify an additional type of document and explain how it would help in assessing Western or non-Western actions and reactions.

## DOCUMENT 1

Source: Charlotte Brontë, English novelist, upon viewing the Crystal Palace at London's Great Exhibition (1851).

Yesterday I went for the second time to the Crystal Palace. . . . I must say I was more struck with it on this occasion than at my first visit. It is a wonderful place—vast, strange, new, and impossible to describe. . . . Whatever human industry has created you find there, from the great compartments filled with railway engines and boilers, with mill machinery in full work, with splendid carriages of all kinds, with harness of every description, to the glass-covered and velvet-spread stands loaded with the most gorgeous work of the goldsmith and silversmith. . . . It may be called a bazaar or a fair, but it is such a bazaar or fair as Eastern genii might have created. It seems as if only magic could have gathered this mass of wealth from all the ends of the earth.

## DOCUMENT 2

Source: Victor Hugo, "This Will Kill That," *The Hunchback of Notre Dame* (1830).

Our readers must excuse us if we stop a moment to investigate the enigmatic words of the archdeacon: "This will kill that. The book will kill the edifice."

First of all, it was the view of a priest. It was the fear of an ecclesiastic before a new force, the printing press. It was the frightened yet dazzled man of the sanctuary confronting the illuminating Gutenberg press. . . . It signified that one great power was following upon the heels of another great power. It meant: The printing press will destroy the Church.

But besides this first thought, there was a second . . . but it no longer belongs to the priest alone, but to the scholar and to the artist as well. Here was a premonition that human thought had advanced, and, in changing, was about to change its mode of expression, that the important ideas of each new generation would be recorded in a new way, that the book of stone, [in which carvings and sculptures had provided the illiterate with a language of images and symbols], so solid and enduring, was about to be supplanted by the paper book, which would become more enduring still. In this respect, the vague formula of the archdeacon had a second meaning: That one art would dethrone another art. It meant: Printing will destroy architecture.

## DOCUMENT 3

Source: Ito Hirobumi, young samurai from Japan, in letter to British official (1866).

Hitherto there have been a great number of stupid and ignorant persons in our provinces, who still adhered to the foolish old learning. They were unaware of the daily scientific progress of the Western nations, being like the frog at the bottom of a well. But lately they have learned. The eyes and ears of the stupid having thus been opened, the desirability of opening our country to foreign knowledge has become clear.

## DOCUMENT 4

Source: Mohandas K. Gandhi, leader of Indian independence movement, *Gandhi: His Life and Message* (1954).

The incessant search for material comforts and their multiplication is such an evil, and I make bold to say that the Europeans themselves will have to remodel their outlook if they are not to perish under the weight of the comfort to which they are becoming slaves.

## DOCUMENT 5

Source: Matteo Ricci, sixteenth-century Jesuit priest, showing a map of the world to the people of Canton during his visit to China (1578).

Of all the great nations, the Chinese have had the least commerce, indeed, one might say that they have had practically no contact whatever with outside nations, and consequently they are grossly ignorant of what the world in general is like. True, they had charts somewhat similar to this one, that were supposed to represent the whole world, but their universe was limited to their own fifteen provinces, and in the sea painted around it, they had placed a few islands to which they gave the names of different kingdoms they had heard of. . . . When they learned that China was only a part of the great east, they considered such an idea, so unlike their own, to be something utterly impossible. . . .

To them the heavens are round but the earth is flat and square, and they firmly believe that their empire is right in the middle of it. They do not like the idea of our geographies pushing their China into one corner of the Orient. They could not comprehend the demonstrations proving that the earth is a globe, made up of land and water, and that a globe of its nature has neither beginning nor end.

## DOCUMENT 6

Source: Swiss author Henri Frédéric Amiel, on European industrialization, as seen at London's Great Exhibition (1851).

The useful will take the place of the beautiful, industry will take the place of art, political economy of religion, and arithmetic of poetry.

## DOCUMENT 7

Source: Ali Akbar Davar, journalist and Iran's Minister of Public Works, editorial in *The Free Man* (1923).

Until we dedicate ourselves to an economic and technological revolution, nothing will move or change. We shall remain a nation of beggars, hungry and in ragged clothing, and we shall continue to suffer. We have six thousand years of history, but that will not translate into factories, railroads, hospitals, or schools. Schools alone without economic reforms will change nothing, as long as the environment outside the schools continues to reek of poverty. . . . When we have at least 5,000 kilometers of railways, 50 factories, 50 roads linking east and west, dams on the Karun River, and have eradicated locusts, we can then attend to the graduation of 1,000 students from institutions of higher learning.

**DOCUMENT 8**

Source: William Blake (1757–1827), English romantic poet, *Milton*.

And did those feet in ancient time
Walk upon England's mountains green?
And was the Holy Lamb of God
On England's pleasant pastures seen?

And did the Countenance Divine
Shine forth upon our clouded hills?
And was Jerusalem builded here
Among these dark Satanic Mills?

Bring me my Bow of burning gold:
Bring me my Arrows of desire:
Bring me my Spear: O clouds unfold!
Bring me my Chariot of fire.

I will not cease from Mental Fight,
Nor shall my Sword sleep in my hand
Till we have built Jerusalem
In England's green and pleasant Land.

## Part B: Continuity and Change-Over-Time Question

**(Suggested planning and writing time—40 minutes)**
**Percent of Section II score—33$\frac{1}{3}$**

---

**DIRECTIONS:** You are to answer the following question. You should spend 5 minutes organizing or outlining your essay.

Write an essay that:
- has a relevant thesis and supports that thesis with appropriate historical evidence.
- addresses all parts of the question.
- uses world historical context to show continuities and changes over time.
- analyzes the process of continuity and change over time.

---

2. Describe and explain continuities and changes in the impact of religion on politics in ONE of the following regions from 600 to 1750.

   Europe
   South Asia

## Part C: Comparative Essay

**(Suggested planning and writing time—40 minutes)**
**Percent of Section II score—33$^1$/₃**

---

**DIRECTIONS:** You are to answer the following question. You should spend 5 minutes organizing or outlining your essay.

Write an essay that:

- has a relevant thesis and supports that thesis with appropriate historical evidence.
- addresses all parts of the question.
- makes direct, relevant comparisons.
- analyzes relevant reasons for similarities and differences.

---

3. Analyze similarities and differences in the modernizing reform efforts undertaken by TWO of the following places during the 1800s C.E.

   Latin America
   Qing China
   the Ottoman Empire

**END OF SECTION II**

# ANSWER KEY
## Model Test 1

## SECTION I

| | | |
|---|---|---|
| **1.** A | **26.** D | **51.** A |
| **2.** C | **27.** C | **52.** B |
| **3.** B | **28.** B | **53.** B |
| **4.** C | **29.** B | **54.** C |
| **5.** B | **30.** B | **55.** D |
| **6.** B | **31.** D | **56.** A |
| **7.** A | **32.** A | **57.** B |
| **8.** C | **33.** B | **58.** C |
| **9.** C | **34.** B | **59.** B |
| **10.** D | **35.** A | **60.** B |
| **11.** A | **36.** D | **61.** D |
| **12.** C | **37.** B | **62.** B |
| **13.** C | **38.** C | **63.** C |
| **14.** B | **39.** A | **64.** D |
| **15.** B | **40.** D | **65.** C |
| **16.** D | **41.** A | **66.** D |
| **17.** C | **42.** C | **67.** B |
| **18.** D | **43.** A | **68.** B |
| **19.** A | **44.** A | **69.** D |
| **20.** B | **45.** C | **70.** D |
| **21.** B | **46.** B | |
| **22.** D | **47.** A | |
| **23.** C | **48.** C | |
| **24.** A | **49.** D | |
| **25.** D | **50.** C | |

# ANSWER EXPLANATIONS

1. **(A)** This question tests comparison and contextualization. Horses did not exist in the Americas prior to the European arrival, making B false, and monotheism and democracy were extremely rare in the ancient world, making C and D unlikely. The cultural legacy of the Sumerians and Olmecs, especially in the case of the former's written script, deeply influenced the societies that appeared after them.

2. **(C)** This question focuses on periodization and use of evidence. Even if A were true, it would not necessarily mean the technology was made of stone, and even though some stone dwellings are evident in the archaeological record, they would have been beyond the abilities of most Stone Age people, or not suited to a hunter-forager lifestyle, making B incorrect. It would be improbable to conclude that Stone Age people would discover the secret of manufacturing stone tools without knowing how to shape them from wood and bone as well, answer C.

3. **(B)** This question involves interpretation and contextualization. Knowledge of the Upanishads' role in the transition from Vedism to Hinduism is helpful, but even without that knowledge, the quotation itself contains nothing to support A or D, and the quotation's emphasis on "the self" favors B.

4. **(C)** This question emphasizes contextualization and, to some degree, continuity and change over time. Answer C is clearly the exception that does not belong because there were no horses in the Andes at this time. However, even if C were not so easy to spot, knowledge of the subject would identify A, B, and D as valid features of Andean societies during this time.

5. **(B)** This question tests causation, contextualization, and, to an extent, continuity and change over time. Answers A, C, and D all caused the movements of people in various times and places, but knowledge of Indian Ocean trade, which motivated many merchant communities to form far from home (such as Indians and Arabs in East Africa, or Jews and Muslims in South and East Asia, to take other examples), should suffice to identify B as correct.

6. **(B)** This question is about continuity and change over time. Most religions adapt to one degree or another to local customs as they spread, and they sometimes blend syncretically with other faiths. Although Buddhism is not without its religious controversies, it is more doctrinally flexible than "religions of the book," such as Judaism, Christianity, and Islam, so D is unlikely, and Buddhism never shed the core concepts of karma and reincarnation, making C false. Answer A presents things in the exact opposite order from how they happened.

7. **(A)** This question tests causation, comparison, and historical interpretation. External pressures famously contributed to the collapse of imperial Rome and Han China, but no one would fault their administrative skills, and both regimes actively tolerated most religions as a way to ease imperial rule (Judaism and early Christianity were rare exceptions in Rome's case), so D and B are false. Knowing the details of how the various empires of this era collapsed—or knowing the history of Eurasian epidemics from this period—is enough to exclude C in favor of A.

8. **(C)** This question requires use of evidence. Be careful in these cases not to pick answers that may be true according to general knowledge, but not proven or indicated by the map (or quotation, or graph, or whichever piece of evidence is provided). The map contains no evidence for A, B, or D, and B and D would seem unlikely in such a densely urbanized area. The proliferation of cities in such a relatively small space makes C the best choice.

9. **(C)** This question is centered on historical argumentation and historical interpretation, as well as causation. The passage's clear purpose is to show that Chinese lack of interest in early gunpowder weaponry was rational and not culturally or economically short-sighted, as Western historians have traditionally supposed.

10. **(D)** This question, related to the one preceding it, involves historical argumentation even more directly. Answer D relates directly to the earlier view described above.

11. **(A)** This question tests continuity and change over time, as it pertains to trade goods and the worldwide diffusion of crops and foodstuffs. Maize (corn) was unknown in Afro-Eurasia prior to the Columbian Exchange, so C is incorrect. From the Neolithic onward, barley was one of the earliest crops known to humankind, excluding D, and while bananas spread outward from Asia at this time, they were not commonly grown in the Mediterranean, making B less likely (in addition, rice took longer to be cultivated outside Asia in any great volume).

12. **(C)** This question involves comparison and contextualization. Both vessels were made principally of wood, and they had nothing to do with each other—the Vikings operated in the Atlantic, the Polynesians in the Pacific—so A and D are false. The Vikings used their longboats to raid over long distances, but while the Polynesians fought wars, their canoes were principally a means of transport, making C a better choice than B.

13. **(C)** This question tests comparison. Although China experienced periods of disunity, it was far less fragmented than Europe became after the fall of Rome, and few states at this time concerned themselves with civil rights, so A and D are false. Religion played a public and political role in both regions, so B is false as well.

14. **(B)** This question calls for contextualization, historical argumentation, and historical interpretation. The passage from the Qur'an presents a cultural norm that religious doctrine sought to enforce—in this case Islam's famous restriction on the consumption of alcohol—while the second indicates that the restriction was not always observed in real life.

15. **(B)** This question involves comparison. Western powers exploited China in many ways during the 1800s, but not by enslaving its people outright, and although missionaries were allowed to proselytize in China after the Opium Wars, the Qing rulership did not convert to Christianity, making A and C incorrect. Answer D does not apply because industrialization was not under way during the 1500s and 1600s.

16. **(D)** This question tests causation and historical interpretation. Answer A runs exactly opposite to the truth—native armies tended to vastly outnumber colonial forces—and even though B played a role in European colonial success, military encounters did not kill nearly as many native Americans, or weaken as many native communities, as

disease did. Answer C generalizes too broadly, failing to account for centralized states like those of the Aztecs and Incas.

17. **(C)** This answer tests comparison. Known collectively as the "gunpowder empires," all three of these states were highly centralized—making B false—and technologically innovative when it came to warfare, pointing clearly to C. Architectural monuments like the Blue Mosque and the Taj Mahal contradict D, and while cotton (referred to in A) was not unimportant in India and the Ottoman province of Egypt, it was not the paramount trade good in any of these empires.

18. **(D)** This question calls for use of evidence, as well as some contextualization. Be careful not to choose answers—right or wrong—for which the map provides no evidence. The map indicates which religion was followed officially or by the majority of the population, not whether it was the only religion in a given region. Therefore A and B cannot be taken for granted (and knowledge of the three-way struggle among Catholics, Anglicans, and Puritans in England and Scotland leads away from B). Because population figures are not given for any region, it is not safe to answer C. The obvious split in the German states lends weight to D.

19. **(A)** This question is comparative and calls for contextualization in the form of general knowledge. Indentured servitude was more common in English colonies, as was settlement by religious minorities, so B and C are unlikely. Russia and France expanded by means of force but, in fact, devoted relatively small numbers of troops to do so, making D unlikely as well.

20. **(B)** This question tests continuity and change over time, as it pertains to global economic developments. Answers A and C do not fit the timeframe, and knowledge of economic life in South Asia is enough to encourage picking B over D.

21. **(B)** This question tests comparison and, to a degree, causation and contextualization. Answer A applies somewhat to the cult of saints, which became part of Latin American Catholicism, but it does not apply to Vodun, and because both religions incorporated elements of Catholicism, D is false. Even though Vodun is associated with the Haitian Rebellion and the Mexican war of independence used Our Lady of Guadalupe as a symbol, neither faith sparked ethnic violence in any noteworthy way.

22. **(D)** This is a comparative question. Since both episodes were linked chronologically, philosophically, and causally, they have much in common. But although violence was hardly absent from the Latin American wars of independence, they did not feature anything like the mass arrests and executions that the French Revolution brought about.

23. **(C)** This question requires use of evidence and historical interpretation, and it also involves causation. If A were true, the number of British troops in India might be expected to rise over time, and there is no evidence in the chart to indicate that B or D were priorities (even though mixing between Europeans and natives was discouraged). Answer C touches on a money-saving strategy used widely by most colonial powers.

24. **(A)** This question emphasizes comparison and some contextualization. In contrast to the thorough Westernization carried out by Japan in the late 1800s, the reforms enacted by Ottoman Turkey and Qing China were famously limited and unsystematic, making A

the best answer. Answer B applies to China but not the Ottomans; C is somewhat true of the Ottomans but not China; and D is true of neither.

25. **(D)** This question tests contextualization. Answer A applies to the Maroons, but not to the Cherokee or Cossacks, and while C has some relevance to the Cossacks' origins, it is not fully true of any of these groups. Answer B relates to none of them. What these groups do exemplify is the tendency during the 1500s through the 1800s of certain societies to take shape on the edge of larger, more centralized, and often expanding states.

26. **(D)** This question involves causation. Answer A describes a trend more relevant to the twentieth century's world wars, and while the demand referred to in B did exist, it did little to bring nineteenth-century women into the university. Especially during the early stages of industrialization, women of the lower classes entered the workforce in large numbers, making C false—but they were more poorly compensated than men, and received no relief from their traditional duties as homemakers and child-rearers, making D the best choice.

27. **(C)** This question tests comparison. All the answers involve racial discrimination, but the White Australia Policy is specifically about restricting immigration by ethnic minorities. Answers A, B, and D involve prejudice against, or segregation of, less-favored ethnicities.

28. **(B)** This question involves use of evidence and contextualization. The photo can date to no earlier than the mid-1800s, by which time the European presence in Africa was growing in scale and exploitation. While answers A and D are not impossible, they are unlikely, and C became increasingly improbable with the passage of time.

29. **(B)** This question tests contextualization. Answers A, C, and D all refer to elements of the Bretton Woods system created in the mid-1940s, whereas B refers to an unrelated development that did not come to full fruition until the 1990s, even though its roots lay in the 1950s. By the time the EU came into being, the gold standard in answer A had long been abandoned.

30. **(B)** This question calls for interpretation, contextualization, and use of evidence. Sukarno's references to peace—sincere or not—make C unlikely, and whatever his feelings about A or D, he says nothing about them. The Bandung Conference was a key moment in the attempt by leaders like Sukarno, India's Nehru, Egypt's Nasser, and Ghana's Nkrumah to create a non-aligned movement in the emerging Third World.

31. **(D)** This question requires contextualization and use of evidence. Nazi propaganda targeted all the topics listed in this question. But the snake in this poster bears the label "Marxismus," a clear clue that the poster's creators consider communism the foe to be fought here.

32. **(A)** This question tests causation. Although the Germans used poison gas during World War I, they did not conduct biological warfare, making B false. Because the flu killed so many people in places like India, which were not directly affected by the war's combat, the factors referred to in C and D can be considered secondary compared to the correct answer given in A.

33. **(B)** This question relates to contextualization and continuity and change over time. Dramatic cultural changes in the late 1900s and early 2000s have involved B and D, and sometimes C, but not A. Cinema and comic art arose in the West, making C irrelevant here, so the remaining question is whether, in these particular instances, Western art forms are overwhelming Indian and Japanese culture, or whether the latter is using the former for their own purposes. Most historians incline to the latter view, making B the best choice.

34. **(B)** This question requires use of evidence and historical interpretation. Although some have attributed gender inequality to C, this passage says nothing about physical weakness and concentrates overwhelmingly on fertility, making B correct. Virtually no feminist thinkers would agree with D, and while some have given credence to A, de Beauvoir does not.

35. **(A)** This related question calls for contextualization and use of evidence. De Beauvoir's emphasis on the biological disadvantages of uncontrolled pregnancy makes A the most sensible answer, even without knowledge of the profound role played by birth control in the trend toward women's liberation in the 1960s and 1970s.

36. **(D)** This question tests historical interpretation and causation. Only D relates directly to mobility. Even if A, B, and C were not unsupportable generalizations, each of them would require more evidence before being chosen.

37. **(B)** This question involves causation. Answers A and D reverse the logic of how settling permanently on the land affects societies, and agriculture supplements animal domestication rather than replacing it, making C erroneous. Even though private property was not unknown among hunter-foragers and pastoralists, it assumed a position of central importance with the ownership of land.

38. **(C)** This question calls for interpretation and contextualization. The passage's focus on parents makes B and D improbable choices. Even without knowing that the names are Chinese or that *The Analects* are attributed to Confucius, the emphasis on ritual obedience and respect to one's parents seems to go deeper than the biblical commandment.

39. **(A)** This question tests comparison and contextualization. The Phoenicians were not Buddhists, and neither they nor the Sogdians developed a truly representative government (although Phoenician city-states were less despotic than was normal for the era), so B and C are incorrect. The Phoenicians are renowned for the importance of their alphabet, but while the Sogdians had a written script, it was not as influential, making D a less preferable answer than A. Phoenician colonies played a crucial role in Mediterranean trade, while the Sogdians did the same along the Silk Roads.

40. **(D)** This question involves causation and requires understanding of continuity and change over time. All of the answers influenced trade in the Indian Ocean, but A, B, and C belong to later centuries.

41. **(A)** This question tests causation and contextualization. Effective administration, as in answer A, along with good infrastructure (not mentioned here) enabled states like Persia to build strong empires. Free-trade zones tend to be more modern institutions, and the Persians warred against the Greeks, so B and C are false, and finally, although

the Persians favored Zoroastrianism, it was only in later centuries that they made it more official, also rendering D incorrect.

42. **(C)** This question relies on use of evidence. Although B refers to a key element of the Roman worldview, it is not alluded to in these laws. The text says nothing of slavery, so D is not correct (a conclusion that can also be reached by knowing that the Romans made heavy use of slaves). The text speaks directly to C and explicitly against A.

43. **(A)** This question tests causation, use of evidence, and interpretation. While B, C, and D are all possible, the letter provides no evidence that they are the cause of the problem at hand. The letter does speak of long separation, a great burden for merchant families prior to industrial-era communications.

44. **(A)** This question involves comparison, as well as continuity and change over time. Answers B, C, and D refer to practices found in specific cultures and places, but not throughout Eurasia.

45. **(C)** This question tests causation and contextualization. Answer D is simply false, and the movable-type printing press was not invented until the 1400s, making B wrong as well. Although gunpowder arrived in Europe during the Crusading era, it did not happen because of the Crusades, as A implies. Campaigns in the Middle East exposed European armies to the region's military architecture, making C correct.

46. **(B)** This question centers on use of evidence and contextualization. In the abstract, all the answers refer to clues that would help with understanding a society's economic activities. However, formal banking was rare in sub-Saharan Africa, and Rome fell many centuries before the time in question, so A and D are not likely. Zimbabwe traded with China and the Middle East, so B and C are both possible, but the former is not only more likely but more directly connected with trade.

47. **(A)** This question involves causation and some contextualization. Islam was brought by conquerors who created a strong sultanate, and while it made its greatest inroads in the north, it did not displace Hinduism, so B and C are incorrect. The caste system did not disappear, making D wrong as well. The process of elimination, plus knowledge of the fact that most Muslim women enjoyed more rights than their Hindu counterparts, makes A the best choice.

48. **(C)** This question calls for use of evidence and contextualization. The lines of movement and the peoples involved make it clear that this map depicts the Polynesian migrations. Knowledge of that subject should be enough to eliminate B and D, which played a part in other campaigns of exploration and expansion, but not this one. Although Polynesian subgroups warred with each other, their migrations were prompted above all by the inability of small islands to support growing populations.

49. **(D)** This question calls for contextualization and historical interpretation. All of the answers allude to factors that must be guarded against when using primary sources. However, both Marco Polo and Ibn Battuta wrote in well-known languages, and while they had political loyalties, they were not an overriding concern in either case, so A and B are not relevant. It is reasonable to consider C, but Ibn Battuta traveled mainly among his fellow Muslims, and so D remains as the greatest potential problem. In the case of

both men, historians have long debated whether they visited every place they said they did or truthfully described everything they saw.

50. **(C)** This question requires historical interpretation and some contextualization, as well as understanding of continuity and change over time. Aside from the text's science-oriented content, which would indicate C, answers A and B refer to episodes that precede the 1690s, and D refers to a cultural movement that appeared roughly a century later.

51. **(A)** This question tests contextualization, as well as continuity and change over time. In the 1600s, the Tokugawa shoguns completed the process, already begun during the late 1500s, of persecuting Christianity and shutting Japan off from the rest of the world—making C and D incorrect. Foreign merchants wished to trade with Japan, but only a few, mainly Dutch, were allowed to, and only via the port of Nagasaki, making B false and A correct.

52. **(B)** This question involves causation and some sense of change over time. With the exception of the Barbary states, African nations rarely possessed strong navies, and they were more likely to make war with each other than to form alliances, so A and D are poor choices. The diseases referred to in C kept Europeans out of the African interior, but not away from the coasts. Answer B correctly alludes to the fact that a number of African states took part in the Atlantic slave trade by selling fellow Africans to European slavers.

53. **(B)** This question tests causation and contextualization. The Mughal emperor Aurangzeb, turning away from his predecessors' policy of religious toleration, alienated many of his subjects—including the Sikhs and Marathas—by pursuing a vigorous Islamic puritanism. This makes B the best answer, even if both groups sought autonomy for other reasons as well. The English were not yet in India in any great force, and the Mughal sultanate faded away gradually in the 1700s and early 1800s, making A and D incorrect. At no point in Indian history would C have been true.

54. **(C)** This question involves periodization and causation. The Arab slave trade persisted in East Africa until the late 1800s, and the Berbers are from West Africa, so B and D are false. Most of the region has never experienced desertification, making A incorrect and leaving C—a major development indeed—as the right answer.

55. **(D)** This question relates to causation and contextualization. Plantation agriculture in the New World gave rise to A, B, and C, but it tended to act directly against D.

56. **(A)** This question tests causation and comparison. As military elites with a vested interest in safeguarding their privileged positions, both samurai and janissaries looked with suspicion upon any changes that threatened to make their military skills obsolete, making D and even the foresighted options in B and C false.

57. **(B)** This question involves use of evidence and historical interpretation. As the leading official in a joint-stock company operating under a government charter, Bentinck was concerned above all with profits and the maintenance of British power, as in B. He was only moved to act on his moral and religious convictions once his main priorities were met. The British East India Company actively discouraged—but did not prevent—Christian missionary activity, and it often ignored local customs it found objectionable,

precisely because it understood how native discontent might destabilize its position. So A and D are incorrect, and Bentinck, although seemingly sincere in disliking the deaths of women caused by sati, gives no indication that he favored women's equality.

58. **(C)** This related question also requires use of evidence and an understanding of historical argumentation. Bentinck's reluctance to interfere with a longstanding Indian custom directly rebuts C, an accusation commonly launched by some historians against colonizing powers.

59. **(B)** This question tests use of evidence and historical interpretation. Answers A, C, and D refer to distinctly one-sided perspectives, whereas de Tocqueville is clearly trying to look at both sides of the issue.

60. **(B)** This question tests historical interpretation and historical argumentation. The historiographical perspectives expressed in A, C, and D are subjective and highly pro-British—especially the last one, which verges on racially stereotyping the sepoys. Answer B does not excuse sepoy violence but attempts to frame it as a native response to a prevailing climate of existing brutality.

61. **(D)** This question calls for use of evidence, historical interpretation, and contextualization. In political cartoons, the image of slicing up a pie is commonly used to indicate the cynical partition of territory, meaning that A and B are very likely *not* what the Asiatic figure in the background is complaining about. Answers C and D are both plausible, although a prominent clue to the country in question is the caption "Chine" (French for "China"). Even without that, the presence of cartoon figures symbolizing numerous countries, not just one colonizer, makes D a better choice than C.

62. **(B)** This question tests contextualization and causation, as well as a sense of continuity and change over time. Transnational banks at this time were heavily involved with economic imperialism, making A and D (more likely in the present day) highly unlikely. Following the course described in C would do a bank no good, so answer B is the most accurate.

63. **(C)** This question tests comparison. Answers A and D apply to State Shintoism, but not to Nazism, and B applies to neither.

64. **(D)** This question relies on use of evidence and contextualization. The map clearly depicts the end result of the "Scramble for Africa" during the late 1800s, carried out by the European powers according to the rules established at the Berlin Conference (answer B), and thanks to military superiority (answer A), improved geographic knowledge of the continent, and medicines that allowed them to penetrate the interior (answer C). The Muslims and slavers referred to in D saw their power diminish quickly and greatly as the Europeans arrived in force.

65. **(C)** This question tests historical argumentation. Answer A would tend to reinforce the traditional view. Answers B and D go a little way toward questioning whether the interwar public was thrust as deeply into despair by World War I as *All Quiet on the Western Front* has led some to believe, but they are not as central to the debate as a pro-war novel like *Storm of Steel* is.

66. **(D)** This question relates to use of evidence and historical interpretation, as well as contextualization. Answers A and B come too early in the 1900s to readily fit the poem's timeframe. Existentialism belongs to the right period, but the poem's celebration of "blackness" is a hallmark of the Négritude movement, of which Senghor was a leading figure.

67. **(B)** This question tests historical argumentation and contextualization. There is no evidence for answer A (and Chamorro fell on the political right), and the fame and visibility of these three women says nothing about how typical or representative they are, making it impossible to choose C. Answer D is irrelevant to the issue of political leadership that the question itself alludes to.

68. **(B)** This question involves comparison. The Indian National Congress relied on non-violence and, while it called loudly during World War II for British withdrawal, it did not collaborate with Britain's enemies, so C and D are invalid. So is A, because India's future friendly relations with the USSR did not involve actually subscribing to communism as a guiding ideology. The ANC wrestled internally over how far to embrace violence as part of its struggle.

69. **(D)** This question tests use of evidence and historical interpretation, as well as causation. Answer A has little to do with population growth, whereas the steadily increasing impact of war on civilian populations makes C false. Answers B and D are commonly given as reasons for population growth, but most historians favor medical improvements as a prime cause.

70. **(D)** This question relies on use of evidence and historical interpretation. Answer A refers to "hard" power (enforced by military and geopolitical might) rather than the "soft" power associated with cultural and economic influence. Even though answer B refers to a trend that has unfolded in many parts of the Third World, it generally involves the nationalization and transformation of Western corporations. Answer C would imply no role at all in the Western world for a corporation like McDonalds, so D is left as the correct answer.

# ANSWER SHEET
## Model Test 2

| | | |
|---|---|---|
| 1. (A) (B) (C) (D) | 26. (A) (B) (C) (D) | 51. (A) (B) (C) (D) |
| 2. (A) (B) (C) (D) | 27. (A) (B) (C) (D) | 52. (A) (B) (C) (D) |
| 3. (A) (B) (C) (D) | 28. (A) (B) (C) (D) | 53. (A) (B) (C) (D) |
| 4. (A) (B) (C) (D) | 29. (A) (B) (C) (D) | 54. (A) (B) (C) (D) |
| 5. (A) (B) (C) (D) | 30. (A) (B) (C) (D) | 55. (A) (B) (C) (D) |
| 6. (A) (B) (C) (D) | 31. (A) (B) (C) (D) | 56. (A) (B) (C) (D) |
| 7. (A) (B) (C) (D) | 32. (A) (B) (C) (D) | 57. (A) (B) (C) (D) |
| 8. (A) (B) (C) (D) | 33. (A) (B) (C) (D) | 58. (A) (B) (C) (D) |
| 9. (A) (B) (C) (D) | 34. (A) (B) (C) (D) | 59. (A) (B) (C) (D) |
| 10. (A) (B) (C) (D) | 35. (A) (B) (C) (D) | 60. (A) (B) (C) (D) |
| 11. (A) (B) (C) (D) | 36. (A) (B) (C) (D) | 61. (A) (B) (C) (D) |
| 12. (A) (B) (C) (D) | 37. (A) (B) (C) (D) | 62. (A) (B) (C) (D) |
| 13. (A) (B) (C) (D) | 38. (A) (B) (C) (D) | 63. (A) (B) (C) (D) |
| 14. (A) (B) (C) (D) | 39. (A) (B) (C) (D) | 64. (A) (B) (C) (D) |
| 15. (A) (B) (C) (D) | 40. (A) (B) (C) (D) | 65. (A) (B) (C) (D) |
| 16. (A) (B) (C) (D) | 41. (A) (B) (C) (D) | 66. (A) (B) (C) (D) |
| 17. (A) (B) (C) (D) | 42. (A) (B) (C) (D) | 67. (A) (B) (C) (D) |
| 18. (A) (B) (C) (D) | 43. (A) (B) (C) (D) | 68. (A) (B) (C) (D) |
| 19. (A) (B) (C) (D) | 44. (A) (B) (C) (D) | 69. (A) (B) (C) (D) |
| 20. (A) (B) (C) (D) | 45. (A) (B) (C) (D) | 70. (A) (B) (C) (D) |
| 21. (A) (B) (C) (D) | 46. (A) (B) (C) (D) | |
| 22. (A) (B) (C) (D) | 47. (A) (B) (C) (D) | |
| 23. (A) (B) (C) (D) | 48. (A) (B) (C) (D) | |
| 24. (A) (B) (C) (D) | 49. (A) (B) (C) (D) | |
| 25. (A) (B) (C) (D) | 50. (A) (B) (C) (D) | |

# SECTION I: MULTIPLE-CHOICE QUESTIONS

**Time: 55 Minutes for 70 Questions**

> **DIRECTIONS:** Each of the questions or incomplete statements below is followed by four suggested answers or completions. Select the one that is best in each case and then fill in the corresponding oval on the answer sheet.

1. Which of the following best justifies the scholarly claim that the period 3500–3000 B.C.E. is a major threshold in world history?
   (A) The glaciers from the last ice age had receded fully by that point.
   (B) The earliest cities came into being around that time.
   (C) The first civilizations are considered to have take shape then.
   (D) The practice of agriculture first emerged during those years.

2. The map below indicates that

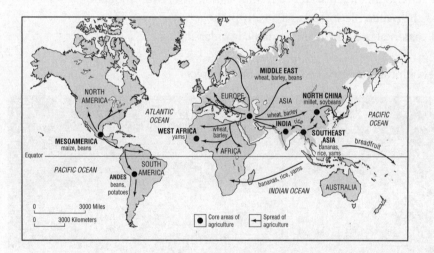

   (A) there was no single point of origin for the domestication of plants.
   (B) barley was unsuitable for cultivation in zones near the equator.
   (C) agriculture experienced an "out of Africa" diffusion similar to early human migration.
   (D) rice was the first crop to be domesticated in Eurasia.

3. The Andean mit'a resembles Russian serfdom in that
   (A) both are forms of coerced labor.
   (B) both used prisoners for large construction projects.
   (C) both involved industrial manufacturing.
   (D) both were imposed by foreign conquerors.

4. "From the mouth of Brahma were produced a thousand pairs of men with the right understanding. From his breast he created another thousand pairs, full of strength and invincible. Another thousand pairs he created from his thigh, full of energy and enterprise. From his two feet he created a final thousand pairs, without beauty and of little understanding. The Lord Brahma then established honor and precedence among them according to their respective rights and obligations."

The Markandeya Purana, compiled ca. 250 C.E.

The passage above reflects which of the following cultural traditions?
(A) Confucian hierarchy
(B) Hebrew monotheism
(C) the Indian caste system
(D) Japanese shamanism

5. A common factor in the downfall of Han China and Gupta India was
(A) a drastic shift in the patterns of transregional trade.
(B) environmental disaster caused by agricultural overproduction.
(C) the pandemic spread of a deadly pathogen.
(D) external pressure from nomadic invaders.

6. The sculpture pictured below most likely depicts

(A) a subject in awe of the divine power of his king.
(B) a slave attending upon his noble master.
(C) an enemy acknowledging defeat before a mighty conqueror.
(D) a performer taking a bow before a royal patron.

7. Rome and Persia each made use of all the following empire-building techniques EXCEPT
   (A) the creation of regional administrative systems.
   (B) the suppression of non-official religions.
   (C) the construction of extensive road networks.
   (D) the standardization of weights, measures, and currencies.

8. Which of the following most complicates the task of historians attempting to understand the life of the Chinese monk and traveler Xuanzang?
   (A) the fact that he may have acted as a spy during his journey to India
   (B) the fact that he is best remembered as a character in a book written centuries after his life
   (C) the fact that he is suspected by many of not having written the books attributed to him
   (D) the fact that different and conflicting versions of his memoirs exist

9. Which of the following is LEAST related to the expansion of trade in medieval Europe?
   (A) the formation of the Hanseatic League
   (B) the emergence of the guild system
   (C) the growth of Europe's urban population
   (D) the rising importance of maize and potatoes as trade goods

10. Which of the following did NOT emerge as a Chinese invention and then spread westward via trade and cultural diffusion?
    (A) the lodestone compass
    (B) the horse collar
    (C) the stirrup
    (D) gunpowder

11. The non-technological factor that MOST facilitated long-distance trade in the Indian Ocean basin was
    (A) the seasonal prevalence of powerful monsoon winds.
    (B) the emergence of a port city to control the vital straits of Malacca.
    (C) the rise of merchant diaspora communities in Malaysia and East Africa.
    (D) the unifying power of Islam and Swahili culture.

12. The map below depicts which of the following?

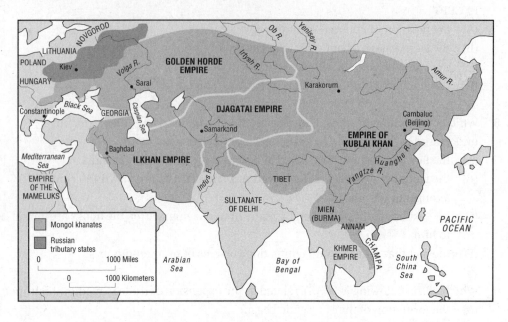

(A) the coalescing of Mongol states into a single empire
(B) the breakdown of the Mongol empire into smaller states
(C) the Mongol empire at the peak of Genghis Khan's conquests
(D) the final defeat of Mongol states at the hands of Muslim forces

13. Between 600 and 1450, the impact of Neo-Confucianism in China and Catholicism in Europe included all of the following EXCEPT
(A) the reinforcement of social hierarchies
(B) the legitimation of political authority
(C) the elevation of the status of women
(D) the provision of spiritual reassurance to worshippers

14. Which of the following would enable a historian to argue that the Mississippian culture was characterized by a high degree of social organization?
(A) It erected large mounds for ritual purposes and built a large city.
(B) It was a highly warlike culture, conquering much of North America.
(C) It was one of pre-Columbian America's first monotheistic civilizations.
(D) It built complex cliff dwellings in the walls of canyons.

15. Shakespearean drama and kabuki theater have which of the following in common?
(A) They appealed to a wider cross-section of society than earlier forms of drama.
(B) They catered exclusively to the aesthetic sensibilities of elite classes.
(C) They rejected poetic forms of storytelling.
(D) They were considered low forms of entertainment in their own day.

16. Which of the following most accurately describes the difference between serfdom and the devshirme system?
    (A) Those recruited by devshirme were coerced by those of their own ethnicity.
    (B) Serfs were used exclusively as agricultural laborers.
    (C) Those recruited by devshirme received more privileges.
    (D) Serfs were freer in a legal sense.

17. Which of the following resulted from the Columbian Exchange?
    (A) the introduction of coffee to Afro-Eurasia
    (B) the introduction of maize and potatoes to the Americas
    (C) the introduction of smallpox to Afro-Eurasia
    (D) the introduction of the horse to the Americas

18. The map below most clearly indicates which of the following?

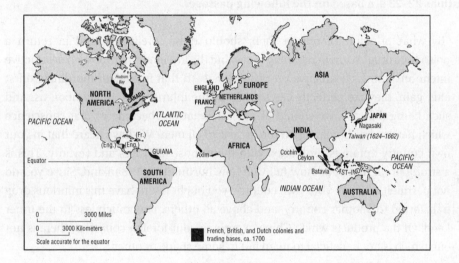

    (A) The English were particularly interested in controlling North Atlantic whaling grounds.
    (B) French, Dutch, and English colonial authority extended only to places easily reached by sea.
    (C) Dutch colonial expansion came in many cases at the expense of the Portuguese.
    (D) The English, Dutch, and French were less interested than Spain in overseas colonization.

19. The circle of justice ideology that legitimated the power of Middle Eastern rulers who acted with virtue, most closely resembles
    (A) Europe's divine right theory.
    (B) the Chinese mandate of heaven.
    (C) separation of powers as outlined in the U.S. Constitution.
    (D) the Enlightenment concept of the social contract.

20. Which of the following did Japanese daimyo and Indian zamindars have in common?
    (A) Both were high nobility.
    (B) Both were religious authorities.
    (C) Both were landholding classes.
    (D) Both were warrior elites.

21. Which of the following played the principal role in widening the impact of the Protestant Reformation?
    (A) the movable-type printing press
    (B) support for Luther among nobles of the Holy Roman Empire
    (C) the propaganda value of Baroque art
    (D) the power of Luther's oratory

**Questions 22–23 are based on the following passage.**

"By what principle of reason then, should these foreigners send in return a poisonous drug? Without meaning to say that the foreigners harbor such destructive intentions in their hearts, we yet positively assert that from their inordinate thirst after gain, they are perfectly careless about the injuries they inflict upon us! And such being the case, we should like to ask what has become of that conscience which heaven has implanted in the breasts of all men? We have heard that in your own country opium is prohibited with the utmost strictness and severity. This is a strong proof that you know full well how hurtful it is to mankind. Since you do not permit it to injure your own country, you ought not to have this injurious drug transferred to another country, and above all others, how much less to the Inner Land! Of the products which China exports to your foreign countries, there is not one which is not beneficial to mankind in some shape or other."

Commissioner Lin Zexu, letter to Queen Victoria, 1839

22. On which of the following arguments does the author principally base his appeal to Queen Victoria?
    (A) It is hypocritical to sell one country a substance banned as harmful in one's own.
    (B) Confucian teachings forbid the use of all narcotic drugs as inherently immoral.
    (C) Addiction is causing China to suffer an unfavorable balance of trade.
    (D) Britain is unwise to risk the wrath of a militarily more powerful state.

23. What background fact about Anglo-Chinese trade—not mentioned in the document—persuaded Europeans to start up the illegal traffic that Commissioner Lin is complaining about?
    (A) China had recently placed an embargo on exports of silk.
    (B) The price of tea had risen higher than European buyers found acceptable.
    (C) The Chinese authorities refused to allow European goods to be sold in their country.
    (D) China's emperor had repeatedly insulted the British ambassador.

24. Which of the following was NOT a consequence of building the Suez Canal?
    (A)  Industrial-era humanity displayed its unprecedented capacity to affect the environment.
    (B)  The volume and patterns of international trade were greatly altered.
    (C)  Nineteenth-century Egypt enjoyed an upsurge in political and economic influence.
    (D)  The geopolitical importance of the eastern Mediterranean increased.

25. A historian seeking to refute the assertion that successful industrialization in the 1800s depended on a *laissez-faire* approach to economics would do best to turn to which of the following examples?
    (A)  Russia and the Ottoman empire
    (B)  Japan and Germany
    (C)  Great Britain and France
    (D)  Chile and Argentina

26. Modern historians are most likely to interpret episodes such as the Sioux Ghost Dance and the Xhosa cattle-killing movement as
    (A)  tactical maneuvers meant to combat invasion by colonizing powers.
    (B)  religious millenarianism triggered by the stress of imperial occupation.
    (C)  a means to deprive foreign settlers of useful economic assets.
    (D)  irrational hysteria psychologically inherent to primitive peoples.

27. "This great purity of the French Revolution is precisely what causes both our strength and our weakness. Our strength, because it gives to us rights of the public interest over private interests; our weakness, because it rallies all vicious men against us. We must smother the internal and external enemies of the Republic or perish with it; now in this situation, the first maxim of your policy ought to be to lead the people by reason and the people's enemies by terror. Terror is nothing other than justice, prompt, severe, inflexible; it is therefore an emanation of virtue; it is not so much a special principle as it is a consequence of the general principle of democracy applied to our country's most urgent needs."

   The above justification of terror, spoken by French revolutionary Maximilien Robespierre in 1794, articulates which of the following political principles?
    (A)  from each according to his abilities, to each according to his needs
    (B)  might makes right
    (C)  the end justifies the means
    (D)  the government is best that governs least

28. The photograph below most likely illustrates an instance of

(A) racial tensions breaking out into open conflict.
(B) the West's imperial strategy of training and deploying native troops.
(C) interregional trade involving the sale of military equipment.
(D) technology transfer of gunpowder weaponry from Africa to Europe.

29. Which of the following did the "space race" have in common with the Olympic Games held between 1948 and 1988?
(A) They each became symbolic expressions of Cold War tension.
(B) They created resentment among poorer nations who could not afford prowess in either.
(C) They both inspired technological innovations that hugely benefited medical science.
(D) They provided numerous opportunities for peaceful U.S.-Soviet cooperation.

30. Which of the following is LEAST associated with religious fundamentalism in the post-1945 era?
(A) rise of the Taliban in Afghanistan
(B) the Iranian Revolution
(C) the Rwandan genocide
(D) advocacy for the teaching of "creation science"

31. "The independence? Nothing of what I hoped for was achieved. I had expected that my children would be able to have an education, but they did not get it. We were poor peasants then, we are poor peasants now. Nothing has changed. Everything is the same. The only thing is that we are free, the war is over, we work without fear—but apart from that, nothing has changed."

> Halima Ghomri, Algerian woman interviewed in the1970s
> after the war of independence

What general observation about national-liberation efforts would Ghomri's comment serve best to support?

(A) Political freedom does not automatically translate to economic improvement.

(B) The former colonial regime is often better than the post-colonial one.

(C) The new liberties gained by decolonization are rarely worth the bloodshed.

(D) Women's concerns are typically given short shrift by national-liberation movements.

32. Examining the chart below, one can safely conclude that

(A) more people in the USSR's Northwest live in cities than in its European Center.

(B) Western Siberia has a larger agrarian population than the Soviet Ukraine.

(C) Central Asia and Belorussia are, by percentage, the least urbanized of the USSR's western regions.

(D) the Baltic is home to more urban dwellers than the Trans-Caucasus.

33. "It's very attractive to people to be a victim. Instead of having to think out the whole situation, about history and your group and what you are doing, if you begin from the point of view of being a victim, you've got it half-made. I mean intellectually."

Indo-Trinidadian novelist V. S. Naipaul, "The Killings in Trinidad," 1974

The above quote seems to undermine which of the following assertions commonly made by historians of decolonization?

(A) that imperial powers inflicted much harm on the parts of the world they ruled
(B) that former imperial powers bear no responsibility for what happens in countries they once colonized
(C) that newly decolonized parts of the world need to assume responsibility for their own problems
(D) that former colonizers are to blame for political and social failings in recently liberated parts of the world

**Questions 34–35 are based on the following passage.**

"[T]he fundamental source of conflict in this new world will not be primarily ideological or primarily economic. The great divisions among humankind and the dominating source of conflict will be cultural. The clash of civilizations will dominate global politics. The fault lines between civilizations will be the battle lines of the future. With the end of the Cold War … a central focus of conflict for the immediate future will be between the West and several Islamic-Confucian states."

Samuel Huntington, "The Clash of Civilizations," 1993

34. Which of the following assumptions appears to be implicit in the above passage?
(A) States during the post-Cold War era will become less stable than ever before.
(B) Conflict between Western and non-Western cultures will inevitably arise during the post-Cold War era.
(C) During the post-Cold War era, global trade will cease to be of great economic importance.
(D) Western civilization is doomed to decline during the post-Cold War era.

35. Which of the following would seem to UNDERMINE the author's contentions?
(A) the U.S.-led war against Islamic terror
(B) close ties between Japan and the United States
(C) friction between Bosnian Muslims and Orthodox Serbians in the former Yugoslavia
(D) diplomatic tensions between the United States and Communist China

36. Which of the following has provided historians with the BEST evidence for a high degree of political centralization among the Indus River city-states?
    (A) the presence of what appear to be public baths
    (B) the uniform layout of streets and public buildings
    (C) the profusion of statues depicting what seem to be political leaders
    (D) the discovery of trade goods from a variety of faraway lands

37. Trade between Egypt and Nubia differed from trade between Egypt and Mesopotamia in which of the following ways?
    (A) The former was greater in volume, the latter was smaller in scale.
    (B) The former involved foodstuffs, the latter centered on precious metals.
    (C) The former was conducted by force, the latter took place peacefully.
    (D) The former traveled by sea, the latter went overland.

38. The Hebrews' adoption of monothestic worship had the effect of
    (A) making them more likely to assimilate fully into other societies.
    (B) strengthening their sense of cultural uniqueness.
    (C) encouraging a pacifist mindset among them.
    (D) fragmenting their population into many small kingdoms.

39. The structure below, erected in Athens during the 400s B.C.E., is an example of

    (A) fanatical and unquestioning devotion to a monotheistic deity.
    (B) political legitimacy gained by building a visually impressive seat of government.
    (C) cultural unity provided by a memorial to those fallen in past wars.
    (D) social cohesion powerful enough to allow a grand expression of religious ideals.

40. Which of the following best explains the many similarities between Buddhist and Hindu spiritual tenets?
    (A) Both imported many concepts from Daoist theology.
    (B) Both have roots in traditional Vedism.
    (C) Both were decisively influenced by missionaries from China.
    (D) Both grew out of the Buddha's original teachings.

41. Which of the following did Andean and Mesoamerican societies NOT have in common?
    (A) states created by conquest
    (B) political rulers legitimated by religious authority
    (C) methods of intensive agriculture
    (D) written scripts

42. Which of the following was a key consequence of Alexander the Great's conquests during the 300s B.C.E.?
    (A) the formation of a Macedonian Empire that lasted for centuries
    (B) the spread of Hellenistic culture through much of Eurasia
    (C) the destruction of the Zoroastrian religion throughout Persia
    (D) the worsening of relations between Europe and the Muslim world

43. Which of the following explains why the spread of Champa rice revolutionized agriculture throughout East and Southeast Asia?
    (A) The ease with which it could be planted and harvested meant higher productivity.
    (B) Its nutritional qualities were far superior to other widely grown crops in the region.
    (C) The labor-intensive nature of its cultivation encouraged the enslavement of peasants.
    (D) Its drought-resistant properties allowed two harvests per year, increasing food production.

44. In what way are the histories of the Bantu and the Polynesians similar?
    (A) Their migrations dispersed a single cultural group over vast distances.
    (B) They cultivated corn and potatoes before most other peoples.
    (C) They navigated the open ocean with great skill.
    (D) They domesticated the horse and pioneered cavalry warfare.

45. "While some theorists in the Middle Ages argued that the jihad was a defensive war… most authorities held that the obligation of jihad did not lapse until all the world was brought under the sway of Islam. The *Bahr* [*al-Fava'id*, or 'Sea of Precious Virtues,' written in the 1150s or 1160s,] insists that the first duty of a Muslim ruler is to prosecute the jihad and bring about the victory of Islam, and if he does not do so and he makes peace with the infidel, that ruler would be better dead than alive, for he would be corrupting the world."

historian Robert Irwin, "Islam and the Crusades," 1995

"It is strange how the Christians round Mount Lebanon, when they see any Muslim hermits, bring them food and treat them kindly, saying that these men are dedicated to the Great and Glorious God and that they should therefore share with them. Likewise, not one Christian merchant was stopped or hindered in Muslim territories."

Ibn Jubayr, Muslim scholar, traveling to Mecca and Jerusalem, ca. 1185

The second passage does not support the first because the second passage

(A) shows how state-level antagonisms in the twelfth-century Middle East were not always reflected in personal or economic life.

(B) shows how Muslims in the twelfth-century Middle East did not take religious obligations as seriously as Christians did.

(C) shows how Muslims were on the whole kinder than Christians in the twelfth-century Middle East.

(D) shows how, in the twelfth-century Middle East, economic factors trumped all other considerations.

46. Which system of coerced labor became associated with the growing of spices and other crops along Africa's Swahili coast?
(A) the exploitation of coolie labor
(B) the East African slave trade
(C) the Ottoman devshirme
(D) the Atlantic slave trade

47. What best describes the relationship between Islamic and medieval European culture?
(A) Muslim scholars and philosophers borrowed from English and French thinkers.
(B) Muslim science and translations from Greek put medieval Europe on the path to the Renaissance.
(C) Muslims learned much about European art and architecture during the Crusades.
(D) Muslim and European cultures did not interact because of intense religious hostility.

48. Which of the following caused Mali's rise as a regional power during the 1300s c.e.?
    (A) its status as one of Afro-Eurasia's key sources of gold
    (B) its sizable and well-trained gunpowder force
    (C) its cooperation with European slave traders
    (D) its success at warding off Muslim armies and missionaries

49. Which of the following best justifies the argument that the aftermath of Zheng He's voyages mark a turning point in Chinese history?
    (A) The gold and silver brought back by Zheng He bestowed upon Ming China a new economic superiority throughout the region.
    (B) By failing to follow up on Zheng He's campaigns of exploration, Ming China missed the opportunity to lead the world in maritime expansion.
    (C) Zheng He's ships brought back bubonic plague, resulting in a medical disaster that permanently weakened Ming China.
    (D) Many neighboring states were forced into Ming China's tributary system by Zheng He's fleet, greatly strengthening it as a regional hegemon.

50. Russia's practice during the 1600s and 1700s of proclaiming native Siberians their subjects and forcing them to hunt furs for them most resembles which of the following systems of labor?
    (A) the encomienda
    (B) indentured servitude
    (C) convict labor
    (D) chattel slavery

51. "The reason produced for condemning [Copernicus's] opinion that the earth moves and the sun stands still is that in the Bible one may read that the sun moves and the earth stands still. Since the Bible cannot err, it follows as a necessary consequence of this argument that anyone takes an erroneous and heretical position who maintains that the sun is inherently motionless and the earth movable. With regard to this argument, I think it is prudent to affirm that the Holy Bible can never speak untruth—whenever its true meaning is understood. But I believe nobody will deny that it is often very abstruse, and may say things which are quite different from what its bare words signify."

    Galileo Galilei, letter to Grand Duke Christina of Tuscany, 1615

    Which of the following best describes Galileo's argument regarding Copernicus's heliocentric theory?
    (A) Any contradiction between the Bible and a scientific theory proves the latter to be false.
    (B) Heliocentrism must be regarded as mistaken and heretical.
    (C) Science is unquestionably superior to the Bible as a way of understanding the universe.
    (D) The Bible may seem to clash with science if its meaning is imperfectly comprehended.

52. The image below most likely represents which of the following?

(A) the importation of Western weaponry into a non-Western social order

(B) an agrarian revolution on the brink of victory

(C) the invasion of a less advanced nation by a more advanced one

(D) the inability of non-Western peoples to adapt to innovative technologies

53. What was the principal means by which okra and rice were transported from Afro-Eurasia to the Americas?

(A) the Polynesian migrations

(B) English colonization

(C) the arrival of African slaves

(D) Chinese immigration

54. Which of the following proved a major source of religious tension between Safavid Persia and many of its neighbors in the Islamic world?

(A) its repudiation of Sharia law

(B) its secularization of public life

(C) its abolition of the jizya tax for non-Muslims

(D) its embrace of Shiite Islam

55. Which of the following would be most useful as evidence for historians researching the number of whales killed by European whalers in the North Atlantic between 1500 and 1800?
    (A) diaries written by members of ships' crews
    (B) tax records in European archives
    (C) ledgers kept by whaling captains
    (D) oral history provided by Inuit and other Arctic natives

56. Portugal's colonial sway over East Africa faded during the 1600s primarily because
    (A) the Portuguese suffered moral qualms over the use of slave labor.
    (B) Dutch armies invaded the Portuguese homeland.
    (C) Portugal concentrated on Brazil as its chief colony.
    (D) Omani Arabs gained dominance over the coast.

57. "Our basic assumptions can be summarized in two words: 'Good-bye Asia.' Japan is located in the eastern extremities of Asia, but the spirit of her people has already moved away from the old conventions of Asia to the Western civilization. The Chinese and Koreans do not know how to progress either personally or as a nation. Their love affairs with ancient ways and old customs remain as strong as they were centuries ago. What must we do today? We do not have time to wait for the enlightenment of our neighbors so that we can work together toward the development of Asia. It is better for us to leave the ranks of Asian nations and cast our lot with the civilized nations of the West."

    from Fukuzawa Yukichi, "Good-Bye Asia," 1885

    Which of the following ideologies forms the core of the above passage?
    (A) Conservatism
    (B) State Shintoism
    (C) Confucianism
    (D) Nationalism

58. How did the United States' relationship with most of Latin America compare with the one it maintained with the Hawaiian kingdom?
    (A) Both regions cautiously resisted U.S. diplomatic overtures.
    (B) Both regions were heavily influenced by U.S. sugar and fruit businesses.
    (C) Both regions were conquered directly by U.S. military forces.
    (D) Both regions entered into firm U.S. alliances on an equal basis.

59. During the first half of the 1800s, the Industrial Revolution was principally associated with the large-scale production of which of the following?
    (A) electricity, chemicals, petroleum
    (B) petroleum, textiles, steel
    (C) chemicals, steel, coal
    (D) coal, iron, textiles

60. Which European event most directly contributed to the outbreak of the Latin American wars of independence?
    (A) the withdrawal of Spanish investments in colonial economies
    (B) British victory at the battle of Trafalgar
    (C) the revolutionary reign of terror in France
    (D) Napoleon's ouster of the king of Spain

61. Which of the following would most strengthen the argument of historians wishing to apply the label "imperial" to U.S. conduct during and after the Spanish-American War?
    (A) the United States' liberation of Spanish concentration camps in Cuba
    (B) the United States' victory over Spain's fleet at Manila Bay
    (C) the United States' occupation of Puerto Rico and the Philippines
    (D) the United States' successful charge during the battle of San Juan Hill

62. Which of the following best distinguishes the causes of global migration in the 1800s from those that prompted it in the 1900s?
    (A) Migration in the 1900s was driven largely by the movement of colonists to newly-established empires.
    (B) Migration in the 1800s was related only somewhat to the search for better work opportunities.
    (C) Migration in the 1900s was increasingly likely to be caused by war-related displacement.
    (D) Migration in the 1800s was forced by repeated medical disasters raging throughout Afro-Eurasia.

63. Which form of coerced labor did the British Empire use to populate far-off colonies like Australia?
    (A) chattel slavery
    (B) corvée labor
    (C) transportation
    (D) serfdom

64. In which of the following ways did India's and Indonesia's foreign policies resemble each other during the Cold War?
    (A) Both enjoyed cordial relations with their former colonizers.
    (B) Both considered Communist China to be their most natural ally.
    (C) Both attempted to remain as unaligned as possible during the superpower conflict.
    (D) Both established close ties with the United States out of fear of the USSR.

65. The map below depicts which of the following?

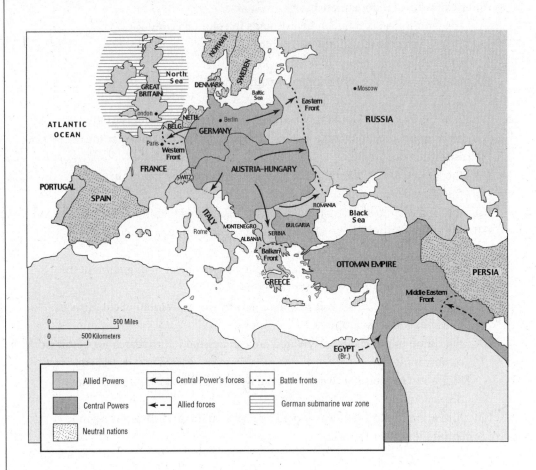

(A) World War I at its midpoint
(B) Europe under Napoleon at the height of his power
(C) the division of Europe by the Cold War's "iron curtain"
(D) Nazi-controlled Europe prior to Hitler's invasion of the USSR

66. "I don't know whether this world has meaning that transcends it. But I know that I do not know that meaning, and that it is impossible just now for me to know it. What can a meaning outside my condition mean to me? I can understand only in human terms."

The above thought, voiced in 1955 by Albert Camus in "The Myth of Sisyphus," expresses which of the following worldviews?
(A) existentialism
(B) religious fundamentalism
(C) new age syncretism
(D) liberation theology

67. Most historians would agree that the period 1989–1991 represents an important break in world history for all of the following reasons EXCEPT
    (A) the end of the Cold War division of Europe.
    (B) the democratization of Communist China.
    (C) the collapse of the USSR.
    (D) the repudiation of apartheid in South Africa.

68. Based on the data presented in the table below, which of the following conclusions can one safely make?

| World's Major Consumers of Primary Energy (1998) Measured in quadrillions of British thermal units (Btu) | |
| --- | --- |
| United States | 94.57 quadrillion Btu |
| China | 33.93 quadrillion Btu |
| Russia | 25.99 quadrillion Btu |
| Japan | 21.21 quadrillion Btu |
| Germany | 13.83 quadrillion Btu |
| India | 12.51 quadrillion Btu |
| Canada | 11.85 quadrillion Btu |
| France | 10.00 quadrillion Btu |
| United Kingdom | 9.75 quadrillion Btu |
| Brazil | 8.08 quadrillion Btu |

    (A) The top energy-consuming nations are to be found mainly in the developed world.
    (B) Brazil has a smaller population than China does.
    (C) Russia is a more efficient consumer of energy than China is.
    (D) Japan has a larger population than India does.

**Questions 69–70 are based on the following passage.**

"Is it not unity alone that can weld us into an effective force, capable of creating our own progress and making our valuable contribution to world peace? Which independent African state will claim that its financial structure and banking institutions are fully harnessed to its national development? Which will claim that its material resources and human energies are available for its own national aspirations? We are fast learning that political independence is not enough to rid us of the consequences of colonial rule. We have been too busy nursing our separate states to understand fully the basic need for union, rooted in common purpose, common planning and common endeavour."

Ghana's president, Kwame Nkrumah, addressing the
Organization of African Unity, 1963

69. In this speech, Nkrumah is espousing which of the following causes?
(A) Nationalism
(B) Socialism
(C) Pan-Africanism
(D) Neocolonialism

70. Which of the following factors was most important in preventing the fulfillment of Nkrumah's political dreams?
(A) a complete lack of common ethnicity, language, or religion
(B) the rapid spread of communism throughout the continent
(C) armed intervention on the part of the Cold War superpowers
(D) Africa's appalling shortage of natural resources

**END OF SECTION I**

**(Suggested planning and writing time—40 minutes)**

**Percent of Section II score—33⅓**

---

**DIRECTIONS:** The following question is based on the accompanying Documents 1–7. (The documents have been edited for the purpose of this exercise.) Write your answer on the lined pages of the Section II free-response booklet.

This question is designed to test your ability to work with and understand historical documents.

Write an essay that

- has a relevant thesis and supports that thesis with evidence from the documents.
- uses all of the documents.
- analyzes the documents by grouping them in as many appropriate ways as possible, and does not simply summarize the documents individually.
- takes into account the sources of the documents and analyzes the authors' points of view.
- identifies and explains the need for at least one additional type of document.

You may refer to relevant historical information not mentioned in the documents.

---

1. Using the documents, compare and contrast European and non-European reactions to encounters with unfamiliar religious beliefs between roughly 1200 and 1900. Identify an additional type of document and explain how it would help in assessing such reactions.

## DOCUMENT 1

Source: Thomas Coryate, English traveler in Turkey, on witnessing Sufi dervishes (1613).

There is a College of Turkish Monks in Galata, that are called [Dervishes], . . . who every Tuesday and Friday do perform the strangest exercise of Devotion that ever I saw or heard of. . . .

A little after I came into the room, the Dervishes repaired into the middle void space, sitting Cross-legged, bending their Bodies low toward the floor for Religion['s] sake, even almost flat upon their Faces . . . the whole company of them were about two and fifty. . . .

[A] certain Singing-man sitting apart in an upper room began to sing certain Hymns, but with the most unpleasant and harsh notes that ever I heard, exceedingly differing from our Christian Church singing, for the yelling and disorderly squeaking did even grate mine ears.... [T]hree Pipers sitting in the room with the Singer began to play upon certain long Pipes not unlike Tabors, which yielded a very ridiculous and foolish Music . . . whereupon some five and twenty of the two and fifty Dervishes suddenly rose up bare-legged and bare-footed, and casting aside their upper Garments, some of them having their breasts all uncovered, they began by little and little to turn about the Interpreter of the Law. Afterward they redoubled their force and turned with such incredible swiftness, that I could not choose but admire it.

## DOCUMENT 2

Source: Council of the Aztec city of Huejotzingo, letter to the king of Spain (1560).

Catholic Royal Majesty!

When your servants the Spaniards reached us and your captain general Don Hernando Cortés arrived, not a single town surpassed us here in New Spain, in that first and earliest we threw ourselves toward you.

. . . we also say and declare before you that [when] your padres, the sons of St. Francis, entered the city of Huejotzingo, of our own free will we honored them and showed them esteem. When they [told us to] abandon the wicked belief in many gods, we did it. Very willingly we destroyed, demolished, and burned the temples. . . .

But now we are taken aback and very afraid, and we ask, have we done something wrong, have we somehow behaved badly, or have we committed some sin against almighty God?

## DOCUMENT 3

Source: Jean Bodin, French philosopher (1530–1596), on Ottoman religious policy.

The King of the Turks, who rules over a great part of Europe, safeguards the rites of religion as well as any prince in this world. He constrains no one, but on the contrary permits everyone to live as his conscience dictates. What is more, even in his seraglio at Pera he permits the practice of four diverse religions, that of the Jews, the Christian according to the Roman rite, and according to the Greek rite, and that of Islam.

## DOCUMENT 4

Source: Photograph of the Shrine of the Twenty-Six Martyrs, Nagasaki, Japan. Dedicated to twenty-six Japanese converts and Catholic priests crucified in 1597 at the orders of Japanese ruler Toyotomi Hideyoshi.

## DOCUMENT 5

Source: Dante Alighieri, Florentine poet, *The Inferno*, Canto XXVIII, 28–36 (ca. 1307).

> I stood and stared at him from the stone shelf;
>   he noticed me and opening his own breast
>   with both hands cried: "See how I rip myself!
>
> See how Mahomet's mangled and split open!
>   Ahead of me walks Ali in his tears
>   his head cleft from the top-knot to the chin.
>
> All the other souls that bleed and mourn
>   along this ditch were sowers of scandal and schism:
>   as they tore others apart, so are they torn."

## DOCUMENT 6

Source: The Regulations of the City of Avignon (1243).

> Likewise, we declare that Jews or whores shall not dare to touch with their hands either bread or fruit put out for sale, and that if they should do this they must buy what they have touched.

**DOCUMENT 7**

Source: Albert Schweitzer, German missionary, doctor, and humanitarian, letter to his sister (April 1913).

Medical knowledge made it possible for me to carry out my intention [of bringing Christ to Africa] in the best and most complete way, wherever the path of service might lead me. . . .

I'm really happy. I feel I've done the right thing in coming here, for the misery is greater than anyone can describe. . . . [T]here are all stages of leprosy. . . . I see a great deal of sleeping sickness. It is very painful for these poor souls. . . . And elephantiasis, that constantly increasing swelling of the limbs. It is dreadful; eventually the legs are so thick that the people can no longer drag them about.

Many heart cases; the people are suffocating. And then the joy when the digitalin works! Evenings I go to bed dead-tired, but in my heart I am profoundly happy that *I am serving at the outpost of the Kingdom of God!*

## Part B: Continuity and Change-Over-Time Question

**(Suggested planning and writing time—40 minutes)**
**Percent of Section II score—33¹/₃**

---

**DIRECTIONS:** You are to answer the following question. You should spend 5 minutes organizing or outlining your essay.

Write an essay that:
- has a relevant thesis and supports that thesis with appropriate historical evidence.
- addresses all parts of the question.
- uses world historical context to show continuities and changes over time.
- analyzes the process of continuity and change over time.

---

2.  Describe and explain continuities and changes in or along ONE of the following transregional networks of exchange between 600 and 1450.

    the Silk Roads
    the Indian Ocean basin

## Part C: Comparative Essay

**(Suggested planning and writing time—40 minutes)**
**Percent of Section II score—33$\frac{1}{3}$**

---

**DIRECTIONS:** You are to answer the following question. You should spend 5 minutes organizing or outlining your essay.

Write an essay that:

- has a relevant thesis and supports that thesis with appropriate historical evidence.
- addresses all parts of the question.
- makes direct, relevant comparisons.
- analyzes relevant reasons for similarities and differences.

---

3. Analyze similarities and differences in the aims and results of TWO of the following modern revolutions.

Mexico (1910–1920)
China (1911–1912)
Russia (1917)

END OF SECTION II

# ANSWER KEY
## Model Test 2

| | | | | | |
|---|---|---|---|---|---|
| **1.** C | **26.** B | **51.** D |
| **2.** A | **27.** C | **52.** A |
| **3.** A | **28.** B | **53.** C |
| **4.** C | **29.** A | **54.** D |
| **5.** D | **30.** C | **55.** C |
| **6.** C | **31.** A | **56.** D |
| **7.** B | **32.** C | **57.** D |
| **8.** B | **33.** D | **58.** B |
| **9.** D | **34.** B | **59.** D |
| **10.** C | **35.** B | **60.** D |
| **11.** A | **36.** B | **61.** C |
| **12.** B | **37.** C | **62.** C |
| **13.** C | **38.** B | **63.** C |
| **14.** A | **39.** D | **64.** C |
| **15.** A | **40.** B | **65.** A |
| **16.** C | **41.** D | **66.** A |
| **17.** D | **42.** B | **67.** B |
| **18.** B | **43.** D | **68.** A |
| **19.** B | **44.** A | **69.** C |
| **20.** C | **45.** A | **70.** A |
| **21.** A | **46.** B | |
| **22.** A | **47.** B | |
| **23.** C | **48.** A | |
| **24.** C | **49.** B | |
| **25.** B | **50.** A | |

## ANSWER EXPLANATIONS

1. **(C)** This question tests periodization, a key part of historiography, or the way historians think about history. Answers A, B, and D refer to developments that took place earlier in time.

2. **(A)** This question requires use of evidence. Answers B and C are contradicted by clues provided by the map, and there is no evidence to support D.

3. **(A)** This question tests comparison. Answer C is too modern, and both systems of labor were homegrown, making D inaccurate. Both were coerced, but neither relied centrally or very much at all on convict labor, making A a better choice than B.

4. **(C)** This question tests use of evidence and historical interpretation, as well as contextualization. Knowledge that Brahma and the Puranas are associated with Hinduism would be enough to answer the question, but even without it, one can assume that it justifies some sort of social stratification, making B and D less relevant. The allusion to several groups favors an interpretation that the passage refers to a number of castes.

5. **(D)** This question involves comparison, as well as contextualization. Empires have collapsed for all the reasons given here, but only D fits the history of both Han China and Gupta India.

6. **(C)** This question calls for use of evidence and historical interpretation. This carving, of the Persian emperor Shapur II, is clearly intended to convey a sense of majesty and military prowess. Answers A and B are not implausible, but C seems most likely, given the humble posture of the kneeling figure.

7. **(B)** This question tests comparison. Answers A, C, and D all refer to methods used by successful empires. Even though some states made use of B as well, both Rome and Persia were culturally cosmopolitan, and their rulers were content to let subjects follow their own faiths as long as they respected imperial authority. (Rome's persecution of Jews and early Christians was due to their monotheistic refusal to recognize the emperor as a living deity—a stance the Romans interpreted as treasonous.)

8. **(B)** This question involves historical interpretation. Important for his travels to India and his doctrinal influence on Chinese Buddhism, Xuanzang also appears as a character in the fictional—and extremely popular—epic *Journey to the West*, where his character is the picaresque Monkey King.

9. **(D)** This question tests causation. Answer D is anachronistic because corn and potatoes were unknown in Europe until after the Columbian Exchange. The factors listed in A, B, and C all played a role in stimulating trade in medieval Europe.

10. **(C)** This question tests contextualization, and requires some sense of change over time. The stirrup is thought to have come from Central Asia.

11. **(A)** This question tests causation and contextualization. Although B and C occurred, they were responses to, not causes of, the trade. The same is true of D, to the extent one can say that unity prevailed in East Africa. Learning how to take advantage of A was crucial to transoceanic voyaging in this region.

12. **(B)** This question tests use of evidence and contextualization. After 1260, the Mongol empire began to split apart into the khanates depicted on the map.

13. **(C)** This question is comparative and requires some contextualization. Both Neo-Confucianism and Catholicism did everything described in A, B, and D. However, like many religions in the premodern era, they both placed restrictions on women's behavior and status, making C the correct answer.

14. **(A)** This question involves historical argumentation and the use of evidence. Answers B and C are not true to the historical record, and D applies to the natives of the U.S. Southwest. Large-scale architectural constructions, as in A, generally indicate the level of social organization alluded to in the question.

15. **(A)** This question tests comparison. Both of these are examples of art forms driven by demand from a number of social classes, including the early version of what can be thought of as a middle class, making A correct. Shakespeare wrote in blank verse and was patronized by England's royal family, invalidating B and C.

16. **(C)** This question involves comparison. Answer D has no historical basis. Even though serfs were most frequently used as peasant laborers, they worked in other capacities as well, and devshirme recruits were chosen by the Ottomans from among Christian subjects, typically European, so A and B are wrong. Although they were technically slaves, those chosen for devshirme service entered elite positions in the military and civil service.

17. **(D)** This question tests causation. All the answers except D reverse the direction in which the exchange worked.

18. **(B)** This question requires use of evidence and some contextualization. As always with this sort of question, be careful not to choose answers that are correct in fact but not supported by the image, map, or chart provided. While the map shows that the territorial extent of French, Dutch, and English colonies was smaller than that of Spain's empire, it says nothing about those countries' lack of interest in colonies, making D wrong. Lack of information about intentions similarly excludes A, nor does the map provide information to support C—even though C describes what actually happened. The map does show that, at least for now, these three nations maintained a colonial presence only where sea power could readily support it.

19. **(B)** This question is comparative, matching conceptually related methods of governance.

20. **(C)** This question tests comparison. Answers A and D apply to the daimyo, who had their origins in the samurai class, but not to the zamindars. Answer B applies to neither of them.

21. **(A)** This question tests causation. Answers B and D worked in Luther's favor, but not as much as the recently invented—and profoundly revolutionary—printing press did. Answer C refers to the use of art as religious propaganda by both Catholics and Protestants well *after* the Reformation was under way.

22. **(A)** This question involves use of evidence, historical interpretation, and historical argumentation. However true B might be, Commissioner Lin makes no reference to it,

nor does he base this part of his letter on threats, making D incorrect as well. Answer C touches on a point of concern for the Chinese, but Lin leaves this unspoken, hoping (in vain) to shame the British by showing that they are acting in violation of their own value system.

23. **(C)** This question tests the same skills as the one related to it above, but it also requires contextualization. Answers A and B are not true, and although British delegates had been treated high-handedly before the Opium Wars, this was not nearly as decisive as European frustration at their inability to sell goods in China, while China happily sold European nations tea, silk, and other products.

24. **(C)** This question tests causation. Answers A, B, and D all resulted from the canal's construction. Only in the 1950s, with Nasser's nationalization of it, did the canal become a truly Egyptian possession.

25. **(B)** This question tests historical argumentation as well as contextualization. Answers A and D refer to pairs of countries that did not make significant industrializing progress during the 1800s and would therefore not serve the historian's argument. Answer C refers to countries that succeeded because of *laissez-faire* economics and consequently support the traditional view that the historian is trying to challenge. Because Japan and Germany successfully industrialized by *not* taking the *laissez-faire* approach, they provide the historian's argument with the strongest ammunition, making B the best answer.

26. **(B)** This question involves historical interpretation. Answer D is an extremely old-fashioned and racially prejudiced view, and while A and C are not implausible, they do not quite fit—in both cases, the colonizing powers were already present, not invading, and while the Ghost Dance movement led to combat and involved a valuable asset (gold mines), neither applied to the cattle killing.

27. **(C)** This question tests use of evidence and historical interpretation. Answer A is a famous Marxist formula, and B is a cynical expression of power politics in the vein of Machiavelli. Robespierre has little to say about the idea contained in D but argues forcefully that, when protecting a noble ideal, terrible times require terrible solutions. The same logic has been applied by many extremist politicians throughout history.

28. **(B)** This question requires use of evidence and contextualization. Answer D gives the wrong direction for the technology transfer in question, and the scene does not seem hostile enough to suit A. The relationship appears deeper than the simple transaction described in C, and so this turns out to be an instance of the time-honored method of deploying native troops—in this case Senegalese trained by the French—as a way to reduce the cost of empire.

29. **(A)** This question tests contextualization and causation. Both technologically and metaphorically, the "space race" was bound up with the Cold War arms race, especially with respect to nuclear rocketry, and although most nations used sports prowess as a marker of nationalistic pride, the superpowers were especially prone to view athletic competition as a thinly veiled substitute for military struggle.

30. **(C)** This question involves contextualization and, to a degree, causation. The Rwandan genocide, mentioned in C, was principally an ethnic conflict, even if religious

difference played some part in marking ethnic difference. All the other answers involve phenomena directly associated with literal and strongly held religious views.

31. **(A)** This question tests use of evidence and historical interpretation. Little if any knowledge of the actual event is needed to sense the author's disillusionment with the effort she helped to support. She does not speak of gender concerns specifically, as in D (although many female revolutionaries do, as with Olympe de Gouges in France), nor does she devalue her new freedoms, as implied in B and C.

32. **(C)** This question relies on use of evidence. Again, as with all graph-, chart-, and map-related questions, be careful to choose only those answers that can be supported by what is provided.

33. **(D)** This question tests historical argumentation. Naipaul, renowned as a contrarian thinker, expresses impatience with the commonly held notion that all or most of the Third World's developmental difficulties can be laid at the feet of former colonial powers, rather than blamed on the new nations themselves. He is not disagreeing with A, and virtually no historians of decolonization would argue B in the first place. (Answer C cannot be chosen, because it expresses exactly the case Naipaul is making, not trying to undermine.)

34. **(B)** This question involves historical argumentation and historical interpretation. Huntington does not speak of C in this passage, nor does he go so far as to argue A or D. However, this passage does seem to indicate the near-certainty of culture-based conflict in the foreseeable future.

35. **(B)** This question tests the same skills as the related one above and also requires contextualization. Answers A, C, and D are instances of conflict between the West and the "Confucian and Islamic states" referred to in the passage, and all these could be used to argue that Huntington's predictions were accurate. The thesis is less useful in explaining how and why countries from clearly different cultures become friends and allies. (Another difficulty with Huntington's essay involves the question of how neatly one can categorize states by "culture.")

36. **(B)** This question involves use of evidence and historical interpretation. Standardization is generally a sign of centralized authority. Answers A and C refer to common fixtures in ancient urban centers, and city-states governed autonomously were capable of developing extensive trade networks.

37. **(C)** This question is comparative and requires contextualization. Both of these exchanges were principally overland and involved a variety of trade goods, making B and D incorrect, and there seems to be no evidence that one was significantly larger than the other, as in A. Answer C, which most historians believe, is left as the best answer.

38. **(B)** This question tests causation, calling for contextualization as well. The ancient Hebrews fought many enemies, and when they split apart, it was into two kingdoms, not many, so C and D are false. A and B contradict each other, but knowledge of how Jewish communities have retained their cultural distinctiveness throughout history leads clearly to B as the correct answer.

39. **(D)** This question tests use of evidence and contextualization. Buildings serving all these functions were built in ancient cities. Monotheism, however, was extremely rare in the ancient world, making A unlikely. General knowledge of the Greeks, and of Athens specifically, should be enough to prompt a correct choice from the remaining answers.

40. **(B)** This question involves comparison and causation. Hinduism preceded Buddhism, and both religions arose in India, so C and D cannot be correct. Daoism is not known to have had any significant impact on India, excluding A and making B—which recognizes the two faiths' common heritage—the best choice.

41. **(D)** This question tests comparison and contextualization. A few Mesoamerican societies developed systems of writing; however, Andean societies relied on quipu knot-tying as a means of keeping records. The things mentioned in A, B, and C were all common to both regions.

42. **(B)** This question involves causation and contextualization. Alexander's empire collapsed very quickly after his death, and Zoroastrianism survived his takeover of Persia, making A and C incorrect. Islam did not exist yet, so D is false. Alexander's great legacy was acquainting a large part of Eurasia with Hellenistic, or Greek-like, culture.

43. **(D)** This question tests causation and calls for contextualization. Answer A ignores the backbreaking effort involved with planting rice, and even though coerced labor was common in Asia, rice cultivation did not necessarily lead to widespread slavery there, so C is not a strong option. The evidence in support of D is far stronger than that in support of B.

44. **(A)** This question calls for comparison and contextualization. The absence of corn, potatoes, and the horse outside the Americas makes answers B and D false. The Bantu were not seagoing people, excluding C in favor of A.

45. **(A)** This question calls for contextualization, historical argumentation, and historical interpretation. The passage discussing conceptions of jihad is more relevant to rulers and political elites, whereas the second deals with the lived experience of people at the lower levels of society, where Crusade-related hostility would not have been as likely to be so heartfelt.

46. **(B)** This question calls for contextualization. Neither the Ottomans' imperial authority nor the Atlantic slave trade extended to East Africa, making C and D irrelevant, and while coolie labor was used throughout the Indian Ocean basin, it was more characteristic of the 1800s—and was tied much less directly to East African spice cultivation than East African slavery, making B a better answer than A.

47. **(B)** This question tests causation and comparison, and, to a lesser extent, the periodization of intellectual history. Most of the intellectual and artistic borrowing between these cultures went east to west, making A and C incorrect. The Crusades did not prevent cultural interaction, making D even more incorrect. Islamic intellectual influences, especially via Moorish Spain, were crucial to Europe's transition from the Middle Ages to the Renaissance.

48. **(A)** This question involves causation and contextualization, as well as some change over time. The Atlantic slave trade had not yet come into being, and neither had

gunpowder warfare to any great extent, so C and B are poor choices. Answer D contradicts the fact that Mali had converted to Islam and was home to Timbuktu, one of the world's great centers of Muslim scholarship. Its role in the Afro-Eurasian gold trade is well-attested, especially during the reign of Mansa Musa.

49. **(B)** This question tests historical argumentation and periodization. China's decision not to pursue maritime exploration and expansion is a turning point not just in its own history, but arguably world history as a whole.

50. **(A)** This question involves comparison and contextualization. The *yasak*, which brought native Siberians under Russian rule and forced tribute and labor obligations on them, can be seen as a close counterpart to the practices followed by Spanish conquistadors in the Americas.

51. **(D)** This question involves historical interpretation. Even when scientists clashed with religious orthodoxy, it did not necessarily mean they were anti-religious—although the danger of opposing established religions in certain times and places can make it difficult to determine true feelings. Copernicus, whose discoveries helped to destroy the medieval Catholic worldview, was devoutly Catholic, and Galileo—supporting Copernicus's ideas in this passage—is doing his best (whether out of political calculation or true conviction) not to deny the Bible's worth. Instead, he is trying to blame apparent incompatibilities between science and the Bible on errors in human interpretation of the Bible, as in D.

52. **(A)** This question requires use of evidence and contextualization. Without seeing the enemy force, there is no way to tell if C is true, and the proof for B is equally limited. Visual evidence strongly suggests that the army pictured here is non-Western (in this case it is Japanese), and although gunpowder was invented in China, muskets of the type shown here were invented much farther to the West, and would have had to be imported from there. The army appears to be using the new weapons adeptly enough to make A a better answer than D.

53. **(C)** This question tests causation and contextualization. English colonists would have been unlikely to possess or transport these crops, and while a few speculate that the Polynesians reached the Americas during their migrations, there is no evidence that they did so, so A and B are wrong. Both crops were present in the Americas before large numbers of Chinese began to immigrate there, and their transportation to the Caribbean and the Americas by African slaves is well documented, making C correct and D incorrect.

54. **(D)** This question relates to causation and requires contextualization. Safavid Persia was as devoted to Islam as its Mughal and Ottoman neighbors, but its shahs embraced the Shiite denomination, as noted in D, and transformed Persia/Iran into one of the great centers of Shiite worship, putting it at odds with the Islamic world's Sunni majority.

55. **(C)** This question involves use of evidence. All of the sources listed here would shed some light on this research topic. But C would provide by far the most concrete detail. Tax records would be indirect; diaries and oral history would also be indirect, as well as anecdotal or impressionistic.

56. **(D)** This question tests causation. The Portuguese empire played a chief role in starting the Atlantic slave trade and relied on slavery for centuries, making A false. Portuguese interest in Brazil did not mean willing surrender of other colonies, and while the Dutch stripped the Portuguese of many colonial possessions during the 1600s, this was not the case in East Africa, so C and B also fail to answer the question. It was at this time that Omani Arabs ventured southward down the East African coast, largely, although not completely, displacing the Portuguese.

57. **(D)** This question involves use of evidence and historical interpretation. The author speaks avidly about change, making A and C, with their connotations of tradition, unlikely. (Elsewhere in the document the author condemns China's and Korea's continued adherence to Confucian ideals.) State Shintoism did build on some of the sentiments expressed here, but religion is not at the heart of this essay, making B less preferable than D as a choice. The unmistakable sense of superiority is a clear indication of aggressive nationalism.

58. **(B)** This question calls for comparison and contextualization. Economic imperialism, more than the outright conquest mentioned in answer C, tended to govern U.S. relations with both regions, and sugar and fruit interests were deeply involved. Latin America could not resist U.S. overtures, as in A, and Hawaii actively sought U.S. protection from the imperial grasp of European powers. In neither case was there much of the equal basis referred to in D.

59. **(D)** This question tests contextualization. The economic foundations of early industrialization were coal, iron, and textiles—all the other goods or sources of power became prominent during the "second" industrial revolution, ca. 1850–1900.

60. **(D)** This question involves causation, with some contextualization. Although Spain's and Portugal's grips on Latin America were already slipping, due to Enlightenment ideals, dissatisfaction with colonial policy and hierarchy, and the example of successful revolutions in the United States and Haiti, it was the sharp blow delivered by Napoleon's invasion of the Iberian Peninsula that shook those grips loose. Answer A is false, and B and C are too early and too indirect.

61. **(C)** This question involves historical argumentation. On its own, answer A constitutes an *anti*-imperial act, and B and D describe purely military victories. It was when the United States persuaded itself to use the occasion of war to acquire territory for itself—a decision bitterly opposed by author Mark Twain and enthusiastically applauded by his English counterpart Rudyard Kipling—that U.S. conduct became "imperial," especially considering the bloody war that had to be waged against Filipino freedom fighters in order to secure the Philippines.

62. **(C)** This question explores causation and requires contextualization as well. All of these answers, including the correct one, involve broad generalizations, but World War II and the innumerable conflicts of the Cold War era—not to mention other conflicts of the 1900s—created millions of refugees needing new homes.

63. **(C)** This question involves contextualization. The British relied on slavery for labor in their colonies until the early 1800s, but the settlement of those colonies with actual Britons was voluntary—except in the case of prisoners and convicts "transported" as

a means of punishment. The American colonies were a common destination until the American Revolution, and then sparsely populated Australia was seeded by the same means in the early 1800s.

64. **(C)** This question is comparative, and also requires contextualization. Answer A did not, for a number of years, apply to Indonesia. Neither B nor D applied to India, which has a hotly disputed border with China and which had amicable relations—but no formal alliance—with the USSR. Both countries were major players in the non-aligned movement.

65. **(A)** This question relies on use of evidence, and also on contextualization. Numerous clues point to World War I as the correct answer, including the zones of military control, the names of certain countries (especially Austria-Hungary, which by itself excludes B, C, and D), and the names of the alliances.

66. **(A)** This question tests historical interpretation. All of the worldviews listed belong to the quotation's timeframe. But even without knowing the identity or prominence of Camus, it can be inferred from the speaker's embrace of uncertainty—and his acceptance of the idea that he must find meaning on his own terms, without the comfort of knowing that life has an external meaning—that this is an existentialist essay.

67. **(B)** This question involves periodization and contextualization. In a very short time near the end of the 1900s, global geopolitics shifted fundamentally with the end of the Cold War, and freedom movements succeeded, nearly simultaneously, in many parts of the world. One exception, however, was Communist China, which repressed the Tiananmen Square demonstrations while the iron curtain was falling in Europe.

68. **(A)** This question requires use of evidence. Since it does not provide population data, this chart does not allow safe conclusions to be reached about efficiency or per capita consumption, making B, C, and D poor choices—even though B is in fact true.

69. **(C)** This question involves use of evidence, historical interpretation, and contextualization. The ideologies named in A and D are diametrically opposed to Nkrumah's worldview, and although he had some sympathy for socialism, it is not the subject of this speech. Nkrumah's great political goal was to persuade the newly liberated countries of Africa to put aside their national differences and join together in a strong, pan-Africanist union.

70. **(A)** This question, related to the previous one, touches on the same skills, but also focuses on causation. Even more so than Nasser's pan-Arab aspirations, pan-Africanism proved limited in potential. The factors described in answers B and C had some bearing on this, but D most certainly did not—Africa is incredibly rich in natural resources, which include gold, diamonds, oil, and uranium. Unfortunately for Nkrumah, Africa is so diverse in terms of ethnicity, language, and culture that pan-Africanists have few if any unifying factors on which to base their movement.

# Appendix: Map of Selected World Regions

## Selected World Regions

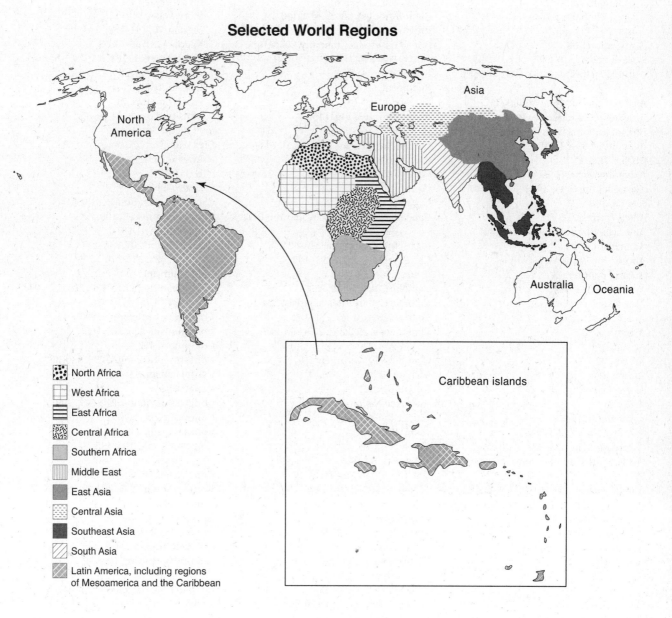

North America

Europe

Asia

North Africa

West Africa

East Africa

Central Africa

Southern Africa

Middle East

East Asia

Central Asia

Southeast Asia

South Asia

Latin America, including regions of Mesoamerica and the Caribbean

Australia

Oceania

Caribbean islands

# Index

Romans
  civilizations, 104–105
  in Middle Ages, 140
  persecution of Christians by, 94–95
Romanticism, 296
Rule, methods of, 107–108
Russia, 209
Russian-American Company, 209
Russo-Japanese War, 278, 288

Schlieffen Plan, 348
Science, 162
Scientific method, 221
Scientific Revolution, 221–222
Scientific thinking, 96
Secularism, 302–303
Seljuks, 143
Seneca Falls Convention, 320
Sepoy Rebellion, 289
September 11, 2001, 370, 390, 392
Serfdom, 73, 139, 235, 238, 240, 316
Seven Years' War, 207, 216–217, 288
Shakespeare, William, 227
Shang Dynasty, 69
Shintoism, 287
Shogunates, 147, 287
Shoguns, 214
Siberia, 209
Siddhartha Gautama, 92
Siegecraft, 108
Sikhism, 226
Silk Road, 100–101, 114, 145, 204, 232
Singapore, 290
Sino-Japanese War, 286, 288
Slash-and-burn agriculture, 115
Slavery, 73, 109, 206, 240–242, 292,
  316–317
Smallpox, 116
Smith, Adam, 308–309
Smith, John, 208
Smoot-Hawley Tariff Act, 406
Social activism, 413
Social classes, 313–315
Social Darwinism, 274, 302
Socialism, 300, 308
Socrates, 96
Song Empire, 145
South Africa, 382
South America
  in 1450–1750, 189–190, 192, 194, 196,
    216
  in 1750–1900, 255, 257, 259, 261, 263,
    291–293
  in 1945–1991, 387–389
  Andean civilizations, 152–153
  early civilizations in, 71
  geography of, 58
  in 1900 to present, 332, 335, 337, 342
South Asia
  in 1450–1750, 188, 190, 192, 194,
    215–216

in 1750–1900, 255, 257, 259–260, 263,
  288–291
in 1945–1991, 385–387
in 1900 to present, 332, 335, 337, 339,
  341
Southeast Asia, 147–148, 288–291,
  289–290, 385
  in 1450–1750, 188, 190, 192, 194,
    215–216
  in 1750–1900, 255, 257, 259–260, 263,
    288–291
  in 1945–1991, 385–387
  in 1900 to present, 332, 335, 337, 339,
    341
Soviet Union, 378–379
Space race, 401
Spain, 140, 204–206
Spanish-American War, 290–291, 293
Spanish Civil War, 363
Specialization of labor, 63, 72
Srivijayan Empire, 147–148
Stalin, Joseph, 354, 399
Stalingrad, 365
Steam power, 306–307
Stock exchanges, 309
Stone Age, 59–60, 63–64
Sub-Saharan Africa
  Islam in, 143–144, 163
  societies of, 163
Suez Canal, 279, 281, 380
Suez Canal Company, 310
Sui dynasty, 145
Suleiman the Magnificent, 211
Sumerians, 66
Sun Yat-sen, 358
Syndicalism, 356

Taiping Rebellion, 285, 315
Tang dynasty, 145
Technology transfer, 115
Terrorism, 330, 378
Thailand, 290
Theory of relativity, 401
Thirty Years' War, 217
Tiananmen Square, 385, 413
Timur, 140, 147
Tokugawa Japan, 287
Tools, 63
Totalitarianism, 329, 354
Trade
  in 1450–1750, 233–234
  in China, 284
  in early civilizations, 73
Transnational businesses, 310–311
Transregional trade routes, 111–114
Trans-Saharan caravan routes, 113–114
Treaty of Versailles, 351–353
Trench warfare, 349
Trojan War, 71
Turks, 143

United Nations, 370
Universal Declaration of Human Rights,
  367
Urbanization, 145, 238, 323
U.S. Constitution, 269

Vedism, 75, 90
Vietnam, 145, 148
Vikings, 139
Virgin of Guadalupe, 225

Wannsee Conference, 367
War crimes, 366
Wars, 108
Water transport, 115
Weapons of mass destruction, 390, 392
West Africa, 164
Western Europe, 411
Whaling, 207, 233, 249
Whitney, Eli, 306
Women
  in 1450–1750, 243–245
  Hinduism views of, 92
  industrialization and, 321
  rights of, in Europe and North America,
    319–320
  in Roman society, 105
  in Stone Age, 60
  suffrage movements, 415
World Trade Organization, 391, 408–409
World War I, 329, 348
  background of, 348
  combat in, 348–350
  Eastern Front, 350
  home front of, 350–351
  map of, 349
  mobilization in, 350–351
  Paris Peace Conference, 351–353
  Western Front, 349
World War II, 329, 362
  combat overview of, 364–366
  Germany in, 364, 367
  globalization after, 406–409
  Holocaust, 329, 362, 366–367
  interwar foreign policy, 362–364
  origins of, 362–364
  regionalization after, 406–409
  women in, 415
Writing, 64, 74

Yalta Conference, 370
Yeltsin, Boris, 389
Young Turks, 278, 302, 357
Yuan Empire, 145–146

Zapata, Emiliano, 360–361
Zheng He, 203, 214
Zhou Dynasty, 69
Zoroastrianism, 75
Zulu, 213, 280

## How to Use the CD-ROM

The software is not installed on your computer; it runs directly from the CD-ROM. Barron's CD-ROM includes an "autorun" feature that automatically launches the application when the CD is inserted into the CD-ROM drive. In the unlikely event that the autorun feature is disabled, follow the manual launching instructions below.

*Windows*®
Insert the CD-ROM and the program should launch automatically. If the software does not launch automatically, follow the steps below.
1. Click on the Start button and choose "My Computer."
2. Double-click on the CD-ROM drive, which will be named **AP_World_History.exe**.
3. Double-click **AP_World_History.exe** application to launch the program.

*Mac*®
1. Insert the CD-ROM.
2. Double-click the CD-ROM icon.
3. Double-click the **AP_World_History** icon to start the program.

### SYSTEM REQUIREMENTS

**Microsoft® Windows®**

2.33GHz or faster x86-compatible processor, or Intel® Atom™ 1.6GHz or faster processor for netbooks
Microsoft® Windows® XP (32-bit), Windows Server® 2003 (32-bit), Windows Server 2008 (32-bit), Windows Vista® (32-bit), Windows 7 (32-bit and 64-bit)
512MB of RAM (1GB of RAM recommended for netbooks); 128MB of graphics memory
CD-ROM drive
1024 × 768 color display

**MAC OS**

Intel Core™ Duo 1.83GHz or faster processor
Mac OS X 10.6 or higher
512MB of RAM; 128MB of graphics memory
CD-ROM drive
1024 × 768 color display